Maximizing Performance and Scalability with IBM WebSphere

ADAM NEAT

Apress™

Maximizing Performance and Scalability with IBM WebSphere
Copyright ©2004 by Adam Neat

ISBN (pbk): 1-59059-130-5

Printed and bound in the United States of America 12345678910

Trademarked names may appear in this book. Rather than use a trademark symbol with every occurrence of a trademarked name, we use the names only in an editorial fashion and to the benefit of the trademark owner, with no intention of infringement of the trademark.

Technical Reviewer: Matt Hogstrom

Editorial Board: Steve Anglin, Dan Appleman, Gary Cornell, James Cox, Tony Davis, John Franklin, Chris Mills, Steven Rycroft, Dominic Shakeshaft, Julian Skinner, Martin Streicher, Jim Sumser, Karen Watterson, Gavin Wray, John Zukowski

Assistant Publisher: Grace Wong

Project Manager: Tracy Brown Collins

Copy Editors: Kim Wimpsett, Nicole LeClerc

Production Manager: Kari Brooks

Production Editor: Laura Cheu

Proofreader: Linda Seifert

Compositor: Gina M. Rexrode

Indexer: Carol Burbo

Artist: Kinetic Publishing Services, LLC

Cover Designer: Kurt Krames

Manufacturing Manager: Tom Debolski

Distributed to the book trade in the United States by Springer-Verlag New York, Inc., 175 Fifth Avenue, New York, NY, 10010 and outside the United States by Springer-Verlag GmbH & Co. KG, Tiergartenstr. 17, 69112 Heidelberg, Germany.

In the United States: phone 1-800-SPRINGER, email orders@springer-ny.com, or visit http://www.springer-ny.com. Outside the United States: fax +49 6221 345229, email orders@springer.de, or visit http://www.springer.de.

For information on translations, please contact Apress directly at 2560 Ninth Street, Suite 219, Berkeley, CA 94710. Phone 510-549-5930, fax 510-549-5939, email info@apress.com, or visit http://www.apress.com.

The information in this book is distributed on an "as is" basis, without warranty. Although every precaution has been taken in the preparation of this work, neither the author(s) nor Apress shall have any liability to any person or entity with respect to any loss or damage caused or alleged to be caused directly or indirectly by the information contained in this work.

The source code for this book is available to readers at http://www.apress.com in the Downloads section.

*To my loving wife, Michelle; my Mum; Dad; and little sister—
thank you for your encouragement, support, and drive over the
past several years, of which this endeavor especially would not
have been without it.*

Contents at a Glance

About the Author ....*xi*

About the Technical Reviewer ....*xiii*

Acknowledgments ....*xv*

Introduction ....*xvii*

Chapter 1   The Need for Performance *1*

Chapter 2   WebSphere Scalability and Availability *33*

Chapter 3   WebSphere 4 and 5 Component Architectures *51*

Chapter 4   WebSphere Infrastructure Design *81*

Chapter 5   WebSphere Deployment and
Network Architecture *149*

Chapter 6   WebSphere Platform Performance,
Tuning, and Optimization *231*

Chapter 7   WebSphere Failover and High
Availability Considerations *291*

Chapter 8   External WebSphere System Availability *343*

Chapter 9   WebSphere EJB and Web Container Performance ...*371*

Chapter 10   Developing High-Performance
WebSphere Applications *395*

Chapter 11   WebSphere Database Performance
and Optimization...................................*411*

Chapter 12   Legacy Integration: Performance
Optimization *453*

Chapter 13   Performance Management Tooling *473*

Chapter 14   Profiling and Benchmarking WebSphere *503*

Index *519*

Contents

About the Author .... *xi*

About the Technical Reviewer .... *xiii*

Acknowledgments .... *xv*

Introduction .... *xvii*

Chapter 1 The Need for Performance *1*

Quantifying Performance *1*
Managing Performance *5*
What Constitutes a Performance Improvement? *7*
Measuring Business Improvements *14*
TCO and ROI Equal TCI: Total Cost of Investment *19*
Managing Performance: A Proven Methodology *24*
Summary *32*

Chapter 2 WebSphere Scalability and Availability .. *33*

Scalability and Availability: A Primer *34*
Costs of Availability, Performance, and Scalability *43*
Summary *50*

Chapter 3 WebSphere 4 and 5
**   Component Architectures** *51*

Component Architecture Overview *51*
Comparing the Versions *79*
Summary *80*

Chapter 4 WebSphere Infrastructure Design *81*

Examining the x86/IA-64/x86-64 Platform
(Intel and AMD) *82*
Examining the SPARC RISC Platform (Sun Microsystems) *94*
Examining the Power4 Platform (IBM) *109*
Comparing Disk Systems *120*
Exploring Advanced Features *145*
Summary *148*

Chapter 5 WebSphere Deployment and Network
Architecture *149*

Overview of Key Components *149*
Topological Architecture *154*
WebSphere Topological Architecture Blueprints *165*
Summary *229*

Chapter 6 WebSphere Platform Performance, Tuning,
and Optimization *231*

The Need for Speed *231*
Performance Testing a Platform *233*
Optimization and Tuning Checklist *251*
Summary *290*

Chapter 7 WebSphere Failover and High Availability
Considerations *291*

WebSphere High Availability and Failover Fundamentals *292*
Web Server Failover and High Availability *307*
Web Container Failover and High Availability *311*
EJB Container Failover and High Availability *334*
Summary *342*

Chapter 8 External WebSphere System Availability . *343*

WebSphere's Reliance on Available External Systems *343*
LDAP Server Availability *344*
NFS Server Availability *347*
Network Infrastructure Availability *352*
Database Server Failover *356*
Summary *370*

Chapter 9 WebSphere EJB and Web Container Performance 371

The Container: An Overview 371
What Do Containers Do? 373
Tuning and Optimization 377
Summary 394

Chapter 10 Developing High-Performance WebSphere Applications 395

The Top 20 List of Performance Development
  Considerations 396
Web Tier Performance 397
Business Tier Performance 400
Data Tier Performance 406
Summary 410

Chapter 11 WebSphere Database Performance and Optimization 411

WebSphere Database Overview 411
Databases Supported 412
J2EE Database Integration 414
WebSphere Database Tuning 427
WebSphere Connection Pool Manager 442
Summary 451

Chapter 12 Legacy Integration: Performance Optimization 453

Legacy Integration: What Is It? 453
Design Considerations for Legacy Integration 455
Summary 472

Chapter 13 Performance Management Tooling 473

Overview of Performance Tooling 473
Monitoring System Utilization 474
Monitoring Disk I/O 485
Monitoring Network Performance 490
Monitoring WebSphere Application Performance 497
Summary 500

Chapter 14 Profiling and Benchmarking WebSphere ...*503*

Profiling and Benchmarking, Revisited *503*
Why Profile and Benchmark? *504*
A Practical Approach to Profiling *505*
Tools Available *507*
Summary *517*

Index *519*

About the Author

Adam Neat, who lives in Melbourne, Australia, is a consulting manager for one
of the world's leading management and IT consultancy firms where he's the
Australian and New Zealand infrastructure and platform lead, focusing on technical architectures such as host systems, storage systems, and operating systems
(and all things in-between), within the communications and technology market
sector.

He's recognized as a global expert in infrastructure and platform architectures, and he provides specialty expertise in technical architectures covering
technologies such as J2EE/Java, various forms of middleware (MQ, CORBA, and
so on), large-scale systems, performance management, and application design
and architecture, as well as the deployment, configuration, and management of
enterprise application servers such as IBM's WebSphere, BEA's WebLogic, and
Sun's Sun ONE Application Server.

Adam continues to be heavily involved in the integration and production
optimization of large-scale Unix-based systems and databases.

Working with a Global 500 client list, Adam has significant experience with
deep technologies and large-scale systems and more than ten years of industry
experience. Adam frequently presents at industry conferences on platform architectures, J2EE and .NET, and open source and Linux topics. He's involved with
several open-source and Linux initiatives and has written for various industry
magazines and publications about these topics.

He's a member of the Australian Institute of Management and has a degree
in Computing Systems from Monash University in Australia.

About the Technical Reviewer

Matt Hogstrom is a senior software engineer with IBM and is currently working for the WebSphere performance team. He joined IBM in 1999 and has conducted performance analysis on all platforms on which WebSphere deploys. He was also IBM's representative to JSR-004 (ECperf 1.0) and JSR-131 (ECperf 1.1). Currently he serves on the OSG-Java subcommittee at SPEC where he works with other vendors (application server, database, and hardware) to develop J2EE-based benchmarks for the performance testing of AppServer configurations. He's generally very boring and late on all assignments.

Acknowledgments

This book has been a true group effort. Many people were involved in pulling this publication together—thank you to you all. There were, however, a few people who worked hard to help me complete this book.

First, thanks to my production team at Apress, lead by Tracy Brown Collins. Without Tracy keeping me on track and up-to-date on what was due and when, this book would have been greatly delayed! Thank you, Tracy, for your patience and perseverance with my sometimes chaotic work schedule, especially given that we had a team working in five different time zones around the globe.

Second, to the rest of the Apress team who worked with me on my book— Laura Cheu, my production editor; Kim Wimpsett and Nicole LeClerc, my copy editors; Jessica Dolcourt, who was involved in marketing the book and convinced me to put my photo on the cover—thank you all for your help and support.

Thanks also to Brian Carr, my photographer, for his much appreciated involvement.

Thanks to Matt Hogstrom from the IBM WebSphere Performance Labs; thanks to you, Matt, and your team at IBM for your validation and support of my recommendations and approach.

Neil Salkind, my publishing agent—thank you for your guidance and help early on in shaping the idea to write this book.

To my family—My Dad, Mum, and sister, Shannon. Thank you for your constant encouragement and feedback.

And to my wife, Michelle, who always puts up with my desire to work long hours, especially the near-ridiculous hours spent writing and reviewing this book. Without your patience, understanding, and constant encouragement, I wouldn't have been able to put this together. Thank you dearly!

Introduction

Welcome to the first edition of *Maximizing Performance and Scalability with IBM WebSphere* from Apress.

Over the past three years, IBM has proven WebSphere's power by molding it into a powerful, scalable, and robust Java 2 Enterprise Edition (J2EE) application server platform. Each major release since 3.5 has included impressive redundancy, scalability, and performance features that continue to put IBM WebSphere at the forefront of high-end J2EE computing.

IBM's persistence in the areas of scalability and performance has paid off. This book is all about that—the science and art of tuning, sizing, and configuring your IBM WebSphere server platform to be optimized to maximize your organization's J2EE application cost-effectiveness.

More and more Internet sites, as well as internal corporate applications, are being built upon the IBM WebSphere platform, and therefore more than ever, it's critical to an organization's Information Technology (IT) excellence to look for ways to optimize and tune its platforms. With the help of this book, you'll see how to approach, plan, and ultimately optimize and tune your WebSphere platforms using structured and battle-proven techniques.

This book covers both WebSphere 4 and 5. As with most enterprise software suites, at any given time, IT organizations may be operating multiple versions of key software products. In WebSphere's case, having a reference guide such as this book, which covers both WebSphere 4 and the newer advanced performance features of WebSphere 5, ensures that organizations not looking to migrate off WebSphere 4.*x* immediately can still reap the benefits of optimization and tuning.

Just as you tune your car to ensure that it runs efficiently and economically, IT managers and Chief Information Officers (CIOs) should use this book to obtain the same positive results for their IBM WebSphere platform.

In summary, with the two versions of WebSphere covered in this book, the optimization and performance characteristics are subtle; however, given that a particular setting in WebSphere 4 may produce a completely different result under WebSphere 5, you'll benefit from this dual-version book.

Who Should Read This Book

This book was written for system managers, platform and J2EE architects, and IT managers. If your job involves designing and or managing WebSphere servers, then this book will be beneficial to you.

Lead and senior Java/J2EE developers can also benefit from this book. Quite often, developers don't get exposed to the important platform-specific considerations and issues when developing applications. HTTP sessions, database accesses, and the combination of failover capability and scalability are several common areas of high-end J2EE application design that often get little focus during design and development.

Therefore, senior developers can gain valuable insight into designing and developing WebSphere-deployed J2EE applications with the strategies and recommendations within this book.

How to Use This Book

This book is broken into 14 chapters. Each chapter covers a specific topic that can be read on its own as a reference guide.

The book alternatively can be read cover to cover to pick up more on the methodology and frameworks that are discussed during Chapters 1 and 2 that, with subtlety, carry through the rest of the book. In this manner, you'll discover the optimal ways to put together a WebSphere platform architecture using a baseline methodology and then design and tune your platform to operate optimally.

The underlying message that the book tries to convey is to always use a methodology and have a purpose in what you're doing.

In **Chapter 1**, you'll explore what performance is all about, why you should care about it, and how to model it. Although this may seem somewhat obvious, it's important to consider performance from the perspective of WebSphere, with a business focus. Too often system managers and architects look at performance as being totally about technology; this chapter explores what performance is really about.

Chapter 2 explores scalability, availability, and performance from the point of view of your architecture. That is, what do you need to consider in terms of scalability and availability when formulating a WebSphere platform design or architecture?

Chapter 3 looks at the WebSphere architecture. In this chapter, you'll explore all the different components and subtle differences between WebSphere 4 and 5. This is an important chapter given that you'll need to be familiar with the definitions of all the components and underlying architecture of WebSphere.

In **Chapter 4**, you'll explore and consider the technologies that make up a WebSphere platform. You'll look at key design considerations for disk systems, networks, and infrastructure concepts. From this chapter, you'll be able to select and model your WebSphere infrastructure design based on my recommendations and guidelines.

Chapter 5 explores key topological architectures that are possible with WebSphere. You'll look at good and bad platform architectures, with recommendations for each model. I provide guidelines to help provide direction for where each different topology is best used and how to understand your requirements.

Chapter 6 starts to explore the fundamentals of tuning WebSphere. In this chapter, you'll explore tuning key components such as the WebSphere Object Request Broker (ORB), networking components, performance optimization for the integration of other systems, and much more. Using the experience and details from earlier chapters, this chapter builds on the strategy and methodology of performance optimization.

In **Chapter 7**, you'll look at WebSphere's clustering and workload management capabilities. This chapter explores how to configure, tune, and optimize your WebSphere platform for high availability and performance.

Chapter 8 looks at ensuring high performance and robustness when you interface your WebSphere platform with external systems such as Lightweight Directory Access Protocol (LDAP) and NT File System (NFS) servers.

In **Chapter 9**, you'll look at optimizing and tuning your WebSphere platform's Enterprise JavaBean (EJB) and Web container components. As you'll discover, these two components are key to your overall performance and availability of your deployed J2EE applications.

Chapter 10 explores 20 best-practice development factors that help you ensure performance, availability, and scalability of your deployed applications. As you'll explore during earlier chapters of the book, high performance and robustness don't start when the WebSphere platform architect or system managers start to model their environment. This chapter looks at some "low hanging fruit" ways to better your application development—ones that quite often cause performance and scalability problems when your applications are deployed.

Chapter 11 explores the tuning and optimization of Oracle 8*i*, Oracle 9*i*, and IBM DB2 for use with WebSphere J2EE-based applications. You'll look at core database tuning approaches as well as some optimization approaches on the WebSphere side of the JDBC-instigated transactions.

In **Chapter 12**, you'll look at what options and strategies exist for ensuring a level of high performance and robustness with your legacy systems. Legacy systems are found in all IT organizations and may extend from something as recent as a COM+ or DCOM environment through to something a little more vintage, such as a VAX-based environment. This chapter explores some methodologies and approaches to ensure a degree of performance and compartmentalization.

Chapter 13 looks at some high-quality commercial and open-source software to help profile, benchmark, and monitor your WebSphere application environment. You'll explore how to implement these types of software tools to understand your WebSphere platform's state of performance and load.

Finally, in **Chapter 14**, you'll use the details from Chapter 13 to look at how to benchmark your WebSphere platform, take those results, and then feed them back into a performance methodology. In this chapter, you'll further explore WebSphere application profiling and look at ways to use the information obtained from benchmarking and profiling tools.

What This Book Is Not

It's important to point out that this book isn't a WebSphere administration manual. Although this book can definitely complement a WebSphere administration guide, its purpose is to provide you with a strategy and methodology for planning your WebSphere platform's optimization and performance.
So often, performance and scalability, as I'll discuss in Chapter 1, is considered achievable by simply purchasing lots of capacity and hardware. This is fundamentally wrong. What this book therefore explores is why you should set certain parameters for your platform's needs.

In Closing

Use this book as a strategy. Earlier chapters provide you with the guidance and approach needed to execute your performance methodology, and later chapters in the book provide you with the know-how, guidelines, and recommendations to implement your WebSphere platform performance management strategy.

CHAPTER 1

The Need for Performance

SOMETIMES, PEOPLE TAKE decreasing hardware and infrastructure costs for granted. System managers typically neglect that to better an application's overall performance (reducing end user–facing response times), it's just as important to look at the *way* something is configured or tuned than it is to add horsepower (hardware) to your platform.

For WebSphere-based Java 2 Enterprise Edition (J2EE) applications, this is an important concept to understand. Poorly performing applications that are simply masked by ultra-fast hardware will undoubtedly be, from a resource utilization point of view, the catalyst for other problems in the future.

This chapter presents several models that exist to help system and application managers understand and appreciate the financial gains and the business benefits from a well-optimized and correctly scaled environment.

Quantifying Performance

What's the definition of *performance* and an *optimized system*, and why are they so important?

Is high performance all about a warm-and-fuzzy feeling we get when our environments and platforms are operating in an ultra-tuned fashion, or is it more about the direct or indirect financial implications of a well-tuned platform? Maybe it's a bit of both, but the quantified and tangible reasons for performance being so important are primarily financial considerations.

Consider the following example: You're operating a 1,000-user environment on a pair of Sun F4800 servers, and the average response time for each user transaction is around five seconds. If your business stakeholders informed you they were going to heavily market the application you manage—with a suggested 100-percent increase in customers—then you'd probably initially think of simply doubling the Central Processing Unit (CPU), memory, and physical number of systems. Or you'd simply look at how the application operates and is tuned.

From personal experience, most people focus on increasing the hardware. System load from customer usage and computing power typically correlate with one another. The problem with this scenario, apart from the de facto upgrade approach being costly, is that it doesn't promote operational best practices. Poor operational best practices (whether it's operations architecture or operations engineering) are some of the worst offenders in spiraling Information Technology (IT) costs today. Operations engineering and performance go hand in hand.

An operations methodology on one side is about the processes and *methodologies* incorporated into the scope of your operations architecture. These processes and methodologies are what drives proactive performance management and optimizations programs, all of which I'll discuss later in this chapter.

The other side of this is a performance methodology. The performance methodology is basically the approach you take in order to implement and drive an increase in application, system, or platform performance.

Figure 1-1 highlights the two methodologies, operations and performance. Although they're both the key drivers in achieving a well-performing system, too much or too little of either can incur additional costs.

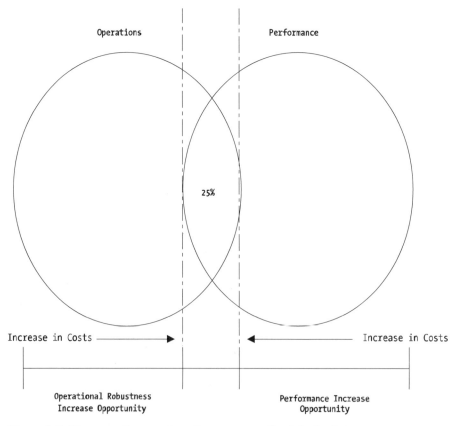

Figure 1-1. The operations and performance methodologies intersect

Figure 1-1 shows a fairly proportioned amount of both operations and performance methodologies. Note the cost scale underneath each methodology.

Let's say that Figure 1-1 represents a model that works to achieve a 25-percent improvement in performance each quarter (every three months). If you wanted to increase this to a 75-percent improvement in performance in a quarter, both operations and performance methodologies would come closer to one another (as depicted in Figure 1-2), and the costs associated with conducting performance management and operational process changes would increase.

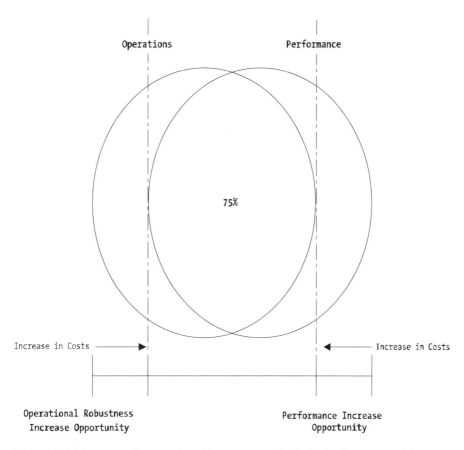

Figure 1-2. The operations and performance methodologies intersect, with an increase in performance

Although there's no problem with attempting to achieve this type of performance increase, costs for both methodologies increase. The question that needs to be answered is, "How much cost is acceptable to achieve a 75-percent increase in performance?"

Would it mean that because of the performance, the volume of transactions could increase, amounting to more customers or users utilizing the application and system? Would this increase potential sales, orders, or basic value to your end users? If this is the case, then the sky is the limit!

Take the following example: Suppose each user transaction netted $100. If your system was able to facilitate 500 transactions per day, then an increase in performance of 75 percent (using Figure 1-2 as the example) would increase the transactions from 500 to 875 transactions a day. This would equate to an additional $37,500. However, to achieve that additional 75 percent of transactions, what does it cost you in additional resources (such as staff hours and staff numbers) and overhead (such as additional time spent analyzing performance logs and models)?

This is the dilemma you face in trying to achieve application and system optimization: How much is too much?

One of the key messages I try to convey in this book is that performance management isn't simply about turbo-charging your environment (applications, systems, or platforms); it's about smart performance management. Sometimes ten seconds is acceptable for a response time for customers and end users; it may cost a further 10 percent of your operations budget to get to six-second response times, but it may cost 90 percent of your operations budget to get to five-second response times.

Therefore, performance management is about understanding the requirements of performance as well as understanding when enough performance is enough.

NOTE This question of "When is enough, enough?" is somewhat analogous to disaster recovery realization analysis. For example, if a company is considering disaster recovery (in its true sense) as a part of its operational effectiveness and availability program, there's little value involved when a particular application or system is used once a month and takes only several hours to rebuild from scratch. The cost associated with utilizing a disaster recovery site may cost less than $1 million, but the financial impact of a "disastrous event" occurring would only be $25,000. In this case, there's little reason to implement disaster recovery planning. In summary, the cost of trying to tune your platform to provide an additional second of response time costs more than the value that the additional performance provides or creates.

Getting back to the earlier thread, not looking at the WebSphere or application platform in order to scale and increase performance opens you up to myriad potential disasters down the track.

Another problem with this kind of de facto upgrade approach is that your developers may fall into the dangerous trap of expecting unlimited processing power if they're used to working in an environment where simply coding to functional specification and practicing for code optimization are the norm.

NOTE   That said, if you've already read later chapters or have previously conducted an optimization and tuning review of your WebSphere environment, upgrading hardware to achieve scalability or boosting performance could very well be the right choice. Just remember, any upgrade to CPU and memory will require changes to your WebSphere application server configuration. As soon as you add either of these two components into a system, the overall system load characteristics will change.

As I've hinted at earlier, negative system and application performance doesn't have just a negative effect on your customers or users, it also has a negative effect on the budgets in your IT department and your manager's perception of your effectiveness.

The bottom line is that poorly performing applications are expensive. The number-one rule in operational effectiveness for managing performance is all about proactive management of your system resources.

Many of you reading this book will be able to tune a Unix or a Microsoft server, but the purpose of you purchasing this book is you wanting (or needing) to be able to also tune, optimize, and ultimately scale your WebSphere environment.

Now that you have a synchronized view of what performance really is, you'll look at the art of managing performance.

Managing Performance

So, what is performance management? The contextual way to answer this is to ask yourself, "Do I have, or have I had, performance problems with an application?" If the answer is "yes," then performance management is the discipline that would've (potentially) mitigated those performance issues.

Depending on whether you're facing this question proactively or reactively, essentially performance management is about the implementation of a performance methodology. It can be further explained as being the execution of the methodology to help identify performance problems (or hotspots); identify an optimization strategy; plan, tune and execute the optimization strategy itself; and, finally, analyze and monitor the system.

There are many industry-specific and even WebSphere-specific performance management models and methodologies. Depending on how fine-grained you like your models, many of these non-WebSphere specific models will suit the task accordingly—one performance model fits all.

As depicted in Figure 1-3, once an optimization and performance management strategy is in place, the performance management model follows an ongoing, proactive life cycle.

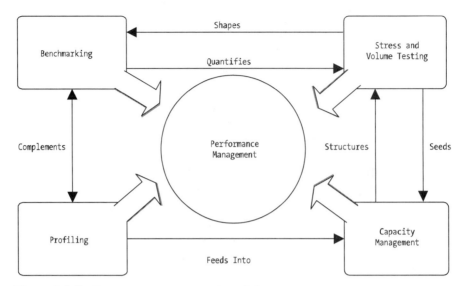

Figure 1-3. Performance management model

Many times system managers implement processes to monitor or tune an environment but don't continue to review, follow up, and make changes where required. A system's characteristics are always changing and growing. Additional customer load, new functionality, and other non-application-specific factors will continuously change the face of your application environment.

It's therefore critical that the process outlined in Figure 1-3 is used continuously to ensure that an ever-changing system is managed for performance.

To highlight this point, Figure 1-4 shows the cost associated with resolving performance problems, both immediately and in the future. As depicted, the longer a performance issue goes unmanaged or unnoticed, the cost associated with resolving or mitigating that performance problem increases drastically.

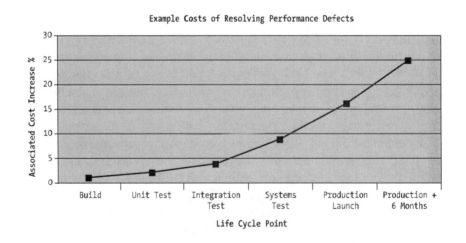

Figure 1-4. Costs for mitigating performance issues, immediate and future

The increased costs come from a number of reasons; the most compelling is associated with the overall life cycle of the platform. That is, if a performance problem becomes apparent yet is left unnoticed or unmanaged, additional layers of application content and functionality will begin to hide the issue. And the longer it takes for you to find and resolve the issue, the more application code you'll probably need to change. Furthermore, the longer it goes unresolved, the more end users, physical systems, and platform complexity that it'll impact.

 NOTE The issue of performance problems going unnoticed over time and the costs associated with resolving them in the future is similar to the timings associated with stress and volume testing during application development. The later in your software development life cycle you perform stress and volume testing, the more costly it'll be to uncover and resolve potential problems. For example, if you perform stress and volume testing after application integration testing and find performance problems, then the cost associated with fixing the issue is significant, compared with the cost in fixing the problem at the unit testing stage.

You'll now look at what's considered a valid performance improvement.

What Constitutes a Performance Improvement?

This is one of those questions that has been argued since the dawn of computing! You can view a performance improvement and what constitutes one in many ways. The following are some of the key indicators that can be attributed to or deemed as performance improvements within a WebSphere implementation:

- A decrease in perceived user or customer application response time (in other words, a decrease in wait time between transactions).

- The ability for the "system" to handle more users or customers (in other words, volume increase).

- A decrease in operational costs associated with either or both of the previous points.

- An ability to scale down infrastructure (or consolidate) because of the higher performance of the application on a lesser-powerful infrastructure.

- The bottom line if Business-to-Business (B2B) activity in any given period will have a direct effect on the revenue-generating capability of the application or system (this typically is connected with the second point).

Although this isn't an exhaustive list, it provides an overview of some of the more obvious and tangible benefits that can be derived from a tuning and optimization strategy.

You'll now explore each of these points in a little more detail.

Decrease in Perceived User or Customer Response Time

A decrease in the perceived user or customer response time is the most obvious of performance improvements. As a system and application management expert, you're exposed to all *those* calls from users or customers who are complaining of poor or substandard application response times.

Although on many occasions this can be because of problems outside the bounds of your control (for example, the many hops and intermediate service provider pops between you and the remote Internet site), a fair degree of an application's performance *is* within your control. Some key components within WebSphere that directly affect performance (and are tunable) are as follows:

- **Queues**: Web server, Web container, database datasource, and Enterprise JavaBean (EJB) container

- **Threads**: The availability and utilization of them

- **Database**: Java Database Connectivity (JDBC) pool, Structured Query Language (SQL) statement controls, and the database itself

- **Transaction management**: The depth of your transaction containment and so on

- **The Java Virtual Machine (JVM)**: Garbage collection, utilization of Java objects within the JVM, and general JVM properties

I'll discuss each of these components—and more—during their respective chapters later in the book. However, these five areas are where you'll focus a fair degree of effort for performance management. Proper tuning and capacity management of these aspects of WebSphere can literally make or break a system's performance, and a little tuning here and a little tuning there of things such as JVM settings and transaction management can increase or decrease performance by more than 100 percent in no time.

Combine this with how well your platform and applications utilize the database pooled connections, Java objects, and other areas of WebSphere such as data and session persistence—and then throw in a well-thought-through methodology—and you can achieve a more than 200-percent improvement in application response time on a poorly performing system.

NOTE   I recently was involved with some performance tuning work associated with a WebSphere 4.02 platform that presented customer invoices online. The response time goal for the application was to have 95 percent of all transactions completed—in other words, backend transactions complete, Hypertext Transfer Protocol (HTTP) transfer to customer commenced—in less than five seconds. Initial testing was showing average response times of 17 seconds, which was a concern. I'll use this example as a case study later in the book; however, after incorporating a performance methodology into the analysis effort and tuning the environment based on this methodology, the response times came down to between four and six seconds per transaction, which was deemed acceptable. The moral is that the sooner you can implement a performance methodology, the faster and more effectively you'll be able to resolve performance problems.

Performance management is a time-consuming process; however, its rewards are high. Given this, it justifies working closely with developers to ensure they're writing code that not only functions according to business requirements but also is written with an operations architecture best-practice mindset.

In summary, time well spent brings large rewards: Do the research, do the analysis, and spend the effort. Follow these three mottos, and you'll see positive returns.

Ability for the System to Handle More Users

When a system manager is propositioned to scale up his or her platform to cope with "y" number of additional users, there are two schools of thought people tend to follow; one is mostly wrong, and one is mostly right.

At first thought, being given a requirement to scale a system up "x" fold to accept more customers is typically met with additional processors, memory, and or physical systems. It's the old vertical versus horizontal scaling question. Where this school of thought is mostly wrong (and I'll explain why it's mostly wrong shortly) is that, with the right tuning and optimization approach, you can substantially increase the life of a system without an upgrade (within fair boundaries).

Before you balk and say that's crazy, I need to point out this only works for reasonably sized increments of load. What constitutes reasonable is driven by the nature and characteristics of the application. I've seen a system architecture implemented for a baseline set of users and the call being made to be able to ensure that it'll cope with nearly three times the original load. Tuning and optimization of the platform made this reality.

That said, with the decreasing costs of hardware from IT server vendors, it may in fact be less expensive to purchase more memory or additional Host Bus Adaptors (HBAs) than to perform a thorough review on the application or environment. This can definitely be the case for the midsize upgrades; however, keep in mind that midsize upgrades come in pairs and trios. Therefore, no doubt in the near future, your stakeholders will approach you requiring additional increases in customer load for another functional or capability change. If you get the impression that you can just keep squeezing more and more out of your system by simply purchasing additional hardware, you'll end up painting yourself into a corner.

What I'm trying to say is this: Hardware upgrades aren't always required for additional load of increased performance. In fact, for two out of three situations, hardware upgrades won't be required for additional load or capability enhancements.

Figure 1-5 breaks down the associated costs for an example platform where an increase in hardware has increased support and maintenance costs to provide a two-fold increase in processing capacity.

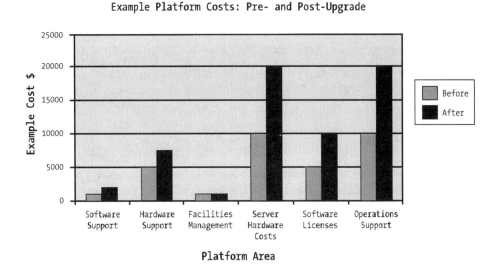

Figure 1-5. Pre- and post-upgrade support costs for an example platform

As depicted in Figure 1-5, the increase in hardware has increased the overall support, maintenance, and license costs for this platform. Because the WebSphere environment hasn't been optimized or hasn't been optimized correctly, the "bang for buck" in dollars per additional transaction is lower.

Figure 1-6, however, shows what can be done in the opposite situation. If a system is optimized correctly, the cost benefit ratio is high. Both these figures are fictitious but do represent the benefits associated with JVM tuning and proper configuration.

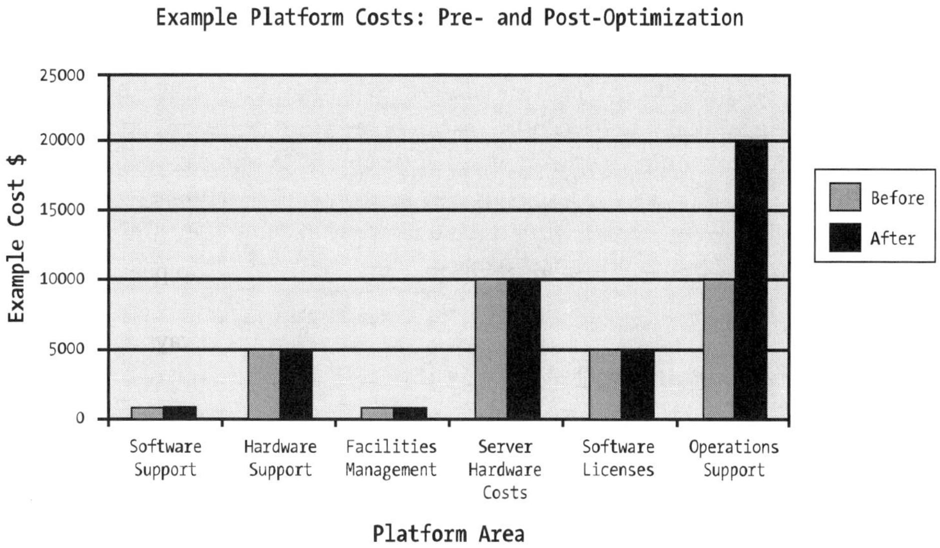

Example Platform Costs: Pre- and Post-Optimization

Figure 1-6. Pre- and post-upgrade support costs for an example platform, the optimized approach

As shown in Figure 1-6, the dollar cost per transaction greatly decreases with optimization, and at the same the time, the overall operational costs associated with the platform remain unchanged.

It's important to understand that the same can be said for the opposite. If you get the impression that "a tweak here and a twist there" can give your business customer a 500-percent increase of application load or performance—without hardware increases—then this can also paint you into a corner.

Setting expectations and providing a clear outline of your methodology and process for the ongoing life cycle of the system, and its application constituents, is critical to your role as an application or system manager.

Decrease in Operational Costs

Operational costs associated with poor or low application performance are one of those financial burdens that, over time, add up and can suck an IT budget dry. Operational costs are typically associated with management and support, the system's "food and water," and ancillary items such as backup tapes, software concurrency, and the like.

A low-performing application that requires heightened management and support because of increased customer inquiries and support calls, additional system "baby sitting," a reduced ability to perform support tasks during operational hours, and so forth will incur costs at a fairly rapid rate. It can be a "slippery slope" under these conditions, and only through proper risk and program management does a system or application in such poor shape survive.

Figure 1-7 indicates the costs involved in an operational budget for a medium-sized WebSphere environment operating on a four-CPU Unix platform with dual WebSphere application servers.

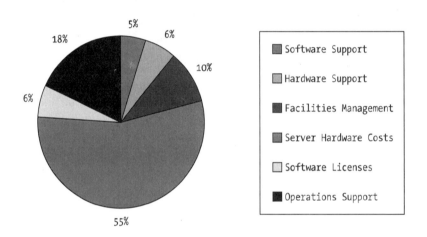

Indicative Operational Costs: Initial Outlay

Figure 1-7. Indicative operational costs, initial outlay

The largest of all cost components in Figure 1-7 is the infrastructure costs, followed by license costs. This breakdown assumes a zero-year horizon on the cost outlays (in other words, upfront cost prior to development).

If you look one year into the future, the most significant costs are the maintenance, support, and licensing costs. Maintenance and support as well as ongoing licensing costs are usually driven by the size and hardware platform you're using. Most vendors work on a license and maintenance agreement where the number of CPUs used in your environment drives the total cost.

You can probably see where this is heading—if you have a well-optimized environment with less hardware, your maintenance costs are reduced and so are your license costs.

In summary, a high-performing application will require less support and baby sitting. Operational tasks can be completed during standard operational hours, and support calls regarding performance and slow response times will be minimized, which reduces the head count for support staff, which in turn directly affects operational support costs.

Ability to Scale Down Infrastructure with an Optimized WebSphere Environment

A system's "food and water"—power, cooling, and hardware maintenance—can also be reduced through WebSphere application optimization and tuning. If fewer physical systems are required, food and water costs are reduced.

This is an important factor in obtaining funding for performance optimization and tuning tasks. As you'll see in the next section, sometimes selling the concept of an optimization and tuning program to business stakeholders (those who hold the strings to the money bag!) is difficult. Unless you reduce the true bottom line costs and can prove that through a structured and clear methodology, these stakeholders will not lay out the funds.

By clearly showing you can reduce operational expenditure costs (by reducing the number of servers, which means less support and management costs), you can easily sell the operational and application optimization and tuning efforts.

The Business Bottom Line

Although some of these points about a businesses bottom line and cost analysis are all somewhat "motherhood and apple pie," the number of installations and environments that can't or won't see the benefits of tuning and optimization is amazing.

Technical people will typically see the benefits from a better-performing system and application. Business people need to see the advantages from a bottom line perspective, and unless you can sell these conclusively, then your optimization plan—or more precisely, its benefits—needs more work.

In some situations, if an application has a transaction response time of ten seconds and the business representatives and customers are happy, do you need to optimize the system further? Unless optimizing the platform will provide a drastic reduction in infrastructure (and all associated costs), then "if it ain't broke, don't fix it."

 NOTE I'm sure we've all faced the opposite of this, which is where a stakeholder or business representative demands unachievable performance requirements such as ensuring that 95 percent of all transactions to and from an IBM OS/390 mainframe complete in less than one second!

Essentially, one of the key aims of this book—other than *how to optimize*—is to attempt to show the business benefits of optimizing and tuning WebSphere. Many readers may already be at the point of having identified the benefits of optimization and even having the concept sold to business sponsors. Possibly, you may now need to know how and what to do to execute the optimization and tuning efforts.

Either way, by reading and using this book, you should be able to build and complete your WebSphere optimization and tuning strategy.

Measuring Business Improvements

It's all well and good to understand the obvious technical benefits of optimizing and tuning, but you need to understand the impact, both positive and negative, that this effort entails. You may be able to tune the JVM settings and notice a difference in the performance of the application or overall environment, but what about the tangible benefits to a business? As discussed, business sponsors and stakeholders will want to see benefits from a business perspective. That is, they'll want to see a decrease in operational, support, licensing, infrastructure, and other costs or an increase in customer usage, satisfaction, and, ultimately, transaction rate (which may or may not drive revenue, depending on the type of application you're tuning).

I'll discuss this topic more, in context, throughout the rest of this book; however, it's worth covering some of the key business impacts that are measurable from optimization and tuning efforts.

The following two scenarios show how business benefits are measurable with performance optimization and tuning:

- Scenario 1 looks at a fairly new application that's in pilot mode. Problems have been found with the application's performance, and failure to improve the performance will most likely result in the application being cancelled.

- Scenario 2 discusses the cost benefits of optimization for a platform that's requiring an upgrade in end user capacity. It explores the alternatives and highlights the bottom line cost benefit from optimization.

Scenario 1: A Pilot Application

As you've seen, the outcome of all optimization efforts for a business is an impact to the bottom line (hopefully a positive one). If WebSphere optimization and tuning is conducted properly, you'll see a positive effect on the budget sheets.

The positive impact may not be so clear initially; however, over time the benefit realization will accelerate and become more obvious. An example of this would be an optimization and tuning effort conducted while an application is new or in pilot phase.

A pilot phase typically includes a small handful of test or trial users testing an application or system. Some people call this a *live production shakeout*, but effectively it represents a pilot phase of the application development life cycle. If the pilot phase, making use of only 10 percent of expected total number of users, showed that the response times were hovering around the 90-percent to 95-percent mark of the acceptable Service Level Agreement (SLA), this would provide an obvious case for optimization and tuning efforts.

For example, let's say an acceptable response time for a WebSphere-based application was five seconds per transaction, and during the pilot, with 10 percent of the targeted application load, pilot users were reporting four-second response times.

Now, unless the application operating in WebSphere had externally controlled constraints that meant four seconds would be the norm even for up to 90 percent of the total projected end user load, typical capacity modeling would suggest that transaction response times increase as the user load does. Given that norm, if 90 percent of the acceptable response time was being reached with 10 percent of the projected end user load, then there's a problem!

NOTE Of course, stress and volume testing should have picked this up in preproduction deployment; however, this doesn't always happen. It's amazing how often stress and volume testing isn't conducted or isn't conducted properly. Never go live (or permit an application to go live) into production without proper stress and volume testing.

At this point, there would be several scenarios that may play out.

If the platform had been sized and modeled by the capacity planners and system architects (typically those reading this book) according to the functional and technical specifications, then this would serve as a baseline for operational performance. However, the input to the platform and application performance modeling is just as critical as the output of the model itself.

In this situation, given that the system performance characteristics are broken, proposing an optimization and tuning exercise of the WebSphere application environment is the only sensible course of action.

Let's assume that some stress and volume testing or profiling had taken place once the performance problem had been realized (I'll go through profiling in later chapters of the book). The output of the profiling would identify poorly operating application code and areas within WebSphere that could be tuned to extend the life of the application in its current state.

The alternative would be to purchase additional hardware and, based on the previous example, lots of it. Mind you, as discussed earlier, it may be a dual-pronged plan—a combined hardware and optimization change.

Measuring the business impact of either solution is straightforward. The baseline cost would be initial implementation. Additional effort to analyze and ensure the application operates within the guidelines set out in the SLA would require funding. Further, depending on the outcome of the analysis, additional hardware or funding for an optimization and tuning effort would be required.

The costs associated with the Scenario 1 project are as follows:

- Initial hardware purchase: $250,000

- Initial development costs: $300,000

- Projected ongoing costs: $50,000 per annum

Let's look at the two options available to this problem: a hardware upgrade or optimization effort. You can assume that to achieve the SLA required with an additional 90-percent load, you'll need at least a 100-percent increase in additional infrastructure or a 100-percent increase in platform optimization (which effectively means a 100-percent improvement in performance capacity).

The following are the costs for Option 1, a hardware upgrade:

```
Additional projected ongoing costs:      $175,000 per annum
    (additional support for
    operations and hardware)
Additional hardware required:            $200,000
_____                        _____

TOTAL                                    $375,000 for year one
```

The following are the costs for Option 2, an optimization and tuning effort with minimal hardware upgrade:

```
Projected ongoing costs:                 $75,000 per annum
    (additional $25,000 per annum
    for increased ongoing
    optimization and tuning program)
Projected costs for tuning effort:       $25,000
Projected costs for code changes:        $50,000
Additional hardware required:            $75,000
_____                        _____

TOTAL                                    $225,000 for year one
```

Figure 1-8 depicts these two options side by side.

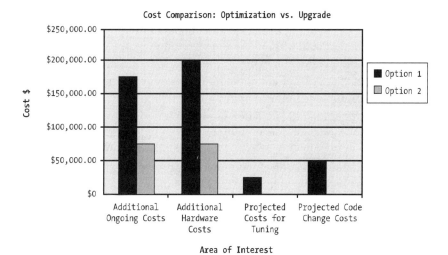

Figure 1-8. Comparing costs of both options

The two options side by side are fairly self-explanatory. Although these costs are examples, they do show the differences in associated costs for a scenario such as this. Specifically, a 100-percent improvement in performance through optimization is in most cases achievable. Even 200 percent isn't a difficult task.

Essentially, the business benefits of improving performance through an optimization and tuning program far outweigh the benefits or costs associated with an upgrade in hardware. The business benefit, although driven by a reactive requirement (in other words, post-deployment cleanup), is $150,000.

Figure 1-9 depicts a second-year view on this scenario. This figure indicates the ongoing savings associated with the initial outlay. The key factor that's driving the increase in cost savings is the ongoing cost for hardware support.

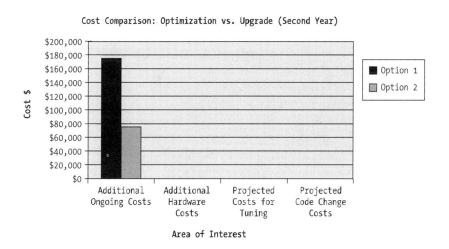

Figure 1-9. The second-year cost comparison of both options

Scenario 2: A Request for Additional User Capacity

Scenario 2 looks at a platform with an e-commerce application, one that has been operating within a WebSphere environment for some time.

In this scenario, if a requirement comes from business sponsors or the company's marketing group that indicates additional users are being targeted through a marketing campaign, you'll need to investigate the state of the WebSphere and application platform to determine the impact and whether any action is required.

As previously mentioned in Scenario 1, two clear options exist in this type of situation. You can undertake a straight hardware increase, based on capacity modeling, or you can facilitate an effort to investigate and ultimately optimize and tune the WebSphere platform.

Typically, you can undertake a baseline of an optimization and tuning strategy quickly and with fewer overhead and impact than a production hardware upgrade. If an optimization and tuning methodology is in place and performance management is a key part of this particular scenario's operations architecture, undertaking a review of the WebSphere platform's performance will incur a minimal incremental cost. Even optimization and tuning that doesn't involve developers can significantly increase the performance of a WebSphere implementation. Modifying JVM settings, transaction management controls, queues, and similar aspects of the environment can result in a large result-to-effort ratio.

In this situation, activating a series of performance monitors that capture the characteristics and workload of the WebSphere environment will provide the key indicators for a review. Once metrics have been captured, then analysis and review can take place. This typically takes one to five days, depending on system complexity and size (at least highlighting several of the key areas of the platform).

Next, planning the WebSphere optimization and tuning effort based on the analysis obtained from the metrics provided by the performance monitors and then planning, testing, and implementing the changes typically requires an additional five to ten days for a midsize system.

All in all, this effort takes approximately ten days; assuming a system manager rate of $500 per day, the outlay would be $5,000.

Again, let's assume an increase in performance of 100 percent was obtained—for this example, let's say the analysis found that several Java database connection methods were serialized, causing all database transactions to queue up behind one another. This is a common problem I've seen in smaller environments where connection pooling within WebSphere wasn't used and a custom-written pool or database connection manager was employed.

Without proper analysis of what was happening "under the covers" using a sound performance methodology, a hardware upgrade would've been costly. A hardware upgrade may not have even resolved the issue, given that the example states the problem is a serialization of the connection beans to the database.

One may have looked at running additional WebSphere instances to allow more concurrent database connections (meaning a higher volume of serialization and bank of database requests but still a higher throughput of queries). This would require additional CPU and memory on the WebSphere application server to provide capacity for running multiple WebSphere application server instances.

Additional hardware costs mean additional licenses and support. Figure 1-8 highlights the difference between the optimization approach and the hardware approach—both options would achieve the same outcome. The hardware costs detailed in Figure 1-8 are based on public pricing details available on the Internet (to be nonbias, I've averaged the cost per CPU and memory between several Unix server vendors, based on entry-level servers). Again, please keep in mind these costs are examples only and are an attempt to show the business improvements and the measurement of these improvements over time; however, their impact and realization is accurate.

Therefore, in summary, measuring business improvement or the effect on a business's bottom line when tuning and optimizing is simply about weighing these tangible costs. I don't want to imply that to gain performance the only option is to optimize and tune and not to perform hardware upgrades. This isn't the case; in many situations—and I'll go through more of these later in the book—a combined approach of hardware and optimization is the most logical.

TCO and ROI Equal TCI: Total Cost of Investment

Now that you've seen the outcome of an optimization and tuning effort, you'll take a step back and look at what other forms of analysis models are available to determine the best alternative for your program.

Total Cost of Ownership (TCO) and Return on Investment (ROI) are among some of the most overly used acronyms within the industry today. Both are high-level, analytical models that provide the unwary system manager with an "all bases covered" methodology hype. Vendors have been flogging their wares for more than a decade now using TCO and ROI statements to quantify the value of their product.

With that said, it's not that either of these two models can't provide value. In fact, used correctly and in the correct context, they're both powerful, independently or together.

Let's take a closer look at both models.

Total Cost of Ownership: An Overview

Since its inception back in 1986 by an analyst at Gartner Research, TCO has been increasingly used as *the* benchmark for determining the overall, medium to long term costs associated with a particular piece of technology. Whether it's software, desktops PCs, servers, or an entire IT project, TCO has been used as the comparative vehicle.

Although TCO has some flaws in its methodology (which you'll see shortly) when used to compare apples to apples, it can provide a well-balanced view of the total cost associated with some form of IT technology investment. This may be a new hardware purchase, a support arrangement, a technology or architectural selection, or an optimization strategy.

By indicating some flaws with TCO, this alludes to the TCO model being an open one. There are little bounds to it, and the outcome is only as good, as valid, or as comprehensive as the input and depth of comparative data used as the basis for the analysis. TCO is also typically only used to model something on a timeframe longer than the implementation itself.

Another example of where TCO breaks is in an example of conducting TCO on the purchase of office desktop PCs. If a TCO analysis on two PC vendors takes into account the cost of the PCs, software, support and installation, and power, how does TCO perform if one vendor's PCs are lower quality yet cheaper? Yes, the TCO based on the purchase price, software, installation, and power is potentially lower, but unless hidden costs can be included into the TCO equation, then it's of little value.

To use a WebSphere-based example, if you attempt to perform a TCO analysis on a WebSphere application platform and attempt to model the TCO based on two differing optimization methodologies, your input must be comprehensive. The inputs should include not only the time and effort to build and design the optimization strategy but also the costs associated with potential changes to hardware, support processes, operational processes, and so forth.

However, if you again use this and change the perspective of time to model two proposed architectures for a new WebSphere installation, you'd include cost items such as these:

- Hardware (physical servers and disk arrays)

- Infrastructure software (initial costs for operation systems and other middleware)

- License costs (WebSphere, operating system, database)

- Support costs (ongoing vendor support)

- Deployment costs (operational staff time and effort)

- Water and feed (power, cooling, fire retardation)

These factors start to provide a good basis for a correct TCO model during implementation.

Another important factor is what I term as *soft costs*. These are TCO aspects such as potential cost reductions through support staff options (for example, lots of lesser-experienced personnel or fewer experienced personnel), maturity of vendors (for example, response times to support calls and professionalism), and availability assurances (from vendors). Most often, these elements don't carry a direct dollar value. Instead, they're used as weighting metrics, and I'll explain this in more detail shortly.

I'll now put all of this into some context.

Tables 1-1 and 1-2 compare two basic systems. This example attempts to model the TCO of a WebSphere implementation to determine the optimal system in terms of performance and scalability.

Table 1-1. TCO Matrix, Hard Metric: Implementation Option 1

TCO Element	WebSphere Implementation Option 1, First-Year Costs
Hardware costs	Two × Intel Pentium 4 servers = $30,000
Infrastructure software	Operating systems and Enterprise Application Integration (EAI) middleware = $15,000
License costs	WebSphere, Oracle, and operating system = $10,000
Support costs	Hardware and software support = $15,000
Operational support costs	24×7 support = $50,000
Deployment costs	Integration team × four personnel = $20,000
Water and feed	Power, air conditioning, and fire-retardant system = $5,500
TOTAL First Year	**$145,500**

Table 1-2. Example TCO Matrix, Hard Metric: Implementation Option 2

TCO Element	WebSphere Implementation Option 2, First-Year Costs
Hardware costs	Three × Intel Pentium 4 servers = $45,000
Infrastructure software	Operating systems and EAI middleware = $20,000
License costs	WebSphere, Oracle, and operating system = $15,000
Support costs	Hardware and software support = $25,000
Operational support costs	24×7 support = $50,000

Table 1-2. Example TCO Matrix, Hard Metric: Implementation Option 2 (Continued)

TCO Element	WebSphere Implementation Option 2, First-Year Costs
Deployment costs	Integration team × two experienced personnel = $20,000
Water and feed	Power, air conditioning, and fire-retardant system = $8,500
TOTAL First Year	**$183,500**

As you can see from Table 1-1 and Table 1-2, Option 1 for the first year is the cheaper alternative—or, it has a lower cost of ownership. If you added scalability as a soft metric and worked on a 75-percent usage growth per annum, the outcome would look different. For example, if these examples were specified to handle 100 concurrent users, the Option 1 (Table 1-1) servers may each be operating at 50-percent load and Option 2 (Table 1-2) at 35-percent load.

If the annual plan to increase concurrent users serviced by the application was an additional 75 percent (an additional 75 users), the Option 1 servers would be nearing 90-percent utilization, or saturation point. The Option 2 servers would be operating at approximately 60-percent load each (getting high but reasonable). Option 1 therefore would require a doubling of infrastructure in the second year, as well as additional software and licensing to service the additional servers.

Figure 1-10 compares the costs of these options for two years.

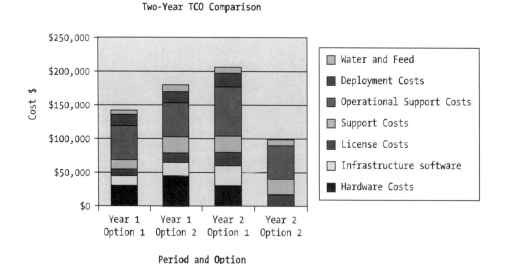

Figure 1-10. A two-year TCO comparison of both options

Therefore, as depicted in Figure 1-10, a two-year view on the TCO, based on the inputs from Tables 1-1 and 1-2, would show that Option 1 would become more expensive over time than Option 2.

The reason is this: Option 2 doesn't need an upgrade in the second year. The costs are fixed and known. When an upgrade is required, this would incur a deployment cost (see Tables 1-1 and 1-2 for associated costs) for each upgrade. To then include soft metrics such as the impact to availability and scalability of the solution, Option 2 starts to pull away from Option 1, boasting an increasingly better TCO. Obviously, three servers are more scalable—albeit to a point—than two servers, and the additional server provides a higher level of availability.

Although this may not accurately represent a real-world scenario, the concept is sound. Projects and people typically underestimate the hidden costs such as development and training when formulating TCO.

This section showed that when performing analysis on an optimization and tuning plan to determine the most cost-efficient or cost-rewarding direction, you should consider the context in which you model the TCO. Use apples-to-apples comparisons, and don't be afraid to use complexity or the perceived value of something (for example, vendor track record) as a consideration.

Now that you're starting to learn about cost rewards or cost efficiencies, you're starting to get closer to the ROI model.

Return on Investment: An Overview

An ROI of a positive of negative nature is an important aspect to be aware of with any system or application implementation. Business cases tend to use a number of derived ROI models such as Net Present Value (NPV).

ROI is best used to predict or model the *future* cost efficiency of an investment, such as the deployment of a WebSphere-based application on a commodity Intel platform versus a higher-grade environment such as a Sun UltraSPARC III platform.

ROI differs from TCO in that TCO was designed to model the outright total cost of something (such as a total WebSphere platform), and ROI was designed to model the financial benefit or return of something in the future.

For example, you may use an ROI model to determine the financial benefits and general return (a.k.a. bang for buck) between two WebSphere optimization strategies—one being to simply install more hardware, such as CPUs and memory, and the other being to physically tune the WebSphere application server engine.

Let's focus on that example for a moment.

Using the set of metrics discussed in the previous section, let's use a scenario where the Chief Information Officer (CIO) has requested an audit of the systems and applications that run within your WebSphere environment. The audit is to perform a review of the cost per transaction for the applications operating within the WebSphere application environment for which you're responsible. The cost for each transaction is made up of system cycles (CPU power), processing capacity of the application server, and time taken to complete the transaction.

The audit is completed, and the results are that the cost per transaction is too expensive—$10 per transaction!

Your next step is then to look at optimizing your WebSphere application environment (using this book, of course). After planning an executing a performance and optimization strategy, you perform an ROI analysis.

In this example, if it took the following to optimize your WebSphere environment, the cost for strategy compilation, execution, and reporting, the program would cost $20,000:

- Ten days to build and test the performance and optimization strategy at $500 per day (you and your team's time)

- Five days to test the strategy in an integration/stress and volume environment at $500 per day

- Two days to implement the solution

- Three days to compile the performance monitoring statistics post-solution deployment

The resulting cost per transaction, after a successful reduction of processing overhead within the WebSphere application environment, was $2.50 (or 75 percent). Therefore, assuming 100,000 transactions per month, you can say, simplistically speaking, the ROI of this effort of $20,000 is 97 percent. That is, for an investment of $20,000, the successful optimization effort produced a monthly positive return (saving) of 97 percent from the pre-optimization platform performance characteristic.

Measuring this type of benefit is important. System managers and architects need to be able to report and represent, as well as view and identify, the bottom line return that will be achieved by investing time and effort into a performance methodology and upgrading hardware.

Managing Performance: A Proven Methodology

Although you can use many approaches to address performance and optimization management with WebSphere, I've found one that tends to synchronize well with the WebSphere platform. It also has the added benefit of being relatively straightforward.

In essence, it's a hybrid of a number of old-style methodologies grouped with newer schools of thought and best practices. For most environments, it'll work well; however, be careful to validate and confirm the approach before diving in. Attempting to overlay complex methodologies with something as complex and large as WebSphere is destined for failure. Instead, a straightforward and logical approach is essential. This methodology is also a living one; that is, you should continue to use it proactively during the lifetime of the system.

Before looking at the methodology itself, you should consider some key points for commencing a performance management program. The next sections highlight these.

Performance Management 101

Like in any testing situation, you can break down the basic scope of effort to the aim, the method, the test, and the results. Although it's a discussion about fundamentals, I believe it's important enough to consider in this context.

Considering these four key points, let's outline a brief performance management approach that the performance methodology, discussed shortly, sits on top of.

Problems found in the results typically can be fed back into the aim of another cycle. Using this aspect of performance management, the model should show the process cycle around continuously, being used proactively to identify and help rectify issues.

The Aim of Performance Management

The aim is sometimes not as obvious as you'd initially think. Consider an underperforming system that needs to be fixed. In this case, the aim is to increase performance by a determined factor. That factor is defined by business sponsors, end user demand, legal agreements, and so forth.

Take, for example, a situation where the aim is to resolve an application performance problem, specific to database-related transactions where a certain query is taking five seconds to respond. This query is fundamental to the application's functionality, and its lengthy delay is causing end users to complain.

The aim is therefore to bring the database response times in under an acceptable threshold. Let's assume that the SLA for the full end-to-end user transaction is five seconds, of which in this example the database query itself is consuming the ensure SLA, leaving no overhead for content composition and so on. It can also be said that the aim is the problem you're attempting to solve.

To get the SLA back under its threshold, the system manager has determined that the SQL query must not take any longer than one second. Therefore, the aim of the performance management approach is to perform analysis on the application environment to bring the database query response time down from five seconds to one second.

The Method of Performance Management

Now that you have the aim, the performance management approach needs to define a method for analysis and testing (quantification). This part of your management approach should address how the analysis will take place and the tools you'll be using.

Continuing on from the example from the aim section, the method of analysis will be to run a SQL query monitor on the database server to determine what's wrong with the query itself as well as to monitor the output from the WebSphere Resource Analyzer to investigate what Java components, if any, are causing the delay.

The method should also include contingency plans for backing out any monitoring components or changes to environments because of an issue in operating the tests.

Testing Performance Management

The test to conduct the analysis will be to run the monitors in the production environment to get the most accurate data set in the least amount of time. This test will operate for 12 hours, during both peak and low utilization periods. The system manager will monitor it continuously to ensure that the monitoring doesn't affect the actual operation of the production system.

The attributed requirements from the aim should be repeatable within the test. This ensures that an averaged result is obtained so that singular uncontrolled events (external issues and so on) don't impact or interfere with the result.

The output will be captured in raw and binary formats—raw from the SQL Query Analyzer and binary from the WebSphere Resource Analyzer tool.

Performance Management Results

The result of the test is the result of the analysis. The result therefore, driven from the output from the test, will be fed into the performance methodology discussed in the next section. Analysis from the test should provide a clear indication of where the problem lies in the environment and will help to provide a guide for where the analysis phase should start.

Now that you've considered this semiformal approach to performance management fundamentals, let's now look at the methodology and walk through how it works, what it covers, and how to implement it.

The Mirrored Waterfall Performance Methodology

Before looking at what the Mirrored Waterfall Performance Methodology (MWPM) is, first you'll see the key areas of a J2EE-based application server environment that affect an application's responsiveness (in other words, its perceived performance) the most:

- Java/JVM memory and object management, queues

- JDBC/Container Managed Persistence (CMP)/Bean Managed Persistence (BMP), pooling, and Java Message Service (JMS)

- The platform components: database, networks, and their configurations

- The physical server configurations (memory, CPU, disk, and so on)

- The operating system: the kernel itself and all associated settings (for example, networks)

I'll go into these five key areas in more detail in future chapters; however, this list is the foundation of what the methodology addresses.

The methodology works using a directional flow rule, somewhat similar to a waterfall (see Figure 1-11). At the top of the waterfall diagram you have the physical server(s) or hardware, followed by the operating system and its associated configurations. The next level down contains the platform components such as databases and network settings, followed by the JDBC, pooling, and JMS type services. Next come the Java and JVM settings and the queues.

Essentially, how this model works is this: If you want to tune the JDBC Connection Pool Manager settings in WebSphere, you must, according to the model, consider tuning and analyzing the configuration and settings of components in the bottom family grouping—the JVM/Java and queue settings. The rule of the model is that if you need to tune or alter something, you must also consider and analyze all component groups down the waterfall. Like water, you can't go back up the model; you must always work down the model on the left side.

The previous example relating to the JDBC settings requiring changes or analysis on the JVM/Java and query component grouping is driven by the fact that altering the JDBC connections will affect on the flow of transactions through the overall WebSphere environment. This is typically associated with what's known as *queues*. I'll discuss these at length in Chapter 9; however, for the purpose of this chapter, understand that the concept of queues essentially relates to the number of open connections at each tier and how those open connections are managed.

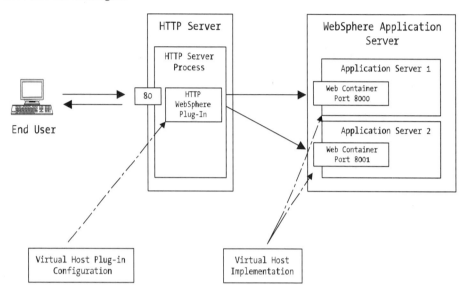

Figure 1-11. The waterfall model

It should be obvious that given the JDBC connections are changing—which will affect either how many or the characteristic of the SQL connections to the database—this will result in a change to the overall balance of the platform tiers.

Secondary to this, because the balance or characteristics of the application platform will change as a result of the JDBC changes, this may change the JVM requirements. How many users (which equates to sessions) will now be required to operate on the platform? Users or sessions drive JVM heap size, so how many concurrent users are on the system, and what type of profile do those customers have?

As you can see, it's all connected.

The second point to make regarding the model depicted in Figure 1-11 is that of the opposite or mirror waterfall model. The right side of the model is the "driver" or mirror aspect. That is, each of the right side component groups drive a change to the next component group up the waterfall, if required.

To put it another way, if after monitoring the HTTP transport queue level in the WebSphere Resource Analyzer it was found that the transport queue was running at 100-percent utilization, then this would therefore mean, based on the model, that the problem with the queues would "drive" the need for a change in the component group one level up the mirror side of the waterfall. In this case, it would drive the need to investigate why the HTTP transport queue was saturated.

Essentially, the right side should only be used as a "finger-pointing" exercise. Use it in the event that something has broken or something is performing badly. It'll help to direct where the source of the problem is.

TIP   Remember that if a particular component isn't performing or is broken, it's not going to always be the fault of that component. In the previous example of the HTTP transport queues reaching maximum capacity, the problem or root cause may not be that the HTTP transport queues are set incorrectly, but it may be that the JDBC settings aren't aligned correctly with the entire platform. In these situations, identify the problem, and then identify the root cause using the right side of the waterfall model.

The pitfall in not conducting these "sanity checks" as part of the methodology is that you end up with a turnip-shaped environment. This introduces potential bottlenecks and will most likely cause more headaches than what you had to start!

The shape of your environment, in terms of incoming requests from customers or users, should be carrot shaped, or a long funnel (see Figure 1-12).

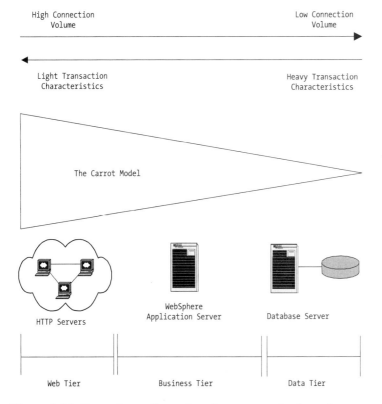

Figure 1-12. Correctly configured environment—the funnel, or carrot-shaped, model

You'll investigate why these environment shapes are important in Chapter 9; however, as a brief overview, you can look at the overall environment from a cost point of view. The pointy end (less volume) of the carrot is the most expensive end, and the larger, less pointy end (high volume) is less expensive.

Most J2EE-based applications will see their environment as having the database tier as the pointy yet more expensive end of the funnel, and the Web tier as the less pointy, less expensive end. Databases transactions are heavy and therefore expensive. Web transactions are lightweight and are somewhat inexpensive.

This boils down to queuing methodologies, a key area of an overall system's performance and one I'll address in detail in future chapters.

Other Considerations

The MWPM (Mirrored Waterfall Performance Methodology) highlighted in Figure 1-11 will be referenced throughout the rest of the book. Therefore, you need to consider a number of other issues with the methodology. Many of these are foundational statements, but many systems managers miss or don't incorporate them formally into their operational models. I'll also cover these in more detail throughout the book; however, they can be summarized as follows:

Educate your developers on the workings of WebSphere—what's a queue, what really is a transaction, what's a small lighter-weight SQL query versus a larger heavyweight query? (See Chapters 9 through 12 for these topics.)

Use this book and best practice development guides to help your developers understand the implications of non-system-friendly code (for example, leaving hash tables open in session state and so on).

Build standards for development, and ensure they're included in the quality assurance and peer review checkpoints.

Implement historic monitoring and reporting. Always ensure you're charting the key components of the system. This should include CPU, JVM, memory, disk, network, and database utilization. I'll discuss some tools to do this later in the book.

Monitor and plan your tuning and optimization approach; in other words, focus on one (problem) aspect of the system at a time. Don't take on too much—conduct the analysis and tuning in small steps.

Implement one change at a time, and monitor. Don't fall into the trap of implementing a whole range of performance tuning changes. Implement one change, monitor for a period of time that gives suitable exposure to system load characteristics (in other words, don't implement on Friday, monitor on Saturday when no one is using the system, and take that as gospel!), and then analyze. If the implementation was successful, roll out the next change.

The final point you should consider isn't a particularly difficult issue, but it's one that's commonly overlooked: conducting performance management and analysis without the testing or monitoring itself, skewing the results, and affecting the outcome.

Measurement Without Impact

Measuring without impact is difficult. I'll first briefly discuss what this means.

How do you measure something without affecting what you're measuring? Take a simple example of a Unix server. If you have a system that's under fairly considerable load, and you run a script every five seconds that performs a detailed ps command (ps -elf or ps -auxw, depending on your Unix of choice) to determine what's taking up the load, you'll affect the very problem you're measuring.

For those who know a little about quantum physics, you can associate "measuring without impact" with the quantum effect attributable to the uncertainty principle. One of the obstacles with science's quantum mechanics is that it's difficult or impossible to directly measure the state of a quantum bit, or some form of *quanta*. This partially has to do with what's known as the uncertainty principle, but it extends to the fact that to measure something directly, you affect it.

Therefore, measuring the state of some *quanta* would make the observation useless. Although this isn't a book on quantum mechanics, the same problem arises in the higher world of WebSphere optimization and tuning efforts!

You can overcome this problem, but it's important to keep it in mind as you go through the WebSphere performance and optimization process in this book. The way I propose to approach this issue throughout the book is to simply minimize the impact. It's not possible (or extremely difficult) to get around the issue; however, through the careful planning and design of your performance management approach, you can minimize the impact.

At a high level, the methodology I'll use in the book considers the following: Whatever you do in production to measure performance, do in all other environments—specifically, development and systems integration. In other words, control your environments. So often I come across sites testing components in multiple environments, with each environment having slightly different software or patch levels.

Furthermore, keep your performance management monitoring system/application/probes constantly running. This provides a standard and common baseline to measure performance degradation and improvements under all situations as well as ensure that if there's a common load characteristic for your monitors, its loading factor on the overall system isn't an unknown.

In other words, keep low-level monitoring continuous but nonintrusive. Understand your environment workload and map your monitoring to that. That is, it's no use running debug or monitoring output on every end user transaction if the data you're capturing is too rich in information. Understand what type of transactional workload is operating on your platform (for example, B2B, consumer-based online shopping, and so on), and tune your monitoring tools accordingly, based on transaction rate, depth, and requirements (such as SLAs and so on).

Summary

Throughout this chapter, you explored different aspects of performance management, including a number of optimization models and optimization approaches. These approaches and models will be beneficial to you through the rest of the book and in your day-to-day work when managing WebSphere environments.

As you explored in this chapter, performance management—and hence performance and scalability—can't exist without performance methodologies such as the examples provided within this chapter. I've worked, and continue to work, on both sides of the developer/system manager fence. I know that developers tend to develop to specification and what they consider a high-performing application design.

More experienced developers (and of course architects) understand that high-performing application design goes beyond good code. Good design needs to extend into design and planning between the system people (the readers of this book) and the developers. Writing code that aligns with the WebSphere system manager's configuration and optimization architecture goes without saying, but on many occasions, I've seen this to not be the case. I cover some guidelines on this particular point later in the book.

In closing, although creating and implementing performance methodologies and managing them against a performance management model can incur some overhead, the benefits of having and using these models will be evident in your WebSphere platform's performance and availability metrics.

CHAPTER 2

WebSphere Scalability and Availability

I TOUCHED ON PERFORMANCE during Chapter 1 but have yet to dive into WebSphere scalability and availability paradigms. Therefore, this chapter explores what it means to have a highly scalable and highly available WebSphere-based implementation.

The terms *scalability* and *availability* are synonymous with high-performance computing. Since the dawn of the computing age, systems have been designed with these two principles in mind, usually alongside their partnering paradigm, performance.

To restate, the three key measures of high-performance computing are the following:

- Availability

- Performance

- Scalability

How well a system rates against any of these three aspects of computing determines the platform's overall compliance to high-end computing platform designs. In other words, there's no sense having a massively scalable system when it's riddled with single points of failure, indicating low availability. That said, as you explore this and subsequent chapters, your application environment may not constitute or demand massive amounts of scalability and availability. For instance, 99.999-percent availability isn't always the Holy Grail; sometimes 99-percent availability is satisfactory.

Size doesn't necessarily come into play here either. Scalability, for example, may mean you can double your log file data easily, but the system may only consist of two application servers, each with a single Central Processing Unit (CPU).

This chapter helps you gauge what these terms really mean and applies them to some example WebSphere implementations. The bottom line is that every WebSphere system will be different. Moreover, every WebSphere system will be subject to different business factors. Again, it may be satisfactory that a WebSphere implementation needs only 95-percent availability! In a case such as this, meeting 95-percent availability may even be deemed as highly available; to another company, this may be a downright time bomb!

You'll now explore these concepts in detail before looking at some case studies.

Scalability and Availability: A Primer

You deploy a WebSphere implementation in order to provide application services to users or business partners. Whether it's a Java thick client, a Business-to-Business (B2B) Web Service architecture, or just a simple Web-based Hypertext Markup Language (HTML) interface, the purpose of a WebSphere application is to serve.

Internet banking, e-commerce, package tracking, and online airline ticketing are all examples of products that WebSphere can serve. As you can appreciate, not all of these services will require large amounts of availability. Furthermore, not all of them will require vast amounts of spare resources or the ability to grow and scale. Of availability and scalability, scalability tends to be an issue (or a design and architectural consideration) for the medium to long term, and availability tends to be an issue for your WebSphere application environment in the short term.

Availability, or *resiliency*, is something that's attributable to how you configure and architect your WebSphere environment (which is why I discuss best practices in detail in Chapter 6). Further, a well-designed, highly available WebSphere platform can actually insulate poorly designed or poorly developed application code. Imagine application code running on a single server (low availability) and a single Java Virtual Machine (JVM) (low scalability) that's buggy and continues to crash.

You could send the code back to the developers, but as you probably know, this can take time and be costly. If your original WebSphere topological architecture has multiple servers or multiple application servers (hence using multiple JVMs), you can insulate, to a degree, bad application code. Of course, if the code is really bad and the JVMs are constantly crashing and restarting, this will undoubtedly affect performance.

It's an age-old question: How much hardware do you add to ensure that your application environment is highly available? There's a point where purchasing more and more hardware to cater for poorly written or designed application code becomes more expensive than changing the code! I'll come back to this later in the chapter.

Scalability: What Is It?

Scalability is the ability of a system to grow, either driven by changes to functionality or technical requirements or driven by organic growth (for example, an increase in registered users over time). When I talk about scalability, you might first think of hardware and infrastructure. Typically, the raw processing power, memory, disk, and network capacity determines how scalable a WebSphere application platform is.

For an application to scale, generally the overall platform housing the application must be able to continue operating under a peak load (or a spike), as well as be able to grow organically as general usage increases over time. What you want to avoid is having to upgrade or alter your topological architecture and your application design every three months to satisfy growth.

On the flip side of hardware, you have software. Software is just as tangible as hardware when it comes to scalability. A classic example of software scalability is a 32-bit platform-specific limitation. In most cases, a 32-bit limitation inhibits memory allocation or file size allocation higher than approximately 2GB. Therefore, you'd need to consider specific platform architectural designs when scaling higher than 2GB for file sizes and memory allocations.

Additional software bounds further limit maximum file and file system sizes, memory allocation sizes, and so forth. For example, most 32-bit JVMs on 32-bit operating systems support up to 2GB of memory heap size. If your environment requires more than 2GB of memory per Java process, then you'll need to go to a 64-bit JVM (64-bit JVMs are in their infancy and only just becoming available) or vertically scale your application architecture by using multiple JVMs (discussed in Chapters 4 and 5).

 NOTE The 2GB limit is the upper bound of the JVM heap size. However, other factors within your operating system and platform will constrain your maximum heap to less than the maximum of 2GB.

In Chapter 5, you'll learn about topological architectures. In that chapter, you'll explore the ways to make your topology scalable so that you can cost-effectively grow your WebSphere environment, with little or no redesign.

Availability: What Is It?

Availability is the measure of a system's or application's processing capability over time. In the case of a WebSphere implementation, this relates directly to how available the WebSphere-managed Java 2 Enterprise Edition (J2EE) application is to users. Simply put, you can model WebSphere availability as follows:

$$WA = \frac{MTBF}{MTBF + MTTR}$$

What this says is that WebSphere Availability (WA) is the measure of the Mean Time Between Failure (MTBF), which is then divided by the sum of the Mean Time Between Failure (MTBF) and the Mean Time to Repair (MTTR).

NOTE There are entire books available on the science of availability; as such, an in-depth explanation of availability is beyond the scope of this book. However, what I do cover in this chapter, and in context within later chapters, is how to understand what availability levels you require.

Availability is a critical key performance indicator for applications. The key to achieving availability is to design and develop good, solid applications, as well as to architect a battle-proven WebSphere-based topological architecture. As such, when measuring availability, there are some important facts to understand.

First, the sum of your overall WebSphere availability is only as good as the mean of the lowest availability component. That is, if you have a WebSphere server cluster with four nodes yet all four nodes are running off the same single power supply that's rated as only having 99.5-percent availability, then all the servers in the world won't provide you with greater than 99.9-percent availability.

At the same time, the more components you have in your environment, the greater chance there is of a component failing. Consider a system with two hard disks, with each hard disk having 100,000 MTBF. This is roughly 11 years of MTBF for each disk; however, as a whole system, you'll have an MTBF on your disks of 100,000 hours divided by 2 (two disks). Similarly, if you have a large system with, say, 200 disks, then the MTBF will decrease to 100,000 divided by 200—or, 500 hours. This equates to approximately one disk failure every 21 days.

Understanding the Business Availability Index

Before actually looking at availability measurements, you'll now consider availability from a risk management and business point of view.

It's possible to break down availability, from an organizational perspective, into five groups. Each group progressively involves more cost, is driven by more management attention, and overall receives more focus from budgetary issues and ultimately customer impact. The five progressive levels of redundancy in an organization are as follows:

- No redundancy

- Data redundancy

- System redundancy

- People redundancy

- Organizational redundancy

Many Computer Science and Business Information Systems university programs teach this model in a common four-step process; what they tend to omit is the fourth point, people. It's great to have a whiz-bang, highly availability WebSphere implementation, but if your key person who knows 95 percent of the system leaves, then your impressive WebSphere cluster can quickly become nothing more than a Christmas tree decoration!

The following sections briefly describe each of the levels in what I call the *business availability index.*

Understanding Level 1: No Redundancy

No redundancy is just that. This level may include rudimentary forms of configuration backup, but essentially a level 1 redundant implementation is a potential disaster waiting to happen. Then again, as you'll see in later chapters, having this level of redundancy may just be all your organization needs.

If, however, you're operating a WebSphere-based implementation that's important or critical to your clients or business needs, then consider levels 2–4.

Understanding Level 2: Data Redundancy

Data redundancy starts to use online or near-online mirrored and redundant data storage technologies. This may be as simple as plain RAID 1 mirroring or something more "exotic" as RAID 5, RAID-S, or some other form of data replication.

It doesn't include replication of data between other hosts because this falls under level 3 redundancy.

Understanding Level 3: System Redundancy

System redundancy refers to multiple load-balanced or hot-standby/failover servers. This is the first availability level you should consider for critical systems. Level 3 relates to all server tiers within a WebSphere environment such as Web servers, database servers, application servers, and other legacy-based systems.

Understanding Level 4: People Redundancy

People redundancy isn't when you're laying off staffers but instead is when you're following some sort of proactive knowledge exchange and skills-transfer program. Similar to some of the concepts from the Extreme Programming (XP) methodology where all development is championed by two people at a time (side by side), this includes daily "handovers," daily knowledge and technology briefings, and so forth. Rotate roles and staff to ensure that all team members get exposure to all aspects of your environment so that when someone leaves your organization, then you're covered and not left standing with a WebSphere-based platform without any experienced employees.

Understanding Level 5: Organization Redundancy

Organization redundancy is all about disaster recovery. If your environment is mission or business critical, this level of redundancy is paramount. It includes active dual-site implementations, hot-standby disaster-recovery configurations, and all forms of data and service replication between two or more sites. This is by far the most complex and expensive of the redundancy levels.

Matching Business Availability with Percentage Availability

To achieve a certain percentage of availability, your application must match one of the previous levels of redundancy. Table 2-1 gives you an overview of common availability percentages, with the corresponding business availability index level.

Table 2-1. Business Availability with Percentage Availability

Availability Percentage	Business Availability Index
98 percent	Level 1
99 percent	Levels 2–3
99.8 percent	Level 3
99.9 percent	Levels 3–4
99.99 percent	Level 5
99.999 percent	Level 5
99.9999 percent	Level 5

Table 2-1 quite clearly shows how the various business availability index levels match up against the availability percentages. For example, if you require 99.99 percent or greater availability, you need to ensure that your operational effectiveness is at level 4 or 5. You can use this table as a guide to ensure that you're matching availability expectations with the correct level of attention.

Understanding the Availability Matrix

The result of availability is measured by a percentage of *uptime*, which is service availability to users. This section describes what it means to be able to provide high levels of availability and what the percentages of availability really mean.

Table 2-2 lists commonly represented availability measurements and their associated downtime per year and per month, depending on how you measure them.

Table 2-2. Availability Measurements

Availability Percentage	Yearly Downtime	Monthly Downtime
98 percent	7.3 days	14 hours, 36 minutes
99 percent	3.65 days	7 hours, 18 minutes
99.8 percent	17 hours, 30 minutes	1 hour, 28 minutes
99.9 percent	8 hours, 45 minutes	43 minutes, 48 seconds
99.99 percent	52.5 minutes	4 minutes, 23 seconds
99.999 percent	5.25 minutes	26.2 seconds
99.9999 percent	31.5 seconds	2.6 seconds

As you can see, as you approach 99.9999-percent availability, the reasonability of this guarantee becomes less and less likely. It's practically impossible to achieve annual availability of 99.9999 percent. However, you can achieve 99.99-percent availability, and even 99.999-percent availability, with a correctly architected WebSphere implementation. The bottom line is that you simply can't guarantee these availability metrics with a single WebSphere platform channel or single-tier application environment. (You'll explore this in more detail in Chapter 5.)

This isn't to say that a system may not be able to meet these availability percentages. That's far from the case. I've seen servers up and available for close to two years without reboots or application failures. Although these systems aren't mission critical, they do serve important purposes in organizations.

CAUTION   Over the years I've witnessed much "chest beating" regarding uptime measurements of servers. Although it's great to know that various operating systems can provide constant availability, never put pride of availability in front of security and bug fixes! And remember, it's not always server availability that's important—it's user-facing or client-facing availability that's key.

Understanding WebSphere Availability

What are the typical or more common causes of downtime for a WebSphere-based platform? There are several key and somewhat obvious ones, but it's important to understand areas of the platform that are susceptible to outages. Table 2-3 lists the key areas within a WebSphere environment that are susceptible to failures and the likelihood of them occurring.

As you can see, outages aren't caused only by software (both infrastructure software and application software) and hardware. Many different reports and estimates present the causes of downtime; more often than not, the biggest availability killer is first the software, then the infrastructure and environment, and then people errors.

Table 2-3. Estimated Causes of Downtime

Area of Impact	Estimated Percentage
Human/operator error	35 percent
Software failures	40 percent
System and environment failures	25 percent

These areas break down even further; for instance, software failures consist of 85-percent application software and 15-percent infrastructure software (for example, WebSphere, operating systems, and so on). In any light, it's possible to mitigate these areas of risk by employing a well-designed and well-architected WebSphere environment.

But what causes WebSphere downtime? Table 2-4 lists various aspects of a WebSphere-based environment that can cause downtime when they fail. It's important to note that the Likelihood column refers to the chance or likelihood of the impact event occurring. The Overall Impact column refers to the damage done from the impact event. Small indicates that the impact event will generally not cause an outage, Medium indicates it may cause an outage (for example, a partial disruption), and High indicates it may cause the entire system to fail.

Table 2-4. Causes of WebSphere Downtime

Impact Event	Likelihood	Overall Impact	Mitigation
Disk failures (system)	Medium	Medium	Use redundant or mirrored disk(s) and arrays.
Memory failure	Low	High	Depending on platform type, use hot-swappable memory or multiple servers.
CPU failure	Low	High	Depending on platform type, use hot-swappable CPUs or multiple servers.
Network interface failure	Low	Medium	Use redundant network interface cards with redundant routes.
Network infrastructure failure	Low	High	Use redundant network infrastructure (switches, hubs, and so on).
Application database failure	Low	High	Use database clusters, High Availability (HA) clusters, or hot-standby databases.
WebSphere 4 repository failure	Low	Medium	Use database clusters, HA clusters, or hot-standby databases.
WebSphere repository corruption	Low	Medium	Split WebSphere domains and cells.
Denial of Service (DoS) attack	Medium	High	Employ firewalls and split WebSphere domains and cells.
WebSphere administrative server failure	Low	Medium	Split WebSphere domains and cells with redundant servers.
Incorrectly installed application software	Medium to High	High	Split WebSphere domains and cells with redundant servers and deploy to one domain or cell at a time (and test!).

Table 2-4. Causes of WebSphere Downtime (Continued)

Impact Event	Likelihood	Overall Impact	Mitigation
WebSphere configuration error	Medium to High	High	Split WebSphere domains and cells with redundant servers to minimize environment cascade failure.
Application software failure/crashing	Medium to High	High	Split WebSphere clones, domains, and cells with redundant servers.
Web server failure	Low	High	Employ redundant Web servers.
Main power failure	Medium	High	Use multiple power supplies with multiple main suppliers for large systems and or use uninterruptible power supplies and generators.
Environment/ air-conditioning failure	Low to Medium	Medium	Physically distribute your WebSphere and backend application servers.
Security breach	Low to Medium	High	Split domains and cells with redundant servers, split firewall environments (consider virtual local area networks), and use different passwords for all hosts.
System crash and failed backups	Low to Medium	High	Take duplicate regular dumps of WebSphere configuration (for example, use compressed installedApps directories after each new deployment to preserve production-deployed application code).
Environment peak load performance problems	Medium	High	Consider updating or increasing servers and consider distributing your different load types to separate servers.

Table 2-4 is in no way an exhaustive list of potential availability killers, but it should give you an indication of what can go wrong and some potential mitigation strategies. If some of the concepts mentioned in Table 2-4 are new to you, don't be concerned at this point; you can come back to this table as you go through the rest of the book. Specifically, Chapters 5 through 8 explore a lot of the availability concepts mentioned in Table 2-4; I'll explain each of them from an implementation and design point of view.

At this stage, if you're planning your WebSphere implementation and topological architecture, use Table 2-4 as a checklist of items to consider.

Overall, WebSphere is a complex beast, and its operational effectiveness is determined by numerous aspects of an operational environment, including infrastructure (both software and hardware), environmental factors, people, and process factors.

Costs of Availability, Performance, and Scalability

Availability, performance, and scalability cost. Although you'd probably prefer to design and manage a WebSphere-based application platform that can scale on demand, perform constant subsecond transactions, and have 99.999-percent availability, the budget and justification associated with those types of requirements are restricted to the likes of NASA!

Table 2-5 shows the average cost per hour of downtime for several industries. The data comes from a Dataquest report from September 1996. Of course, the average cost per hour of downtime is more than likely higher in 2003 than in 1996. However, Table 2-5 provides an indication of these costs.

Table 2-5. Costs of Downtime

Industry	Business Operation	Average Downtime Cost per Hour (in U.S. Dollars)
Financial	Brokerage operations	$6.45 million
Financial	Credit card/sales authorization	$2.6 million
Media	Pay-per-view TV	$150,000
Retail	Home shopping (TV)	$113,000
Retail	Home catalog sales	$90,000
Transportation	Airline reservations	$89,500
Media	Telephone ticket sales	$69,000
Transportation	Package shipping	$28,000
Finance	ATM fees	$14,500

If, for example, you're operating a brokerage-based WebSphere implementation and you need to ensure that you have greater than 99.95-percent availability, your business justification is that by not having a high-availability WebSphere-based system, the costs of downtime are approximately $6.45 million. In most cases—and obviously it depends on your sizing requirements—$6.45 million will get you a number of high-performance, high-end servers from one of the leading server manufacturers!

In other words, if the downtime costs are so large, then the business case for spending the money proactively to ensure that you have a highly available system is well justified. In fact, you can graph availability in such a way that depicts it as an exponentially growing trend. The exponential factor in it is the cost of ensuring that availability. As availability nears 100 percent, the cost in providing that guarantee soars (almost exponentially).

For the most part, providing availability guarantees of 99 percent is fairly straightforward. Typically speaking, most single-server implementations will support this level of availability as measured over a period of a year. Measuring availability of a server or WebSphere implementation is about measuring the WebSphere availability index (see the "Availability: What Is It?" section) for each component within your environment.

These components include the following:

- Disks

- Memory

- Network controllers (interface cards)

- Motherboards and main boards

- Other controllers, such as Input/Output (I/O), Small Computer System Interface (SCSI), and so on

- Power supplies (internal)

- Environmental systems (air conditioning, main power)

- System cooling

- CPUs

- Software

The overall value of the WebSphere availability index is the mean of all those components. Typically, a system will only guarantee between 99-percent and

99.9-percent availability; in order to exceed that range, you need to go with multiple servers (I'll discuss that in Chapter 5).

Calculating the Cost of Downtime

As you'll see in this and the following section, calculating the cost of downtime is relatively simple if your requirements are simple. Generally speaking, calculating downtime cost is as hard or simple as you need (want) it to be based on your input factors. If you have a great deal of intangible impacts caused by downtime (for example, goodwill), then calculating downtime cost will be harder.

Table 2-6 lists some cost impact factors that can help determine downtime cost.

Table 2-6. Example Downtime Cost Impact Factors

Impact Factor	Relative Cost Impact	Example
Impact to sales	Variable ($1 million to $6 million per hour)	Impacts Amazon.com online book sales.
Impact to services	Variable	Customers unable to watch Webcast of a sporting event.
Impact to goodwill	Intangible	New hot product goes on sale, and the platform fails. There are many upset customers.
Impact to staff	Variable	Long hours during system instability can impact morale of staff members.
Impact to infrastructure	Variable ($100 to $1 million)	Constant power cycling, thrashing, and overloading of disks will shorten their life spans.

Using Table 2-6 as a guide, along with additional site-specific impact costs, your formula for calculating the cost of downtime can take one of several forms. First, if your WebSphere implementation is specific to sales or financial transactions, you can take the mean or average transaction cost and the transaction rate per hour and use that as a per-hour impact cost.

Chapter 2

For example, let's say you're operating an online bookstore and selling about 5,000 books per hour at an average cost of $50 per book.

You could do an easy calculation as follows:

```
Books sold per hour × Average book cost = Outage cost per hour
```

For this example, the calculation is as follows:

```
5,000 × $50 = $250,000 per hour
```

In this case, your downtime cost is $250,000 per hour.

Add on top of this other aspects such as loss of goodwill for those customers who get so annoyed at the outage that they go elsewhere to purchase the book and possibly won't come back. You could apply a *churn* or goodwill percentage to this equation of, say, 0.5 percent per hour for all registered customers you'll lose because of these annoying outages.

If you then knew each customer would purchase a single book per month and you had one million customers, you'd know that your annual sales amount will decrease by $3 million. For example:

```
(Customer base - (Customer base - Outage churn rate percentage)) = Set A
Average number of books per customer per year × Average book cost = Set B
    Sales lost through lost goodwill = Set A × Set B
```

The calculations are as follows:

```
(1,000,000 - ( 1,000,000 - 0.5%) ) = Set A
                 12 × $50 = Set B
  Sales lost through lost goodwill = $3,000,000
```

So, as you can see, the cost of outages is expensive. And although these are fictitious figures, they represent the types of costs your company can incur. Your estimates and calculations may be simpler or more complex, but at the end of the day you need to research all your business and technology cost impacts. Furthermore, based on a per-hour outage during either peak or average utilization periods, calculate your hourly downtime costs.

Understanding Your Availability Needs

What is it you need for your organization? Are you running a mission-critical environment and need less than 99.99-percent availability? Or does your organization just need to have a service available that can be batch based and can be down several hours a day without impacting the bottom line?

46

In fact, understanding your availability needs is one of the easiest parts of designing a highly available WebSphere environment. First, you need to determine the financial impact of the WebSphere platform's downtime to your organization. (The previous section explained some example calculations.) Second, you need to determine how much downtime (outage cost) your company can withstand.

Using the example from the previous section, the total hourly outage cost that included both loss of sales and loss of goodwill came to $3 million per hour. Although this is a high figure, it does illustrate the point well. If this was your company and you were asked to calculate and understand the impact of outages, you'd need to consider this hourly outage period. You'd also need to consider MTTF, which may make the minimum average downtime two hours and not just one. Either way, this is a big figure.

The decision you need to now make is what it'll cost to ensure that your WebSphere implementation doesn't go down! Chances are, with $3.25 million for hourly outage, you'd want to aim for an availability percentage of greater than 99.99 percent. As you saw in Table 2-2, 99.99-percent availability is a small fraction of downtime. Furthermore, as highlighted in Table 2-1, it requires your WebSphere topological architecture to conform to level 5 of the business availability index.

NOTE   Incidentally, the example has the need for a split site configuration and the highest level of platform redundancy—redundant servers, split WebSphere domains and cells, and clustered data services.

Therefore, you can now understand your availability needs using these two tables (Tables 2-1 and 2-2). If your downtime costs are large on a per-hour basis, the only way to minimize your downtime—according to Table 2-2—is to ensure greater than a certain level of availability. At this point, you need to "sign up" for the business availability index that's best suited (according to Table 2-1) to your WebSphere availability percentage requirements.

In summary, this business availability index provides a guide for meeting your availability of service agreements.

Understanding Your Scalability Needs

As you saw earlier in the chapter, scalability is closely associated with availability. More times than not, by virtue of a highly available WebSphere environment, you'll have a highly scalable one.

Scalability, as you've seen, refers to how well (in cost and effort) and how easily (a modular and extensible application) your application platform can grow into existing or additional hardware or infrastructure software changes.

A common error with scaling application platforms is that people purchase too much infrastructure or "overscale" and "overspecify" their topological configuration. This is bad. Overscaling a platform, although great for running extra processes and reducing your capacity management workload, can hide problems and make developers lazy when implementing their application code.

Furthermore, I've seen implementations where a system has been so overspecified that it was in fact hiding all sorts of fundamental application code issues such as memory leaks and poorly performing business logic. The extra capacity insulated the problems from view, and as you know, the longer a problem or bug goes unnoticed or goes through the development life cycle, the more expensive it gets. With this particular application being in production, the cost to fix it would've been large.

It's important to weigh purchasing hardware and infrastructure for scalability versus that of availability. My recommendation is get availability before investing in scalability. My reasons are simple:

- First, as I said before, scalability tends to inherently come with availability. Two servers provide a more scalable solution, off the cuff, than a single server (ignoring technicalities, two times more scalable in fact!).

- Second, a highly scalable single-server solution isn't much good if it doesn't insulate you from single-server outages! A highly available server farm will provide insulation from external and internal impacts that may have the potential to initiate a platform failure in a platform that's not highly available.

- Third, in most cases, you can deploy another server (thus providing more redundancy/availability) and add another line or two to your load-balancing mechanism to point to the new server, and you instantly have additional scalability.

At the end of the day, I could list many reasons why it's more advantageous to spend funds on high availability rather than scalability. There may in fact be legitimate reasons to purchase additional hardware to scale your application. For example, you may already have three WebSphere application servers, and your existing J2EE-based deployed applications require more memory. The solution is to purchase more memory in each of the three WebSphere application servers because this is a vertical scaling requirement (more memory per JVM process). In this case, there's little benefit from purchasing an additional server over that of purchasing additional memory.

In summary, use these tips when considering your scalability and availability requirements side by side:

- If you want to ensure scalability, implement high availability first (either additional servers, additional interfaces, additional disks, or so on). A system isn't scalable if it's nonredundant.

- If your application JVMs require more memory, scale up vertically.

- If your deployed applications require more processing capacity (CPUs), scale vertically first, horizontally second.

- Don't overscale your environment—if you have cash to spend, invest it in high-availability purchases before you scale a nonredundant system.

- Don't overspec your environment to insulate developers from badly written or badly performing code—fix the root cause.

Ten Rules to Live By

The following are ten items I always live by when using WebSphere. These availability tips are ones that, if followed, should point you in the right direction for availability success:

- Mirror your disks.

- Use redundant network interfaces on your servers.

- Use redundant network switches, hubs, and routers.

- Consider systems capable of hot-swappable disks, power supplies, memory, CPUs, and peripheral cards.

- Horizontally scale your environment with multiple physical servers.

- Vertically scale your environment to obtain more scalability of your application components (for example, more memory equals more memory buffer and head room).

- Cluster your platform services such as databases and Lightweight Directory Access Protocol (LDAP) servers.

- Consider disaster recovery and split site deployment for critical systems.

- Split your application environment into two or more WebSphere administrative domains or cells.

- Partition your application and platform environment (for example, utility services, and customer-facing services) to compartmentalize differing workloads.

Summary

This chapter defined what performance and scalability mean in a WebSphere environment and discussed the costs of implementing availability versus the costs of downtime.

This chapter serves as a primer to the rest of the book, providing you with a construct to measure the financial return on undertaking performance management profiling and optimization efforts. The "Ten Rules to Live By" sidebar serves as a solid foundation for your performance and scalability approach. Throughout the rest of this book, you'll explore each of these ten rules in more detail.

WebSphere 4 and 5 Component Architectures

THROUGHOUT THE BOOK, I talk about the major components of WebSphere for versions 4 and 5. It's therefore important to highlight and detail these key component areas, which in later chapters are the focal points, or performance levers, used for tuning and optimizing WebSphere.

Component Architecture Overview

Both versions of WebSphere are complex software platforms, comprised of many components and differing technologies. Ensuring that users are being offered the fastest response times and greatest availability of your application are the most obvious reasons why WebSphere performance and optimization is so important, especially given the myriad component setting combinations.

For a single software platform to be able to efficiently handle hundreds of thousands (and quite probably millions) of user transactions per day with maximum availability—and given the sheer number of interface possibilities available with WebSphere—you need a good optimization strategy.

It's important, however, to understand the two platforms from a component level. Although at the end of the day both WebSphere 4 and 5 perform the same tasks, by virtue of ever-evolving application software, they're different.

So you don't confuse the high-level components and to gain a clear view of the subtle differences in each platform, the followings sections explore the major components of the two versions and their differences.

WebSphere Common Components Between Versions 4 and 5

The following sections give you an overview of the major components that are common between WebSphere 4 and WebSphere 5. Please note, however, that although at a high level the components in this chapter are the same, there are subtle differences between version 4 and version 5. Be sure to read the notes and cautions in subsequent chapters regarding specific features.

CAUTION   One setting used in a component of WebSphere 4 may have disastrous effects if used blindly in WebSphere 5!

Session Database

One of the most useful capabilities associated with server failover and general load-balanced performance is the ability to share user sessions between application servers, server groups, domains, cells, clones, and nodes.

The session database is used for what's known as *session persistence*, which allows a user's session details to be *persisted,* or stored, on a common, accessible database. Within WebSphere, you can tune and optimize session persistence in many areas, as well as the database used to store the persisted user session details.

Not all applications can take advantage of session persistence; however, if you're looking to better support users during failover situations, session persistence is a sound solution.

I'll address session databases in detail during later chapters.

Virtual Hosts

The virtual host capability of WebSphere is somewhat analogous to virtual hosts in a static Web server world. A *virtual host* is essentially a configuration that provides the system manager with the ability to house multiple, logically defined virtual hosts within the same physical server. By default, WebSphere provides several base configurations such as `http://YourLocalServerName:9080/` and `http://YourLocalServerName:9443/` for testing and example purposes.

 NOTE   The term *virtual hosts* is a concept that allows you to configure a single physical machine to appear, listen, and process requests to multiple logical (as opposed to physical) servers. Depending on the underlying technology, this may be multiple logical server instances, or it may be a single server process. In WebSphere, virtual host configurations allow you to make your WebSphere server appear as multiple servers. For example, it could appear as both `www.mydomain.com` and `www.theotherdomain.com`.

The invocation process is the same as it is for static Web server requests; basic content routing—through the Hypertext Transfer Protocol (HTTP) plug-in or by other means—sends the user request for a particular Uniform Resource Locator (URL) to the WebSphere node associated with the URL (for example, YourLocalServerName). WebSphere is configured through the virtual host configuration to listen on the configured port and act on it.

In essence, virtual hosts give WebSphere the ability to house multiple Web-based application domains on a single physical WebSphere application server, and they, combined with WebSphere server groups, allow for vast clusters of WebSphere servers to operate and process requests in a WebSphere farm-type configuration.

Virtual hosts simply allow a more compartmentalized management and operational model for your WebSphere application server environment.

What this means is that when combined with the server group capability, virtual hosts allow the system manager to isolate and manage—in a compartmentalized manner—any Web-based application on a WebSphere cluster.

Administrative Consoles

The system manager has several standard options and interfaces to control and manage the vast number of components available via the administration consoles. Generally speaking, however, there are not many options available to tune these aspects of WebSphere. Furthermore, given that they don't tend to be user facing, they don't rank high in the list of potential areas of performance improvement!

It's important to remember that WebSphere version 4 is managed via a Java/Swing-based Graphical User Interface (GUI), and WebSphere version 5 is managed via a Web-based console. These consoles are where a great deal of your performance and optimization work will occur, so it's best to be familiar with them if you aren't currently.

HTTP Server

The HTTP server is an external-based server, facilitating HTTP requests and redirecting them to the appropriate backend WebSphere application server host and port. Operating a stand-alone Web server can be advantageous in many respects (which you'll see in Chapter 5), but it may introduce unnecessary complexity or security risks into your environment. Obviously, this is an architect's issue and requires resolution prior to implementation!

That said, when you use an external HTTP server, the common topology design is to operate one or more (for redundancy and performance) static Web server, which is configured to use the WebSphere HTTP plug-in (see the next section). This model is typical because it allows integrators and system managers to house their business logic and data behind protected firewall environments, leaving noncritical, commodity Web servers within a secured Demilitarized Zone (DMZ).

By using this approach, traffic coming into the Web server traverses a firewall (or series of firewalls) through port 80 or 443 for Secure Sockets Layer (SSL)/Secure HTTP (HTTPS) to the specific Web server Internet Protocols (IPs). The WebSphere HTTP plug-in, configured using Extensible Markup Language (XML)–defined rules, then takes the HTTP requests from the customer browser and directs them to the configured backend server IP and port number.

The external HTTP server can be one of several third-party HTTP server platforms, including the following:

- The Apache Web server

- The IBM HTTP server

- The Microsoft Internet Information Services (IIS) server

- The Netscape Web server

- The SunOne/iPlanet Web server

WebSphere HTTP Plug-In

The WebSphere HTTP plug-in is a key component in a Web-based WebSphere environment. The plug-in routes and directs user requests from one or a number of Web servers to backend WebSphere application servers.

Essentially the plug-in controls where a user request goes—which port, which server, and so forth—so it doubles as a load balancer, routing requests to the most appropriate application server based on the configured settings.

Figure 3-1 shows a basic load-balanced topology that utilizes the WebSphere HTTP plug-in to distribute requests between multiple back-end application servers.

To achieve load distribution to more than one HTTP Web server, typically you can deploy a hardware-based load balancer in front of the HTTP server to farm out inbound HTTP requests to all configured servers.

Each HTTP server is configured with a copy of the WebSphere HTTP plug-in configuration file, which details the various URL and Universal Resource Identifier (URI) context path names, the associated route group, and the associated server and port to which the HTTP request should be routed.

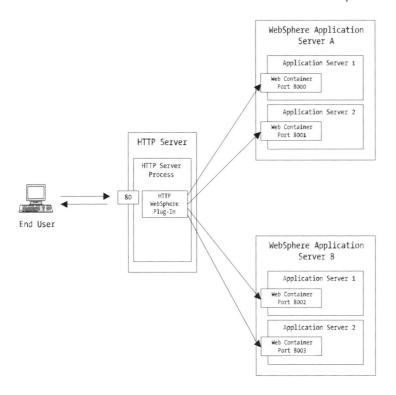

Figure 3-1. Example WebSphere HTTP plug-in topology

Listing 3-1 shows an example WebSphere HTTP plug-in configuration file.

Listing 3-1. Example HTTP Plug-in Configuration File

```xml
<?xml version="1.0"?>
<Config>
    <Log LogLevel="Error" Name="/opt/WebSphere/AppServer/logs/native.log"/>
    <VirtualHostGroup Name="default_host">
        <VirtualHost Name="*:80"/>
        <VirtualHost Name="*:5500"/>
    </VirtualHostGroup>

    <UriGroup Name="MySampleApplication/myApplication_URIs">
        <Uri Name="/myJsps/examples/*"/>
    </UriGroup>

    <ServerGroup Name="mySampleAppServerGrp">
            <Server Name="MyApp">
                <Transport Hostname="AppServer1" Port="5500" Protocol="http"/>
```

```
            </Server>
    </ServerGroup>

    <Route ServerGroup="mySampleAppServerGrp"
        UriGroup="MySampleApplication/myApplication_URIs" ⤵
        VirtualHostGroup="default_host"/>

</Config>
```

The WebSphere HTTP plug-in configuration file shown in Listing 3-1 has five main sections. Let's now look at the important parts of this file.

Section One

The first section is the noncontext configuration section. In the example, it's as follows:

```
<Log LogLevel="Error" Name="/opt/WebSphere/AppServer/logs/native.log"/>
```

I'll discuss the meaning of the various directives in later chapters; however, for the purpose of this chapter, know that this line declares the location for the plug-in log file and the debug or logging level required.

Section Two

The second section lists the directive that specifies the default virtual host. Again, I'll discuss this in more detail later in the book; however, for now, know that the following directive establishes the default host name and the ports that are applicable to the backend WebSphere application server:

```
<VirtualHostGroup Name="default_host">
        <VirtualHost Name="*:80"/>
        <VirtualHost Name="*:5500"/>
    </VirtualHostGroup>
```

This directive lists two virtual host ports: port 80 and port 5500. Port 80 is the default port implemented, and port 5500, as you'll see shortly, is the port for the example application.

What this directive means is that for the default host (whatever that may be), two ports are valid and configured.

This configuration must also match that which is configured in the HTTP Transport settings of the backend WebSphere application server node.

NOTE I discuss the WebSphere application server HTTP `Transport` settings in more detail in later chapters. Briefly, however, the HTTP `Transport` settings, along with other parameters, manage the queue and connections from into the WebSphere application server port (in other words, port 5500).

Section Three

The third section declares the possible URI groups. The `UriGroup` directive declares the URL contexts that this WebSphere plug-in should trap as part of user requests. A URL context is defined as being the nonhost component of the URL. For example:

```
http://www.mysite.com/myJsps/examples/HelloWorld.jsp
```

The URL context is the defining characteristic of what the HTTP plug-in should do with the request.

A `UriGroup` directive looks like this:

```
<UriGroup Name="MySampleApplication/myApplication_URIs">
        <Uri Name="/myJsps/examples/*"/>
    </UriGroup>
```

This directive basically defines a URI group with the name of `MySampleApplication/myApplication_URIs` and declares that any URL context that matches the expression of `http://…./myJsps/examples/*`, such as the previous URL, will be trapped and associated with this URI group.

Section Four

The fourth section has the responsibility of setting up the routing of the requests. That is, now that the plug-in has the user's URL request, a route association needs to be defined so that the user request can be forwarded to the appropriately configured server.

The `Route` directive looks like this:

```
<Route ServerGroup="mySampleAppServerGrp"
        UriGroup="MySampleApplication/myApplication_URIs" ↵
        VirtualHostGroup="default_host"/>
```

What this is declaring is that a server group known or defined as mySampleAppServerGrp is associated with a URI group name of mySampleApplication/myApplication_URIs. As noted previously, there's a URI group defined with the group name of mySampleApplication/myApplication_URIs. Therefore, this Route directive associates the server group name with the URI group name.

This is then used for the final section.

Section Five

This final section of a basic WebSphere HTTP plug-in configuration file sends the user's request, based on the data built up over the four previous sections, to an appropriate application server and port.

This final section is a server group definition, and it looks like this:

```
<ServerGroup Name="mySampleAppServerGrp">
    <Server Name="MyApp">
        <Transport Hostname="AppServer1" Port="5500" Protocol="http"/>
    </Server>
</ServerGroup>
```

Because there can be (and most like will be) many ServerGroup directives in a HTTP plug-in configuration file, the ServerGroup directive name is matched via the Route directive as detailed in the fourth section.

To summarize, the final action on the part of the plug-in itself is to match the server group name with the route, as defined by the Route directive, and then forward (proxy) the request to the application server and port, defined by the Transport declaration, within the ServerGroup directive.

Depending on your configuration and how many application servers are operating in your backend, there may be multiple Server or Transport declarations defined (for example, multiple Hostname, Port, and Protocol statements).

NOTE   Please note that this is a basic plug-in configuration file. You'll need to configure this plug-in file specifically for your environment—the previous example will not function in your WebSphere server environment.

Application Server

The application server is the key component of any WebSphere implementation.

The application server is the encapsulating construct that the Java Virtual Machine (JVM) provides the runtime from for deployed Java 2 Enterprise Edition

(J2EE) and Java-based applications. The application server comprises various containers, such as Enterprise JavaBean (EJB) and Web containers, as well as other communications-based components. Further, the application server services requests for other WebSphere and J2EE technologies such as the following:

- Tracing services

- JavaMail services

- Java Database Connectivity (JDBC) and pooling

- Messaging interfaces—for example, Java Message Service (JMS)

- Java Management Extensions (JMX) administrative services

- CORBA Object Request Broker (ORB) services

- Java Naming and Directory Interface (JNDI) services

- JVM Performance Interface (JVMPI)

Essentially, the application server calls on these services as the deployed application components request them. Although many of the services listed aren't technically operating within the JVM space that the application server is operating within, the client, or *stub,* components exist for the purposes of service request and activation when needed by your deployed applications.

Given the overall platform importance and centralization of the WebSphere application server, this is one of the key areas I'll focus on for optimizing, tuning, and configuring WebSphere.

Finally, the application server also manages the key containers that are central to J2EE environments, including the EJB container, the Web container, and, for WebSphere 5, the Java Connector Architecture (JCA) container.

I'll discuss each of these containers in more detail in later sections of this chapter.

Web Container

The Web container is one of the well-known components of a J2EE environment.

Quite simply, the Web container is responsible for processing presentation-based components such as Java Server Pages (JSPs), servlets, and other types of presentation such as static content from Hypertext Markup Language (HTML) and Extensible HTML (XHTML) files.

Because the Web container operates in its own JVM (to which you can have multiple), it provides several Java object management services such as garbage collection and object allocation/deallocation for servlets and JavaBeans.

Although the Web container is synonymous with *Web-based technologies*, it's capable of running standard Java technologies such as JavaBeans and data connectivity services such as JDBC. In smaller environments, many application architects choose not to use EJBs—and hence the EJB container—and elect to operate all code and functionality from within the Web container.

There's nothing technically wrong with this approach; however, a few limitations from both a performance and an application functionality point of view affect this decision. These mainly relate to application distribution and integration to legacy systems. This type of approach is acceptable because you can use several alternative application and platform design options.

Figure 3-2 shows an example Web container implementation within WebSphere.

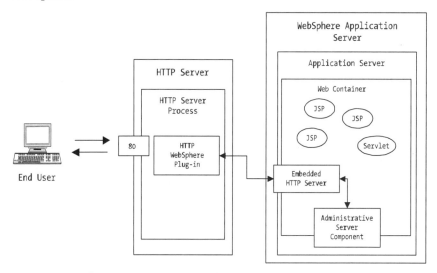

Figure 3-2. Web container services within WebSphere

As depicted, the system manager configures the Web container with options and settings such as ports, type and setup of connectivity between the Web server and the Web container (for example, queuing and threads), and session management.

Embedded HTTP Server

Within the application server exists an embedded HTTP server. This component provides a good platform for testing code during deployments as well as in the event that connectivity is lost between the front and static Web server(s) and the application servers.

CAUTION Although the embedded HTTP server makes Web server–like services available, you shouldn't use this component alone as the frontend Web server. This should be handled by something such as SunOne/iPlanet Web server, Apache, or IBM HTTPD. Essentially, the embedded HTTP server doesn't have the configuration capability or performance to manage the vast numbers of incoming connections that are synonymous with static Web servers. Security is also another reason not to operate the HTTP server in this manner. Always use a standard Web server (or many) to rate limit and control the inbound connections to your Web containers.

EJB Container

The EJB container is synonymous with the Web container in that it provides and facilitates the runtime requirements and services for operating EJBs.

One of the big selling points of EJBs is that an EJB container handles all the low-level work that the developer typically needs to do. This includes what I like to call the *plumbing*, and it includes all the things that relate to file management, database connectivity (this depends of course on CMP, BMP, or JDBC direct), threading, transaction management, and so on. This type of development is typically the most developer-intensive aspect of coding applications that require any of these services.

The other important point to note is that the EJB container operates from within the application server. Essentially, the EJB container provides an operational construct for the EJBs.

The EJBs communicate to the outside world via an intermediate layer. Figure 3-3 shows the way in which EJB clients communicate to EJBs within the EJB container.

It's important for system managers to get an overview of the EJB technology in the context of the WebSphere EJB container. Therefore, as a high-level overview of how the EJB works in relation to the WebSphere EJB container, you'll look at a simple EJB transaction.

As depicted, once the client has obtained a reference to the business components' home object (Point 1), the client/client application requests the home object to find (Point 2) or create (Point 3) an EJB.

The home object creates or finds the EJB, and a reference to the remote object (in other words, the remote EJB object) is returned to the client (Point 4). The client then calls a business method to the EJB object. This EJB object works with the container to manage the transaction, the communications, and the thread between the client and the EJB itself. The EJB object at this point proxies the business method call and the associated values to the bean for processing.

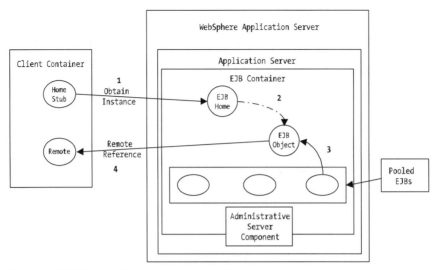

Figure 3-3. EJB container insulation and implementation

The EJB itself then processes the request using properties and values stored in the JNDI context, and then, once processing has been completed, the return values are proxied back to the EJB object, which, in turn, returns the values to the client.

The stage where the proxy between the client, EJB object, and the EJB itself takes place is a fairly complex phase of the transaction. You can tweak many performance levers at this point, both in code and in the EJB container and application server, to optimize or tune the transaction.

Overall, EJBs are one of the more complex areas of J2EE application development. The bulk of the complexity lies in the application code itself; however, the system manager should be familiar with what's actually going on in the EJB container for obvious reasons!

Application Database

The application database, or databases, provide the deployed applications with their long- and short-term application storage. This could be anything, including application configuration, profile information, customer information, or application data. I'll cover the myriad parameters and options available for managing performance with these application databases in later chapters.

Although the application database isn't specifically a WebSphere component, it's important to note that the application database (or the accessing of it) is one of the main causes of poorly performing WebSphere application environments. Poorly modeled data schemas and poorly tuned database configurations can quickly be the demise of a deployed WebSphere application's performance.

Session Database

The session database is the critical data storage mechanism for multiapplication server environments. User session information—that is, information pertaining to a user's environment and session state—needs to be persisted or distributed so multiple application server instances or nodes can reference that data. If you're looking to load balance users between multiple nodes or if you're simply operating multiple application servers within a singular node, you need to use session persistence if the information that a user builds up in their session is important for using the application.

Typically, the data is persisted to a database such as Oracle, DB2, or Sybase. Through the JSESSION session ID, which is the standard session identifier, the WebSphere environment can re/dereference information that's persisted from multiple nodes or application servers that are configured to interface with a common session persistence data store.

Obviously, if the relational database that's used to maintain this persisted data isn't tuned correctly, or the JDBC parameters on the WebSphere end aren't correctly configured, then user response times will degrade almost exponentially as the load increases.

WebSphere 5 provides a new technology known as the Data Replication Service (DRS). It's possible to use this memory-to-memory type replication capability between multiple application server nodes in place of using a relational database to persist the session information. Depending on your availability requirements (and needs), a hybrid solution may be the chosen option where session information is persisted and published onto the configured DRS queue.

I'll discuss more of these options in later chapters.

Web Module

WebSphere 4 introduced a new component definition, known as a *Web module*. The Web module is effectively a WebSphere representation of a Web Archive (WAR) file. A Web module provides an ability to stop, start, and manage Web-specific applications (contained in WAR files) independently of an entire Enterprise Application Resource (EAR) file.

Even when you deploy WAR files that are contained within a J2EE EAR file, the WAR files are extracted and can be managed via the Web module services. The Web module allows a system manager to change settings specific to a WAR file's contents without affecting the rest of the application (for example, EJBs, other WARs, and so on). Within each Web module or WAR, you'll typically house servlets, JSPs, and static HTML content.

EJB Module

The EJB module isn't unlike a Web module. The EJB module is used to compartmentalize one or more EJB. Typically, the module is encapsulated as an EJB Java Archive (JAR) and includes all the deployment descriptors and the EJBs themselves.

By compartmentalizing EJBs into EJB modules, it allows the system manager to stop and start specific, usually associated, EJB groups during runtime.

How you package the EJB modules has some bearing on the operational integrity of your system, so, therefore, there are best practices associated with this. There aren't a great deal of performance options associated with the EJB modules themselves; however, given they operate within the EJB container, I'll focus on this aspect of EJB technology within this book.

WebSphere 4-Specific Component Architecture

IBM WebSphere 4 arrived on the market boasting some significant architectural differences from its predecessor, WebSphere 3.54. With the large number of fairly fundamental changes from version 3.54 to version 4 came the added benefit of a much improved platform in the way of performance and robustness.

Prior to version 4 of WebSphere, BEA WebLogic's application server was the market leader, touted as having the best high-availability features. With version 4 of WebSphere, the gap closed significantly, and now both BEA WebLogic and IBM WebSphere are on an equal playing field.

As discussed in earlier chapters, WebSphere 4 follows the standard J2EE component architecture. This is good for J2EE compliance, and IBM has been able to obtain market differentiation from other vendors with WebSphere's underlying engine components (a.k.a. containers) and some proprietary features such as domains, server groups, and clones (which I'll discuss later in this chapter).

The following sections present the major components specific to WebSphere 4.

WebSphere Control Program

As an alternative to the graphical administration console of WebSphere, WebSphere 4 offers a command-line management interface known as WebSphere Control Program (WSCP). WSCP is a command-line interface providing access to all settings and commands available under the graphical-based consoles.

You'll realize the power of WSCP for tasks such as deployment and bulk work. You can write scripts to interface with WSCP that allow you to noninteractively install, modify, or manage your WebSphere environment.

For example, if you wanted to install a new EAR at 3 a.m., you could create a script, Unix shell, or Windows/DOS batch and trigger the shutdown of a particular application server, the removal of an existing EAR, the installation of a new or updated version of the EAR, and a restart of that EAR. From time to time in the book, I'll refer to using the WSCP interface for its ease of changing parameters. If you haven't used WSCP before, I highly recommend you try it. You can find it in your WebSphere bin directory under the Windows (`<WebSphere_HOME>/bin/wscp.bat`) or Unix (`<WebSphere_HOME/bin/wscp.sh>`) platforms.

XMLConfig

The XMLConfig tool in WebSphere provides an alternative system management facility to the WebSphere administration console. You can configure all the components of WebSphere 4 in a batch-like mode using this tool. You can't do much to tune or optimize the performance of this component, but I mention it here for completeness.

Server Groups

WebSphere 4 improved the concept of server groups, and it provides additional management capabilities of the server group platform capability over that of version 3.54.

A *server group* is a logical grouping of near-identical copies of an application server and its configuration, deployed applications, and resources. In fact, a server group consists of the same structure and constructs as a normal application server. That is, the server group, like an application server, consists of components such as EJB and Web containers and the deployed configuration that's part of an application server (see the "Application Server" section for more details).

The key difference between a server group and an application server is that a server group isn't associated with any particular node. The logical representation of an application server through a server group provides the system manager with the ability to maintain groups of application servers distributed across multiple nodes.

The grouping also allows the system manager to stop, start, and make changes to common application servers distributed across a WebSphere cluster of common components, rather than having to configure similar application servers on disparate physical nodes one by one.

Figure 3-4 depicts the association between server groups and other components within WebSphere 4.

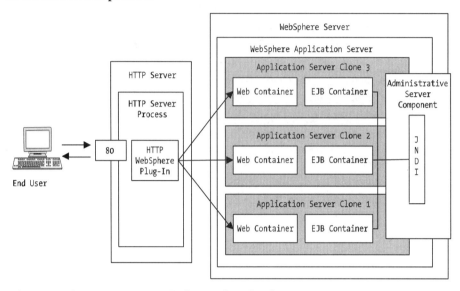

Figure 3-4. Server group association with WebSphere 4 components

A server group consists of a single application server configuration template; however, it can be operating or distributed to multiple WebSphere nodes. In Figure 3-4, there are three application server clones within a single application server group. The server group is a logical template and configuration mapping construct for cloned application servers (JVMs).

Each application server operating in the environment can be configured as a clone (see the next section), which allows the association to extend to one server group consisting of multiple application server clones, all operating on multiple physical nodes. This capability within WebSphere provides the ability to distribute common WebSphere components—that is, application servers—to multiple physical nodes, hence providing greater levels of availability and heightened performance.

The server group is the key component in giving WebSphere 4 its ability to scale both vertically and horizontally. I'll discuss the various options of WebSphere server groups in greater detail throughout the book.

Clones

Not unlike version 3.5, WebSphere 4 provides the ability to clone components of an environment. With WebSphere 4 cloning, system managers can create clones of server groups based on preconfigured operating instances. The key difference between a clone and a server group is that a clone—unlike a server group—consists of actual operating processes and components.

When used in conjunction with server groups, system managers are able to change the master server group configuration, and via the server group capability, the configuration change is then replicated (or synchronized) to all other clones operating within that server group.

What this capability allows the system manager to do is distribute application servers, or clones of an application server, across multiple servers to provide horizontal scaling or create multiple clones of an application server within a single node to provide vertical scaling.

Cloning supports both horizontal and vertical cloning simultaneously.

NOTE   It's possible to use clones without server groups; however, more effort is required to maintain multiple independent configurations. Server groups provide the encompassing, centralized management control of multiple clones.

One of WebSphere's key features in workload management is the ability to load balance (a.k.a. workload management) between multiple servers and clones. For example, Figure 3-5 shows a high-level process of how you can use cloning (via server groups) to extend the load-balancing capability of WebSphere.

Figure 3-5 shows the flow of an inbound request from the frontend Web server HTTP plug-in. The request, based on a context of /myApplication/logon.jsp, is routed through to one of the clones on the application server. Clone 3 responds with the result of processing logon.jsp.

If clone 3 in Figure 3-4 became unavailable (for example, if the JVM crashed), clones 1 and 2 would continue to operate. The HTTP plug-in on the front of the Web server would detect the "dead" clone and route further requests through to either clone 1 or clone 2 available in the Work Load Management (WLM) pool.

CAUTION   It's possible to modify a clone directly; however, in doing so you immediately introduce risk into your environment with having clones operating with different configurations. You should make changes to clones through the server group settings. This method then synchronizes the changes down to the associated clones.

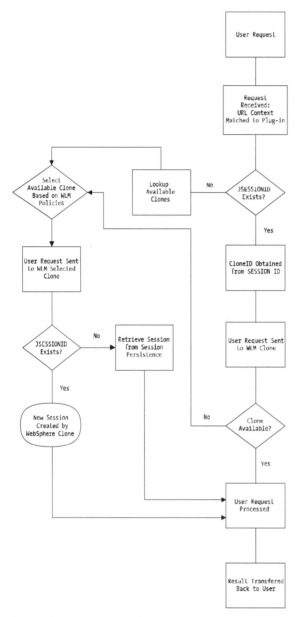

Figure 3-5. WebSphere 4 cloning and workload management flowchart

Administrative Repository

WebSphere 4 operates using an administrative repository to store and facilitate global WebSphere configuration settings. Unless you operate many WebSphere 4 nodes within a domain, the repository database doesn't require a high-performance database environment. It does help, however, to ensure that it's operating on a highly available database, typically a high availability or active cluster.

In a basic WebSphere environment, the repository can operate on the local server; however, larger environments should look toward operating the repository on a dedicated database server or, preferably, a high-availability database cluster.

I'll discuss options for tuning the repository in later chapters of the book; however, the basic topology for a repository is almost trivial and can operate on Microsoft SQL, Oracle, DB2, Sybase, or Informix database platforms.

Administration Server

The WebSphere 4 administration server is the centralized management server for WebSphere.

The administration server is a critical component of WebSphere. It provides, among other features, functions such as stopping and starting application servers, nodes, server groups, and so forth. The administration server is also responsible for controlling, operating, and facilitating the operational runtime of the workload management and the general runtime control of the WebSphere server.

In a multinode deployment of WebSphere 4, each node operates an independent administration server that also manages the interaction and state of the other nodes in a WebSphere domain.

WebSphere 5-Specific Component Architecture

As mentioned earlier, WebSphere 5 includes some fairly significant changes in its architecture from that of WebSphere 4. The most noticeable changes pertain to JMS services, data stores (repositories and so on), and the concept of a cell, node, and deployment manager.

Overall, there are essentially two WebSphere 5 server implementation types. The first, as shown in Figure 3-6, is the standard WebSphere 5 and is typically associated with simple, single server installations.

The second implementation type, as shown in Figure 3-7, is the WebSphere network deployment configuration. This implementation type is used for multi-server configurations or when your environment requirements become more complex (horizontal and vertical scaling).

Like WebSphere 4, version 5 follows a standard J2EE deployment architecture but also includes some additional advanced proprietary features to extend key features such as high availability, clustering, and redundancy. Through the following sections, I'll discuss the various key components of the WebSphere 5 platform.

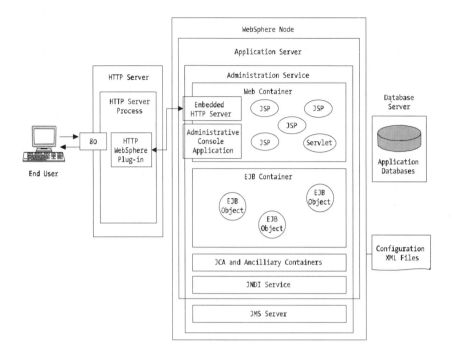

Figure 3-6. WebSphere 5 standard deployment component architecture

Cell

The *cell* is a new technology in WebSphere 5. It provides one of the key combined high-availability and management (administrative) features of WebSphere 5. Basically, a cell is analogous to a WebSphere 4 domain. In WebSphere 4, a domain was a grouping of associated application servers in a commonly administered group, or *domain*. This group capability allowed system managers to effectively split their WebSphere environment into separated administrative zones that removed single points of failure associated with common administrative repositories.

The technology allowed a system manager to shut down a section of an operating WebSphere environment and upgrade that section independently of the still-functioning environment.

The alternative is to have a single domain environment. In that case, regardless of how many application servers, clones, and server groups are configured, if the WebSphere 5 environment is configured as a singular administrative domain, then an outage in the administrative repository (in other words, in a deployment manager, node agent, or something in between) would mean the entire application environment would fail. Therefore, for WebSphere 4, it's advantageous for larger environments where horizontal as well as vertical scaling is used for multiple administrative domains.

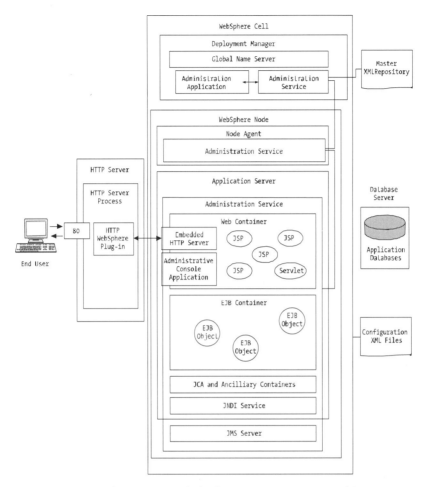

Figure 3-7. WebSphere 5 network deployment component architecture

In WebSphere 5, the concept of a domain has been replaced with a cell and has a few additional features over that of a domain. A WebSphere cell encompasses the entire WebSphere 5 environment from an administrative point of view.

A cell is an autonomous administrative WebSphere zone; because of this, if you increase or partition your WebSphere operating environment into more administrative cells, you'll incur management overhead.

What this means is that because each cell is administered independently, you must deploy software to each cell, hence requiring more checks and effort for each application change. Obviously, the trade-off, albeit positive, is that you can isolate hardware and software failures using cells. With the alternative, each major software or hardware fault in a common component (for example, the repository database) will cause a total outage.

You can extend the multicell approach to more than two cells, but as indicated previously, the more cells, the more overhead.

NOTE You can reduce this management overhead associated with multiple cells by configuring WebSphere semi/automated scripts (which I'll also discuss in this book). I've seen one WebSphere 5 implementation configure a local administrative portal page, which allows operations staff to administer and manage a multicell environment from a single location. Without this approach, management of the environment increases proportionally to the number of cells!

If the deployment manager process for one particular cell failed, on most occasions those particular WebSphere application servers in the fault cell would also fail.

NOTE This isn't always the case; I'll cover the details regarding this in future chapters.

However, all application services (for example, the applications themselves, the WebSphere application servers, and so on) would continue to operate as normal, within the remaining cell.

CAUTION For this type of environment topology to function correctly, you must ensure that if cell A failed, all physical servers in cell B would be able to continue operating, conducting business as usual, with the extra load. Furthermore, you'll need to ensure that as part of your server capacity modeling, you capture not only the runtime load but the added overhead of the initial failover load (in other words, servers in cell B handling the additional peak requests as all traffic and load is diverted).

This is an important configuration and tuning aspect of WebSphere and therefore will be discussed in more detail during later chapters.

Node

A *node* is typically associated with a physical server entity that operates, on that physical server, WebSphere application servers, and other common server processes. A node will contain the following:

- One or more application servers, possibly consisting of multiple Web, EJB, and JCA containers

- JMS server(s)

- Administrative services

- JNDI server(s)

- Security services

In a network deployment configuration, a node will also consist of a node agent (see the next section). A network deployment implementation of WebSphere will also consist of multiple nodes, with each node consisting of one or more application servers, all managed and orchestrated within an administration cell by a deployment manager.

Node Agent

A *node agent* is the coordinating agent process for a network deployment configuration of WebSphere. The node agent has no management services available to applications, essentially making it transparent to deployed J2EE components. The node agent also facilitates performance monitoring (used by JVMPI) and deployed configuration management (synchronization between nodes for the deployment manager). The agent communicates to the application, JMS, and other servers, as well as the deployment manager, to manage and coordinate the operations of the node on which the agent resides.

This should highlight the agent's role in configuration synchronicity between the various application servers within a node.

Deployment Manager

The deployment manager, like the node, is fundamental in a network deployment configuration of WebSphere. The deployment manager in essence provides the sole central point of control for all administrative functions pertaining to all components within a cell.

The deployment manager governs the content mastered within the various repositories on each node within a call. The synchronization is managed via the node agent operating within each node in the cell.

Given that the deployment manager governs many of the centralized administrative functions in a cell, it therefore hosts the administration console.

Web Service Engine

The Web Service engine provides J2EE draft–compliant Web Services. It's important to briefly discuss the status of the Web Service components on the WebSphere 5 platform.

Because Web Services, at the time of writing this book, weren't completely ratified, only draft specifications of the technology exist. Therefore, IBM—in my opinion, correctly—used an open-source series of Application Programming Interfaces (APIs) available from the Apache Axis project.

Axis is a series of APIs that provide Web Services, such as capabilities that provide the key ingredients to a Web Service implementation. They include the following:

- Universal Description, Discovery, and Integration (UDDI)

- Simple Object Access Protocol (SOAP)

- Web Services Inspection Language (WSIL)

- Web Services Description Language (WSDL)

- Web Services Invocation Framework (WSIF)

The Axis framework APIs and components are instantiated, on request, within the Web container. Future releases of WebSphere will possibly operate the Web Service engine in some other form (for example, either as a Web Service container or as a Web Service server analogous to the JMS server).

UDDI Registry

Given the hype around Web Services and their potential increased integration into the enterprise, IBM has included a UDDI Registry as part of WebSphere 5 to help sites better use and integrate Web Service technologies into legacy environments.

The UDDI Registry is in fact a J2EE application developed by IBM that the system manager needs to deploy into each application server for custom or third-party applications to use.

 NOTE   If you're not familiar with what UDDI is, think of it as the *Yellow Pages* for SOAP or any of the Web Service protocols. UDDI is somewhat analogous to NIS/NIS+ in Unix environments.

JCA Container

The JCA container is a lesser-known component of the J2EE world. JCA allows components to communicate, primarily from EJBs, to myriad legacy systems typically associated with enterprise information systems. One example is to communicate from an EJB to some form of transaction processing–based legacy mainframe.

IBM and other J2EE application server vendors provide many forms of connectivity solutions such as JDBC and MQ Series; however, there may be a case where an enterprise houses disparate legacy backend systems that include specialized schemas or highly normalized database systems such as when working with Online Analytical Processing (OLAP) cubes.

In essence, the JCA container is a "catch all" for connectivity within a J2EE environment where native drivers may not exist.

Name Services Server

The name services server is pivotal to J2EE environments. JNDI provides a distributed contextual tree for storing all types of information relevant to J2EE resources such as JMS queues, general application properties, EJB states, JDBC locators, and much more.

Each application server operates its own JNDI namespace and stores the previous information.

Distributing JNDI information between multiple nodes is an area of interest for performance and scalability. I'll go through the options in later chapters of this book.

Security Services Server

WebSphere 5 has a number of security services available to developers. The security server provides the hooks between applications and the WebSphere application containers to facilitate authentication and authorization into varying levels of the WebSphere environment (in other words, administration, application access, fine-grain and coarse-grained access control, and so on).

JMS Server

JMS is a technology that allows communication on both a point-to-point and publish/subscribe model. The key areas in WebSphere 5 where JMS is used are internal communications (messages) within the components of a WebSphere cell and when using message-driven beans.

JMS has a multitude of uses—it integrates well with IBM MQ Series, and many Enterprise Application Integration (EAI) vendors use JMS as the entry protocol into their proprietary EAI bus architectures.

The JMS server also is integrated into the transaction management services provided by WebSphere. This provides the integration layer into heavy transactions such as MQ Series. In context, when a series of MQ requests makes up an entire transaction, one failing will cause the transaction management service to roll back the entire transaction.

In a network deployment configuration, the JMS server operates under its own JVM space, independent of the application server JVM where, under a base configuration of WebSphere, the JMS server operates within the same JVM as the application server.

Administrative Services

The administration service provides the interface and capability for all the configuration services within WebSphere. Under a base configuration deployment, an administration service runs within the core application server, differing from a network deployment whereby the administration service operates in each of the four key servers: the node service, the deployment manager, the application servers, and the JMS server.

The administration service stores the WebSphere configuration in a set of XML files stored natively on the operating server's file system. This is different from the WebSphere 4 platform where the repository or configuration information is stored in a relational database.

You can also configure the administration service to use differing levels of access to the service. Please see your WebSphere administration manual for more information about this.

 NOTE   As discussed in the "Deployment Manager" section, once under a network deployment configuration, the deployment manager takes control of all administrative functions. So, although an administration service may be actively operating on each of the four key servers (in other words, JMS, application, node service, and deployment manager), under a network deployment configuration the deployment manager will transparently manage the administrative functions on all four servers via the deployment manager.

Data Stores and Repositories

An environment such as WebSphere has several needs for short- and long-term storage of information. The following four sections present an overview of the key repositories used in WebSphere 5.

Configuration Repository

The configuration repository is the replacement for the WebSphere 4 relational database-stored configuration repository. IBM has chosen for WebSphere 5 to replace a relational schema with flat-XML configuration files.

These files are managed by the administration service operating under the deployment manager (under a network deployment configuration) and by the administration service operating under the core application server (under a base deployment configuration).

All aspects of the server's configuration are stored in these XML files.

CAUTION   Although it's technically possible to edit the XML-based repositories by hand, unless you're completely sure about what you're editing, you should use the Web-based administration console to manage these configuration repositories.

Master Repository

In a network deployment configuration where one or more cells exist, the master repository maintains the entire cell's configuration information.

As discussed in the "Configuration Repository" section, the configuration repository stores all relevant configuration data for a particular node's environment. Under a network deployment configuration, the configuration repository changes to maintain a synchronized view of the master repository with the deployment manager of each cell mastering all data.

Node-specific information is still mastered in the configuration repository; however, the changes for node-specific items are routed via the cell's deployment manager and then synchronized back down to each node. Under the network deployment configuration mode, the local configuration repositories are read-only, and only the deployment manager can write to the configuration repository.

NOTE Throughout the book I use both the terms *configuration repository* and *node repository*. When I talk about a configuration repository, I'm referring to the configuration repository of a WebSphere implementation using a base configuration model. Node repository refers to a configuration repository under a network deployment implementation model to highlight that I'm referring to the node-specific configuration rather than the cell or master repository.

Other Components

A number of products are available from IBM and other vendors that can aid in promoting high availability and robustness. Load balancers, content distributors, and content proxy solutions are just some of the available platform tools. You'll look at some of them now.

IBM Edge Components

IBM's Edge components include software-based network services such as load balancers and caching servers. In this book, I briefly cover some design and environment considerations relating to Edge components; however, because these aren't technically WebSphere, I've excluded the finer details.

Effectively what this method achieves is to load balance user requests between multiple frontend Web servers. Common alternatives to this software option are to use hardware appliances from vendors such as Cisco Systems/ArrowPoint (for example, the CS-11500 content switch), Radware, Intel, and many more.

In summary, there are many ways to fulfill your frontend load-balancing requirements; IBM WebSphere Edge components can provide you with a near turnkey solution to do this if you're happy with operating these layer 4–8 services (of the Open Systems Interconnection (OSI) model) via software on low-end systems. Chapter 5 covers the concept and technology associated with frontend load balancers such as the Edge server.

WebSphere Cluster Environment

In WebSphere 5, the notion of a WebSphere cluster has somewhat dwindled because the concept of a cell and the services pertaining to cells.

In WebSphere 4, server groups and clones are the foundation of a cluster. In WebSphere 5, server groups and clones have been replaced with other technologies; however, the term *cluster* is still loosely attributed to a situation where you have a cluster of physical servers, all operating the same J2EE applications. These physical servers in the cluster aren't necessarily aware of one another. The glue that allows them to be termed a *cluster* is typically mastered through frontend standard or geographical load balancing. The session state may or may not be persisted in this situation.

In summary, the term *cluster* in WebSphere 5 is a logical grouping rather than a capability. It's the same as a cell of nodes participating in application workload management, without the umbrella management of the cell and deployment manager. I'll discuss this in detail in Chapter 5.

Comparing the Versions

Now that I've discussed the high-level component architecture of the two versions of the WebSphere platform, Table 3-1 summarizes the key differences between them.

Table 3-1. WebSphere Platform Comparison

Component Type	WebSphere 4 Offering	WebSphere 5 Offering	Notes
Frontend HTTP plug-in	HTTP server plug-in (uses HTTP)	HTTP server plug-in (uses HTTP)	Both platforms offer the same capability via the plug-in.
Workload management/ high-availability capabilities	Domains, server groups, clones, HTTP plug-in	Cells, nodes, deployment manager, HTTP plug-in	Version 5 does away with server groups and clones.
Data storage	WebSphere administration repository, application database, session database	XML-based configuration repository, XML-based master repository, application database, session database, DRS	The key difference is in configuration storage medium in version 5.
Administration capabilities	X-based GUI, WSCP, XMLConfig	Web-based console, wsadmin	Version 5 has greatly expanded on the management control interfaces.
Server-to-server replication	Custom application, shared session database, load-balanced JNDI contexts	DRS, custom application, shared session database	DRS is a powerful tool featured in version 5. It provides memory-to-memory object replication technologies.

Summary

As you can tell, WebSphere 4 and 5 are similar in their baseline architectures. WebSphere 5 has, however, a different underlying technology in the areas of high availability and distributed platforms. Cells and DRS are two key examples of the advanced features of WebSphere 5.

This isn't to say, however, that WebSphere 4 doesn't stand up in the areas of high availability and redundancy—quite the contrary. As you'll see during later chapters, WebSphere 4 can function within about 90 percent of the high-availability capability of WebSphere 5.

If you're thinking about upgrading from WebSphere 4 to 5 based on some of the points in this chapter, my recommendation is this: Unless you have a compelling reason to do so, such as the need to take advantage of newer J2EE component technologies or there's a licensing or support complication in not upgrading, then stay where you are on version 4. IBM continues to support WebSphere 4 by releasing new versions, fixing bugs, and adding features.

This chapter has given you a good foundation of the major components within both versions of WebSphere. The chapter has summarized each of the components discussed in later chapters. It's these areas or components within WebSphere that allow you to tweak, tune, and optimize the environment to achieve a highly stable, robust, and high-performing environment. Use this chapter as a reference while you explore the performance and optimization capabilities of WebSphere.

CHAPTER 4

WebSphere Infrastructure Design

IN THIS CHAPTER, YOU'LL LOOK at the three most common platform architectures onto which you'll deploy WebSphere application servers. Specifically, you'll look at the x86 from Intel/Wintel and Advanced Micro Devices (AMD), the SPARC from Sun, and the PowerPC from IBM. For example, why choose an Intel Xeon over that of a Pentium 4?

This chapter's aim is to provide you with a fairly in-depth understanding of the three platforms and provide guidelines for the configuration best suited to your specific environment when deploying or designing a WebSphere implementation.

I've approached this chapter in the following way: Each main section—covering Intel/AMD, Sun SPARC, and IBM PowerPC—discusses the three platforms in some detail. I'll discuss the most recent processors available from each platform and their advantages and disadvantages. I'll then present the CPU models in each platform family that should be used for specific purposes—for instance, I'll present the model of processor in the Intel family that should be used for small, medium, and large WebSphere environments. I'll also present other important system architecture components, including network and disk technologies.

By the end of the chapter, you should understand the best-practice topology or platform architecture choices best suited to a WebSphere environment and be versed in the platform of your choice from the point of view of the Central Processing Unit (CPU) architecture, storage, network infrastructure, memory and Input/Output (I/O) controller, and interface.

This chapter isn't intended to provide you with a deep architectural understanding of the different processor models and families. Instead, it's a guide to what model is best in the three families of platform architectures, and it'll help you appreciate why one processor—usually affiliated with a certain level of server—is recommended over another processor.

Examining the x86/IA-64/x86-64 Platform (Intel and AMD)

The following sections discuss the x86 family.

Platform Overview

The x86 platform is probably the best-known processor architecture. Starting as far back as 1980, the x86 platform has been manufactured in numerous guises by many companies, most notably Intel and AMD.

Intel currently has a larger install base for the x86 platform, but AMD's recent high-quality processor families have taken a bite out of Intel's market share. AMD was founded in 1969 and used to produce various non-CPU based products. In 1979, AMD commenced manufacturing 8086 and 8088 processors for Intel and continued doing so with the 80286 through 1986 when Intel and AMD parted ways.

Up until the mid-1990s, AMD produced clones of the 80386 and 80486 processors. In 1995, via a series of corporate purchases, AMD commenced manufacturing its own x86-compatible CPU family. The first product off the line was the AMD-K5, a direct competitor to the original Intel Pentium.

Most of you know the history of the x86, with its inception into the mass market thanks to the 8080 in the late 1970s, shortly followed by the 8086/8088 processors that were used to power the first IBM PCs.

NOTE Previous Intel-manufactured processors, the 4004 and 8008, were available but not deemed "mass market" in the early 1970s. These processors were available as part of computer kits.

The x86 is quite possibly the driving reason for the computer revolution because it brought low cost (to the consumer) and microprocessing capacity to end users.

Platform Architecture

You can find the x86 architecture in many flavors. Three companies have produced x86 processors in the past 30 years: Intel, AMD, and Cyrix, with some input from NEC, National Semiconductor, and more recently Transmeta.

Unlike a SPARC-based processor, there isn't a standard for the x86. What makes the x86 a leading processor architecture is its low entry cost. You can pick up basic-level Intel and AMD CPUs for less than $35, which makes them a bargain for anyone wanting to set up test or low-end systems.

Although you can't compare a Power4 or UltraSPARC III to a lower-end x86 processor, the cost indicates why x86 is so popular. Some have compared it to Linux versus the commercial Unix systems. That is, Linux—being more or less free—means that anyone (those without big budgets) can download Linux, install it, and use it and perform pretty much the same tasks as someone who operates a commercial Unix such as Tru64, Solaris, or AIX.

To focus on the most relevant x86 processor line-up, I'll compare only the processors released since January 2002 from Intel and AMD. This in no way represents a view on other manufacturers' processors, however; AMD and Intel are the most commonly used x86 vendors for WebSphere implementations on the Linux and Windows NT/200x/XP platforms.

You'll now see some of the key processors commonly found in x86 server platforms.

NOTE   Over the years, the nomenclature of x86 platforms has been fairly well publicized. The *IA-32* term is essentially Intel's convention of the x86 platform architecture and refers to *Intel Architecture—32 bit*. The term *IA-64* stands for, as you can probably guess, *Intel Architecture—64 bit*.

NOTE   x86-64 is AMD's answer to IA-64, with the important and clever distinction of the x86 preceding the *64-bit* term. In other words, x86-64 means an x86 platform on a 64-bit architecture. Incidentally, AMD has code-named the x86-64 the AMD *Opteron*.

What Makes an x86/x86-64/IA-64 Processor Fast?

Like all processors, many factors make up the reasons why one processor is fast and another is slow.

Back in the 16-bit versus 32-bit days, it was fairly straightforward. The AMD 80386DX-40 processor was a step ahead of the market, with true 32-bit in, 32-bit out bus-processing lanes. You may recall that some manufacturers dabbled in hybrid 32/16-bit processors, which were termed *SX processors*, such as the 80386SX-33.

Nowadays, the processors are an order of magnitude more complex. They include internal threading, dual-core engines, superscalar technologies, multi-pipeline approaches, and preemptive processing. The clock rate is still in there, but it's masked significantly by the quality and architectural implementation of the previous factors.

Cache is another big hitter in these types of processors (as it is in most processor architectures).

You'll revisit this question of what makes a fast processor after you've explored all the recent CPUs in this group of processor architecture.

Intel Pentium III Xeon: 900MHz Version

The arrival of the Pentium III Xeon 900 megahertz (MHz) processor was possibly the first sign of Intel's real entry into the high-end workstation/server market. The initial Pentium III Xeon processor was designed to operate in systems with up to eight-way processing. Each CPU came with 2MB of advanced transfer level 2 cache, which was a large upgrade from the standard 256KB level 2 cache found in other Pentium III–based processors.

The core CPU was interconnected to the system bus at 100MHz with an address width of 64 bits. This processor also directly supported up to 64GB of memory.

Intel Pentium 4: 1.7GHz–2GHz Version

Although not the first release of the Pentium 4 processor, the 1.7GHz–2GHz versions were the sign of things to come with the Intel line-up. Pentium 4 was the first new CPU architecture for Intel since its Pentium Pro, which was made available in mid-1995.

This range of Pentium 4 processors operated on a 400MHz system bus speed, and level 2 cache was supported by 256KB cache memory. This initial batch of Pentium 4 processors was based on what's commonly known as the *Willamette* core.

Intel Pentium 4: 2GHzGHz–2.6GHz Version

This second family of Pentium 4 processors arrived in January 2002, all based on the new Northwood "A" processor core. Among other things, the new core is developed with a 0.13 micron process as opposed to the 0.18 micron in the previous Pentium 4 processors.

Intel Pentium 4: 2.26GHz–3.2GHz Version

Pentium 4 underwent another change in April 2002 when the Northwood "A" processor was replaced with a "B" model. The biggest change for the newer post–April 2002 Pentium 4 processor was with the system bus interconnect or, as Intel has coined, the Front Side Bus (FSB). The previous Pentium 4s came with a 400MHz FSB, and the newer Northwood "B" models came with a 533MHz FSB.

What's more, the 3.06GHz version of the Pentium 4 introduced a feature known as *hyper-threading* into the mainstream Intel product line-up.

Previous Intel CPUs such as Xeon processors came equipped with the hyper-threading technology, which essentially provides a dual-processor core. Although hyper-threading doesn't provide 100-percent twin-CPU capabilities, it does come close. Nonexecution areas within the CPUs are duplicated. Areas such as the processor scheduler are duplicated, which allows for multiple system threads to be scheduled simultaneously. Symmetric Multiprocessor (SMP) operating systems will see the logically split processors and multithreaded applications (such as WebSphere-deployed applications) and will be able to take advantage of the feature.

If you're looking to use an Intel x86 platform architecture, the Pentium 4 3.2GHz is a high-quality and high-performing processor.

 NOTE   At the time of writing this book, Intel has announced a pending 1,000MHz FSB version of the Intel Pentium 4 processor family.

Intel Xeon

As well as the Intel Pentium III Xeon processor, Intel provides the Xeon processor in its Pentium 4 family. Although the latest Xeon is quite different from the Pentium 4 processor, there are some similarities. The Xeon is probably the closest, architecturally speaking, to the Pentium 4. It's a server-targeted processor in several forms. To continue with the generational breakdown of processors, you'll see that the Intel Xeon comes in a number of flavors.

The first generation of the current family of Xeon processors is supplied with 256KB of level 2 cache, interfacing with the system bus at 400MHz. The clock speeds range from 1.4GHz–2GHz. This Xeon doesn't support hyper-threading

(Intel's dual-execution CPU core technology) but does directly support dual-processor configurations.

The second generation of Xeon processors support a slightly higher amount of level 2 cache at 512KB, the 400MHz system bus interconnect speed. This generation of Xeons does support hyper-threading, and like the first-generation Xeon, it directly supports dual processors. Clock speeds for this Xeon range from 1.8GHz–3GHz.

The third generation of Xeon processors introduces a faster 533MHz system bus interconnect speed and similar characteristics to the second-generation Xeon, such as hyper-threading, native dual-processor support, 512KB of level 2 cache, and clock rates from 2GHz–3.06GHz.

Intel Xeon MP

The Xeon MP is Intel's high-performance (computing bandwidth) x86 processor. Similar to the Xeon in some respects, the Xeon MP is targeted at implementations and computing requirements of more than two Xeon CPUs, with direct support for up to eight-way configuration. Proprietary chipsets can support greater than eight-way configuration for Xeon MP processors.

The key point about the Xeon MP is that it comes with a level 3 cache, as well as the standard level 1 and 2 caches. The level 3 cache is touted as the *integrated cache*, effectively placing an abstraction caching layer between the CPU (level 2 cache) and the off-CPU activities.

The Xeon comes with clock rates of 1.4GHz–2GHz. The level 2 cache comes with up to 512KB of cache memory, and the level 3 cache can be supplied with up to 2MB of cache memory with all cache memory operating at the clock rate frequency.

The other key design aspect of the Xeon MP is that the I/O bandwidth is faster than the standard Xeon processors, capable of up to 4.8GB per second using the PCI-X architecture standard.

As you'd expect, hyper-threading comes standard. It's important to note that the Xeon MP also is limited in its chipset usage, so selection of main boards is important. The Xeon MP supports only the ServerWorks GC-HE chipset or any proprietary chipset that a main board manufacturer chooses to design and implement.

Intel Itanium and Itanium 2

The Itanium is Intel's flagship 64-bit computing platform. It, unlike previous generational CPU architecture upgrades from Intel, doesn't provide native backward compatibility with the x86 architecture and instead uses an IA-64 architecture.

This is unlike the AMD Opteron, which follows the same path that the x86 architecture has for the past 20 years. That is, as each evolutionary change in data and CPU sizing has taken place (8-bit to 16-bit to 32-bit and so on), the next processor model in line is always backward compatible with the previous data set.

The Itanium does in fact provide limited non-native support for legacy x86 code by means of an emulation mode in which the processor can be run. This is implemented through firmware capability on the processor.

The Itanium and Itanium 2 processors are Intel's new-world server processor platforms. The Itanium 2 supports a three-layer cache system—layer 1, layer 2, and layer 3 cache of up to 6MB.

Intel markets the Itanium in a "workstation" and a "server" flavor. The key difference between the two target platform offerings essentially boil down to better support for dual or more processors in the server incarnation of the Itanium 2.

The Itanium 2 DP processor is primarily a dual processor–optimized Itanium 2 offering. The Itanium 2 MP is a multiprocessor version, which is targeted to servers with more than two processors. A third flavor exists that's targeted toward high-density computing platforms such as supercomputer-type implementations. This third flavor of the Itanium 2 is powered by a smaller cache size and processor clock speed, driving down the voltage level.

AMD Duron

The AMD Duron is a lighter-weight processor than the Athlon and somewhat analogous to Intel's Celeron family of processors.

Duron is soon to be retired by AMD, but you can still order systems and parts for the Duron.

The Duron is essentially the same processor as the Athlon—it uses the same core, with the main exception being the amount of level 2 cache. The Duron comes with a level 2 cache of 64KB, and the Athlon's are 256KB and upward.

The Duron has been produced based on three cores, first commencing in 2000. The original core, the Spitfire, was based on the Althon's Thunderbird core and provided clock speeds of 600–950MHz. The more recent, or second-generation, core—known as the *Morgan* core—was based on the Althon XP Palomino core and is what today's Durons are based on.

Duron processors are available in speeds up to 1.3GHz.

AMD Athlon, Athlon XP, and Athlon MP

The Athlon AMD processors are the primary competing models of the Intel Pentium III and Intel Pentium 4 processors. Over the past few years, Pentium and Althon have both been the leader for the fastest (in processing terms) x86-based CPU.

Athlon

The original Athlon, operating on the AMD-K7 core, was limited to speeds of 1GHz. These initial Athlons were more in line with the Intel Pentium II processor family than the Pentium III.

Athlon started to improve its place in the microprocessor world in mid-2000 when it released the Thunderbird core. Interestingly, the Thunderbird core–based Althon's level 2 cache is half the size of the original K7-based Althon. The Thunderbird has 256KB of level 2 cache where as the K7 has 512KB of level 2 cache. The key difference, other than the size of the cache memory, is that the Thunderbird reverted to having the cache physically on the Thunderbird processor die where as the K7 has the memory externally mounted. This comounting or cohousing the level 2 cache on the processor die improved the performance of the level 2 cache; and in cache memory terms, faster is typically better than more!

Athlon XP

The Athlon XP is essentially AMD's third-generation of Althon processor. Released in mid-2001, the Athlon XP included a number of new capabilities, as well as performance improvements. The key architectural differences of the third-generation Palomino core–based Althon were an additional two instruction sets, SSE and 3DNow, and an increase in the initial clock rate up to 1.73GHz.

A reduction in power consumption of the Palomino core meant that the stock processor can be clocked faster.

Two additional generations of Althon XP are available—one based on the Thoroughbred core and the more recently released Barton core. These processors are essentially clock rate and instruction core optimized versions of the Palomino-based Althon XP. The clock rate of the two processors weren't the same as the offerings from Intel Pentium 4, however. Depending on who you talked to, the type of processing you were undertaking, the lower clock rate Barton and Thoroughbred-based AMD processors were faster than the Intel Pentium 4 processors.

You'll notice that AMD now names its processors in the form of *Athlon XP 2800+* and *Athlon XP 3000+*. The number at the end of the processor name (for example, 2800+ and 3000+) is an attempt to compare each processor against the relative speed of the Intel Pentium 4 processors. AMD uses that rating as an indicator of the relative speed of the Intel Pentium 4 equivalents.

Athlon MP

The Althon MP is a modified Althon processor that has been designed specifically for multiprocessor-based systems. Several features are present that allow better utilization of pipelining and cross CPU cache coherency. These concepts are quite sound, and many of the off-CPU functions that are associated with SMP-based main boards are incorporated into the CPU itself. The more manufacturers can pack onto a CPU rather than traversing a bus, the faster the overall performance of the CPU will be.

AMD Athlon 64

Code-named *ClawHammer*, the Athlon 64 is one of two CPU branches that AMD is manufacturing for 64-bit computing. Although not available commercially until late 2003, there's a fair amount of information available about the new family of AMD engines.

Although I could (happily) talk about CPU architecture all day, I'll try to highlight some of the key points of the new Athlon 64. Obviously, it's a 64-bit CPU that's capable of running 32-bit (and 16-bit) applications natively. AMD has cleverly taken the x86-32 specification and extended it to allow for seamless 64-bit computing. Additional registers and some extensions to the existing ones in the core provide the extra 32 bits.

The Athlon 64 also incorporates an on-CPU memory controller and a new bus known as *HyperTransport*. The on-CPU memory controller greatly reduces latency when communicating with the memory itself as the memory controllers actually operates at the same frequency, or clock rate, as the CPU. The HyperTransport bus is a concept that allows multiple AMD CPUs and or other bus-connected technologies such as I/O interfaces—Universal Serial Bus (USB), Integrated Device Electronics (IDE) devices, and so on—and graphics devices to be interconnected. Similar in theory to the on-CPU memory controller, having the HyperTransport bus technology colocated on the CPU means that the HyperTransport bus is operating at the ultra-high frequencies at which the core CPU is operating. A 32-bit HyperTransport bus interface with a 1600MHz clock rate will allow it to operate at 6.4GB per second.

AMD Opteron

Similar to the Athlon XP, the Opteron is the server, or high-end workstation, version of the x86-64 AMD offering (in other words, the Athlon 64). Based on the SledgeHammer core, the Opteron provides some clever performance features. Essentially, the Opteron is AMD's competitor to Intel's Xeon server processor family.

The Opteron comes in three models—the Opteron 1*xx*, 2*xx*, and 8*xx*. The first digit represents the validation certification of the CPU, or what its platform design is intended for—one-, two-, or up to eight-way systems. The next two digits represent the AMD performance index of the particular processor.

Where Opteron is different from AMD's Athlon 64 CPU powerhouse is primarily in the cache and number of HyperTransport interfaces. Opteron has been designed using the SledgeHammer core to provide more and potentially faster on-CPU cache than the Athlon 64. The Athlon 64 also supports one HyperTransport interface where as the Opteron supports up to three HyperTransport interfaces.

Quite simply, the need for a workstation or desktop to have vast amounts of cache and on-CPU hyperlevel interconnects is probably not required (given the typical use of a desktop or workstation). Obviously, in a server configuration, the more cache and number of meshed interconnects for SMP is important.

Comparison Chart: x86/IA-64/x86-64/ Processors

Now that you've gotten an overview of the most common server-oriented x86 processors that are used for WebSphere implementations, Table 4-1 provides recommendations for different CPUs.

The definition of each system type is fairly high level but indicates the suggested use. Workstation could be either a development workstation or a development server for environments where budgets aren't as large and therefore lower-end systems must suffice. Although there's no rule for what constitutes a production or development server, I've used the guide of one to two CPUs constituting a workstation or a midrange server environment where horizontal scaling may be more extensively used. Furthermore, *high-end server* refers to a larger production environment where more than two CPUs will be required with an emphasis on vertical scaling.

Table 4-1. CPU Comparison Chart: x86/x86-64/IA-64 Platform

CPU Name	Workstation	Midrange Server	High-End Server
Intel Pentium III Xeon	†	✓	✓
Intel Pentium 4 Generation 1	✓	✓	†
Intel Pentium 4 Generation 2	†	✓	✓
Intel Pentium 4 Generation 3	†	✓	✓
Intel Xeon Generation 1	†	✓	†
Intel Xeon Generation 2	†	✓	†
Intel Xeon Generation 3	†	✓	✓

Table 4-1. CPU Comparison Chart: x86/x86-64/IA-64 Platform (Continued)

CPU Name	Workstation	Midrange Server	High-End Server
Intel Xeon MP	†	†	✓
Intel Itanium	†	†	✓
AMD Duron	✓	†	†
AMD Athlon Classic	✓	†	†
AMD Athlon Generation 2	†	✓	†
AMD Athlon XP	†	✓	✓
AMD Athlon MP	†	†	✓
AMD Athlon 64	†	✓	✓
AMD Opteron	†	✓	✓

32-Bit or 64-Bit Computing?

The computing industry is at the crossroads of 32-bit versus 64-bit computing. Many, if not all, of the high-end server platforms such as SPARC, Alpha, and PowerPC are 64-bit architectures. The x86 world is slowly but surely catching up with AMD's Opteron and Athlon 64 and Intel's Itanium processors.

The argument of 32-bit versus 64-bit computing is also an old one. The 16-bit versus 32-bit argument was definitely not as prevalent as the 64-bit one, but over the next two to five years, desktop computing will demand it. Right now, people can get away with 32-bit desktops—who has a personal computer with the need for more than 4GB of memory? Intel's Xeon processor is a 32-bit CPU but actually addresses memory through a masked 36-bit address space, thus supporting up to 64GB of memory.

Typically, at least in the past, if someone required more than 4GB of memory, 64-bit CPUs (and operating systems) were available from IBM, Sun, and Digital/Compaq/Hewlett-Packard (HP). Sun now can supply 64-bit processors for less than $2,000 with a decent amount of memory and internal hard disk space.

The bottom line is that the choice of 32-bit versus 64-bit computing is a nonissue for the Reduced Instruction Set Computer (RISC) players such as the SPARC, PowerPC, and Alpha systems. They're all 64 bits. The issue gives rise to the x86-based system managers. The question therefore needs to be asked—do you require bigger than 2GB files, and do you require more than 4GB of memory?

As you'll explore in later chapters, different WebSphere topologies allow you to get around the 4GB memory issue if you decide to use a commodity CPU system architecture. And if there's a need for large database file and or memory support, then an Intel Xeon configuration may be the obvious choice (getting you to 64GB of memory).

My personal recommendation is this: Take a serious look at the AMD Opteron and Intel Itanium processors. Both are 64-bit, and if you're implementing a new environment where no Java/Java 2 Enterprise Edition (J2EE) code porting will be taking place to migrate from 32-bit to 64-bit, then Itanium is a breeze. AMD Opteron, on the other hand, natively supports x86 instructions, with no translation of abstraction layers. If you're porting from a 32-bit to 64-bit environment and want your application code to access more than the stock amount of memory, then Opteron may be the easiest approach.

 NOTE At the time of this writing, Itanium supported 32-bit computing through a firmware-based emulation layer. Intel has been hinting that some form of direct or native support for legacy 32-bit instructions may become available later.

That all said, the Java Virtual Machine (JVM) runtime should take care of this memory referencing issue for you. As the Opteron and Itanium processors become more prevalent and more support is made for them, investigate the available JVMs that may take better advantage of the 64-bit platform for you.

You'll explore JVMs more in later chapters.

So, Which CPU?

You'll now look at the best CPUs. Using Table 4-1, you can break it down to low-end requirements such as desktop machines or development nodes, production servers, and high-end mission-critical servers.

Development and Desktop Needs

AMD Athlon and Intel Pentium 4 processors are the best choice here. If your budget allows, get the maximum amount of cache you can and, as always, the fastest processor rating.

What you'll find, however, is that if you're running a low-end environment for personal development needs, basic environments typically suffice. In my home lab, I still have a number of 266MHz Intel Celerons and Pentium III machines running a mixture of operating systems (Linux, BSD, and x86 Solaris).

As long as they have enough memory (typically for personal or development use, 384MB is probably the least you want to have for a WebSphere and a database server environment), you'll find that almost any processor will perform the task.

Generally, it's a bit of a "how long is a piece of string?" question. If you're writing, testing, integrating, or developing a new Java/J2EE-based application that's somewhat large with multiple JVMs and so on, then it may pay to have more grunt.

In later chapters, you'll compare JVM threads to CPUs to Kernel threads—this will also help you understand the CPU requirements.

That said, if you're running a fairly complex application with several JVMs, investigate the hyper-threading features of the Xeons or Pentium 4 3.06+GHz processors. Busy JVMs typically perform best with their own CPUs. Again, you'll investigate this further in later chapters when I discuss operating systems.

Server and High-End Server Needs

As I hinted in the previous section, one of the key drivers of selecting a CPU, other than pure performance, is the number of threads that are active on it, driven by the JVM.

As a guide, JVMs can have an operating system thread to JVM thread ratio of anywhere from 1: 1 to 1:25. Depending on how your Java applications are transaction weighted (for example, how many threads are used per client or user transaction), your JVM threads may be long running and require more Kernel threads. Kernel threads are basically what drive the need for additional CPUs or additional CPU performance.

For servers, cache, memory interconnect speed, interleaving factors, and general memory type are the four key factors. All of these factors typically correlate to the speed of the CPU itself. The faster than CPU, the faster the cache and memory interconnect speed (because of architectural CPU releases and general CPU performance). That is, you're not going to find 533MHz Double Data Rate (DDR) memory on a Pentium 4, 1.7GHz processor. The main reason is that 533MHz DDR wasn't available when the Pentium 4 1.7GHz became available.

That's not the say that the Pentium 4 1.7GHz isn't a good choice of CPU—for lower-end or horizontally scaled environments, the Pentium 4 1.7GHz may be a good choice. You'll look this point in the next chapter when I discuss topologies.

In summary, if your WebSphere applications are referencing large amounts of memory from the Java heap (the memory allocated to the JVM), the DDR memory or the newer Intel 800MHz FSB memory interconnect technologies are a good choice. Large and fast cache will improve the overall performance of the application but will noticeably impact calculation-intensive applications.

Table 4-2 summarizes and rates each of the more prominent CPU features from low to high in terms of preference or overall performance improvement for the example implementations.

NOTE   Of course, if a large budget is available, get the fastest, largest cache-based CPU available!

Table 4-2. Example Application Implementation CPU Choice

Application Type	Memory Interconnect	CPU Speed	Cache Size	Threading/ Dual CPU
Java Server Page (JSP)/ Hypertext Markup Language (HTML)– based WebSphere application	Medium	Medium	Medium	Low
JSP/servlet-based WebSphere application	High	Medium	Medium	Medium
JSP/servlet/Java Database Connectivity (JDBC)–based WebSphere application	High	Medium	Medium	Medium
Small Enterprise JavaBean (EJB)– based WebSphere application	High	High	High	Medium
Multi-JVM EJB- based WebSphere application	High	High	High	High

Examining the SPARC RISC Platform (Sun Microsystems)

The SPARC platform is considered to be one of the driving forces in the expansion of the Internet in the late 1990s. You'll now take a closer look at the SPARC platform.

Platform Overview

The SPARC platform has been available for many years now. Since its inception, myriad CPU architectures have come on the market, including the more recent Sun UltraSPARC Is, IIs, and IIIs and the TurboSPARC, MicroSPARC, and SuperSPARC architectures.

For the purposes of this book, you'll focus on the UltraSPARC II and III and other members of their lines. Further, you'll focus on the SPARC processors from Sun Microsystems. Although there are a number of other vendors still producing SPARC-based processors, from a WebSphere implementation perspective, the Sun SPARC processors are the most common (95 percent of the market share).

The range of systems you can find the UltraSPARC II and III in are endless. Sun has produced a vast range of platform choices in the past 10 years, all of which have been high-quality systems.

This list includes server models such as the Ultra series (5, 10, 20, and so on) workstations to Enterprise series servers including E240R, E250, E450, E480R, E3500, E4500, E5500, E6500, and the ominous E10000. Previous models of the Enterprise series also included the E3000, E4000, E5000, and E6000 systems with a range of submodels in-between.

More recently, Sun's UltraSPARC III processor has been found in a vast range of systems, many of which I'll discuss in this chapter. They, however, include volume workgroup or departmental servers such as the V480, V880, and V1280 systems and the SunFire range of the F3800, F4800 (and a short-lived F4810 rack-based version of the F4800), a F6800, F12000 (F12K), and an F15000 (F15K).

Sun's more recent SunFire Enterprise class servers (F3800 upward) provide split system domain capabilities and a vast array of redundancy and high-availability features. I'll discuss these at length in upcoming sections.

You'll now look at Sun's SPARC platform in more detail.

Platform Architecture

As noted previously, the SPARC platform is somewhat vast, but it essentially revolves around the SPARC Compliance Definition, created by the International SPARC Organization. Sun Microsystems originally invented the SPARC architecture and codeveloped it with Fujitsu in 1986.

In 1989, Sun transferred ownership of the SPARC design to the International SPARC Organization, a nonprofit organization that provides an open specification of the SPARC architecture to any organization that wants to use it to build microprocessors. Nowadays, you can find SPARC processors in everything from digital cameras all the way to some of the world's largest Unix superclusters.

As hinted at earlier, this chapter focuses on the UltraSPARC II and III CPUs that are applicable to V and F series SunFire-based servers, such as the V880 and F4800, and E-based enterprise servers, such as the E480R.

 NOTE The letters following and preceding each of the Sun-based server models depict the type of server (family) and physical characteristics of the servers. For example, in a V880 server, the V stands for *volume* or *volume workgroup* server, the E in an E6500-based server stands for *enterprise* server, and the F in a F4800 server depicts that it's a *SunFire* class server. The R in server model names declares them to be rack based as opposed to data center or pedestal based.

Out of the UltraSPARC CPUs available, the most commonly found models are the following:

- UltraSPARC IIe

- UltraSPARC IIi

- UltraSPARC II

- UltraSPARC III

- UltraSPARC IIIi

Each of these CPU models offer differing capabilities, specifically in the areas of CPU clock speeds, bus interface and bus interconnect speeds, and level 1 and 2 cache sizes (and in some cases, level 3 cache).

What's important to note is that both the UltraSPARC II and UltraSPARC III processors are based on the SPARC V9 RISC architecture, as set out by the International SPARC Organization. Both models support 64-bit computing, both in slightly different forms, which I'll discuss shortly. It's important to understand the differences between these processors at this level in order to understand the differences in areas such as addressable memory, performance (not just clock speed), and scalability features.

Unlike the Complex Instruction Set Computing (CISC)–based processors from AMD and Intel, the RISC-based UltraSPARC processors provide high-processing throughputs, with lower clock rates. In many cases, the bus transfer rates of the UltraSPARC processors (even those running at one-third the clock rate of the Intel Pentium 4 processors) can sustain bus transfer speeds (I/O, memory, and so on) far in excess of the x86 counterparts.

I've found that people who are less familiar with or who haven't had as much exposure to high-end processors such as the offerings from Sun, HP (formerly Compaq, which was formerly Digital), and IBM often scoff at the costs of the RISC-based processors. Generally, the costs for comparable lower-end RISC processors are comparable to the CISC or x86 processors.

The flaw to many people's argument over x86 versus RISC is that it's all about clock speed. This couldn't be any further from the truth. The clock speed is more of a marketable term these days, and although it does have some bearing on the end result of the performance of the processor, it's no longer the absolute.

In the old days of 386s and 486s, there wasn't a great deal of complex features in those processors. The legacy of "faster clock speed means faster processing" can be attributed somewhat to those days where the difference between a 386DX33 and a 386DX-40 was a whopping 7MHz, and that 7MHz made a world of difference! However, nowadays, RISC and CISC processors are both complex technologies.

Furthermore, the power consumption of the UltraSPARC processors is far less than that of the x86 equivalents. The UltraSPARC II consumes 19 watts of power, and the Intel Pentium 4 2.8GHz processor consumes approximately 68 watts. Things start to heat up considerably when you have a few processors in a server operating at high wattage levels.

One final point to make about UltraSPARC processors is that all UltraSPARC processors are superscalar, essentially allowing several executions to be active on the CPU at any time. Although this is slightly different to outright pipelining, because of the nature of the simplified instructions on a RISC-based CPU, the outcome is that there's more chance that the CPU can accommodate a superscalar design.

The problem with superscalar design is that if two instructions are being executed at any one time, and instruction A requires the result of instruction B, there will be latency in the CPU core. For this reason, simplified instruction sets work best, and therefore RISC is the outright winner here.

The more recent x86-based CPUs from Intel and AMD both support basic superscalar design but aren't as effective, given the more complex instruction sets.

Given the subtle differences between the UltraSPARC II and the UltraSPARC III family of processors, you'll now take a closer look at four processors in more detail.

Sun UltraSPARC II

The UltraSPARC II was a major step for Sun when it was released. Ensuring Sun was a firm competitor in the RISC-Unix market, the UltraSPARC II is probably what gave Sun its success in the late 1990s as Internet usage became more widespread.

The UltraSPARC II is a 64-bit based CPU that, like more recent Sun SPARC CPUs, includes features such as on-CPU I/O and memory controllers. It's interesting to note, as you saw in the x86 section, that the x86-based processors are only just now starting to incorporate these on-CPU features. You'll explore the advantages of having these features onboard the CPU shortly.

The UltraSPARC II comes in four speeds—360MHz, 400MHz, 450MHz, and 480MHz. The performance of the UltraSPARC II, despite its lower clock speeds, is quite good. It performs at a rate equivalent to other forms of processors with double its clock speed, and it's able to hold up in the system bus transfer ratings.

The processor comes with a level 2 cache, like most processors, that Sun coined as the *e-cache*. The size for this cache varies from processor to processor but is essentially available from 2MB–8MB. The 2MB version was the de facto standard in larger systems such as E450s and higher.

Bus transfer speeds were reasonable and for CPU to memory transfers, the processor could sustain 960MB per second when the Ultra Port Architecture (UPA)–connected bus was operating at 120MHz.

At the upper end of the processor models, the CPU to level 2 cache transfer rate could peak at 1.92GB per second when fitted with a 480MHz processor.

The UltraSPARC II also employed pipelining capabilities and had a good instruction per clock cycle ratio. The processor essentially supports four-way pipelining, and basic instructions are processed in one clock cycle. More complex instructions such as square-root calculations aren't pipelined and take between 12 and 22 clock cycles depending on single or double precision.

Note these numbers for the future CPU models.

The CPU also provided the ability, through the solid architecture baseline that it sits on, to interconnect with systems of up to 1024 processors. Of course, proprietary hardware implementations could extend this to an almost limitless number.

Sun UltraSPARC IIi

The UltraSPARC IIi was an upgraded version of the UltraSPARC II processor that became available in two models—the 440MHz and the 650MHz versions. Like the UltraSPARC II processor, the IIi supported 4GB of memory per CPU. Additional CPUs provided additional address space to reference (or associate) additional memory.

Although the UltraSPARC-IIi processor's clock rate is higher than that of the UltraSPARC II processor, the e-cache (level 2 cache) is somewhat smaller than the UltraSPARC-II. Level 2 cache available on these CPUs was a de facto 512KB, which, although providing good throughput and performance, does force the recommendation of these CPUs to more mid-level production systems. Both 1MB and 2MB versions were available in design but not common in implementation.

One of the reasons (if not the only reason) for this reduction in cache size is that the level 2 cache in the UltraSPARC IIi was more tightly integrated onto the processor itself, reducing latency and increasing performance. Given that real estate on the processor die is limited, the trade-off is that the cache memory has to be reduced in size in order to fit.

At the time the UltraSPARC IIi became available, the UltraSPARC III processor family was being released. Sun marketed the UltraSPARC III to servers while the IIi was marketed to more commodity-based or workgroup-based systems and servers. The CPU provided the ability to interface with more commodity-based memory technologies such as PC100/133 Synchronous Dynamic Random Access Memory (SDRAM) commonly found in x86-based systems. The CPU found its way into products such as Sun's rack-based servers and high-end workstations such as V100s and V120s.

The IIi has a CPU to memory transfer rate of 800MB per second, as compared to 960MB per second of the UltraSPARC II. Overall, the performance of the UltraSPARC IIi, even at 650MHz, isn't as high as the UltraSPARC II 480MHz processor but is more cost-effective for lower-end systems.

Sun UltraSPARC IIe

The IIe is a model of Sun SPARC CPUs that are targeted to the low-end server or workstation market. They're more comparable to the x86-based CPUs that you'd find from Intel and AMD and cost a great deal less than the II, IIi, or III processors.

The IIe only supports 2GB of memory per CPU and comes with 256KB of level 2 cache. Memory to CPU transfer speeds are the same as that of the IIi, and therefore, for most low-end applications, it'll provide a solid base for either development, low end, or possibly highly horizontally scaled WebSphere implementations.

I don't recommend servers operating with these CPUs for medium- to large-sized WebSphere implementations because of their low memory capability and small level 2 cache size.

Sun UltraSPARC III

The UltraSPARC III is Sun's answer to the increasing pressure from IBM's PowerPC platform and the Intel/AMD push into the 64-bit market.

The III is, like the II family, a 64-bit SPARC v9–compliant processor supporting greater memory sizes (up to 16GB per CPU) as well as a greatly increased clock speed. Advanced features such as memory-level prefetching (providing memory to core data parallelism) and a redesigned level 2 cache that's accessed via what's known as *associative referencing* rather than via direct-mapped cache are also included. This associative referencing introduces a level of abstraction that increases the amount of cache that can be easily referenced by the CPU.

Another key feature that helps to increase the performance of the CPU without the concept of simply increasing clock speeds is a new on-CPU component called the Instruction Issue Unit (IIU). The IIU manages where each instruction is routed to within the CPU. That is, the IIU takes instructions and routes them to the integer execution unit, floating-point execution unit, or the load/store execution unit.

Unlike previous UltraSPARCs, the III works within a switching-based architecture. All components within the realm of the processor are interconnected to one another via a Fireplane bus.

You can break the key components of the UltraSPARC III down to four main groups:

- Instruction component such as IIU

- Pipeline processing units such as Floating Point Unit (FPU) and IPU Instruction Processing Unit (IPU)

- Level 1 cache management such as prefetch and data caches

- Auxiliary unit such as an interface to level 2 cache and memory controller

It's probably worth familiarizing yourself with this processor architecture (albeit at a high level) if you don't already understand how processor architectures work. The UltraSPARC III uses a surprisingly straightforward (and logical) high-level architecture for the major components within the CPU itself.

The pipeline services within the III are basically the same as that of the UltraSPARC II in terms of number of pipelines. The number of instructions per clock cycle is the same for the basic operations with division and square-root type instructions being slightly higher (40 to 70 cycles depending on precision).

A key feature of the UltraSPARC III is that it provides a data prefetching capability. This technology essentially allows for increased memory parallelism, which helps to mask the issue of latency when an instruction misses the cache. Without it, the processor would simply wait until the entire instruction to complete before executing any other instruction.

Another key point of the III is that it supports up to 16GB of memory per CPU, as opposed to the 4GB per CPU maximum of the UltraSPARC II. The memory is controlled by an on-CPU memory controller unit that interfaces with another key CPU component known as the System Interface Unit (SIU). This SIU is responsible for all communications between other components off the CPU (such as other CPUs, the main system memory, and the system bus communications).

As discussed earlier, pipelining is an important topic for CPUs. Pipelines essentially allow more things to be happening (or executing) on the CPU at any given time.

Things are no different for the UltraSPARC III. It has a six-stage pipeline, which in my opinion is a good size. As you saw, pipelines that are too big can create latency when a cache miss occurs, and pipelines that are too small will only be marginally better than a CPU with no pipeline. Therefore, the UltraSPARC III with its sic-stage pipeline provides a good result for performance.

In larger systems, the SIU ensures coherency between multiprocessor system caches. Because the UltraSPARC III was designed for both single and multi-CPU systems, it supports a variety of operating modes. However, each UltraSPARC III is essentially the same, with the difference being on the main and logic boards on which the CPU sits. That is, the logic (or *uniboard)* that the UltraSPARC III CPU sits on is different depending on the system family in which you install it.

The V880, for example, supports up to eight UltraSPARC III CPUs, and although an 8MB e-cache UltraSPARC 950MHz CPU would have the same processor as one installed in an F15K, the interface board that the CPU sits on is different. I'll go into this in some more detail—it's an important part of Sun's system architecture.

In a dual-CPU configuration, such as in an E280R, UltraSPARC III CPUs are connected via a 128-bit, 150MHz Dual CPU Data Switch (DCDS). Given that there's a limitation on memory per CPU (16GB per CPU), the DCDS is connected to the banks of SDRAM (two banks in a dual-CPU configuration) via a 512-bit bus operating at 75MHz. The DCDS in turn interfaces with the rest of the system over what Sun terms the *level 1 data switch* via a Fireplane data interconnect at 256 bits.

In four-processor systems such as V480s, the system operates essentially as two dual-CPU systems. Each pair of CPUs is connected, like the dual-CPU configuration, via a DCDS. The two pairs of DCDS are then in turn interconnected via a level 1 data switch. You can probably see where this is going.

Much larger systems start to involve a level 2 data switch as the systems go beyond six processor inboards, and after this limit is reached, a level 3 layer is introduced, known as the *Fireplane crossbar*, which support systems with more than six inboards.

At the end of the day, however, the same physical CPU remains, but a series of integrated switches are used to extend the size of the system to an almost limitless number. Essentially the design works like a lattice framework—common components are repeatedly interconnected to build larger and larger systems.

Finally, the Fireplane is a fairly integral part of Sun's larger systems. It's a two-part component, with one part consisting of the point-to-point data interconnection service and the second part being a hierarchical bus for control messages and component addresses.

Sun UltraSPARC IIIi

The UltraSPARC IIIi is a similar incarnation of the UltraSPARC III as the UltraSPARC IIi is to the UltraSPARC II. You'll find that the UltraSPARC IIIi is an update to the UltraSPARC IIi processor, and yet again, it's different from the standard III chip.

Designed for smaller systems of up to four CPUs, it incorporates a smaller level 2 cache (up to 1MB) and 1GHz clock speed. Overall, it's a solid processor for the lower-end systems and is definitely worth looking at if your per-server configurations aren't going to exceed four CPUs or 64GB of memory.

Comparison Chart: Sun SPARC v9 Processors

Of the five UltraSPARC CPUs I've covered, you can categorize each of them in a best-use model. Therefore, the following sections detail where each CPU best fits.

Sun UltraSPARC II

The UltraSPARC II is slowly being phased out but is still available for existing customer systems. Therefore, it's an interesting model of CPU. The Sun E10K is still available and operates with UltraSPARC II CPUs, as do smaller systems such as E450s and so forth.

Overall, the UltraSPARC II is a well-performing CPU but should be avoided for your WebSphere implementation operating on a Solaris environment.

Sun UltraSPARC IIi

The UltraSPARC IIi CPU is readily available on lower-end systems. This includes a variety of models such as V100 and V120 systems. These servers are typically rack based and operate with one to two CPUs per system.

They're best suited for lower-end production systems or if you're able to scale your application horizontally rather than vertically. Given that the V100 and V120 support 2GB and 4GB of memory, respectively, there's not a great deal of memory "head room" for larger or vertically scaled applications.

However, I've seen environments where massive distribution of load is possible through some smart Java Naming and Directory Interface (JNDI) or Remote Method Invocation (RMI), and in these cases, V100s and V120s aren't a bad option. Further, it should be noted that the V120 is supplied with SCSI-2 drives that have 10,000 revolutions per minute (rpm).

For midrange or high-range systems where memory and scalability are issues, then the systems housing UltraSPARC IIi CPUs should generally be avoided. If you're operating a small WebSphere implementation with, let's say, just JSPs and servlets, these servers with this CPU will provide you with a solid base.

 NOTE These two servers, the V100 and V120 servers, are designed for data centers where racking of servers is a key factor. They come standard with lights-out management and remote console capabilities. Further, they're well priced with base systems available for only a few thousand dollars.

Sun UltraSPARC IIe

The UltraSPARC IIe is an entry-level CPU designed for workstations. For production-based WebSphere platform demands, I recommend you avoid these systems. However, for development workstations operating WebSphere, systems based on this CPU (such as Sun Blade 100s) are good performers.

Sun UltraSPARC III

The UltraSPARC III is the workhorse of the current UltraSPARC processor family. As you saw in earlier sections, it's a fast, powerful, and scalable CPU technology.

Given this CPU comes in servers of all sizes, from a single CPU up to the Sun E15K with 106 CPUs, it can be used in any WebSphere environment—production or development.

Sun UltraSPARC IIIi

After the UltraSPARC III comes the IIIi, which is a good-performing entry-level CPU that can be used for smaller-sized to medium-sized production environments. With the ability to support 16GB of memory per CPU and operating at 1GHz, the CPU can offer a well-balanced performance-to-cost ratio for smaller production environments. Limited to four CPUs per server, you can find the CPU in Sun servers such as V210 and V220 servers.

If you don't believe your production environment (or development for that matter) will exceed four CPUs and you don't have a processing-complex application (in other words, a cryptography or data mapping application), then the IIIi-based servers are a good choice. Given the CPU is based on the III, it also supports up to 64GB of memory on a four-CPU server such as a V220—for small to medium environments, sometimes this is more than required.

Again, if you can architect your WebSphere-based J2EE application to be horizontally scalable (processor-wise) and take advantage of the large amount of available memory, then this processor will suit you well.

Selecting Your Sun SPARC-Based Server Platform

You've looked at the various CPUs available in the Sun UltraSPARC family, so you'll now look at some of the more common Sun-based servers and try to apply them to differing types of WebSphere implementations. As you've seen, there are four primary CPU choices to select from, all of which are fairly aligned with increasingly more powerful and high-performing systems.

Table 4-3 gives an overview of the Sun server model in each you can find each of the four main CPUs.

Table 4-3. CPU and Server Comparison Matrix

Sun Server Model	UltraSPARC III	UltraSPARC IIi	UltraSPARC IIe	UltraSPARC IIIi
Sun V100		550MHz–650MHz		
Sun V120		550MHz–650MHz		
Sun V220				1GHz
Sun V480	900MHz			
Sun V880	900MHz			
Sun V1280	900MHz			
Sun F3800	900MHz–1200MHz			
Sun F4800	900MHz–1200MHz			
Sun F4810	900MHz–1200MHz			
Sun F6800	900MHz–1200MHz			
Sun F12000	900MHz–1200MHz			
Sun F15000	900MHz–1200MHz			

Table 4-3 focuses on the newer range of servers from Sun, which are mostly based on the UltraSPARC III and IIIi processors.

So, Which CPU?

How long is a piece of string? Seriously, "So, which CPU" is one of those questions. I think the question should be more like "So, which server?" You need to make several decisions to answer this question:

- What are your scalability requirements?

- What are your availability requirements?

- What are your performance requirements?

- What are your disaster recovery and dual-site requirements?

Once you've made these decisions, then you'll know what size and type of system you need. However, as a guide, the following sections contain some pointers for the servers that work well for certain WebSphere implementations.

NOTE I'll talk about topologies in the next chapter—this section may be clearer after you've read Chapter 5.

Small Production Environments

In this size of environment, let's assume your small production environment is based on a single WebSphere channel and the application is operating mostly JSPs and servlets but with a small handful of EJBs and a JDBC connection to a backend database. From a user size (in other words, concurrent users and sessions), the number of concurrent users would be from 50 to 250, depending on the characteristics of your transactions. That is, you could have 10 transactions per second that are small and lightweight (for example, a basic select column_name from a table query) or you could have 10 transactions per second that are heavyweight (for example, the same select statement but with joins and unions).

If you're looking for a solution that just works and works with reasonable performance, then the decision process is somewhat easier. However, if you're looking for something that's highly available (in a single chassis), then the costs increase quickly (as you'd probably guess).

The Sun V series of servers are best suited to smaller, not necessarily mission-critical, systems. Typically they're used in WebSphere environments where more than one WebSphere application server is being used, which helps overcome the single server point of failure issue.

The V880 server is probably the "sweet spot" in the V series range. It's an eight-CPU system with the ability to scale to 64GB of memory. It also comes with an internal 12-bay Fibre Channel Arbitrated Loop (FCAL) disk cabinet, allowing for fast FCAL 10,000rpm drives to be installed (six by default).

As I'll discuss in a moment, the V series doesn't have internal redundancy other than the basic components such as power supplies, multiple disks, and possible multiple interface cards. For this reason, if you're budgeting on the V series of servers and availability is a concern, look to purchase two or more application servers.

On the database side of things, the V series is also a solid choice. Obviously, if your database requirements exceed eight CPUs and 64GB of memory, then these may not be what you need. In that case, consider the 12-way V1280 server.

Never discount looking at database clusters or hot-standby servers either. It's good to have a dual redundant pair of WebSphere application servers; however, if you're operating a WebSphere 4 platform or your application requirements are fairly database intensive and then your database goes down, you could have all the application servers in the world, but your environment would stop working without an active database.

Medium Production Environments

A medium-sized environment is one that hosts between 100 and 500 concurrent user sessions. Furthermore, a midsize production WebSphere environment will carry high-availability requirements.

Based on this, there are two schools of thought you could apply. First, you could look at a horizontally scaled system (to get physical redundancy) and V-class systems with plenty of memory, such as a V880 (64GB of memory) or a V1280 (96GB of memory). You could apply this model to both the WebSphere and database tiers.

On the other hand, it's possible to look at the enterprise or SunFire range of Sun systems such as the F4800 or F6800 servers. As I'll discuss shortly, the SunFire class of Sun servers come with myriad redundant and high-availability features.

With the SunFire family, just about every component is hot-swappable and or has a redundant part. This includes the following:

- Redundant CPUs (and hot-swappable)

- Redundant memory (and hot-swappable)

- Redundant CPU and memory boards

- I/O assemblies

- I/O adaptors

- System controllers

- System clock

- Fireplane interconnect switches

- Power supplies

- Redundant transfer switches (for power supplies)

With the SunFire range of servers, it's also possible to use *domains* (explained in the following sections in more detail). Domains allow you to split a physical frame into logical domains. These domains act as separate servers, sharing some common components, but are essentially self-contained.

For this reason, it's possible to purchase something such as an F4800 that supports two domains and operate your redundant pair of WebSphere application servers within each of the domains. The same applies for database servers.

You should note that WebSphere has no hard limitation on the number of nodes in a WebSphere cluster. For this reason, it's possible to gain a high degree of what I term as *soft availability* from massively horizontally scaled environments using smaller systems.

 CAUTION It's a common falsity that you can always achieve performance, scalability, and availability simply by building environments with smaller commodity systems. I'll discuss this in detail in the next chapter, but don't get caught up in the bad practice of purchasing 20 or so small servers (such as Sun V100s or single CPU x86-based servers), meshing them all into a WebSphere cluster, and believing you'll gain performance and scalability.

Large Production Environments

A large production environment is one operating with between 500 and 5,000 concurrent users. In this environment, availability and performance are critical. The WebSphere application could be for e-commerce, or it could be for a back-office task, such as a telemarketing system interfacing to something such as a PeopleSoft Customer Relationship Management (CRM) environment.

NOTE My definitions of small, medium, and large environments has no science behind them other than that, based on experience, companies that have 500 or more users actively participating in transactions are typically large and complex environments.

There are several options for this type of environment. Although a Sun model such as the V1280 is a well-performing system, compared with the similar-sized (CPU and memory-wise) F4800, the F4800 outperforms the V1280. It's another misnomer that a 12-CPU V1280 provides the same performance as a 12-CPU F4800.

Mainly for availability and redundancy, I recommend SunFire-class servers for larger environments. Consider single or multiple F4800s or even F6800s if your processing demands require it.

The F4800, as I've hinted at, is a 12-way CPU with the capability of 96GB of memory. It has two domains, allowing it to operate as a single server or with two active domains (servers) using Sun domain technologies.

The F6800 is a 24-way CPU with the capability of 192GB of memory and supports up to four domains per chassis.

If site or chassis redundancy is a requirement for your WebSphere environment, then a pair of F4800s or F6800s (depending on budget) can be split over sites easily with WebSphere clustering and system mirroring.

The F6800 provides the ability to fully segment the chassis down the "spine" and operate different sides of the spine on different power grids.

If 24 CPUs in a single server isn't enough, alternatives to the F6800s include the E10K with 64 UltraSPARC II CPUs and the E12K and E15K that support up to 52 and 106 CPUs, respectively.

Furthermore, memory on these systems, or the availability of it, isn't an issue. The E12K supports 288GB of memory, but the E15K supports more than half a terabyte. The E15K also supports up to 18 domains inside the chassis, effectively providing the ability for 18 servers to be hosted in a single chassis.

Platform Summary

In the previous sections, you've looked at what the Sun UltraSPARC processors have to offer. WebSphere and Solaris mate well together, and as you'll see through the upcoming chapters, other than IBM's AIX operating system, Solaris is probably the next best operating system for your WebSphere implementation.

Sun offers a solution for any WebSphere environment size and complexity. From the baby V100s to the flagship SunFire E15K, WebSphere operates well on all available models—the decision will come down to purely a performance and capacity requirement and a scalability and redundancy requirement.

Examining the Power4 Platform (IBM)

The IBM Power4 processor family consists of some of the industry's most powerful single-die CPUs. In the following sections, you'll take a closer look at the fundamentals of the Power4 processor.

Platform Overview

IBM isn't one to go without a formidable RISC-based 64-bit processor platform. The Power4 platform is IBM's competitor to the likes of the UltraSPARC and the Alpha processors from HP/Compaq.

Essentially, the latest model of the Power4 processor is 64-bit, namely the PowerPC 970. This is IBM's mainstream PowerPC-based 64-bit processor and one that's now found in many of the more recent server offerings from IBM.

I should note that IBM also produces x86-based servers that compete with the likes of the HP/Compaq and Dell server markets. These systems are aimed at the Windows and Linux markets. However, I'll focus on the PowerPC systems for this chapter.

 NOTE   Linux will also run on the PowerPC processors, and IBM has vocally backed Linux for the past year and a half.

The birth of the PowerPC platform is one of those great stories of the Information Technology (IT) industry. In the early 1990s, IBM attempted to build a PowerPC-based processor architecture for less cost because of the Power platform found in the popular RS/6000 servers.

To make a long story short, IBM teamed up with Apple, which was looking for RISC-based processors to incorporate into Macintosh systems, and Motorola, which was a company that had a long-term affiliation with Apple and a reputation for building high-quality processors.

By the mid-to-late 1990s, the consortium, known as AIM (for Apple, IBM, and Motorola) had produced quality 32-bit and 64-bit processor designs, including the 603 and 604 models and the 620 that was a 64-bit processor.

The processors that IBM supplies nowadays for its Unix servers extend from the well-proven 604e 32-bit processor up to the flagship 64-bit Power4+

processor. In-between, there are a number of processors including the 64-bit Power3-II, Power4, RS64-II, and RS64-IV.

As you'll see shortly, the IBM and Sun SPARC processor families closely resemble one another in terms of their associated clock rates and features. Although Sun and IBM defiantly have a different view on the world according to the processors that they make and what constitutes good performance, there's an interesting line-up of features in the common vertically tiered processor market.

Platform Architecture

The processors I'll focus on include the processors available in today's IBM Unix server market. Some of these processors are a number of years old but still are well performing.

The processors I'll focus on from IBM are as follows:

- 32-bit 604e

- 64-bit PowerPC 750

- 64-bit PowerPC 750GXe

- 64-bit PowerPC 750FX

- 64-bit RS64-III

- 64-bit RS64-IV

- 64-bit Power4

- 64-bit Power4 970

Before looking at each processor in more detail, you'll see an overview of the processors at a high level and the systems in which they come.

NOTE   IBM builds WebSphere. As you can imagine, there are some benefits to using IBM hardware when it comes to using WebSphere-based applications. This extends to several features typically found in the operating system level (in other words, a tighter integration of the JVM and AIX operating system) and in the IBM JVM itself.

IBM PowerPC 604e

The IBM 604e processor is one of IBM's most successful processors. It's a 32-bit CPU for the lower-end server market and for high-end workstations. The 604e is similar in target market to that of the lower-end UltraSPARC II processors, with the main difference being its 32-bit implementation. The 604e supports 4GB of memory per CPU and has 32-byte level 1 data and instruction caches.

The processor operates at 250, 300, 333, 350, and 375MHz. These days, you can only find the 604e on IBM systems such as the RS/6000 B50 (a rack-mounted Telco/utility server) and the RS/6000 150, which is a small business server.

Although the 604e is a quality processor, for a production WebSphere-based environment with the atypical needs of an online application, the 604e isn't the processor of choice.

As you'll see, the 64-bit Power4 processors are a big step ahead in terms of performance and scalability.

IBM PowerPC 750

The PowerPC 750 is where IBM's Power architecture began to be seen as a formidable player in the high-end RISC market. There were several models of the 750, most notably, and the ones I'll discuss are the PowerPC 750, the 750Cxe, and the 750FX. You'll look at each of these in further detail.

PowerPC 750

The PowerPC 750 was a 32-bit RISC processor that was released in the late 1990s by IBM. Based on the success of the Power-based CPU architecture, the 750 provided high performance. Even though the processor was effectively a 32-bit processor, it performed well alongside 64-bit CPUs as the time.

The PowerPC 750 comes with a 32-bit address bus (used for memory addressing and pointing—32-bit data types) and a 64-bit data bus for moving data. Also, it comes with an independent on-CPU 32KB instruction and 32KB data level 1 cache as well as an expandable level 2 cache supporting Static Random Access Memory (SRAM) expansion in 1MB increments.

The PowerPC 750 provides the ability to execute up to six instructions per clock cycle for some data types when most other instructions only take single clock cycles to execute.

Like most of the PowerPC/Power-based processors, the PowerPC 750 can support both big and little endian modes, allowing multiple manufactures such as Apple, Motorola, and IBM to use the same common processor platform.

Other than the 32-bit factor, the only other major limitation of the PowerPC 750 is that, like UltraSPARC II processors, it only supports 4GB of memory per

CPU. Overall, the mainstream PowerPC 750 supports speeds of 233MHz–500MHz.

The system bus clock speed starts from 66MHz for the lower-end 233MHz versions of the PowerPC 750 and continues up to 100MHz in most versions. There's a landing point for some of the PowerPC 750 models with system bus speeds of 83MHz.

PowerPC 750Cxe

The PowerPC 750Cxe at a high level is similar in architecture to the "stock" PowerPC 750 model. With the same amount of level 1 cache, the PowerPC 750Cxe changes from the PowerPC 750's design of having a large, off-processor level 2 cache. The PowerPC 750Cxe's on-processor design supports up to 256KB of level 2 cache.

Processor or clock speeds are nearly double that of the "stock" PowerPC 750 processor; the PowerPC 750Cxe supports up to 700MHz with the entry-level models coming in at 400MHz. System bus speeds for the 750Cxe start at a higher rate than that of the "stock" PowerPC 750, commencing at 100MHz with the highest being 133MHz.

Power 750FX

The PowerPC 750FX is, like the PowerPC 750Cxe, similar to the "stock" PowerPC 750 processor. The key differences for this processor are the additional level 2 cache of 256KB, taking level 2 up to 512KB, and the ability for the process to scale up to and faster than 1GHz.

IBM made other internal upgrades to this processor such as various internal bus expansions, including the level 1 data cache. The stock PowerPC 750 processor operated a 64-bit bus to this particular cache; however, the 750FX has been upgraded to support 256 bits.

IBM RS64-III and RS64-IV

The RS64 processor family is a 64-bit RISC platform that was originally designed for the AS/400 and RS/6000 systems from IBM. These processors are both high-performing processors that, although originally produced a few years ago, continue to provide high-performing options for various models of IBM systems such as the p660 and p680 systems.

I won't present the RS64 range of processors in great detail because of its limited use in the WebSphere application server market. However, as a high-level overview, the processors range from speeds of 262MHz (for the RS64-III) to more than 750MHz (for the RS64-IV).

Both processors support fairly large independent level 1 data, instruction caches of 128KB, and level 2 off-CPU caches up of to 8MB in size for the RS64-III and 16MB for the RS64-IV.

IBM Power4

Industry analysts once considered the IBM Power4 processor architecture an ambitious project, but IBM came through and released the Power4 core architecture. This was because the Power4 processor boasts 170 million transistors as compared to the Pentium 4 processor having 52 million transistors.

Essentially, the Power4 core is a dual-core CPU with three levels of cache (a level 1, a level 2, and a level 3 cache). Because of all the added complexity within the Power4 core, IBM added a number of other components to the processor architecture to facilitate the additional data flow.

The twin processor cores (which hold the standard processor-type components such as issue and execution units and the instruction and data level 1 caches) operate together yet share a level 2 cache and a component known as the *fabric controller* (discussed shortly).

A key point is that the Power4 level 2 cache memory operates at the same speed as the clock rate. Therefore, with a standard processor clock rate of 1.3GHz, the level 2 cache is being accessed at the same cycle rate as the core. The two cores in the Power4 can communicate with the level 2 shared cache memory at more than 100GB per second.

The fabric controller is essentially a switch that's responsible for switching and managing the data flow around the processor. It also supports the processor-to-processor communications for SMP-based multiprocessor systems.

The fabric controller also interconnects the processing engines to the rest of the system via what's known as a *GX controller*. Although the fabric controller switches the traffic and data around the processor itself, the GX controller is responsible for the messaging and controlling of data in and out of the processor.

Another component worth mentioning is the level 3 cache component. The level 3 cache is a whopping 32MB in size per Power4 processor. As you add additional processor modules, you effectively increase the amount of level 3 memory available to the processor modules, and you also increase the available bandwidth. As level 3 cache memory is shared across process modules and managed by the level 3 memory controller on each processor module, you gain physical size and bandwidth to level 3 shared cache as you add more processors.

When adding in additional CPU modules to make use of larger multiprocessor systems, the CPU modules will connect via a ring topology and be controlled by the intermodule bus controller. This design allows for the sharing of level 3 cache memory.

The level 1 and level 2 cache memory in the Power4 supports 64KB of level 1 instruction cache and 32KB of level 1data cache. The level 2 cache is supported with 1.5MB of cache memory and is shared between both cores on a dual-core based Power4 chip.

Multiple CPU modules can be interconnected to form 8-way, 16-way, 24-way, and 32-way configurations.

Each processor core can support up to 16GB of system memory, with the memory-to-processor data transfer rate supported at a peak rate 205GB/s with the 1.3GHz cores. Compared with the high-speed FSBs of the high-end Intel Pentium 4 processors of 800MHz, the Power4 currently operates at a slightly lower 433MHz between system memory and processor cores. Although the bus clock rate is lower in the Power4 than it is with the high-end Intel processors, the transfer rate is still comparable.

The Power4 processor comes in two primary versions (as opposed to the PowerPC/Power4 derivatives discussed next). The first Power4 version is touted by IBM as being optimized for data-intensive applications (for example, scientific, financial modeling, and so on); it's the Power4 HPC processor.

This model of Power4 processor operates at 1.3GHz and operates with only one core instead of the much-touted dual-core model. The level 2 cache, therefore, is shared by a single core only, providing essentially double the cache memory for level 2 cache.

The second version of the Power4 is the Power4 standard. This model of Power4 is primarily what I covered previously. It comes with the standard dual-core design and shared level 2 cache and is the more general-purpose processor (if such a processor can be called that!).

The high-end IBM pSeries 690 server can operate both these Power4 processor models.

From a core-processing perspective, each core (in the Power4) or single core (in the Power4 HPC) can execute a multiply/add instruction each cycle or four floating-point instructions per clock cycle per core. In summary, each core is capable of executing up to eight instructions per clock cycle. The Power4 has a large 12-stage pipeline, one that definitely helps it compete alongside that of the deep Intel and AMD pipelines (up to 20 stages for the Pentium 4).

The Power4 is considered to be the most powerful single processor in the IT industry today.

IBM PowerPC 970

The PowerPC 970 is essentially a trimmed-down version of the Power4 processor architecture.

The PowerPC 970 is a 64-bit 1.4GHz–1.8GHz superscalar processor that offers most of the features of the Power4 processor architecture, with a few modifications.

The main difference is the change from a dual-core design from the Power4 back to a single-core design. The resulting clock speed of the single core is higher; however, with the implementation of the PowerPC 970 on a smaller die, the processor has done away also with the level 3 cache. Also gone is the complex fabric controller found in the Power4 flagship processor.

The PowerPC 970 is essentially IBM's much-anticipated mainstream version of the Power4 processor. The target markets for the PowerPC 970 are entry-level servers and high-end workstations. Because of the addition of many new Single Instruction/Multiple Data (SIMD) instructions, it makes the PowerPC 970 popular for workstation-based computing as well as server-based computing.

The make-up of the PowerPC 970 includes a 64KB level 1 instruction cache, a 32KB level 1 data cache, and a 512KB level 2 cache.

From an internal perspective, the PowerPC 970 boasts similar features to that of the UltraSPARC III. The impressive feat is that the PowerPC 970 incorporates a 900MHz processor bus (somewhat equivalent to the Intel/AMD FSB). This delivers peak transfer rates of more than 6.5GB per second, making the FSB speeds of the PowerPC 970 very impressive.

The PowerPC 970 also consists of a number of graphical instruction sets, all of which make no difference to the operational performance of a WebSphere-based environment.

The PowerPC 970 does, however, come close to that of the Pentium 4 super pipelining capabilities, boasting a 16-stage pipeline for integer instructions and slowly scaling up to a 25-stage pipeline for SIMD instructions.

Comparison Chart: IBM PowerPC Processors

From a WebSphere application server perspective, the PowerPC processors offer good performance. And, like the other three vendors you've looked at (AMD, Sun, and Intel), the differences in performance from the older model processors to that of the newer model processors truly shows how Moore's law is working.

 NOTE   Moore's law states that processor performance will double every 18 months.

The following summarizes the IBM processors:

PowerPC 604e: This is an aging processor from IBM. It was a quality, 32-bit processor when it was first released; however, unless you have a specific need to utilize a WebSphere server with this processor, I recommend looking at the 64-bit processors first.

PowerPC 750/750Cxe/750FX: The PowerPC 750/750Cxe/750FX is, again, a quality family of processors. They're hard to find nowadays, and therefore I only recommend using them for WebSphere-based implementations if you must. Ideally, you should look at the higher-end and more recent PowerPC-based processors instead.

PowerPC RS64-III and RS64-IV: Several systems are still available from IBM with these processors. The IBM p620 servers are supplied with the RS64 processors and will run WebSphere application environments well. The class of servers operating these processors are best for small to medium WebSphere implementations.

IBM Power4: The Power4 processors are by far IBM's best-suited processor for server tasks. Obviously, if your server requirements just don't dictate large-scale processor power and copious amounts of memory, the Power4 may not be the best choice. In this case, consider the RS64 processors as an alternative. However, the Power4 is available in many models of IBM systems from small to the largest IBM Unix system, the p690. The p630 IBM server is a low-end system that will support up to 32GB of memory for a WebSphere-based application environment. Using WebSphere clustering, a combination of Power4 processors, and these lower-end IBM servers, you'll achieve high levels of availability and performance with a decent price tag.

PowerPC 970: The PowerPC 970 is a processor that will become quite popular and will possibly overtake the server models using the older 604e-based and 750-based CPUs and, quite possibly, the RS64 platforms. Although it doesn't have a large level 2 cache like most high-end processors, it's still a good performer, especially if your WebSphere application is suited to this type of architecture.

Selecting Your PowerPC Platform

Now that you've seen the more common IBM-based processors at a high level, you'll get an overview of where each of them would fit in different-sized environments.

Again, like the previous SPARC and Intel/AMD sections, these recommendations are based on approximate sizes. You should ensure proper capacity planning so that the processor performance and characteristics match those you require for your WebSphere environment.

So, Which CPU?

Based on at the CPUs you've seen so far, the following sections offer some guidelines and recommendations on where you could use the IBM-based processors and servers within a WebSphere environment.

Small Production Environments

For smaller WebSphere production environments where either a single WebSphere application server or dual or more small servers are required, there are several choices.

First, I recommend the Power4 processor for all WebSphere-based needs unless there's a compelling reason to go with an older processor such as a PowerPC 604e or PowerPC 750, or even an RS64.

Based on this recommendation, consider the IBM p630-based servers. These servers support up to four-way configuration with up to 32GB of system memory. These systems are capable of Dynamic Logical Partitioning (DLPAR)/Logical Partitioning (LPAR) partitioning with up to four partitions, thus allowing you to build a WebSphere cluster using internally partitioned components within a single frame. The p630 also supports hot-swappable internal drives and up to six Peripheral Component Interface (PCI) interface slots.

One processor I didn't speak about in detail in the previous sections is the Power3 processor. If budgets are constrained and IBM is your vendor of choice, the RS/6000 server costs less with a Power3-II processor.

Check with your local IBM vendor representative or reseller about the support and service availability of these model servers and CPUs.

Medium Production Environments

A medium-sized WebSphere environment will typically host between 100 and 500 concurrent users and require a high degree of availability and redundancy.

As you saw with the Sun SPARC platforms, you can take two paths here. First, it's possible to take the servers listed in the "Small Production Environment" section and horizontally scale them (in other words, use more smaller servers) to a point where, instead of having two p630 servers, you have four p630 servers. This would provide a high degree of processing power (up to 16 Power4 CPUs) and up to 128GB of memory between all the systems.

However, as I touched on previously, you must be confident that your WebSphere application requirements from a processing and memory point of view don't exceed your lower-end servers.

Remember the earlier discussion on the ratio of operating system threads to JVM threads? As a guide, one CPU per running Java application JVM is a safe starting point. I've been involved in environments where the ratio of JVMs to CPUs is higher—in the vicinity of one JVM per three CPUs. Typically this is caused by applications that are memory hungry, where there's a constant need for garbage collection. Remember, like most of these guidelines, your mileage is going to vary depending on the structure and characteristics of your application. It'll also vary depending on your platform of choice—Power4, Intel, SPARC, and so on. Based on a rule of one JVM per CPU, a fully featured IBM p630 server should operate, at maximum, with four WebSphere-based applications.

 NOTE   This ratio of JVMs to CPUs isn't a WebSphere-specific requirement guide. It's more driven by how the Java JVM operates. And, depending on your Java JVM vendor, this will also vary!

If your pure processor power, number of active JVMs, or amount of memory required exceeds something like a p630 or another smaller, lower-end server, the next models up from IBM will support up to 8-way and 16-way processing and up to 256GB of memory.

The 16-way processor systems are leaning toward the larger WebSphere environments, especially if you're operating multiple nodes.

Two key systems that IBM produces that are well suited to medium-sized WebSphere environments are the p650 and p655. The p650 is a rack-mounted system that supports up to eight-way Power4 processor capability and 64GB of memory. Like other IBM systems operating the Power4 range, the p650 and p655 support DLPAR/LPAR partitioning, so, again, you could deploy one or two of these and partition the servers to meet your requirements. The p655 is a chassis-based server that's eight-way and supports 32GB of memory. This server also supports both Power4 HPC and Power4 standard processor modules.

Large Production Environments

For large Power4-based WebSphere environments operating anywhere from 500 to 10,000 concurrent sessions, there are two primary choices: the p670 and the p690. The p670 has up to 16-way processor support and 256GB of memory, and the p960 has up to 32-way processor support and 512GB of memory.

Again, like other IBM Power4-based systems, these two servers come with all the partitioning capabilities to be able to split them down to multiple nodes per chassis.

Where Are the Large IBM Servers?

A question I regularly get asked is, "Why does IBM only support up to 32-way in a single chassis?" IBM has a slightly different architecture plan than that of Sun: In order to obtain more processing power per physical server (in other words, more than 32-way), IBM has a number of advanced clustering solutions that allow you to cluster your servers.

However, at the end of the day, considering WebSphere as your platform engine, I don't recommend architecting your WebSphere or J2EE applications to require more than 32 JVMs in a single server.

In future chapters, I'll cover running multiple groups of servers or partitions to keep your maximum CPU count per server (not per chassis), domain, or partition down to 24–28 CPUs.

For WebSphere to be able to support this many active JVMs is an immense task. The better option is to split your servers into common tiers such as a utility tier, a batch tier, and an Enterprise Integration Layer (EIL) tier.

Using this model, you could purchase a pair of IBM p690s and partition them like so:

- Partition A: 12 CPUs

- Partition B: 12 CPUs

- Partition C: Six CPUs

Partition A may be the utility tier, Partition B the batch tier, and the Partition C the EIL tier. Then you'd mirror this configuration to the second p690 for frame redundancy.

Should you find that the 24 CPUs of processing power for partitions A and B isn't enough, purchase an additional p690 or lower-end p670 and add them to the WebSphere cluster associated with the first two partitions (in other words, the utility and batch tiers).

I'll cover this method of WebSphere platform architecting in greater detail in Chapter 5.

Platform Summary

As you've seen, the IBM PowerPC and Power4 range of processors are high quality and high performing. Without a doubt, the Power4 processor is one of the market leaders in terms of its performance and scalability capabilities. Remember, when considering Power4 processors, each Power4 chip effectively has a dual core.

Although it's not a 100-percent performance improvement over having a single Power4 processor, it does provide a large advantage in terms of performance given the dual cores are cross-connected via high-speed buses, greatly reducing the latency between processor cores. This is unlike that of other SMP-based processor architectures where latency can sometimes, but not always, be an issue for large-scale SMP performance.

Comparing Disk Systems

Any platform you'll use will require some form of disk storage. Like processor cores, disks come in many shapes, forms, and make-up. As you'll see, there are a vast array (no pun intended) of disk technologies available, and most have their place and purpose in a WebSphere environment.

In the following sections, you'll look at the various disk technologies common to AIX (PowerPC), Solaris (SPARC), Linux, and Windows (Intel/AMD x86). After that, I'll discuss the pros and cons of each disk technology and provide support for selecting your disk technology.

Disk Technologies

You're probably familiar with the terms *IDE* and *SCSI*. Both of these terms refer to the leading disk technology or architecture on the market. There are several other disk architectures available, including Fibre Channel, Serial ATA (S-ATA), and the lesser-known FireWire models using the IEEE 1394 FireWire standard.

Disk technology—or, more specifically, the choice and implementation of disk technology—is important for your system. Next to CPU performance, the disk's subsubsystem is probably the next most important aspect for a WebSphere environment (or any environment for that matter).

How you lay out your disks (partitioning and so on), how you implement your disk layouts—such as Redundant Array of Inexpensive Disks (RAID), Just Basic Old Disk (JBOD), and so on— and what technology or architecture your disk subsystem is made up of will greatly affect the performance of an application.

You'll now go through the major disk architectures currently available.

ATA: IDE, EIDE

In 1990, the American National Standards Institute (ANSI) ratified an IDE-like standard, now known as ATA-IDE, or just ATA (which stands for *Advanced Technology Attachment*). IDE for years now has been the leader in low-end servers and desktop workstations. It's a cheap and effective technology that provides quite good performance for general use.

IDE was really the first of the high-performing, low-cost disk technologies on the market. Not long after IDE appeared, an enhanced version, Enhanced Integrated Disk Electronics (EIDE), was released. The EIDE version is more commonly found in today's PCs, desktops, and notebooks in some form or another.

SCSI: SCSI-2 and Ultra SCSI

SCSI has long been touted as the leader in the storage market for servers. Competing closely with Fibre Channel, the various SCSI standards since SCSI-1 in 1981 all operate with a SCSI protocol and language.

SCSI is a mature and stable disk technology and provides a robust disk attachment platform for higher-end computing. SCSI drives—or, more specifically, SCSI-2 and more recent SCSI implementations—support a higher sustained throughput than the typical IDE-based drives. "Disk bandwidth" is higher in a relatively sized SCSI drive than a high-end IDE drive and therefore is better suited to more than one concurrent disk request.

As discussed previously, the majority of IDE drives can come fairly close to the more mainstream SCSI-based drives; however, because of the overall SCSI architecture, there's more growth potential—in terms of performance—in SCSI than there is in IDE.

Table 4-4 highlights some of the most mainstream SCSI drive configuration types.

Table 4-4. Common SCSI Implementations

SCSI Type	Bus Width	Bus Speed	Cable Length (in Meters)	Maximum Devices
Wide Ultra SCSI	16 bits	40 megabits (Mb) per second	1.5–3	8
Ultra2 SCSI Low Voltage Differential (LVD)	8 bits	40Mb per second	12	8
Wide Ultra2 SCSI (LVD)	16 bits	80Mb per second	12	16
Wide Ultra3 SCSI (LVD)	16 bits	160Mb per second	12	16

LVD was an important step in SCSI's evolution when it was introduced. Basically, pre-LVD SCSI implementations were limited by a number of factors, including the number of drives (or devices) that could be placed on a SCSI bus and how long the cables were.

As you can imagine, trying to squeeze eight SCSI drives onto a 1.5-meter cable is near impossible. Then came LVD, which essentially provides a differential-based bus technology. A second set of data lines is provided that allows for signals to be driven with the opposite electrical polarity as the original lines. If a 1 bit is represented by +5 volts in the standard data line, that same 1 bit is echoed on the supplemental data line as -5 volts.

As such, there's a higher overall voltage switch to represent the data. There's also redundancy in the transmission paths, and any outside noise that might enter the lines will be canceled out at the receiving end. Further, the resulting differentiated bus provides a boost in cable lengths to 25 meters.

Ultra160 and Ultra320

Ultra160 and Ultra320 are two technologies that are based on the core SCSI technology command set. Ultra160 supports the same speed as Ultra3 SCSI, with a reduced command set. Recently the Ultra320 SCSI flavor was released, which supports a maximum transfer speed of 320MB per second.

Ultra160 and Ultra320 are sound technologies; however, because of their implementation of a reduced SCSI command set, some features may be made available from your selected storage vendor. Be sure to validate the command set used in your Ultra160 and 320 implementations.

iSCSI

iSCSI is the Network Attached Storage (NAS) lover's pinnacle storage architecture. iSCSI is a network or Transmission Control Protocol/Internet Protocol (TCP/IP) implementation—or, better put, an embedding of SCSI-3 into a protocol level (the TCP packet). In essence, it's an IP-based disk attachment technology.

iSCSI uses the same SCSI protocol commands used in standard SCSI, but the medium isn't a SCSI cable per se. Best of all, iSCSI is device independent. Imagine being able to mesh your data center storage systems and be able to access any data from any system—long gone are the days where you wonder how you're going to get data off a mainframe when its only disk-connect technology is Escon!

Another obvious benefits of iSCSI is that data centers can now truly start to consolidate storage devices. Coupled with any of the various third-party storage provisioning (storage on demand) software packages, iSCSI can allow system architects and operation managers the ability to truly share disks and tape storage systems from anywhere. Consolidation of backup devices is another benefit of the iSCSI technology.

Some of you may be saying that it's like NAS. Well, it's kind of like NAS; however, it continues where NAS stops. NAS is still a semiclosed technology. You need specialized switches and potentially specialized Host Bus Adaptor (HBA) interface cards. With iSCSI, it's all TCP/IP, and it uses your existing network fabric of routers and switches. It also can share the existing TCP/IP-bound network adapter in your servers.

Obviously, if your data center storage I/O requirements are large, you may need to lay new cable and deploy additional switches to cater to the additional IP load. Networking vendors are also getting on the bandwagon. Companies such as Cisco are embedding iSCSI protocol handlers and offloads into their switching and routing gear. Although this type of hardware isn't required for a straightforward installation of iSCSI, it does appear to require skilled network engineers! Figure 4-1 highlights a typical iSCSI implementation.

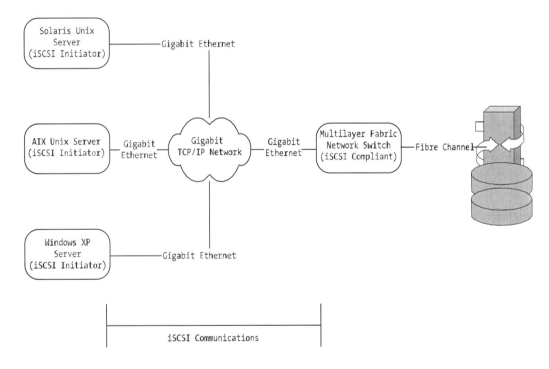

Figure 4-1. High-level iSCSI implementation

iSCSI is a fairly new network implementation and looks to have a long future. Many experts are touting iSCSI to be the replacement for FCAL given the theoretical no-distance limitation of iSCSI and the commodity-based iSCSI interfaces—in other words, TCP and commodity Fast Ethernet/gigabit+ network infrastructure. There are now several vendors supplying 10GB Ethernet networking infrastructure, which makes the business case for iSCSI quite strong.

Currently, the market is fairly limited in terms of iSCSI, and therefore, I won't focus on this area a great deal. However, within the next year or two, iSCSI will gain a lot of momentum among the leading storage-connect technologies.

SAN and NAS

Although the Storage Area Network (SAN) and NAS technologies aren't technically at the same level as SCSI or ATA, they play an increasingly important part of data center and e-commence systems.

Storage Area Network (SAN)

SAN provides the ability for systems to interface with disk or storage devices over a Fibre-based switching infrastructure. SAN uses SAN switches, which are somewhat similar to that of a IP network; however, SAN is closer in fundamental architecture to FCAL than IP.

SAN provides for the interconnection of commodity-type storage units to many systems. Many large enterprises are using SAN to create an enterprise storage array where all the host systems can interface with the centralized enterprise storage array over a SAN mesh.

Figure 4-2 shows a high level overview of how SAN could be implemented.

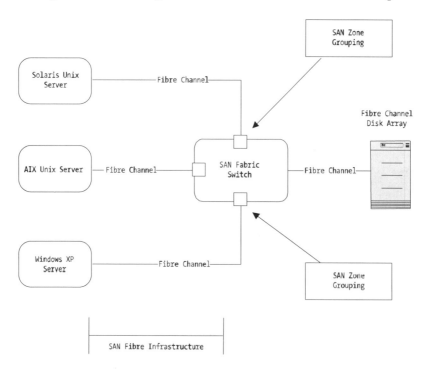

Figure 4-2. High-level SAN implementation

As you can see from Figure 4-2, the SAN allows for a many-to-many or a many-to-one relationship with hosts to storage devices. SAN supports a one-to-one relationship but unless you're trying to obtain some level of cost scalability by using SAN, one-to-one storage to host relationships is best implemented using straight Fibre Channel.

In Figure 4-2 the SAN infrastructure depicted represents a Fibre SAN interconnection that could be over any distance from several meters, or yards, to several hundred kilometers, or miles. There are important design considerations you need to be aware of if you're trying to extend your SAN over distances greater than several hundred kilometers, or miles. Several vendors supply technologies that help extend a SAN to long distances. However, when latency starts to impede performance, other technologies may be better choices such as NAS and iSCSI.

The idea behind SAN is really about storage consolidation and easy integration and management. It provides a wire interface speed of 100MB per second, similar to that of FCAL. However, the method of implementation can reduce or increase this figure greatly—such as in a situation where you have four hosts interfacing via a SAN to a central disk storage array, with one SAN interconnect from the storage array to the SAN fabric. This would have four hosts sharing a single 100MB per second SAN interconnect from the SAN switch to the storage array.

Network Attached Storage (NAS)

NAS is SAN's counterpart in the enterprise storage market. Essentially, NAS is an IP-based storage network. Where SAN allows the sharing and meshing of storage systems via Fibre-based connections at FCAL-like speeds, NAS provides the sharing and meshing of storage systems via IP-based networks. That is, speeds such as 100Mb per second and 1000Mb per second are the current mass-market speeds in which you can connect your storage array to your hosts over NAS.

Of course, with appropriate bridges and switching hardware, you can increase these speeds via multiplexing and other wide-area technologies such as OC-12, OC-48, and beyond (655Mb per second, 2048Mb per second).

NAS is a great alternative to applications that aren't I/O intensive. In a WebSphere-based environment, unless your deployed J2EE applications require access to data stored at a great distance away (more than approximately 500 kilometers, or 300 miles), then NAS probably doesn't have a place in your high-performance WebSphere environment. With NAS, you get all the TCP/IP overhead you'd get with normal networking.

NOTE I don't want to give the impression that NAS isn't a good technology. I've seen it used in J2EE environments, and it can be a good choice under the right circumstances. At the end of the day, 99.9 percent of all systems can talk via IP. Therefore, it's currently the ultimate technology for interfacing one system type to another system type. Think of how easy it would be to interface a WebSphere-based application on a Sun Solaris system to an IBM MVS system when there's a need to access files on the mainframe from the WebSphere-based application on the Solaris system. Other options exist such as MQ Series, but NAS is a good alternative here.

Fibre Channel Arbitrated Loop (FCAL)

Fibre Channel–based storage systems have been the high-end computing disk-connect technology of choice for the past 5–10 years.

FCAL, using the Fibre Channel communications standard, operates in an arbitrated loop configuration whereby all nodes or devices in the loop must "arbitrate" to communicate onto the loop. FCAL most commonly operates using a 100MB per second interface speed, faster than most SCSI implementations and, despite its name, can operate on optical fiber or twisted pair mediums.

For higher-speed FCAL implementations, optical fiber is required. Fiber also has the advantages of being able to operate for longer distances than that of twisted pair. And remember, I'm talking optical fiber. It's not as easy to manipulate as its twisted pair or even SCSI counterparts. That's the trade-off for excellent performance.

Although FCAL is associated with a looping bus topology, it's possible to use Fibre Channel hubs, which allow the loop to be collapsed to individual loops between the end device (such as a disk) and the hub or switch. Like the old days of coaxial-based bus networks, in a full arbitrated loop configuration where all end devices are connected via a loop, if a single device is unplugged or fails, the entire loop fails. As you can imagine, if you have a great deal of data housed on disks with a legacy loop configuration and one disk fails, the resulting effect is disastrous. Figure 4-3 provides a high-level overview of how FCAL operates.

FCAL-based disks are available and are high performing (more than that of their SCSI counterparts at similar levels of capability and spindle speed). However, many storage vendors nowadays are providing FCAL interfaces to controllers within disk storage cabinets, and the disks themselves are connected to the FCAL "heads" or exposed controller interfaces. This helps reduce the costs of the disks themselves because you can use commodity SCSI or other forms of disk technology in place of FCAL disks while at the same time obtaining the same performance. You'll also get the added benefit of being able to house the disk cabinets away from the servers.

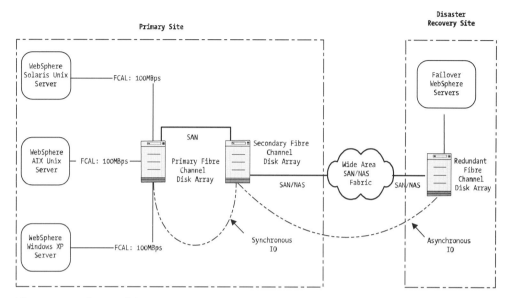

Figure 4-3. FCAL architecture

Unless your WebSphere-housed applications are referencing large amounts of data on disk at great frequency, or your disaster recovery data center architecture or other storage requirements require that your disks are located away from the host systems, FCAL could be an overkill for your needs. From a price to performance comparison, they're at the upper level of disk technology costs.

This is an important consideration and one with which many systems engineers and architects need to contend. Therefore, it shouldn't be displaced as an alternative, but remember that the investment is high compared to more standard SCSI implementations. Figure 4-4 depicts the method of locating your disks at a distance from your host's systems while using more standard disk technologies such as SCSI.

Remember also that Ultra3 SCSI (Ultra160) can support 160MB per second, and the recently released Ultra320 is also becoming available from a number of vendors. These native SCSI-based technologies are typically better performing for the price and storage capacity you can obtain from FCAL.

On paper, the ATA-100 and ATA-133 are faster than standard FCAL but aren't suitable for large-scale deployment because of architecture limitations, such as the number of drives or devices on the bus. FCAL can still support 127 devices on a single arbitrated loop. If you multiplex your loops, you can get an order of magnitude more devices—most high-end storage vendors support this.

Although FCAL is limited in performance to 100MB per second, many high-end storage vendors allow you to multipath and, as such, multiplex your storage connections to either SAN, NAS, or Direct Attached Storage (DAS) devices. EMC, one of the world's leading storage array vendors, is a prime candidate for this technology. I've been involved with systems implementations that required multiple DAS zonings to support more than 100MB per second disk I/O and, as such, utilized designs that used four 100MB per second FCAL interfaces, supporting a combined I/O performance rate of 400MB per second.

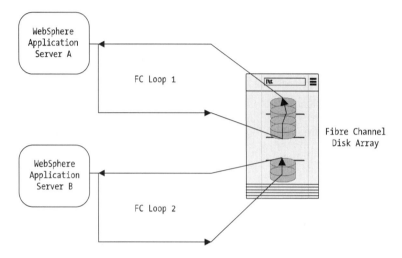

Figure 4-4. Distributed storage architecture example

That all said, it's rumored that the 10GB per second FCAL standard isn't too far away. This technology will outpace anything else on the market. Being able to transfer approximately 1,000MB per second isn't a small measure. Many lower-end systems will struggle to support these speeds.

Even with today's fastest systems, I/O bandwidth (or system bus bandwidth, depending on your architecture of choice) will be in the order of 1.2GB per second and up to 9.6GB per second for sustained, nonaggregated performance.

In summary, FCAL is the Rolls Royce of storage technologies. It scales, can be highly distributed (cross-city and cross-country depending on your I/O characteristics), and has a clear technology growth path into higher-end speeds such as 10GB per second. If you're after top-performing technologies with good growth, FCAL is a good choice.

Serial ATA (S-ATA)

S-ATA is a relatively new disk-connect technology and one I highly recommend you watch. Unlike traditional ATA, which is Parallel-ATA (P-ATA), Serial-ATA (S-ATA) operates using a serial protocol layer, using a seven-wire flat connector, looking not unlike a USB connector.

With the serial interface, a smaller and easier cable design, and an overhauled power interface supporting three voltage levels (as is found in the 2.5-inch drives typically associated with laptops and other portable devices supporting 2.5-inch hard disks), the overall physical implementation is far easier to use.

Current S-ATA technology is targeted to the low-end market such as desktop PCs and workstations but may eventually gain share in the server area. At the end of the day, the drives are still in essence using standard IDE/ATA technologies and, as such, are similar in performance to Ultra SCSI versus that of IDE/ATA.

Being a new standard means that many of the proven concepts from other disk technologies over the years have been incorporated into the standard. As such, the S-ATA standard will surely become the leading commodity or workstation disk technology in the coming 12–18 months.

Furthermore, S-ATA is fast. The initial specification supports 150MB per second as standard per drive, and upcoming S-ATA 2 standards will see this speed increase to 300MB per second. Although it's initially only slightly faster than the current standard ATA standard (better known as ATA-133) that operates at 133MB per second, there's a clear and healthy growth path because of the use of a LVD signaling interface, similar to the high-speed Ultra160 and Ultra360 SCSI specifications.

Given the relatively low cost of S-ATA disks, you can purchase almost four S-ATA disks in place of one SCSI-based disk of relative size. Theoretically, this can produce top performance because the load is distributed over four spindles rather than the one. There are downfalls to this approach, however. Bus, HBA (if using an external device), and controller bandwidth may become saturated under this type of load while controlling the I/O and communications of many more disks.

At the end of the day, good solid capacity planning will prove whether this is possible.

"Way Out There" Disk Technologies

Before summarizing the various technologies associated with disks and their impact on a WebSphere implementation, I'll make a few final points about some upcoming disk interfacing technologies.

USB and FireWire are two connection technologies found mostly in desktop-based systems. Currently, they support speeds of 480Mb per second and 400Mb per second, respectively, and USB and FireWire do support low-end disk technologies.

At these speeds, used in a WebSphere server environment, especially one with lots of log file writing, opening files, and closing files (images, JSPs, servlets, and so on), they'll operate at sufficient I/O rates.

The roadmap for FireWire looks quite good. Currently operating at 400Mb per second, recently released draft specifications suggest speeds of 800Mb per second, 1.2 gigabits (Gb) per second, and 3.2Gb per second (I'm talking here megabits and gigabits per second, not megabytes and gigabytes per second).

Another interesting disk or storage technology I've seen is with the use of RAM disks. A small handful of sites I've worked on have implemented RAM disks. While booting the WebSphere application server, the contents of the `installedApps` directory where the deployed J2EE applications resided and the WebSphere cache directories have loaded into RAM disk. This provides quite a good degree of performance. The downfall is that any contents of the RAM disk are flushed after any system reboot. The need for a script that operates every five to ten minutes is essential to copy back changes and updates made to cache.

RAM disks aren't for everyone and should only really be used in a environment where many small I/Os are taking place to specific areas. I'll discuss this further in later chapters.

Summarizing Storage Technologies in WebSphere Environments

You've looked at a fair number of disk technologies in this chapter. What's important to you now, if it wasn't already, is to look at what is the best disk technology for your WebSphere environment. As you'd expect, there's no "one size fits all," but the following sections will provide some support for deciding on a disk technology.

These sections will break up the disk technologies and rate them in terms of their value or effectiveness in a J2EE WebSphere-based environment. The sections cover individual disk speed, overall architecture performance, architectural complexity, and cost.

Storage Technology: Disk Speed

Disk speed is obviously one of the most important points of any system. From a default position, disk speed in a WebSphere environment doesn't have a major impact on the overall performance of the application unless the application components are performing a lot of I/O to the storage technology.

Databases connected to your WebSphere application server for either repository information (for WebSphere 4) or application information will quickly become the failure point of your environment if you have slow or poorly configured disks.

Imagine a situation where your WebSphere-deployed applications are regularly making requests to a database to retrieve information. Let's assume it's something such as an online order and sales system.

Each page click would require some form of database query to retrieve the information. Using this example, you'll now look at the disk technologies and which ones work and which ones don't work.

 CAUTION As I mentioned earlier, there's no one size fits all; however, this example should indicate the best practices for the various disks.

Figure 4-5 shows the disk technologies. The ranking is performed based on future speed as well current speed.

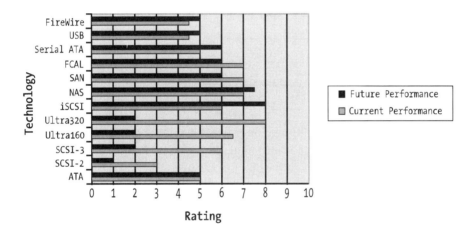

Figure 4-5. Disk performance overview

As you can see, the Ultra320 technology is the highest-performing disk technology. It's important to note that although Ultra160 and Ultra320 are theoretically faster than FCAL, direct FCAL–based disks are the best disk technologies. They offer fast onboard disk caches and quite often come with a great deal of onboard intelligence for real-time tuning and management of the disk I/O logic.

Storage Technology: Overall Performance

Like most things, overall performance consists of many components working together harmoniously. You can't strap a big Chevrolet engine to a budget family sedan and expect it to perform well. The same applies to storage technologies. You can have an array of IBM 73.5GB 15,000rpm drives yet a poorly performing storage bus, thus reducing your expensive disk array to nothing more than a bunch of perceived low-speed storage devices.

It's important to choose the right storage architecture for the "big picture." For this reason, it's important to plan and understand what your WebSphere applications will require. You need to ask questions, if they aren't already obvious, of application designers and architects, preferably before they commence development. The following questions are examples of what you can ask your developers or application architects to discover the fundamentals of the software architecture from a file I/O point of view:

- If there's file I/O occurring, what's the nature of the I/O? (Is it random or sequential? How many concurrent requests will there be? What's the size of the I/O requests? What's the I/O transaction rate?)

- Do the application components expect the resulting I/O to be completed within a certain timeframe?

- Are the application components associated with the file I/O multi-threaded? Specifically, are requests made to a file I/O factory in a separate thread, ensuring that I/O delays don't freeze the main thread of the application?

Let's look at those points in a little more detail.

Specifically, you should identify what the nature of the file I/O is. This will help determine what technology is viable for your system. For example, if the architects and software planners state that the requests are far and few between, such as simply logging information to an ASCII log file, then the I/O rate is minimal. Technologies such as NAS and the lower-end ATA-based technologies will perform the role sufficiently if the I/O transaction rate is low.

For ATA (S-ATA or P-ATA), the current technology standards support a fair amount of I/O. In the SCSI and FCAL worlds, you can roughly pin the number of I/Os for a particular disk on the number of revolutions per minute of the disk, divided by 100. For example, a 10,000rpm SCSI-2 disk will allow approximately 100 I/Os per second.

This rule doesn't always work, but it's a good guide. An ATA-based drive is somewhat slower, and the rate of I/O varies greatly. Depending on your manufacturer of choice, this reduction in performance can be anywhere from 20–50 percent less than that of a similarly sized SCSI-based disk. This is primarily because of the actual ATA disk having slightly lower-performing onboard logic and chipsets.

Therefore, if your application architect states that with 5,000 concurrent users on your system, you'll be performing 500 file I/Os per second, or a

10 percent I/O to active session ratio. For this case, you'd want to have at least five SCSI-2 or SCSI-3 drives or five native FCAL or mixed/native FCAL and SCSI-2/3 drives. SAN would perform the role sufficiently as long as your fan-out ratio (the number of disks presented versus the number of systems interfacing to them and the number of host Fibre Channel connections to number or disk cabinet connections) is at worst 1:4 (one disk cabinet to Fibre Channel connection per four host-based Fibre Channel connections).

Of course, if you're looking to increase I/O performance and or provide some buffering to the five disks, look at striping your disks with either something such as RAID 5 or RAID 0 (or RAID 0+1 to gain mirroring). Doing this increases your number of spindles, which effectively increases the available file I/O rate— more disks equal more I/Os per second.

Some disk vendors such as EMC provide proprietary mirroring and striping capabilities. EMC provides a similar technology to RAID 5 and RAID 0+1 known as RAID-S. Consider these types of capabilities if the storage vendors aren't offering the disk technology you're looking for (in other words, FCAL, SCSI-3, and so on).

From a database perspective, I/O rate is one of the biggest killers of database performance. Without getting into database fundamentals, the most important point I can make about databases and their system architecture is this: Distribute your I/O load! Whether you do this via a distributed database technology such as Oracle 9*i* RAC or you simply lay out the database files on separate individual disks and then mirror and stripe them, it's imperative to do this from a high-performing database point of view.

Generally speaking, the further down the physical tiers you look, the more disk I/O is important. If I had to rate the importance of file I/O or, more specifically, disk I/O from Web tier to application server tier to database tier, the weighted requirement would be low for Web tier, medium for application server tier, and high for database tier. Also, don't be afraid to mix and match your disk technologies.

For this reason, for larger implementations, my preference is this:

- Use onboard SCSI-based drives for thin Web servers (for example, Ultra160 or Wide Ultra 2).

- For application servers where file I/O is at a medium level and only standard logging is taking place that's properly threaded, use SCSI-based disks such as Ultra160 or Wide Ultra 2 (and always mirrored and typically stripped),

- Or use FCAL-based interfaces to external disk cabinets operating either native FCAL disks or higher-end SCSI-based disks such as SCSI3 or Ultra160 and Ultra320.

For the database tier, I always use the fastest possible disks available in the budget. Again, Ultra160 SCSI disks or FCAL technologies work well. Many of the bigger Unix vendors supply low-end systems with onboard FCAL connections and disks. The Sun V880 server supports up to 12 FCAL disks internal to the chassis. If it's only your database that requires high-speed disks, these servers make a great cost-effective alternative to having external storage cabinets.

The other points in the first question such as the concurrency of the file I/O and transfer size of the I/O are also important. In some cases, slower technologies such as ATA and NAS can provide fairly good I/O; however, if you're I/O size is high, then bus bandwidth can be a problem. If your application is requesting 800 I/Os per second yet the block transfer size is 32KB, then this would require approximately (not taking into account bus overhead and so on) 25MB per second of bandwidth.

Calculating Disk Performance: Disk Transfer Time

It's probably worth briefly explaining some calculations on disk I/O performance characteristics. I'll use the previous example to show how to do the calculations. You'll first want to select some disks. For the comparison, I've selected two disks from IBM (it's easy to find full disk specifications from IBM):

- The first disk is a 34.2GB ATA-based disk with an average seek time of 9 milliseconds (ms), a track-to-track read time of 2.2ms, an average latency at 4.17ms, and 2MB of cache. The average transfer speed that this disk is capable of is 18.35MB per second.

- The second disk is a 36.9GB SCSI-2 disk with an average seek time of 6.8ms, a track-to-track read time of 0.6ms, an average latency at 4.17ms, and 4MB of cache. The average transfer speed that this disk is capable of is 25.7MB per second.

These disks are a few years old and are provided as an example only. Both disks are also 7,200rpm.

The method to therefore calculate the time-to-transfer speed, based on 512KB worth of data, is to use an equation as follows:

```
[Seek time / Latency] + [512KB / Disk average transfer rate] = Time to transfer
```

Therefore, using these two disks, you can calculate that the transfer time for 512KB of data is as follows:

```
Disk 1: [9 / 4.17]   + [512K / 18.35] = 30.05 milliseconds
Disk 2: [6.8 / 4.17] + [512K / 25.7]  = 21.55 milliseconds
```

You'll look at what happens if you add additional disks, but before you do that, you need to be sure the bus you've chosen can support the speed.

Calculating Disk Performance: Bus Bandwidth

Before looking at the impact of adding additional disks, you should know that adding additional disks alone won't always provide you with the increase in performance you might expect. There's obviously only a finite amount of bandwidth on your disk bus. Whether this is the system bus or the disk bus itself (SCSI, FCAL, ATA), there's always a limitation. Most of the time, the way to get around the limitation is to simply add another bus. For SCSI, FCAL, SAN, NAS, and iSCSI, it's relatively easy to add additional buses (just add another HBA!). However, with ATA and IDE, it's sometimes trickier. This is because standard main boards supporting ATA or SCSI only have four ports, and in the x86 world, each pair of IDE ports require a dedicated Interrupt Request (IRQ). With the x86 limitation on IRQs, you need to consider this if you're choosing IDE as your disk.

More recently, vendors have been bringing out expander and daughter boards in a variety of mixtures, where the daughter board (the non-onboard IDE controller) handles the IRQ masking for you, and you essentially use just one IRQ for the entire bank of IDE disks.

To calculate your bandwidth's performance, or the point at which x number of disks will saturate your disk bus, you can use the following equations. You have an idea of how long it takes one disk to transfer 512 kilobits (Kb) worth of data, so you can assume the following:

```
Transfer speed of 512KB = [ Transfer size / Transfer speed ] = Transfer rate
```

The calculation for the example is as follows:

```
Disk 1: = [ 512 / 30.05 ] = 17.04MB per second
Disk 2: = [ 512 / 21.55 ] = 23.75MB per second
```

Now, if you wanted to understand what this equates to in terms of utilization of the two buses, ATA and SCSI, you'd use the following equation:

```
Bus utilization = [ Transfer rate for 512KB / Bus bandwidth ] = Utilization
```

Therefore, the calculation is as follows:

```
Disk 1: = [ 17.04 / 100 ] = 17% ATA bus utilization (ATA-100)
Disk 2: = [ 23.75 / 80  ] = 29% SCSI-2 bus utilization (SCSI-2)
        = [ 23.75 / 160 ] = 14% Ultra160 bus utilization (Ultra 3/Ultra160)
```

It's important to note that these calculations are guides. There are other per-system factors that need to be included in the calculations if you're looking for a truly scientific outcome. However, what these results are saying is this:

- ATA-100 has more bus bandwidth available than SCSI-2 (100MB per second versus 80MB per second).

- A similarly sized SCSI disk with the same rotational speed is faster, transfer-wise, than an equivalent ATA disk.

Now you'll look at the effect of adding disks to your bus.

Calculating Disk Performance: The True Effects of Striping Disks

When you look to distribute load across many disks or spindles, you need to be careful that the total data transfer doesn't saturate the nominated bus. To calculate this, I'll assume you've deployed a WebSphere implementation and have noticed that a file system that's sitting on a particular disk, which houses WebSphere log files, is becoming overloaded.

You've decided you need to distribute the load better by striping two to three disks. The simple calculation you can assume is this: If that particular disk bus is doing nothing else other than handing the I/O associated with your log files, it's a matter of dividing the per-disk transfer speed and rate by the number of disks in the stripe set. I typically add 10–15 percent overhead to this to account for the slight overhead associated with striping.

Note, however, that adding disks to perform striping doesn't decrease the bus utilization. Again, the simple calculation is to divide or multiple your I/O factor by the number of additional disks. If you're still transferring 512KB, but the 512KB of data is being sourced from a stripe over three disks instead of a single Just a Basic Old Disk (JBOD), the utilization of the bus still remains relatively the same. There will be a slight overhead of 5 percent per additional disk to counter for the additional bus-level commands of talking to three disks instead of one.

However, if one of your deployed applications got word that there was additional storage available and started to use the stripe set that housed your WebSphere log files, this would obviously affect your transfer rate and bus utilization.

For example, say another application started performing debug dumps on your newly created three disk stripe set, originally intended to house WebSphere logs. Being a debug dump, the I/O was fairly high and, as such, would frequently store 4KB of data to your stripe set.

The disk calculations would now look like this:

```
Disk 1: Transfer time = [9 / 4.17] + [512K + 64K / 18.35]  = 31.38 milliseconds
Disk 2: Transfer time = [6.8 / 4.17] + [512K + 64K / 25.7] = 22.41 milliseconds
```

Then, to understand the transfer rate over time, you calculate this:

```
Disk 1: Transfer rate = [ 512 + 64 / 31.38 ] = 18.35MB/s
Disk 2: Transfer rate = [ 512 + 64 / 22.41 ] = 25.70MB/s
```

This is the calculation for the bus utilization:

```
Bus utilization = [ Transfer rate for 512KB + 64KB / Bus bandwidth ] =
Utilization
Disk 1: = [ 18.35 / 100 ] + 5% = 23.35% ATA bus utilization (ATA-100)
Disk 2: = [ 25.70 / 80 ]  + 5% = 37.12% SCSI-2 bus utilization (SCSI-2)
        = [ 25.70 / 160 ] + 5% = 21.06% Ultra160 bus utilization (Ultra160)
```

As you can see, the additional 64KB of data doesn't produce a massive amount of overhead; however, it's increasing. Furthermore, 512KB of data isn't a large amount—consider the same calculations if your application server is handling large files in excess of a megabyte.

What all this means is that although technologies such as SCSI and FCAL support quite a number of disk, all having them operate on a singular bus can lead to bus saturation.

Storage Technology: Cost

Cost is always a major driver of any architecture. This is unfortunate but true, and WebSphere implementations are no different. From a storage cost perspective, there's vast difference between costs for an ATA-based implementation versus something such as a SAN or Fibre Channel implementation.

In the IT world, fast is best, and best costs. For storage, the costs of your chosen architecture should be driven by the technology—that is, what technology bests fits your implementation needs as determined by capacity planning and systems engineering? Then you need to look at the cost of the preferred storage technologies.

As explored in Chapter 2, Total Cost of Ownership (TCO) is a good measure of a technology's total cost. This will, or should, include items such as management and support costs of the technology, implementation costs, upgrade and scalability costs, and technology availability costs.

You'll now look at those in some more detail.

Management and Support Costs

Supporting any technology will cost money. Depending on the technology, the support costs will differ. There are several reasons for this, but generally the more complex the technology is, the more specialized the support services are. This drives up support costs. Complexity—and managing it—further increases costs.

For this reason, the supporting costs of ATA-133 disks in a lower-end WebSphere server will undoubtedly cost less to support and manage than that of a storage cabinet running Fibre Channel disks. Figure 4-6 shows the support costs associated with the storage technologies covered.

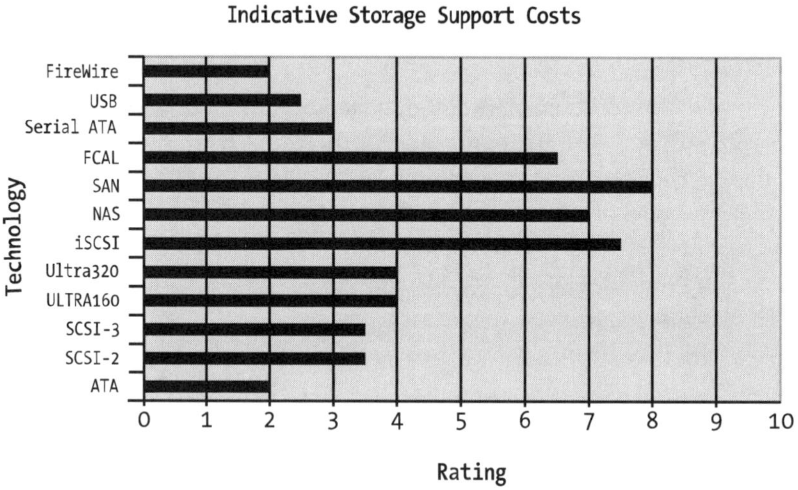

Indicative Storage Support Costs

Figure 4-6. Storage support costs

As you can see, the NAS, SAN, and iSCSI implementations are the most costly to support and manage. However, they're among the fastest of the disk storage technologies (refer to Figure 4-5). That said, as enterprise storage solutions such as SAN grow within an organization, the costs for support decrease steadily over time while the SAN's storage "mass," or size, increases.

Implementation Costs

The costs associated with implementation are also driven by the complexity of the technology. SAN and FCAL are examples of this. Closely followed behind these two flagship disk technologies, SCSI, NAS, and iSCSI are the next most costly of storage technologies to implement.

The implementation costs driven by the technology complexity are caused by the size of the implementation. That is, it's rare for anyone to install mission-critical WebSphere servers requiring high storage I/O throughput to use ATA-based disks.

The implementation costs consist of design and architecture costs and physical deployment and configuration costs that include personnel and resources. The more complex the technology, the more costly the resources will be. Figure 4-7 shows the costs associated with the implementation of the storage technologies discussed.

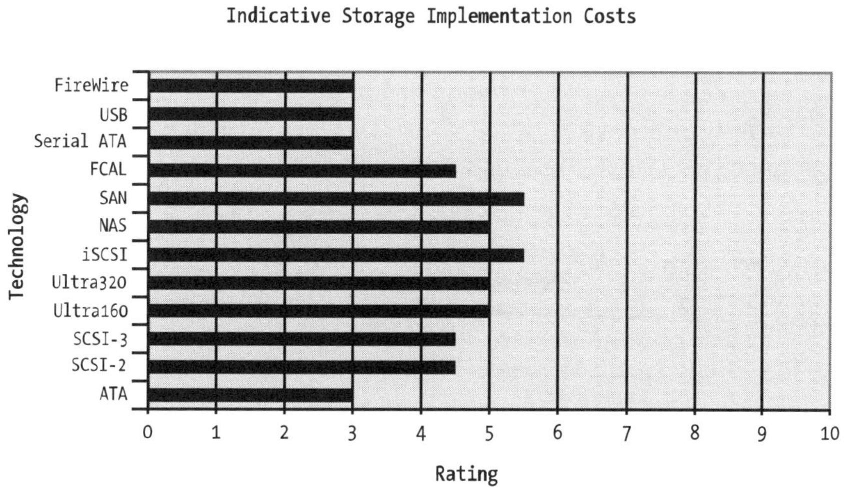

Indicative Storage Implementation Costs

Figure 4-7. Storage implementation costs

The distributed storage technologies such as NAS, SAN, and iSCSI incur the highest implementation costs. Point-to-point implementations are typically the least costly to implement.

It's important to note that these implementation costs assume a new installation. If the tables were turned and the example WebSphere environment was being plugged into existing NAS, SAN, or iSCSI storage fabric, the implementation costs would be greatly reduced for these technologies.

In summary, if your organization is using something such as an enterprise SAN or a preexisting Fibre Channel storage farm, the majority of the implementation costs are already covered, and therefore the implementation costs will be closer to that of SCSI, ATA, and other simpler storage technologies. This is predominately because you'll be initiating an additional connection to an existing enterprise storage solution.

Upgrade and Scalability Costs

A sometimes hidden cost in the selection of a technology is the future upgrade-ability and scalability costs. If, for example, you select an ATA disk-based storage technology that's typically limited to a small number (typically fewer than six) of interfaces, and you need to upgrade to additional disks, you'll find that there may not be enough interfaces for you to add disks.

Although there may be other solutions to get around this problem (daughter board IDE controllers and so on), it does illustrate the need for scalability.

What about your prized high-performing proprietary FCAL-based disk cabinet? It may come with 100 FCAL bays for storage, but exceeding 100 disks may require the purchase of another external disk storage cabinet. This increases costs for the physical cabinet purchase itself (sometimes 70–80 percent of the total solution cost), and you'll incur other costs incurred such as feed and water (for example, power, air conditioning, and so on). You'll need to know whether it would've been cheaper to go Ultra160 SCSI and take the hit on the SCSI bus overhead when connecting vast numbers of drives to a host system.

Storage Technology: Architectural Complexity

As mentioned in the previous section, architectural complexity is an important factor in the selection of the storage technology choice. Although it shouldn't be the most important aspect of your selection, you need to be mindful of it.

Storage Technology Summary

In summary, the storage technology you choose for your WebSphere system architecture should be based on an as-needed basis. That is, don't get FCAL for an implementation if you don't think there will be much in the way of high I/O. Of course, consider something such as high-end SCSI or FCAL for your database server tier. However, unless your applications running within WebSphere are regularly writing or reading data to disk, the lower-end disk technologies will suffice.

Network Controllers and Interfaces

Networking is another of the key components of a WebSphere environment—one that can break or make the performance or availability Service Level Agreements (SLAs) of an application. WebSphere, like any network or distributed-type application environment, benefits greatly from fast, robust, and resilient networking architectures.

I've found you can break down WebSphere networking requirements into three sections:

- WebSphere cluster networking (node-to-node communications)

- WebSphere-to-database (repository) networking

- WebSphere-to-customer (or frontend Web server) networking

You must carefully plan, design, and implement each of these requirements for your WebSphere application environment to operate within nominal performance boundaries. The design should also incorporate availability as a requirement.

You'll now take a look at these three key points in more detail.

NOTE   in the next chapter, I discuss WebSphere topologies in detail. Topologies typically involve network design, so the following sections act as an overview.

WebSphere Cluster Networking

This is a topic that won't apply to you if you're operating a small or lower-end WebSphere environment where you're running a single WebSphere application server node. If, however, you're operating a multinode or multiapplication server WebSphere environment, this will be of importance to you.

Like many J2EE application servers, WebSphere will communicate between application servers for a variety of items. This includes things such as a distributed JNDI tree or data replication (for WebSphere 5+). You may also have internal application communications between nodes for some form of higher-level load balancing. This type of application design will also be affected by slow or high-latency networking infrastructure.

So what does this type of networking requirement entail? I highly recommend you have two WebSphere application server nodes connected via some sort of medium. For availability reasons, you may have these two WebSphere application servers located in different cities approximately 1,000 kilometers, or 620 or so miles, away from one another. Because of this distance, there's an increased latency overhead associated with networking, and depending on the type of networking technology you use between your WebSphere nodes, this may be an unworkable design.

For example, if you were to use a 56Kbps modem to communicate between the two nodes, your latency would be approximately 240ms. Putting aside the fact that 56Kbps wouldn't be able to handle the amount of traffic that would be generated between two WebSphere nodes, the response time your users and customers would experience with the application would be atrocious.

 NOTE Don't use satellite (which I've seen being used before!) for this because it too has a high-latency factor associated with it. If you're distributing your WebSphere nodes apart from each other, use the fastest, least overhead technology you can afford.

You could use ATM, Packet over SONET (PoS), SONET, Frame Relay with a decent Committed Information Rate (CIR), or Digital Data Service (DDS), or, in a pinch, you could use a Virtual Private Network (VPN) over the Internet if your last-mile connections to your Internet Service Provider (ISP) were fast enough and your ISP had sufficiently large and well-performing internal network links.

If you're locating your servers together, then your task is far easier.

Look at using Gigabit Ethernet for the internal connections, even if you don't think you'll come close to using 1Gbps of bandwidth; the low latency of Gigabit Ethernet makes it a good choice.

Further, 100Mb per second Ethernet has a fairly good latency measure against it and is also fine for the role. However, capacity plan your requirements—if your 100Mb per second becomes overutilized by internal application-to-application or WebSphere-to-WebSphere traffic, you'll quickly see the latency increase.

These days, you can pick up Gigabit Ethernet interface cards for most systems fairly cheaply. Even if you build a point-to-point network (in other words, direct server to server) and use a standard switching network topology for a backup, this will be a low-cost solution.

In later chapters, you'll learn about the tuning of these interconnection links. Depending on your requirements, different TCP settings on your WebSphere hosts can make a big difference to the overall performance.

WebSphere-to-Database Networking

If you're operating a WebSphere 4 platform with a repository or if your applications are using a database for application data, this part of your WebSphere networking environment is critical from a proper network design point of view.

Database communications via something such as JDBC typically follow a fairly random characteristic in terms of size and frequency of the requests. That is, you may have a burst of small queries going to the database from the applications and small result sets. On the other hand, you may have a mixed bag of big and small result sets and few and many queries.

Either way, this part of your WebSphere environment can cause headaches for your users if it's not designed correctly.

Some basic recommendations, and ones I'll cover in more detail in later chapters, are as follows.

Redundancy Paths

Always have redundancy paths from the WebSphere tier to the database server tier. This may be via basic level 2 or 3 load balancing (or switching) or could be something such as the Solaris IPMP (IP Multipathing) software. Apart from a gain in performance (through a possible decrease in latency), this redundant path will result in higher availability.

At worst, for larger environments, use two links from each WebSphere server with different weighted metric values for each interface. This way, if one link goes down, a secondary link is available.

Number of Application Servers

Ensure that the sum of all WebSphere application servers connections don't flood a single database server connection. That is, be mindful of how many WebSphere application servers you have interfacing with the database server. It may be worthwhile, based on your capacity modeling, to have the database server hooked into a switch at gigabit speed and the WebSphere application servers all interfacing to the network at 100Mbps. This will ensure that any one WebSphere application server can't flood the network to the database server with requests should the application become unstable.

If you're using the connection pool manager within WebSphere (which I'll discuss in later chapters), the probability of this occurring will be reduced. However, for good practice, follow this rule.

Location of Application Servers

Locate your database server or cluster physically near your application servers. The purpose of this is to reduce latency. If you're looking to gain some form of disaster recovery, my recommendation isn't to locate the database tier any farther away than 200 kilometers. This will only increase your latency by a number of milliseconds, as opposed to 20–30ms for a digital line extending 1,000 kilometers.

Database Server Node

Don't try to gain performance from housing your database server on the same node as your WebSphere application server. Albeit not purely a networking issue, housing the database on the same server as the WebSphere engine itself will gain you some performance because of communications going via the local host interface as opposed to out on the wire. However, you'll find that the load and characteristic of the database server on the same node as the WebSphere engine will cancel out most performance architecture you've included as part of your server design.

Unless either your database server requirements are exceptionally small or you have large application servers, steer clear from this topology.

WebSphere-to-Customer (or Web Server) Networking

Given the nature of the traffic generated by the WebSphere HTTP plug-in sitting on the frontend Web servers, you'll find that a high-performing network architecture between the HTTP servers and WebSphere backend will ensure a fast-responding application.

The WebSphere HTTP plug-in talks to the WebSphere backend via HTTP. If you were to look and monitor the traffic exiting from the Web server and destined for the WebSphere engine, you'd see that it's all simple HTTP commands.

Given that your application will, like most HTTP/HTML interfaces, be made up of many components (GIFs, JPEGs, text, frames, and so on), each element that makes up the output on the customers browser will result in additional HTTP requests to the backend. The more elements that make up your output, the more individual requests that will be requested to the WebSphere server.

For this reason, you'll find that traffic quickly increases as customer load increases. Complex user interfaces can be made up of 100 elements; if there are 500 users online, each averaging several page clicks per second, the transaction rate will be quite high.

If the individual requests are delayed because of the latency issue, then the perceived performance of the application will grind to a halt.

Ensure that the link between your Web tier and backend tier is high speed—at least 100MB is recommended; for redundancy and potentially performance, consider multiple links and routes.

Because the HTTP server will probably be located within a firewall environment, consider the additional latency overhead introduced on the wire transaction by elements such as firewall devices, switches, and routers.

Again, you'll investigate topologies in the next chapter; however, if you're geographically locating your HTTP and WebSphere servers, consider the overhead and traffic requirements associated with delivering HTTP payload over a wide-area infrastructure.

In summary, it's important that your networking infrastructure in this zone of your topology supports a high request rate—in other words, the lower the latency, the better the overall performance.

Exploring Advanced Features

There's a range of advanced capabilities that each vendor tries to use to differentiate themselves. In the following sections, you'll look at some of these advanced features for the key platforms.

Sun SPARC Platform Features

In the preceding Sun SPARC section, I touched on some of the advanced features of the Sun platform. You'll now look at these features in more detail and see how they apply to a WebSphere environment.

Dynamic System Domains

Dynamic System Domains (DSDs) are a Sun technology found in its SunFire family of servers and the enterprise E10K server. Basically, domains provide the ability to split a physical frame (chassis) into separated servers. Each server is essentially its own machine, with dedicated CPU and memory, PCI interface cards and buses, and so forth.

There's a common component shared across multiple frames of the system—this component, known as the *Fireplane*, is the overall system interconnection bus and operates in the fashion of a switch.

Domains allow you to effectively run an entire platform in a single chassis. If your requirements state that you need processing power across your tiers of up to 24 Sun UltraSPARC CPUs, then through the use of domains and an F6800, you can partition your frame into several servers.

The domains can be arranged within the chassis so that if you were to operate two WebSphere application severs as part of your domain configuration within a particular F6800 frame, the two WebSphere application server domains could be split so that they wouldn't share any common components. That is, it's possible to design the layout so that each common or clustered application server (which is a domain) would operate on differential power supplies, memory and CPU boards, system controllers, and I/O controllers. Further, you can configure the system so that the Fireplane interconnect is segmented down the spine of the frame.

When you partition domains in this manner, you're effectively building two independent servers (for two domains) or a pair of servers (for four domains).

The other benefit of the domains is that most components within the SunFire family of servers are hot-swappable and hot-pluggable. If your data center operates a capacity-on-demand model or you use computer virtualization, SunFire servers and domains allow you to add and remove capacity and components in real time, without any customer or operational impact.

Hot-swappable components include the following:

- CPUs and memory boards

- Power supplies

- The Fireplane interconnect switch (hot-pluggable only)

- I/O assemblies

- PCI adaptors

This type of configuration can allow you to operate a configuration such as a dual-node database cluster and a dual-node WebSphere application server cluster within a single chassis.

Although the entry costs of this sized frame are higher for lower-end configurations, the cost benefit starts to be realized when you take into account the power and flexibility associated with the advanced domain and SunFire technologies. Facilities management costs can be greatly reduced with this type of configuration, and should a multisite option be a consideration, you could opt for a dual, lesser-powered F6800 configuration split over two sites or a dual F4800 configuration, which supports up to 12 CPUs and 96GB of memory.

Grid Computing

Grid computing is starting to become more apparent in the finance and scientific/engineering markets. Although it can't be implemented via WebSphere (without some serious development effort), WebSphere environments can interface with a grid-based computing environment.

Essentially, *grid computing* is a form of parallel clustering. This type of clustering was made famous by the cluster farms associated with the graphical rendering of the film *Titanic*, whereby clusters of hundreds of servers are connected together through a certain topology and with some specific application coding and server software, allowing all servers in the cluster to operate as one.

It's not possible to use WebSphere in this fashion—WebSphere uses its own clustering technologies (which I'll continue to focus on). However, if you're involved in a site that requires vast amounts of computing power, you'll need to interface with a grid-based environment.

NOTE   Grid computing isn't necessarily a Sun concept. Many commercial vendors, including IBM and HP, have their own versions of grid computing. Various standards are starting to emerge that allow grid-computing environments to share resources across multiple vendor systems. Furthermore, Linux has a number of open-source implementations that are along the same lines as grid computing. The most common one is the Beowulf cluster—an open-source parallel computing framework giving the ability to interconnect vast numbers of commodity Linux servers together to operate in a parallel cluster environment.

IBM PowerPC Platform Features (pSeries)

The PowerPC/Power range of IBM servers exhibited a number of technologies that provided high availability and other advanced computing options. You'll look at two that are similar to those you've explored for the Sun platform range.

Logical Partitioning (LPAR) and Dynamic Logical Partitioning (DLPAR)

IBM's system partitioning technology is called DLPAR. LPAR, on the other hand, is the predecessor of DLPAR and is a fixed version of DLPAR. Essentially, LPAR allows an IBM pSeries server to be partitioned. This partitioning, like SunFire domains, allows you to distribute CPUs, memory, and I/O adapters across multiple logical servers within a single chassis. DLPAR is an advancement of LDAR and allows the components within the various logically portioned servers to be dynamically allocated (or deallocated) to and from partitions while they're active.

This extends the notion of computing on demand to a new level by allowing unused resources to be allocated to a production environment during peak times and deallocated during off-peak times for testing or other purposes.

Another popular use of this technology is to house a spare set or pool of resources (in other words, CPU, memory, and I/O adaptors such as network interface cards and so on), which are available to any of the other live partitions in the frame. In the event of component failure or adverse peak loads, DLPAR can let you absorb unforeseen peaks and problems with the performance of your WebSphere applications.

The inner workings of LPAR and DLPAR are beyond the scope of this book; however, I'll discuss DLPAR again throughout later chapters when you delve into AIX operating system tuning during Chapter 5.

Summary

As you learned in this chapter, there's a great deal of design and decision making required when choosing your system platform. The approach you take is important because your platform choice will have a lasting effect on your J2EE application design.

The reason for this is that different platforms have differing limitations and capabilities. If, for example, you choose an x86-based processor from Intel that has a 4GB memory limit, then your application design needs to follow a horizontal system architecture model—that is, you need many smaller servers to get over memory limitations.

Also, consider the costs associated with going for smaller model servers in your chosen platform; with the saved costs, you can obtain further benefits from high-availability features previously out of your budget's reach.

It's better to have a redundant system than a system that has too much headroom and scalability capability that may never be required.

WebSphere Deployment and Network Architecture

IF TUNING WEBSPHERE constitutes the micro view of your tuning and performance methodology, then the deployment and network architecture (aka the topologies) is the macro view. Throughout this chapter, you'll take a detailed look at the various network and deployment architectures that you can use with WebSphere.

Each topology has its place and its pros and cons, mostly dependent on or driven by three key factors: scalability, reliability (availability), and performance. In this chapter I examine each topology from a top-down perspective and focus on what each design entails, cover what its benefits and trade-offs are, and suggest different WebSphere implementations that would benefit from each of the topological architectures.

Like most topics I've discussed so far in this book, cost is the most prohibitive factor. If cost wasn't an issue, I'm sure most of us would go for the most scalable and reliable system. However, as we all know, cost benefit realization is an important analytical process that should be weighed against each design to essentially determine whether paying 50 percent more for your infrastructure costs is really worth the fourth 9 in the magic availability measurement (i.e., 99.99 percent versus 99.9 percent availability).

Overview of Key Components

You've looked at several of the components covered in this section in some detail already, but not as part of a heterogeneous system in the context of an overall platform architecture.

A WebSphere implementation, from the physical view at the highest level, can be broken into four main components:

- Web server or Web tier

- Application server or application/business tier

- Database server or data tier

- Network infrastructure

These four parts are the highest level view of a single-site WebSphere implementation. From those four key components, you're able to extend and expand your design both horizontally and vertically to achieve the exact mix of scalability, reliability, and performance that you need. Let's consider a brief example.

Suppose your application server was operating at greater than 70 percent utilization and customers were starting to notice a performance degradation. You could scale your application or business tier either vertically (i.e., add more CPUs, memory, disk, network interfaces, etc.) or horizontally (i.e., add more servers). As you'll see in detail in this chapter, both approaches have pros and cons, and although the choice may appear to be simple for resolving your performance issues, the answer isn't always straightforward.

Not all applications that operate under WebSphere can be simply scaled either way. With the onset of technologies such as blade servers, it's a common but incorrect assumption that scaling your application environment can always be achieved simply by throwing more servers, or blades, into your WebSphere or J2EE application server farm.

Yes, this works for smaller applications, which may happen to be mainly JSPs, servlets, and static HTML content. For these types of applications, serving this type of content and processing this type of load can be minimal. If you introduce heavy workload components such as CPU and or memory-bound application modules, or if your application consists of many parts (e.g., many EJB-JARs, WARs [Web Archives], etc.), then you'll quickly run out of memory and CPU cycles on lower-end systems. For this reason, larger systems are needed and vertical scaling starts to become a necessity rather than a choice.

In the following sections, you'll look at vertical and horizontal scaling in a little more detail, especially in the context of WebSphere.

Horizontal Scaling with WebSphere

Horizontal scaling of a system or a system's components essentially means that you're looking to increase, in some way, the capacity of your environment by adding in additional servers. For example, you may have an x86-based platform with a memory limit of 4GB, and a number of your application's users are in need of more memory for session-based data. To extend beyond the 4GB limit and allow your customers to still be able to use the application, you would add in an additional node with 4GB of memory. The sum of total session memory available to your application will then be 8GB of memory. Although a single process can't extend beyond 4GB of physical memory, it does allow you to cater for additional growth.

Figure 5-1 illustrates an example of horizontal scaling.

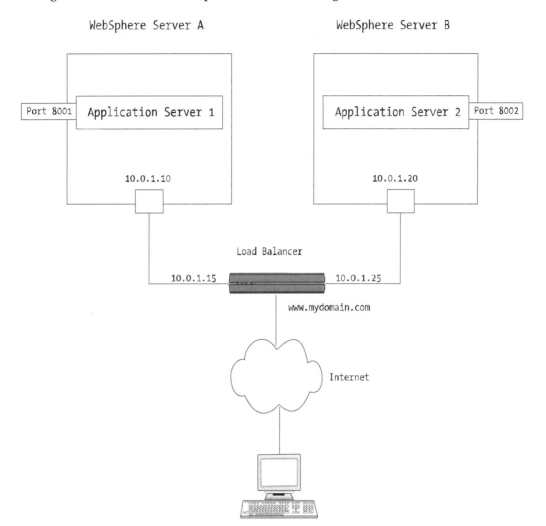

Figure 5-1. Horizontal scaling example with WebSphere

As you can tell from Figure 5-1, horizontal scaling is a relatively straightforward approach to extending a WebSphere environment from the point of view of a basic or noncomplex J2EE application running within WebSphere. However, once you start to need to look at ensuring that users' data is maintained across all nodes, for varying levels of application code, and for even more varying levels of legacy and data tier integration, horizontal scaling can become a nightmare if it isn't properly designed.

You'll explore the concepts of cells, server groups, and clones in more detail later in this chapter, but for now you should know that these options provide the ability to drop in additional servers and further distribute the WebSphere load. The same "drop in" approach be used for vertical scaling, and although it's similar to horizontal scaling in terms of basic environment implementation, vertical scaling does introduce several additional headaches for your application and system architects.

Vertical Scaling with WebSphere

Vertical scaling involves scaling "upward" within your existing servers. That is, you add in, or upgrade, additional processing power, memory, disks, and so on within existing servers rather than purchase additional servers (which is what is involved in horizontal scaling). This form of platform scaling is best suited to large applications that require centralized, workhorse-type servers to be able to process large numbers of requests.

Vertical scaling is also the optimal choice for sites that are short on support resources. Generally speaking, the more servers that you have to manage, the more support processes and resources you need to have in place to adequately manage your many horizontally scaled servers. More infrastructure can also cost more from a facilities management point of view—more rack space, more power requirements, more networking infrastructure, and so on. Therefore, the decision to vertically scale or horizontally scale may be based on factors other than application architecture requirements.

You'll need to consider vertical scaling in the way you configure your WebSphere server and, depending on your application architecture, in the way you design your application. What this means is that it's all very well to purchase a server with plenty of memory, but you need to specifically tune and configure your WebSphere platform to take advantage of memory. You need to consider such factors as maximum JVM heap space, JVM threads to kernel thread ratios, and so on. Most 32-bit JVMs have memory heap limitations of 2GB. Therefore, unless you design the rest of your WebSphere application environment correctly to be able to load balance with more than one servicing J2EE application (which is effectively a JVM), you won't be able to take advantage of large amounts of memory. (You'll look at these types of limitations and rules of thumb in more detail throughout the rest of this chapter.)

The same considerations apply to CPUs. There's no benefit to having a system with ten CPUs and, due to some form of application design limitation, only being able to operate a single JVM instance of your application and effectively wasting nine CPUs!

One downside to vertical scaling for the majority of WebSphere implementations is that, with a less distributed environment (i.e., a less horizontally scaled environment), you may be exposed to risks associated with a less redundant environment. Having fewer physical servers for complex and mission-critical environments can lead to downtime risks in the event of a system or site failure. For this reason, vertical scaling alone isn't a good choice for critical or customer-facing systems. Ever more so in today's global climate, disaster recovery and geographically split site configurations are essential for mission-critical systems. For these types of systems to work, you must employ horizontal scaling alongside vertical scaling.

Combined Horizontal and Vertical Scaling with WebSphere

At the end of the day, the best design uses a mixture of horizontal and vertical scaling. This satisfies availability requirements as well as scalability and performance requirements for application environments:

- Multiple servers support redundancy and availability, and aid in scalability.

- The servers can be upgraded or vertically scaled to support growing application-processing demands.

A mixture of horizontal and vertical scaling can also provide the best of both worlds from an operational and facilities costs point of view, with fewer, higher capacity servers keeping the water and feed costs down for the majority of application environments and data center housing.

Figure 5-2 highlights a basic vertically and horizontally scaled application environment.

Figure 5-2 illustrates how customer traffic and requests are distributed to a two-node WebSphere application server cluster, which uses multiple application-servicing JVMs to provide performance, availability, and redundancy. This type of configuration could be labeled as the basic production-ready WebSphere platform architecture. My recommendation is that this type of configuration is the basic building block for any WebSphere environment—anything less in a production environment leaves the door open to myriad problems.

That said, if you're looking to roll out a smaller WebSphere implementation, you should conduct a return on investment (ROI) analysis on the costs associated with the additional infrastructure. In Chapter 2 you looked at some examples for ROI analysis. When lined up against the costs associated with actually having downtime, the result from the ROI model may suggest that it isn't cost-effective to employ additional infrastructure for redundancy when the platform requirements are small.

I know systems managers who are responsible for small WebSphere production environments running on x86 clone machines. Their train of thought is that, if the server dies, all they need to do is run down to the local PC shop and pick up the new replacement part(s), install it, and then restore the data from the last backup. The cost for that replacement part may be only a few hundred dollars, and given the general low complexity of these types of systems, installing the part and bringing the system up again may take only as long as 30 to 90 minutes.

For this reason, having additional servers to cater for redundancy may not be an issue for some sites.

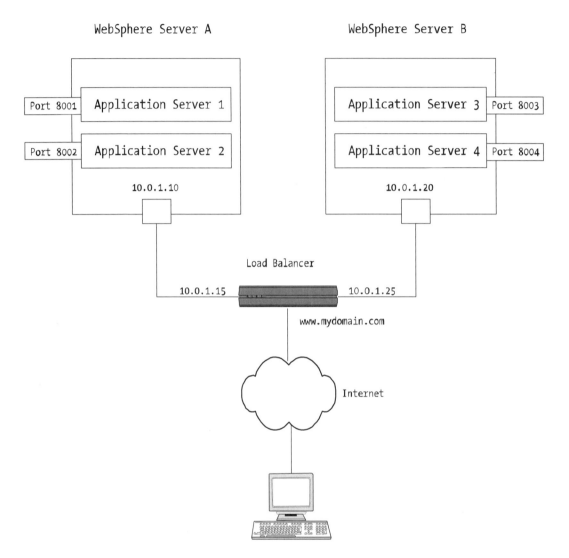

Figure 5-2. Example of a horizontally and vertically scaled environment

Topological Architecture

Topological architecture is the combined design of networks, systems, platforms, and storage architectures. Some call this area *physical architecture*; however, I personally feel that the term *topological* infers topology, and WebSphere performance scalability is very much about topology selection.

WebSphere performance is just as much about how your physical components interact. If you treat a WebSphere platform as an onion and you peel the layers away, when you get to the innermost components you're looking at a distributed environment. Everything in the environment is object-oriented and, therefore, is indirectly (or directly, depending on how you perceive the analogy!) distributed.

Even in a single node system, components talk to one another via a distributed mechanism. In most cases, this communication takes place via EJBs over RMI/RMI-IIOP or legacy Java components such as CORBA objects and the like.

Either way you look at it, stuff is distributed. There are IBM extensions in WebSphere that provide the capability for EJBs to communicate over a quasi-local interface instead of remotely. This capability is known as *Call-by-Reference*, and you can set this during application deployment in the Application Assembly Tool (AAT). The default EJB specification is to call EJBs via a mechanism known as *Call-by-Value*.

 NOTE   In J2EE 1.3, the EJB 2.0 specification provides for a local interface that allows EJB clients to communicate to EJBs via a "local" interface instead of via a remote network call. This can help decrease overheads associated with having to call EJBs internal to EJB containers by not having to invoke a network call.

For this reason, how you plug your physical components together to form your topological architecture is very important.

WebSphere Building Block Rules

The WebSphere topology that you select should roughly follow a capacity modeling equation that you can apply over and over again. I tried to stay away from using the cliché of portraying it as blocks of LEGOs, but this analogy truly fits the bill in this example!

When you play (or played) with LEGOs, you always knew that to build something, you have to choose among fixed, defined pieces. In my experience, the same idea can be applied to designing and building WebSphere platforms. You should select a basic model that's based on architectural design driven by capacity modeling and analysis, which will enable you to easily scale and grow your WebSphere application environment in any way needed, without a major redesign of your application.

For example, one of my personal building block rules is to always roll out components (i.e., CPU, memory, disks, I/O cards, etc.) in even numbers. I've found that, when I initially build the basic components of my WebSphere platform, by rolling everything out in even numbers I'm inherently introducing redundancy in everything I do.

Another rule I follow for WebSphere servers is this: For mission-critical systems, I always roll out WebSphere servers in combinations of three or more (to the extent to which there are obvious cost benefits). I then factor into my design a rule that states that any two servers in a three-way WebSphere server cluster must be able to handle the full load of the application utilization, with no more than 60 percent load any one host. This promotes a WebSphere platform that can run with a downed server through either a server crash or a scheduled outage period during nonpeak times. Two servers provide redundancy but not always performance under a 50 percent operational condition (i.e., where one server has crashed).

Example Building Block

To put this concept of "building blocks" into context, for medium-sized WebSphere environments an example of a WebSphere topological building block model would be to use Sun V880 servers. As I discussed in the previous chapter, Sun V880 servers provide the ability to take eight CPUs and 64GB of memory.

You may decide that, based on an application architecture in which there will be four deployed Enterprise Archive Resource (EAR) files (used to contain and structure J2EE applications) on each server, each WebSphere J2EE application Java server would require between 512MB and 1.5GB of Java heap memory. As a rough guide, each Java JVM should have—in the majority of cases—at least one dedicated CPU. This helps to cater for garbage collection, as garbage collection effectively stops more than 98 percent of requests from being serviced by the JVM while the garbage collection process is taking place.

NOTE *Garbage collection* is the term used to describe a Java JVM regularly going through its heap (allocated memory) and cleaning out unused objects and space. During this time, the JVM appears almost frozen to the servicing applications that are operating within it. Therefore, there's a delicate tuning process that needs to take place to ensure that the JVM doesn't spend its entire life garbage collecting.

From a redundancy point of view, you'll look to clone two of the J2EE application servers for WebSphere version 4 or use cells and nodes for WebSphere version 5. More than one physical WebSphere server will also be included. Based on these requirements, you can state the following basic requirements:

- Each physical server will require at least six CPUs (one for each JVM plus operating system overheads, or you can assume that the two uncloned/non-cell-configured JVMs are low weight).

- Each physical server will require at least 7GB (4×S1.5GB and 2×512MB) of memory for the JVMs plus operating system overhead (3GB), totaling approximately 10GB of memory.

To achieve redundancy across multiple servers, you will require a second Sun V880 server of equal capacity, given that you'll want to provide 100 percent processing ability during a node failure. The basic building block, therefore (excluding disk, network, and other peripherals at this stage), is a Sun V880 server with six CPUs and 10GB of memory. Each time you want to add in new capacity—given that the V880 is only an eight-CPU chassis—you would look to deploy another server (block) of equal capacity.

Essentially what I'm saying here is that you should select your topological architecture before anything else, and when you've confirmed it, lock it in. Changing your topological architecture midstream generally is a complex and expensive task because you may need to alter the application architecture and there's a potential for several high-risk outages for hardware upgrades.

Considerations for Scalability and Performance

In the land of J2EE, and specifically with WebSphere-based implementations, two areas of your overall application infrastructure determine its ability to scale and perform. The first is the application design itself, which I cover later in Chapter 10. The second is the way that the physical layers are designed and constructed.

As I've touched on in earlier sections, WebSphere can scale both horizontally and vertically to achieve performance and scalability. In the upcoming sections, you're going to look at some key topological architectures in detail and examine the pros and cons of each. To summarize the various approaches, this section presents some considerations before you start planning the infrastructure components of your WebSphere environment.

JVM Memory Characteristics

The JVM is the central component in any Java-based application. The JVM is the virtual machine that the Java application threads operate within, and it provides the bytecode interpretation for your nominated platform. Over the years, JVMs have evolved somewhat in terms of their performance. Back in J2EE 1.1, JVM performance, while good, suffered all sorts of weird anomalies, most of which have been addressed in subsequent versions.

One of the main aspects of a JVM's role involves managing the memory space allocated to the Java applications operating within it. The memory allocated to the JVM at JVM bootstrap time is known as the *heap*. At the time the heap is allocated during JVM initialization, there are two primary settings used to set memory requirements: the initial heap and the maximum heap. The *initial heap* is the starting point for allocation, and the *maximum heap* is the maximum amount of memory space that the JVM can or will reference during its lifetime.

Java is based around objects, and these objects need to be resident in memory until their use has expired. One of the selling points of Java is that it manages the memory allocation and deallocation for you, and for this reason you need to tune the JVM carefully so that it knows what it can and can't reference.

Those of you who have used languages such as C and C++ know that programming in those languages involves the use of the `malloc()` library to obtain memory for your runtime. C and C++ runtime compilers don't automanage the memory for you and, as such, it is up to you to manage the memory space. Therefore, in Java you need to plan around the area of memory allocation prior to sizing a system.

I've noted two Java JVM settings that are specific to memory usage. There are, in fact, many more. Most of them you'll never need to use, but from time to time, and on large environments, you may find a need to use them. It's important to note at this stage that there are several JVM vendors on the market. IBM, Sun, and BEA are just three vendors that produce their own JVM implementations. Each of these JVMs has the majority of the primary settings available to it, but if you do have a need to use a JVM other than the one that comes with WebSphere, study the release notes carefully. A setting on an IBM JVM may have an adverse affect on a BEA JRockit JVM.

Because the JVM manages the memory allocation and object heap space for your J2EE and Java applications, it needs to clean itself and its workspace periodically. How frequently this occurs is dependant on how busy your application is and how much memory you've allocated to it.

I've referred to garbage collection many times during the book so far, but now I'll cover it in more detail. Essentially, garbage collection is the JVM's way of cleaning out unused and unwanted objects from its heap. Quite often, applications don't clean up and dereference objects from use. This includes items such as arrays and vector lists, which are used frequently by applications but may not always be removed after use. Garbage collection takes care of this.

However, there is a downside to this paradigm of software development. As the JVM is providing the runtime for your applications as well as garbage collection for your applications' unused objects, there is a clash. When garbage collection occurs, the JVM is almost 100 percent dedicated to the task of garbage collection. This causes applications to mostly freeze during this housecleaning exercise. Excessive (i.e., constant) garbage collection can cause an application to appear to not respond. Therefore, it's important to size and tune your JVM correctly.

Here are some JVM rules of thumb to follow:

- Because of 32-bit limitations (or complications—whichever way you look at it), don't allocate more than 2GB of heap space per JVM. Unless your JVM is one of the new 64-bit JVMs that are soon to be commonplace, trying to use more than 2GB of JVM space can cause problems. This is why you may want to look at using multiple JVMs to run multiple instances of an application (I discuss this later in the chapter).

- Keep to the rule of initially setting your JVM maximum heap size to half of the physical amount of memory or half the physical amount of system memory allocated to the JVM's purpose.

- Keep the minimum or initial heap size to half of the maximum heap size until tuning tells you otherwise.

- Avoid (like the plague) allocating more memory to your JVM (or more JVMs if you're running multiple instances on the same server) than you have physical memory. Don't let the JVM eat into swapping and memory paging danger areas.

- Be aware that large heap sizes will require longer garbage collection cycle times, so, if you believe you need large amounts of memory allocated to your JVM, either tune the JVM (see next the section for more information) or allocate a smaller amount of heap and look into using multiple JVMs.

- If, after testing, you find that the JVM is garbage collecting more than 10 to 15 percent of the time, there is something incorrect with your JVM heap settings.

Garbage Collection Monitoring

Checking for how much time your JVM spends garbage collecting is a fairly simple task. Within your WebSphere console, or manually through wscp, XMLConfig, or wsadmin, add in the bootstrap property to your JVM startup parameters of `-verbosegc` and restart the JVM. If you then monitor the log file associated with the application server that you've modified with the `-verbosegc` parameter, you'll see entries starting with "GC" appear when garbage collection occurs.

With the current JVM versions available, the current method of garbage collection is typically conducted in a multithreaded fashion; however, when garbage collection occurs, the JVM attempts to defragment the heap and compacts it. This compacting or defragging is a single-threaded operation and tends to be the main cause for application freezing during garbage collection. This is why you'll generally want to avoid long periods of garbage collection or frequent garbage collection.

Figure 5-3 shows an example of what garbage collection looks like on a system that is exhibiting memory leaks. The ever-growing heap memory usage is a giveaway of this situation or of a system that has had its initial heap set too low. The time period is 5 minutes, with a garbage collection occurring about once every 30 seconds or so.

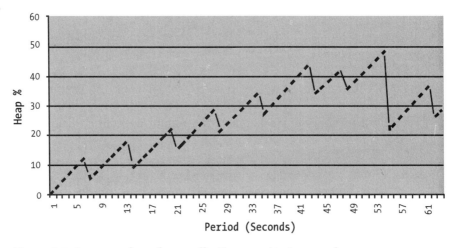

Garbage Collection Frequency Graph

Figure 5-3. An example garbage collection monitoring graph

I discuss tuning in more detail during later chapters, but it's worth noting here that the output of this graph suggests that I'm able to increase the initial heap size a little. This won't necessarily decrease the frequency of garbage collection, but it will reduce the time that garbage collection takes.

This type of profiling and tuning exercise should be a normal part of your capacity management program. In Chapter 13, you'll look at other ways to monitor the JVM and its operational characteristics, plus you'll learn about ways to tune it.

Other JVM Memory Issues to Consider

Although I've discussed garbage collection, I haven't touched on what can cause it. Two key factors can drive a JVM to be a painful part of your architecture: memory leaks and Java object overuse.

Probably the nastiest of all Java-based problems is memory leakage. Although Java insulates developers from a memory allocation and deallocation, there can still be problems within your application code that cause certain types of objects to build up over time and not get swept up in garbage collection. Hashtables and vector lists are common causes of memory leaks, as they can continue to exist without application references to them. Over time, they'll build up and the available heap will become less and less, yet the JVM will try more and more frequently to garbage collect as its available heap becomes exhausted.

The most obvious sign of a memory leak is a Java "out of memory exception." If you see one of these, it's a sure sign that either you've grossly underspecified your Java JVM heap settings or you have memory leaks. You'll look at how to identify these exceptions and fix them in Chapter 13.

Another memory-related problem is the overuse of Java objects. That is, instead of using pooled or cached instances of the specific object, your application instantiates a completely new instance of the object on each and every request.

CAUTION   Although the approach of pooling Java objects will help with Java heap management, it does have the potential to introduce other problems that can lead to poor performance and issues associated with threading. Be sure to design your application architecture carefully if you're using manual Java object pooling (i.e., you're not letting the WebSphere containers take care of it).

Again, you'll look at this problem and how to identify it in more detail in later chapters. The obvious sign of this problem occurring is that the time to garbage collect is taking longer on each request. A quick remedy to this problem is to run multiple JVMs (which I discuss later in this chapter), but this is a temporary solution and it does not address the problem's root cause.

JVM Threading Characteristics

When you're capacity planning your WebSphere topological architecture (your server platform), you need to consider the number of CPUs you'll require for your application to perform at adequate levels. There are a number of rules of thumb relating to the allocation of Java JVMs against CPUs that you can follow but, once again, nothing beats good solid modeling of your application against your chosen hardware platform.

The first rule of thumb is this: For every CPU you have within a system, my general recommendation is that you allocate 1.5GB of memory per JVM (for JDK

1.2/1.3) and 2GB to 2.5GB of memory per JVM (for JDK 1.4). For each medium-
to high-operating JVM, you should allocate a single CPU.

In Chapter 4 you looked at sizing your application environment based on
the perceived number of threads operating concurrently within your J2EE application. At a higher level, you can use the preceding guide for memory per JVM or
work within the guideline of one CPU per JVM in a medium-sized environment
or two CPUs per JVM in a larger production environment in which the JVM is
heavily used. Therefore, for an application server that has four applications, two
of which are heavy-operating JVMs and the other two of which are low-operating
JVMs, you should look for a system with 6GB of memory and three CPUs.

Each Java JVM that's a medium- to high-operating JVM will undoubtedly
conduct a fair amount of garbage collection. Therefore, you don't want other
JVMs affected by the cleanup processes of another application.

 CAUTION   These recommendations in this section are intended as
general guides and rules of thumb. Your mileage may vary with
these ratios. It goes to prove that you must perform capacity modeling, but use these recommendations as a starting point.

You'll recall that in Chapter 4 you looked at the ratio of threads per JVM. This
varies on how your deployed application is architected, but it's an important part
of sizing your environment. At the end of the day, the number of Java JVM
threads compared to the number of operating system or Kernel threads is going
to vary based on the particular vendor's JVM you use as well as your chosen
operating system. Recent operating system versions come with more advanced
thread libraries that marry better with the platform-specific Java JVM.

There are a number of ways to monitor and tune threads within your JVM
and the application itself. You'll also look at this in Chapter 13.

Local Network Environment

I touched on network architectures in the previous chapter and which ones are
better suited to WebSphere platforms. Although there's no hard-and-fast rule
here for the right network architecture for WebSphere (how long is a piece of
string?), there are a few considerations that you should either include as standard in your architecture or use to build off of.

You can break a network within a WebSphere environment into three main
categories, as shown in Figure 5-4.

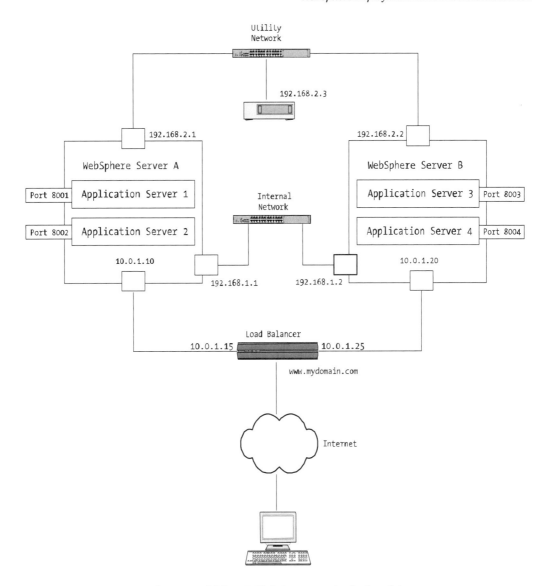

Figure 5-4. Major network types within a WebSphere topological architecture

First, you have the external network components. These network links and interfaces typically handle the traffic to areas outside the application space. These include, for example, the link through which customer traffic traverses. This network is depicted in Figure 5-4 as the 10.0.1.*x* network.

The second network type is the internal private network "mesh." This network is the 192.168.1.*x* network depicted in Figure 5-4. This network is for internal WebSphere-to-WebSphere communications. Depending on your physical architecture, this may or may not be the network in which traffic from your Web servers to your application servers traverses—the Web servers may be located at a physical distance from the WebSphere application servers. Typically, however, this internal private network would be used for WebSphere nodes to be able to communicate to one another (e.g., for workload management, JNDI tree spanning, database queries to database servers, etc.).

The third type of network is the utility network, depicted in the diagram as the 192.168.2.*x* network. This network should be used for all backup (e.g., tape backup) and administrative functions. The driver behind this network is so that backups and administration/operational functions don't interfere with the user-facing operations and vice versa. Consider the situation in which you may be receiving a denial of service (DoS) attack and your application is under load from the excessive traffic. If your network is saturated, then it's going to be difficult to administer the WebSphere server components. Therefore, you should always consider this third network type as a requirement.

NOTE You could do away with the third network interface and look at serial-based communications. These are out-of-band and are not subject, in most cases, to typical DoS attacks and other forms of network storms. The only downside to this approach is that graphical tools aren't available, and neither is the ability to easily transfer files back and forth and use the medium for backups.

I'd also always recommend at least a backup route to be shared between the customer- or user-facing network requests and the internal private network traffic. Intelligent routing and/or switching can make this a trivial exercise to set up and configure.

A note on Gigabit Ethernet versus Fast Ethernet: I've been witness to some odd discussions over the past 12 months or so, in which Gigabit was dismissed simply because it was Gigabit. Comments such as "We don't need 1000Mb/s" were common. My qualm with this is that Gigabit Ethernet is only fractionally more expensive than Fast Ethernet. For an extra 10 to 15 percent of the cost of hardware and switches, you get an extra (theoretical) 10 times the throughput performance! My recommendation is that if you have the infrastructure in place, or you have spare funds, go for Gigabit. Simple things such as file transfers and WebSphere clustering will be noticeably faster and will result in a better, higher performing application platform.

WebSphere Topological Architecture Blueprints

Now you've learned some of the key elements associated with topological architecture considerations. In this section, you'll move on to look at some blueprints for WebSphere topological design, their pros and cons, and where you might choose to use one of them. I also discuss the configuration aspects of each topology that you need to consider. Remember, your application architecture must marry up with the topological architecture—neither of the designs can be done in isolation.

The approach to this section of the chapter is as follows. First, I discuss some key points that are common to both single and multichannel environments. Following that, I discuss the factors associated with either a single-channel or a multichannel system. Each subsection has information that you should read if you're considering either of the solutions.

Common Elements to Consider in Your Topological Architecture

In the next few sections, I discuss some high-level design attributes common to all topologies, including the following:

- Web servers (thin versus thick models)

- Application servers

I should also point out that in this chapter, I'm making an assumption in all the topologies that you'll be operating a firewall environment (of at least two tiers). Therefore, all topologies will be based on environments in which firewalls exist. I also discuss and lay out the various topologies based on real-world use cases. There are several other combinations of WebSphere topology that you can use, but those topologies I present here are the most common and provide the best features.

Web Server

The Web server in any topology can be implemented in one of two configurations, from a component delivery point of view. First, it can be installed as simply a Web server configured with the WebSphere HTTP plug-in. Second, it can be "fattened" to also run WebSphere and serve presentation components such as JSPs, servlets, and static HTML content, while the application server also operating on WebSphere facilitates connectivity to backend or legacy systems and runs more advanced J2EE components such as EJBs.

The choice of whether you opt for a "thin" or "thick" Web server should be based on several considerations:

- How strict are your firewall rules?

- Is security a big concern for your application environment?

- How much static content are you likely to be running?

- Is your firewall located in a separate location from your backend application and database servers?

- Do you have an operational preference for server sizes and configurations? (That is, do you prefer to operate large processing application servers versus many smaller servers?)

- Does your application architecture have any special considerations for protocols or logic between the Web container (presentation components) and the application server (business components)?

Let's look at those questions in more detail.

How Strict Are Your Firewall Rules?

The first question relates to your corporate security policies for your firewalls. This question attempts to derive the sort of firewalls you have in place. I've worked with the most basic of firewalls, which are simply Network Address Translation (NAT) firewalls (if they can be called that), up through to the more complex four-tier firewalls. Your WebSphere platform needs to be architected differently for each, and each is driven by the protocols and transaction rate between presentation components and the business components.

For example, you would notice a performance impact on your application if you were running a heavy firewall configuration and had a thick Web server running WebSphere for presentation components (JSPs, servlets, etc.) in the first or second tier of your firewall, yet your backend application servers were residing out on your corporate network.

For most medium-sized and larger WebSphere application environments, the transaction rate between the presentation tier and the business tier will be high. With servlets and JavaBeans communicating to backend JavaBeans and EJBs, as well as other service provider types, the applications' overall performance will be impacted by the translation and interrogation conducted by the various firewalls.

Figure 5-5 illustrates the issues associated with a thick frontend Web server (running WebSphere) talking to a backend application server and database tier.

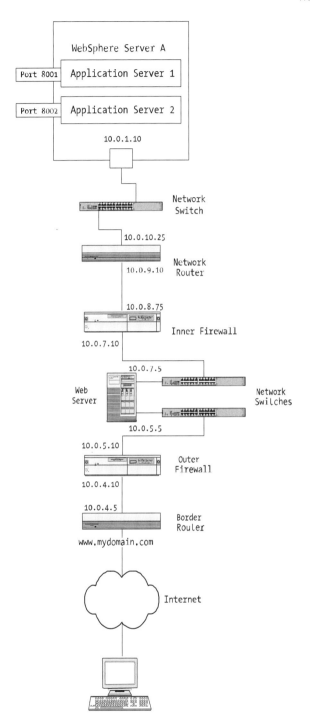

Figure 5-5. Overhead associated with communications via a firewall for heavy transaction data

As you can see, each hop through the firewalls may introduce an additional 2 to 5 milliseconds of latency. By the time the packets get to the backend, they may have had an increase in latency of up to 30 milliseconds, and if each transaction is consuming some 100 network I/Os, this becomes expensive (network payload–wise).

The network diagram in Figure 5-5 shows a somewhat "heavily engineered" firewall environment. Although the network addressing in the example is cumbersome (in reality, a more efficient network address design would be used), the firewall layout is one that isn't uncommon in larger environments. Consider that at each level there would be virtual LANs (VLANs) and other demilitarized zones (DMZs) hanging off the various firewall tiers. This may not always be an issue for all sites. Typically, this is the case for medium-to-large organizations that may have quite complex firewall requirements and many tens or hundreds (or thousands) of servers to protect. In these cases, the firewalls will be several tiers deep.

You may also find that, depending on how you communicate between your frontend and backend tiers, firewalls may not be able to route the traffic correctly. An example of this is Internet Inter-ORB Protocol (IIOP) and RMI-IIOP. These are what I term *intelligent protocols,* as they aren't simplistic like HTTP and HTTPS. IIOP-like protocols typically carry source and/or requester address information in their payload and the destination system receiving the protocol data will typically attempt to do something intelligent with the return protocol based on the contents of the payload, rather than simply follow standard IP source and destination headers.

For this reason, my recommendation is to use a thin Web server environment and use the WebSphere HTTP plug-in to route requests from the Web server in the firewall out to the backend application servers. Figure 5-6 highlights this recommendation.

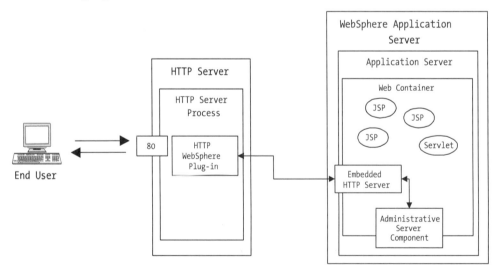

Figure 5-6. A thin Web server configuration

As the HTTP plug-in communicates via pure HTTP, it's easy to route and handle through firewalls.

Is Security a Big Concern for Your Application Environment?

The second question relates to security—essentially, this is in line with the first question relating to firewalls. The answer to this question may simply back up the answer to the first question.

The stricter your corporate security is, the further away from the public Internet you would want your business logic and data tiers. For example, you wouldn't want to house your Web, application, and data tiers all within the first tier of a firewall, which is typically known as the *demilitarized zone* (DMZ). This type of data housed on the database servers is typically sensitive in nature, so having it close to your Internet borders is risky because there's only one firewall to traverse to obtain access to that data. This reinforces the notion of a thin Web server redirecting traffic via the HTTP plug-in to backend application and database servers.

Some sites go so far as to place firewalls between each of their tiers. That is, the setup looks something like Figure 5-7.

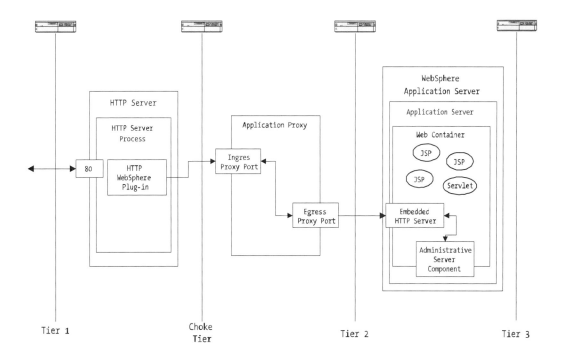

Figure 5-7. A 3-tier firewall topology

These types of firewalls are typically used to house 3-tier and n-tier applications, but they do have the capability to fast-track the request through the firewall tiers through the use of networking solutions such as VLANs.

In the high-level diagram in Figure 5-7, there are clearly three "tiers" of servers separated by various firewalls and a single *choke,* which is a scaled-down firewall that typically operates on access control lists (ACLs).

How Much Static Content Are You Likely to Be Running?

If your application is Web based and is delivering a lot of static content, it maybe worth considering housing a small WebSphere or static HTTP server environment on tier 1 of your firewall to reduce the HTTP I/O rate between the frontend and backend components.

NOTE Many organizations make use of third-party content providers to host noncore content such as static HTML and images.

Some Web-based applications have many GIFs, JPEGs, and static HTML included within the output that is being delivered to the customer's screen. If this is the case, the I/O rate on incorrectly sized backend servers can sometimes create large amounts of overhead, as each connection request for a particular image or HTML file generally spawns a new HTTP thread on the WebSphere backend. For this reason, if the content is truly static, consider housing it on the Web server on the frontend.

Is Your Firewall Located in a Separate Location from Your Backend Application and Database Servers?

This question relates to proper network design but it's something you need to consider alongside the system architecture for your backend application server(s). If your site is highly distributed, most likely geographically, then this is an important point.

In some situations, it may be worth considering having the backend application server simply processing business logic requests such as JDBC database and EJB type requests. If you're able to push the content delivery closer to your customers, then this creates a less expensive infrastructure model to operate. That said, you need to weigh the cost and security pros and cons associated with having possibly too much "logic" on the frontend Web servers.

As I discussed in relation to the first question, best practice states that no business logic should ever be directly accessible by customers. The best situation is for your application architecture to have an abstraction layer between the Web tier and the application/business tier. This provides the ultimate level of application security, while at the same time allowing for you to push nonbusiness logic (i.e., presentation logic) to the frontend Web servers. Figure 5-8 shows an example of how this abstraction layer model could work.

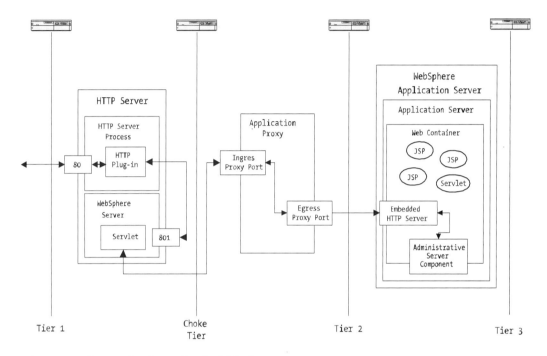

Figure 5-8. Abstraction layer for the Web tier

As you can see, the initial request that comes into the Web server from the customer is routed by the plug-in to a WebSphere application server, which is running a lightweight servlet process. The request is processed by a servlet that somewhat proxifies the customer request, rewrites it into an application-native message request, and delivers it to the appropriate backend services. The middle firewall tier may operate a secondary application proxy, or the WebSphere instance operating on the first tier, the HTTP server, can be installed on the middle firewall tier, replacing the "application proxy." This prevents customers from hijacking the Web server and pushing requests through the firewall, which may have previously been plain native HTTP requests.

In this example, the Web server, operating WebSphere, takes the requests within a servlet and proxies the request to the backend application servers in a form not readable by the clients or anyone else in between. An example of this may be to encapsulate all the requests into hashcode with some identifier codes within the request that follow a paired-key approach to ensure that the backend application servers know that the inbound request is in fact legitimate and from the frontend server.

CAUTION   No amount of clever logic within an application is better than solid firewall and security. Eight times out of ten, security break-ins to applications are due to poor or insufficient security infrastructure rather than application design.

The outcome of this question is this: If your WebSphere-based application is heavily made up of static content, then consider placing the static content on the frontend Web server or WebSphere application server (under the defaultApp, for example). If, however, your application doesn't have many static images and components, and/or many of those components are dynamically generated by business logic, then consider the thin Web server approach.

Do You Have an Operational Preference for Server Sizes and Configurations?

This question relates to the preferences of your organization's CIO in terms of server models. Some companies prefer the many, smaller or blade approach, whereas other companies prefer the fewer, more consolidated server approach, which may follow some type of utility model. WebSphere can operate all its major application components on a single node, or it can be distributed to a very fine level.

One way to quickly answer this question is to understand what your application processing demands are. If your application requires a lot of "processing horsepower" to compose output, result sets, and so forth, the answer to this question may be that you need to operate large servers on your backend rather than more, smaller servers.

If, on the other hand, your application is lightweight and isn't processing intensive, then the more, smaller servers approach may be the best option for you here. In this case, with regard to your Web server, you need to understand that whatever option you go for, you should consider how the previous four questions may affect the server model you use.

NOTE   I discuss the application server processing demands and what the considerations are in the next section.

Generally speaking, however, Web server models suggest that the optimal approach is to use the more, smaller model. In this section, though, we're focusing only on the single-channel approach—the basic building block or model should remain the same.

Does Your Application Architecture Have Any Special Considerations for Protocols or Logic Between the Web Container (Presentation Components) and Application Server (Business Components)?

This last question ties in closely with the first question in the discussion about traversing your firewall environment with weird and exotic protocols. If your firewall policies are well tied down, then you may not be able to get anything more than SMTP and HTTP over your firewall. In this case, having a thin front-end Web server is possibly the only model that you can use without a redesign of your firewall.

If, however, your firewall does allow for changes and sometimes nonstandard protocols, and your application requires unusual protocols to go from the frontend to the backend, then it's an either/or question that should be answered with the help of the other five questions.

The reason for this line of thought is that firewalls typically only allow a handful of protocols to traverse them. Nowadays, the list commonly contains HTTP and sometimes HTTPS, SMTP, and some form of VPN or encrypted tunnel protocol such as SSH or IPSec. This isn't to say that other protocols can't traverse firewalls; rather, the point here is that if you're communicating from a non-thin Web server operating WebSphere on the frontend to a backend WebSphere application server using something other than one of the aforementioned or other similar simple protocols, you may find that there are compelling reasons to go back to a thin model.

In the thin model, all the traffic from the Web server operating a HTTP WebSphere plug-in (to provide routing and context management rules) to the backend WebSphere application server(s) will communicate via plain HTTP. This makes for a simple and easy-to-manage configuration for your firewalls. In this model, however, all your exotic protocols would operate on the backend server environment.

From this, you should be able to see the emerging power of technologies such as SOAP and Web Services. These application protocols allow you to communicate between disparate, diverse, and distributed systems over plain protocols such as HTTP and HTTPS, using a controlled and managed application protocol framework. The remote systems communicate via a standard, exposed "context" within your WebSphere application server. The requests from the remote systems are routing via the HTTP plug-in on the frontend Web application server—like any other application context request—and are routing through to the WebSphere application server on the backend for processing.

Single-Channel Topologies

The single-channel topologies are the most simplistic of all WebSphere topologies. The term *channel* refers to the primary path available between tiers. With a single-channel topology, the Web server(s) tier communicates to a single WebSphere application server and a single database server. Figure 5-9 highlights this concept at a high level.

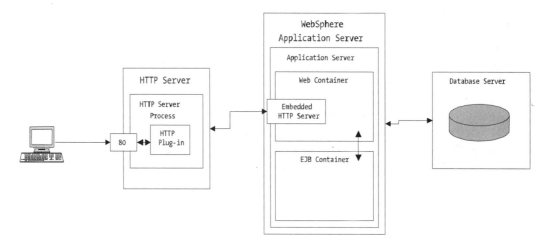

Figure 5-9. An example high-level single-channel topology

As you can see, traffic is restricted to one WebSphere application server instance on the application server and only one database server exists.

This single-channel topology is unlike a dual or multichannel topology, in which multiple independent paths are available between the various tiers. Typically, this involves two or more Web servers, two or more application servers, and two or more database servers. As you can imagine, it's a far more complex design, but it does provide a higher availability guarantee, better scalability, and generally a better performing system.

Single Web Server, Combined WebSphere Application and Database Server

The most simplistic single-channel WebSphere topology that should be considered for a production environment is a single Web server, either thick or thin, and a combined WebSphere application and database server.

I have a few initial points to make about this topology. First, you should only consider this topology if—and only if—you're 100 percent sure that your database load will be minimal to none. As I discussed earlier in the book, database and WebSphere processing characteristics are quite different, meaning that you can't tune or specify your server based solely on one or the other. Given this, having both components operating at the same time will undoubtedly cause you performance issues of several types.

That said, some application architectures just may not require large amounts of database I/O; therefore, this model is quite possibly sufficient for smaller environments. It does not, however, follow what I'd classify as a best-practice design approach of compartmentalizing all of your differing application services into separate server tiers—that is, Web server services in their own server, application-processing services in the application server, and a dedicated database server.

Figure 5-10 illustrates this most basic form of WebSphere topological architecture.

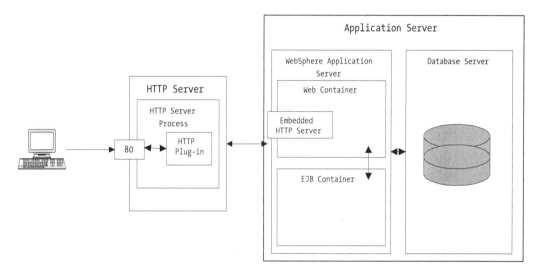

Figure 5-10. A high-level, single-channel, 2-tier topology

Figure 5-10 highlights a high-level 2-tier WebSphere topology. As you can see, it quite clearly has a stand-alone Web server, operating in a thin mode, and a combined backend WebSphere application server and Oracle database server.

Let's take a look at each major section in more detail. First, you'll notice that in this single Web server topology, only a single HTTP Web server instance exists. This can be an HTTP Web server operating Microsoft IIS (for Windows platforms), Apache, IBM HTTPD, or iPlanet/SunOne Web server.

As I discussed in previous chapters, in this thin Web server model, your Web server is just providing you with a redirection layer. This is facilitated by a WebSphere HTTP plug-in that operates within the HTTP Web server process space. The plug-in is configured and tuned via a file known as the `plugin-cfg.xml` file and it's hand editable. This plug-in configuration file maps out what and how requests will be routed through to backend WebSphere application server instances. As you'll see in later sections, this plug-in provides a good level of WebSphere-aware load balancing or workload management.

The second major component in this topology is the combined WebSphere application server and database server. The database server software can be running any of the major Relational Database Management System (RDBMS) packages such as DB2 and Oracle, and it's used, depending on which version of WebSphere you're running, primarily for two purposes. First, in a WebSphere version 4 world, the database is used for the administration repository. This is where WebSphere deployed applications' configuration and setup information is stored. Remember that in WebSphere version 5, the repository has been replaced through facilitation of XML configuration files resident on each of the WebSphere application servers and managed through a series of WebSphere components such as the Deployment Manager. The second use for the database server is for the storage of application data. Anything that your applications may need to persist or store on a database would be stored here. Customer data, profile information, logging, and transaction information are some examples of what may be stored here.

In this simple 2-tier WebSphere topology, you must assume that there won't be any "smarts" behind the database server, such as clustering and hot standby.

The WebSphere application server, operating on the same physical node as the database, is where all the applications are deployed. In this topology, the configuration of this WebSphere application server is very straightforward and doesn't maintain clones or clustered application instances, and is therefore low in complexity. This is the most basic of all WebSphere configurations, short of housing the Web server on the same node as the WebSphere and database services.

Advantages

We need to put a stake in the ground and assume that this topology is only used by very small production environments or, more likely, development and testing environments. The advantages of this topology are as follows:

- **Low cost**: There's little cost associated with this deployment because there are no complex components such as shared storage or clustered database servers. The fact that there are only single instances of applications running infers that there isn't a lot of memory or CPU power required and, as such, a dual CPU machine with 2GB to 4GB of memory would be sufficient for something of this size. Ironically, as you'll see in the next section, splitting out the database and WebSphere components into dedicated servers will result in a similar overall net size of environment processing and memory capacity.

- **Low complexity**: As only one application instance is running at any time and there aren't any high-availability requirements associated with this topology, the database and WebSphere configurations are simple, which keeps down deployment, integration, and operational management costs.

- **No need for load balancing**: This topology reduces costs by removing the need to run additional load-balancing hardware on the frontend of the firewall.

Disadvantages

The disadvantages of this topology are as follows:

- **Little or no redundancy**: Because so much of the application is residing on a single backend combined WebSphere and database server, there's little redundancy available to these components in the event of a hardware failure. A hardware failure of almost any type on any of the server tiers will result in a complete application outage.

- **No service compartmentalization**: If the database server starts to grind the backend server to a halt through a database-intensive process (e.g., archiving), this will affect the rest of the overall application by having a direct effect on the WebSphere applications.

- **Low scalability**: With the backend server assumed to be small (you probably wouldn't purchase a single large system in place of a cluster of smaller systems!), there's little or no scalability available in this topology.

- **Updates and upgrades require outages**: Any upgrades to hardware, application software, or capacity will result in an application outage, as there is only one instance of anything operating at any one time.

- **Possibly low in performance**: With a system of this size, you could assume that the performance may be suitable for a fixed small number of users; however, any wayward processes would instantly impact the overall application performance. Then again, the system may be so small that the usage and utilization of the environment is minimal, and the impact between multiple sessions may go unnoticed.

Final Considerations

The only additional recommendation that I can make about this topology to try and help mitigate some of the risks associated with it would be to consider ensuring that your servers in each of the tiers are internally redundant. Servers of the size that would typically be housed in this kind of topology won't provide redundant, hot-swappable CPUs and memory, so the best you'll be able to do is to use mirror disks (stripped for the database files), redundant network interface cards, and redundant disk controllers. If the vendor of your hardware choice offers it, opt for redundant power supplies and cooling systems too.

In summary, this topology should only be used for small, non-business-critical production systems or for development environments. If you use this topology, I advise that you either invest in hot-standby servers or plan to upgrade to a multiserver 3-tier environment down the track.

Single Web Server, Single Application Server Topology

As you've seen several times throughout this book, these are the key components of a WebSphere physical implementation. In this configuration, physically separate servers are operated that distribute the frontend Web server, the WebSphere application server itself, and the database server. This is different from the first topology you looked at in which the database and WebSphere application server reside on the same physical server. In this topology, the database server sits by itself out on its own dedicated hardware.

Figure 5-11 shows an example of this topology.

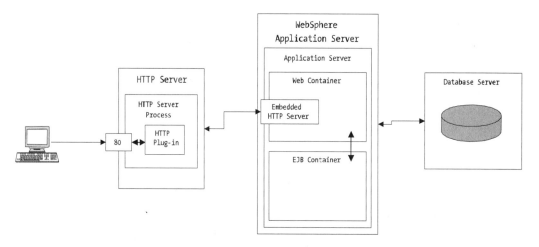

Figure 5-11. A high-level, single-channel, 3-tier topology

As you can see in Figure 5-11, this topology quite clearly shows the 3-tier model: physically separated and dedicated Web, WebSphere, and database servers. The Web server and WebSphere application server interact in the same manner in this 3-tier model as in the first 2-tier topology you examined. Traffic or customer requests are routed through from the Web server HTTP plug-in to the WebSphere application server instances.

Let's take another look at how this plug-in would work in a 3-tier environment. Putting this into context, on your WebSphere application server, you may be running three J2EE-based applications (three EARs):

- A portal application providing basic login screens and navigational logic

- An interactive application for sales and order management

- A customer self-service administration application for customers to update and alter their personal settings, details, and preferences

These three application components, all operating in their own separate JVM or WebSphere application server instance, are configured with their context within the HTTP WebSphere plug-in on the Web server. The context is essentially the URL after the host URL component. That is, with the URL of `http://www.mydomain.com/someContext`, your context would be `/someContext`. This element is used to "route" the customer request to the appropriate application server instance on the WebSphere application server.

You may (and do in this example) have three contexts:

- `/applicationPortal`

- `/theApplication`

- `/selfServiceManagement`

In the plug-in file, you'll configure each of these URLs in such a way that has them coupled with a "route group" to identify to the plug-in to which you eventually send the request. In your basic 3-tier server model, you have only one server of choice to "route" the request through to. However, the way in which J2EE application servers function in this form is to operate the HTTP interfaces to JVMs on separate TCP ports.

So, with your three WebSphere J2EE-based application servers (i.e., the portal, the sales and order management application, and the customer administration application), you have three ports configured within WebSphere. Let's assign the ports as follows:

- `/applicationPortal` as port 10000

- `/theApplication` as port 10001

- `/selfServiceManagement` as port 10002

If you want to, you can access the applications directly on these ports by pointing your browser to the WebSphere application server and the port number directly. For example, pointing your browser to `http://myWASbox.`
`somedomain.com:10000/applicationPortal` results in your being able to use the application directly on the port allocated to `/applicationPortal`. This is not of

much consequence in single server, single instance implementations but, as you'll see in the next section, it has a major effect on what gets load balanced and how it gets load balanced.

To conclude the overview of the operations of the plug-in file, the final step is to attempt to access the applications via the global domain, which you've allocated and configured on the frontend Web server. That is, www.mydomain.com would be configured in the mydomain.com DNS zone files to point the "www" to a host name. In the example here, the host name may be "myHTTPbox"; therefore, pointing the browser to www.mydomain.com or myHTTPbox.mydomain.com will result in the request being sent to the Web server running on the frontend Web server instance.

In this case, the Web server first passes the request through to the HTTP plug-in to determine whether the context in the user's request matches any of the configured contexts in the plugin-cfg.xml configuration file. If it does, the plug-in redirects the request to the server and port, as configured in the plugin-cfg.xml file.

Back on the 3-tier model itself, generally the choice of this model will be the result of one or two things. Either the risks or disadvantages of the shared infrastructure design will result in a need for an additional or dedicated database tier, or the production database transaction load will mandate a dedicated database server.

In most cases that I've seen, the resulting decision for the 3-tier versus 2-tier setup has been mostly driven by the fact that the database transaction load is too high for a shared server environment. The next section deals with that point because I've mentioned it several times now.

Database Transaction Load Considerations

Databases typically have the characteristic of high disk I/O. Because the purpose of a database is to store data and allow you to query against it, the data storage has to be done on some persisted data form via a long-term storage medium such as a hard drive.

As I discussed in the previous chapter, selecting hard disks isn't as simple as looking at capacity or RPM rates. Although these factors have a strong bearing on the final performance indices, the capability for a disk to perform is far more than that. Databases need fast, high-performing disks. As you can imagine, a database that's conducting many queries to its storage files (on the disks) will result in a high I/O rate. If you have just one disk servicing your database files, then you'll notice I/O contention on a medium to high query rate database environment. Striping disks to average down or smooth out the I/O spikes on select physical disks is one popular method of keeping this load under control.

In a shared database and WebSphere application server environment, you may be able to get away with having a separate disk controller and several disks dedicated to database I/O. The problem still remains in the areas of process space and processing capacity, however. Databases will still require memory I/O and CPU capacity to perform queries, indexes, and all the administrative functions that databases need to perform under the hood.

This goes back to what I noted earlier in this chapter about the load characteristics of a database being completely out of tune to those of a WebSphere application server. WebSphere-based applications require memory and CPU cycles—the drivers behind this are pretty simple. Putting aside the processing overhead of the transactions themselves (e.g., a financial management system written in Java), Java/J2EE applications store objects in memory. The JVM is responsible for the management of those objects, including maintaining them, cleaning them out of memory, and accessing them.

All this requires CPU and memory capacity—the same capacity that a database requires. Therefore, a given WebSphere application server will manage itself within its bounds and those in which it is designed to operate within, and it will have no care for the operational needs for a database server and vice versa. There will be system contention from both applications to obtain system resources, and therefore the contention is enough of a reason for not maintaining these two types of applications on the same physical server.

Because the 3-tier model is similar in internal capability to the 2-tier model, in the next sections I cover their advantages and disadvantages.

Advantages

Although the 3-tier model is similar to the 2-tier model component-wise, it has some advantages over the 2-tier model:

- **Generally low cost**: Although the cost of an additional server does make this a more expensive option than the 2-tier single-channel WebSphere topology, the bang-for-your-buck factor is higher in this 3-tier topology.

- **Low complexity**: Because only one application instance is running on the WebSphere application server, and because this is still a single-channel, single-JVM instance topology, it's a low-complexity option for a WebSphere topology.

- **No need for load balancing**: This reduces costs by removing the need to run additional load-balancing hardware on the frontend of the firewall.

- **Limited redundancy**: Although there are still single points of failure in the model due to the single-channel servers (one path), the additional tier does provide for greater redundancy.

Disadvantages

Although this topology is what I consider to be the first true production-ready model of those I discuss here, you'll still need to take the following disadvantages into account:

- **Single path point of failure**: Although you've now increased the number of servers in the model by adding in a dedicated database server, you still have a single path. This model does help reduce the odds of a failure, yet the sum of the system's availability is still affected by the single point of failure within the topology.

- **Low volume-capacity management**: Somewhat similar to the preceding point is the inability for this type of environment to handle unexpected peak volumes. Unless the servers in this basic 3-tier topology are specified to quite a large degree with plenty of processing overhead, they typically won't be able to handle unforeseen volumes, peak loads, or more sinister things, such as DoS attacks, with transparent ease.

- **Inability to perform upgrades that don't impact customers**: This may not be a high priority on everyone's list, but some environments just can't go down, even for capability upgrades. For medical systems, global finance systems, or air-traffic management systems, taking the application offline for an upgrade is, in most cases, unacceptable. As you'll see in the next few sections, having additional channels or application paths starts to provide the ability for systems managers to deploy new capabilities without affecting existing production and, hence, existing customers. This basic 3-tier model doesn't provide this capability, so my recommendation is that you not use it for mission-critical systems.

- **System geographies**: With this topology, because only one channel exists, the systems can't be geographically load balanced or distributed. This is in line with general scalability, and if your application is servicing a wide range of geographic locations, choosing this topology initially may not provide a straightforward upgrade path down the track to distribute out additional servers.

 CAUTION If you're licensing Java from Sun, be sure to review the end-user license agreement. The Java license prohibits the use of Java in environments deemed "high risk," such as nuclear power plants, air-traffic control systems, and life-support machines.

Final Recommendations

This topology does provide a solid, albeit basic, model for smaller, less mission-critical WebSphere implementations. Use this topology if greater than 99.9 percent availability isn't required or you've purchased systems that support internal redundancy and hot-swappable components (e.g., HP Superdomes and Sun SunFire systems). Note that these classes of servers aren't cheap!

Multiapplication JVM, Single-Channel Topology

There are two primary reasons to use multiple JVMs in a WebSphere (or any J2EE server) environment. The first is to gain more processing ability. As I discussed earlier in this chapter, more JVMs means more threads can be processed, which means more customer or application transactions can take place. The second reason for using multiple JVMs is to instigate another level of redundancy. With two or more JVMs, you reduce the risk of having a single JVM application crashing and leaving you with a downed application. That said, not all applications can be simply be "cloned" to use multiple JVMs. You need to consider things such as user sessions, data persistence, transaction management, and so forth.

As I discussed earlier, your application environment may simply need more than one JVM to operate in order to gain more than the limitation of available memory per JVM. Either way, there are many sound reasons why you'd look to use this topology. Let's look at some points you'll need to consider when architecting this kind of topology.

Essentially, the key difference between this topology and the previous topologies is that it incorporates multiple JVMs for each specific application. That is, the application is "cloned" in order to meet one or both of the previous reasons for using multiple JVMs.

Figure 5-12 clearly shows the multiple JVM configuration.

As noted in the first topology presented in this chapter, for Web-based applications that are operating within each of the JVMs depicted in Figure 5-12, requests are sent to each of the JVMs via the use of the frontend HTTP WebSphere plug-in on the HTTP server.

Up until now in this chapter, in a thin Web server configuration the HTTP plug-in has simply been routing requests through to the backend application server. For the first time in this topology, you can see how the HTTP plug-in can be used to provide a level of load balancing. Figure 5-12 shows how an inbound user request is trapped by the HTTP plug-in on the Web server. The HTTP plug-in then, based on its routing rules defined in the HTTP plug-in configuration file (also located on the Web server), will deliver the user request to the most appropriate backend application server. The request is routed based on one of several workload management policies, with the most common being to reroute pre-setup requests with active sessions to the original server process.

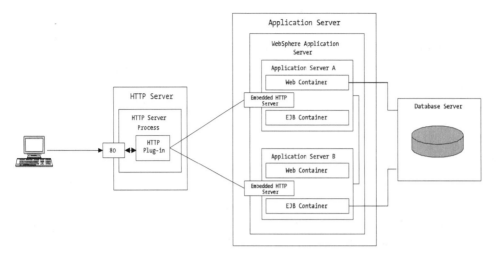

Figure 5-12. A high-level, 3-tier, multi-JVM topology

For example, say that the customer had originally logged into the Web-based application and the HTTP plug-in had decided, based on a pure round-robin load-balancing policy, to send the request to JVM A on the application server. With a concept known as *server affinity* being active, all subsequent requests made by that same user session (as defined or identified by the active session ID) would be delivered to the original server process which, in this case, would be JVM A.

If the configuration had been set up to accommodate session persistence, the two JVMs would be persisting the user's session object to the backend database to ensure that in the event of a JVM failure (e.g., JVM A), the subsequent user request would be routed through to JVM B and that JVM would be able to access the existing session details that JVM A persisted. The features that handle load balance and failover between differing JVM instances are typically, but not always, managed by server groups and clones in WebSphere version 4 and Dynamic Replication Service (DRS) in WebSphere version 5. (Sound confusing? In Chapter 7 I discuss in detail the configuration and design considerations associated with workload management.)

With this ability to round-robin, load balance, and support failover scenarios, you have a situation now in which your topology starts to exhibit traits of redundancy and high availability. Let's examine the considerations of this topology in more detail.

Considerations for Multiple JVM Environments

As I alluded to previously, an application can't always just be incorporated into a multi-JVM architecture. You'll need to consider various design points relating to the application architecture prior to going down this path:

- Do you need to control user sessions? That is, are your transactions sticky and, once a customer logs into the application, does the application need to track items and details about the user's session?

- How are you going to handle transactions that span multiple JVMs?

- Are you going to use file system–level or database-level persistence for storing certain types of data?

These questions can't typically be answered right away; however, let's briefly look at the details of each. First, session state for customers or users accessing the application may be used to store various bits of information. This may be items as straightforward as the user's login name or it may extend to information that has been retrieved from a database relating to data such as the user's past spending history. Therefore, if you're using session state to store this type of information, you'll need to ensure that if JVM A crashes or some form of load balancing pushes the customer requests to another JVM, the other JVM can access the customer's session with no or little fuss.

Second, if your application design makes use of large (long-timed) transactions that may span several JVMs, operating multiple JVMs without some consideration for the application architecture in this type of situation could result in many headaches. It's a common mistake to not design how applications are broken up at a J2EE component level early enough in the design phase of a project. Component modeling and the interaction between components within a design phase are just as important in J2EE architecture as threading design and data transformation. The output of component modeling should leave you with an application design that doesn't have an issue with transactions over multiple JVMs, thus eliminating this issue from your checklist.

 NOTE Component modeling can come in many forms in the J2EE world. In this section's context, component modeling is all about what is contained within each of your J2EE packagable component types—EARs, WARs, EJB-JARs, and JARs—and how it is contained. Each of these components communicates to methods and interfaces with other components differently, and there are boundaries for all four components as to what and how they communicate.

The last point relates to the age-old issue of persistence. If you have multiple JVMs operating an application, how does the application operating under WebSphere manage accessing the same piece of information or data? For databases, generally speaking, this isn't as much of an issue if you're operating something fairly straightforward such as JDBC. Once you get into the world of

Container Managed Persistence (CMP) and Bean Managed Persistence (BMP), however, things can get a little hairy. For file-level persistence, in which multiple JVMs may access file system–level files, for example, persistence and data integrity are almost completely in the hands of the developer. Not all application designs may incorporate or even have considered this as a factor.

The bottom line is this: If you're modifying an existing application environment to incorporate multiple JVMs, test, test, test. Speak with the application developers to ensure that this type of event is well covered. If the application is new, ensure that the integrity management of the persistence layer is well designed and tested.

Other Considerations

With additional JVMs operating, you might assume that the server load will increase. If you're performing an upgrade to a multiple JVM environment in which previously a single JVM configuration existed, you must assume that the load will be evenly split between the two JVMs, 50/50, plus a small amount of overhead. This is a straightforward concept to manage. If, however, you're adding in additional JVMs to cater for load issues, there are a few issues you need to consider.

First, you should understand what adding in the additional JVMs for a particular application instance will do to the overall load characteristics of the application environment. That is, although you may gain additional memory to be able to perform and process certain logic, this will have a direct result on your server platform. Depending on what type of server platform you have chosen or are currently using, this effect will vary somewhat. Different platform types and memory configurations will perform in different manners. I use a rough rule that says if the load of a system is x with one JVM, and that JVM is using greater than 80 percent available JVM memory, additional JVMs will introduce load to the factor of the following:

Overall System Load = ([$x \div Nj$] × [Nj × 1.1])

This formula adds roughly 10 percent additional overhead per JVM process to the overall loading of the application environment. This will vary depending on the type and version of JVM you're using, the platform type you're using, and how many CPUs you'll run.

As I noted earlier, if you're running single or dual CPU systems for your application server, carefully plan what impact running multiple JVMs will have on your overall platform. Just adding in additional load-balanced or workload-managed JVMs that are under a fair degree of load (greater than 40 percent) will make a system's performance actually go backward.

Looking back to the earlier discussion, JVMs operate and manage threads for the applications that your developers write. These threads correlate to system-based threads or kernel threads. At any one time, a finite number of threads can operate on a single CPU. If you're attempting to get 1.5 or 2 times the amount of transaction performance by adding in an additional JVM without sufficient CPU power, then all that you're doing is pushing the thread handler in your operating system's kernel harder. This will work up until a point at which, after a while, the thread manager will start to become saturated with requests and the system's performance will start to stagger. Figure 5-13 highlights how this load issue can become a problem.

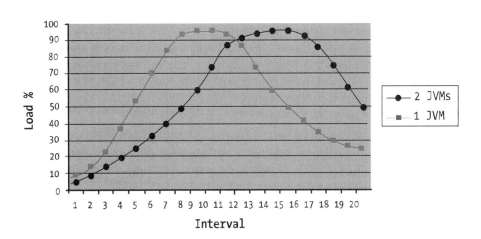

Figure 5-13. *Multiple JVM transaction considerations*

As you can see, up until a point, the dual JVM configuration outperforms the single JVM configuration. However, as the total threads being processed by the system's threading engine begin to near the maximum capacity of what can be pushed through the single CPU, the second JVM starts to buckle.

Though this may seem obvious to those readers who are better versed in these areas than others, it needs to be said that the performance impact could also be the result of other factors. Most of the time, the issue will come back to system load, but not all transactions are CPU-hungry and tie down clock cycles. Consider distributed transactions, network load, throughput, and other such factors. Consider the case if your JVM processes were writing to disk, and by adding in an additional JVM, the additional processing load from the additional JVM doubled the disk I/O and saturated the disk bus. Consider simple things such as network load if your application is network bandwidth intensive. I've seen sites in which an application's purpose was to obtain data from an EAI bus, massage it into HTML-based output, and deliver it to the client. The resulting output was very large, and with this type of transaction, the JVMs were well utilized transforming data off the EAI call into objects and then delivering them down to the client browser. Remember that intensive network operations will consume CPU cycles—this consumption will result in less available computing power for your JVM(s).

Advantages

As I noted, this topology is the first that is exhibiting traits of high availability and limited application redundancy. This provides a number of advantages:

- **High application redundancy**: With the capability to now load balance and round-robin, and with failover between multiple application JVM instances, you can ensure greater availability of the applications. Although this topology is limited physically to a single path, if the decision was made to purchase servers that consisted of high levels of internal chassis redundancy, with the use of multiple JVMs, the topology would be able to meet quite high availability SLAs.

- **Increased application performance**: With the additional JVMs now configured and active in this topology, you can extend the available memory to by using multiple JVMs to distribute memory or object space. In turn, the JVM itself doesn't need to garbage collect as frequently (assuming your capacity modeling is solid!), given that the object space is distributed between more than one JVM. That said, for this topology to operate efficiently and as discussed here, your system will need to be running multiple CPUs when using memory- and or process-intensive applications.

- **High application availability**: Similar to the first point, with the additional JVMs that can operate within the same physical application server, it's possible to perform limited upgrades to application code while the system is still running. This is limited to certain components—the applications operating within the JVMs will be under workload management (e.g., server groups) and, as such, will be mastered by the parent WebSphere processes. Any changes to one JVM instance can and may have an effect on the other. However, items that can be easily hot-deployed, for example, can be managed in this way and tested independently of the main production processing scope.

- **Low-cost option for medium levels of single system redundancy**: Considering the low costs associated with having a basic 3-tier model, the ability to operate a multiple JVM configuration does provide a low-cost option for basic application redundancy. Don't become too complacent with this design, however—there are still single points of failure, but it's a big step up from the previous single JVM topologies.

Disadvantages

I've discussed a few of the design considerations of this topology that could be labeled as disadvantages (i.e., multiple JVM considerations and so forth). Most, if not all, are manageable. Additional disadvantages to this topology are as follows:

- **Servers are still single points of failure**: I've covered this one in all topologies so far. The same applies to this 3-tier topology in that although you have additional redundancy built into the application through the use of multiple JVMs, all it takes is a CPU to panic and you could run as many JVMs as you like yet the system and application will still fail. The only caveat here is if you're running a high-end Unix system such as a SunFire server, which is capable of hot-swapping and management of bad CPUs. In this case, the offending CPU will be deallocated from the CPU pool and the application will continue operating.

- **Lack of scalability**: Once again, similar to previous topologies, the single machine model still generally lacks adequate scalability for medium to large WebSphere environments. You must not become complacent with the ability to internally scale (application vertical scaling) as a replacement or substitute for true physical scalability.

- **Single repositories and memory spaces**: Because the WebSphere implementation is operating singularly, with a single series of governing administrative processes and object spaces (session stores and so on), as with the previous single-channel topologies, there is a chance the process space within WebSphere could become unstable and cause a total crash. The same applies to the fact that there is only one administrative domain (WebSphere version 4) or cell (WebSphere version 5). Given this, the applications operating within these domains and cells can in themselves suffer failures. As you'll see shortly in more advanced topologies, when you design mission-critical WebSphere topologies, you should consider splitting their infrastructure into multiple domains or cells.

Final Considerations

As you're moving through these WebSphere topologies, you should be starting to see their best practices. Although some of these topologies and concepts in theory aren't uncommon in large-scale platform engineering and architecture, they do map slightly differently to WebSphere environments due to the way in which WebSphere functions.

This 3-tier topology represents the first of what I'd class as production ready or production safe. It presents limited vertical and horizontal scaling, as well as limited application and server redundancy through the use of the multi-JVM approach.

Even if your needs don't require the use of a secondary JVM, consider this approach for redundancy purposes. As discussed, by workload managing your application into multiple JVMs, you acquire not only a performance improvement or the ability to scale, but also application redundancy.

Dual Web Server, Single Application Server Topology

The dual Web server topology is the first of the horizontally scaled topological designs. In this approach, you gain the ability to obtain performance and availability improvements on the frontend Web server, whether it is thin or thick in design.

Common uses for this topology may be to simply handle and manage requests from geographically distributed sites and route the requests to backend WebSphere application servers (see the section "Geographically Distributed Application Servers" in this chapter). Or, if your topological architecture makes use of a thick Web server model in which the Web server is running WebSphere as well as the static HTTP server, this can be a good approach to gaining server redundancy for presentation components.

Figure 5-14 shows the thin Web server model for this topology.

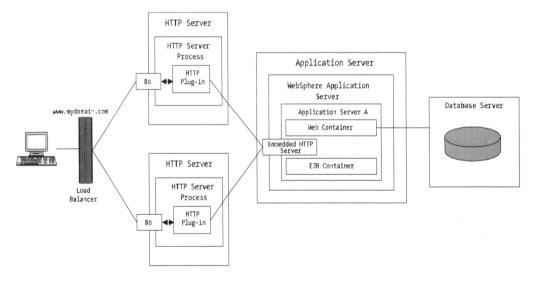

Figure 5-14. The dual Web server thin model

Figure 5-14 provides an overview of how this type of topology can service the needs of geographically distributed requirements for Web serving. As you can see from this example, the model depicts two Web servers operating with the HTTP WebSphere plug-in routing requests to a backend WebSphere application server.

In this model, the Web servers can be located side by side (i.e., in the same data center), or they can be distributed at key locations on a corporate network or on the Internet. For example, if an online ordering application receives requests from Australia and the United Kingdom, design considerations may include locating each of the two servers in, say, Sydney and London.

Another consideration is to locate each of the servers at entry points into corporate firewalls or networks. For example, suppose a company based on the West Coast of the United States has its corporate firewall entry points distributed between Los Angeles and Seattle. A good design choice is to locate one server in each of the geographically distributed firewall centers to gain both sites' redundancy but also allow a level of Internet interconnection redundancy. With these types of distances, the servers aren't located far enough away that the distance (equaling latency) starts to become a problem.

The other design consideration for this topology is if your application architecture allows or requires a thick Web server model. In this case, predominantly your presentation layer is located on the Web servers and only business logic (i.e., data tier integration, EJBs, JMS, and legacy systems integration) is located on the application servers. Both tiers are operating WebSphere.

Figure 5-15 depicts a thick Web server WebSphere topology.

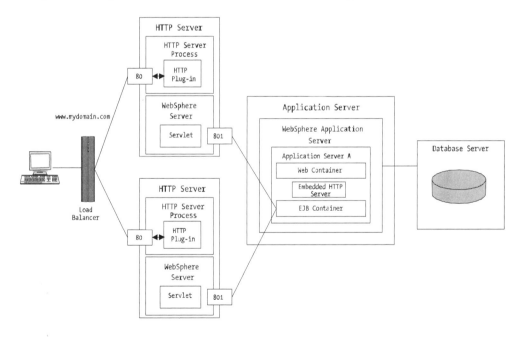

Figure 5-15. The dual Web server thick model

This modified version of Figure 5-14 is the first of the topology designs that incorporates server or horizontal redundancy. In this model, the Web server operates both a static Web server application, such as Microsoft IIS or SunOne

Web server, as well as the WebSphere application server for presentation layer components (e.g., JSPs, servlets, etc.). This topology provides the ability to load balance the presentation components of your WebSphere application. That is, components such as JSPs, servlets, xHTML, and so forth can be distributed for both performance and redundancy purposes.

This type of model starts to prove itself quite powerful for those application architectures that don't have a great deal of business tier components—those components being EJBs and legacy systems integration. For example, you may have an online ordering system in which the presentation components are used to perform the interface to the backend system as well as the formatting, composition, and display of the output retrieved from the backend database and application servers.

To further illustrate this concept, Figure 5-16 places some components into the topology of Figure 5-15 that help explain what can be achieved here.

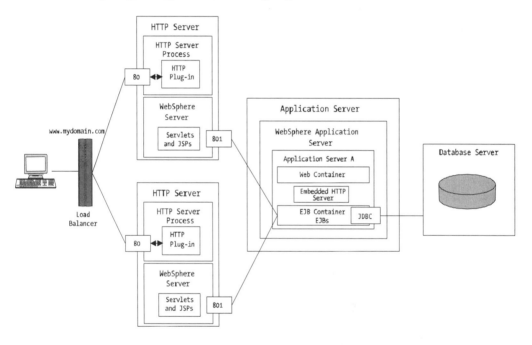

Figure 5-16. Component mapping for a thick Web server topology

Figure 5-16 shows an architecture in which JSPs, servlets, EJBs, and JDBC integration is used. Table 5-1 discusses each of those components and how it fits into this topology in more detail.

Table 5-1. Overview of Example Components

Component Type	Example Purpose
JSP	Used to compose and display the data retrieved from servlets and, ultimately, the backend database servers. They are lightweight and highly distributable. In this application example, the JSPs format the HTML and placement of dynamic data.
Servlets	Used to perform the controlling of the data retrieval to the backend components (EJBs) and massaging of data returned from the EJBs. In the example, the servlets communicate to the EJB methods directly.
EJBs	Used to perform the workhorse functions of the application. The EJBs communicate to the database server by binding to JDBC data sources configured within WebSphere.
JDBC classes	Used to enable you to communicate from your container or application components, via JDBC. JDBC classes are simply Java classes (JDBC Type 2 or Type 4, primarily) that are provided by your database vendor. In this example, the JDBC classes are used only on the application server and are referenced indirectly by the EJBs components via the use of a WebSphere data source.

NOTE A term I've used several times in this chapter and haven't discussed in much detail in previous chapters is *data source*. "Data source" is typically the name given to data tier provider components. That is, ODBC or JDBC classes that are provided by your database vendor will be used to create a specific data source to your data tier. This may be an Oracle database, DB2 database, or any other of the multitude of data tier engines available on the market (e.g., RDBMS, OO-DBMS, LDAP, etc.). Essentially, a data source is a construct that you create within WebSphere that manages the pools of connections for each instance of your data tier interface for your application components. In your applications, you will typically bind to the named data source via a JNDI lookup, and WebSphere will in turn, via your configured data source components, provide your application with a pool of connections.

This type of topological architecture is a good solid design, both from an infrastructure and an application architecture point of view. The key to this topology is that components are split or tiered correctly in that presentation components are on one tier, business components are on another tier, and database services are on the data tier. This is an architectural purist's and the J2EE specification's preferred base model.

Why Split the Components into Their Own Tiers?

Apart from providing a clean design, distributing components in this fashion provides a more modular system. You can complete upgrades and software changes easily as you distribute your components more, and redundancy starts to become inherent in the design. As you'll see in upcoming sections, the more you distribute your design, the more you're able to gain performance benefits and redundancy, albeit to a point.

Also, with general J2EE design, the JSPs and servlet components are typically used more. In many cases, it may just not be necessary to use EJBs for each and every user transaction. You may only use a call to an EJB once or twice in a user's session, because it may be possible to load up the required information on the user's initial login via a call to the EJB (and hence the database). As you saw in earlier chapters, the aim in performance is to keep the loading model as a carrot or funnel, with the small or pointy end referring to the small amount of connections and transactions (the database) and the large or wide end referring to the large amount of connections and transactions (HTTP and JSP connections).

EJBs are heavyweight elements of an application. They are expensive to maintain through infrastructure; therefore, if you can ensure that the design of your topology (and your application!) only uses EJBs when required, you'll find that the platform will operate far more efficiently.

It's worth noting some further points here on the schools of thought surrounding EJBs. You may read or hear some developers or architects say, "Don't use EJBs—they're expensive and they're kludgy." My personal opinion is that, yes, in previous version of J2EE (1.1 and, to a far smaller degree, 1.2), EJBs had some serious questionable design elements that made them almost a nightmare to deal with.

In more recent J2EE versions, such as 1.3 and 1.4, EJBs have come a long way and are now powerful components. But, like any piece of the model, they need to be used where and when appropriate. You wouldn't use them for presentation construction (don't laugh, I've seen it), and you wouldn't purposely design them in your application just because they're distributable.

The other end of the spectrum is that some people tend to use EJBs too much. I feel that many people believe that they must use EJBs because EJBs are considered to be a major part of J2EE. Again, to a degree, EJBs are a major part of J2EE, but as you learned in Chapters 2 and 3, J2EE is made up of many components and the EJB specification is just one of them.

My generalized rule is as follows: If you need to expose something, whether it be tables in a database, directories from an LDAP cluster, results from an MQ call, or data from a SAP financial system, EJBs are a very sound way to achieve this. It's technically possible to perform this via servlets and other presentation components, but EJBs were designed to provide and perform distributable business integration logic.

Advantages

As you've seen, this topology starts to show the beginnings of a sound and highly available platform design. Here are the key advantages of this platform:

- **Load-balanced frontend tier**: This is a good model for thin application environments, but if your budget is constrained and your firewall and business rules allow for it, using a thick Web server model to place JSPs and servlets (under WebSphere) on dual-node Web servers provides a sound design for high availability.

- **Overall increase in platform performance**: Performance improvements will start to be apparent in this design over that of the previously covered topologies. Again, based on a thick Web server model, you'll be able to operate between 70 and 100 percent more load due to the dual-node Web servers. The reason the load improvement isn't always 100 percent is that the factor of performance for your presentation components operating under WebSphere are still at the mercy of the business tier (EJBs and the like also operating under WebSphere). If every user transaction requires a database lookup, then you're limited to the performance of the backend tiers, which are single-node only. If one large transaction comes through, chances are it will have an effect on the overall performance of the application, whereas with a multinode backend system, the likely impact of an abnormally large transaction will be somewhat smoothed because of the separate physical processes.

- **More resiliency to DoS and abnormal transactions**: I touched on this in the previous point. Additional servers (or single servers with multiple CPUs and multiple JVMs) can assist systems managers and capacity planners with tackling abnormal transactions. In today's software industry, regardless of how good the capacity modeling may be, there will always be a superfluous transaction that gives a server a pounding. Likewise, with worms and DoS attacks almost as common as spam e-mail, it's important to ensure that production and business-critical systems are resilient to these types of issues. Therefore, the dual frontend Web server configuration will help contain unusually large or abnormal transaction in most cases. Although there are still single nodes on the backend (application server and database), this topology does introduce a solid design principal in J2EE applications (and almost any online applications, for that matter).

- **Cost-effective availability when using the thick model**: In this topology, the cost of the implementing dual backend application servers may be beyond many budgets, the reason being that in most cases, servers that operate EJB containers are typically more expensive than those that operate servlet containers. Therefore, if you use a thick Web server model, you achieve a sense of high availability with a good return on investment (see Chapter 2).

Disadvantages

You've seen that this topology does provide some solid design principals and the measurement of these is high performance and a good level of availability/ redundancy. However, you're still faced with some disadvantages in this configuration:

- **Possible false sense of redundancy security**: Although I've stated that this topology provides a fairly solid level of redundancy in the presentation tier, you shouldn't be too complacent and believe that this topology is completely sound from a redundancy perspective. As I mentioned earlier in this chapter, if your budget can afford it, double everything.

- **Limited scaling in the application tier**: Because this topology has only a single application server, the implementation of components on the application server tier may not support high distributability. That is, although the application tier is typically associated with EJBs, not all software components on the application tier are EJBs. Don't fall into the trap of thinking that because the components are sitting on an application tier they're EJBs and/or distributable. Standard JavaBeans, serialized objects of many sorts, and other associated Java components aren't typically distributable, or at best they may require code changes to support a fully distributed platform.

- **The database tier is a single point of failure**: Continuing on with the last point, the database server is still a single point of failure. It's all well and good to ensure that the presentation tier is load balanced, but my belief is that 80 to 90 percent of applications will use a database for application data storage, and for WebSphere version 4 the repository may sit on the database tier. Therefore, if the database is down, chances are that the application is down.

- **Security with a thick model**: Consider the points I made about firewalls earlier in the chapter. Your application architecture and your security policies may forbid having JSPs and servlets in a DMZ in which those types of application components may need to be behind a firewall. In this case, you'll typically lean toward using a thin Web server model (there are ways around this, but moving to a thin model is the most common and recommended method).

Final Considerations

As you can see, in this chapter's coverage of topologies so far this model is the most advanced. It also offers the best availability and performance, but it still lacks, in my opinion, the true scalability, availability, and performance that medium- to large-scale mission- or business-critical applications require.

However, this topology is a very sound and well-priced model for applications that are heavily based on JSPs and servlets. If your application only accesses the backend tiers (application and database) on an infrequent basis, then this model is a good choice.

Multiapplication JVM, Dual Web Server, Single Application Server Topology

The next "step up" in topologies is to look back at the use of multiple JVMs for the various containers. When I discussed this concept earlier in this chapter, I didn't discuss at length the use of multiple JVMs in thick models. This topology explores the concept further and looks at ways of splitting up your application so that you can make better use of split JVMs.

 TIP   Remember that in most cases, the use of multiple JVMs on a single server is only beneficial if the server has multiple CPUs. Smaller environments can get away with single CPUs and multiple JVMs if the workload is low; however, as a rule of thumb, any contained application should operate on its own JVM.

Firstly, let's look at a standard application operating on a single application server. Figure 5-17 highlights a basic J2EE application design that contains both business and presentation components.

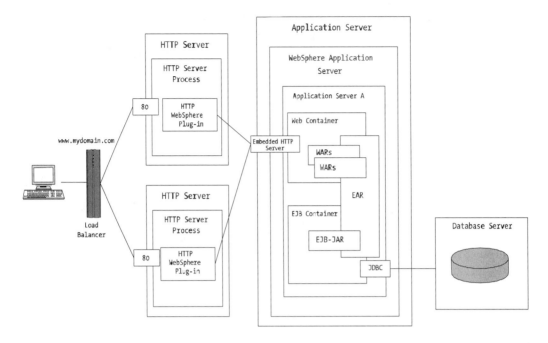

Figure 5-17. A basic J2EE application operating under WebSphere

As you can see in Figure 5-17, a single WebSphere instance is operating, and within the singular WebSphere instance is a single J2EE application server—a JVM. Inside the JVM is a deployed application bundled within an EAR file. That EAR file contains a WAR file containing all the JSPs, servlets, and static components (GIFs, HTML, etc.), and the EAR also contains an EJB-JAR, which contains EJBs classes and descriptor components.

The EJB and servlet containers can both use split JVMs independently of one another. That is, an application can be broken up into its Web-based and EJB-based constituents. It is then possible to run an application with two JVMs under the servlet container, operating the Web components (i.e., JSPs, servlets, etc.) and two JVMs under the EJB container operating the backend components (i.e., EJBs, standard JavaBeans, etc.).

NOTE   Remember that the use of multiple JVMs should be coupled with the use of multiple CPUs. Basically, if you're considering using multiple JVMs to gain performance, you should include an application server with multiple CPUs.

This seems straightforward and, in fact, it is. When you deploy your application EARs into your WebSphere environment, the deployment tools that you're using (as provided by WebSphere) take care of scoping where the different parts of the application need to go, how they're interfaced back into WebSphere itself, and how they run.

Figure 5-18 shows a slightly different view of a standard WebSphere deployment. The difference here is that the Web and EJB components are actually deployed into different application servers, which results in the components operating in different JVMs.

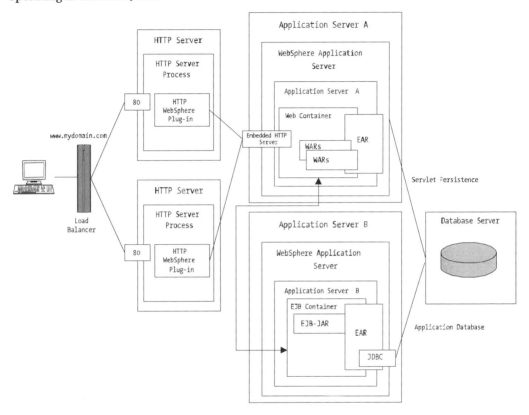

Figure 5-18. A split Web and EJB container JVM configuration

Figure 5-18 shows the concept of a split configuration for the servlet container and the EJB container. Although this alone doesn't provide a large increase in performance, it does aid in the operational management aspects of a WebSphere implementation.

Like most of the designs you've seen and the recommendations I've provided in this chapter, the more you can compartmentalize your application environment, the better. There may be some extra overhead during development to cater for this, but it's only an incremental amount, and the payoffs are great. Consider the benefits from a dual application server configuration with a split Web and EJB container configuration. The ability to mesh the communications between the multiple application servers and to turn on and off specific components and services at will makes for a resilient and manageable WebSphere environment.

What's most different in this configuration is that the deployment of the application components to WebSphere is split into two EARs. One EAR contains the application WAR file(s), and the other EAR contains the EJB-JAR and standard JAR packages that may contain standard JavaBeans and associated components. This can provide a slightly increased level of redundancy because in the event that, for example, the EJB-based JVM/application server crashes, the Web-based JVM/application server will continue to operate.

Of course, if your Web components are dependent on the backend components, then only a dual tier or redundant application servers (i.e., redundant application JVMs) will make this configuration beneficial. If this is the case, and your frontend components (e.g., JSPs and servlets) are dependent on backend components (e.g., EJBs), then the use of server groups and WebSphere clusters with multiple nodes (depending on which version of WebSphere you're operating) is a sound solution.

Let's now take a more detailed look at the dual Web, single-application server, dual JVM configuration, as shown in Figure 5-19.

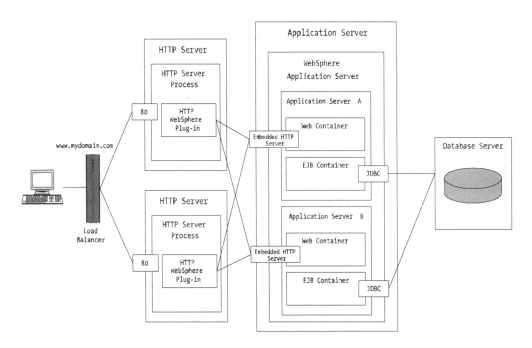

Figure 5-19. A dual Web, single application server, dual JVM topology

The most obvious difference here is with the additional JVM instances operating within the application server. In this example, the dual JVMs are operating both. So as to not confuse the differences between WebSphere 4 and WebSphere 5, this diagram doesn't show the underlying detail associated with workload management on both versions of WebSphere.

In WebSphere version 4, the multiple JVMs can be configured into a single server group and operate as clones. As I discussed in Chapter 4, server groups provide the mechanism to group multiple application servers, or clones, into a single administrative group. Primarily, server groups provide a way of implementing workload management (WLM) for J2EE applications under WebSphere. Application server clones are literally clones of one another. They coexist and operate within different JVMs and are managed by the server group WLM process (e.g., configurations, status, stop and start, etc.).

In WebSphere version 5, this concept of multiple JVMs is slightly different. The definition of a WebSphere cluster is more evident within WebSphere version 5, and it essentially replaces the concept of a server group. Node agents and the Deployment Manager are new components that join to make WLM function within WebSphere version 5.

At a high level, the way in which the two JVM application servers operate is dependent on whether the application environment is using Web-based or thick-based Java clients. Assuming for the time being that you're considering only Web-based architectures, the way in which this topology operates is simple, yet effective.

The frontend Web servers maintain a list of application servers via the implementation of the XML-based HTTP server plug-in file. This plug-in file lists multiple server entries for each available service. In a WebSphere version 4 world, the plug-in file will contain multiple Transport entries for each of the application servers or JVMs operating on the single WebSphere server. Each entry has a clone ID associated with each of the application server clones. This provides a way of allowing the plug-in logic to route the user request to the appropriate application server. If server affinity is used, the affinity is achieved by attaching the clone ID of the originating application server clone to the end of the session ID.

 TIP   Be sure that you have WebSphere generate the plug-in file and cut and paste it to the location on your Web server. Removing and or changing the names of clone IDs can result in your users' sessions being nuked.

In this fashion, the frontend Web servers will receive requests, confirm the URL context is valid (e.g., `http://somesite.com/MyContext/`), query the route path (found within the plug-in), and then deliver the request to the backend application server clone.

NOTE The plug-in allows for several methods of routing requests through to the backend application server clones. Round-robin, weighted load-balancing, and variants associated with server and session affinity are possible. Consider the selection of these carefully as each of routing types has plusses and minuses. I discuss this in more detail in Chapter 8.

WebSphere version 5 operates in a similar manner. Slight changes are evident in the plug-in file configuration (I discuss these changes in Chapter 7), but the basic concept is the same. The key difference is that the requests sent from the one of the Web servers on the frontend to the backend application servers aren't going to clones but instead are being directed to application server instances.

It's important to note that routing requests to non-Web-based components such as EJBs and so forth also fall under the WebSphere WLM system. I discuss this topic in more depth in Chapter 7, so for the purposes of covering this topic in the context of topologies, let's briefly look at non-Web-based WLM.

Non-Web-Based Workload Management Topology Considerations

For non-Web-based WLM, the differences in topology design considerations are somewhat varied. WebSphere version 4 provides WLM of non-Web-based components, such as EJBs, via the use of an ORB plug-in that understands WebSphere WLM. The ORB plug-in, like the HTTP Web server plug-in, maintains a list of available components (e.g., EJBs and JavaBeans) and directs requests to the appropriate service when requested.

WebSphere version 5 has a slightly more advanced implementation of non-Web-based WLM. Through the use of the Deployment Manager, client requests bootstrap against the Deployment Manager and within the resulting IOR exists a route table available to backend services and servers. The Deployment Manager continuously integrates the WLM-available components, such as EJBs, and maintains the list for subsequent client ORB requests.

As noted, I discuss this aspect of WebSphere WLM in greater detail in Chapter 7. For now, let's look at the advantages and disadvantages of this specific topology.

Advantages

It should now be clear that WebSphere is a very powerful application platform when it comes to distributed applications. This topology starts to open up WebSphere's powerful WLM capabilities. As you'll learn in Chapter 7, WebSphere's almost seamless integration of WLM features into the core platform makes it a market leader in the area of highly resilient and scalable application platforms.

That said, the topology you've just looked at is a solid performer in the areas of availability and potential application performance. Here are some of the key advantages of this topology:

- **High levels of availability**: Through the use of WLM capabilities within WebSphere, the topology allows for a very scalable model for platform availability. The use of multiple JVMs as well as multiple entry points helps to promote very high uptimes. This topology may be able to provide greater than 99.9 percent availability with the use of high-end servers from the likes of IBM, Sun, and HP. These vendors, as you learned in Chapter 5, all offer advanced system-availability capabilities (e.g., SunFire servers from Sun). These types of systems may provide an alternative to more expensive multiapplication server topologies, which we have yet to look at.

- **High levels of performance**: With the compartmentalization and splitting up of applications into multiple JVMs, you gain a level of performance over that of singular JVM applications.

- **Solid return on investment/good price for the performance**: This topology provides a good baseline for performance at a reasonable price. This topology could be achieved for under US$30,000 using Intel CPU systems, assuming two Web servers, an application server with multiple CPUs, and a database, also with multiple CPUs.

Disadvantages

The disadvantages of this topology are somewhat similar to the other multiple JVM-based topologies. The extra requirement of a JVM typically means that one or more extra CPUs are required, and the architecture of your environment can quickly go down the path of a very vertically scaled solution.

This is fine from a performance point of view. An application architecture that can operate within a vertically scaled environment is good, but there are still limitations to the architecture's availability. In my view, an environment isn't designed for or capable of high levels of availability if there is limited or no use of horizontal scaling present in all tiers.

I suppose what I'm getting at is that although this topological architecture is sound, you shouldn't become complacent and believe that it's foolproof from an availability or redundancy perspective. As I've said many times before, availability and/or redundancy above 99 percent may just not be required by some

installations. This specific topology will support greater than 99 percent availability, but it won't guarantee greater than 99.9 percent availability.

You may argue that if your single application server is an IBM iSeries 960 or
a Sun SunFire F6800, for example, both of which have very sophisticated levels
of internal hot redundancy, it doesn't matter how many servers you have in your
application tier. To a point, this is correct. Where the argument breaks down is
that you're still limiting yourself to a single WebSphere instance and a single
physical server. A physical server can only be in one place at any one time; therefore, if that sole server is located in a site that suffers a catastrophic failure, then
the application will cease to operate.

At the same time, IBM WebSphere versions 4 and 5 are, after all, just software. Like any software, they're susceptible to glitches and bugs. Therefore these
versions contain within themselves a single point of failure.

Final Considerations

Like most of the multiserver topologies you've examined in this chapter, this
model is well suited to implementations that require greater than 99 percent
availability but don't require greater than 99.9 percent guaranteed availability. I
recommend that you use this topology for non-mission-critical systems. It will
work well with a small- to medium-sized production system that can get away
with a few hours of possible downtime per month.

Consider using highly redundant servers for the middle tiers to help with
availability. You'll find that for the price of the more sophisticated hot-replication
server technologies available from companies such as HP, Sun, and IBM, you're
better off for small- to medium-sized environments to go down the path of a
fully scaled, fully redundant topology such as one from the upcoming sets of
architectures.

Multichannel Topologies

Multichannel is the term I use for the deployment of two or more application
paths within an application environment. Essentially, it refers to the paths that
the application can take.

In the previous sections, you looked at single-channel and hybrid single-
channel architectures in which one primary WebSphere application server
operated for the business application tier. As noted, this type of single-channel
configuration is fine for small- or medium-sized application environments,
which may just not need the guarantees of high availability. However, for those
production application environments of any size that are deemed business or
mission critical, the only choice is to make use of a multichannel topology.

In this part of the chapter, you'll explore the major components of several
topological architectures that are based on a multichannel model.

Multi-Web Server, Multiapplication Server Topologies

As this section's title implies, I discuss the design considerations around multi-application server topologies in this part of the chapter.

The key difference in this topology is the inclusion of an additional server, which operates the core WebSphere application services. Not unlike a multi-JVM installation, this topology almost appears, from a WLM perspective, to be similar to a dual Web server and multi-JVM topology.

Figure 5-20 shows an overview of the architecture of a multiapplication server implementation. The most obvious feature is the second WebSphere application server, which services requests from the frontend Web server environment.

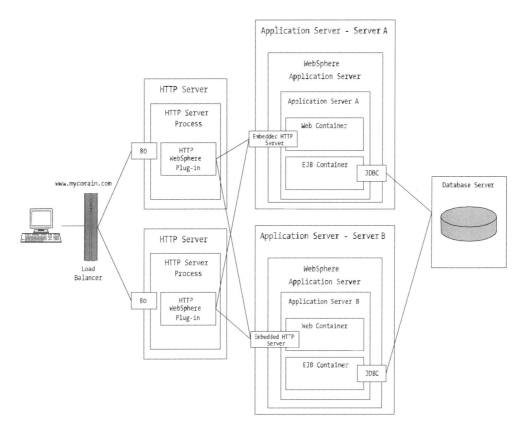

Figure 5-20. A multi–Web server, multiapplication server topology

Traffic or user requests are routed through to one of either of the application servers, just as if they were two JVMs on a single application server. For all intents and purposes, the HTTP plug-in doesn't know the difference between the two topologies.

This topology provides a solid base for a very scalable and high-performing application server environment. With the additional application server operating, there are myriad additional operational management capabilities available to you. For example, depending on how you decide to design your end topology, it's possible to have the two WebSphere application servers operating as two independent applications, or WebSphere domains for version 4 or WebSphere clusters for version 5. That is, from a WebSphere perspective, you may have two separate WebSphere domains or clusters (WebSphere versions 4 and 5, respectively) which, although operating the same application components, don't share administrative or internal WLM space.

This is a hybrid of the multiapplication server topology that I discuss in more detail shortly. The point that I'm trying to make here is that the inclusion of an additional WebSphere server (a physical node) paves the way to a whole range of possible options in your architecture.

Let me reiterate the two primary goals for platform resiliency: remove all single points of failure and remove all interdependent components. Having a second WebSphere server (a physical server) satisfies these two goals. Figure 5-21 illustrates this concept.

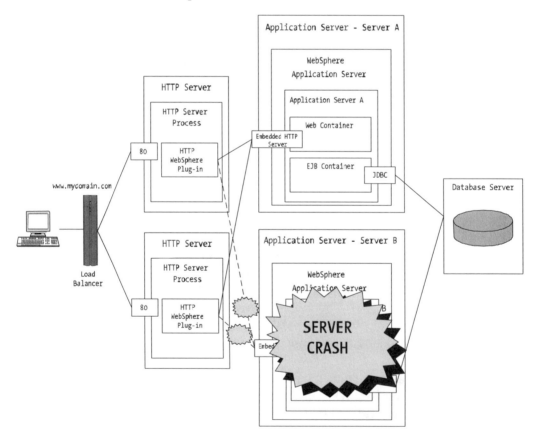

Figure 5-21. Single points of failure in a WebSphere environment

At the most simple level, if server B failed (e.g., via CPU panic or server freeze), the HTTP plug-in on both of the frontend Web servers would realize this, mark server B as dead, and push all requests through to server A. In this case, the single point of failure has been eliminated because you have a secondary server. Simple, right?

If you have the same environment as Figure 5-21, and if you're running a WebSphere version 4 cluster and the database repository on the database server became corrupted or crashed, the entire environment will fail. This highlights a single point of failure.

Split-Brain WebSphere Configuration

I mentioned earlier that you might consider splitting the environment into two separate WebSphere domains or clusters. This can introduce some extra overhead from an application development and possibly a network traffic point of view, but it does promote an ultra-high-availability environment.

Essentially, in this case, the only component that would need to be shared would be user sessions. That is achievable by still having the WebSphere servers split into separate domains and clusters, but if you need user sessions to be available from both sides of the environment, you would share the session repository database that you would create within the WebSphere main console for each WebSphere application server.

The other way to help provide this is to use sticky routing or server affinity for sessions. In this way, once a user logs onto a WebSphere application server, the user remains there until he or she logs off or until the server crashes and the request is forced over to the secondary server.

Depending on how you persist your sessions (i.e., manually, through an end-of-service update, or periodically), the session may be preserved or it may need to be re-created. If it's the latter, this typically suggests that something isn't right within your application (e.g., your application is unable to handle session failures) or the WebSphere environment isn't configured correctly.

All this depends also on how dependent your applications are on the session being up to date. Consider this situation: Your application developers may use the session to store things such as credit card information and payment details. A payment transaction is presented over several pages, and on each page more and more detail is built up about the payment transaction. If, let's say, server B fails midstream during the user clicking through to set up his or her transaction, one of the following three things will happen:

- The entire transaction will fail because your application isn't able to handle session failures of any type.

- WebSphere won't persist the last session update. This is configurable within WebSphere, so it may be caused by a misconfiguration, or if your site is high volume, your database server may not be keeping up with all the requests.

- The next page presented to the customer will be slightly delayed while the WLM process kicks in and the session details are obtained by server A.

Application Server Capacity Considerations

It's all well and good to have two or more load-balanced application servers operating within your WebSphere environment, but I'd consider your design flawed if your customers are impacted by poor performance if in the event of a server failure the remaining load-balanced infrastructure is unable to keep up with the load.

The rule I always follow is this: In a high-availability environment with two servers in a singular tier, no server should ever exceed 40 percent utilization. The reason for this is that if one of the servers in your specific tier crashes and the remaining load is all placed on the other server, that other server will theoretically need to—almost instantly—handle twice its load. You'll need to add in some additional overhead, especially for the failover period. Therefore, if you have two servers operating at 50 percent utilization and one fails, the remaining server will need to double its load, effectively taking it over 100 percent utilization. You'll soon end up with two dead servers!

As you add in additional servers, this becomes less of a concern. For example, if you have three servers, each server should not exceed 50 percent load. This is worked out by saying, if one in three servers failed, with all servers operating at 50 percent load, then the remaining two servers would theoretically need to handle an additional 25 percent load. This would take the operating load of each server to 75 percent plus overhead.

My rule of thumb is that, in a single server environment, no OLTP or online server should ever exceed an average 60 percent utilization. Go beyond this and there's a mismatch in your capacity model. Consider upgrading to faster CPUs or adding in additional CPUs (then again, it could be that your server is swapping madly due to insufficient raw memory, and you need to upgrade your memory). When you have more than one server, such as the previous three-server example, in a failover scenario in which you may have one server crash, the remaining servers should not exceed 80 percent load.

So, stick to a threshold of less than or equal to 60 percent load for maximum average utilization for a single server and less than or equal to 80 percent load for maximum average utilization for multiple servers during a failover scenario. The 80 percent rule is only valid during unusual operating periods, such as a failover.

CAUTION   The golden rule is that you should never run your system at 100 percent utilization. It amazes me how often I see sites that let their server operate at 100 percent utilization. There is a big difference between 100 percent effectiveness of your operational platform and 100 percent utilization of available resources. At 100 percent utilization, an operating system isn't doing what it should be doing, and instead it's working madly trying to handle an unworkable load with limited resources.

My guess is that during a failover situation, you'll want to focus on fixing the dead server, not trying to diagnose the load on the other remaining servers. You don't want to be at a command prompt (for Unix) or in your Services Manager (for Windows NT/2000/XP) and have to wait seconds for a response to issued commands and requests.

From a J2EE JVM perspective, remember that when a JVM conducts garbage collection and other housecleaning routines, most of the processing and thread work ceases for a second or so (depending on the size of the cleanup and the amount of memory consumed). During this time, your application will freeze until the garbage collection completes. Now consider what will happen if your JVM is attempting to contend with basic operating system threads—we all know which process will get priority, and your application will stand still for a long time during excessively high system utilization.

Database Considerations

I discuss this in a little more detail in the upcoming sections, but just briefly, designing your WebSphere topological architecture in this fashion is only going to be worthwhile if you're able to build in some redundancy to your database server tier.

Consider hot-standby databases or database clusters in either high-availability/active-standby or active-active configurations. Failover times between active-standby servers varies, but you'll need to ensure that the failover time doesn't exceed that of any HTTP session time-out, user browser time-out, or any other form of idle or I/O time-out value.

This concept also obviously applies to the application databases. Unless you use a sophisticated database caching system or you have low-update data tables all depersisted by CMP or BMP, chances are that your J2EE applications will be unable to operate without being able to retrieve data from a database.

You'll take a more detailed look at the WebSphere database architecture at the end of this chapter.

Advantages

This topology is a true high-availability WebSphere server environment. As you've seen, at least two Web servers, two application servers, and a database server are available, all of which provide high levels of redundancy.

This topology can be extended greatly to more than two Web servers and two WebSphere application servers. Once you've designed your base architecture, adding on three or more application servers is almost trivial. Minor changes to the frontend HTTP Web server plug-in files provide the ability to scale out horizontally to any number of backend servers. Here are some of the key advantages of this topology:

- **High availability in the WebSphere application tier**: The addition of a secondary WebSphere application server in the business tier helps to provide redundancy. If your topology is a thick Web environment (i.e., WebSphere operating as a Web/servlet container on the Web servers, and an EJB container operating on the main WebSphere application servers), your application environment will be highly available. Redundancy in all tiers is the Holy Grail of a J2EE application environment, and this topology comes very close.

- **The cost isn't necessarily high**: If you're running a smaller production environment and you're using Intel/x86 systems for your servers, you'll find that this topology, though highly available and scalable, is in fact not overly expensive. Depending on how high you spec your servers and the level of advanced features you include in your server specifications, you could get away with a full environment of this topology for under US$30,000. Of course, if you're more inclined to build your own x86 systems (i.e., clones), then you'll be able to roll out a system like this for possibly 50 percent less.

- **Ability to conduct in place upgrades for 90 percent of your application changes**: Because this topology incorporates redundancy and load balancing at both of the application logic tiers, it allows you to shut down one channel of the application environment at a time and upgrade the application on that specific channel, without impacting customers and production load. This only works, however, with two provisos: first, as long as your application logic isn't upgrading or altering the shared database application schema on the database, and second, so long as you've designed your application so that one channel can handle the entire load of the production load. As I've discussed, there's no use having a load-balanced application topology if, in the event that one channel or server goes down, the remaining infrastructure is unable to maintain the load and service level response times deemed required.

Disadvantages

Obviously, as you add in more hardware, costs are going to increase. Hopefully in the business case that you've put together, the benefits to your business and the costs associated with additional servers are outweighed by the benefits of higher availability.

The other disadvantage with this level of environment is that it starts to become more complex. You and your team will need to build up operational skills to ensure that people are aware of what to do during outage periods, to manage the system during upgrades so that there is no outage, and to ensure that everyone on your team is clearly aware of how everything hangs together. You don't want to spend a great deal of money on a high-availability WebSphere system and then find that it's coming down often because of "operator error."

Final Considerations

As with most network-based and distributed computing platforms, as you add in additional servicing components such as WebSphere applications servers, the complexity or interconnection of components increases constantly in direct proportion to the number of components. For this reason, carefully consider things such as interconnects and backup networks, and their impact on your topological architecture specific to your network topology.

It's all very well and good to have high-speed E1/T1 links and ATM-type connections for distributed systems, but if the distances involved are such that the latencies are high, no matter how many servers you have and how big they are, you'll encounter problems with so many transactions trying to go over high-latency pipes. Design your topology to be compartmentalized. Plan it as if you were designing many separate applications in different locations, and consider sending data over long distances only when or if required.

Multiple JVMs with Multiapplication Servers

As you've seen, the use of multiple JVMs within WebSphere application servers serving the same application provides a very healthy platform design of high availability. To recap, the use of multiple JVMs within WebSphere allows you to run more than one instance of your deployed J2EE application, whether it be a Web or EJB container deployment.

You'll recall that in a Web-based environment, the HTTP plug-in on the Web server tier is configured to route the user requests through to the backend Web container within the WebSphere application server, based on a predefined load-balancing setup (e.g., round-robin, session affinity, server affinity, etc.). This design allows for high levels of redundancy and performance, given that not just one virtual machine is doing all the work. Remember, though, that the use of multiple application JVMs will need to be considered along with multiple CPUs in order to gain a performance improvement.

NOTE I've also noted in this chapter and in earlier chapters that for small applications the need for multiple CPUs with multiple JVMs may not be required after you've conducted performance modeling. My rule of thumb is to always start out with the notion that for each JVM you have, you operate at least one CPU.

If you take this model for multiple JVMs a step further and apply it to the previous topological architecture that you looked at (multiple application servers), you have a recipe for a high-performing, high-availability, and high-scalability WebSphere platform. Consider Figure 5-22.

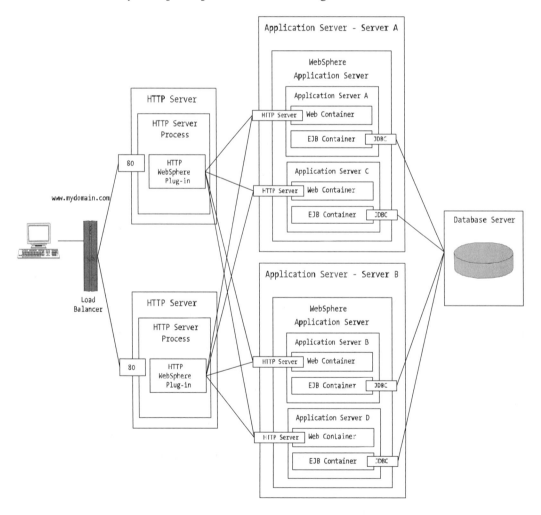

Figure 5-22. Multiple application servers with multiple application JVMs

Figure 5-22 illustrates a topology that uses a dual thin Web server model and two backend WebSphere application servers, each operating two J2EE application server clones (in a WebSphere version 4 environment) or application servers (in a WebSphere version 5 environment) in a server group or server cluster (WebSphere version 4 and 5, respectively) configuration. The two thin Web servers are both operating static Web servers with the HTTP WebSphere plug-in. The plug-in would be configured so that it traps the configured context for the backend applications (those in the clones and or application servers) and routes the request accordingly based on whatever the chosen load-balancing rule is. The request is routed to the most appropriate backend JVM process, based on the configuration settings within the plug-in file.

In this type of configuration, you have a platform that can withstand server outages (both Web server and WebSphere), application failures (e.g., crashed JVMs), failed network components, and many other WebSphere and operating system problems.

In the upcoming chapters, I discuss the benefits of using a high-availability database. The only component missing from this topology in order to guarantee greater than 99.9 percent availability is the redundancy in the database.

Non-Web-Based Application Considerations

While continuing to focus on the Web-based aspects of WebSphere topologies, I need to keep noting the benefits associated with these topologies that are associated with the backend components such as EJBs and so forth. I discuss this in more detail in the next chapter (Chapter 8), but I'll note here that this specific type of topological architecture provides a great deal of high availability and performance benefits for non-Web-based components such as EJBs.

As I've touched on several times, EJBs' "homes" are obtained through context lookups to the WebSphere JNDI tree. The actual act of the lookup and the internal management of this "tree" is slightly different between WebSphere versions 4 and 5, but for the purposes of this section assume that a JNDI lookup for a particular EJB is not different between versions.

The key point to note here is that if you go down the path of a split-brain architecture, in which the two WebSphere instances on the two channels are independent of one another, the ability to access multiple EJB homes on different servers isn't possible within the standard framework that WebSphere provides. For that reason, using mechanisms such as multiple JVMs per WebSphere instance provides the ability to "cluster" EJB and other data tier services.

If, on the other hand, your topological design doesn't use a split-brain approach, the resulting architecture with multiple JVMs means that you can cluster EJB and data tier services across multiple physical servers. This greatly increases your business logic availability, which most of the time is critical to the application operations.

One you should remember is that EJBs are considered "heavy." That is, they exhibit a fair amount of network traffic for all the *transaction* setup (e.g., location of the home interface, instantiation, passivation, etc.). The more recent EJB 2.0 J2EE 1.3 specification provides a more environment-conscious EJB framework, whereas previous versions of the EJB specification (e.g., version 1.1 in J2EE 1.2) were ghastly and caused headaches for network engineers on large J2EE-based application environments.

Although things have improved, there is still a degree of transaction overhead necessary for EJBs to work. My belief is that this is just a part of the use of EJBs and therefore shouldn't pose a problem. If you need distributed components within your application architecture, then by all means, use EJBs, but use them wisely. Consider using EJB facades to standard JavaBeans if possible, which will reduce overheads.

These days, the cost of 1Gb Ethernet over that of 100Mb Fast Ethernet is trivial. For the majority of WebSphere applications, the costs associated with 1 hour of downtime due to the nonuse of EJBs, will be greater than or equal to 5 times the cost of implementing gigabit-based switches.

Extensions to This Topology

You can do a number of things to help improve the redundancy of this specific topological architecture. Consider design aspects, such as ensuring that the WebSphere application servers are themselves highly available. That is, if budgets permit or your application is truly mission critical and just can't go down, look into the advanced hardware capabilities from IBM and Sun that provide hot-swappable, hot-upgradeable, and highly redundant server chassis.

As I discussed in the previous section, split-brain or split-WebSphere-universe configurations add another few notches to your net availability. Consider the model in Figure 5-23.

Figure 5-23 shows a topology similar to that of Figure 5-22, with the main difference being that the WebSphere repository database (for WebSphere version 4 administrative control) or the WebSphere cell (for WebSphere version 5 administrative control) is split. That is, there are two separate application environments coexisting and serving as one (as seen from the frontend Web server plug-in).

This configuration insulates the application from cascade JNDI tree failures and other forms of whole application data failures. This will only limit the impact of things such as DoS attacks—it won't completely insulate a system from one, but it does help insulate the application from cross-contamination from misconfigurations in a server group for WebSphere version 4 or a cell or a cluster within a WebSphere version 5 environment.

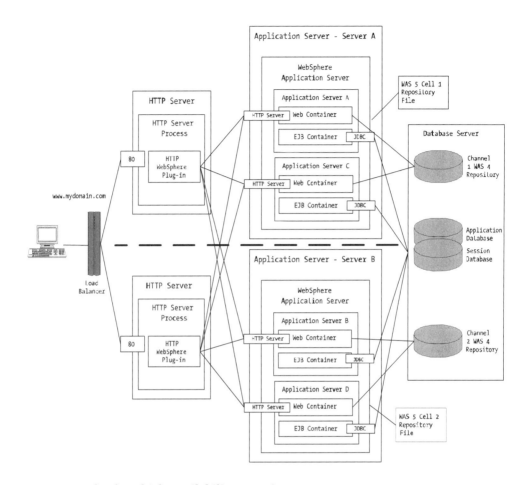

Figure 5-23. WebSphere high-availability extension

Database and Other External Interface Pooling

WebSphere provides a number of connection pooling managers for various resources. These resources include JavaMail components, ODBC, and JDBC-based database interfaces.

Using multiple JVMs has an added advantage in that each additional application JVM is bootstrapped against its own instance of a pool manager. For example, if you have an application that interfaces with a relational database, you'll use a JDBC resource created within WebSphere to access the database. By using connection managers within WebSphere, you get the advantage of a whole range of features such as connection pooling, connection management, and transaction monitoring.

When you go to configure a JDBC resource, you configure a number of parameters (I discuss this in detail in Chapter 11) for settings such as the minimum number of connections in the pool, the maximum number of connections in the pool, the idle time-out, and so forth.

NOTE   The reason pool managers are used for interfacing with systems such as databases is to help reduce the load and overhead associated with establishing new connections for every request. Pool managers also increase performance as the connection is already established, and therefore the time to conduct a transaction is not impacted by load or unavailable ports on your database.

Part of the tuning life cycle and your initial capacity modeling of your application environment should also include modeling how many connections your applications will need to the database. Remember, however, that at the end of the day, your database can accept a finite amount of connections and is limited by both CPU and memory in terms of how many simultaneous connections it can handle.

From time to time, however, failures in your application can occur when a database JDBC resource runs out of available connections in its pool. This causes a `StaleConnectionException` on your JDBC pool manager and, as such, no new connections can be established. If you happen to have only a single JVM application server running, this would cause the application to cease running until an available pooled connection becomes free.

The advantage of having multi-JVM applications is that each application JVM instance obtains its own instance of the JDBC pool manager. As such, if your JDBC resource in WebSphere was originally configured to support a maximum of 75 pooled connections, then each application instance would be provided a pool manager resource containing 75 pooled connections. This compartmentalization helps to insulate each JVM application server from resource exhaustion, which may be a result of buggy application code, excessively long transactions (caused by a badly performing database), or incorrectly modeled settings.

If one JVM exhausts all of its available pooled connections, it doesn't affect the operation of the other application instances.

NOTE   Be wary of making the maximum pooled connection setting too high. Although it's tempting to set it to something high, such as 200, you'll do more damage than good with this approach. In Chapter 11, I discuss these settings and how to tune them. Note also that if you set the maximum pooled connection setting too high, you may not have enough connections on the database itself to support all the connections.

Overall, model your database requirements carefully and plan to understand what sort of transaction characteristics your applications will have. It's a costly exercise to have to go back and resize your database or trudge through Java code to fix problems after your application has gone into production.

Advantages

The advantages of this architecture should be clear as day! Although there are additional costs associated with the operational aspects of the environment due to the increased complexity, the overall benefits far outweigh those costs.

Most important, this topological architecture provides a high-performing, highly available environment. The advantages are as follows:

- **High performance**: With the introduction of multiple JVMs on multiple servers, your applications' performance should be an order of magnitude higher than that of single server, single instance JVM topologies.

- **High availability**: Although the topology isn't dissimilar to the previous topology in the way of net redundancy, the introduction of the additional JVMs does further reinforce the robustness of the application environment. The chances of JVMs crashing are rare these days, yet it does still happen, and other performance-related complications can be just as damaging on a systems performance and availability, as is a JVM crash (e.g., excessive garbage collection).

- **In situ upgradeability**: The multiple JVMs provide a way to test and shake out application upgrades without affecting customer or user availability. Although the previous topology could also do this, the testing aspect of a multiple JVM environment wasn't possible and unforeseen complications with sessions and session failovers can cause a verification tests to be nulled.

Disadvantages

The disadvantages to the architecture simply relate to the added complexity of the topology. There should be no application architecture changes required as a result of this topology, but operations staff need to be well trained on the multiple JVM configurations and the methods by which components of an application environment such as this can be brought up and down.

There are additional costs associated with this type of architecture also. These are unlike the costs of the previous single-JVM topology because, as you have multiple JVMs, the rule of thumb states that for every application JVM operating, a dedicated CPU is required.

In a pinch, and for smaller applications, a two application-JVM based WebSphere platform could make do with each server operating just two CPUs. If your application environment is larger, you should consider one CPU for all core process functions (e.g., operating systems, core WebSphere internals, etc.) and a JVM per application.

Given this, the costs increase for CPU hardware, as do license fees for WebSphere (for the majority of cases). However, as I've noted on numerous occasions, if an application environment has been sized and modeled to need multiple JVMs, you could take a punt and say that the very driver behind needing multiple JVMs should be equally applicable to the qualification of having additional CPUs.

Final Considerations

For the majority of all WebSphere environments that I deal with personally, this is always my starting point. My experiences with WebSphere have typically involved large organizations with large customer or user bases; therefore, the needs of these higher availability requirements are fairly obvious.

The one area that you should consider for higher availability designs is the data tier. Essentially this is because, although it's all good to have umpteen levels of redundancy in your application, application servers, and network, as I discussed earlier, if the database goes down, so does the application if it is database dependent.

High-Availability Database Server Topologies

I've noted on several occasions over the past two chapters the importance of a database in a J2EE application. Of course, not all applications will talk to a database for either application- or WebSphere-orientated data, but it's common knowledge that databases are found in the majority of J2EE applications. If databases aren't use for data storage, they're used for persisting various objects and data such as session information or even operational auditing and logging information.

If your application just doesn't need a high-availability database, but it does need to be able to log some data, it may be most cost-effective to operate a stand-alone database environment and ensure that your application code can support and handle the various types of SQL exceptions that may be thrown from the WebSphere or your own custom pool manager. In this case, the application just keeps on operating and ignores the fact that the database is down. However, for those in the majority who need databases and whose applications are critically dependant on databases, in this section you're going to explore some of the topological considerations that are important to database tiers.

First, please note that this section doesn't attempt to explain how to configure or manage a database. Instead, I discuss various architectural considerations and best practices for databases from a high-availability point of view, as well as some of the options and features available in the leading databases available on the market.

When you talk about database services, at least from a relational database point of view, you can break them down into four primary groups of availability architecture:

- Stand-alone (single database server)

- Hot-standby

- Active-standby

- Active-active

As you can probably tell, the complexity of each of those database availability types increases (almost dramatically) as you go down the list. First, let's examine each of them at an architectural level.

Stand-Alone Databases

As its name implies, a stand-alone database server is simply a database operating by itself, on its own. This is the most simplistic view of a database installation and is the quasi-default for any database deployment. A fair majority of database installations operate within this model. It's a time-proven solution, given that the market leader databases in themselves are quite stable, and this solution will suit the purposes of approximately 80 to 90 percent of all installations.

The only issue with this configuration is that it's a single point of failure. As you've seen in previous sections, it's not much use buying several high-availability servers for your application server tiers and having a glaring single point of failure in your database tier.

My recommendation is simple: Use this topology if your application doesn't necessarily need a database to be actively running or if your application is not a mission-critical environment and the costs of something more robust aren't warranted (e.g., a single-channel topology).

Hot-Standby Databases

Again, the name is fairly self-explanatory, but the concept of a hot-standby database can come in several flavors. Essentially, the idea is that you have a two database servers: one is the master and the other is a standby. The configuration is set up as such, so that all changes to one database are synchronized with the second, hot-standby database.

This configuration is a sound solution given the robustness of databases in today's market. Quite often you'll see a database operate without problems for well over a year, with the only reason for downtime being to apply service packages and bug fixes.

The solution has a downside, however. In the event of a primary database server outage, the act of failing over to the hot-standby server is typically a manual one. More recent JDBC drivers from various vendors support connect-time failover and the like, which will connect to the primary database, and if the primary database fails, the JDBC pool manager will automatically attempt a failover connect to the standby. Different database vendors support this in various ways, so take a careful look at your vendor documentation. I discuss this in some detail in Chapter 7.

Overall, this type of configuration is sound and is suitable for production environments of any size. You'll need to consider the final synchronization, synchronization integrity, and failover times associated with a hot-standby server environment. That is, how often do you synchronize the hot-standby with the master? Consider what may happen to your application environment if the failover took place, yet the databases haven't synchronized within the last few minutes. Would this pose a problem for your application integrity and user experience? If so, then hot-standby servers may not be the best choice for your application environment.

Active-Standby Databases

Active-standby database solutions operate typically under some form of clusterware. *Clusterware* refers to software that manages a whole raft of system-level components such as disks, disk volumes, applications, and other various resources.

Clusters and clusterware is a complex field of software. As such, if you're considering going down this path, you'll need to ensure that your operational staff and engineers are fully trained in the ins and outs of your chosen clusterware.

From a database perspective, however, your database vendor will (or should) have specific cluster-aware versions or management agents of their database platform. In the active-standby configuration, you would typically have two (or more) database servers, each aware of the other and interfaced by private networking connections. The database platform itself would only ever operate on one node at any given time but would interface to a shared storage medium.

The clusterware keeps an eye on the life signs of the database and monitors it for problems and critical issues. If the clusterware layer recognizes a critical failure, it will shut down the suspect database instance on one server node and attempt to bring it up on the secondary node. Because the database files and medium is shared via a shared storage mechanism (or a replicated intelligent storage solution), the newly activated instance of the database should continue on from where the other database instance (the failed one) left off.

Unlike the hot-standby configuration, this model is considered a proper high-availability database architecture. The failover is mostly transparent and general failover times are in the order of 5 to 30 seconds, depending on the level of activity and possible need to shut down in-flight transactions, the load of the database instances, and the state of the overall cluster.

Figure 5-24 shows a typical database configuration when using a clustered active-standby configuration.

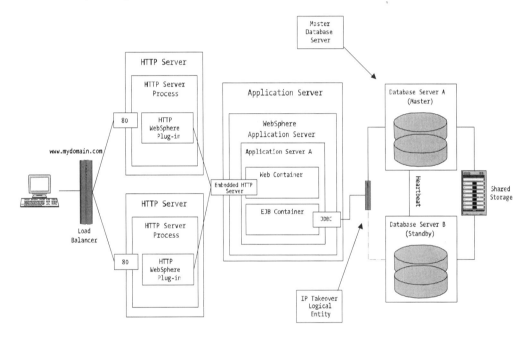

Figure 5-24. An active-standby database failover

In Figure 5-24, you can see how both database instances share a common data storage device, with only one database having access to it at any one time (the active node). You can also see that there are interconnection network interfaces that are used for internal communications between the two nodes, as well as private IP or proprietary networking communications.

JDBC interfaces to databases will, the majority of the time, understand the failover mechanism and through configuration, tuning, and possibly exception handling within your application code handle the failover and reconnect to the new database instance once it becomes available. However, you'll find that in-flight transactions are generally not failed over, and neither are things such as open cursors. Any outstanding queries will be terminated, and it will be up to your application code to be able to understand the specific exceptions being thrown back and retry the SQL transaction.

This type of configuration is generally considered to provide greater than 99.9 percent availability, and this configuration is one considered valid for a business-critical applications (but not necessarily mission-critical applications).

Active-Active Databases

What I consider the pinnacle of database server technology is the relatively new emergence of true active-active database environments. If you take into account the complexity of a database engine—transaction management, query management, data file handling, locking, I/O management, and myriad other areas of architecture under the hood of a database—you should be able to understand why active-active databases are rare.

Oracle has had a product available for a few years now known as Oracle Parallel Server (OPS), and more recently the company has released its Oracle9*i* Real Application Clusters (RAC) system. OPS is a parallel server, and although it appears to be active-active, it isn't fully active-active. Oracle9*i* RAC, on the other hand, is. Through a sophisticated architecture, Oracle9*i* RAC now allows systems architects to have more than one database server servicing database requests. What's very powerful about this is that the queries are load balanced against any one of many databases in the RAC cluster and, as such, if one of those nodes goes down, the outage is 99.9 percent transparent to the application. In-flight transactions, open cursors, and queries are all safeguarded, and transparent failover to another node is possible.

It probably goes without saying that Oracle9*i* RAC is a truly sophisticated piece of software. Many things are different in a RAC Oracle database than in a hot-standby or active-standby configuration. The same applies for the clusterware. Clusterware is still required for RAC to operate, as the clusterware manages all the life support systems for the RAC layer (e.g., disks, volumes, resource groups, adaptors, etc.).

IBM DB2 enterprise coupled with the Parallel Sysplex provides a similar capability to the Oracle9*i* RAC solution.

Figure 5-25 gives a very high-level view of how an active-active database configuration operates.

The database (in this example, assume it's Oracle9*i* RAC) is servicing requests via both database server A and database server B. Whether you're using thick or thin JDBC drivers will depend on just how transparent this database communication is.

If you're using thick JDBC drivers, you have very little visibility regarding which database instance (which node) you're communicating. For this reason, you would consider that you're communicating with a logical database SID (let's call it MYDB1). If the database instance of database server A fails, all connections, queries, and transactions can be transparently failed over to the other instance operating on database server B. To the application, there is no impact. This configuration is tunable and based on a number of available considerations. You may decide that you don't want failover to be so transparent, because full transparency requires more hardware (because of additional load and connections).

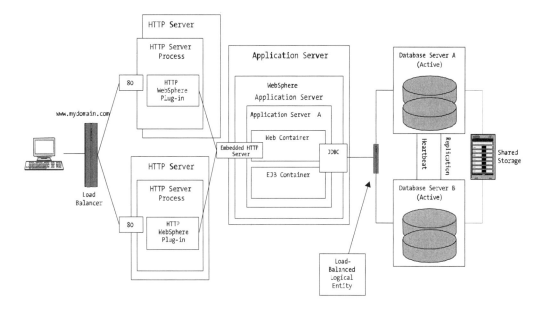

Figure 5-25. An active-active database configuration

If you're using thin JDBC drivers, you're more limited in terms of your ability to failover and load balance between nodes. However, the services still do exist, and they're almost just as transparent as in a thick connection. If you're using JDBC pool managers such the Pool Manager that comes within WebSphere (and you should!), the JDBC driver within WebSphere will throw a StaleConnectionException when the currently connected database becomes unavailable. Within a second or two, the connection is failed over to the other (or any available) remaining database instance within the RAC cluster.

As you can imagine, this configuration provides very high levels of redundancy and availability. If your WebSphere platform requires greater than 99.9 percent availability, then active-active database configurations are the way to go. If you're operating a mission-critical environment that just can't go down, then an active-active database architecture is almost mandatory.

NOTE   Imagine NASA launching the space shuttle and all of its controlling systems operating under WebSphere suffer a 30-45 freeze while the active-standby database system fails over! You'd want and expect that the database failover is completely transparent to the controlling systems.

Geographically Distributed Topologies

Because J2EE inherently is a distributed platform, it's possible to extend that concept to the *n*th degree. Many large Web-based applications geographically locate their systems (frontend and backend) to multiple locations in order to help distribute load, as well as provide an added level redundancy (some would say disaster recovery).

A common model is to locate servers on the West Coast and East Coast of the United States. Another model is to locate server into areas (i.e., cities, countries, and continents) in which there is a clear load distribution.

The method to which traffic is distributed is achievable via several ways. The most common method is to distribute load based on source IP. There are various lists and databases available around the Internet that provide a fairly good status of where IP ranges are allocated, such as country or company. Using this mechanism, it's possible to distribute the inbound request to the most appropriate server farm, typically the one located the closest to the requestor. Organizations such as eBay and Google make use of geographic load balancing, and although they're considered to be "mega sites," the concept is still very valid for any organization that deems it a requirement.

WebSphere itself doesn't provide the capability to do this type of traffic distribution. However, several of IBM's products can aid in the distribution of geographically load-balanced systems.

If you're looking to make use of a geographic load-balanced environment, there are some architectural considerations you need to be aware of for your environment to function properly. In the next sections you'll look at some of the aspects of WebSphere that would be affected by load balancing on such as scale and I'll discuss how and what approach should be taken in order to ensure both performance and reliability.

Multiple Web Server Topologies

Probably the most common of the all the geographically load-balanced components of a large system is the frontend Web servers. Figure 5-26 below shows a topology in which a farm of Web servers is located in London, another is located in New York, and another is located in Hong Kong.

As an example, say that this WebSphere-based application was an online ordering system. Customers would be logging in to order products. Assume that the request rate is relatively large—somewhere around 10,000 orders per hour. Also assume that behind each Web server farm is a WebSphere-based application server farm consisting of three WebSphere application servers and an Oracle9*i* RAC–based triple-node database cluster. So the entire farm consists of the following:

- Four Web servers per site, totaling twelve Web servers

- Three WebSphere application servers per site, totaling nine WebSphere servers

- Three Oracle9*i* RAC servers per site, totaling nine database servers

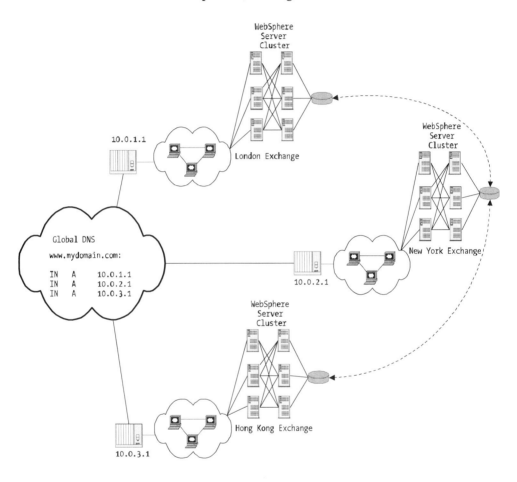

Figure 5-26. Geographically distributed Web servers

With this model, there are several key issues to consider from a design point of view. First, how do you synchronize sessions over such long distances? Although it may not be a common task that needs to be fulfilled, in the event of a site failure, the remaining sites would need to take on board users' sessions (the sessions would contain the users' shopping baskets, login details, personal profiles, and so forth). Second, how would you synchronize the databases? Over such distances, it would be difficult to replicate the databases in order for them to be able to keep in sync.

The answers are fairly simple. Before reading on, based on what you've learned in this chapter and possibly from some personal experience, consider what you would do.

Now let's look at some ways to get around these issues. There's little need to be able to ensure 100 percent continuity between all three sites for any one customer's session. However, in the event that a site fails, you would need to cater for session failover. Therefore, you would do two things. First, if you were using WebSphere version 5, you would set up weighting rules within your HTTP server plug-in file so that the local systems would have a high weighting and other sites would have a low weighting. Second, you would configure each site's WebSphere application servers into PrimaryServerCluster within the plug-in file and all other servers at other sites in a group called SecondaryServerCluster. Setting this directive means that only servers local to the specific Web server farm will be in use. Only when all local servers are down would the Web servers attempt to redirect requests to WebSphere servers at other sites. In WebSphere version 4, this capability doesn't exist. However, through the use of a product such as IBM Edge Server and or Network Dispatcher, you're able to obtain some of this functionality.

If the entire site was down, the geographic load-balancer device would cease sending requests to the downed site until it determined that servers were up. One way to extend this is to make use of a feature in most high-end load-balancers whereby they can periodically access specific URLs and look for positive results. A good way to take advantage of this for WebSphere version 4 would be to use the geographical load-balancer to ping a custom-built JSP or servlet. This JSP or servlet would only respond with an "OK" if the backend server was up and running. Easy solution.

Geographically Distributed Databases

Replication of database information is a hard one. Three possible scenarios exist:

- First, the data is deemed not to be needed to be replicated.

- Second, the data needs to be replicated, but it can be done in an asynchronous fashion.

- Third, the data needs to be replicated in almost real time.

You can do away with the first scenario. You can achieve the second in several ways. IBM DB2 and Oracle8*i* and 9*i* support database replication with myriad tunable and configurable options. You can use third-party solutions such as Veritas Volume Replicator (VVR) to perform the geographic synchronization. Another alternative that I've seen work, although it's a little clunky, is to have the backend WebSphere applications duplicate all database updates, deletes, and inserts. These duplicated SQL statements are performed in another series of threads so as to not slow down the main thread of the users session.

The third way to replicate the database in a real-time fashion would be to use something such as VVR or the features within Oracle9*i* RAC, which would allow asynchronous updates to be made to the remote database servers. High-speed data pipes would be needed to make this reality—whether it is back over the Internet via a VPN or via dedicated back-of-house data pipes to each site (or a mixture of both).

All of the options within the last two scenarios would provide session and data replication. The response time for the updates is a measure of cost for the bandwidth as well as any licensing that may be required by third-party products.

Geographically Distributed Application Servers

Consider the scenario of an application thread at one site wanting to access a method within an EJB at another site. One possible reason for this would be to send a packing request to the closest site, geographically speaking. A person who is in London may want to send a package to a friend who is located in Hong Kong. In this example, the order would be facilitated in London but either in or out of thread, a request would be made to another site to place the packing request.

This may be just a batch job, but due to the demand of the products being sold online, the company operating this WebSphere-based environment may deem it too time-sensitive. This being the case, with WebSphere version 5, dynamic data replication could be used to globally distribute packing center information or on both versions of WebSphere, a separate administration process could be set up on each WebSphere node that maintains an out-of-bounds location service daemon (LSD) or bootstrap list of where to access these highly distributed methods from.

Additional Application Server Topology Considerations

Another way to compartmentalize your application platform is to split your WebSphere application server into subtiers. I've discussed operating thick Web server models, in which the Web server operates both a static HTTP server and a Web container, processing and servicing all JSP, servlet, and other presentation based requests. You can extend this concept to support tiers such as utility or servlet/Web container tiers.

It's a computing industry dilemma: Do you make your environment more complex by compartmentalizing it but gaining performance, scalability, and availability improvements, or do you keep everything close and tightly bound? My personal preference is to keep same or similar service-based components together, but if there are differences in business logic, operational placement (e.g., utility services versus customer or user-facing services and operational characteristics such as batch versus online), then I recommend splitting them up. Figure 5-27 illustrates this concept.

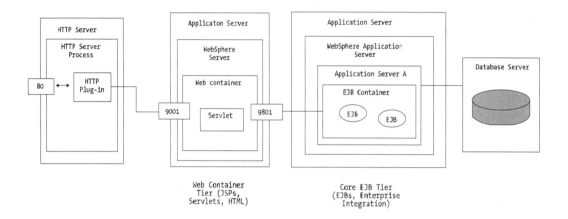

Figure 5-27. A compartmentalized server approach

As you can see from Figure 5-27, the concept of compartmentalization is obvious, with a presentation utility tier serving JSP and servlet requests, and a core application tier serving business logic requests.

Spitting up servers like this can actually make sizing them slightly easier. The theory behind this is that by planning to include all components (e.g., servlets, EJBs, JavaBeans, JSPs, etc.) into a single server, you need to be more precise about your impact calculations between all the components. Whereas, if you have your J2EE components split out to different tiers, your design calculations are easier due to the fact that you're modeling common yet compartmentalized components—presentation versus business logic.

You may ask about additional network latency decreasing the performance. Although it's true that there will be some additional latency on the servlet container to EJB container requests, you're only talking about below 3 millisecond latency, assuming the two tiers are next to each other (i.e., they're connected via a LAN, not a WAN). At the same time, the splitting of the components into different JVMs will typically result in an increase in network latency, canceled by the decrease in processing time.

As you can see, because different types of services have the potential to work against one another (i.e., they have different load and operational characteristics), it's sometimes good practice to compartmentalize. Consider that a batch type process that goes berserk won't affect user-facing performance.

Summary

In this chapter, you saw a diverse range of potential topological architectures that will work well with WebSphere. Although this list was by no means exhaustive, it should provide you with a solid starting point in understanding how modular WebSphere is.

Modularity and the ability to compartmentalize help the areas of redundancy and performance. The side effect of this is that you inherently obtain scalability from the distributed nature of the platform.

I presented many rules of thumb and common practices in this chapter, but nothing is as valuable as solid design and capacity modeling. The number of times I've seen applications designed around infrastructure that was previously decommissioned is astonishing. Identify and design what you need, and then model your topology.

CHAPTER 6

WebSphere Platform Performance, Tuning, and Optimization

IN THIS CHAPTER, YOU'LL get down and dirty with WebSphere performance. You'll look at the top issues associated with WebSphere performance and learn how to extract the most from your platform. You'll also look at WebSphere from an architectural viewpoint and see how to best deploy and optimize your applications (post-development) to ensure maximum operational performance.

The Need for Speed

I'm one of those people who get a warm-and-fuzzy feeling inside when I see high-performing, well-optimized, and well-tuned environments. It says to me that the people responsible for this environment take care and pride in what they do, and chances are that everything about the environment (not just the performance) is nicely designed and managed.

You could liken the art of optimizing a computer system to spending your weekends polishing and tuning a sports car. Specifically, the WebSphere performance methodology you explored during Chapters 1 and 2 is akin to polishing and tuning your sports car. It's this methodology that helps you ensure a constantly high-performing and well-tuned WebSphere application environment.

Things change over time within your environment. To use the sport car analogy, the oil level changes, the weather changes, your driving habits change, and so forth. All of these factors affect the level of optimization of the car itself. WebSphere is no different. Although this analogy somewhat oozes cliché, there's a close similarity between WebSphere and a sports car because they both need constant monitoring. You should be able to set up some scripts and tools (which I'll discuss in later chapters), and WebSphere should tell you when things are becoming a little rough around the edges.

What kind of things will change over time? How long is a piece of string?

In the world of Internet-based applications and e-commerce, trends and usage change constantly. Although there's some cyclic trend to most of the load characteristics from a microworld perspective, over time, 99 percent of applications will need to be tuned. Additional customers, additional system load, increased amounts of data requiring more and more Central Processing Unit (CPU), memory, disk storage, and so forth are all aspects of a system that need constant management and care.

The Methodology for Optimization

In Chapter 1, you saw a methodology that you can use to tune and manage the performance of your WebSphere environment. It's important that you follow a methodology even if it's not the one I suggested. Although there's some overhead in following a methodology, it does promote a controlled and managed approach to optimization. You need to know and track what settings change what factors of performance in what ways. Furthermore, you need to be able to start to plot the changes and the impact of those changes over time.

I tend to look at a tuning and optimization strategy as a large panel of switches and knobs. Each turn of a knob and each flick of a switch will cause a different result. Because of the vast number of combinations that are possible from the huge array of setting options available within WebSphere, it's imperative that the approach for tuning is controlled. Following the methodology each time makes sure that what you're tuning (and ultimately changing) doesn't affect other dependant components.

The methodology, known as the Mirrored Waterfall Performance Methodology (MWPM), works in such a way that it helps you know what dependant components may be affected by your tuning efforts. For example, you can't change your application's data persistence layer or database reliance without looking at what the effects will be on components such as the Java Database Connectivity (JDBC) pool manager. This is even more evident if you're using something such as Container Managed Persistence (CMP). With CMP, you rely on a well-tuned WebSphere platform, so any poor results in performance are the result of an incorrectly sized system or incorrectly tuned and optimized settings.

Finally, if you do change a setting in WebSphere and the results are favorable, it's prudent to check all downward components (down the model) even if the initial results seem promising. You may make the changes inadvertently during a quiet period, and although the results of your changes to, let's say, a JDBC connection pool manager are promising, you may have thrown the whole queuing model of your environment out of whack.

So, plan, test, plan, test...and then implement.

Know What You're Changing

I have a problem with managers who attempt to manage something they don't understand. This is similar to architects who attempt to architect something that they themselves can't or shouldn't develop. The same applies to systems managers and environment specialists such as those reading this book. Although you may be a developer or have been a developer in the past, don't fall into the trap of being a system manager/administrator and not being fully versed in Java code.

That's not to say that you need to be a developer guru, but you should be able to understand or at least read the Java code and understand the basic fundamentals of the Java 2 Enterprise Edition (J2EE) stack, what each piece means, and why each piece is used.

Most of this is well beyond the scope of this book, but I suggest you get your hands on a good J2EE/Java architecture book (`http://www.sun.com/j2ee`) or attend a course to understand more about Java and J2EE.

Performance Testing a Platform

Performance testing a WebSphere-based application is as much about testing as it is about actually conducting the testing. You'll need to consider several factors before commencing any platform testing. Typically, these factors include your expectations or your business sponsors' expectations on the level of performance and the response times of your application.

There's no magic rule, but the following sections provide some good starting points for determining your expectations of the testing results.

The Approach: Setting Your Expectations

What is it that you're trying to achieve? Your expectation of the testing is what drives the approach (to a point). The following are examples of expectations that are typical to online-based applications (the following sections discuss them in more detail):

- Response times

- Concurrent and registered users

- Transaction characteristics

- Transaction rates

- Application availability

At this stage, you should detail what your expectations are for your WebSphere platform; at least try to do this prior to setting up your profiling and benchmarking tests (see Chapter 15).

Response Times

The most obvious factor is response time for an application. Your application sponsors may infer that your response time for the user transactions must be completed within five seconds. That is, from click to result, the end-to-end response time must not exceed five seconds.

Initially, this is seems fine. However, what does *end-to-end* really mean? Does it mean that clients who are on the back of slow dial-up 56 kilobits per second (Kbps) modems are included in that test? Or, does it mean your tests should only encompass network activity—in other words, from the time the frontend Web server receives the transaction request until the time that the first byte of the request results are sent back to the user?

For example, Figure 6-1 shows a fairly standard WebSphere environment, with some additional components. These additional components refer to the network elements within your WebSphere environment, such as routers, switches, and firewall infrastructure.

You'll need to understand and determine whether your testing is conducted from a response time perspective (from the Web server to the database server) or whether it encompass the transfer time from the user all the way through back-end (for example, the database). This is important to determine your requirements. Are you spending too much time trying to improve the performance of something you can't control (for example, the Internet), or should you focus on the things within your control, such as the WebSphere application server and the database server?

My recommendation is stick with the things that are in your "circle of influence." However, you should be at least aware of the big picture. It's important to ensure that all elements are included or considered with your performance methodology. Get the right people with the right skills involved with your tuning efforts, especially in areas of your environment with which you may not be 100 percent comfortable.

In your optimization strategy, you may decide that you want to go down a level or two and state that different tiers must have certain response times. This would be typical for larger environments where there are a mix of asynchronous type transactions going off to legacy mainframe systems or batch and report runs that may take several hours to complete while providing online, interactive response times for real-time data.

Consider elements such as firewalls, load balancers, switches, and other infrastructure-related items that may not be in your direct control but that affect your WebSphere application's overall performance. There can be hundreds of components within an enterprise-class WebSphere environment that'll need to operate efficiently for a WebSphere application to perform well.

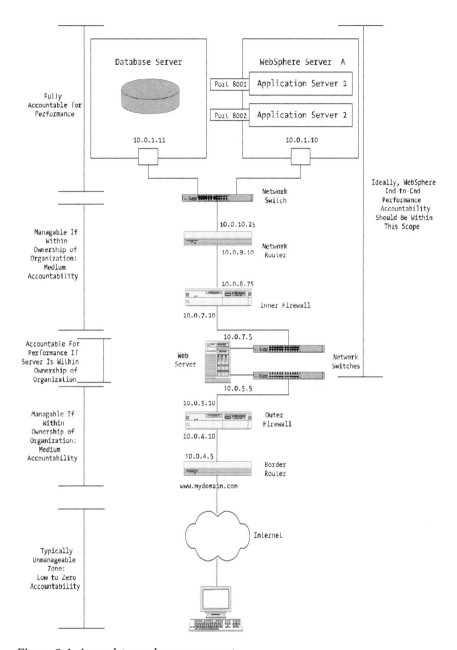

Figure 6-1. An end-to-end measurement

Many of these components, such as firewalls and switches, are beyond the scope of this book. However, this shouldn't discourage you from including them in your plan for overall platform optimization. You, as the application or system manager, need to set expectations for these aspects of your platform's performance.

In Figure 6-1, there are scope guides on the left side, which indicate the boundary of accountability in terms of managing response times. What the figure is attempting to show is the different areas within your WebSphere environment and a breakdown via the scope guides as to who or what is in "scope" for end-to-end response time accountability. Obviously, if in your organization you're only responsible for managing the immediate WebSphere environment systems, you may have little area of influence in the design and performance of the firewall. Then again, you may be working for a smaller organization where you're responsible for more than just the WebSphere environment and may in fact also have accountability for the firewall and network components!

Concurrent and Registered Users

How many users will be using your application environment (for example, how many registered users?), and how many will be concurrently using the application? There's a big difference between the two, and it's one I have to explain often.

Your application may have one million registered customers, but you may be providing a service that only sees them using the application once per year. Therefore, your concurrent user count is low. You can work out or at least surmise what your approximate concurrent user rate will be by understanding the operational hours and the frequency of usage.

For example, if your application is open 24×7 but is only used during normal business hours local to your time zone, you can infer that, based on ten-hour days for a week, you should expect approximately 45 concurrent users based on a ten-minute session time. This isn't much at all and could be easily handled by the most modest of WebSphere installations.

On the other hand, if you expect your registered user base of one million customers to use the application daily, then the figures look a lot different. The resulting load would be an approximate 165,000 concurrent users online at any one time, and the WebSphere environment to match would give any hardware enthusiast a level of adrenalin!

Sure, these are extreme cases, but they do happen; I've seen both ends and all points in the middle.

Transaction Characteristics

You can further spread that spectrum of user load in the previous section. What if those 165,000 concurrent users were using the WebSphere-based platform to simply obtain an account balance for their savings account? This would infer a fairly lightweight transaction characteristic.

The other end of the spectrum would be if all users, in both scenarios, were coming to perform online tax returns. This would be a heavyweight transaction characteristic per session, given the amount of underlying logic that would be needed. All the checks and balances, the storing, the validation, and the dynamic presentation based on user input are examples of the business logic that would be included in a system such as this.

In earlier chapters, I touched on the topic of transaction characteristics and how you'd model with them. As mentioned, a transaction characteristic has more of an impact on a system's response time and load than does the number of users using the application environment. The only paradox is that it takes users to drive the transaction characteristic effect, not the other way around.

However, if you were to graph different levels of concurrent users using a system against differing levels of transaction characteristics (for example, low, medium, and high), then this transaction characteristic effect would be far more profound. Another way to look at this is this: If you have a lightweight transaction–based system, had 20 users concurrently online, and tested 40, then 80, and then 160, then you'd probably see the utilization graph of the overall environment increase quite smoothly if your system was able to handle the increase in concurrent users to 160.

However, if you performed the same test, with the same amount and increasing number of concurrent users on a system that had heavyweight transactions, you'd quickly see the system start to be affected far more than that of the lightweight transaction–based system.

To explain this further, Figure 6-2 shows lightweight versus heavyweight transactions.

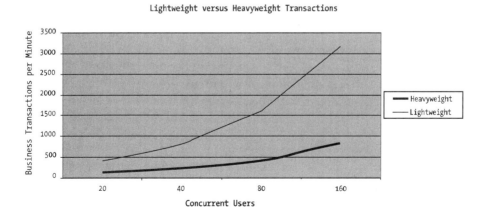

Figure 6-2. Lightweight versus heavyweight transaction characteristics

As you can see from Figure 6-2, the first test with the light line is the light-weight transaction test, and the other test, the heavyweight transaction, is in the darker color. The left axis is the total number of transactions at each level, and the horizontal axis is the number of users online.

As you can see, the lightweight transactions are increasing at a far faster rate than the heavyweight transactions. This seems somewhat obvious, but you need to understand that one of your expectations is that you're aware of and know what the transaction characteristic of your application environment is.

The reason for the transaction characteristic to be higher in a lightweight transaction environment is that heavyweight transactions are just that—they're heavy (in other words, they take up more system resources). The heavier the weight of the transaction, the more effort and processing power is required within the environment.

Transaction Rate

Not completely separate but definitely different from the transaction character-istic expectation is the transaction rate. Transaction rate is almost a reverse of what you just looked at. It's another way of understanding what the load of your application may look like.

Transaction rate plus transaction characteristic equals your transaction pro-file. That is, it determines how many transactions your users will be performing on the WebSphere platform when they use the system. If they're logged in for, let's say, ten minutes at a time, they may perform five clicks.

Those five clicks drive the number of transactions. Within your environ-ment, you need to understand how many function transactions (user clicks) take place per user and per session and, of those function transactions, what the underlying application transactions are that take place.

Remember that if your Web-based User Interface (UI) is made up of not only dynamic content—driven by JavaServer Pages (JSP) or Hypertext Markup Language (HTML)—but also many images such as JPEGs and GIFs, then this will increase the time to display your UI. For example, displaying one 200-kilobyte (KB) image displayed within a Web UI will be faster than displaying ten 25KB images. The more images and components you have within your UI, the more interactions occur between the user browser and the Web or application server.

The perceived response time for displaying a Web UI increases as the band-width between the user's browser and the Web or the WebSphere server decreases in capacity. This is important to remember when designing and tuning your presentation framework—consider a best fit rather than trying to tune for all specific bandwidth types.

Of course, if you're implementing a WebSphere application purely for Local Area Network (LAN) or even high-speed broadband users, then your job is easier. The effects of the multiple page "component composition latency" on broadband or LAN speed networks can be somewhat masked because of the high speed of the networking medium.

NOTE   Don't get mixed up between Java/J2EE transactions and the transactions I'm talking about in this chapter. They're two separate concepts and unfortunately are commonly misunderstood!

Consider this example of transaction rate: If your users or customers are using the application to look up movie times, this could be perceived as having a fairly low transaction rate. The user logs in (one functional transaction), chooses the date they'd like to see a film (one functional transaction), selects the cinema of choice (a one functional transaction), reads a synopsis (one functional transaction), and then logs out (one functional transaction). There are four functional transactions. Therefore, the functional transaction rate per customer is an average of four per session.

But what happens under the hood? Each of those functional transactions may have to perform complex database queries, validation against the user profiles to make sure they're able to view synopses of movies allowable for their age group (for example, the G, PG, PG-13, and R ratings), and so forth. Each of these transactions may average to be five application transactions per functional transaction. This would lead to an average of 20 application transactions per user session (in other words, four functional transactions multiplied by the number of application transactions, which equals 20).

The expectation you need to consider here is the number of transactions taking place, both as an average functional transaction and as an average application transaction. These figures will help you build up a performance profile of your application—one that will help you better model for future capacity.

You'll look at profiling and benchmarking in more detail during Chapter 15.

Application Availability

Although application availability is a service level in itself, it's not a performance measurement per se. It may be deemed a performance "yardstick" in the context of a contractual agreement or legal binding between a developer and a company, but, at the face of it, it's not directly in the path of system performance.

However, I've seen application availability cause an impact on the performance of an application in the case of buggy software or unstable hardware. Imagine for a minute that you have a complex application environment with several database nodes running in a High Availability (HA) cluster. For some reason, the clusterware is unstable and is causing the database nodes to failover to one another.

Given that an HA database may take up to a minute to failover to one of its constituent nodes, this will result in a decreased transaction rate potential, and therefore, overall performance will be lowered (with performance measured by the number of transactions per minute or per second).

The Outcome: Measuring Your Expectations

Once you've determined what your expectations are, you need to understand how you're going to test. I also touched on this point back in Chapter 1, and it's an age-old problem with performance modeling, monitoring, and analysis. Quite often, your testing will drive load onto your application. How are you going to test your WebSphere application so that you cause as little impact on it as possible? It's almost impossible to do any form of monitoring without impacting your customers or users.

As soon as you implement user experience monitors (in other words, test harnesses that access key function points of the WebSphere-based application and time the result speed), you impact your overall application environment. The impact may only be small, but it's still an impact, and your results are skewed (albeit, potentially only a small amount).

One method to avoid this is to build into your application response time monitors. This way, each transaction will be timed, and there will be no impact to your perceived application response time because the small overhead associated with the extra application timing code will be considered "business as usual" for your application.

Therefore, you need to define the method of monitoring and testing that both suits your specific application and that provides you with the best results in terms of being able to match them against your expectations.

The following are some words of wisdom:

Don't write timing markers into your code and output them to the WebSphere standard out (in other words, <WebSphere_HOME>/logs/ <application_name>.stdout.log) or standard error (in other words, <WebSphere_HOME>/logs/<application_name>.stderr.log) logs if you're trying to achieve a fine level of optimization. I've seen this being done a lot. Although it's probably safe to use this form of logging once for analysis or for specific debugging tasks (rather than for performance management), running these types of timer outputs can skew your results. An incorrect implementation of the custom-built timer class may be single-threaded in nature, and as such, the whole application has to wait for it to complete assigned time stamps to variables. Although this may not impact a small application with only a handful of customers or users online, if every user had to wait 300 milliseconds for a static thread to complete on a 500 concurrent user system, it'd slow the overall performance down considerably.

Be aware that different operating systems have different timing resolutions when using standard Java timing classes. This resolution variance can be as much as 15 milliseconds (ms) for Windows-based applications.

Do consider placing time stamps in logging entries within your database. This can incur a small amount of overhead, but far less than that of the previous item. In this case, you'd schedule weekly or nightly jobs to run through the database and run a report the various time stamp and thread ID combinations. For example:

```
SQL> select txn_entry_type from operational_log_t where txn_entry_type ⤸
' START' and 'STOP';
```

Although this puts load on the database during the report time, you can schedule the task to run during off-peak or nonoperational periods.

Another design consideration in using this approach is to cache the timing figures into some form of memory or cache storage area and periodically persist the information to the database. If you have 5,000 concurrent users with hundreds of page clicks per second, your database will be quickly consumed with timing data inserts rather than serving customer-facing application requests.

You may want to consider using the Performance Management Interface (PMI) timing hooks available within the WebSphere application server. These interfaces allow you to access various timing measurements and can avoid overheads associated with issues such as the one mentioned previously (database insertion overhead). You'll look at PMI in Chapter 13.

Do operate user experience monitors. That is, use any number of the product suites on the market that allow you to simulate a user using the various key functions of an application.

This does increase load by a factor indexed against the frequency of the test and what sort of functional tests are involved; however, given the test is testing live functionality, you should have an idea from your initial setting of expectations what the impact will be. Therefore, you could run the test and extrapolate backward, calculating for the discrepancy of the test user.

Don't run technical tests behind the scenes unless you really must. That is, don't run scripts that periodically hit the database or specific methods within the application from the command line or batch-driven processes that "probe" certain aspects of the application. If you do, you'll need to make sure you compensate for the load you're introducing. You'll need to be careful that you don't skew your results by not following through on a complete business transaction. For example, if you're trying to hit a method within an Enterprise JavaBean (EJB) Java Archive (JAR) that will time the response to query all movie sessions at a particular cinema, your transaction test may not factor in predecessor variables that might be applicable when the true transaction is executed by a real live user or customer. For example, what if your test is simply hitting a null field in order to obtain method invocation and execution time. However, although this may give a result of "x," the true value of "x" may be quite different when you obtain "x" through a live transaction (for example, session setup, presentation tier delays, and so on).

Do baseline your WebSphere-based application in a controlled and scientific manner. Baselining and profiling are your friends when it comes to performance optimization. They're the key performance (no pun intended) indicators that'll determine if the optimization approach you're performing is working. In Chapters 13 and 14 you'll look at the tooling and baselining of WebSphere and WebSphere-based J2EE applications.

Although this isn't an exhaustive list, the basic premise is that monitoring and testing application software impacts the net response curve for all users. Table 6-1 summarizes the various testing types.

Table 6-1. Monitoring and Probe Impact Matrix

Monitoring Type	Test Accuracy	Potential Impact to Performance	Overall Test Result Quality
Intrusive probes	Medium	High	Low
Method timings output to logs	Medium	Medium	Medium
Database reports based on transaction time markers	High	Low	Medium
User experience monitors	High	Medium	High

As you can see, the best result of testing is a true user or customer simulation test. It provides an overall test result that gives accurate performance indicators for the testing that you're trying to achieve. It doesn't, however, provide an ability to test each specific method of interface during the overall user session without more sophisticated software.

I'll discuss this in more detail in Chapter 14.

Tools for Testing

With all the discussion about what to test and how to test it, it's worth discussing what tools are good for testing your WebSphere environment.

Essentially, you can break down testing tools into three main groups:

- Profilers and benchmarkers

- Monitors and probes

- Stress and volume suites

The following sections explain each of these.

Profilers and Benchmarkers

This group of testing tools builds a baseline of your application's performance. Typically these are used before and after optimizing as part of your strategy.

For WebSphere, there are a number of free, open-source, and commercial profilers that help with this. Table 6-2 summarizes some of the tools that work well with WebSphere-based environments. Again, this list isn't exhaustive, but it includes tools I've found to work well within WebSphere-based environments. The table provides an overview of the various packages, and I'll discuss their use and implementation in more detail in Chapter 14.

Table 6-2. Recommended Testing Applications for WebSphere

Tool/Application	License Availability	Tool Type
Grinder	Open source	Profiling and load testing
WinRunner, Mercury Interactive	Commercial	Profiling and load testing
Jprobe, Quest Software	Commercial; demo availale	Profiling

Table 6-2. Recommended Testing Applications for WebSphere (Continued)

Tool/Application	License Availability	Tool Type
HPJMeter, Hewlett-Packard	Freely available download	Profiling
Custom-built packages using operating system tools	Included in your operating system	Profiling

I've provided links to these software packages in Chapter 14. All of these applications provide value on their own; however, WebSphere comes with a Resource Analyzer package that allows you to monitor the operational aspects of your applications.

Resource Analyzer includes features such as the number of active threads, the number of connections, the number of sessions, the number of EJB cache hits, and so on. All these tools will help to provide a picture for the operational status of your application, as well as give you a good understanding of the state of your application under certain loads (for example, during load testing or during normal operational production load).

Monitors and Probes

Monitors and probes are typically associated with operational alarming and the likes. For example, you may have a specific function that needs to be regularly tested (probed) to see that its response time doesn't exceed "y" number of seconds.

The monitors may also be a way to understand availability and uptime of your components. That is, how often does a Java Virtual Machine (JVM) crash or how often does a JVM garbage collect? The latter will definitely impact the overall performance of your application. If you're able to monitor and plot this, you may be able to identify a trend in your WebSphere-based applications, such as too little heap space.

You can find some of the most useful monitoring packages in the opensource arena. Furthermore, a range of commercial products allow you to feed information from WebSphere into them. You may also be at a site that has an enterprise systems management suite that you're able to hook into.

Table 6-3 describes some common tools that are useful as monitors and probes.

Table 6-3. Recommended Monitors and Probes for WebSphere

Tool/Application	License Availability	Tool Type
Multi Router Traffic Grapher (MRTG)	GNU/open source	Monitoring tool (Graphing)
RRDtool	GNU/open source	Monitoring tool (Graphing)
Lynx	GNU/open source	Command line Web browser with some nifty features
Curl	GNU/open source	Powerful command line tool for probing Internet services
Custom-built Java applications		Provide any form of analysis and monitor desired
Big Brother	Open source/commercial	Monitoring and alerting

I tend to use these packages a lot given that they're open source and readily available. Again, you'll look at their implementation in later chapters.

Stress and Volume

Stress and volume testing is a bit of a science. It's not as simple as running a `while true` loop and pounding away at an application for a designated time-frame. Many commercial offerings exist in this field, and all of these are sophisticated software application suites, capable of everything from simple stress and volume testing to ongoing capacity and resource management facilities.

It should be a golden rule that prior to any production system going live, formal stress and volume testing should be undertaken. When conducted properly and at the right stage during software development, stress and volume testing will help both the developers and architects identify if there are any hot spots or bottlenecks within the application and, more importantly, how the application operates under load and volume.

I'll briefly discuss what stress and volume testing is. *Stress testing* is a test to identify whether there are any issues with the application or platform when a level of computational or derived load is placed on the aforementioned components. This is different to *volume testing*, which tries to identify what the upper limits are in terms of resource utilization from a volume perspective.

For example, volume testing checks to see how many concurrent transactions a particular (or a whole) component will be able to handle. For example, you may want to volume test your database connections from your WebSphere environment to understand how many concurrent queries can be sustained before the performance and response times of those queries go beyond your expected results.

Stress testing is more of a peak load test. If you have two WebSphere application servers operating and one of them crashes, requiring the remaining application to server to take over the load, will the secondary server be able to handle the additional peak load, or the stress, of double the connections all within a short period?

Ninety-five percent of the time, you'll conduct stress and volume testing together. If your application is large and complex and has countless components, you'd want to test specific components and elements in specific ways.

Table 6-4 shows some of the stress and volume tools available.

Table 6-4. Available Stress and Volume Tools for WebSphere Applications

Tool/Application	License Availability	Tool Type
LoadRunner, Mercury Interactive	Commercial	Stress and volume testing
Microsoft Web Application Stress Tool	Free	Stress and volume testing
PerformaSure, Quest	Commercial	Stress and volume with application management
Curl/Perl/Lynx	GNU/open source	Combination of software to help custom build stress and volume testing suites
Custom-built packages		Custom built to your site's requirements

Stress and volume testing is a complex area of operational architectures and software delivery. It's a science within itself, and there are many books dedicated to the planning of stress and volume testing.

You'll learn how to best test WebSphere and WebSphere-based applications using stress and volume testing methodologies that'll focus on planning and understanding what you want to test and then map those expectations to a plan to achieve your desired testing outcomes.

Measuring the Effects of Tuning

Recording the results of testing is just as important as testing is. Most of the commercial packages have plotting and data presentation tools that allow you to make graphics and historic models of the testing. Some of the other software, such as those from the open-source industry or under the General Public License (GPL), needs to have its results interpreted by something. This is especially the case when you develop your own probes and tests, which simply output numerical data that, on its own, presents no information at all.

My preference for occasional graphing or plotting is to use a spreadsheet program such as Microsoft Excel. These types of spreadsheet applications provide an enormous amount of mathematical facilities for plotting and analyzing all kinds of data. With Microsoft Excel, you're able to plot and analyze almost any form of input data you can think of, and you can correlate any number of data types within a single graph.

If, however, you're keen to use automated tools that run from your Windows scheduler or a Unix Cronjob, applications such as MRTG and RRDtool provide great solutions. Both of these products are the creation of Tobias Oetiker, and both are high quality and fast. In the case of RRDtool, it's a very powerful graphical plotting application.

 NOTE   You'll look at MRTG and RRDtool in more detail in Chapter 13 and 14.

However, part of the process of performing optimizing and tuning on a WebSphere-based application environment is being to plot and determine the results. Further, if you're six months into an operational cycle within a WebSphere-based environment, you should have continued monitoring and probing occurring against your application environment. The reason for this is so you can build up both a historic reference and a model for growth. The historic reference is a safeguard to help ensure that you have a clear view, with historic perspective, of any trend for the component of your environment you're monitoring.

A classic usage for this type of monitoring is network utilization. Over time, theoretically, if your application is increasing in load and usage (usually driven by additional functionality, bug fixes, and so on), you'll have a situation where your network traffic will also be increasing.

Like most things in the computing world, networks of any size have limitations on their capacity, and, with the increase in load, there will be an increase in network utilization. Using a combination of a network interface monitor (which could be something as simple as a `netstat -i` command periodically outputting to a text file or an `snmpget` command on your network interface) and a graphing or plotting tool such as MRTG or RRDtool, you'll see an increase in usage over time.

Some additional scripts could output the results of the `netstat -i` command or `snmpget` command to a centralized alerting tool for operator notification.

A common test I implement to monitor WebSphere JDBC connection pool usage is an external Perl script that, using Perl DBI modules, periodically logs into various databases and understands how many and which users are logged in. With this, I know how many times a specific user is logged in and plot that against how many user logins there should be. I can correlate that with the WebSphere JDBC Resource settings—via either an XMLConfig dump or WebSphere Control Program (WSCP) output for WebSphere 4 or wsadmin output in version 5—to determine whether I'm close to the threshold.

Figure 6-3 shows an example of what the output of a database connection script would look like, once plotted.

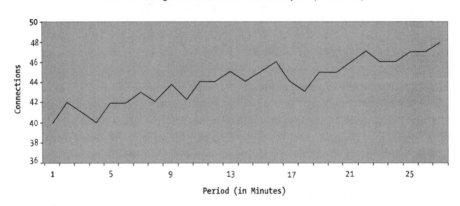

Figure 6-3. Database connection usage

Quite clearly, you can see the trend is increasing over time for the JDBC connection pool usage. If you had the JDBC connection pool maximum connections set to 50, the graph would clearly show that the JDBC provider is about to hit its upper limit and exhaust all available pooled connections (not a good thing).

NOTE You'll walk through creating these types of scripts later in Chapters 13 and 14.

In this example, the trend is suggesting some sort of code-related problem with not closing off connections to the database. As you can see in this figure, the number of connections is slowly increasing over time, somewhat analogous to a memory leak. Although this upward trend of increasing connections to the database may simply be that of an organic increase in connection load (in other words, as load increases toward peak periods), these sorts of trends invariably lead to code-related problems.

Either way, historic trend analysis is important when already operating a WebSphere application environment and while conducting an optimization strategy.

In the case of the optimization strategy, your time frame or historic data will be compressed and therefore will more likely result in profiling or baselining runs. For example, let's say you're attempting to tune a JVM for an application server operating on a WebSphere platform.

The initial settings for the JVM may be set at 768MB of the initial heap and 1024MB for the maximum heap size. If your application environment is under constant load, it's best to set the minimum and maximum JVM heap sizes to be the same. In my experience, it's better to set these values the same in a high-load environment, slightly higher than what you may actually require, to avoid garbage collection.

As discussed several times in the book so far, garbage collection is a heavy hitter for overall application performance degradation in Java/J2EE environments. Your garbage collection is believed to be occurring too frequently, so let's assume you've attempted to look at this problem by analyzing the output in the standard WebSphere application server log file (a standard out file).

 TIP   In order to obtain verbose garbage collection output from your JVM, you'll need to include the -verbosegc directive in your JVM startup parameters.

If you were to watch the log files for this example JVM, you may see some garbage collection occurring via the following types of output messages:

```
[GC 983301K->952837K(1021216K), 0.0207301 secs]
[GC 983301K->952837K(1021216K), 0.0222956 secs]
[GC 983301K->952837K(1021216K), 0.0234131 secs]
[GC 983301K->952837K(1021216K), 0.0246168 secs]
[GC 983301K->952837K(1021216K), 0.0230762 secs]
[GC 983301K->952837K(1021216K), 0.0222828 secs]
```

This output, from a Sun Solaris JVM, is indicating a line for every JVM garbage collection occurring for your specified application server.

 NOTE   Other platform JVM garbage collection output will vary slightly. Generally, they'll exhibit the same amount of basic information.

The first column after the [GC is the amount of heap space allocated *prior* to garbage collection. The second field is referring to the amount of memory allocated *after* garbage collection has taken place. The number in parentheses is the currently allocated heap, which in this case is 1,024 megabytes (MB), or 1 gigabyte (GB), of memory.

 TIP If your system has Grep, Sed, and Awk installed—such as all Unix servers—the following command will allow you to quickly obtain garbage collection information from your log files:
`grep / | awk '/^<GC/    {print ($12); }' | sed "1,\$s/>//".`

The last number in the previous code is the time taken for the cleanup to occur. As you can see in this example, the time taken is relatively small; however, what's not shown here is the time between collections.

This data by itself isn't too useful. You may get a feeling that there's excessive cleanup occurring if you see either large cleanup amounts (greater than 50 percent of the heap) or that the time taken to clean up is longer than one second.

However, if you're analyzing a performance problem and trying to log that there may be errors, you can't beat good historic reference data.

The previous numbers provide data but not information. If you were to graph that data, you'd see something like Figure 6-4.

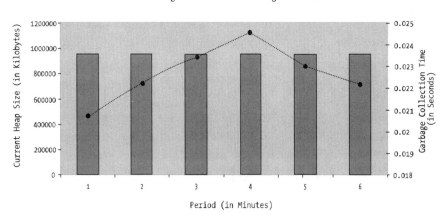

Figure 6-4. Example logging of garbage collection

As you can see, Figure 6-4 shows a fairly uninteresting story. There's neither a linear reference nor anything to correlate it with (for example, no load or utilization indices to indicate if the system was under load).

If, on the other hand, you had collected the garbage collection information over time, Figure 6-5 shows what you can infer from good data.

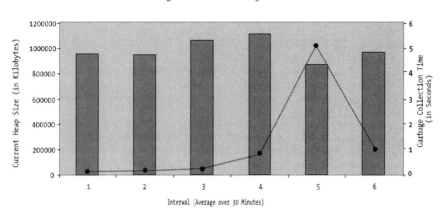

Figure 6-5. Historic garbage collection logging

As you can see, there are some pretty significant cleanup points in Figure 6-5 that indicate some heavy object utilization. This may not be necessarily a problem in itself; however, given that the heap is nearly 100 percent allocated for a good proportion of the time, it's definitely worth looking at the object utilization and even the amount of heap allocated to this JVM.

Optimization and Tuning Checklist

I'm a strong believer in checklists. It's amazing how many times things don't go according to plan because simple things don't get completed or done correctly. That's why a checklist is a good thing. Checklists should be living artifacts that get updated before and after each change or deployment or integration that you perform with WebSphere-based applications.

Given the myriad of configuration options and combinations of settings available within WebSphere, changes and deployments can be complex activities. This is especially evident when you're dealing with production systems and deployments are being carried out live—in situ—while not affecting existing traffic!

Although this chapter doesn't go into details about deployment checklists, it provides a performance tuning checklist. I use a checklist similar to the one presented in this chapter each time I deploy a new WebSphere system or new application. It allows you to check off pieces that need to be looked at, tuned, or optimized based on the application being deployed.

Many of these settings and recommendations are based on best practices, proven baselines, and battle-tested platforms. Most of the recommendations aren't WebSphere specific; however, they, when combined with a WebSphere-based application environment, do provide a fair degree of performance and optimization improvements.

Your mileage may vary depending on a range of factors regarding your hardware (for example, based on your bus, network controllers, disk and disk technologies, and memory types). However, for the most part, you'll find these recommendations invaluable for your WebSphere-based application environments.

Operating Systems

Given that WebSphere will always sit on top of an operating system of some sort, the operating system therefore forms a crucial part of the WebSphere environment. Further, WebSphere can operate on many different operating systems, including anything from a Pocket PC 2003 operating system on Personal Digital Assistant (PDA) to a zSeries IBM mainframe.

However, you'll focus on some of the more mainstream operating systems on which WebSphere is most commonly deployed:

- Windows NT, 2000, XP, and 2003

- Linux

- Solaris

- AIX

Many of these points are non-WebSphere specific in that you can apply them in any instance for distributed-type computing applications. However, there are a handful of them that are known and proven to work well with WebSphere.

Windows NT, 2000, XP, and 2003

Microsoft's server platform operating systems—Windows NT, Windows 2000, Windows XP, and Windows 2003 (supported as of WebSphere 5.02)—are popular for smaller- and medium-sized environments. Although the Windows server market has been coming under fire from Linux over the recent 12–24 months, the well-known Graphical User Interface (GUI)–based operating system can provide a good solid platform choice for use with WebSphere.

Most of the tuning aspects of the Windows server operating systems can be applied across all these server types. You'll look at these in the following sections and then see the specific Windows server tuning and optimization tips for WebSphere.

General Windows Server Operating System

Windows systems use a registry-based tool for centralized configuration information. Using the Registry Editor tool, you'll be able to change the settings within the registry as you see fit.

 CAUTION   The Windows registry is the centralized configuration area for your Windows server. As the administrator user, you can change any setting within the server. Be careful about what you change, however, and always make backups of the registry before you commit any changes.

Maximum TCP Port Number Assignment

This setting allows you to bind WebSphere to ports beyond the default range. This additional registry setting will help with larger WebSphere installations on a Windows-based server where you may have a need for many ports.

To make the changes, follow these steps:

1. Load your Registry Editor (in other words, regedit).

2. Go to the registry directive of \HKEY_LOCAL_MACHINES\SYSTEM\ CurrentControlSet\Services\TCPIP\Parameters.

3. Most likely, the registry entry of MaxUserPort won't be present. Create a new entry, and set the value to be greater than 32,768 but less than 65,536.

4. Restart the system.

This setting is essentially allowing WebSphere's dynamically allocated ports to go beyond the default number. Although this may not be a problem for all installations, Windows-based WebSphere implementations that are large and have many connections from a Web tier or many internal application servers may receive a performance boost from this.

The complication of this sitting not being high enough is that application instances or network connections attempting to bind to a higher port or a port that's not available will result in errors.

This setting can be tied to end user Web browsers and Hypertext Transfer Protocol (HTTP) keepalive configurations. The more your environment and ultimately your end users' browsers can take advantage of keepalives, the more efficient the use of system network points associated with this setting will be.

TCPTimedWait Delay

The TCPTimedWaitDelay value within Windows NT, 2000, and XP defines the time between when a connection has ceased (closed) and when the operating system can relinquish the connection handle to other resources (such as new connections).

The telltale sign of this setting not being correctly tuned for your WebSphere application environment is when running the `netstat` command and seeing many TIME_WAIT entries in the STATE column of a `netstat` command's output.

The TIME_WAIT state is a period between when the Transmission Control Protocol/Internet Protocol (TCP/IP) stack has closed a connection between a client and server but hasn't released the connection itself. This is somewhat analogous to file handlers—if you delete a file that's opened by an application, the file isn't really gone if the application has an open handle to it. The application needs to be cycled or forced to drop the handle in order for the file to be released.

You should change this setting if you've noticed that new connections between a client and the WebSphere server (for example, thick Java clients, lots of external socket connections, and so on) were sluggish and operating at a low throughput.

This doesn't always mean that the WebSphere application server or the operating system are operating or performing badly, and you may even find that the transactions, once established, operate at normal speed. It's a stress versus volume issue—poor volume capability versus good stress capability.

Essentially, you need to decrease the TIME_WAIT interval time from the default of 240 seconds (which is four minutes) to a lower amount.

To make changes to this setting, follow these steps:

1. Load your Registry Editor (for example, `regedit`).

2. Go to the registry directive of `\HKEY_LOCAL_MACHINES\SYSTEM\CurrentControlSet\Services\TCPIP\Parameters`.

3. Similar to MaxUserPort, most likely the registry entry of TCPTimedWaitDelay won't be present. Create a new entry, and set the value to be between 30 seconds and 60 seconds. The value needs to be entered in hexadecimal format with 30 seconds equaling 0x0000001e and 60 seconds equaling 0x0000003c.

4. Restart the system.

After you've restarted the system, monitor the output of `netstat` and track (using some form of graphing or plotting tool) the frequency of TIME_WAIT values. You should see the amount of TIME_WAIT instances drop. You should, however, see a noticeable increase in new connection transaction rate to your WebSphere server.

Linux

Linux is undoubtedly the fastest growing operating system on the market. Since its inception in the early 1990s, Linux's acceptance and installed user base has been increasing almost exponentially.

IBM embraced Linux several years ago and invested significant amounts of funding and resources in the emerging operating system. Now, with Linux ported to more hardware platforms than any other operating system, it's set for a long history within the Information Technology (IT) industry. It didn't take IBM long until it ported the WebSphere platform to Linux.

For what it's worth, I'm a Linux enthusiast, so I take great interest in that I can install WebSphere on an old desktop that may be laying around my house and, within an hour or so, have Linux installed and WebSphere applications up and running.

You'll now look at some of the settings available for a high-performing WebSphere environment running under Linux.

NOTE These tuning and optimization recommendations are correct for 2.2.*x* to 2.4.*x* Linux kernels. With the rapid pace of Linux kernel development, please check the errata and README instructions in your kernel source tree to determine whether these settings are still required in your potentially newer version of Linux. That said, these settings should apply to newer kernel versions without any adverse performance degradation.

Linux TCP/IP Stack Optimization: Turning Off Unnecessary Features

Most of the time, your WebSphere application will operate fairly network-intensive applications. Some WebSphere installations will notice or deem this setting as a priority more so than others, but for the most part it's prudent to look at optimizing your network settings as much as possible.

Two features of the Linux TCP/IP stack, although "cool" features, can impede performance in a WebSphere environment.

CAUTION The following settings will need to be updated in your startup scripts to preserve the new settings after a reboot.

TCP Selective Acknowledgment Disabling

The first setting to deactivate is the TCP Selective Acknowledgments setting. This feature alters the way in which select acknowledgment messages are handled for TCP communications, which is a feature that's not required for WebSphere optimization or functionality.

To deactivate the feature, run the following command as root on your Linux-based WebSphere application server:

```
[root@somenode: /home]  echo 0 >/proc/sys/net/ipv4tcp_sack
```

A powerful feature of the Linux kernel is that you can modify many of its settings and features dynamically by directing commands to the proc file system.

 NOTE   The proc file system on the Linux operating system (and to a degree, Unix in general) is a file system view of the active processes and elements in memory. Linux extends this further by loading kernel parameters into this memory space and allowing elements and options to be changed on the fly.

TCP Time Stamp Disabling

Another on-by-default feature of Linux is TCP time stamping. This TCP feature is primarily meant for, but not limited to, long-distance routes where Round Trip Time (RTT) and other similar algorithms are calculated to aid in proper routing and TCP protocol framing and transmissions.

Unless your Linux-based WebSphere application environment is doubling as a host-based router (!), then you can safely turn this feature off.

To deactivate the feature, run the following command as the root on your Linux-based WebSphere application server:

```
[root@somenode: /home]  echo 0 >/proc/sys/net/ipv4/tcp_timestamps
```

Problems with TCP Keepalive

The Linux kernel by default has a TCP keepalive value of two hours, which, on a busy WebSphere-based system, can cause problems with long-held TCP sockets.

This can be a feature or near requirement on certain systems, but for WebSphere-based applications (or any J2EE application server for that matter) that tend to exhibit smaller transactions (in other words, higher transaction rate, small transaction characteristic), there's little or no need to manage keepalives beyond a few minutes. Essentially, there are other ways in which this can be managed at the application level.

To deactivate the feature, follow these steps:

1. As root on your Linux-based WebSphere application server(s), you'll need to edit the kernel source and recompile it.

 NOTE Recompiling the kernel is beyond the scope of this book; however, a good Internet resource for kernel recompilation is http://www.kernel.org.

---

2. Using a text editor (for example, vi, emacs, joe, and so on), open the file to edit:

   ```
   $SOURCE_BASE/include/net/tcp.h
   ```

3. Search for this line:

   ```
   define TCP_KEEPALIVE_TIME (120*60*HZ)
   ```

4. Change the value to this:

   ```
   define TCP_KEEPALIVE_TIME (5*60*HZ)
   ```

5. Save the changes, and exit.

6. Recompile, deploy, and reboot your server(s).

Increasing Socket Buffer Memory Allocation

The socket buffer is the context that's used for all new TCP-based connections within WebSphere. Like most things, the more memory you can allocate to the buffers, the better performing your WebSphere-based applications should be.

There are two settings you need to change to optimize the socket buffer, or there are four to change if your application environment is making a lot of outbound connections to other systems.

As root on your Linux based WebSphere application server(s), run the following command:

```
[root@somenode: /home]  echo 262143 > /proc/sys/net/core/rmem_max
[root@somenode: /home]  echo 262143 > /proc/sys/net/core/rmem_default
```

This setting increases the buffer space enormously from the default values. Be aware that this buffer increase needs to be calculated during capacity modeling. You'll always want to make sure you have sufficient memory available and allocated to these types of buffer spaces.

If your WebSphere applications are performing a lot of outbound connections, issue the following commands as root on your Linux-based WebSphere application server:

```
[root@somenode: /home]  echo 262143 > /proc/sys/net/core/wmem_max
[root@somenode: /home]  echo 262143 > /proc/sys/net/core/wmem_default
```

Given that the settings are instantly active, you should be able to perform testing or profiling again.

Increasing the Amount of Open Files

This setting is of most use to those sites that have many Web presentation components. That is, for a UI with many components within it, such as GIF and JPG image files, this setting will affect the volume of traffic your WebSphere system can support.

An example symptom of what this fix will achieve is where you have a Web-based interface and images are missing within the output. Although this isn't always caused by an open file limit issue, chances are that it will be!

This setting really just allows your WebSphere-based applications to access and reference more files. If you have a larger site or a high-volume site, this setting is a must for your Linux server.

Depending on which versions of the kernel you have, there are two approaches to this setting.

Pre-Linux 2.2

Pre-Linux 2.2 such as 2.1 and even possibly 2.0 systems (which aren't always necessarily supported by WebSphere) provide the ability to change the number of open files on the system via configuring the proc file system.

To make the updates, run the following command as the root on your Linux-based WebSphere application server:

```
[root@somenode: /home]  echo 8192 > /proc/sys/kernel/file-max
```

This sets the value to be 8,192 open files available to your WebSphere server.

Keep in mind that the more files you have open, the more buffer space (memory) is used. A rough guide to how much you should set this to is 4,096 for every 64MB of memory.

You'll also need to increase the number of inode handlers that are possible. *Inodes* in Unix are a reference or handle to a file. Depending on how you configure your file system, your files on your disk may require several inodes. For this reason, I recommend setting your maximum inode value to four times that of your open files.

To change this setting, run the following command as root on your Linux-based WebSphere application server:

```
[root@somenode: /home]   echo 32768 > /proc/sys/kernel/inode-max
```

The value of 32,768 is four times that of the value 8,192 from the previous example.

Linux 2.2+

Changes to how the proc file system was structured were made between Linux kernel versions 2.0/2.1 and 2.2+. As such, the proc elements that need to be configured and changed are different.

The same setting recommendations and guidelines mentioned previously apply for Linux 2.2 and higher.

To change this setting on Linux 2.2 and higher, as root on your Linux-based WebSphere application server(s), run the following command:

```
[root@somenode: /home]   echo 8192 > /proc/sys/fs/file-max
[root@somenode: /home]   echo 32768 > /proc/sys/fs/inode-max
```

Linux and Lightweight Processes (LWPs)

A mechanism in several Unix variants, including Linux, exists called Lightweight Processes (LWPs). LWPs are units of operational runtime that exist between user-level threads and kernel-level threads and provide a different paradigm for running applications and processes from that of more the more traditional kernel and user-level threads and processes.

LWPs can be useful for providing a more granular method of system (memory predominately) management within a Linux server. However, be cautious of getting confused when seeing process tables. LWP-based threads don't operate in the same nature as a standard process under a user-level thread does.

One of the key reasons for using LWPs is that (if you recall back to earlier discussions on context switches within a server CPU) the LWP, because of its lightweight model, can be context switched faster on and off a CPU than a standard process. For this reason, it can be advantageous for performance to use LWP libraries within your Linux or Unix server.

LWPs can be of great assistance for smaller environments that may have only a single processor. Because the LWP libraries provide a quasi-multithreaded construct for applications to operate within, you can obtain increases in WebSphere application performance on single-CPU systems through the more efficient use of system resources.

Before you use LWPs, however, be sure you understand their implementation and system architectural implications.

Sun Solaris

Sun Solaris, once known as *SunOS*, is Sun Microsystems' long-time Unix-like operating system, developed and available for both the SPARC and x86 platforms. Over the past 12 months, Sun has been toying with the Linux operating system. Indications from reviews, reports, and insider information are that Sun sees Solaris as an enterprise operating system while supporting Linux (previously a Red Hat variant) on lower-end systems (such as the x86).

Like Linux and AIX, there's a plethora of best practices regarding tuning the Sun Solaris operating system for various applications.

For WebSphere-based applications, again like Linux and AIX, the tuning and optimization is based mostly around the networking side of the operating system. This is primarily because of the sometimes not so obvious fact that J2EE applications are inherently network-centric. EJBs by their nature are distributed (networkable) objects, and, as such, optimizing your networking layer for both hardware and software will always give you positive gains.

In the following sections, you'll first take a look at the networking tuning that I recommend for your WebSphere-based servers. The networking optimization recommendations for Solaris aren't too different from that of the other operating systems discussed in this book.

Proper TCP resource utilization is really the key to high WebSphere performance. You could have a massively scaled Symmetric Multiprocessor (SMP)–based server with tens or even hundreds of CPUs, but if your networking settings aren't correctly tuned, WebSphere and your J2EE applications won't function in the way you want.

On smaller systems, you can get away without these settings. That is, development nodes and quite small production environments wouldn't notice the difference, in most cases, if these up coming recommendations aren't applied. However, you'll notice a performance impact if they're not correctly set for higher-end environments. If you have the luxury of a solid stress and volume testing environment, try it out for yourself.

CAUTION The following settings that use the ndd command aren't permanent and are only active for the duration that the server is up and running. To preserve them after a reboot, look at including them in your startup scripts on boot.

TCP Keepalive Settings

Similar to the Linux operating system recommendation, the TCP keepalive setting can be helpful in some networking scenarios; however, for the atypical WebSphere-based implementation, especially a fair-sized one (medium to large), keeping TCP connections open for too long in the hope that a client will continue to make requests down the same keepalive connection will exhaust the available TCP sockets.

This will also result in a memory usage problem because each additional connection consumes memory as well as CPU cycles. You should aim, as a rule, to ensure that as many CPU cycles as possible can be provided to process application and user requests, rather than unnecessary house cleaning.

You'll now look at the current TCP keepalive setting to determine what your final setting should be. First, to find out what the current setting on your Solaris box is, issue the following command:

```
[root@labserver1: /home]  ndd -get /dev/tcp tcp_keepalive_interval
```

A number should come back; if you haven't already changed this number, it should be set to the default value of 720,000 (seconds), or 12 minutes.

Based on your application characteristics, you should be able to calculate what the maximum window should be. The interval window should be small enough to ensure that connections are being managed efficiently yet, at the same time, not so large that your environment or your TCP stack is running out of available connections.

For WebSphere on Solaris, my recommendation is to set this value between 2.5 and 5 minutes, with the values of 150,000 and 300,000.

To make changes to this setting, as root on your Solaris-based WebSphere application server, run the following command:

```
[root@labserver1: /home]  ndd -set /dev/tcp tcp_keepalive_interval 150000
```

The setting at this point is made, and no reboot is required.

TIP   After making changes such as this one, it's worthwhile to keep track of what difference the setting change makes to your environment. A simple method is to continuously count the number of established connections before and after the change over a period of time using a small script. You'll look at this in Chapter 14.

TCP TIME_WAIT interval

This setting is similar to the TIME_WAIT setting discussed for the Windows-based server configurations. Following along the same principles, the TCP TIME_WAIT interval setting relates to a situation where connection handles are maintained or, kept open, for too long a period once a connection has in fact ceased.

This affects a system because the server will start to become sluggish and poor performing while TCP connections remain open, unneeded.

If you're able to test this situation in a stress test environment, you'd find that the WebSphere application server starts to become bogged down with system-based processing tasks, and user space application tasks (when looking at vmstat, for example) will decrease rapidly while the operating system attempts to manage all the connections.

In extreme cases, you'll find that connections can be refused if the active list of connections is too high.

This setting is in fact set up by default in the WebSphere startup scripts; this only works if you run your WebSphere server as the root user (which you shouldn't). To view what the current setting is, run the following command:

```
[root@labserver1: /home]  ndd -get /dev/tcp tcp_time_wait_interval
```

The returning value, if it's set as default for Sun Solaris, will be 240,000 (milliseconds). This value is a little high; for large or high volume sites, you should look to decrease it.

Solaris lets you set the value as a minimal 30 seconds (30,000 milliseconds). Depending on your application usage and volume levels, this value should be set no longer than 90 seconds.

I recommend you start at 60 seconds and profile your environment from there. To make changes to this setting, as root on your Solaris-based WebSphere application server, run the following command:

```
[root@labserver1: /home]  ndd -set /dev/tcp tcp_time_wait_interval 60000
```

No reboots or restarts are required; the changes are instantly active.

FIN_WAIT_2 Problem with Solaris

With similar consequences to not correctly tuning the TCP_WAIT setting in Solaris, the FIN_WAIT_2_FLUSH_INTERVAL setting is also important.

The FIN_WAIT_2 state is a TCP state that occurs when the server running WebSphere attempts to close the connection with the client. The sequence of events for a connection closure is the server sending the client a FIN bit directive. The client is meant to respond with an ACK packet, indicating that it has received the connection termination request (in other words, the FIN packet). The client then sends a FIN packet directive to the server, which in turn sends back an ACK packet.

During the period that this is occurring, the server places the connection into a state of FIN_WAIT_2. Of course, if the network path between the server and client is overutilized or there's some performance degradation somewhere in the middle (or on either of the servers), this period of FIN_WAIT_2 can continue indefinitely.

Some operating systems such as Solaris allow you to cap this interval period.

The consequences of not having a correctly set timeout value is that the server will continue to try to maintain the handle on the nonterminated connection resource and could eventually run out of new connection handlers or cause the server to run out of memory in extreme cases. Remember, the operating system will consume system resources (CPU and memory) for each open connection. Given that these resources have finite capacity, you want to be sure that they're operating efficiently.

To view the current setting, run this command:

```
[root@labserver1: /home]  ndd -get /dev/tcp tcp_fin_wait_2_flush_interval
```

The default Solaris setting is 675,000 milliseconds, or approximately 11.5 minutes.

As you can appreciate, if a close connection request is attempting to take this long, there's surely a problem!

You can decrease the setting to anything you desire; for WebSphere-based environments, my recommendation is to consider starting at 30 seconds but using nothing longer than 90 seconds.

Note that the settings are set, like other Solaris settings, in milliseconds. To make changes to this setting, as root on your Solaris-based WebSphere application server, run the following command:

```
[root@labserver1: /home]  ndd -set /dev/tcp tcp_fin_wait_2_refresh_interval 60000
```

No reboots or restarts are required; the changes are instantly active.

Solaris TCP Time Stamp

Identical to the Linux TCP time stamp directive, disabling this feature can provide a slight improvement of network communications for high-volume WebSphere applications. Again, be sure that you really don't need this; in more than 95 percent of the cases, you won't.

To determine the current setting, run this command:

```
[root@labserver1: /home]  ndd -get /dev/tcp tcp_tstamp_always
```

If the result is 1, the setting or feature is enabled. To disable it, run this command:

```
[root@labserver1: /home]  ndd -set /dev/tcp tcp_tstamp_always 0
```

This will take effect immediately and won't require a reboot.

Solaris Maximum TCP Buffer Size

In the WebSphere networking environment, if your platform is operating on a LAN or other form of high-speed network as opposed to over a Wide Area Network (WAN), changing this setting can improve the performance for WebSphere components talking to other fast-connected systems.

Essentially this is the maximum TCP buffer size available for data transmission. The more you can buffer into memory, the faster networking performance typically is. This value is somewhat dynamic, and WebSphere uses libraries that can change this on the fly. However, this doesn't always occur in the manner you may want.

To determine the current setting, run this command:

```
[root@labserver1: /home]  ndd -get /dev/tcp tcp_max_buf
```

The result will be a number between 8,192 and 1,073,741,824. The easiest way to set this directive is to match the configuration against the link speed of your network. If you're operating a 100 megabits per second (Mbps) network infrastructure, use the value of 104,857,600. For example, use this command:

```
[root@labserver1: /home]  ndd -set /dev/tcp tcp_max_buf 104,857,600
```

This is a setting that can have a fairly adverse affect on performance, so be sure you've tested it adequately before running this in a production environment.

Solaris TCP Connection Hash Table Setting

The TCP connection hash table is useful for large sites that have thousands or tens of thousands of connections to their WebSphere application servers. The problem with large connection environments is that not only do you require plenty of processing and memory capacity for the application runtime, but you'll also need a degree of overhead to cater for Input/Output (I/O) and networking load.

The flip side of this is that if you allocate a huge TCP connection hash table size, you'll waste valuable memory resources and CPU cycles to maintain this hash.

You set this differently than those you've seen so far. The setting is one that changes in the system file. That is, it's in the /etc/system file, which is used by the kernel to set system-based properties at boot. As such, when you change this value, you'll need to reboot the machine for the changes to take effect.

You may already have this value set; you can qualify this by opening the /etc/system file and looking for an entry that looks like this:

```
set tcp:tcp_conn_hash_size=512
```

The value 512 is the size of the TCP connection hash table. The setting must be a number of the power of 2. Essentially, the default of 512 will support a few thousand connections. However, if your system is going to be many thousands of connections, increase the figure appropriately.

The setting range is between 512 and 1,073,741,824. As a rough guide, start at 512 for every 2,000 connections. For example, for 10,000 connections, set the value to 2,500.

You should test this setting along with the previously discussed settings prior to implementation.

Solaris Process Semaphores

Processes and threads within Solaris use *semaphores* for a range of per-process reasons. Semaphores play a big part in shared memory synchronization and under Solaris. Because of the memory-intensive nature of Java, the reason why semaphore parameters may be important to tune for your environment should be obvious!

Under a WebSphere-based environment where there can be many thousands of active threads operating (on large systems), the relationship between the JVM and operating system at the process level can quickly overwhelm a system with default values for these semaphore settings.

If you're running a system-based process analyzer in conjunction with a thread analyzer within your JVM space, you'll be able to see how these two correlate and where the hotspots appear under load. Therefore, to help ensure that semaphore locking isn't causing the operating system to lag, you should consider the following settings.

The first option you should consider sets the number of operations per semaphore `semop()` call. This setting allows the semaphores to not be serial in nature (in other words, to process more).

The default setting for Solaris is 10; I recommend you change this to 200 to 500 depending on your system's size. Start at 200, and if you believe that isn't sufficient, increase it by 50 each time. The upper limit is 2,147,482,637. To change this setting, look for the following line in the `/etc/system` file:

```
set semsys:seminfo_semopm
```

If it doesn't exist, add it and set to the value to be as follows:

```
set semsys:seminfo_semopm = 250
```

The second entry sets the number of maximum number of semaphore undo entries per system process. This setting is set to 10 by default and is far too low for a WebSphere environment. You can determine if the entry is set in to the `/etc/system` file by looking for the entry as follows:

```
set semsys:seminfo_semume
```

The option may or may not have a value set, and it may be commented out. You should set this to at least 512 for midsized systems or 1,024 for larger systems. Again, use the recommended values as a baseline and then test to determine if you need to alter the settings.

Chances are that the value of 1,024 will be sufficient for most medium and large systems. Therefore, to change this setting, open the `/etc/system` file and either change or add the line as follows:

```
set semsys:seminfo_semume = 1024
```

Save the file, and you'll then need to reboot for both settings to take effect.

AIX

AIX is IBM's long-time enterprise Unix operating system that, like Sun Solaris, was its pride enterprise Unix operating system for mid-range systems (in other words, nonmainframes). AIX appears to slowly be integrating closer and closer with Linux; however, for the meantime, AIX is its own entity.

For WebSphere-based systems, AIX has a number of optional parameters that you can set and tune to optimize the performance of a WebSphere-based application environment.

You may be noticing a pattern emerging between the operating systems discussed so far. Several common optimization strategies are common between all four platforms—those regarding the network configurations.

TCP Timewait Value

Operating the same as the TIME_WAIT settings for both Solaris and Windows, the AIX Timewait setting should be changed for WebSphere-based implementations. To recap why this is recommended, the Timewait interval helps to prevent excessive termination delays between the time when connection handles are maintained, or kept open, once a connection has in fact ceased.

With AIX, the same symptoms can occur—connection lists can become too large and trigger any number of system resource exhaustion problems.

To identify what your setting is at, you use the AIX no command (which stands for *network option*). To find out the current setting for the Timewait interval, use the following command:

```
[root@aixserver1: /home]  no -d tcp_timewait
```

This will return a result that will display a value. If the default value is set, the command will return 1. The value is read as 1 for every 15 seconds, whereby setting the value to 4 will increase the time wait interval to 60 seconds.

As a guide, you should use a value of 4, which equals 60 seconds, for your AIX WebSphere implementation. I suggest you shouldn't increase this value to longer than 90 seconds (a value of 6).

To set the value to 4, use the following command:

```
[root@aixserver1: /home]  no -d tcp_timewait=4
```

These settings take effect immediately with no reboot.

 CAUTION Changing these settings doesn't mean they're permanent. You'll need to include this command in your startup scripts during boot.

Delay Acknowledgment

This setting provides the ability to delay the acknowledgment, or ACK directive, in your TCP startup and shutdown communications. Altering the setting from the default allows the ACK directives to almost "piggyback" the next packet in the transmission sequence.

By changing this value, you can gain a performance improvement with Web clients communicating to your Web tier or your WebSphere application server by decreasing the amount of overhead associated with the transaction.

NOTE   To use this command, you must use it in conjunction with the delayackports directive. I'll discuss this in the next section.

There are four settings to this command:

0: No delays; normal operation

1: Delays the ACK for the WebSphere or HTTP server's SYN

2: Delays the ACK for the WebSphere or HTTP server's FIN

3: Delays both the ACKs for the SYN and FIN directives

I suggest you use the option of 3 for the delay acknowledgment setting because this appears to achieve the best results for a WebSphere-like environment.

To determine the current setting value, use the no command with the following attributes:

```
[root@aixserver1: /home]  no -d delayack
```

This will return the currently set value for the delay acknowledgment setting. To set the values, you must use the same no command, as follows:

```
[root@aixserver1: /home]  no -d delayack=3
```

Like I mentioned in the previous optimization recommendation, this setting isn't persistence and should be included in your system's startup scripts to ensure that it's fixed.

Delay Acknowledgment Ports

To use the delay acknowledgment directive in the previous section, you must configure the AIX networking stack to set the ports on which the delayack is valid.

The ports you choose to use with this setting on are both the Web ports to your Web containers, your HTTP server ports, and possibly the ports used by the EJB container in each of your WebSphere application servers. This ensures that you don't affect any other ports on the system, which may not benefit from changing a setting such as delay acknowledgment.

To determine what the currently configured ports are, use the no command to query the attribute of delayackports as follows:

```
[root@aixserver1: /home]  no -d delayackports
```

To set the ports you want to use, you can first clear the current settings by issuing the following command:

```
[root@aixserver1: /home]  no -d delayackports={ }
```

This wipes the existing ports from the configured list. To add ports, you must enter them between the curly brackets; you can specify up to 10, separated by columns. For example:

```
[root@aixserver1: /home]  no -d delayackports={8080,8111,443}
```

You've now set two ports on our WebSphere server, plus a third port that's a local HTTPS Web server.

 CAUTION   I don't recommend changing any other port settings other than those in WebSphere and the HTTP server. Altering other ports on the system may have an adverse effect on the operations of other processes and services (in other words, non-WebSphere processes).

AIX TCP Send and Receive Buffer

The TCP send and receive buffer attributes are simple to modify but are somewhat significant settings. They help provide more memory buffer for the TCP stack to help facilitate higher network throughputs.

The default settings are 16KB, or 16,384 bytes. In a WebSphere-based environment where network traffic is a key to overall performance, this default setting is too low. I recommend increasing this value to 64KB, or 65,536 bytes.

To check what the value is set to, use the no command to query the two send and receive buffers:

```
[root@aixserver1: /home]  no -d tcp_sendspace
[root@aixserver1: /home]  no -d tcp_recvspace
```

The sendspace attribute refers to the output buffer, and the recvspace attribute refers to the receive input buffer.

To change these settings, use the following commands:

```
[root@aixserver1: /home]  no -d tcp_sendspace=65536
[root@aixserver1: /home]  no -d tcp_recvspace=65535
```

Increasing the value may have a further positive result for your WebSphere-based application; however, the larger the buffers are, the more buffer scanning the operating system needs to perform. There will be a point where this setting can be set too high and ultimately cause performance issues. I suggest you use the 64KB value; if you're not satisfied with the performance, change the setting and profile.

TCP Maximum Listen Backlog

The TCP maximum listen backlog setting is a simple attribute change that provides the ability to increase the scope of the listen queue on waiting or pending TCP connections. For a WebSphere environment with a high transaction rate, this can help greatly because the transfer of information from the listen queue to the TCP input/output buffer space is transferred with little overhead to the TCP stack. With a smaller value, there's more connection processing overhead because of a higher connection establishment time (in other words, new connections can't commence until the listen backlog has sufficient resources).

To view the current setting, use the following no command and attribute query:

```
[root@aixserver1: /home]  no -d somaxconn
```

The AIX default is 1,024 bytes (or 1KB). This is a small but sufficient setting for smaller environments. As a rule of thumb, for every 500 concurrent users, increase this by 1,024 bytes; with lightweight connections (simply presentation), increase this by 2,048 for every 500 concurrent connections. Lightweight connections rather than Remote Method Invocation (RMI) connections tend to tear up and tear down more often, causing more overhead. Test this setting carefully with your application transaction characteristic.

As a guide, you could safely set this value to 10,240 (ten times the original value) without adversely impacting memory or CPU while still obtaining a good result in increased performance.

To make the changes to this setting, use the following no command and attribute:

```
[root@aixserver1: /home]  no -d somaxconn=10240
```

TCP Hash Table Size

Similar to the Solaris TCP hash table size, this AIX directive provides some improvement for TCP-based connections, which is the case under WebSphere. The TCP hash table maintains the hash list for TCP Protocol-Control Blocks (PCBs). PCBs, briefly, are the socket-abstracted entities used to maintain things such as TCP socket options, send and receive sequence numbers, windows, segment sizes, and other important information. As such, its ability to handle more information typically means that more information is being buffered or, indirectly, cached.

The default value or size of the TCP hash table in AIX is 24,499. This value is an integer value of the number of hash elements available within the hash table itself.

To confirm the size of the TCP Hash table on your AIX server, use the following command:

```
[root@aixserver1: /home]  no -d tcp_hashtab_size
```

I recommend increasing this to a value of more than 100,000; however, try to stay at a value less than 150,000. Therefore, to set the value, use the following command:

```
[root@aixserver1: /home]  no -d tcp_hashtab_size=120000
```

As always, save and test this value with a load-testing tool to ensure that it doesn't interfere with or disrupt other vital system components or processes.

System and Hardware Tuning

Hardware tuning is one of those ambiguous phrases that refer to a wide range of do's and don'ts, specific to the close relationship between the operating system and physical hardware. Given this, this section doesn't cover all aspects of this field of expertise but instead covers specific hardware performance tuning and optimization concepts that benefit WebSphere.

Chapter 5 covered some of these aspects of platform optimization at a theoretical level and showed the platform design options available to three popular WebSphere platform architectures (Sun SPARC, IBM PowerPC/Power4, and x86/x86-64/Itanium). In the following sections, you'll look at several important aspects of system-level tuning and optimization that can significantly improve the overall stability and performance of a WebSphere-based platform.

You'll look at the following items:

- Disk layout approaches

- Memory allocation and optimization

- Network configuration

- File system configuration and selection

Although these aspects may seem somewhat trivial, you'll be surprised at how many WebSphere installations don't always follow them and just how much a difference some of these settings can make.

Disk Layout Approaches

No doubt you've heard, read, or used file system layout structures such as the Oracle Filesystem Architecture (OFA) standard. WebSphere and the underlying operating system can benefit from a similar approach. Although the necessity for WebSphere-based environments to be structured in as methodical manner as the OFA standard isn't needed, there's still a great deal of value to be found in logically laying out your environment.

 NOTE This approach isn't endorsed by IBM as a recommended layout; however, it's one I've found to be useful for WebSphere servers.

You'll first look at what data types you have in a WebSphere environment. You can break down the data types as follows:

- Core operating system (for example, kernel and libraries)

- Logging and auditing information

- WebSphere itself (the binaries and libraries)

- WebSphere installed applications

- WebSphere application usage directories

- Third-party applications

- Administration home directories (for example, user directories)

If you look at those seven data types within a WebSphere server, you should notice that the breakdown is split not only on data types but also on usage patterns. For example, once a server has booted, typically the core operating system files aren't frequently accessed (as opposed to WebSphere application files such as JSPs and Java classes).

You'll also notice that there's an obvious split between WebSphere binaries and libraries (in other words, the core WebSphere package) and application data.

The reason for this is fairly simple: The recommended approach attempts to split up components to the point where if one file system filled up because of a core dump or a runaway process dumping lagging information and so forth, the chances for the WebSphere-based applications failing would be minimal—or, one chance in seven if using this approach.

J2EE and Java applications by nature can quickly dump logs and auditing information to a file system. It's not uncommon with large applications that may have verbose logging activated to dump several hundred megabytes every few minutes.

Other than the sheer amount of disk space to support this rate of file I/O, your WebSphere-based environment needs to be able to identify the vast amount of I/O and then somehow control and manage the rotation of that data.

What happens, however, if your application logs consume too much disk space in too short amount of time, causing a file system to fill up—one that's shared with applications, WebSphere, and logging information? If WebSphere attempts to passivate EJBs or compile Java code and the file system is full, your application will cease functioning correctly. Further, your customers will start to see an impact on the application's performance.

You need to split log files from application temporary storage, away from file systems that may create things such as file-based semaphores and the like so that you have an almost uninterruptible operating environment or one that's close to it.

Unix File Systems

My recommended approach for a WebSphere environment is to lay out a system using the following structure:

Root and swap on a separate physical spindle (disk) to all other file systems and mirror them.

Although slightly dependant on your Unix variant, the root file system should consist of /, /etc, /kernel, /bin, and /sbin.

Possibly on the same disk, create another mount point for the following data types:

- Application data mounted as /usr

- Another mount point for optional or third-party applications under /opt

- Another mount point for /var

- Another mount point for /tmp

The WebSphere package should sit under something such as /opt, which is separated from the rest of the system data.

The WebSphere logs directory should reside also on its own mount point or file system. Given that this directory can easily become massive with auditing logs and application dumps, it's important for operational support as well as for system continuity to ensure that the logging information is maintained for as long as viably possible. From a performance perspective, if your application is producing a lot of logging data, it may be prudent to log this information to another set of disks. As you know from Chapter 5, you only have a finite amount of I/O available per physical disk. You need to be consistent of this, especially when considering high write-based data requirements such as the activation of debugging and tracing within WebSphere.

Separate onto another file system all user directories. This should be restricted to operational support people (those in your team and who you control or manage). Consider using quotas to help ensure that even people within your team don't go filling up the /home or /export/home directories, causing grief for all other system support people.

If disk space and budgets prevail, consider splitting up the WebSphere installedApps directory. In the previous examples, this would be located in somewhere such as /opt/WebSphere/AppServer/installedApps. This directory houses all your deployed applications. Given that a lot of compilation can occur here, it's wise to try to split this out to another file system for continuity.

I'll summarize these points with a real-world example. Let's suppose you're operating WebSphere on a Linux platform. In this environment, you have several Linux-based WebSphere application servers that operate in a highly horizontally scaled environment.

An example file system layout should provide an extensible and robust layout of file systems. Each file system is extended to a point where it's succinctly separate from the rest of the system, greatly minimizing impact to your operational platform.

Windows-Based File Systems

Windows-based file system layouts are somewhat more simplistic but do follow the same methodology to that of the Unix file systems. The key is to ensure compartmentalization of differing data types. In a Windows world, there are two ways of achieving this breakdown. The first is via the standard C, D, and E drive mapping nomenclature, and the second is the method of using Server Message Block (SMB)–based file systems via the \\machine\mount convention.

The latter method isn't recommended for high I/O requirements such as logging and virtual memory; however, for storing shared application binaries between multiple clustered WebSphere servers, SMB provides a sound solution, both performance-wise and cost effectively.

The basic premise with Windows-based file systems is to ensure that, where possible, each component of the WebSphere environment is compartmentalized.

Although Windows enthusiasts may disagree with me, Windows standard file systems don't yet provide the level of functionality and adaptability as is provided with the standard Unix-like file systems. My recommendation is therefore to extend, while keeping your sanity, the Unix-type layout to be separate drive names. Let's consider that point for a moment.

You should look to ensure that Windows itself, the core operating system, and its virtual memory counterpart are located on a disk that's separate to the application and logging disks.

At worst, you should have four drives—all mirrored—and one pair containing the root and swap (virtual memory) services and another pair supporting all the application data such as logs and installed applications directory (installedApps).

If you're fortunate to have a RAID array on your Windows-based WebSphere application servers, look to strip these two components as much as you can. Don't be afraid to have a dozen or so drive letters if it's going to help you compartmentalize your operations. Remember, what would you rather have—a system that falls over because it's out of disk space or a system that has a few more drive letters?

Network Configuration

As I've discussed earlier in this chapter, memory within WebSphere and J2EE applications is a critical part of the overall performance. You've seen how to tune the configuration of networking within the various operating systems; however, you'll now look at some ways to gain more performance from networking within a WebSphere environment at a physical level.

In Chapter 5, I talked about good network architecture. Like most things, fast, redundant connections are always the best way to go.

If your WebSphere environment is an exceptionally high-loading environment that makes a mockery of a 100Mbps network infrastructure, you may be considering not only upgrading to Gigabit Ethernet but some form of multipathing infrastructure.

All Unix-based operating systems support some form of multipathing technology that allows you to effectively load balance—or, multiplex multiple network links together—to gain orders of magnitude increases in your overall networking performance. The beauty of this approach is that you can gain massive amounts of bandwidth for usually only the cost of additional network interface cards and cabling.

For example, Solaris supports a feature called IP Multipathing (IPMP). This essentially uses multiple network interfaces of whatever speed you desire and binds them together to form a single logical interface. This feature is only supported currently on Solaris and Solaris-based servers, but you'll be able to bind two interfaces together with little trouble and gain an 80–90 percent improvement of the original speed.

For example, binding two 100Mbps interfaces together will provide you with approximately 180Mbps of theoretical bandwidth. That's a fair increase in performance for some extra cabling and another fast Ethernet port! You can tie several of these links together that, theoretically, would allow you to support multigigabit Ethernet networks between hosts.

One thing to note about this technology is that, unlike jumping from 10Mbps to 100Mbps to 1000Mbps where you get a decrease in latency as you step up each level of technology, this doesn't apply the same way as bonding multiple network links together with IPMP.

Both Linux and AIX have similar features that allow you to do the same.

Intelligent Routing

Another feature I've seen work quite well is that of intelligent routing via multiple interfaces. Through the use of somewhat small Time to Live (TTL) values in routing tables, you can set up routing between redundant/multiple switches and redundant/multiple network interfaces so that if a particular network interface appears overloaded, then the operating system will attempt to send the request via redundant paths.

You can also achieve this via a combination of Work Load Management (WLM) with EJBs within WebSphere. I'll discuss this in more detail in Chapter 8 when you'll look at WLM.

If you're looking at operating well-distributed WebSphere components, you can also look at smart routing protocols such as Border Gateway Protocol (BGP) and Open Shortest Path First (OSPF). These protocols, among others, provide sophisticated routing capabilities. These capabilities include intelligent, self-healing routing capabilities, which pretty much do what the previous example suggested by default.

SSL Considerations

Within the WebSphere HTTP Transport configuration, it's possible to configure WebSphere so that it'll communicate with clients or the HTTP plug-in on a Web Server via Secure Sockets Layer (SSL). This may be a necessity for your application environment if communications between various tiers need to be secure.

You need to be cognizant that there's a performance penalty you'll be imposed with on the WebSphere application server. The degree at which this impacts overall application response time and general transaction performance is driven by two factors: first, the type of SSL cipher you want to use and, second, how powerful your application server is (how many CPUs you have, what type they are, and how fast they are).

The following sections discuss a few options that may help you increase your application environment's performance if you're using SSL-based HTTP communications.

Increase Number of Requests per Connections

One of the big hitters for SSL performance difficulties is the initial SSL handshaking for an SSL-based connection. Once the connection in an SSL session has been established, generally speaking, the performance is fine. Depending on your cipher level and type, as well as the specification of your system's CPU(s), you should only notice a small decrease in overall transaction response time with SSL transactions, once established.

On loaded systems or systems where the CPUs aren't as suited for encryption/de-encryption, the bottleneck is in the handshake.

NOTE x86-based CPUs tend to outperform their more expensive Reduced Instruction Set Computer (RISC)–based CPUs such as the Sun SPARC and IBM PowerPC-based processors. There's nothing wrong with having SSL offloaders or Web servers operating on an x86-based platform with the rest of the application environment working from RISC-based CPUs.

Therefore, the goal is to try and push as many requests down an existing connection.

In WebSphere, you're able to set up HTTP keepalives within the HTTP `Transport` settings. This setting allows you tune the number of requests coming in from the HTTP plug-in on the Web servers so that they (the requests) are contained within the scope of a single connection, up until the point where the maximum requests per connection has been reached.

At that point, WebSphere will drop the connection, and the HTTP server and plug-in will re-establish another one. This helps prevent denial of service attacks; however, it also helps to decrease the setup time for each transaction (the handshaking).

The key with this range of settings is to increase the requests per connection to a reasonable limit. By default, this setting is set to 100 requests per keepalive connection; however, if you're using SSL, look to increase this to 250 and test.

CAUTION Be aware that by changing this setting you're affectively changing the queuing model of your WebSphere environment. I'll discuss WebSphere queuing later in this chapter.

SSL Crypto Interface Adapters

Another option for increasing SSL-based performance is to consider SSL crypto interface cards. These adaptors plug into your server and, via system-level device drivers and plug-in agents to supported applications, allow the SSL encryption and de-encryption to be offloaded to special hardware-based crypto processors. This reduces the impact to the core CPUs and increases overall performance.

Be aware that the crypto card drivers will need to be able to support WebSphere if you're looking to terminate the SSL connections at the WebSphere server or your chosen HTTP(s) server if you're looking to operate them on your HTTP servers.

SSL Ciphers

As you're no doubt aware, there are many SSL ciphers available: DES, RSA, 3DES, MDx, and so on are just a few cipher implementations available.

Different ciphers are processed in different ways, and these different approaches to encryption can affect the performance of your application. Many ciphers also allow for different key lengths to be configured. Unless you're operating a military or high-security WebSphere implementation, there may not be a need for long key lengths.

WebSphere Queues: A Queuing Theory

WebSphere queues are an important part of WebSphere performance and capacity management. WebSphere operates, or can be tuned to operate, with what's known as a *queuing network*. What this essentially means is that each tier within your application environment is configured to handle a certain amount of requests or transactions or connections at any one time.

WebSphere supports the two key queuing models: open and closed. By default, the closed queuing model is implemented. In this configuration, all the queues within the environment are tightly controlled and more importantly, capped. By setting up your different tiers to have a finite number of connections in a closed queue model, you control and curve runaway processes (such as denial of service attacks) and manage your resources more intelligently.

The open queue model that exists is basically a free-for-all. In this model, the different tiers aren't constrained. My recommendation is not to use an open model. By using the closed queuing model, you can manage your environment with more accuracy and better plan and manage your capacity model.

In Chapter 1, I discussed the carrot and the turnip models whereby your WebSphere environment is meant to accept many connections on the frontend (the Web server) and fewer proportionate connections on the backend. Figure 6-6 shows the carrot model discussed in Chapter 1.

As mentioned, your environment needs to appear like a carrot in that the thick end (of the carrot) relates to the size of the pipe or the queue at the Web server tier, with the smaller, pointier end relating to the proportional queue size at the data tier.

Between the Web tier and the data tier are several other components, all of which you're now familiar with. Other than the Web and database servers, these components are also essential to making up the overall queue:

- Web server

- Web container

- EJB container

- Object Request Broker (ORB)

- Data sources

- Database

- If implemented, legacy systems integration components (resource connection manager)

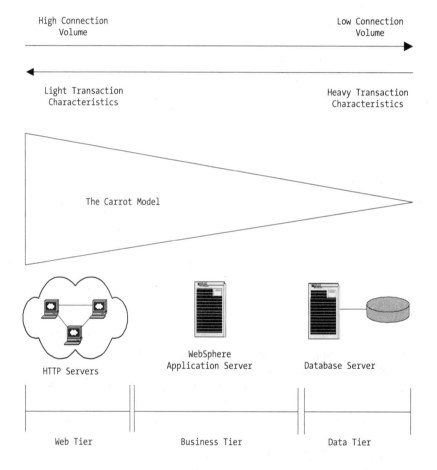

Figure 6-6. Correct queuing configuration, the Carrot model

You'll now see how a queue operates in a real-world example.

Suppose you had a Web-based application, deployed and operating within WebSphere. For the purpose of this discussion, consider it to be a fairly high-volume site (a high transaction rate and lightweight transaction characteristic) that provides customers with delivery tracking information.

Figure 6-7 later in the chapter shows a queuing network model for the example application. As you can see, the application deployed has a Web tier (thin model web server), a Web container, an EJB container, and a JDBC data source to a backend database.

The size of the bars in the model indicate how many open connections are possible within each tier. For example, the Web container is configured to accept 200 connections at any time.

Why Do You Do This?

Looking at Figure 6-7, you're probably saying, "So what?" The benefits from what this can achieve are really a two-fold return. First, queuing network models such as this allow you to model your environment and understand how many connections are required through your tiers. This translates into dollars per transaction or sizing estimates for your physical architecture.

Second, queuing models help to manage the WebSphere application and servers correctly. You can rate limit the number of inbound connections to any one tier to ensure that all users and customers of the application are experiencing maximum performance.

The method in which queues are meant to function is that the heavier the transaction cost, the less or smaller the amount of concurrent load you want to have as you get deeper into your model. That is, for a large system, you may want to allow for 1,000 connections coming into the Web server, 750 at the Web container, 250 at the EJB container, 100 at the JDBC connection manager, and 75 at the database server.

The key is to try and reduce or minimize the number of requests within the WebSphere application server at any one time. The aim is to try and keep the pending requests in the network, usually out front of the Web server. This approach works best when you have multiple channels or WebSphere application servers.

By keeping requests pegged at a certain measure, it allows for a more stable environment where customer or user requests aren't bogging down a system. That is, you have a fixed number of requests in each component or tier at any one time. This is controllable and manageable.

Overall, this progressive queuing approach promotes solid system design and management as well as ensures response times are optimal.

That all said, you may actually find that there's a need in your environment to have a one-to-one relationship between Web container connections, EJB container connections, and database/data source connections. This is still using a queuing model and is valid, but it isn't a "lean" model. If you have large resources, this approach is achievable, but you should still ensure that you model and baseline the queue settings—whatever they may be—so that there's a control and capacity modeling measurement.

You'll now look at how to calculate the queue sizes.

Determining Queue Sizes

Determining the size of each of the queues is a several-stage process. It can be summarized as follows:

1. Understand and identify your user requirements (for example, concurrent users and so on).

2. Set an initial estimated queue overlay on the overall system.

3. Test and measure the initial overlaid figures to obtain a baseline.

4. Analyze the results of baselining and the undertaking of a tuning effort to configure the queues to the optimal size.

The first question you need to answer, and the one you should know already, is how many concurrent users are you expected to have online at any one time?

Let's assume that 500 users is the magic figure, with each session lasting ten minutes on average, and five functional transactions are completed throughout that ten minutes.

You could make an initial assessment and say that at any one time (or within the space of a minute), there would be approximately 250 concurrent functional transactions taking place (for example, 2,500 transactions over a period of ten minutes).

You'd know that each transaction would require resources from the Web server and Web container and one in every two transactions would require database query or updates.

The model would look like that in Figure 6-7.

This initial assessment for a WebSphere environment is sufficient from a starting point, but you haven't taken into account the actual latency between each tier.

 CAUTION Figure 6-7 is an example only, and the settings shouldn't be transposed or used directly within your environment. Be sure that you follow the guidelines within this chapter to ensure that your queuing model is correctly configured.

For example, what if a basic transaction that was made to the database (such as a query of some sorts) took 5,000 milliseconds (five seconds) to respond? This would limit the transaction throughput for your overall application and cause requests to "bank up" in front of the EJB container.

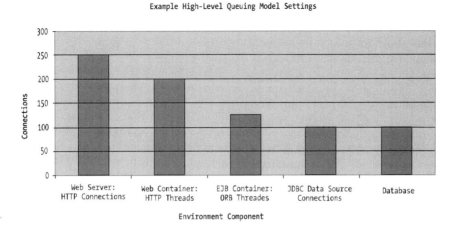

Figure 6-7. Example queuing model

To a point this may be acceptable; however, given that each tier in front of the EJB container would need to manage how it handles the queued connections, you'll need to understand what will happen with those queued connections.

If you had a load balancer in front of the Web servers, the request could be queued in the network, further back in a Web proxy, or even at the user's browser. This queuing helps to ensure that each piece of your application environment is operating at a level that's adequate to meet Service License Agreements (SLAs), and no one piece is or can be overloaded (in theory).

Looking back at the initial baseline queue configurations, it's important that the right tools are used for the task of profiling and baseline identification.

I'll cover the topic of profiling and tooling in Chapters 14 and 15. For usage and detailed information about these tools, how to use them, and the methodology for profiling, review those chapters. For the purposes of this chapter, I'll discuss what items need to be monitored when profiling.

Queue Configuration Baselining

After you've configured the various components within your environment with the chosen baseline queue settings, it's time to profile your application to see how they—the settings—respond. For the most part, this type of monitoring and testing works best using the WebSphere Resource Analyzer (WebSphere 4) and Tivoli Performance (WebSphere 5) tools.

In both tools, what you're looking at is the specific element within the environments that corresponds to the queues. For each application server, Table 6-5 highlights the components that need to be monitored to obtain the data.

Table 6-5. Queue Modeling: Items to Monitor

Queue Component	WebSphere Element to Monitor	Level of Monitoring Setting
Web container	Servlet `Transport`: available threads, active threads	High
EJB container	EJB container: active threads	High
Data source provider	Chosen data source provider: connection pool used, connection pool free	High

NOTE Because these measure only the WebSphere application server, you'll need some tool or tools to monitor the Web server and database server for their concurrent connection rates and resource exhaustion rates. I'll discuss the tools for Web and database servers in Chapters 13 and 14.

You'll now look at the configuration items for each of the main components and what you should look for in terms of correct tuning and optimization techniques.

Updating and Configuring the Queues

For the WebSphere-based components, you can make the changes to the various queues via the administration console. As I've mentioned throughout the book, these changes need to be made in a logical and structured manner. Make a single change at a time, test, and change the next setting—if required. Never change several settings a time. The reason for this is so that you know what each setting change has done and how it affects your system. In this fashion, you can measure the effect, which allows you to better understand the characteristics of the environment.

By also changing one setting at a time, you avoid the chance that one of your tuning changes results in negative performance. If you change several settings at once, you won't have any idea which setting change affected the performance negatively.

I'll discuss making changes to the queues and modeling their performance in Chapter 14. You'll now look at some example settings for the primary tiers in a queuing model.

HTTP Web Server

The Web server queue settings amount to the number of connections that the Web server will accept or process concurrently. All the HTTP servers I've discussed in this book allow you to configure the maximum number of concurrently processed requests.

This setting should be larger than the maximum number of concurrent sessions (for example, logged-in users) to your WebSphere-based applications. For example, if your capacity model states that during peak periods, your environment will have to support 500 concurrent users, this setting will need to be approximately 10 percent more than 500 (for example, 550 sessions).

The additional 10 percent will cater for unforeseen peak loads or issues where those impatient users click Stop on their browser and quickly rerequest the page. You may also have an application that requires (or drives) users to open multiple concurrent sessions. This will also increase your concurrent session usage.

WebSphere Web Container

The next major tier component within the queue is the Web container. The key to this queue setting is to the minimum and maximum HTTP thread pool values within the Web container settings.

As you explored in earlier chapters, this setting should reflect the number of concurrent connections active from the HTTP Web server (via the plug-in) to the Web container. This needs to reflect the number of concurrently accessed servlets, JSPs, and other content components such as HTML, images, and so forth.

Therefore, you should determine this setting using the following:

```
Maximum Threads =
Average_Number_of_Components_per_Client_Transaction × ↵
Number_of_Concurrent_Sessions
```

Using the Resource Analyzer or Tivoli Performance tool (WebSphere 4 and 5, respectively), you can monitor this queue setting via the Active Threads counter. This will provide you with a real-time view of how many threads are being used within this queue tier.

If this counter is constantly hovering or constantly at the maximum thread pool size value (as configured in the Web container services settings), this value may be too low. Ideally, you want this counter to sit at approximately 80 percent of the total pool size.

WebSphere EJB Container

The EJB container queue tier settings aren't different from that of the Web container thread settings. The EJB container's primary queue setting is derived from the ORB thread pool. This setting, as you've seen, is the number of concurrently active requests being processed by the EJB container. Not unlike other thread settings, this value is derived by understanding the average number of requests per client transaction that will be accessing the EJB container.

For example, if for every two Web container–based requests, a resulting EJB container request for an EJB object took place, with a Web container configured with 200 queues, the EJB container would be configured, initially, with 100 available queues. Of course, if your environment isn't running a Web-based UI and is running a thick-Java based UI, this queue value is predominantly the primary "throttle control" into your WebSphere environment.

The equation to set this queue setting within a thick-Java UI environment isn't complicated—essentially you're calculating the average number of concurrent EJB requests against the concurrent users in your environment. Be aware that, assuming you're only accessing your data tier from the component within the EJB container, setting the queue value for this tier too high may affect the performance (in other words, overload) the database.

Use the queue settings of the JDBC connection pool manager to help rate limit this problem.

Using the Resource Analyzer or Tivoli Performance tool (WebSphere 4 and 5, respectively), you can monitor this queue setting via the ORB Thread Pool counter. Like the Web container, as you tune and test these settings, use this counter to understand how this queue setting is working against the maximum thread pool size.

Again, like the Web container, my recommendation is to set the queue setting to be 80 percent of the modeled maximum number of concurrent threads.

JDBC Connection Pool Manager

The data source or JDBC pool manager queue is the next queuing tier in the overall model. By now, you're probably seeing a similarity between all the different queuing tiers in that the way to tune and monitor them all is via the respective pool sizes. In the case of the JDBC pool manager, or data source manager, the key setting to test and tune is the Maximum Pool Size setting within the pool manager configuration sections of the WebSphere console.

Prior references to the JDBC pool manager settings within this book have suggested that this value of the maximum connection pool size should be derived by adding 5 to 10 percent on top of the value of the ORB thread pool value. Other references suggest that this value should be simply the ORB thread pool size plus one. I don't agree with this rule because it limits or reduces the ability for the container to properly handle peak loads efficiently.

When you're tuning and modeling this value, within the Resource Analyzer or Tivoli Performance Viewer tool (WebSphere 4 and 5, respectively), you can monitor the queue setting via the Average Pool Size counter.

You should monitor this value to remain under the maximum pool size value for 80–90 percent of the period in which your testing is performed.

Tuning the JVM

The JVM is one of the most important parts of your overall WebSphere environment from a performance perspective. You can tune WebSphere to an inch within perfection, and yet still, a poorly configured or tuned JVM will bring a system to its knees.

Through the optimization efforts discussed so far and those coming in later chapters, you can somewhat insulate a badly performing JVM. However, over time, it'll catch up with you.

The JVM is, as discussed, a virtual machine environment, specific to each platform. The JVM is responsible for all matters dealing with things such as memory allocation and deallocation (but don't let this make the developers become complacent!), object creation and life cycle management, and runtime control of the Java byte code.

Given that Java is an object-relational language, it's structured around the premise that live objects exist and are managed in memory. Although object-orientated environments provide powerful architectural paradigms, they also exhibit a fair degree of memory-intensive characteristics.

I've discussed in earlier sections and chapters that for the JVM to support a managed memory allocation/deallocation model, it must ensure that regular housekeeping is conducted. The JVM is therefore a sophisticated runtime engine, providing a great deal of autoplumbing and execution capabilities that would normally be managed by the developer in other object-oriented languages.

One of the side effects of having a self-managing environment such as this is that the JVM, as configured, doesn't provide a one-size-fits-all model. Each different application will require, or should require, different memory allocations and configuration setups. What's known as the *Java heap* is the memory space that's allocated for runtime for your WebSphere-based applications. This heap space is where runtime code is managed as well as where data and objects are stored. Your application type and ultimately its load will determine what sort of configuration your JVM will require.

To further complicate matters, there are many vendor-specific JVMs on the market. Generally speaking, the primary setting or available configurations are standard; however, there are a number of unique capabilities and options that each individual JVM supports.

JVM Tuning Options

You'll now look at the primarily used JVMs on the market. Each of the three featured JVMs support the core JVM functionality, but each also supports its own specific tuning and performance options.

I'll cover the following JVMs:

- Sun HotSpot JVM

- IBM JVM

- BEA JRockit JVM

Sun HotSpot JVM

The Sun HotSpot JVM is the JVM offering from Sun Microsystems. It offers a generational garbage collection mechanism that considers object lifetime. Essentially, the heap is split into the New Heap (also known as *Young Heap*) and the Old Heap.

The New Heap is then split into three subsections: the first known as Eden and the other two are Survivor heap spaces. The way that this JVM object life cycle works is that the new objects are created in the Eden space. As the objects move through their usage life cycle, they're moved out of the Eden space into the Survivor spaces and, ultimately, into the Old Heap.

It's important to note that when the New Heap fills up, a minor garbage collection takes place in the New Heap space. In this minor collection, all surviving heap-based objects are moved into the Old Heap. Once the Old Heap fills up, a major collection takes place—this is analogous to a normal garbage collection.

The JVM bootstrap parameters that affect these settings are as follows:

- **-XX:SurvivorRatio**: This value determines the Eden to Survivor ratio.

- **-XX:NewRatio**: This value determines the Old to New Heap ratio.

- **-XX:NewSize**: This value determines the new initial bound.

- **-XX:NewSizeMax**: This value determines the new maximum bound.

You need to carefully consider these values if you're determined to change them. My recommendation is that for 80–90 percent of all cases, managing the minimum and maximum heap sizes for this JVM will provide sufficient tuning capability for your JVM sizes.

What these values do provide for is the ability to fine-tune garbage collection for application environments that are object "savvy." That is, if your application shows characteristics of heavy object creation and usage, these settings may help by fine-tuning the frequency of garbage collection.

IBM JVM

The IBM JVM offering supports a number of parameters that can improve performance of object allocation within the JVM heap. There are several available options to set; the following list provides an overview and several recommendations of when and where to set these optional parameters:

-Xgcthreads: This value allows you to set the number of threads for garbage collection. It allows you to get around the standard single-threaded model that pre–Java 1.4 JVM's have. As a guide, this value can be set to the number of CPUs that your system has. For example, if your system is a quad-processor system and you expect your JVM to have moderate load, configure this value to be 2 to 4 depending on your collection frequency and demand.

-Xml: This value defines the maximum object size for limiting the size of objects to be allocated and referenced from the local cache. The key is to use the local object cache as much as possible rather than the general JVM heap for small- to medium-sized objects.

These values, when tuned appropriately, tend to drive performance improvement by up to 20 percent for fairly standard Java environments.

As discussed many times in this book, be sure that you size your object allocation and memory usage carefully to ensure that settings such as these are optimized appropriately for your specific WebSphere application environment needs.

The BEA JRockit JVM is a Wintel platform (x86 Intel Itanium) optimized JVM. Originally developed by a European company, JRockit was recently released by BEA (the makers of the BEA WebLogic J2EE application server). Some developers and system architects say it's the "world's fastest JVM."

JRockit is an unusual JVM implementation and is quite different from others; it offers an advanced garbage collection architecture via four different collection methodologies. Two of the key garbage collection facilities within the

JRockit JVM allow for simultaneous collection and object cleanup in parallel to the main Java JVM threads. This can dramatically increase the overall runtime performance by not pausing the JVM runtime for the garbage collection thread. Of course, this capability only really makes a real impact with multiple CPUs, but the improvement in performance is evident still via a single CPU system.

The second major difference between JRockit and other JVMs is that JRockit also provides an advanced Just In Time (JIT) compiler. The feature essentially precompiles all methods within all classes within your application when bootstrapping, and it provides a continual background optimization function that constantly removes bottlenecks. Lastly, the JVM's optimization thread capability constantly tunes frequently used methods and interfaces within deployed Java code.

In summary, if you're running an Intel-based or AMD-based platform (32-bit or 64-bit), then consider the JRockit JVM if your application is memory intensive (heap usage and object allocation).

Summary

This chapter explored myriad performance and tuning possibilities and options. It goes without saying that although you've explored many options and optimization approaches in this chapter, you need to plan, model, and test your proposed optimization and setting changes carefully.

Too often I've see environments where systems managers have had the right intentions to optimize their environment, but the sizing and proper modeling has left them short on results. In the worst case, your performance can actually decrease in some cases. Classic examples of this are the JVM settings that you explored several pages back. Therefore, use the options and approaches in this chapter in conjunction with an overall methodology such as one discussed in Chapter 1.

WebSphere Failover and High Availability Considerations

IN THIS CHAPTER, YOU'LL dive into high availability configuration and considerations associated with WebSphere implementations. You'll explore what is possible in terms of failover and high availability with WebSphere and expand on what you learned in Chapters 5 and 6.

Over the past two major releases of WebSphere (i.e., versions 4 and 5), WebSphere has come a long way in the areas of high availability and failover. It's quite possible to configure a WebSphere application environment to be 99.99 percent (or higher) available within a reasonable budget on commodity hardware.

In Chapters 5 and 6 you looked at topological architectures and best practices for selection of platforms and platform designs that foster high availability. In this chapter, you'll delve further into high availability and WebSphere, and you'll be provided with the context you'll need to design a WebSphere environment which ensures high levels of availability.

This chapter covers the following topics:

- Failover and high availability fundamentals

- Disaster recovery

- Clustering

- Web server failover configurations

- Web container failover configurations

- EJB container failover configurations

- Database server failover configurations

By the end of this chapter, you should have a good understanding of WebSphere's high availability and failover features and be in a position to architect and configure your platform to provide maximum uptime for your customers and users.

WebSphere High Availability and Failover Fundamentals

Because of WebSphere's logical and modular design, just about every key server feature is clusterable and supportive of failover configurations. This allows you to implement highly available configurations that promote uptime for your end users.

Essentially, what we mean by *high availability* is designing and then building a WebSphere-based platform in such a way that it eliminates single points of processing and failure of the environment. This not only includes adding in additional servers to gain high availability, but also ensuring environment aspects, such as data and application software, are implemented and developed with a modular and distributable model in mind.

Consider the following example for a moment. Suppose you have a WebSphere-based application that is reliant on a data store of some sort (e.g., an RDBMS). Within this application, there is a single component that manages data concurrency (such as a ID generator or an incrementor). If this is the case, you'll have difficulty deploying that application into a distributed or highly available environment if there is a single application component responsible for data concurrency. How are other cloned application instances able to make updates to a centralized data store without corrupting the data?

Another aspect of high availability, and something I touched on in Chapter 3, is the question of what is really high availability in terms of your organization. Do you really require 24/7/365 availability or would something closer to 20/5 be satisfactory? To achieve 24/7/365, you'll need to spend extra money and effort in ensuring you've removed all (within reason) single points of processing and failure and, most likely, you'll need to distribute your processing site over two or more locations.

You also need to consider the difference between operational availability and service availability. In most cases, when we talk about high availability, we're really talking about service availability—availability of the application and services for end users. However, you can't have service availability without operational availability. On the other hand, you can have operational availability but not necessarily service availability.

Consider a scenario in which you have 15 application servers, a highly available database server tier, clustered Web servers, and actively redundant network infrastructure. You may have a data integrity issue that has caused your application or your service to become unavailable, but your operational platform is still fully online. This is the quandary of application availability. Where do you draw the line to ensure that you have suitable amount of availability at a cost that is not prohibitive? Again, consider the discussions in Chapters 2 and 3 relating to the notion of estimating your downtime and uptime costs. If you're total downtime costs are only $100 per hour, then purchasing an additional $20,000 server isn't cost justifiable (unless you have very deep pockets!).

The following sections summarize what forms of availability there are within a WebSphere environment.

WebSphere High Availability

WebSphere platform high availability, as opposed to application availability (i.e., operational availability versus service availability), can be achieved via one or more of the following methods:

- Clustering (software, hardware, WebSphere)

- Disaster recovery

- Failover

Each of these concepts is supported by WebSphere, and in the next several sections, you'll explore each of these in more detail. Each method description is followed by an implementation explanation.

Clustering

Clustering is the form of availability assurance configuration in which key components are duplicated to some degree with the aim of reducing single points of failure. Although you can use clustering to achieve performance improvement by having more components processing more requests, clustering is essentially a high availability concept.

As you'll see, clustering comes in three forms in the context of WebSphere: software clustering, hardware clustering, and WebSphere internal clustering.

Software Clustering

Software clustering boils down to the implementation of what I term *proprietary clustering*. Proprietary clustering is usually facilitated via product- or application-specific clustering components that allow you to span out a particular service to one or more physical servers.

Some examples of software clustering implementations are as follows:

- HTTP server clustering

- Lightweight Directory Access Protocol (LDAP) server clustering

- Database server clustering

The actual engine or software that drives the clustering is typically part of the product you purchase. For example, Oracle provides a "clustering" layer as part of the Oracle Parallel Server (OPS) product. Crystal Enterprise, a product that provides Web reporting capabilities, comes with its own internal clustering software.

This isn't to say that you can't use a hardware clustering solution instead of or in conjunction with any of the proprietary software clustering solutions. In fact, in many cases, a combination of the two will provide you with a linear improvement of your potential availability measurements.

Hardware Clustering

Hardware clustering is, in most cases, the more costly of the three WebSphere environment clustering solutions. However, it typically provides you with the highest form of service availability. The reason for this is that hardware clustering, as its name implies, uses redundant components (e.g., servers, networks, etc.) to provide clustering solutions.

Hardware clustering is also the most complex of the three WebSphere environment clustering technologies because it involves many parts and complex software that I tend to refer to as *clusterware.*

Clusterware is third-party software that you use to cluster your components. Clustering in this form usually involves more than one server, and the clusterware sits "on top" of the physical environment and overlooks key processes (e.g., databases, Web servers, etc.) and key hardware components (e.g., network devices, hard disks, storage groups, and the servers themselves).

Some of the more well-known and WebSphere-supported clusterware solutions are as follows:

- Microsoft Windows Internal Clustering (Windows NT, 2000, XP, and 2003 Server editions)

- Veritas Cluster Server (most operating systems, including Solaris, Linux, AIX, HP-UX, and Windows)

- Sun Microsystems SunCluster (Sun Solaris systems only)

- High Availability Cluster Multiprocessing (HACMP, IBM AIX systems only)

- MC/ServiceGuard (HP-UX systems only)

- Compaq/HP TruCluster (Digital/Compaq/HP Tru64 Unix systems only)

Each of these clustering solutions provides varying levels of functionality and reliability that allow you to cluster servers running on their respective operating systems.

Essentially, the architecture of a hardware clustered solution is that the clusterware is configured to own and manage key aspects of the environment. As mentioned earlier, this includes peripheral hardware components as well as software processes (daemons and server processes).

There are two primary forms of hardware clustering:

- Active-standby clustering

- Active-active clustering

In active-standby clustering, typically two servers are configured in a cluster and one server is the master until the clusterware determines that the second server takes over. The reason for the takeover may be a faulty disk, a dead daemon process, or some other critical hardware component failure (e.g., CPU panic).

Figure 7-1 shows a before shot of a basic active-standby cluster configuration, and Figure 7-2 shows the same environment after an event triggered the cluster to failover from server A to server B.

In Figure 7-2, some form of failure took place on server A. The clusterware sits on both servers (or all servers) in a clustered configuration, and each node is continuously informing the remote server of its status. This "heartbeat" can be as simple as a network ping through to something more complex such as running a small application periodically on each remote host to understand the state.

In this case, server A failed (let's say a database process crash occurred) and server B, via one of its continual status requests, was informed that a process was dead (or missing) on server A. This would have triggered server A to shut down all its managed processes and failover to server B, or server B may have found a missing process and told the clusterware on server A to shut down and, subsequently, server B took over as master.

Because there is a failover concept involved, there is a period in which the cluster can't service requests. This period can be anything from a second or two through to several minutes or more, depending on the cluster complexity and clusterware configuration.

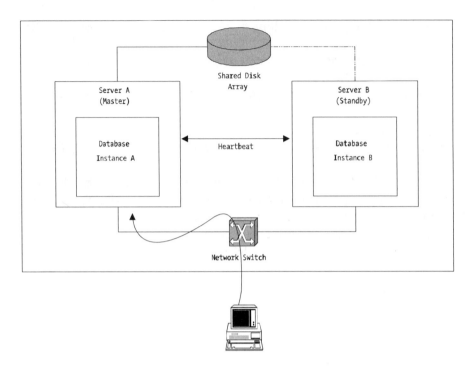

Figure 7-1. An active-standby cluster configuration before failover

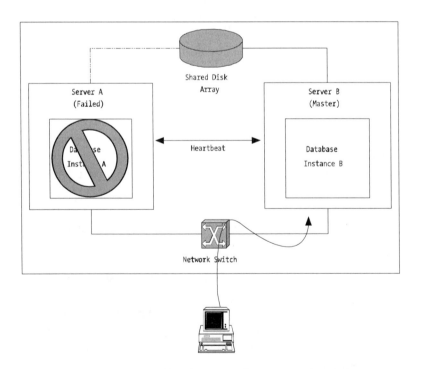

Figure 7-2. An active-standby cluster configuration after failover

The second type of hardware clustering solution is the active-active cluster. This is a far more complex clustered environment, but at the same time, it provides greater availability as well as the advantage of usually providing more performance (you can use all nodes in the active-active cluster to process requests rather than have one lie dormant for lengthy periods). Active-active clusters are more complex because of the data and process management issues surrounding access.

Consider for a moment a database on a single node. When you make updates to a database, there is a whole layer of data locking, I/O, and process management that ensures there is a high level of transaction integrity. Then consider placing two or more nodes into an active-active database cluster and what level of control and management would be required to facilitate that same update, but to a database that is located on multiple physical servers. This is the degree to which hardware clusters in an active-active configuration need to be carefully designed and implemented.

The following two diagrams show an active-active clustered database configuration. Figure 7-3 shows an operational active-active cluster servicing requests. You'll notice that there are three databases operating over the two physical servers, each operating with a single instance on each node. Figure 7-4 shows the same environment, with the difference being that server A has failed in some respect, and server B has taken over all operational load of the environment.

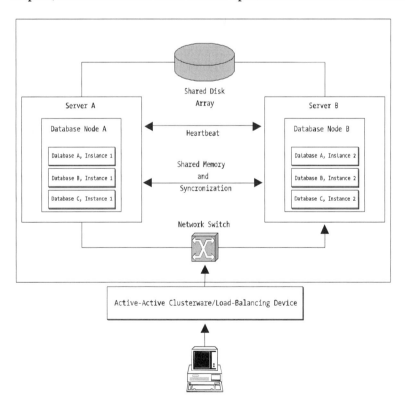

Figure 7-3. An active-active cluster configuration before failover

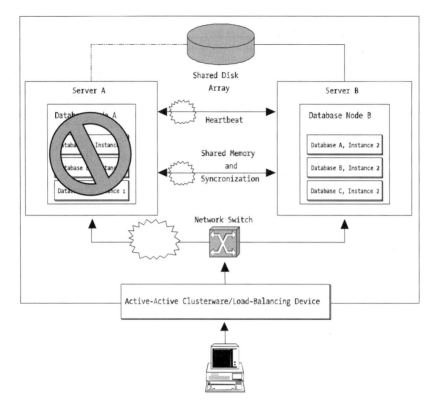

Figure 7-4. An active-active cluster configuration after failover

As there is no pause or delay during a failover scenario—the cluster services are still servicing requests to users or other applications. Therefore, unlike in active-standby clusters, the availability of an active-active configuration is typically higher.

The software driving your cluster will affect how you communicate to your cluster. Your interface to the cluster may be as simple as a hardware load-balancing switch, or it may be software driven.

 CAUTION Be wary of committing yourself and your active-active cluster to being able to handle 100 percent of the overall cluster load when half of your cluster is down. It's possible to build an active-active cluster in which half of the cluster can handle the entire load.

WebSphere Clustering

WebSphere itself also provides several forms of clustering, all of which could be considered the same as software clustering. The reason I've split discussion of this clustering out into its own section is that this is where you'll specifically focus your attention in this chapter—and besides, WebSphere clustering and high availability is what this book is all about!

So what then is WebSphere clustering? In essence, WebSphere clustering relates to the clustering of components operating within the application server, usually among a number of servers. The nomenclature does differ slightly between WebSphere version 4 and version 5 with respect to clustering, but essentially the concept is the same. WebSphere clustering provides the ability to distribute load and services over one or many physical nodes operating WebSphere.

As I expressed earlier in the chapter, it's important to remember that not all application components can be clustered. Think of situations (hopefully not too common!) in which you have had singleton objects in your application or some form of socket-based I/O happening on the backend. There are ways around this, but your application will quickly become cumbersome and overly complicated.

Disaster Recovery

Disaster recovery is an overly used business imperative that involves having a secondary site or tertiary sites (or more), and locating mirrored hot or cold standby infrastructure in a ready operational state. It's primarily used to prepare for disaster-level events such as earthquakes, floods, and other natural disasters; power and environmental outages; and, unfortunately more common nowadays, terrorist or war-based events.

Disaster recovery is an expensive undertaking by any organization, regardless of size. Correctly done, it typically involves duplicating all processes and infrastructure at one or more other sites, and either having the sites operate simultaneously (and gaining geographical load-balancing as a positive side effect) or operating the disaster recovery site in a hot or cold standby configuration. True disaster recovery requires locating your data centers in different cities to avoid power grid contention or naturally occurring events (e.g., earthquakes, inclement weather, etc.).

In years gone by, especially during the Cold War era, disaster recovery was used by computing sites to avoid nuclear attack on cities. In today's world, in which terrorism is a major threat, this may start to become a new motive for opting for disaster recovery depending on the criticality of data.

Simultaneously operating disaster recovery sites are becoming a commonly implemented solution when employing disaster recovery over recent years. These solutions are primarily driven by the notion that if you have a second or *n*th site operating, why not harness some of the computing power to increase performance and scalability?

Implementing a disaster recovery solution for a Web site that is fairly simplistic—one that may not have a vast amount of dynamic presentation or complex backend interconnections (e.g., legacy and/or EIS systems, databases, etc.)—is fairly straightforward. There are few moving parts, so to speak. If, however, you attempt to run a simultaneous solution among multiple sites and have legacy and backend services required at all sites, then your complexity indices very quickly increase. For example, how would you synchronize synchronous writes to multiple clustered database solutions over vast distances without affecting performance? It's possible to do so, and there are solutions available on the market from vendors such as Veritas and EMC, but there is a cost.

A "hot" disaster recovery site is slightly different from a simultaneous or split-site implementation. In the truest sense, a hot disaster recovery site is typically what comes to mind when people think of disaster recovery. A hot site operates by having the same hardware located at alternate sites. Should the primary site fail, for whatever reason, the secondary site immediately kicks in. The "hotness" works by a constant synchronization of data in an asynchronous or batched synchronization manner. That is, the data being replicated isn't necessarily written bit for bit on the remote hot site for each write I/O occurring on the primary site. Although sites that are close to one another (within 50 kilometers of each other) can get away with this form of data synchronization, sites that are distributed over a few hundred to a few thousand kilometers may suffer performance issues with write updates and synchronization from the primary to the backup site due to latency.

Figure 7-5 shows a dual-site topology in which site A is the primary site and site B is the secondary site.

In Figure 7-5, the example active-active database cluster environment is distributed over two sites, Seattle and Washington. With the increased distances between the two servers comes additional latency to the tune of ~45 milliseconds. Now on a basic IP network this isn't anything to be too worried about, but consider the performance hit if your database nodes were constantly trying to synchronize cache, distribute queries, and synchronize the I/O to a shared storage array.

In summary, a hot disaster recovery site is a sound solution for having a secondary, ready-to-operate operational environment. However, you need to consider how you're going to get the data synchronized between the two sites and at what frequency. How much data loss can you sustain before your application is unusable: 1 second, 5 seconds, 15 seconds, or 2 minutes? That is, you may be able to get by with a hot disaster recovery site such as the one in Figure 7-5 if you can survive with having a delay between data synchronization between the two sites. This form of disaster recovery solution may be a cheaper and more viable option if your recovery service level agreements allow for a delayed data synchronization.

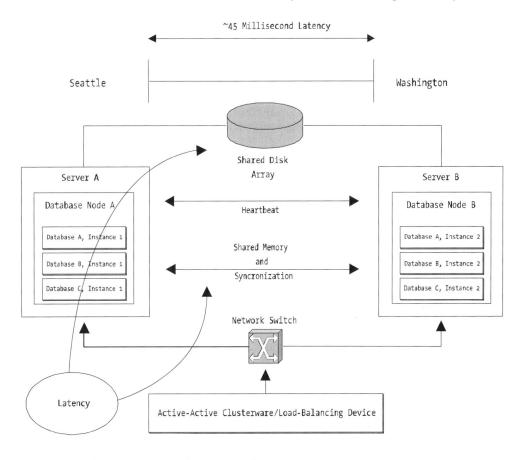

Figure 7-5. A disaster recovery hot site topology

Cold disaster recovery sites are typically implementations in which a secondary site sits almost dormant until the need arises to failover to it in a disaster. In some cases, the cold site works by only synchronizing data and application configurations at the time that it's needed from the archive or backups. Other approaches include deploying all application changes and configuration to both sites at each "software release" and then synchronizing data at the time of a disaster.

In summary, cold disaster recovery sites are far less costly to maintain than hot disaster recovery sites, but there is a greater time period between restoration of data and application availability. This period may be anywhere from 1 hour to 72 hours or more.

Failover Techniques with WebSphere

WebSphere is able to take advantage of all the previously mentioned clustering and site implementation architectures. Figure 7-6 shows a complex WebSphere environment that has incorporated many different implementations of clustering and high availability facilities.

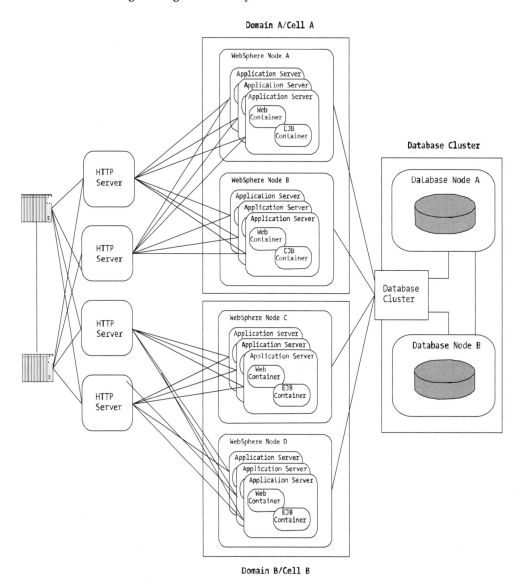

Figure 7-6. A complex WebSphere high availability environment

Figure 7-6 includes the following levels of high availability:

- Database clustering

- WebSphere domains (WebSphere version 4)/cells (WebSphere version 5)

- Cloned WebSphere application servers

- Vertically scaled environment (multiple JVMs per WebSphere server)

- Horizontally scaled environment (multiple physical WebSphere servers)

- Redundant, load-balanced frontend HTTP servers

- Dual redundant load balancers

In this example, it would be possible to make this configuration into a split site (simultaneous processing centers) or a hot disaster recovery configuration due to the split domain/cell configuration. The concept of a split domain or cell configuration is almost like the environment in Figure 7-6: two separated application environments glued together.

This type of configuration, which I refer to as a configuration *split down the spine*, helps to prevent cascade failures within your application code from bringing down the entire environment. In the case of a configuration split down the spine, if the domain A or cell A applications "rupture" and cause a cascade failure on WebSphere application server A and B, the resulting effect shouldn't affect the second domain or cell, because they're split down the lines of the administration boundaries.

Let's look at the different components in more detail and put into context how each tier and key component of a WebSphere environment can be implemented in such a way that it provides a high degree of failover or clustered capabilities (and hence, high availability).

Web Server Tier: HTTP Servers

The Web server tier or HTTP servers that facilitate the transfer of HTTP/ HTTPS-based requests to and from the WebSphere application servers are one of the more straightforward components in a WebSphere topology that can be implemented in a high availability form.

As you saw in Chapter 6, distributing Web servers gives you high availability of the servers that distribute requests through to the backend WebSphere application servers via the WebSphere HTTP plug-in that sits on the HTTP server. By having multiple Web HTTP servers, you achieve a very high level of redundancy in your ability to service more requests, thanks to multiple servers, and you also increase the number of possible paths through to your backend application servers.

Recall that you'll need some form of load balancer in front of your Web HTTP servers. This can be a hardware appliance from a company such as Cisco or a software product such as the WebSphere Edge Server. Both of these products, and the many more available on the market, will distribute the requests to the appropriate Web server based on your desired configuration (i.e., lease loaded, load balanced, round-robin, random selection, etc.). This will provide you with the Web HTTP server availability, and the WebSphere HTTP plug-in will distribute the user requests to any of the configured backend WebSphere application servers.

Web Container

In most cases, the next component that will service requests in the environment is the Web container, which is part of the WebSphere application server. The WebSphere HTTP plug-in passes requests to the appropriate application server clone on one of the configured backend WebSphere application servers. Once the request has made its way to the WebSphere application server, the targeted Web container will service the requests.

In the event that the application server the particular Web container is operating under fails, the next request made by the end user will be directed to the next appropriate application server clone, and the session details will be, if configured, retrieved from the user session database.

Therefore, for the Web container to be highly available, the following components need to be void of single points of failure:

- Physical application server

- Database server(s)

- Network infrastructure

Once the user request has hit the particular application server (Web container), the subsequent user requests will stay with the application server, in most cases. This factor is dependent on your application architecture (e.g., do you need sessions?). The WebSphere clustering will handle all failover capabilities if the originally targeted application server (Web container) fails.

EJB Container

The EJB container, not unlike like the Web container, receives its requests from somewhere in the WebSphere environment. This maybe a Java object within the Web container, such as a servlet or JSP, or it may be another EJB somewhere else in the environment, either local or remote.

The EJB container is less bound to servicing its own originating request. For valid reasons, your application code, specifically EJBs operating under the EJB container, may call other EJBs that happen to be on remote servers. This may be accomplished through forceful remote calling (e.g., calling services on other remote systems) or through workload management (WLM).

When EJBs are participating in WLM, their reference is maintained in the global JNDI tree. Therefore, when a client Java object makes a lookup to obtain the reference to a specific EJB, that client may be calling an EJB on a remote server rather than the local one. This is configurable in how you set up local versus remote calls, and the setup is somewhat similar to that of the Web container.

Given the nature of EJBs, there are, however, many more options available for how you may want to distribute their services. This provides a high degree of control of your EJB workload at a very granular level. The different levels of WLM availability that you can configure your EJBs with are as follows:

- Random selection

- Round-robin

- Random prefer local

- Round-robin prefer local

It's important to note that these WLM settings are overridden by EJB server affinity settings, which are as follows:

- *Process affinity:* All requests from a Web container Java object are serviced by the EJB container operating in the same application server. Requests are never routed outside the application server.

- *Transaction affinity:* All requests from a Web container–based Java object, for example, are serviced by the referenced JNDI EJB context. All subsequent requests in the same client transaction are bound to that EJB container.

I discuss these settings in more detail in the section titled "EJB Container Failover and High Availability."

Database Server Tier

As you've seen, the database server is an immensely important component of most WebSphere application server topologies. Because of the database's importance, a number of clustering and failover configurations are available for the database server tier.

Here's an overview of the database availability options, which I discuss in more detail later in the chapter:

- Database server clustering (active-active or active-standby)

- Stand-alone database instances (no replication)

- Database replication

- Hot-standby databases (nonclustered)

Remember, the key to database availability is to first prevent database "services" from becoming unavailable through an active-active cluster or a highly distributed database environment (e.g., hot replication to many nodes), or minimize failover times. There's no use in having a hot-standby database or an active-standby database topology if your failover time exceeds that of your thread pool or JDBC connection time-out values!

Administrative Functions

Administrative functionality is more prevalent in WebSphere version 4 because of the Administration Repository database. There are capabilities within the administrative services that act similar to those of the standard EJB WLM functions. For the WebSphere version 5 platform, distributing the Deployment Manager functionality ensures that master-update and replication functions for cell configuration are available at all times.

It's important to note that stand-alone Java applications may not be privy to the WebSphere administration services. In this case, it's important that for bootstrapping your developers provide a full list (such as in a properties file) of all WebSphere administration nodes. This will provide a failsafe mechanism for the Java client to rotate different WebSphere application servers until it finds one available.

Consider using Java Application Clients (JACs). These components, although similar to stand-alone Java clients, provide the ability to hook into the WebSphere core services from outside WebSphere itself (i.e., not within a standard application server container). I discuss the implementation of JACs and Java clients and how to maximize their availability later in this chapter.

In any case, failover support for JACs, administration services, and Java clients is all provided within the bounds of the WebSphere application server architecture.

Network Components

Without the network, your WebSphere platform is broken. The network infrastructure is essential to the operational capabilities of your WebSphere environment. It's therefore imperative that you use redundant network paths and network infrastructure for critical WebSphere application environments.

Always use at least two paths between your WebSphere application servers to other tiers, and consider segmenting your networks to help prevent DoS attacks. The preferable approach is to have WebSphere and database servers communicate with one another via a private network, different from that of the "customer traffic" network. This will help prevent bottlenecks and impacts when your applications are moving large amounts of data around the network, in between nodes.

More on network availability later in this chapter.

Recap of Topologies Suitable for High Availability

In this section you examined a number of features that WebSphere supports to aid in high availability and redundant application server environments. Two key components to a WebSphere application server are the EJB container and the Web container. To obtain or promote high availability with your applications, these two components need to be clusterable.

As I discussed, WebSphere clustering through server groups, domains, cells and other features allows for increased availability of your WebSphere services. Essentially this all boils down to being able to support both vertical and horizontal clustering and load distribution, or WLM.

Using vertical clustering capabilities such as server groups, clones, or multiple application servers (depending on your version of WebSphere), you will be able to ensure that your application environment is insulated from single JVM performance issues or memory constraints that may cause poor performance or outages in a single JVM or application server environment.

Horizontal clustering will ensure that a single server outage won't cause a complete failure of your application environment, by having multiple physical WebSphere servers operating redundant instances of your application JVMs.

The (near) ultimate in high availability assurance is to use both horizontal and vertical clustering. You can further extend this, as I discussed in Chapter 5, by splitting your environment into separate administrative domains or cells (WebSphere version 4 and version 5, respectively) to ensure that there isn't cross-contamination of incorrect data or cascade corruption of configuration or JNDI tree data.

Web Server Failover and High Availability

As I discussed earlier in this chapter, the Web server is a critical component in any Web-based WebSphere environment. In Chapter 5 I discussed possible topological architectures that involve multiple load-balanced Web servers. In this section you'll look at what options are available to facilitate those topological architectures presented in Chapter 5.

Web Server Overview

Due to its inherent application and protocol simplicity, the Web server tier is a noncomplex environment to work with. Because of the technology's inherent simplicity, it provides an easy platform for implementing solutions in high-availability forms.

In the most basic form, you'll have a single Web server servicing requests from end users. Through the use of the WebSphere HTTP plug-in that is installed into your chosen Web server product, you'll be able to route requests to the backend application servers with ease. To achieve failover and high availability with this component of your topology, as discussed in Chapter 5, always use more than one Web server.

Web servers are commodity systems and don't need to be high powered if you're using a thin WebSphere model. Many Unix vendors are now producing low-end machines below US$1,500 that can perform this job perfectly fine. All you need is 256MB to 512MB of memory, a pair of redundant mirrored disks, a couple of Fast Ethernet or Gigabit Ethernet ports, and you're off and running.

It's possible and quite valid to mix your platform vendor for your environments. That is, there's nothing wrong with using x86 (Intel/AMD)-based servers running Solaris x86, BSD, or Linux, mixed in with higher-end Unix-based systems for the backend servers. This can reduce costs considerably or provide a budget to purchase more commodity-based Web servers.

Web Server Implementation

Figure 7-7 shows an approach to Web server high availability.

The configuration in Figure 7-7 uses a mixture of DNS round-robin, hardware-based load-balancers, and the WLM (clustering) aspects of WebSphere via HTTP Web server plug-ins.

The DNS round-robin configuration is a very simplistic approach to achieving redundancy in your load balancers. It's a common issue I see in which sites have purchased a load-balancer device (e.g., a Cisco CS series, Alteon, Radware, etc.), but it poses as a single point of failure (how very ironic!).

Best practice in this configuration is to use something such as DNS round-robining, which is a simplistic but robust mechanism for sending requests to more than one ingress point in your network. Essentially, in your DNS you configure your site name to have multiple "A"-type entries in your zone files so that when a request is made for www.mysite.com, for example, the DNS responds with an IP or host name that is contained as one of the A entries in your www.mysite.com zone file.

Another approach is to use distributed or geographically load-balanced sites, in which there is more than one pipe or connection into your network. Using Internet routing protocols such as Border Gateway Protocol (BGP) and Open Shortest Path First (OSPF), you can distribute your traffic to multiple locations, based on availability and serviceability.

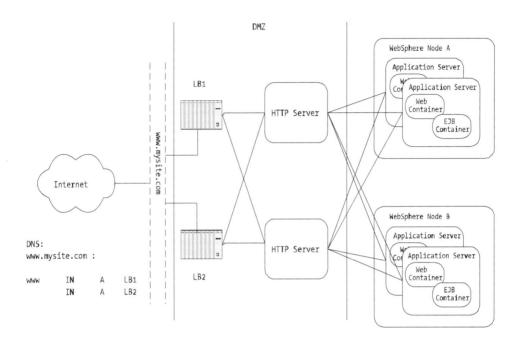

Figure 7-7. Web server failover and high availability model

Figure 7-8 shows an example of two businesses accessing a Web site (frontend to a WebSphere application platform) via two different geographically distributed border sites, Seattle and Washington. This method provides quasi–load balancing. It's fairly static most of the time, but the load is distributed. The value in this approach is that there's a high degree of failover capability within the design.

As you can see, each business goes through a different route path to get to the www.mysite.com environment. If, however, ISP N failed, OSPF and BGP routing would immediately reroute the traffic to another route path, and ultimately direct all traffic via ISP P (see Figure 7-9).

Let's now look at the next most common tier in a WebSphere platform: the Web container.

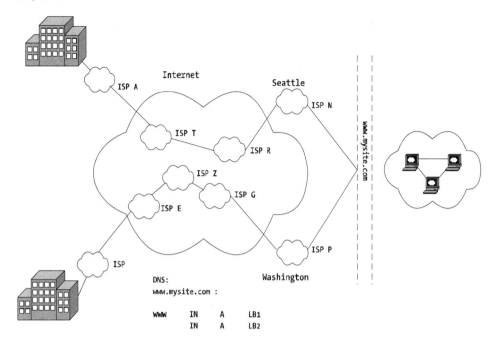

Figure 7-8. Global routing example

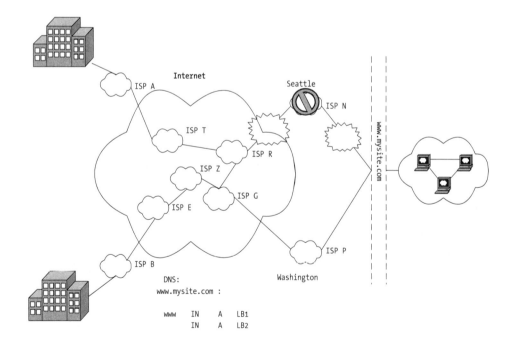

Figure 7-9. Global routing example failover scenario

Web Container Failover and High Availability

The Web container is a critical component in any Web-based WebSphere environment. In a nonfailover or non-Web container clustered configuration, should the Web container fail, all end user transactions will typically cease.

Let's look at the various options offered to improve availability within the Web container and the WebSphere application server WLM functions.

Web Container Overview

The Web container operates within the WebSphere application server JVM space for each configured application server. You'll recall from earlier chapters that the application server will operate both a Web and an EJB container under a single JVM.

The key to improving availability of your Web container is to configure the Web container to participate in WLM with other cloned application servers as well as configure the distribution of load via a WebSphere HTTP plug-in on your Web servers.

Let's first take a look at the HTTP plug-in file.

HTTP Web Server Plug-in

As you learned in Chapters 4 and 5, the WebSphere HTTP plug-in file is an XML plug-in configuration that provides you with the ability to configure WLM or load balancing of your user requests to your Web containers.

Let's look at an example plug-in file that isn't configured for failover support. The first configuration file, shown in Listing 7-1, is based on a WebSphere version 4 format. The second configuration file, shown in Listing 7-2, is based on a WebSphere version 5 format.

Listing 7-1. WebSphere Version 4 Example HTTP Plug-in File

```
<?xml version="1.0"?>
<Config>
    <Log RefreshInterval="10" LogLevel="Error" ⏎
Name="/opt/WebSphere/AppServer/logs/native.log" />
    <VirtualHostGroup Name="default_host">
        <VirtualHost Name="www.mysite.com:80" />
    </VirtualHostGroup>
<!-- ### Start of Main Section #### -->
<!-- Portal Application -->
```

```
    <ServerGroup Name="portalApplication Server Group">
        <Server CloneID="uk396h0g" Name="portalApp">
            <Transport Hostname="serverA.mydomain.com" ↵
Port="10000" Protocol="http" />
        </Server>
    </ServerGroup>
    <UriGroup Name="portalAppEAR/portalApp_URIs">
        <Uri Name="/portal/*" />
    </UriGroup>
    <Route ServerGroup="portalApplication Server Group"
        UriGroup="portalAppEAR/portalApp_URIs"
        VirtualHostGroup="default_host" />
</Config>
```

Listing 7-2. WebSphere Version 5 Example HTTP Plug-in File

```
<?xml version="1.0"?>
<Config>
    <Log RefreshInterval="10" LogLevel="Error" ↵
Name="/opt/WebSphere/AppServer/logs/native.log" />
    <VirtualHostGroup Name="default_host">
        <VirtualHost Name="www.mysite.com:80" />
    </VirtualHostGroup>
<!-- ### Start of Main Section #### -->
<!-- Portal Application -->
    <ServerCluster Name="portalApplication Server Group">
        <Server Name="portalApp">
            <Transport Hostname="serverA.mydomain.com" ↵
Port="10000" Protocol="http" />
        </Server>
    </ServerCluster>
    <UriGroup Name="portalAppEAR/portalApp_URIs">
        <Uri Name="/portal/*" />
    </UriGroup>
    <Route ServerCluster="portalApplication Server Group"
        UriGroup="portalAppEAR/portalApp_URIs"
        VirtualHostGroup="default_host" />
</Config>
```

The key line item in these example HTTP plug-in files is highlighted in bold in each listing. This line, known as the Server or ServerCluster directive, provides a way to determine how the user requests via the frontend Web server will be routed through the environment.

> **NOTE**   Both WebSphere 4 and 5 plug-in files require the `CloneID`
> directive to be present for session management to function.
> However, if your environment doesn't require session manage-
> ment or server affinity, you can remove the clone ID from the
> plug-in file. Keeping it there creates overhead for the Web server
> to try to process the ID for each request.

In these two configurations, there is no failover or secondary available clones
or servers to service the end user requests. Therefore, if `serverA.mydomain.com`
fails or isn't available, then the service will be unavailable. Therefore, you need
to look at operating multiple Web containers on your WebSphere application
servers.

You saw in Chapter 5 various ways that topologies can be deployed, and one
of the common traits among high-availability topological architectures is to
employ multiple application servers, which entails multiple Web containers.
Consider for a moment that you added in an additional physical server to your
topology, server B. Your topology would look like the diagram in Figure 7-10.

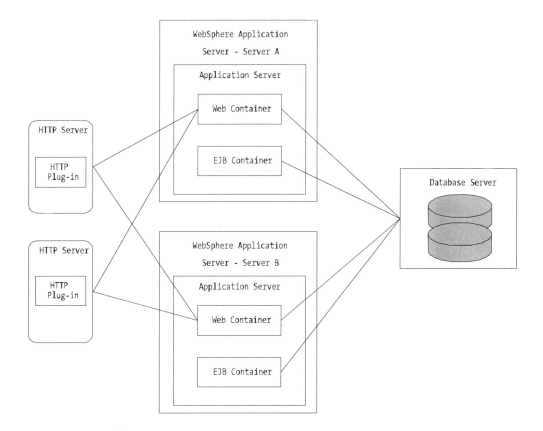

Figure 7-10. Dual application server configuration

You'll want to configure each HTTP plug-in file on the HTTP servers to route requests to all available, or configured, WebSphere Web containers on both server A and server B.

Now consider for a moment the two code examples, Listings 7-1 and 7-2. The key lines are the server group and server cluster directives. These two lines, which represent different nomenclature for WebSphere version 4 and version 5, are the drivers behind the routing process. Consider the following snippet of configuration code:

```
<ServerGroup Name="portalApplication Server Group">
    <Server CloneID="uk396h0g" Name="portalApp">
        <Transport Hostname="serverA.mydomain.com" ↵
Port="10000" Protocol="http" />
    </Server>

</ServerGroup>
```

Also consider this snippet:

```
<ServerCluster Name="portalApplication Server Group">
    <Server Name="portalApp">
        <Transport Hostname="serverA.mydomain.com" ↵
Port="10000" Protocol="http" />
    </Server>

</ServerCluster>
```

These lines basically state that should a route request be made to either the ServerGroup or ServerCluster "portalApplication Server Group," then send the request to the server entry, as defined in the Transport directive.

If you want to map this configuration to that of the dual instance Web container configurations, you'll need to make the following changes. First, the changes for WebSphere version 4 are shown in Listing 7-3.

Listing 7-3. WebSphere Version 4 Example HTTP Plug-in File

```
<?xml version="1.0"?>
<Config>
    <Log RefreshInterval="10" LogLevel="Error" ↵
Name="/opt/WebSphere/AppServer/logs/native.log" />
    <VirtualHostGroup Name="default_host">
        <VirtualHost Name="www.mysite.com:80" />
    </VirtualHostGroup>
<!-- ### Start of Main Section #### -->
<!-- Portal Application -->
    <ServerGroup Name="portalApplication Server Group">
```

```
        <Server CloneID="uk396h0g" Name="portalApp">
            <Transport Hostname="serverA.mydomain.com" ⏎
Port="10000" Protocol="http" />
        </Server>
        <Server CloneID="ao356hib" Name="portalApp">
            <Transport Hostname="serverB.mydomain.com" ⏎
Port="10000" Protocol="http" />
        </Server>
    </ServerGroup>
    <UriGroup Name="portalAppEAR/portalApp_URIs">
        <Uri Name="/portal/*" />
    </UriGroup>
    <Route ServerGroup="portalApplication Server Group"
        UriGroup="portalAppEAR/portalApp_URIs"
        VirtualHostGroup="default_host" />
</Config>
```

The changes for WebSphere version 5 are shown in Listing 7-4.

Listing 7-4. WebSphere Version 5 Example HTTP Plug-in File

```
<?xml version="1.0"?>
<Config>
    <Log RefreshInterval="10" LogLevel="Error" ⏎
Name="/opt/WebSphere/AppServer/logs/native.log" />
    <VirtualHostGroup Name="default_host">
        <VirtualHost Name="www.mysite.com:80" />
    </VirtualHostGroup>
<!-- ### Start of Main Section #### -->
<!-- Portal Application -->
    <ServerCluster Name="portalApplication Server Group" RetryInterval="15"
LoadBalance="RoundRobin">
        <Server Name="portalApp" LoadBalanceWeight="5">
            <Transport Hostname="serverA.mydomain.com" ⏎
Port="10000" Protocol="http" />
        </Server>
        <Server Name="portalAppCloned" LoadBalanceWeight="5">
            <Transport Hostname="serverB.mydomain.com" ⏎
Port="10000" Protocol="http" />
        </Server>
    <PrimaryServers>
        <Server Name="portalApp"/>
    </PrimaryServers>
```

```
<SecondaryServers>
      <Server Name="portalAppCloned"/>
  </SecondaryServers>
    </ServerCluster>
    <UriGroup Name="portalAppEAR/portalApp_URIs">
        <Uri Name="/portal/*" />
    </UriGroup>
    <Route ServerCluster="portalApplication Server Group"
        UriGroup="portalAppEAR/portalApp_URIs"
        VirtualHostGroup="default_host" />
</Config>
```

Considering for a moment the WebSphere version 4 example in Listing 7-3, the essential changes to this file are those line items in bold shown in Listing 7-5.

Listing 7-5. WebSphere Version 4 Key Clone ID Changes

```
      <Server CloneID="uk396h0g" Name="portalApp">
          <Transport Hostname="serverA.mydomain.com" ↵
Port="10000" Protocol="http" />
      </Server>
      <Server CloneID="ao356hib" Name="portalApp">
          <Transport Hostname="serverB.mydomain.com" ↵
Port="10000" Protocol="http" />
          </Server>
```

The CloneID directive is a unique identifier that WebSphere associates with cloned application servers. The other change, the secondary Server directive, is fairly self-explanatory.

 NOTE   The CloneID directive is generated by WebSphere when you create application server group clones. Don't change this value from the WebSphere-defined one.

The WebSphere version 5 example is a little more in depth. Listing 7-6 highlights the changes.

Listing 7-6. WebSphere Version 5 Example Clone ID Changes

```
<ServerCluster Name="portalApplication Server Group" RetryInterval="15"
LoadBalance="RoundRobin">
```

```
        <Server CloneID="uk396h0g" Name="portalApp" LoadBalanceWeight="5">
            <Transport Hostname="serverA.mydomain.com" Port="10000" ↵
Protocol="http" />
        </Server>
        <Server CloneID="zm791h0b" Name="portalAppCloned" ↵
LoadBalanceWeight="5">
            <Transport Hostname="serverB.mydomain.com" ↵
Port="10000" Protocol="http" />
        </Server>
    <PrimaryServers>
        <Server Name="portalApp"/>
    </PrimaryServers>
    <SecondaryServers>
        <Server Name="portalAppCloned"/>
    </SecondaryServers>

    </ServerCluster>
```

The addition of another server requires an additional directive to indicate the existence of another servicing server. The notable change here, though, in the WebSphere version 4 structure is the introduction of the `PrimaryServer`, `SecondaryServer`, and `LoadBalanceWeight` directives.

The `PrimaryServer` and `SecondaryServer` directives can be used to help support failover configurations (but this isn't mandatory). Essentially, these two directives allow you to support hot-standby or disaster recovery sites. With these directives in place, the configuration in Figure 7-10 will only see server A being used. Should server A fail and not respond to requests, the servers identified by `SecondaryServer` will be sent requests.

Without these `PrimaryServer` and `SecondaryServer` directives, the two servers, server A and server B, will receive requests from the HTTP plug-in based on the value of the `LoadBalanceWeight` directive. In the example case, the setting is 5 for each server. Given this, both servers will receive equal distribution of load.

As a rule of thumb, always keep this directive the same if you're using single-site configurations. That is, if you have all your backend WebSphere application servers located in the same server room or data center, keep the value the same and try to avoid distributing weight differently to different servers.

This value can be helpful in maintaining a good distribution of load where you may have a split-site configuration simultaneously processing requests. In this case, you may want to have the two HTTP servers configured opposite one another in terms of their `LoadBalanceWeight` setting. For example, if you set up a HTTP server plug-in file in Seattle, where server A is located, you set the `LoadBalanceWeight` value to be, for example, 2. However, server B is located in Washington; therefore, you may want to set the `LoadBalanceWeight` directive to, say, 5. The Washington-based HTTP server would be configured with the mirror configuration of server A, such as server A's LoadBalanceWeight being 5 and server B's LoadBalanceWeight being 2.

A common setting in both WebSphere version 4 and 5 plug-in configurations is the LoadBalance directive. This directive allows you to set up the master load-balancing configuration type for your environment. The options available are round-robin with weighting and random. WebSphere version 5 has a more sophisticated load distribution system than WebSphere version 4, which I discuss this further shortly.

By default, round-robin is the type of load distribution used if there is no LoadBalance directive implemented.

 NOTE   The round-robin value is overruled when you define session affinity settings. That is, in most cases, this value is only valid if you don't have any active sessions and all requests are stateless or the request is a new connection without a session.

WebSphere 5 Weighted Load Distribution

WebSphere version 5 introduced a sophisticated load distribution model that favors session affinity. Remember that by not having session affinity (in which your subsequent requests aren't sent to the server or clone that initially set up the session), you'll incur additional load overhead while your Web containers retrieve persisted session data from the session database or from in-memory replication.

Suppose, for instance, that you have an environment with only one Web server but two backend WebSphere application servers. With the LoadBalanceWeight setting, as each request that isn't sessionized (i.e., it isn't a user request that contains an active or valid session cookie) is sent to a server, the plug-in decrements the LoadBalanceWeight ratio by 1. This occurs until the value reaches 0. After all servers have had their ratio decremented to 0, the plug-in resets all weighted ratios to their original value and starts the process again. Let's look at an example.

Say you have a plug-in file on the Web server that is configured in a way that has the following directives set as follows:

- The LoadBalance directive is set to RoundRobin

- For server A, LoadBalanceWeight is 5

- For server B, LoadBalanceWeight is 2

As a user request initially comes into the Web server, the plug-in randomly picks the first server to send the request to (regardless of the `RoundRobin` setting). Here's the process:

1. If the plug-in selects server A for the first request, the `LoadBalanceWeight` value for server A is decremented by 1 to 4.

2. Another request comes in, and this request is sent to server B, which has its ratio decremented by 2 to 1.

3. The next request comes in and this request has a session cookie tagged to server A. This request is therefore sent to server A, but server A's `LoadBalanceWeight` value doesn't get decremented on this request.

4. The next new request comes in and is sent to server B, whose `LoadBalanceWeight` value is decremented by 1 to 0.

5. The next request comes in and has a valid session cookie tagged to server B. Server B handles the request and its `LoadBalanceWeight` value isn't decremented.

6. The next request is new and is sent to server A. The `LoadBalanceWeight` value for server A is decremented by 1 to 3.

7. The next request is new and is sent to server B. The `LoadBalanceWeight` value for server B is unchanged; it stays at 0.

8. The next request is new and is sent to server A. The `LoadBalanceWeight` value for server A is decremented by 1 to 2.

9. The next request comes in and has a valid session cookie tagged to server A. Server A handles the request and its `LoadBalanceWeight` value isn't decremented.

10. The next request is new and is sent to server B. The `LoadBalanceWeight` value for server B is unchanged; it stays at 0.

11. The next request is new and is sent to server A. The `LoadBalanceWeight` value for server A is decremented by 1 to 1.

12. The next request is new and is sent to server B. The `LoadBalanceWeight` value for server B is unchanged; it stays at 0.

13. The next request is new and is sent to server A. The LoadBalanceWeight value for server A is decremented by 1 to 0.

14. The next request arrives and triggers all values to be reset back to their original settings. The request is deemed new and is sent to server B.

15. And on the process goes.

As you can see, this method of weighting your requests can provide a powerful mechanism for distributing your load. As you add in additional HTTP servers, this distributing mechanism becomes even more powerful.

An important point is that WebSphere 5.0.1 was released with changes to the operation of this weighting. Effectively, the change is that valid session cookie–based requests also decrement the value, but, as the value passes 0 and goes negative, this doesn't trigger a reset or any other state. Each time a request is sent to a server that has a negative value, the server will check to see if the other server had reached 0. If so, then the plug-in checks to see if by adding the original value of LoadBalanceWeight to the negative number it will increase beyond 0. If it does, the plug-in performs the operation and increments the LoadBalanceWeight of the once negatively valued server to the *negative_value + original starting value of LoadBalanceWeight*.

For example, if server A has its value at –3 and server B is at 0, the plug-in will attempt to take server A's value and add into the initial LoadBalanceWeight, which is 5. Because this takes the value back over 0, the process continues until both servers are at 0 (or the value of one of the servers is at negative something, and the *negative_value + original value* check is performed again).

If the value of server A is in fact –7, for example, then adding the initial value of a LoadBalanceWeight of 5 won't increase the value above 0. In this case, both servers will have their result of *current_value + initial_value* multiplied by another HTTP plug-in directive, maxWeight. By default, this is set to 2, so both servers will be reset to the following:

Server A: $(-7 + 5 \times 2) = 3$

Server B: $(0 + 2 \times 2) = 4$

Let's take a look at another key WebSphere version 5 HTTP plug-in directive that you can use to support external software or hardware-based load-balancing gear.

WebSphere 5 and External Load Balancers

On occasions, there may be a valid reason why you may not want to use the load-balancing capabilities supported within the HTTP plug-in. There's another plug-in directive, `ClusterAddress`, that allows you to force non–session affinity requests to an external load balancer.

The `ClusterAddress` directive is located at the top of the `ServerCluster` group directive as follows:

```
<ServerCluster Name="portalApplication Server Group" RetryInterval="15"
LoadBalance="RoundRobin">
        <ClusterAddress Name="myCiscoLoadBalancer">
                <Transport Hostname="myLoadBalancer.myDomain.com" ⏎
Port="80" Protocol="http" />
        </ClusterAddress>
        <Server Name="portalApp" LoadBalanceWeight="5">
                <Transport Hostname="serverA.mydomain.com" Port="10000" ⏎
Protocol="http" />
        </Server>
        <Server Name="portalAppCloned" LoadBalanceWeight="5">
                <Transport Hostname="serverB.mydomain.com" Port="10000" ⏎
Protocol="http" />
        </Server>
   <PrimaryServers>
        <Server Name="portalApp"/>
   </PrimaryServers>
  <SecondaryServers>
        <Server Name="portalAppCloned"/>
  </SecondaryServers>
</ServerCluster>
```

This directive works as follows: For all new requests that don't have an active session cookie, the plug-in will route the request to the `ClusterAddress` device—myLoadBalancer.mydomain.com in this example—for the external load balancer to handle which server the request should be sent to. Subsequent requests or requests that do have active session cookies will be sent to their affinity server.

Why use this directive? Consider for a moment all the discussion about load balancing and availability around the HTTP plug-in to date. In all cases, you've only been able to route requests to backend servers based on a rule (e.g., a defined route group) or an already established link via a session cookie.

This form of "soft" request distribution can fall down, however, in the case in which the next selected server, based on `LoadBalanceWeight`, is heavily loaded. This may be due to one large request that's consuming a lot of system resources or there could be a DoS attack or something else that is slowing the environment down (e.g., a bad network). Although it's possible to tweak the `RetryInterval` to lower values (under 5 seconds), which may provide a "quasi–server load litmus test," this doesn't provide an accurate test of server load.

Many of the high-end load balancers, and even many of the feature-rich software load balancers, allow you to configure them to do one of two things. First, you can configure them to probe the remote WebSphere application servers with a basic HTTP GET call and time the response, distributing the load accordingly. Second, you can install the load balancer's software on your WebSphere application server host and configure it so that the load balancer will continuously interrogate to determine the true load on the server. The load balancer will then route the initial request in a session to the least truly loaded server.

WebSphere 5 ConnectTimeout Setting

In Chapter 6, you explored various tuning options and settings associated with various operating systems' TCP/IP stack configurations. One key point that I discussed related to decreasing the TCP/IP time-out values within the operating system of your choice. I also discussed the risks associated with this, especially because your server that is hosting your WebSphere application server instance may be supporting other TCP/IP-based services. In this case, the setting changes would affect all TCP/IP-based services on the physical node.

To get around this, WebSphere version 5 supports a setting called ConnectTimeout that is accessible and tunable within the HTTP plug-in file used by your chosen HTTP server.

 NOTE This setting has no bearing on your environment if you're using a thick UI-based model in the place of a Web-based UI.

Within the Server directive of the HTTP plug-in configuration file, you can declare the ConnectTimeout setting and value as shown in Listing 7-7.

Listing 7-7. WebSphere Version 5 Example HTTP Plug-in File: ConnectTimeout Value

```
        <Server CloneID="uk396hOg" Name="portalApp" LoadBalanceWeight="5"
ConnectTimeout=10>
            <Transport Hostname="serverA.mydomain.com" Port="10000"
Protocol="http" />
        </Server>
```

As you can see from Listing 7-7, the ConnectTimeout value is set to 10, which refers to 10 seconds. This setting sets the plug-in manager to use a nonblocking TCP connect sequence with a timeout of 10 seconds. There isn't a rule of thumb for this setting. The best way to determine its value, if required at all, is to perform testing. Of course, the setting should be lower than that of the TCP/IP time-out value to be of any use.

If the server defined in the Server directive (to which the ConnectTimeout directive is associated) doesn't respond with a TCP connect within the defined value period (e.g., 10 seconds), the plug-in will mark that server as down for the retry period. The setting needs to be set based on your network bandwidth (i.e., speed, capacity, and latency) and the load of the remote server. If you're happy with 15 seconds of lag between client transactions because of a heavily loaded WebSphere application server, this ConnectTimeout directive should be set accordingly.

Finally, this setting can be very useful if you have frontend HTTP servers distributing user requests to backend WebSphere application servers that are located both locally and via WAN (e.g., such as servers located in another city for disaster recovery purposes). For remote servers, you may want to increase the value of this time-out directive, whereas as for local servers, you may want the setting to be lower (e.g., 10 to 20 seconds). For this reason, it's possible to set a different ConnectTimeout value on each server.

Session Failover and Persistence

Session persistence is an integral part of most Web-based applications. Because the primary protocol that Web transactions are conducted over, HTTP, is essentially stateless, there is no default mechanism for storing state. This is different from thick client environments, which may have a Java GUI operating on end user desktops. In this case, the application, or Java GUI that operates on the desktop, stores state in its memory space, like the majority of other client/server-based applications.

The way to get around the stateless environment situation is to employ a mechanism that binds itself to the user's session. There are several ways to implement this "stickiness," but the crux of the solution works by creating a token or identifier that is maintained by the Web client through each URL transaction and having that identifier associate itself with an object on the backend server.

In a Web-based Java world, this works by having a value, known as the session ID, tagged for each active end-user session. That session ID is then maintained by the Web container operating the WebSphere application server. The Web container builds up a session object that incorporates all the session attributes required for the user to use the Web-based application.

You'll need to take into account a number of performance and operational considerations with implementing failover and high availability when session objects are used. Here are a few of them:

- The J2EE Servlet specification requires that all requests for any one particular session is routed back to the originating Web container.

- Session objects can become large. Failing them over and maintaining them in memory can present a performance issue.

- If session persistence is used, consideration needs to be given to the database impact.

Within WebSphere, there are three forms of session affinity and persistence:

- No sessions—no affinity and no persistence required

- Session affinity with no persistence

- Session affinity with session persistence

The important point to remember is that once a session has been created, all subsequent requests made by that particular session will go back to the originating WebSphere application server (Web container). This is important to remember when modeling and designing your topological architecture. Consider it from an application perspective.

Let's say the application that you're serving on a WebSphere platform is some form of online payment system. You may have three pages to get through in order to make your payment. That is, page 1 is where you enter in your invoice or bill number, page 2 would be your personal details such as delivery address and so forth, and page 3 may be where you enter in your credit card details. Each page click will most likely store the preceding built-up information into a session object. Going from page 1 to page 2 will store the tax and invoice details into the user session, going from page 2 to page 3 will add in the personal details of the user, and so on.

Consider what will happen if between page 2 and page 3 the application server crashed. If you had no session persistence, your user would have to start all over again. This is only an annoyance, but it's something that users don't like (a studied, proven fact). If your application is more critical than for producing payments, then the consequences of a lost session could be higher.

Session persistence is therefore the key to surviving Web container failovers within WebSphere. The version of WebSphere you're running will determine your options for session persistence. With WebSphere version 4, the only option available is a database as data store. For version 5, you have the option of either using a database or using the WebSphere memory-to-memory replication or Dynamic Replication Service (DRS).

Before moving on, let's look at how a session failover would take place, as shown in Figure 7-11.

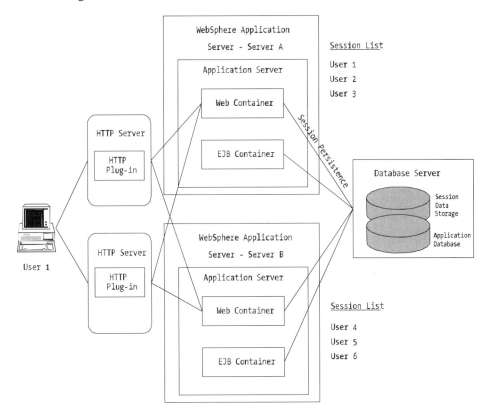

Figure 7-11. An example of session management with WebSphere

Figure 7-11 shows a user, user 1, logging into a WebSphere-based application. The heavier thick lines show the path user 1's requests would take after establishing a session with server A. You'll also note the session lists for both server A and server B, which depict what sessions are active on each server, on the right side of the image.

If server A failed, for whatever reason, the way in which persistent sessions work is that the subsequent request will be redirected by the plug-in to the next available server in the ServerGroup or ServerCluster list.

NOTE It's at this point that tuning the RetryInterval is important, because you don't want clients timing out in their browsers while the plug-in continues to attempt to send requests off to dead clones or application servers. I discuss this setting in more detail in the next few sections.

Figure 7-12 shows how the plug-in redirects all user requests away from the dead server to one of the remaining active servers, which in turn retrieves the session objects from the database.

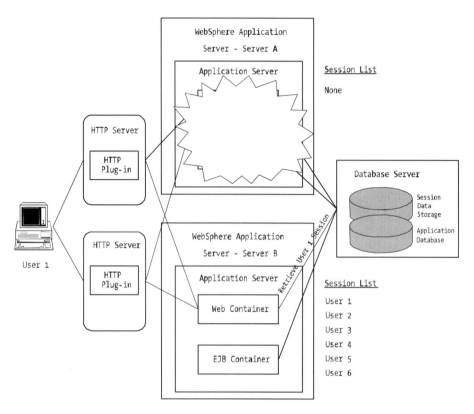

Figure 7-12. An example of session management with WebSphere in a failover scenario

As you can see, the session failover is transparent to the user with the caveat that there may be a slight delay (a couple of seconds) while the session is retrieved.

It goes without saying that persisting user sessions to a database introduces extra load onto the database tier. Be sure that you account for this type of load, as well as peak load periods when failover events are taking place. It's worthwhile assuming that during a peak period such as a failover situation, your load on specific components of your environment may increase threefold during initial transaction cutover.

You'll need to factor in a few other considerations into your design when you implement sessions or, more specifically, persistent sessions. That is, how do you ensure that your developers or the applications you're deploying into WebSphere support your chosen method of gluing sessions to requests?

WebSphere Session Identifiers

To make your sessions sticky and have them routed to the correct or desired application server, you need to configure your WebSphere Session Manager to support a specific session identifier type. WebSphere versions 4 and 5 support three types of session identifiers:

- Cookies

- URL rewriting

- SSL ID

WebSphere supports a new session management scope that is available as of WebSphere version 5. Unlike in WebSphere version 4, in which session identifiers were configured for the entire scope of the active Web container, it's possible with WebSphere version 5 to configure session management at a far more granular level. For example, it's possible to now configure session management at the following three levels:

- **WebSphere application server level**: Default configuration and settings are applied to all WAR/Web modules within the WebSphere application server.

- **Application level**: This setting allows configuration to be set for all WAR/Web modules in the deployed application.

- **Web module level**: This setting specifically sets session management properties at the WAR/Web module level.

Keeping all of this in mind, let's look at each of the session identifier types in more detail and examine their pros and cons.

Cookies

Standard *cookies* are the most popular way of managing sessions within J2EE applications or, more specifically, WebSphere. Cookies provide an easy method of hooking applications into sessions via the use of a servlet standard session construct called JSESSIONID.

The downside to cookies is that the user must support them in his or her browser—more specifically, the user must allow cookies. The upside to cookies is that they work well with WLM and session replication during failover events. They also don't require specific coding in your deployed applications to be supported. Unlike URL rewriting, which requires modification to application code to use it, cookies use standard get and set methods to obtain and store information into the session object.

URL Rewriting

URL rewriting is a form of managing sessions via placing a cookie ID blatantly in the URL string.

My personal preference is to avoid this option wherever possible and use cookies as the first alternative. Having the cookie ID in the URL opens the door to problems through URL correction and exposes some of the workings of your applications to the world.

URL rewriting is, however, the best choice when/if your end users don't use or support cookies. By placing the cookie ID in the URL, you can get around security issues and blockages imposed by personal firewalls and browsers.

The biggest downside to URL rewriting is the need for your developers to modify their application code to support the URL rewriting. URL rewriting also can't be used in static sites. You'll always need to push the cookie ID along from page to page and link to link to preserve the hook back into the session. As soon as one page is moved that doesn't have a URL rewrite in the linkage, the cookie ID is lost.

NOTE URL rewriting is a sound backup solution to standard cookies. If you configure WebSphere to use cookies and URL rewriting, WebSphere will use cookies as first preference and, if it isn't supported by the remote browser, it will revert back to URL rewriting for that session.

SSL ID

SSL ID session linkage is the least used of all session identifier types. It's provided as an absolute last-chance option for application environments to support sessions. Because of this, it does have many limitations, some of which may be acceptable to you if this is your last chance to use sessions.

Essentially, SSL ID session linkage works by requiring that you configure your Web server as an HTTPS- or SSL-based server. WebSphere in turn can access the SSL session ID (different from the WebSphere user session ID) and use that SSL session ID to generate a user session ID.

The downside to SSL ID–based configurations is that you must employ some form of stick load-balancer in front of the Web servers to ensure that subsequent users requests go back to the originating Web server (not necessarily WebSphere). Because the SSL ID is generated via the SSL engine within the Web server, as soon as the user accesses the backend WebSphere application server via a different Web server, the SSL ID will change and the user session will be lost.

Not all Web servers support SSL ID–based tracking. Currently, WebSphere only supports iPlanet Web server/SunOne Web server and IBM HTTPD server. As previously mentioned, to support the SSL ID sticky routing requirement an intelligent hardware or software load-balancing switch is also needed, such as products from Cisco and Alteon (now owned by NortelNetworks), and the IBM WebSphere Edge server.

If you also want your user sessions to participate in workload management, you'll need to employ either URL rewriting or cookies to attach the `CloneID` directive to the session identifier. Without this, the requests can't find their way back to the appropriate application server.

Web Container Failover

The Web container failover is a fairly simply affair with the control and responsibility for container failover being that of the HTTP plug-in. Via specific IP network responses (or lack of response), the HTTP plug-in will determine that a specific Web container is dead.

Table 7-1 outlines some likely reasons why a Web container would fail in a typical environment.

Table 7-1. Web Container Primary Causes for Failure

Reason	Failure Type	HTTP Plug-in Response Time to Problem
Physical server unavailable (i.e., it's being shut down)	Physical	Lengthy
Environment overload—incorrect queue settings, DoS attack	Software	Variable; can be lengthy
Application JVM crash	Software	Fast
Network infrastructure problem—broken NIC or cable	Physical	Lengthy
Manual intervention—stopping application for deployment or upgrade	Software	Fast

These causes may seem fairly obvious and are typically the reasons why most Java components fail or cease to work. They are all, however, factors that I've touched on or will touch on during this book; therefore, they shouldn't be a problem or cause (a large) impact to your WebSphere platform.

Removing single points of failure such as adding in additional cluster members (WebSphere application servers) and using redundant hardware components is the best advice for big-picture platform availability. However, to ensure your Web container is able to sustain outages and failover user transactions to other nodes, you must use ServerGroups (for WebSphere version 4) and ServerClusters (for WebSphere version 5).

You explored the definition of these two concepts back in Chapter 4, and you've covered them again at length in this chapter with respect to HTTP plug-ins and WLM. Essentially, the result of a container failover is handled by the HTTP plug-in configuration. It is this small but vital piece of your WebSphere platform that handles the interface to your Web container's WLM functionality.

If a Web container fails, the Web container doesn't "failover" to the remaining WebSphere application servers (all operating their own clustered Web containers), the HTTP plug-in determines that a server has died and there's a need to divert all subsequent requests to another server.

Failover Process

In the event the HTTP plug-in identifies that a Web container has stopped listening, the HTTP plug-in will perform one of many functions. Referring back to Table 7-1, the third column suggests approximate times for how long it will take a HTTP plug-in to acknowledge that a Web container is unavailable, mark that server as dead, and move on to the next available server. This is important because all the backend application servers in the world won't help you out if you're banking up connections waiting for response times on your user requests.

The "lengthy" time interval items, being "Physical server unavailable" and "Network infrastructure problem," are probably the worst offenders to user transaction delays. The reason for this is that the plug-in will continue to try to connect to the host system until the local host system's TCP connection time-out threshold has been reached. This is different from the "Application JVM crash" scenario. In this case, the operating system of the WebSphere application server, while functional, doesn't have an active listening port on the specific port that the HTTP plug-in is attempting to connect to. In this scenario, the operating system responds back immediately with a connection refused message (no different from a connection refused message if you try to telnet into a server in which the telnet daemon has been shut down or deactivated).

As you saw in Chapter 6, you need to undertake changing these types of settings with great care. If you're running WebSphere version 5, there is a HTTP plug-in feature to get around this problem, which I discuss shortly. If you're running WebSphere version 4, you may want to consider reducing the TCP connection time-out setting on your operating system if you have stand-alone Web servers.

 CAUTION Unless you know exactly what you're doing, don't change the TCP connection time-out settings on your WebSphere application server if you're running a combined HTTP server/WebSphere application server on the same physical node. Also note that changing the connection setting on some operating systems may affect both inbound and outbound connections.

There are several settings configured in the WebSphere version 5 HTTP plug-in on the Web servers that can help you eliminate delays between when servers are made unavailable. Unfortunately, these options are only available in WebSphere version 5. The settings that you can change to help eliminate delays in recognizing dead or unresponsive clones are as follows:

- RetryInterval

- ConnectTime

In the next sections you'll examine these settings in more detail.

WebSphere Version 5 RetryInterval Setting

The RetryInterval setting is a HTTP plug-in directive that allows you to specify the time between when a marked clone or application server is down and when the HTTP plug-in will try again to connect to it. Having this setting too low will result in a "flip-flop" situation in which servers may not respond fast enough after the interval has expired, and the HTTP plug-in will simply continue to mark it bad. There maybe in-flight transactions currently active on the specific Web container or application server that are marked as bad, yet it takes just one failure to cause them to be marked as bad. If this setting is set too high, cascade failures in your environment in which one of two servers is down and the other server is faulting because it's overloaded by full peak load of all transactions will occur.

Consider a situation in which you have two clones on two servers (four clones in total). Server A crashes and requires a reboot. In this scenario (see Table 7-1), the plug-in keeps sending requests to the downed server's clones because it (the plug-in) is still waiting for a response back from the downed server. Instead of there being a response of any kind, there is nothing, so the plug-in assumes that the server is simply bogged down.

If this setting then is set to a value that's too low, say 120 seconds, and it takes 180 seconds to reboot a server, you'll be waiting for up to 4 minutes for the clones on server A to be available again. All the while, end users are experiencing what they see as poor performance and time-outs unless they've persisted session affinity to the clones on server B. New requests will either connect randomly or round-robin between the servers, in which case up to 50 percent of all new requests will suffer time-outs and delays.

You should also be conscious of the fact that if server B becomes overloaded with too many connections, the plug-in will mark all of its clones as bad also. If this happens, it could be several minutes before any user transactions take place. Therefore, as a guide, you should set the `RetryInterval` value quite high, in the vicinity of 300 to 900 seconds, depending on your environment configuration.

The reason I recommend setting the value high is so that you can help to eliminate lengthy delays for customers as much as possible. If you set this value to 600 seconds, and your TCP connect time-out value is 45 seconds, the most your users will have to wait is 45 seconds until the plug-in realizes that the remote clone is down and marks it bad for 10 minutes. In most cases, a downed server or application server will be rebooted or brought back up within 10 to 15 minutes, so long as there are no critical failures.

One alternative here is to reduce time-out waiting periods is to decrease the TCP time-out value which, as I mentioned, is only recommended if you know what you're doing and this occurs preferably only on a dedicated HTTP server. To set this value, insert the directive `RetryInterval=<value>` in the `<ServerCluster>` line (e.g., `<ServerCluster name="MyCluster" RetryInterval=900>`). The other alternative is to look at the `ConnectTime` value, as discussed in the next section.

WebSphere Version 5 ConnectTime Setting

The `ConnectTime` setting is another HTTP plug-in directive that helps to alleviate the problems presented in the previous section with relation to connection time-outs for downed servers.

Because the plug-in operates at an application layer rather at the IP layer, it's not able to directly detect a server's operational network status. As such, scenarios like those discussed in the previous section can occur.

The `ConnectTime` directive allows you to override the HTTP plug-in server's TCP time-out values by clocking the time it takes to actually perform a connection from the plug-in to the desired clone or application server. This value shouldn't be set to a level so low that it's disadvantaged by moderately loaded systems, and it shouldn't be set so high that it becomes ineffective. My belief is that if a WebSphere application server or clone can't respond to a connect within 15 seconds, there's something wrong other than load (and you should dust off your performance management models!).

The setting can be tied in with the other WebSphere version 5 settings you've looked at such as `RetryInterval` and `LoadBalanceWeight`, as well as using round-robin load-balancing. As an example, consider an environment in which if you had two servers operating four WebSphere clones in total (two clones per physical node), you could set the plug-in file up as follows, in this order:

First clone	Clone A, server A, `ConnectTime=10,` `LoadBalanceWeight=5`
Second clone	Clone B, server B, `ConnectTime=10,` `LoadBalanceWeight=6`
Third clone	Clone B, server A, ConnectTime=12, `LoadBalanceWeight=7`
Fourth clone	Clone A, server B, `ConnectTime=15,` `LoadBalanceWeight=8`

Configuring your environment in this fashion means that you're distributing your load "odd-even" between your servers to eliminate single server overloading and, as a safety blanket, you slightly increase the connection time-out in the plug-in as you go along to cater for potential extra delays should you start to have an unstable environment.

This is a very conservative approach. If you're comfortable with your stress and volume testing, and the overall sizing of your environment, the plug-in file would be better tuned as follows:

First clone	Clone A, server A, `ConnectTime=10,` `LoadBalanceWeight=5`
Second clone	Clone B, server B, `ConnectTime=10,` `LoadBalanceWeight=5`
Third clone	Clone B, server A, `ConnectTime=10,` `LoadBalanceWeight=5`
Fourth clone	Clone A, server B, `ConnectTime=10,` `LoadBalanceWeight=5`

Keeping all servers equal helps squash any slight load distribution differential that may creep in.

In summary, Web container failover is simply a configuration item in your WebSphere administration console. The control and management of the transitions affected by the failover are managed by the HTTP plug-in. As you've seen, there are a vast number of optional strategies that you can employ to help with Web container failover and availability.

EJB Container Failover and High Availability

The EJB container and the Web container are probably the two most important application parts of the WebSphere environment. In this section, you're going to look at promoting high availability and failover capabilities within your application server's EJB container.

EJB Container Overview

The EJB container sits within the same JVM space as the Web container within your WebSphere application server. The EJB container is responsible for managing the runtime and operational life cycle of your application's EJB components. The way in which you ensure that the EJB container is highly available and is failover solid isn't too different from that of the Web container and, in fact, many settings and issues are the same, just simply transposed to an EJB world.

Like many components in WebSphere version 5, there are many differences between the WebSphere version 4 EJB container and the WebSphere version 5 EJB container. Both versions 4 and 5 provide a location service daemon (LSD) to provide a level of indirection for accessing EJB home lookup. Used for non-WebSphere-based object request broker (ORB) as well as other proprietary interfaces, the LSD can also be used directly for other WebSphere components, in which case the ORB doesn't have the WLM flags set for the period of the transaction.

Workload Management

Workload management of EJBs is an inherent feature of WebSphere's EJB container. Since version 4 of WebSphere, no implicational changes were required to take advantage of EJB WLM.

The way in which this works is that the ORB that facilitates object brokerage services in the container is configured with a WLM plug-in specific for the EJB container. When lookups are made by clients trying to obtain references to EJBs in the EJB container, the ORB identifies via a WLM flag that a particular EJB is part of a WLM server group. This allows the ORB to understand that if a request comes for the EJB again from another client but finds that it can't service the request because the initial EJB container has become unavailable, then the ORB will obtain the reference to an EJB in another clone via a list it maintains. It also provides the ability to load balance or round-robin between other available cloned EJBs.

Just like with the Web container, you can implement different routing methods for the EJB container to better support your type of WebSphere environment. The four primary forms of EJB request routing are as follows:

- Weighted round-robin (default)

- Prefer local

- In process

- Affinity based

Let's look at each in more detail.

Weighted Round-Robin

The *weighted round-robin* routing algorithm used within WebSphere version 5's EJB WLM routing is quite similar to the weighted round-robin method used by the Web container and the plug-in during Web-based WLM.

In essence, weighted round-robin WLM allows you to set routing weights on requests to EJBs on both local and/or remote EJB containers. For example, say you have two servers, both with two EJB containers, all of which are operating in a WLM EJB container cluster. The server A EJB round-robin configuration is configured with weighted round-robin values of 5, while server A is configured, via the ORB configuration and properties settings, with a value of 10. This allows all requests to source EJB objects from the local server, rather than going out on to the wire to access EJB objects from server B.

Prefer Local

The *prefer local* algorithm allows you to have your EJB clients access WLM EJB services local to the node that the client is operating from as a preference. If there are no EJB resources available in any local server groups on the local node, the EJB client, via the WLM-aware ORB, will attempt to gain access to EJB resources on remote nodes participating in WLM.

The weighted round-robin algorithm is used to select desired EJB clones on the local server if they're available. Similar to most of the EJB and Web container routing algorithms, the specific EJB clones participating as part of a server group still decrement their weighting until they reach 0, at which point they reset to their initiating weighting.

In Process

In-process routing works by ensuring that the request for an EJB is routed to an in-process EJB clone or an EJB clone local to the application server.

This is the least resource-intensive algorithm of all options available, because the requests from client to EJB are maintained within the same application server space. Therefore, no network or RMI calls are required to remote server groups or other JVMs.

If the EJB clone is down within the specific application server, weighted round-robin is used and the WLM-aware ORB is queried for the next best weighted EJB container clone.

Affinity Based

There are two types of affinity-based routing within the EJB-based server groups. Essentially, affinity routing, as its name implies, allows you to route based on one of two affinity strengths.

The first affinity type is known as *applied affinity*. This affinity type is typically used for EJB clients requesting IORs via the LSD. During the course of the transaction between the EJB client and the EJB itself, the linkage and routing between the two is maintained. All subsequent requests to the EJB are maintained along the initially defined routing when the transaction was initially set up. This model uses the weighted set approach, and each request decrements the weighted value by 1 until it reaches 0. However, because the ideology behind this routing algorithm is to maintain the linkage between the EJB client and the chosen EJB clone, the EJB client will continue to make queries to the EJB clone even while it has a weighted value of 0.

The second type of affinity-based routing is called *transactional affinity*. This form of routing follows container transactions, and all requests for EJB methods and interfaces are maintained to the initial EJB clone at the beginning of the transaction until the transaction completes. You need to be cognizant of transactional affinity and be sure that your application code has been developed with the ability to "clean up" after a failure in communicating to a remote EJB clone.

EJB Container Failover

Like Web container failover, when we talk about container failover scenarios, we're not necessarily talking about abstracting the failover technique of the container itself. Instead, we (and WebSphere) focus in on how to get the next client request to the next working or available container instance, fast. As you'd expect, WebSphere versions 4 and 5 operate slightly differently when it comes to EJB container failover.

WebSphere version 4 works simply by the client ORB maintaining a list of workload managed EJB homes across multiple WebSphere application server clones. In the event of a failover scenario, the Java client will experience a time-out for accessing the remote EJB and reattempt to look up the context. With the

`MaxCommFailures` setting set to the default of 0 (meaning that as soon as there is any communication failure, an exception is thrown to the ORB), the ORB will reroute the EJB request to the next available EJB container clone. Figure 7-13 shows how the WebSphere version 4 model works.

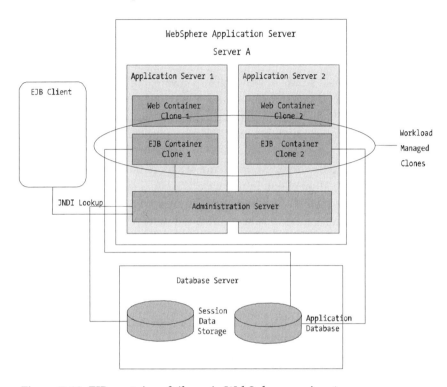

Figure 7-13. EJB container failover in WebSphere version 4

If the ORB goes through all available EJB container clones (clone 1 and clone 2 in Figure 7-13) in the list and they're all marked unavailable, the ORB will rerequest an updated list of available EJB container clones from the administration server. This may loop until a clone becomes available or your EJB clients and ORB will be presented with a `CORBA.NO_IMPLEMENT` exception. I discuss this further shortly.

In the case of the WebSphere version 5, the failover scenario and events that follow it are a little different. There are two possible courses of action. One is if you're running native WebSphere-based application code under a WebSphere application server (as opposed to using legacy CORBA code), and second is if you're running native WebSphere-based application code via any other non-IBM EJB implementation. If, however, you're using non-WebSphere-running applications (such as CORBA or non-IBM J2EE implementations) and you need to access local WebSphere-based EJBs, WebSphere version 5 has support for LSD.

The LSD is kind of like a route map that maintains information about specific application servers that are exposing EJB containers (and EJB homes). With the LSD approach, clients (Java, C++, or otherwise) obtain an IOR to the LSD as opposed to the specific EJB that they're after. The LSD then provides an IOR to the best available EJB container clone for the client request. This sort of connection is deemed to be non-server-group-aware and, as such, the request isn't directly aware of load balancing and WebSphere-specific WLM policies active within the containers. Because there is limited ability for non-WLM-aware clients to automatically participate in load balancing, there are limitations in what is available in terms of failover for your application code, although it's still somewhat seamless!

For clients that are not WLM- or server group–aware, if a request is made to an already obtained EJB IOR reference, but that EJB container or application server has failed or crashed, the client receives an error (a commFailure) and goes back to the LSD to rerequest another active EJB container clone to interface with.

If the client is said to be server group–aware, it's more than likely that it is a WebSphere-based application client. In this case, the client still may go via the LSD to obtain the initial IOR. Within the return response of the initial IOR of the first available EJB container clone has been provided to the client. If the client is, in fact, WLM-aware, it now has a list of available server groups and EJB container clones to communicate to directly. Because the client is WLM-aware, subsequent calls are made using the list of available server groups and EJB container clones it was passed by the LSD.

Handling Failovers

When errors occur with your EJB communications, you're EJB application components will react the much the same way as the plug-in does when various events occur. To be more specific, Table 7-1 explores five different scenarios within a WebSphere environment and labels their "response time to problem." This is an important table for both Web components and EJB components.

EJB components follow the same rules of time-outs and delays when it comes to failures with the server groups and/or servers. Essentially, there are five key messages that will be thrown to your EJB clients:

- CORBA.COMM_FAILURE

- CORBA.NO_RESPONSE

- CORBA.COMPLETE_STATUS

- CORBA.INTERNAL

- CORBA.NO_IMPLEMENT

Those familiar with CORBA will understand these messages well, but essentially, they're the basic communications status messages that the ORB and EJB clients handle. These are also the hooks in which your EJB clients will use to failover, change server clones, or retry during the course of the failures depicted in Table 7-1.

COMM_FAILURE is just that—a CORBA communications failure of some sort. If your EJB client is making an initial request to the ORB or LSD to obtain an IOR for an EJB home, and it is thrown a CORBA.COMM_FAILURE exception, the WebSphere ORB will determine what state the transaction is in. From this, the ORB will determine that it is an initial lookup request and simply resend the request to the LSD to locate another server clone to direct the EJB client request to.

If the exception is thrown after the initial context has been found, the WLM components of the ORB will handle the CORBA.COMM_FAILURE exception. The ORB will then mark the problem EJB container clone as bad and resend the request to another operating EJB container or server group (based on your routing algorithms).

NO_RESPONSE is an exception thrown typically when there is a server down or something is internally wrong with the remote ORB (wherever or whatever vendor ORB that may be). The handling of a NO_RESPONSE exception is much the same as the COMM_FAILURE, and the same process of redirection to another working, EJB container clone will be the resulting action by the ORB.

COMPLETE_STATUS is a resulting secondary exception message that is thrown when a COMM_FAILURE or NO_RESPONSE exception is thrown to the EJB client and/or WebSphere ORB. There are three basic state messages that will accompany the COMPLETE_STATUS exception:

- COMPLETED_YES

- COMPLETED_NO

- COMPLETED_MAYBE

If a COMM_FAILURE message is received by the EJB client and/or ORB after an initial context lookup has been made (and the active list of server clones is present with the EJB client), and COMPLETE_STATUS is COMPLETED_YES, then everything continues on. In this case, there was some form of error somewhere in the transaction pipeline, but the transaction completed successfully.

If COMPLETE_STATUS is COMPLETED_NO, then the request is rerequested via another available EJB container clone.

If COMPLETE_STATUS is COMPLETED_MAYBE, then nothing can occur. The EJB client or client code must handle this exception itself and include logic to rerequest the request from the beginning of the transaction.

In the `COMPLETED_MAYBE` state, the CORBA ORB isn't sure whether the transaction completed cleaning. Therefore, it doesn't deem it safe to continue on with the transaction (consider double payments as a reason this makes good sense).

The `INTERNAL` exception is thrown when all remote ORBs aren't available. In this scenario, the total environment is down and a full restart is required.

The final exception type is the `NO_IMPLEMENT` exception. This exception is thrown by the ORB when all attempts to make requests to all EJB container clones in the once-accurate server group list are unavailable. The ORB can be tuned using the `RequestRetriesCount` and `RequestRetriesDelay` values for this scenario.

There are no golden rules for these settings, but you should set them to a value that isn't so low that your environment doesn't retry enough times to get over transient problems, but you shouldn't set them so high so that the components continually retry.

At some point, your environment may be simply broken and will require a restart. I've discussed ways to mitigate these single points of failure in the environment through split WebSphere domains and cells, multiple servers, distributed environments, and so forth. Using these design considerations, you need to model the optimum setting that suits *your* environment.

Workload Management and EJBs

This chapter has mainly focused on the ORB aspects of the EJB container failover and support. Now you'll go over some key considerations that need to be made or understood with regard to EJB clients. In this section, you'll look at how failover affects the different forms of EJB caching.

 NOTE   You'll explore more aspects of EJB performance and availability best practice development in Chapter 10.

Chapter 9 looks at ways that EJBs can be cached by the EJB container. Caching can greatly improve performance by using design principles, such as EJB pools, that provide a construct for EJBs to stay activated until they're called on by EJB clients rather than starting up and shutting down at the beginning and end of each transaction.

Without wanting to repeat Chapter 9's discussion, there are essentially three states that your EJB caching settings can be in. These are referred to as caching options A, B, and C. If you don't want to use any specific EJB caching, option C is the default setting for EJB caching and is automatically enabled when you go to deploy your EJBs via the Application Assembly Tool (AAT).

NOTE I discuss in Chapter 9 that once you've set up the EJB caching in AAT prior to deploying your EJB-JARs, you can modify and change the EJB caching settings in the IBM extension's deployment descriptor.

To recap how to cache EJBs, how they operate, and how they fit into a failover scenario, consider the fact that during a single transaction, WLM ensures that the client is directed to the EJB container that was involved at the beginning of the transaction. If your EJB is an entity EJB maintaining a persistence layer between your application logic and the database, you don't want entity EJBs to be managed correctly in the event of a failover situation.

However, once the transaction is completed, and potentially a new one commences, the request can go to any available WLM-based EJB container clone. In this case, the entity EJB can be reloaded at will and no harm is caused to data integrity or your persistence layer. Specific to entity EJBs, as long as you use EJB caching option C or B, then entity EJBs can happily (and safely) participate in WLM.

Option A EJB caching is what I call a *full cache*. Once the EJB is loaded (via ejbLoad()), it stays loaded for the whole time. This means that other EJB clients can access the EJB construct and break the model. In Chapter 9, I discuss the fact that option A caching isn't recommended in a clustered environment because WebSphere requires that no other changes to the persistence layer (the database) can take place during a transaction unless it's managed via a singular EJB container.

Therefore, EJB caching for entity EJBs can only be done via option B and option C caching. That said, it's possible to workload-manage just the home interfaces of entity EJBs under option A. This provides a middle ground for WLM of entity EJBs and provides some limited support for failover. Note that the entity EJB itself using option A isn't clusterable—just the home interface.

When you consider stateful and stateless EJBs, stateful EJBs cause headaches when you try to give them the ability to failover. WebSphere doesn't support this, but I've seen cases in which sites have tried to implement stateful EJB failover capabilities. The rule here is to use stateless EJBs as much as you can. Due to their nature, it's easy to have them failover to other servers and clones without having to worry about maintaining transient states.

Table 7-2 summarizes the EJBs available in WebSphere versions 4 and 5, and notes which ones are clusterable and can partake in WLM environments.

Table 7-2. Summary of Clusterable EJBs in WebSphere 4 and 5

EJB	Type	WebSphere 4	WebSphere 5	Clusterable
Session bean	Stateless	Y	Y	Y
Session bean	Stateful	Y	Y	N
Session bean	Home interface	Y	Y	Y
Entity bean	Container managed (option A)	Y	Y	N
Entity bean	Bean managed (option A)	Y	Y	N
Entity bean	Home interface (option A)	Y	Y	Y
Entity bean	Home interface (options B and C)	Y	Y	Y
Entity bean	Container managed (options B and C)	Y	Y	Y
Entity bean	Bean managed (options B and C)	Y	Y	Y
Message-driven beans		N	Y	Y

As you can see from Table 7-2, despite the inherent complexity of EJBs, there is a fair degree of cluster support for them in WebSphere. The only EJB that isn't clusterable is the full failover of entity EJBs under option A. In this situation, with option A, you wouldn't want to use it anyway because it doesn't properly support clustering due to restrictions with the data integrity of the persistence layer mechanism.

Option A, as discussed in Chapter 9, is one I recommend everyone stay away from. Option B is the number one choice for performance of EJB components. More on that in Chapter 10.

Summary

In this chapter, you explored the many facets of WebSphere high availability. By this point, you should have a clear idea of what WebSphere can provide and what options exist for your highly available WebSphere environment.

Always remember, there are many ways to "skin the cat," and you should now understand that there are many ways to configure WebSphere to be highly available. Horizontal clustering, vertical clustering, domain clustering, and even component clustering all promote availability and scalability within your WebSphere application server.

CHAPTER 8

External WebSphere System Availability

IT'S ALL WELL AND GOOD that you may have a highly available, high-performing WebSphere environment, but if your critical network infrastructure component and external systems aren't performing well, then you may as well run your production WebSphere environment on your home PC!

In this chapter, I'll discuss some guidelines for high availability in external systems and components such Network File System (NFS) and Lightweight Directory Access Protocol (LDAP) servers, firewalls, and database components.

WebSphere's Reliance on Available External Systems

WebSphere's power is its ability to interface with myriad external systems to provide a centralized application delivery platform. Like many enterprise application systems, WebSphere's value is its ability to obtain data from almost any source and, through smart application development, combine that data to form value-driven output.

Because of this ability to interface with many third-party systems, it's important to understand and recognize the implications of interfacing with systems that may themselves be single points of failure or lack any solid performance or availability architecture mechanisms. Although this book isn't a book about how to best architect a Java 2 Enterprise Edition (J2EE)/WebSphere-based application, it is about ensuring that you have a guide when interfacing WebSphere with other non-WebSphere platform products.

Therefore, in this chapter, you'll look at a few of the more common platform derivatives:

- LDAP servers

- NFS servers

- Network infrastructure (routers, firewalls, and load balancers)

- Database failover considerations

By the end of this chapter, you'll understand what to consider if you have to interface any of these non-WebSphere systems with your core platform. This chapter isn't about necessarily *how* to configure those systems but about what aspects of the platform, systems, or technical architecture you need to be wary of when integrating with WebSphere.

LDAP Server Availability

LDAP is a data store–based system that's somewhat like a database but instead of being object-orientated or relational, it's directory based. The key to an LDAP environment is that it's a high-read, low-write infrastructure. Tuning an LDAP environment is about ensuring that Input/Output (I/O) is distributed across many disks and that caching and network infrastructure are optimized and sized correctly.

WebSphere supports several LDAP servers:

- IBM Secureway Directory Server

- Novell eDirectory server

- Lotus Domino Enterprise Server

- Sun ONE Directory Server

- Windows 2000 Active Directory (with LDAP extensions)

You'll now look at some LDAP servers and how they integrate with WebSphere.

Options and Considerations

In this chapter, I'll assume you have a working understanding of each of these platform technologies. I'll focus on what to consider when integrating WebSphere with these technologies in a highly available manner.

Too often I've been involved with WebSphere implementations that are pear-shaped because of poorly performing or low-availability third-party systems. Although an external interfacing system with long transaction times (for example, greater than five seconds) isn't necessarily a bad thing, solid application architecture and design needs to insulate the online WebSphere applications from the slower performing external application. An example of this is having a splash screen that presents a message to the user saying "Please wait…" or prefetching the required information, if possible, while the user is logging into the application and thus hiding (masking) any high-latency transactions.

In a LDAP and WebSphere mixed environment, if your WebSphere applications require constant access to the LDAP environment, then the LDAP servers should be clustered. Like WebSphere clustering techniques, there are three forms of clustering available for LDAP environments:

- Hardware clustering

- LDAP server clustering

- A combination of both

As you saw in earlier chapters, hardware clustering is the use of third-party "clusterware" products that provide failover and active-standby (or active-active) clustering solutions. By using a clusterware solution such as Hewlett-Packard's MC/ServiceGuard, Veritas Cluster Server, or something similar (see Chapter 7), you're able to set up a high-availability cluster with a master/slave configuration. Should one of the nodes fail, the clusterware would "Internet Protocol (IP) address failover" the LDAP service to another, working server. WebSphere clients would autonomously switch over to the remaining server.

LDAP server clustering is a byproduct of the LDAP technology. LDAP lends itself to being a highly available and robust technology at a fundamental level. Because it's a high-read, low-write technology, the synchronization sophistication isn't as complex and involved as it is for relational or object-oriented database systems such as Oracle, DB2, and ObjectStore.

Therefore, the inherent nature of LDAP means that you can gain some availability advantages when using it. In LDAP vendor-speak, an LDAP server is predominantly either a master or a replica (there are other subtypes, but I'll leave these out for the moment). If you're running an LDAP server that's being relied on by WebSphere online-based applications, use master/replica configurations to ensure that you have a failover device available should the master fail.

The third form of implementing LDAP availability is to use a combination of both IP failover clusterware and the inherent or built-in LDAP master/replica availability features.

You'll now look at the implementation of a highly available LDAP cluster in a WebSphere environment.

Implementation and Performance

It's important to remember that like any failover-capable system, there's a need to be able to control and manage transactions that may be "inflight" during the point of failure. The application developers need to write application code that supports LDAP connection failure exceptions and timeouts and that handles transaction failures and transaction rollbacks.

It's not uncommon nowadays to use LDAP over Secure Sockets Layer (SSL), meaning that you'll also need to employ some form of SSL engine on both sides of your LDAP server. This form of LDAP (sometimes referred to as LDAPS) will incur a performance hit with the overhead of SSL. Consider using SSL offloaders or SSL-compatible crypto cards that are available from most leading server vendors.

If your application is a distributed application, such as the example of a site in Seattle and a site in Washington, configuring an LDAP farm using LDAP master/replica data replication techniques is probably the best option to use for failover. This way, you're not only implementing a failover-supportive LDAP environment, but you're also employing a design that promotes performance with each site potentially having its own local LDAP replica server.

In terms of maintaining a master across all the LDAP servers in your environment, either you can use a load balancer that'll simply redirect your LDAP requests from your WebSphere hosts to the most appropriate LDAP instance or you can use the hardware-clustered solution to support a derivative of IP failover.

In this scenario, you can set up the LDAP cluster to have a master and replica LDAP architecture, as well as a master and secondary configuration in the clusterware layer. Your cluster can then expose a generic server name such as myLDAPCluster.mydomain.com, which, using IP address failover cluster configurations, will only need to communicate to myLDAPCluster.mydomain.com. Figure 8-1 illustrates this approach.

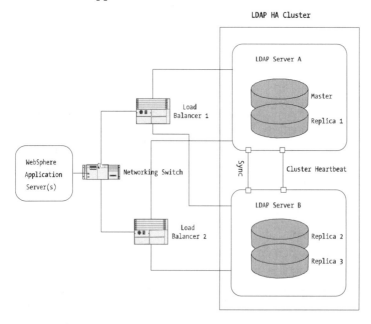

Figure 8-1. High-availability LDAP implementation

The model used in Figure 8-1 provides a solid performing and highly available LDAP farm for your WebSphere-based applications. In this example, the load balancers distribute the requests to the most appropriate LDAP instance. The configuration also supports the ability to distribute requests based on a master-secondary configuration that's mastered by the active-standby cluster. This provides the ability for clients to interface either via a global name (for example, LDAPCluster.mydomain.com) using the cluster or by having LDAPCluster.mydomain.com as a virtual IP managed by the load balancers.

You can configure your WebSphere application to talk to the closest LDAP node first (the local node), which may be a replica, or you can configure it to communicate with the cluster-assigned primary. You could take the implementation a step further and set up weighted round-robin connection management so that all requests are sent to the local LDAP server first (high weighting), and if it times out because it's down, the request is sent onto the master LDAP server in the cluster.

NFS Server Availability

NFS is Sun Microsystems' technology that provides the ability to expose server file systems to other servers. Originally developed for Unix systems to be able to remotely mount other Unix server file systems, it has now come to be used widely by systems and application architects. NFS is also now available on Windows-based platforms and is interoperable with Unix and Windows servers and clients.

NFS has its issues. There are performance trade-offs and security implications for using it, but when tuned correctly and implemented in the right way, it can serve as a powerful solution to share data between multiple nodes—a cheaper option than using Network Attached Storage (NAS)—and, in many cases, it does the job just as effectively.

NFS is widely used to provide a shared file system mountable across many Unix (or Windows) servers. You'll now look now at some implementation options where people are using NFS within WebSphere environments.

NFS Options

NFS is essentially a shared file system technology. Similar in function to NAS, Storage Area Networks (SAN), and Session Message Block (SMB)—which is a Windows-based file system network protocol—NFS provides a simple and cost-effective way of sharing data between hosts.

Prior to the likes of NAS and Samba (using SMB), NFS was the main network file sharing technology available. Even now, NAS has limitations in being able to share common data (shared data) with multiple hosts in a read-write configuration, but NFS supports it well. Figure 8-2 shows a typical example of a NFS solution.

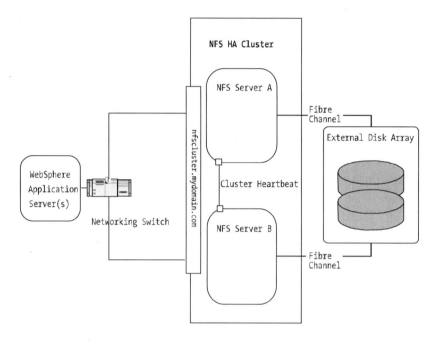

Figure 8-2. Basic NFS implementation

The difficulty with NFS configurations is that there's a fair amount of file locking and I/O management that takes place within the NFS server itself. Because of this, it's not easy to load balance or cluster NFS without some solid design considerations.

Consider for a moment that you have a cluster of WebSphere application servers, all accessing data files present on a remote NFS server. If you're wondering what you could use NFS for in a WebSphere environment, consider some of these options:

- WebSphere operational log directory sharing

- Commonly deployed Enterprise Archive (EAR)/Web Archive (WAR)/Enterprise JavaBean (EJB)/Java Archive (JAR) files directory

- Application data area—for example, temporary files and images created on the fly such as Portable Document Format (PDF) files, and so on

- Raw data being read into the WebSphere applications

If the NFS server went down, what would happen to your WebSphere application servers? If your WebSphere environment was using the NFS server for operational purposes, chances are things would get wobbly pretty quickly. If it was an application-related area or data store, then your applications would most likely cease functioning. You need some form of load balancing or clustered NFS solution to ensure that your data is always available.

There are several options available for highly available NFS solutions. The following are some of the products that provide solid, robust solutions for WebSphere-based applications using NFS:

- EMC Celera HighRoad (a hybrid NFS/Fibre/SCSI solution)

- Microsoft Windows internal clustering (NT, 2000, XP, and 2003 Server editions)

- Veritas Cluster Server (most operating systems, such as Solaris, Linux, AIX, HP-UX, Windows)

- Sun Microsystems SunCluster (Sun Solaris systems only)

- High Availability Cluster Multiprocessing (HACMP) (IBM AIX systems only)

- MC/ServiceGuard (HP-UX systems only)

- HP TruCluster (Digital/Compaq/HP Tru64 Unix systems only)

- Polyserve Matrix Server

All of these, and many more on the market, provide solid NFS cluster solutions. In fact, NFS is one of the easier forms of clustering available given that it's what I term a *quasi-stateless* technology. That is, imagine that you have two NFS servers, both unplugged from a network yet both configured as the same host (in other words, with the same IP address, the same host name, the same local disk structure and files, and so on). If you have a third Unix server that's an NFS client and remotely mounted to one of the NFS servers, you'd be able to happily access files and data over the network to the NFS server.

If you pulled the network cable out of one NFS server and plugged it into the secondary Unix server, nine times out of ten, your NFS client wouldn't know the difference—apart from a possible one- to two-second delay. Of course, if you did this during a large, single file I/O, depending on how you tuned your NFS server and clients, it may result in additional latency and the file I/O being retried (retrieval would start again).

NFS is inherently a resilient technology. For this reason, it's a solid and cost-effective data sharing technology for J2EE-based applications.

Implementation and Performance

Using one of the NFS cluster offerings mentioned, you can easily set up an automated network file sharing service that's highly available. The Unix vendor cluster technologies such as SunCluster, MC/ServiceGuard, and so forth provide solid solutions for high availability.

You need to consider the following, however, when looking at your highly available NFS implementation:

- Network infrastructure performance

- Failover time

- File I/O locking and management

You'll now look at each of these in some more detail. Figure 8-3 shows a highly available NFS implementation.

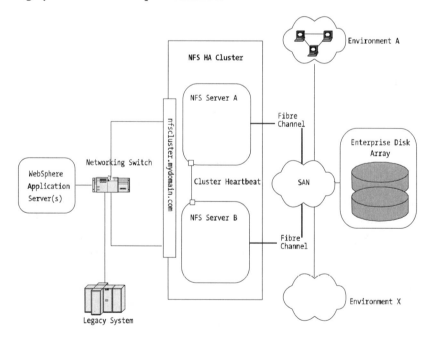

Figure 8-3. Highly available NFS implementation

In Figure 8-3, a NFS cluster exists as well as a number of WebSphere-based hosts. This implementation is advanced given that it shares storage behind the NFS servers via a SAN. A highly available NFS environment doesn't need this. However, if you're sharing more than one NFS server node, you'll require this type of technology or something similar to it.

Many system vendors manufacture dual-headed disk arrays that allow two hosts to connect to the array at the same time. It's then left up to the high-availability cluster to determine which node sees those disks and controls them. In most cases, only one server can directly connect to a disk array volume group at the same time.

NOTE There are advanced technologies available from EMC and Veritas that provide high-end data clusters that can expose shared disk volumes via clustered file systems with up to eight nodes serving as active-active data bearers. This level of environment is beyond the scope of this book.

Given that the NFS technology is communicating on a standard Transmission Control Protocol/Internet Protocol (TCP/IP) network (also one of NFS's values), it's bound by normal network related issues such as routing, Denial of Service (DoS) attacks, poor performance, and so forth.

As you'll see in the next section, with something as critical as your WebSphere NFS-based data store, always ensure there are multiple routes between the client and servers.

Consider using a private network that's internal to your WebSphere cluster and NFS cluster that's used for both internal WebSphere traffic and NFS traffic only, and leave customer-facing traffic to a separate network. This will help mitigate any chance of DoS attacks that directly impact your file I/O. It'll also ensure that any large NFS I/O that takes place doesn't impact customer response times.

Furthermore, use the fastest network technology available. For example, 100 megabits per second (Mbps) Ethernet is essentially the same speed as an old 10 megabytes per second (MBps) Small Computer System Interface (SCSI). This may be sufficient for many implementations, but remember the earlier discussion of disk I/O when you saw how quickly a SCSI bus of 80MBps can be fully consumed! Consider using Gigabit Ethernet, which will operate, in theory, at the same speed as Fibre Channel (100MBps). In practice, you'll see speeds closer to 50MBps. Still, it'll burst and is better than 5MB–10MBps!

Failover time within your NFS cluster is another important issue. You don't want to run a cluster that takes 30 seconds to failover. When configuring your NFS cluster, ensure that the cluster is only operating a highly available NFS agent and not servicing other components within the same cluster. Most well-configured NFS cluster solutions will failover within a matter of seconds. Any longer than this, and some of the WebSphere timeout settings discussed in other chapters will start to kick in and cause problems for your users.

File locking and I/O management is another important issue. Although NFS is versatile, it can introduce some quirky problems with environment integrity if you try to force it to perform double-file I/O locking. This situation occurs when you have two NFS clients trying to write and update the same file at the same time. Although technically this is possible, there are well-documented situations with NFS where this will cause NFS server daemons to go into an unhappy state for a short period while they try to manage the file I/O.

Avoid having your WebSphere-based NFS application clients writing to the same file at the same time. If you need to write to one particular file from many locations, consider developing a distributed file writer service within your application and have all WebSphere application clients communicate to it for file writing I/O.

If your WebSphere applications are simply writing to their own files (or reading) but are on the shared NFS storage, then this is fine and there will be no I/O latency issues.

Network Infrastructure Availability

I've discussed network availability in a fair amount of detail in this book. What I haven't discussed or focused on, however, is general network infrastructure—switches, routers, and multiple network interfaces from the servers. In the following sections, you'll look specifically at firewalls and load balancers and some methods to improve their availability.

Overview

Firewalls and load balancers are critical components to any online-based, business-critical system. Firewalls are key to security, and load balancers are key to availability. Ironically, both of these components can form a single point of failure in your environment.

If your firewall infrastructure must be traversed for each data packet entering or exiting your WebSphere environment, what happens if the firewall goes down? It's the same for load balancers—if your load balancer becomes unavailable, what happens to traffic flow? Some load-balancing appliances have support to fail into a limp home mode where they revert to a dumb hub or dumb switch that simply passes packets back and forth, but this doesn't work well if you have complex Virtual Local Area Network (VLAN) or private IP configurations set up within your environment.

You'll now see some ways to ensure availability of your WebSphere environment with firewalls and load balancers.

Firewalls

Firewalls are typically hardware appliances or some form of software service running on a server. Many medium and large businesses will operate a fully formed Demilitarized Zone (DMZ) that operates between two or three firewalls.

What happens, however, if your firewall becomes unavailable? Does traffic to your WebSphere environment stop? There are a number of schools of thought on this scenario: Some people believe that if the firewall ceases to work, then so be it. You lose processing availability of your applications, but it's better to be safe than sorry. I don't agree with this approach. If you've spent a zillion dollars on building up a WebSphere environment that's highly available, you don't want a single point of failure such as a near-commodity network device (your firewall) to be the cause of your application going down. Therefore, the simplest way to move forward and provide high availability is to have a standby or active-active firewall configuration that has two or more firewall devices at your network borders.

Consider an example where there are two firewalls at the border of a DMZ. These two firewall devices are routing traffic from frontend routers or switches (in front of the firewall devices), which are in turn routing traffic via global routing protocols, such as Border Gateway Protocol (BGP).

If one of the border routers goes down, BGP routing would redirect all traffic to the secondary router.

Most of the high-end switch and routing device vendors have their own form of internal high-availability capabilities that could also be used in a situation to make switches such as these highly available. Cisco, for example, has a technology called Hot-Standby Routing Protocol (HSRP).

Cisco PIX firewalls, for example, are hardware-based appliances that support HSRP capabilities.

These types of firewall devices have an inbound and an outbound interface (or several) and simply interrogate traffic as it traverses, denying and accepting traffic based on defined rules.

If the firewall device becomes unavailable, the frontend routers would detect that a firewall device had gone down—because of network failures being returned from the broken or downed firewall—and redirect it to the remaining firewall device.

If you're using software load balancers that operate on servers, then you can take advantage of IP takeover-based clustering using one of the clustering technologies discussed in this chapter and earlier chapters.

This provides a highly available firewall environment but does have a limitation in that it's a failover configuration. In times when the failover is taking place, there will be a delay while the failover takes place and routing resumes on the new master firewall host.

You can achieve this in many ways, and dozens of firewall vendors and products support these types of situations. This example should provide you with some ideas when considering your design.

Load Balancers

Load balancers are another common component within the online world of WebSphere-based applications. As you've seen, load balancers provide the ability to distribute traffic between WebSphere application server hosts as well as many other forms of application hosts within computing environments.

Load balancers themselves, like firewalls, are prone to failure. Some load-balancer vendors, such as firewall vendors, provide limp home modes for their products that allow a load balancer to revert into a switch/hub or straight-through configuration. This is a "better than nothing solution," but it doesn't help those sites that are more complex. Also, as discussed before, they may use more complex network architectures such as VLANs, Network Address Translation (NAT), and so forth. These technologies will typically not support a pass-through configuration from a load balancer when or if they fail.

The best way to combat load-balancer availability is to load balance the load balancer! It sounds like overkill, but the approach is the same as that for firewalls. If your budget allows, high-end routers and switches support load-balancing capabilities. In these cases, your border routers or switches would perform the load balancing for you to your firewalls, and they may provide inner load balancing within your secured area or in the inner DMZ.

I tend to approach load-balancer and firewall implementations the same way. I picture the method of routing traffic to each tier within the firewall (which will consist of firewalls, load balancers, switches, and routers) like sifting sand. The sifter is cone-shaped with the border routers or switches being the large cone end and the inner DMZ firewall (between the DMZ and your application's servers) being the pointy end.

The large cone section where the border routers are allows the coarse-grained traffic to flow through, and the pointy end only allows fine-grained traffic to flow through. The coarse-grained traffic is routed via coarse-grained routing mechanisms. In this case, it may be BGP or Open Shortest Path First

(OSPF). As the routing of traffic nears the inner DMZ firewall, the routing mechanism is all point-to-point IP (using VLANS) or some other form of private IP routing.

Your approach, therefore, may look something like this:

1. Traffic is routed through the Internet (or intranet) via BGP or OSPF to the BGP/OSPF-selected router/switch on the border of the firewall.

2. One of the two frontend routers receives the packets and sends them to either of the firewalls based on basic weighted routing rules (simple load balancing).

3. The firewall device interrogates the packets and sends them out the egress interface to standard load balancers (lb1 or lb2).

4. The load balancers send the traffic to one of the servers in the Web server farm for processing.

5. One of the servers in the Web server farm processes the request and then sends the result into a backend WebSphere application server via the rules defined in the HTTP plug-in file (load balancing happens at this point for the backend WebSphere application server's selection via the plug-in).

6. The Web servers send the request out to the backend using standard weighted metric routes on each server, or using routing rules, via inner-router-01 and or inner-router-02.

7. Either of these routers then sends the request onto the WebSphere application servers via their own local switches.

This is a complex area of networking, and these short guidelines should be only taken as that—guidelines. It's important, however, to consider these issues of WebSphere environment architecture because as a WebSphere manager, architect, or senior developer, you'll need to understand the end-to-end picture of your environment.

Some other considerations of your firewall and load-balancing environment are as follows:

*   Additional firewall tiers may be required if security is a concern. Options exist for the additional firewall to be placed between the Web servers and the inner routers or on the egress-side inner routers before hitting the WebSphere application server's local network.

- Investigate your vendor's end-to-end capabilities. It's possible that the vendor can provide an end-to-end model for your highly available firewall needs.

Database Server Failover

I've said several times throughout this book that databases and WebSphere are almost synonymous with each other in an online J2EE environment. For the most part, placing a user-oriented application on the Internet requires some form of backend database. If not only to provide tracking or logging services, databases are pivotal to a WebSphere-based platform. For that reason, in this section, I'll focus on several ways to implement or, more specifically, support database failover within WebSphere applications.

You've already focused on the performance of database interconnection with WebSphere. The other side of the equation is failover. It's important to realize that sometimes performance and failover can cancel each other out or, at the very least, impact each other.

The following sections cover these areas of failover support:

- WebSphere 4 repository database failover

- User application database failover support

- Session database failover support

- Considerations when using Oracle 9i Real Application Clusters (RAC) and Oracle Parallel Server (OPS)

- Considerations when using other databases that support clustering and failover

You'll first look at WebSphere 4 and its repository failover support.

WebSphere 4 Administrative Repository Considerations

As discussed in earlier chapters of this book, WebSphere 4 maintains a repository on a relational database. The repository itself stores runtime and configuration information about WebSphere application servers and or domains.

Configurations for server groups and other associated configuration areas within WebSphere are stored and maintained within the WebSphere 4 repositories.

However, it's important to note that the repository is managed by the WebSphere 4 administrative server. This administration server maintains and supports a lot of the functionality that the WebSphere 5 deployment manager and node agents support, such as Java Naming and Directory Interface (JNDI) failover and support, centralized application server runtime support, and so forth.

In Chapter 7, I discussed WebSphere 4 administration server failover but focused on the specifics of the administration server runtime failover. Because there are elements of the administration server that rely on the database during database failover, the specifics of repository failover have been left for this section.

Consider for a moment what happens to the repository during a failover event. The answer to this question depends on the state and status of your application environment. If, for example, you have two WebSphere server nodes running, with a handful of application servers and clones running in each node, and your repository became unavailable, nothing would happen. The repository is only critical during WebSphere application server failover, startup, shutdown, or configuration changes. Most of the configuration that you set up via the administration console or the WebSphere Control Program (WSCP) command line tools can only take effect after restarting an application server.

If your repository goes down for a period of a few minutes, and there's no need for your applications or WebSphere itself to query information about its constituent components, then the impact to a repository failover (or downtime) is minimal. Therefore, configuring or tuning the availability of the repository during a failover involves minimal effort.

If you're using a database that supports connection time failover (such as Oracle), then you can configure your administrative server Java Database Connectivity (JDBC) settings in your <WAS_HOME>/bin/admin.config file to support JDBC thin-driver connection time failover. This will provide your administrative server with the ability to connect to alternative repositories if you're running static or standby database servers where data replication is manual (via loading of redo and archive logs), semimanual (via data replication), or multinode configurations in an active-active database configuration.

If you're running an active-standby configuration, your JDBC Uniform Resource Locator (URL) will be already pointing to the "cluster" address. In most cases, you'll configure, with your database cluster (active-standby), a Domain Name System (DNS) entry that's the IP address takeover host name for the cluster.

That is, if you have two servers in an active-standby configuration—one with IP address 10.0.0.1 and the other with 10.0.0.2, you'll also then have another IP address such as 192.168.1.1, which refers to the "cluster" address. Through the clusterware configuration that supports and manages the IP address takeover configuration, you configure a mechanism to facilitate the takeover and reactivation of the 192.168.1.1 address as nodes failover back and forth.

The cluster DNS name, which may be something such as yourDBCluster.mydomain.com, will refer to 192.168.1.1 in the zone file. At one point, during initial booting, the host name of 10.0.0.1 will have been configured on another network interface, 192.168.1.1, which refers to yourDBCluster.mydomain.com. If 10.0.0.1 fails, the clusterware takes over the IP address of 192.168.1.1 (yourDBCluster.mydomain.com) and tells 10.0.0.2 to activate it on one of its configured network interface cards. In this way, the host entry of yourDBCluster.mydomain.com is pointing to the same IP address the whole time, meaning that you can configure your JDBC URL settings for your repository to be yourDBCluster.mydomain.com.

As the database nodes failover back and forth, your repository still connects to what it thinks is the same node each time. As long as whatever mechanism you use in your database availability model supports solid and up-to-the-millisecond data synchronization, you won't have a problem. If your database replication or failover model is a little less diligent with synchronizing data, you may have a problem if you failover to stale data.

The repository updates the data store from time to time as nodes, application servers, server group, and so forth start up and shut down (enter and leave WebSphere clusters). You can probably appreciate what kind of mess would occur if you had recently fired up a WebSphere server that updated the shared repository between all the nodes in the WebSphere 4 domain, and, shortly after, the repository database had to failover to a state version of the repository that didn't have the recently booted WebSphere node in its repository data store. As soon as another WebSphere node attempted to join the cluster (or any constituent part of any of the existing nodes), the dirty or stale information in the repository would cause problems with your cluster's host maps and synchronization.

So, as you can see, maintaining the repository doesn't require a complicated failover model as long as data is always synchronized. Failover times of up to several minutes can usually be handled by most WebSphere environments with the only exceptions being changes (configuration or state) to the components within the WebSphere domain.

User Application Data Sources and Databases

Applications that use databases to store data using JDBC are well supported by WebSphere when it comes to database failovers. The JDBC Application

Programming Interface (API) in both WebSphere 4 and 5 supports a range of exception messages that WebSphere as well as the application itself can use to perform certain events.

What am I talking about when I mention *application databases*? Essentially, this is where your application is binding itself to a data source (in this example, a JDBC data source) that in turn pools connections to a relational database (such as DB2, SQL Server, Oracle, and so on).

Failover of these databases is a situation that can cause great headaches for both systems managers as well as application architects. So, what can happen? Well, consider a standard query to a database. The sequence of events is something like this:

1. Application code usually performs a JNDI context lookup to get the JDBC data source binding.

2. Once the application code has the reference to the data source, it'll request a connection from the connection pool.

3. Once the connection object has been obtained, the application code will then perform some sort of query via Container Managed Persistence (CMP), Bean Managed Persistence (BMP), Data Access Objects (DAO), or straight JDBC calls.

4. Once the result set has been returned, the application code, or a factory class that supports the opening and closing of connections, closes the connection to the database pooled connection object, and the pooled connection object returns to the pool manager's available connection list.

 NOTE   This is an example of a connection to a database. There are other ways you can achieve this, but this example uses this simplistic yet legitimate approach.

At any point in these four steps, a database failover could occur; the result is different for each step and needs to be handled differently. You'll now go through each step and look at what can happen and what to do in the event of a failure.

Step 1: Application Binding

This step doesn't involve the database at all. In fact, it relies on the JNDI construct being available that's managed and supported by the administration servers in WebSphere 4 and the node agent or application servers in WebSphere 5.

Always bootstrap against the administrative server in WebSphere 4 for JNDI failover and application servers in WebSphere 5. Your JNDI lookups can then support failover.

Step 2: Pooled Connection Request

Requesting a connection to the database from the connection manager will perform satisfactorily each time within an application given that the request for a connection from the pool manager will result in a query to the local application server data source provider. As each application server instance obtains its own data source (and connection pool manager), if the pool has failed, then the application has failed. The resulting recovery steps in this process are handled in a different area within WebSphere.

If a query is performed (see the next section) via a pooled connection and the connection fails because of a downed database, then at this point one of two things can happen: First, if the application JDBC pool manager is interfacing with an active-standby database, then the pool manager's connection timeout settings will affect the outcome of what may happen. Second, if the connection timeout settings are set too low and the cluster fail takes longer than the timeout settings, then the connection will fail and either a StateConnectionException or a ConnectionWaitTimeoutException will be thrown.

Step 3: Query Performed

Once the query is performed, the data source has obtained the connection to the database and the query is made to the database. If the database suffers a failure in midflight of the query, again, depending on your database configuration and architecture, your query may fail, or it may be retried. Best practices suggest that your application query and capturing your database exceptions should be managed within a single method.

Developers should be creating their application code so that the calling method that pushes the query to the database also captures any resulting exceptions. If the resulting exception is either a StateConnectionException or a ConnectionWaitTimeoutException, then the application code should be able to handle the situation by retrying the client requests the number of times defined by the application.

If the number of retries defined in the application code is exceeded, then the application should give up and assume there's a failure in the failover process (assuming you've coded your timeouts appropriately with your database failover period). Listing 8-1 shows an example of this implementation.

Listing 8-1. Handling Database Errors in Application Code

```
int retryMax = 3;
int waitValue = 5000;

Public void someConnectionPool () {
    // assume all appropriate java classes are loaded
    try {
        // assumes that the JNDI data source binding has already been made
        conn = datasource.getConnection();
        statement = conn.createStatement();
        statement.execute("select * from my_table where user_name = 'adam'");
        retry = false;
    } catch (staleConnectionException s) {
        // commence management of error
        if (retries < retryMax) {
            retry = true;
            retries++;
            sleep(waitValue);
        } else {
            retry = false;
        }
    } catch (SQLException se) {
        // manage general SQL exception types here
    } finally
{
        // close of connections and statements here
    }
    } while (retry);
}
```

As you can see from Listing 8-1, some fairly simple logic implements some robustness in the application code. Although this doesn't necessarily support the failover of the database, it does support the ability to insulate applications from failover delays. Essentially, the application could throw an error message to the customer, asking the customer to retry his request in a few moments—by which time you hope that the database failover has taken place.

If you're using transactions within your application code, you need to be aware of the additional overhead of performing queries and updates to a database that may fail at some point because of a failover situation or, worse, a total database environment failure. You can implement transaction control using standard Java Transaction API (JTA) or similar Java/J2EE transaction management functionality, or your developers can develop transaction management using custom-built transaction managers.

If you're using transactions within your environment, you'll need to ensure that if a situation arises where after a number of retries to a database, a request or update fails and the entire transaction needs to be rolled back. The development of this application code is beyond the scope of this book, but it's something you should consider.

If your applications are using CMP, then the EJB container will manage the retrying of the queries to the data source without the application being involved.

This discussion so far has only focused on databases that are active-standby where there's a failover period involved. If your database environment is something that's multiheaded or active-active, then you can further insulate your applications from outages. As you've seen in other chapters, an *active-active* database is one where there are two or more nodes, actively participating and serving in database queries. This is different from a load-balanced environment in that the load distribution is handled by the database cluster software rather than a hardware or software appliance distributing requests to multiple nodes (as in a Web server farm).

In this type of database configuration (which you'll see in more detail later in the chapter), you'll still be faced with StaleConnection and ConnectionWaitTimeout exceptions if all nodes are down. However, with an active-active database environment, you'll always have more than one node actively running and servicing requests. In most cases, the distribution mechanism is handled by the JDBC driver with specific database vendor settings that help distribute load accordingly.

In summary, follow the same rules as discussed for Listing 8-1, but be aware that your environment availability will be higher and more robust than it'd be with an active-standby database cluster.

Step 4: Closing the Connection

Closing the connection is similar to the second step where the application processes and connection pool manager are operating almost within the same space (definitely the same JVM). When the application code requests that statements and connections are closed, this doesn't affect or involve the database at all, but it helps to release unused objects from memory.

Session Database

The session database is a key part of your overall WebSphere availability strategy. This service within WebSphere ties into the HTTP plug-in mechanism discussed at length in this book. The session database essentially backs up the session manager by persisting the session object (and its contents) to a database. This provides the ability for the user session to not be lost during a failover scenario (see Chapters 6, 7, and 9 for more discussion on session management and persistence).

You'll now look at the implementations and configuration options that can help improve availability of your user sessions during database failover scenarios.

In Chapter 7 when I discussed configuring and tuning of the session persistence process, you learned about the three forms of session persistence that come standard with WebSphere 4 and 5:

- Time-based persistence

- End of servlet service method

- Manually via the sync() method (an IBM extension)

Essentially, you need to choose from two options when implementing your persistence of sessions. Do you want to tune your environment to be potentially higher performing (a lower impact on your database) and less supportive of failovers or more supportive of failovers yet have a higher impact on your database because of more persistence writes? Of course, you can always be sure to model your database so that it supports the high-persistence model (highly synchronized), in which case you're already aware of the managed load that'll be put onto your database.

WebSphere 4 and 5 both differ in terms of their options for session persistence. Because this chapter focuses on failover of external systems, you'll only see the persistence to the database option here. Please refer to Chapter 7 for a discussion about memory-to-memory and in-memory persistence options available in WebSphere 4 and 5.

So what is it that you're trying to achieve Simple—if you've gone to the trouble and expense of implementing a high-end WebSphere environment and are using session management, you'll want to be able to recover, as transparently as possible, from situations where an application server has failed and the user session needs to be available from another application server clone or instance.

Figure 7-11 from the previous chapter highlights a situation where a user, User 1, is logging into a WebSphere environment. The session is managed by Server A. Figure 7-12 shows the same diagram after a failover scenario has occurred with the application servers. All user sessions are now available from the remaining Server B node. However, if the database server is what fails rather than an application server, the situation is slightly different.

If you have a single database server, you'll find that your session will be lost if you can't failover to another database node that has access to the user session tables. For this reason, my recommendation is that it's nearly pointless to have multiple WebSphere application servers and only have a single database server if the reason for having multiple application servers is redundancy or high avail-ability. If the database server goes down, all the application servers in the world won't keep you up and running!

Then again, if your J2EE/Java-based application that happens to be running on the multiple WebSphere application servers isn't overly database-centric, then there may be a fair case for there not to be a clustered database server envi-ronment (active-standby or active-active). A failover within an active-standby database cluster environment is, like application databases, easy to recover from. The session persistence manager is supported via the Web container con-struct within WebSphere.

A nice feature of the WebSphere session manager capability is that when you configure the session manager to use a persistent model, you have to specify a data source. This data source is the same type of JDBC data source that your normal WebSphere applications use to communicate to their database. Therefore, the settings associated with WebSphere application data source usage can be applied to the session manager data source.

Remember, you want to ensure that if you have a failover configuration (active-standby), then you'll need your connection timeout setting to be longer than that of your tested failover period; otherwise, your session manager will timeout prior to the recovered or newly failed-over node becomes available.

If your database is an active-active architecture, the JDBC settings are no different except for the format of the URL (see the next section). In the extended JDBC URL format, you can support thick-based JDBC drivers that supply time-out and failover connection details in the JDBC URL. I'll discuss this in more detail in the next section.

In summary, if you require a high-availability WebSphere application, my recommendation is to consider what and how frequently the persistence of session objects is required. Remember, large HTTP sessions are expensive to persist to the database. As discussed in Chapters 4, 5, and 6, try to keep your HTTP session objects per user less than 8 kilobytes (KB), with a preference to maintain them at under 4KB if you're looking to utilize session persistence for session failover. Anything greater than 8KB starts to become increasingly inten-sive to persist to a database. You can take the blanket approach by persisting all session information at the end of each servlet method call, or you can persist session information at a defined period (for example, every 60 seconds).

There's a final approach, which is either to manually persist the session data using the sync() method call (which is an IBM extension) at the end of key session updates (for example, via a custom-built session store class) or to store information onto a database manually and avoid the session manager alto-gether. I suggest staying away from the latter approach unless there's some limiting factor why you can't use the WebSphere session manager. Although implementing your own session manager is possible, it does introduce a whole level of complexity that WebSphere itself does a good job doing.

Finally, by using the sync() method, persisting data at the end of key functions and methods allows you to persist information at a more granular level than at the end of each servlet call. Remember that a servlet method call may entail a whole range of backend EJB-based transactions, each of which may build up return objects that will ultimately be stored in the user session. There may be a design consideration for your application platform where the cost of performing these backend transactions warrants the need for you to be ultra-sensitive to the cause and force the persistence of session information at key strategic points of a large transaction.

Considerations When Using Oracle 8i OPS, 9i OPS, and 9i RAC

As I've discussed already in this book, Oracle is one of the popular database platforms being used globally by WebSphere platforms because of its flexibility, scalability, and performance capabilities. OPS and RAC are both high-end, highly scalable relational database platform products from Oracle. Both provide active-active configurations, with Oracle 9*i* RAC being the flagship of Oracle's highly available database platform technologies.

I've discussed OPS and RAC in earlier chapters in terms of general implementation considerations. In this section, I'll give you an overview of how to ensure that your WebSphere applications are insulated from failover scenarios with both products.

As you've seen, WebSphere supports JDBC access via type 2 and type 4 drivers when used with Oracle. The key for ensuring that applications aren't impacted by Oracle failover situations and for taking advantage of the advanced features of Oracle RAC is that you can use a number of JDBC driver and URL settings.

With Oracle technologies, there are two types of high-availability feature you can use. The first is Oracle Connection Time Failover (CTF). CTF is a simple JDBC driver setting that allows you to configure, in their tnsnames.ora or in their JDBC URL, values that provide failover capabilities during connection. The second option is Transparent Application Failover (TAF). This is a more advanced option and not all WebSphere implementations and models support this. This form of capability requires the use of an Oracle Call Interface (OCI) or thick-based JDBC driver (type 2).

Oracle Connect Time Failover

How this works is that a global service name is created for your Oracle database. Within the scope of the global service name for your OPS and or RAC database, you configure the various database nodes that participate within the cluster.

In this section, you'll look at a sample tnsnames.ora file first and then at an example of an extended JDBC URL that provides CTF. Listing 8-2 shows an example tnsnames.ora file that has the CTF extensions in it. DBServerA and DBServerB are the two nodes in this OPS or RAC cluster.

NOTE   The syntax of the tnsnames.ora file is a standard Oracle implementation that's used to support and find listeners within your environment. The configuration and syntax details of this file are beyond the scope of this book. Please refer to your Oracle administration and installation guides for more information on the syntax of these files.

Listing 8-2. Oracle Transparent Network Substrate (TNS) Names Configuration File for Server Failover

```
MyDBCluster.mydomain.com=
    {description=My DB Cluster
        (load_balance=off)
        (failover=on)
        (address=
            (protocol=tcp)
            (host=DBServerA)
            (port=1521))
        (address=
        (protocol=tcp)
            (host=DBServerB)
            (port=1521))
        (connect_data=
            (service_name=MyDBCluster.mydomain.com))))
```

The key lines to this tnsnames.ora file are the load_balance and failover directives. As you can see, this example shows that load balancing is off and failover is on. You can have both active by setting them both to on. If your environment is tuned to service requests in a true active-active configuration, then ensure that the failover setting is on.

If you have a topology where you may have two WebSphere "channels," you may consider having each channel with the `tnsnames.ora` file configured differently, with the `load_balance` directive turned off. That is, channel 2 would have DBServerB first, and channel 1 would have DBServerA first. With the load-balance directive off, the driver picks the first server from the list to which it can connect.

The load balancing isn't true load balancing. Instead, it's a randomness of connectivity to one of the hosts. This is good—what you don't want to have is a situation where all your applications bootstrap and connect to the first working database server. In this case, DBServerA would be taking all the requests, and the load differential would be skewed between the database server nodes.

You can use the same configuration in a JDBC URL. The previous line could be placed in a JDBC URL as shown here:

```
JDBCDriver="jdbc:oracle:thin:@ {description=My DB Cluster (load_balance=off) ⤷
(failover=on)  \(address= (protocol=tcp) (host=DBServerA) (port=1521)) ⤷
(address= (protocol=tcp)  (host=DBServerB) (port=1521)) (connect_data= ⤷
(service_name=MyDBCluster.mydomain.com))))"
```

In implementation, this URL would typically be one long line. As you can see, it's quite an ugly-looking string. Configuring this in your JDBC data source provider is a little sore on the eye, but the end result is robust failover support.

How this JDBC configuration works is this: If DBServerA fails, the JDBC driver tries to connect to the DBServerB. The driver will keep trying each server until one becomes available, should both servers be unavailable.

Oracle Transparent Application Failover

Oracle TAF is a more advanced version of CTF. Essentially, this capability provides a completely transparent failover and connection layer to application and WebSphere databases. Using a thick-based JDBC driver implementation, TAF provides the same functionality that CTF provides, but it supports active connections rather than new connections (at startup or through a failover).

Similar to the CTF implementation, TAF is implemented through the `tnsnames.ora` configuration file on each WebSphere host. Much of the syntax is the same, except for some extensions that provide more advanced redundancy and robustness in the application connections to the database.

Listing 8-3 shows a TAF-based `tnsnames.ora` file, which takes the same configuration file from Listing 8-2 and adds directives that are the TAF-specific settings. These are highlighted in bold.

Listing 8-3. Oracle TNS Names Configuration File for Transparent Application Failover

```
MyDBCluster.mydomain.com=
    {description=My DB Cluster
        (load_balance=on)
        (failover=on)
        (address=
            (protocol=tcp)
            (host=DBServerA)
            (port=1521))
        (address=
            (protocol=tcp)
            (host=DBServerB)
            (port=1521))
        (connect_data=
            (service_name=MyDBCluster.mydomain.com)
            (failover_mode=
            (type=session)
            (method=basic)
            (retries=5)
            (delay=5))))
```

These additional lines provide directives to the JDBC driver to direct it to load itself up in a specific manner. That is, in Listing 8-3, the main lines of importance are the type and method lines.

The type defines the type of failure required. For this directive, there are three options: Session, Select, and None. They can be summarized as follows:

- **Session**: The Session type provides a high level of failover support. Specifically, this type fails the application's pooled connections to the *other* host. There's no query failover supported within this option.

- **Select**: The Select type is more thorough than the type Session. In this option, all queries and open cursors are maintained across failover, and generally no impact is found noticed with this option.

- **None**: The None type, as it suggests, doesn't attempt to failover any active queries or cursors.

The `method` directive defines how the failover should occur. There are two settings available for this directive: Basic and Preconnect. They can be summarized as follows:

- **Basic**: The Basic method provides the capability for the failover connection to the failover node to occur at the time it's required—a failover. There's no overhead in maintaining this form of failover method.

- **Preconnect**: The Preconnect method supports an advanced failover capability that sees that all connections established on one host (for example, DBServerA) are opened and maintained on the second host (for example, DBServerB). This, as you can appreciate, introduces overhead on the secondary server but provides an ultra-transparent failover configuration for your applications.

From these details, if you're looking for an ultimate failover design, the best options to choose are the Select type and Preconnect method. There have been reported problems in various Internet-based discussion groups on the Select type with WebSphere. For this reason, ensure that if you want to use this type, test failover thoroughly during stress and volume testing. Alternatively, you can opt for the Session type, which will guard against most failures and, in this case, have the application code rerequest the query.

If you use a Session type and a failover occurs with an inflight query, your applications will be thrown a `StaleConnection` exception. As discussed earlier in this chapter, implement application logic to retry the query or request, or if your applications are using CMPs, the container will rerequest the query automatically.

Using Other Active-Standby or IP Takeover Clustering Systems

You can summarize all database failover events and resulting environment states in three parts:

- Complete and total environment failure after a database server/cluster fails

- Semimanaged, semitransparent failover where inflight transactions will most likely need to be retried

- Fully transparent database failover to applications

The first possible scenario is something that'll likely only occur when there aren't remaining nodes available in a cluster or when there's only a single database server operating. The second scenario will occur in an active-standby or hot-standby database configuration where there may be an unusually long period of failover that causes, or requires, the applications to retry their queries several times. The third scenario is where something such as an Oracle 9i RAC or DB2 Enterprise Edition database (with Parallel Sysplex) is being used to transparently serve requests between multiple hosts.

Of all the databases supported by IBM WebSphere, each of them supports at least the second scenario where you can implement basic clustering to support failover with hot-data replication (via a shared or mirrored storage system).

In this form of clustering, the databases are clustered and are exposed to your network and WebSphere environments via a clustered IP address or host name. As discussed in earlier sections, typically this form of IP-takeover clustered solution simply shuts down and starts up network interfaces between one or more nodes, which makes the database appear as though it's always available, with slight delays or pauses in query services.

If you're concerned about high availability and must have some form of always-available database platform, be sure to implement your database environment with, at the very least, IP-takeover clustered solutions (for example, active-standby). If your WebSphere-based applications are mission critical and just can't go down (or the costs of them going down is hugely expensive), then consider one of the active-active database platforms available such as Oracle 9i RAC and DB2 Enterprise Edition database (with Parallel Sysplex). Each of these databases is available on all supported WebSphere operating systems.

Summary

In this chapter, you explored external systems that, at some point in time, you may need to integrate with WebSphere. This chapter provided a level of detail that gives you an architectural view on what approaches are available and what approaches are the best.

It's important to remember that each of the external systems discussed in this chapter will potentially have books (similar to this one) that are dedicated to them and that cover performance tuning, scalability, and availability architecture.

WebSphere EJB and Web Container Performance

A KEY COMPONENT FOR all J2EE application servers is the container. The container essentially compartmentalizes certain aspects of the operational runtime of your J2EE engine. Specifically in this chapter, you'll look at the EJB container and the Web container (sometimes referred to as the servlet container).

The Container: An Overview

As I've discussed in earlier chapters, the container is essentially a runtime environment in which the J2EE-based applications operate. The container also provides hooks into the application server interfaces, as well as distributes computing logic between external enterprise application and various services available from and within the local runtime.

J2EE tech-speak calls this a "federated API view, providing a common, yet maintainable framework for the deployment and runtime of J2EE- and J2SE-based application environments." Sound complex? It's not, really. Consider the diagram in Figure 9-1 to get a better understanding.

Essentially, Figure 9-1 shows a high-level view of a WebSphere implementation. There are three main components shown here. The first component is the outer box, which is the WebSphere application server itself. This area, or governing engine, provides all of IBM's implementation of the J2EE API stack and the associated services. The application server includes things such as the communications stack, administration functionality (e.g., JMX), and distributed computing services such as clustering and WLM functionality.

Within the WebSphere application server, you have the container (among other things). The container encompasses such things as enterprise application management services, J2EE application service interfaces, and distributed computing logic. It also contains deployment and configuration services for the J2EE applications that will be deploying and managing within your WebSphere environment.

The last major section in the diagram shows the J2EE application itself. This component or group of components contains all the Web Archives (WARs), Enterprise JavaBean Java Archives (EJB-JARs), and standard components such as external Java Archives (JARs) and stand-alone classes.

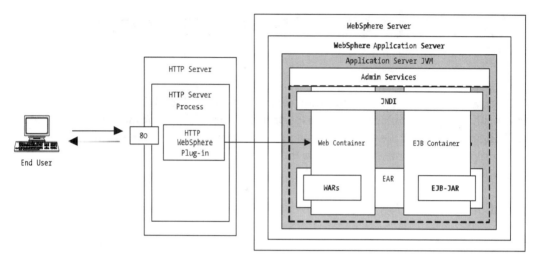

Figure 9-1. High-level application server framework container view

All of this is typically bundled up into an Enterprise Archive Resource, or EAR, file. Within the EAR file, you have all the components included into a tarball-like structure, governed and mastered by an enterprise application deployment descriptor (i.e., `ejb-jar.xml` files) and vendor-specific deployment descriptors.

The enterprise application deployment descriptor is the master descriptor for your J2EE application. It includes all important information associated with your EAR and its internal components. Bootstrap information, initial JNDI context information, and proprietary vendor information specific to each vendor's implementation of an application server are all included within the enterprise application deployment descriptor.

Each of the constituent parts, such as the WARs and EJB-JARs, has deployment descriptors specific to it and the code and logic within it.

NOTE Technically speaking, there are actually several different containers within WebSphere. Not only are there the standard or more commonly known containers, the Web and EJB containers, but also there are others, such as the application container (for application clients). These secondary level containers are pretty much self-managing and don't offer a lot in the way of performance-tuning capability.

What Do Containers Do?

A common misconception about containers is that they operate within their own JVMs. This isn't the case, especially according to the J2EE EJB and Servlet/JSP specifications. Technically speaking, the containers are nothing more than vendor-provided (IBM, in this case) class packages that offer, among other things, deployment and runtime support for the specific application types that they're designed to support (e.g., EJBs and servlets).

However, the containers operate within the application server JVM. That is, as you've seen, you'll have one or many application servers running either clones or separate instances, and in each of those application servers, you'll have either a Web container or an EJB container, or both.

Let's look at each container in a little more detail.

The Web Container

The Web container, as noted previously, is the configuration and runtime engine for presentation layer type components, such as JSPs and servlets. Its role is to provide the plumbing for all the dynamic presentation components, such as the Request and Response objects, and manage the life cycle of each servlet as it is loaded and unloaded, finishing up with garbage collection by the application server's JVM.

Figure 9-2 shows how the Web container operates within the application server JVM space and how it communicates with the outside world.

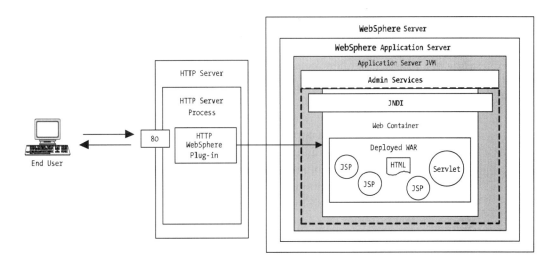

Figure 9-2. Web container view

The application server itself is used to configure environmental settings such as the port that the Web container should listen on and a range of performance and operational settings that help to tune and optimize the runtime of this aspect of the application server.

As Web components (Web modules) are deployed to a WebSphere application server, part of the deployment process includes the absorption of configuration details located within the deployment descriptors of the Web modules (i.e., the WAR files). Included among these details in the deployment descriptors are directives such as the root context of the WAR and other specific types of information relating to the files to be referenced within the WAR file (e.g., servlet configuration and so forth).

As the application server "deploys" the WAR file, various other settings are configured through the deployment process. This covers settings such as HTTP transport configurations. Of these settings, the target HTTP port, Secure Socket Layer (SSL) configuration (if required), minimum and maximum threading allocation, time-out values, and a whole range of settings associated with the internal servlet engine (e.g., caching, session linkages, etc.) are configured during the deployment process.

Of note, the Session Manager is an embedded component within the IBM WebSphere application server's Web container. The Session Manager is also highly configurable, as you saw in Chapter 7.

The EJB Container

The EJB container is a little more complex than the Web container because of the nature of the components that operate inside it. Let's take a look at the EJB container (see Figure 9-3).

The key point to make about the EJB container is that, similar to the Web container, it sits in between the application server and the operational runtime components—in this case, the EJBs. EJBs don't communicate directly to the outside world; instead, they communicate to the application server via the container interfaces. Like the Web container, the EJB container is a logical entity and not operational (as in an application server). Through vendor-provided classes, based on the application server, EJB, and EJB container specifications of the J2EE architecture, the container provides threading and transaction support as well as a bunch of other plumbing features.

An EJB is a complex beast. EJB technology builds on the philosophy that the application programmer shouldn't have to worry about the infrastructure, but merely about the application. This means that the server that deploys the EJBs must provide a number of services to EJBs in order to manage them properly. As such, there are a vast number of configurable combinations available within the EJB container aspect of the application server.

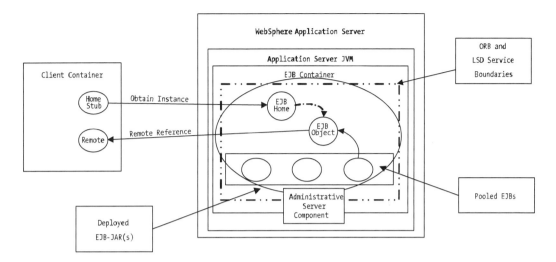

Figure 9-3. EJB container view

In order for the management of EJBs to be handled by the application server correctly, a client (i.e., a servlet, Java client, etc.) must access the EJBs through a conduit that is proxified. The conduit, or proxy, is provided by the EJB container. Ensuring that the outside world doesn't see the inner workings of the EJBs allows the EJB container to control persistence, security, caching, and connection management with no knowledge (or care) by the EJB client. To facilitate this, client access to EJBs is managed by multiple instances of the EJB home and EJB object interfaces. These interfaces are fundamental aspects of the EJB specification and are pivotal to the correct operation of the EJB container.

These interfaces are created by developers during development (e.g., within WebSphere Studio Application Developer or whatever Java/J2EE IDE the developers or you choose). This allows the application server to perform management tasks under the hood, by mapping the calls to these EJB interfaces to the appropriate calls to the EJB itself.

The role of the EJB home interface is to provide a way for clients to find and create EJBs as needed. For entity EJBs, the home interface includes methods for finding single beans or groups of beans, based on certain criteria, including at least one method that allows the location of a bean in a database using a primary key class (e.g., FindByPrimaryKey).

For both entity EJBs and session EJBs, the home interface includes methods to create new instances of an EJB inside the EJB container and then return the reference to an instance of the EJB object interface for the specific EJB type.

NOTE   There is only ever one EJB home interface instance per class of EJB in an EJB container, but there may be many EJB object interface instances, depending on how many actual instances of the EJB class are active in the EJB container.

Session and Entity EJBs

It's worth breaking here for a moment to briefly explain the distinction between session and entity beans, as well as the difference between the types of session beans (i.e., stateful and stateless beans).

As I've touched on in previous chapters, entity beans are essentially EJBs used for representation of persistent data. An entity bean can be accessed by multiple clients concurrently, unlike a session bean, which is typically associated with a singular client transaction. The session bean is created for use by a client request in which the transaction updates and alters the state of the session bean.

Both types of EJBs contain logic. In the case of the entity bean, it will contain logic to persist and depersist data to and from the data source (e.g., an Oracle database), as well as finder and other data query methods. The session bean more likely includes business logic such as application and integration logic.

As I alluded to previously, session beans consist of two types of enterprise beans: stateful session beans and stateless session beans. Stateful session beans are a heavier incarnation of the session bean flavor. This type of enterprise session bean has a tightly bound relationship with client transactions.

Stateless session beans, on the other hand, are reusable distributed object constructs. This form of session bean is higher performing than the stateful session bean and isn't as tightly bound to the client transaction as the stateful session bean is.

As a development or architectural recommendation, try to avoid using stateful session beans. Due to their tightly bound client transaction relationship, they don't offer a highly scalable solution. Stateless session beans provide a scalable and higher performing solution than stateful session beans. Primarily, this is due to the fact that stateful session beans need to have their state passivated, which increases load within certain components of your environment.

The final component, the EJB object interface, is responsible for providing access to the method operations of an EJB. Any call to an EJB object interface instance is associated with a corresponding call to an EJB instance by the EJB container. Because of this separation from the actual EJB, the container is free to release resources used by the EJB as it deems necessary. These resources include database connections or even the EJB instance itself, yet the container restores the EJB instance when a client makes a new call to it.

In the next section you'll look at the approach for tuning the EJB and Web containers. Be mindful of the previous sections—it's a good thing to understand what it is you're tuning!

Tuning and Optimization

Let's now look at actually tuning the EJB and Web containers. Because of subtle differences between WebSphere versions 4 and 5, I've broken the discussion out by version. Generally speaking, both versions are quite similar, but WebSphere version 5's interface is different from WebSphere version 4's interface.

Before I begin, remember the golden rule about optimization: Tune/change one parameter at a time, test, document, and then start again. The worst thing you can do during a tuning and optimization effort is to go in and change a whole range of settings, save, restart, and test. This not only tunes settings that you may not need to tune (if it ain't broke, don't fix it), but also removes any clarity around what setting may have made *the* difference. For future reference, you want to be able to know what settings attributed to what performance improvements (or degradations!).

In the next section you'll examine the EJB container. It's important to note that the object request broker (ORB) is a key part of the EJB container's overall performance. This is primarily because client transaction requests are queued by the ORB (and routed) before being delivered to the EJB container itself.

EJB Container Tuning

To a point, you should really only bother with the EJB container if you are, in fact, using EJBs or EJB-JARs within your deployed applications. There are only a handful of "EJB container" settings, with most of the performance tuning from an EJB container perspective being carried out in other parts of the WebSphere configuration interfaces.

 NOTE Remember that there's no use tuning something that's not being used—it's a waste of your time!

In fact, the ORB itself plays a key role in the performance of the EJB container. The ORB receives requests from EJB clients and the requests are queued in the ORB thread pool (which I discussed in Chapter 7).

The next sections cover the minimal tuning aspect of the EJB container for WebSphere versions 4 and 5. I discuss the settings, what they mean, and where they're located. Following that, I discuss the tuning aspects of the various settings, most of which are common between WebSphere versions 4 and 5.

WebSphere Version 4 EJB Container Tuning

The EJB container in WebSphere version 4 doesn't provide a vast range of available options. As I noted before, the EJB container is really not optionable. Most of the settings that affect EJB performance are driven by the JVM. Further, remember that one of the powerful features about EJBs is that they allow the developer to focus on the development of application code, rather than the plumbing. Therefore, in theory and in line with the transparent, automagical EJB container layered interface between EJBs and EJB clients, the WebSphere "engine" should take care of the plumbing and dynamic tuning for you.

Let's first look at where to find the settings. Figure 9-4 is a screen shot of the WebSphere version 4 administration console. Notice on the right side of the screen the section highlighting the EJB container option under the Services selection tab.

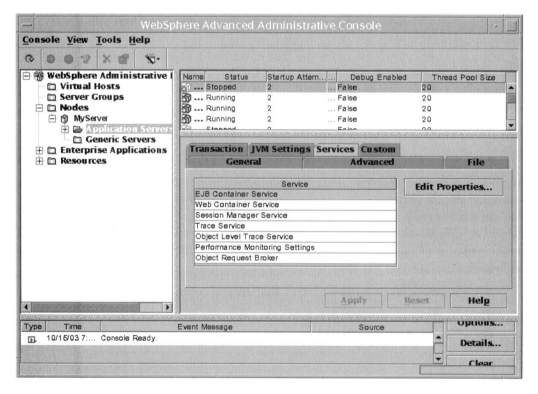

Figure 9-4. WebSphere version 4 administration console

You'll note that you can access the EJB container for any application server by following these steps:

1. Right-click the application server you want to view or modify.

2. Select Properties from the pull-down tab or click the desired application server, which changes the right administration console pane to offer the main configuration items available.

3. Select EJB Container Service.

4. Click Set Properties.

Once the EJB Container Service dialog box appears, you'll notice just how few settings there are, as shown in Figure 9-5.

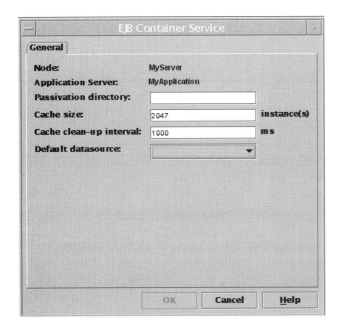

Figure 9-5. EJB Container Service dialog box in WebSphere version 4

As you can see, there are three settings available. Table 9-1 lists these settings and provides a brief description of each.

Table 9-1. EJB Container Service Options

Option	Description
Passivation directory	Directory used by WebSphere to store passivated session enterprise beans
Cache size	Value that determines how many cached EJBs can be resident in the local EJB cache at any one time
Cache cleanup interval	Value that determines the threshold when cache cleanup will occur by the EJB container cache manager

I discuss tuning these settings shortly. Let's now look at what is available and where in the WebSphere version 5 EJB container settings.

WebSphere Version 5 EJB Container Tuning

WebSphere version 5 operates in much the same way as version 4 in terms of the EJB container. Most of the tuning and dynamics of the container are managed by the application server itself, which is in turn managed by other defined settings, such as those from the ORB, the JVM, and so forth.

To access the EJB container settings in WebSphere version 5, simply follow these steps:

1. Ensure that the server's node is expanded and showing the link to Application Servers.

2. Click the application server item of your choice.

3. In the right pane, select the application server you want to modify.

4. Halfway down the screen, you'll see a link labeled EJB Container. Click this link.

5. You'll then be presented with the various options for the EJB container.

Figure 9-6 highlights the WebSphere version 5 console after the preceding selections have been made.

Let's now look at what to tune and when.

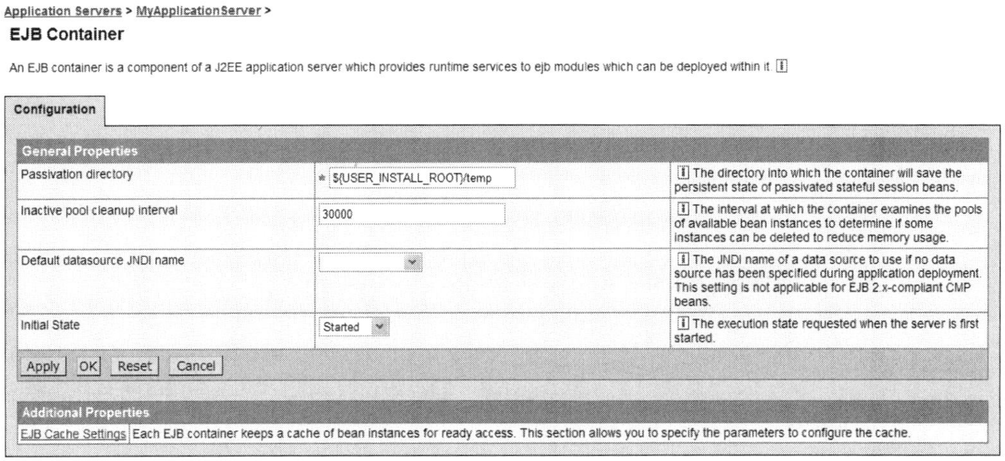

Application Servers > MyApplicationServer >
EJB Container

An EJB container is a component of a J2EE application server which provides runtime services to ejb modules which can be deployed within it. ⓘ

Configuration

General Properties

Passivation directory	∗ ${USER_INSTALL_ROOT}/temp	ⓘ The directory into which the container will save the persistent state of passivated stateful session beans.
Inactive pool cleanup interval	30000	ⓘ The interval at which the container examines the pools of available bean instances to determine if some instances can be deleted to reduce memory usage.
Default datasource JNDI name	▼	ⓘ The JNDI name of a data source to use if no data source has been specified during application deployment. This setting is not applicable for EJB 2.x-compliant CMP beans.
Initial State	Started ▼	ⓘ The execution state requested when the server is first started.

Apply   OK   Reset   Cancel

Additional Properties

EJB Cache Settings Each EJB container keeps a cache of bean instances for ready access. This section allows you to specify the parameters to configure the cache.

Figure 9-6. EJB container services in WebSphere version 5

Tuning the EJB Container

Both versions of WebSphere are fairly similar in their EJB container configurations. Essentially, you have four primary options you can use to optimize or tune the container:

- Passivation directory

- Inactive pool cleanup variable

- Cache size

- Cache cleanup interval

Let's look at each option and the most appropriate ways to optimize it.

Passivation Directory

The passivation directory is the location or directory where WebSphere will persist (save) stateful session EJBs.

When the EJB container needs to reclaim memory space, the container spawns a thread that serializes the appropriate session EJBs and persists them to a file on disk. In the event that a request is made to reuse the passivated session EJB, the EJB container deserializes it and pushes it back into the EJB container cache.

The key performance point here is where those persisted EJBs are stored and what they're stored on. If you set this option to use slow spinning disks or disks that are already heavily used by other I/O-intensive processes, you'll find that your EJB container, when under load, will perform badly.

Some rules of thumb for using the passivation directory are as follows:

- Ensure that this directory is on a relatively low-load disk or series of disks.

- Configure your file system, if possible, to use small file byte size allocations (e.g., in Unix, smaller bytes-per-inode are good for this setting, such as 1024 or 2048). This setting really depends on the size of your passivated session EJBs. Try to match them up if you're expecting a high passivation rate.

- Don't store this directory on a shared file system, such a Network File System (NFS) or Server Message Block (SMB) file system.

You should avoid having a high passivation rate. This means that there's some sort of memory shortfall somewhere, most likely in the cache settings for the EJB container. Memory is faster than passivation, so look to increase memory rather than rely on passivation.

At the end of the day, passivation is analogous to swap or virtual memory. It's good to have and useful to implement, but you want to avoid using it on a regular basis. Doing so means that there is a shortfall elsewhere and overall performance will be degraded.

Inactive Pool Cleanup Variable

Over the course of an EJB container or application server operating, you'll invariably build up junk that isn't needed. This includes enterprise bean instances that may be left lying around for one reason or another. You use this setting to help reclaim memory space by clearing out pooled bean instances that aren't used or haven't been used within a period of time.

This setting has an effect on the utilization of passivation. If bean instances—specifically, session bean instances—are lying around in container memory space, they'll be persisted, which will consume processing resources. It's best to set this value to an integer setting greater than 0 milliseconds to make sure that housecleaning is performed.

The catch is that you don't want to set this value too low, which will clear out instances that will only be re-created from scratch again shortly. At the same time, though, you want to ensure that you do clean out the space so that you don't consume valuable cache memory.

As a rule of thumb, set this value to be 10 times that of the cleanup interval setting. For example, if you set your cleanup interval to 5 seconds

(5,000 milliseconds), you should set your inactive pool cleanup variable to 50 seconds (50,000 milliseconds).

NOTE Because of the transactional nature of stateful EJBs and the manner in which the EJB container will passivate their state, it's important to consider time-out settings. Understand that incorrectly setting a time-out value will affect the capability of the EJB container "reaper" thread to satisfactorily clean up unwanted stateful session beans. You can set the time-out value within the Application Assembly Tool (ATT) prior to deployment of your EJBs or via manual modification of the EJB deployment descriptors once the stateful EJBs have been deployed.

Cache Size

The cache size setting refers to the number of cacheable objects in memory at any one time. WebSphere terminology refers to this as *buckets*, with buckets indicating the number of buckets being consumed by cached EJBs. This bucket list is, in fact, a hash table of sorts. Each bucket is just an entry to another EJB in the so-called cache.

As you can appreciate, the more buckets you have, the more memory is consumed by cached EJBs. If you set this value to, say, 5,000, and it's full, this will consume a great deal more memory than if you set it to 2,000. This comes back to the need for careful capacity planning and modeling. If you know that your EJBs will consume 200KB of memory each, and you have 10,000 of them in memory, you'll need at least 1.9GB of memory to store these EJBs.

The way to work this value out is to determine how many concurrent users you'll have active on your system at any one time and then multiply that number by the number of EJBs required or used within each user's functional transaction. If you're using session EJBs, add into this figure the number of active session EJBs at any one time. For example, you may have 1,000 concurrent users, and each standard transaction uses two EJBs. Occasionally, other EJBs are used, so you can use a value of three EJBs per functional transaction, which with 1,000 concurrent users would require 3,000 buckets in the cache size.

Cache Cleanup Interval

The cache cleanup interval is analogous to garbage collection within the JVM. This interval setting is used to clean out unwanted (as opposed to unused) items from the EJB container cache. Similar to the previous settings, this directive should be run only when appropriate—that is, not too frequently, but frequently enough so that when the job operates, your container isn't spending too much time processing old cache data.

As a guide, this setting should be 10 times less than the inactive pool cleanup variable. Therefore, if the inactive pool cleanup variable is set to 50,000 milliseconds, the cleanup interval setting should be 5,000 milliseconds.

You may find that tuning this setting slightly by 10 times either side of the value (e.g., 10 times less or more) may make subtle differences to the operational performance of your platform, but for most cases this thumb rule will work well.

Web Container Tuning

The Web container provides several more configuration items as standard, with the Session Manager settings being a separate component. Compared with the basic settings of the EJB container, the Web container provides more options for tuning the performance and processing characteristics.

The main types of elements that the Web container allows you to alter are directives around network queues and associated settings. These types of settings allow you to limit and control (and ultimately tune) how many connections your Web container should handle and what sort of transaction characteristic it should expect.

Let's take a look at the various options and configuration items available within the Web container.

WebSphere Version 4 Web Container Tuning

The WebSphere version 4 Web container settings are found via the same path as the EJB container settings. There are two ways to access them (through the console). Note that you can access the Web container for any application server by following these steps:

1. Right-click the application server you want to view or modify.

2. Select Properties from the pull-down tab or click the desired application server, which changes the right administration console pane to offer the main configuration items available.

3. Select Web Container Service from the list components.

4. Click Set Properties.

At this point, a dialog box will appear with three tabs at the top, as shown in Figure 9-7.

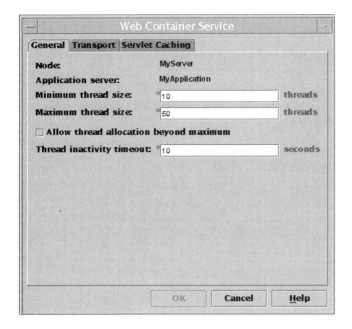

Figure 9-7. The Web Container Service dialog box in WebSphere version 4

The tabs General, Transport, and Servlet Caching provide the links to the main controls of the Web container configuration. I discuss the optimization and tuning approach for these settings shortly. First, though, the next section presents an overview of the WebSphere Web container settings for WebSphere version 5.

WebSphere Version 5 Web Container Tuning

Like the WebSphere version 4 configuration dialog box entry screens, the WebSphere version 5 HTTP-based console provides an easy way to configure your Web container settings. The key difference is that the Web container settings for WebSphere version 5 now encompass the session management settings. This section, however, excludes the session management settings, as I discussed them in Chapter 7.

Let's look at how you can access the container settings. Figure 9-8 shows a screen shot of a WebSphere version 5 console.

Figure 9-8 shows the right side of the WebSphere administration console after drilling down to the example application server's Web container settings. Follow the next steps to access the Web container settings. Use Figure 9-8 as a guide and use the breadcrumb navigation at the top of the right pane to help you understand where you're situated within the console.

1. Click the Application Servers link in the left pane.

2. Click the application server whose Web container you want to view or modify.

3. Scroll down the screen. In the right pane, you'll see a link labeled Web Container. Click this link.

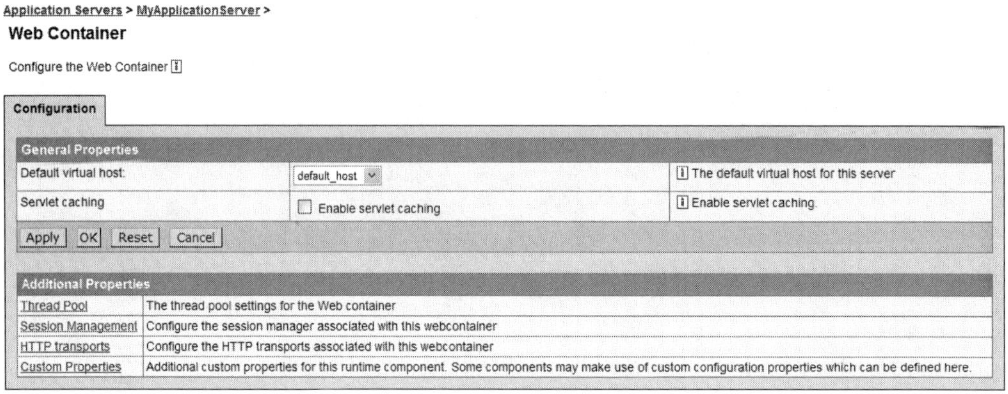

Application Servers > MyApplicationServer >
Web Container

Configure the Web Container ⓘ

| Configuration |

General Properties

| Default virtual host: | default_host ▾ | ⓘ The default virtual host for this server |
| Servlet caching | ☐ Enable servlet caching | ⓘ Enable servlet caching. |

Apply OK Reset Cancel

Additional Properties

Thread Pool	The thread pool settings for the Web container
Session Management	Configure the session manager associated with this webcontainer
HTTP transports	Configure the HTTP transports associated with this webcontainer
Custom Properties	Additional custom properties for this runtime component. Some components may make use of custom configuration properties which can be defined here.

Figure 9-8. Web container services in WebSphere version 5

At this stage, you're located in the Web container for your chosen application server. Keep an eye on the breadcrumb navigation at the top of pane to orientate you.

Instead of tabs, as in WebSphere version 4, you have four option links that provide access to Thread Pool, Session Management, HTTP Transports, and Custom Properties. I'll focus on the Thread Pool and HTTP Transports settings here.

Let's now look at modifying and optimizing the Web container.

Tuning the Web Container

As discussed earlier, the Web container is a fairly tunable component within your WebSphere application server. In this section, I discuss several key items that you should tune in order to maximize performance for Web-based components.

Keep in mind that because the Web container is "up the line" from heavy components such as EJBs and the database, if the Web container is performing poorly, then the rest of the environment will also perform poorly.

There are four key items you should tune to improve Web container performance:

- Thread size/thread pool

- Maximum keep-alive connections

- Maximum keep-alive requests

- Keep-alive I/O time-out

Configuring these four items is slightly different in each version of WebSphere. In the following sections, I highlight the configuration method for each of the settings.

Thread Size

As I discussed in earlier chapters relating to queues, *thread size* refers to the number of threads that are being processed by the Web container. In theory, this value is the number of elements, such as servlets and JSPs, being processed by the Web container.

With the value set to 25, your Web container can be processing a maximum of 25 JSPs and/or servlets at any one time. This value is arbitrary by itself and can only be set while within the context of your application's performance and transaction characteristics. This means that setting this value is about understanding the results of the queue modeling you did back in Chapter 6 as well as understanding your concurrent user load.

If you have a single WebSphere application server operating a single application server (hence, a single Web container), this value will be straightforward to set. If, on the other hand, you're running multiple WebSphere application servers, all of which are operating multiple cloned application servers (hence, many Web containers), this thread size value will be harder to set because you'll need to understand your total transaction rate, the rate at which requests are being sent to each server (e.g., are you using a weighted configuration in your HTTP plug-in?), and the length of time that the transactions are taking place.

To understand this value better, ensure that you use the Resource Analyzer (WebSphere version 4) or the Tivoli Performance Viewer (WebSphere version 5) to monitor both the Percent Maxed and Active Threads values.

 NOTE   See Chapters 13 and 14 for information on how to use the Resource Analyzer and Tivoli Performance Viewer tools.

My recommendation is to set this value to a setting 50 percent greater than your estimated number of concurrent users and, by using the Resource Analyzer or the Tivoli Performance Viewer, work your way down until your active threads are within 80 percent of the maximum thread size. Operating at 80 percent thread pool size means that you have room to move if you have an unforeseen peak, but at the same time you aren't wasting previous CPU cycles or memory.

As a rule of thumb, if your thread size looks like it will exceed 100, consider cloning and running multiple application servers instead. Trying to push too many threads through your Web container (i.e., your JVM) could result in bigger picture performance issues.

Keep in mind that your EJB container, with a setting of 100 threads in your Web container, will typically require between 50 and 75 threads. Therefore, with 100 threads active in your Web container and up to 75 in your EJB container, plus in-flight threads from the ORB and other resources, your JVM will be fully occupied.

To set the thread size value in WebSphere version 4, follow these steps:

1. From the Web Container Service dialog box, select the General tab.

2. In the Maximum thread size directive entry section, enter your desired value.

3. Select OK and then Apply. You'll need to restart your application server for the changes to take effect.

To set the thread size value in WebSphere version 5, follow these steps:

1. From the Web container section in the right pane, click the Thread Pool link.

2. In the Maximum Size directive entry box, enter your desired value.

3. Select Apply and OK, and ensure that you save your settings.

You'll notice a check box that allows you to let the threads go beyond the maximum limit. I recommend you never use this setting. Doing so will only open up your applications to bigger problems, and it's better for your customers to be able to sit in the network queue than experience a flaky or crashed environment.

 CAUTION   In WebSphere version 4, the default manner in which the ORB handles threads is to let them grow uncontrollably—there's no limit. To ensure that the threads don't run away and bring a system down, you can use specific JVM parameters to curb this undesired characteristic. The value for curbing this problem is `-Dcom.ibm.ws.OrbThreadPoolGrowable=false`.

TIP You can use an additional WebSphere version 4–specific parameter to help improve the ORB performance: `-Djavax.rmi.CORBA.UtilClass=com.ibm.CORBA.iiop.Util`. This parameter will essentially replace the standard `UtilClass` that comes as part of the core J2EE class packages with an IBM optimized version.

Maximum Keep-Alive Connections

This setting drives the number of keep-alive connections held open between the Web server plug-in and the Web container, or any other direct connecting Web-based interfacing client. Using keep-alive connections means that your server operating system (and, to an extent, WebSphere) isn't having to open and close connections constantly between the Web server tier. The purpose here is to ensure that connections are maintained for as long as possible. The key is to avoid having your server bogged down with TIME_WAIT states.

A rule of thumb here is to ensure that the number of TIME_WAITs between your Web tier and your application server doesn't exceed 15 to 20 percent of the total Web container thread pool. For example, if your thread size is set to 50, you shouldn't see any more than ten connections in a TIME_WAIT state.

TIP You can find out the value of how many connections are in TIME_WAIT state by using the `netstat` command in both Unix and Windows. Make sure you select values only from the output between your Web server(s) and your application server.

This setting works similarly to pooled connections to engines such as databases and legacy systems, in which the opening and closing of connections is expensive (resource-wise). Therefore, the best approach is to try to keep connections open for a longer period of time and reuse them.

Overall, this value can't exceed 80 to 90 percent of your Web container thread size. Each connection will consume a thread, and to ensure that you always have spare threads available, keep this value within those bounds. For example, on a system with a thread size of 50, the maximum keep-alive connections value should be set between 40 and 45 (80 percent and 90 percent, respectively). For a system with a thread size of 75, this value should be set between 60 and 67.

To set this value in WebSphere version 4, follow these steps:

1. From the Web Container Service dialog box, select the Transport tab.

2. In the Maximum keep-alives per request option, enter your desired value.

3. Select OK and then Apply. You'll need to restart your application server for the changes to take effect.

To set this value in WebSphere version 5, follow these steps:

1. From the Web Container section in the right pane, click the HTTP Transports link.

2. Select the Host Line Entry applicable to the Web container you want to modify.

3. Scroll down the right pane and select Custom Properties.

4. If you don't already have a value in the right pane labeled MaxKeepAliveConnections, click the New button. If you already have the value there and want to change it, click the MaxKeepAliveConnections setting.

5. A new screen will appear with three empty boxes. In the Name field, enter the directive property **MaxKeepAliveConnections**.

6. In the Value field, enter the setting for this option (e.g., **60**).

7. Click Apply and OK, and then save your settings. You'll need to restart your application server for the changes to take effect.

This is an easy setting to monitor and test using the Resource Analyzer or Tivoli Performance Viewer tool. Ensure that you've stress-tested and volume-tested this setting before moving into production.

Maximum Keep-Alive Requests

This setting ultimately determines how many connections can be open to process and transfer data, such as HTML, images, and so forth. Over each keep-alive connection, it's possible to send many requests.

After the defined number of requests has been sent over the keep-alive connection, the connection is terminated and reestablished. This helps to ensure that resource or connection starvation doesn't take place and that there isn't an "open door" to resource utilization. Indirectly, this also helps prevent various DoS attacks, by ensuring that there isn't a constant open connection available.

If you're able to ensure that only requests from a specific Web server and plug-in will connect to your Web container (via the use of port blocking, stringent controls, etc.), this setting can be increased to quite a high value to improve performance. By default, the value is set to 100, which means that at full utilization, there will be x number of keep-alive connections active, with y number of requests, or x multiplied by y.

If your WebSphere applications are fairly Web intensive and have a lot of components within the presentation such as images and other items, increasing this setting will increase the performance, because the container won't be closing the keep-alive connections down as frequently.

My recommendation is to use a rule of setting this value to 2.5 times that of the thread size—meaning that with a thread size of 50, you would set this setting to 125. There is no upper recommended limit. However, be aware that the higher this value is, the more requests can come through from a DoS attack. Be sure to consider port and or route blocking so that only known servers can connect to this interface.

You need to be aware also of the fact that if your presentation consists of many images and elements in your interface output, you may need to look at the number of open files available to the operating WebSphere user process (e.g., ulimit on Unix). If this setting is too low and there are too many requests being made over the keep-alive connections, your output will quickly become broken with missing images and elements.

To make the changes to this setting in WebSphere version 4, follow these steps:

1. From the Web Container Service dialog box, select the Transport tab.

2. In the Maximum requests per keep-alive directive entry section, enter your desired value.

3. Select OK and then Apply. You'll need to restart your application server for the changes to take effect.

To make the changes to this setting in WebSphere version 5, follow these steps:

1. From the Web Container section in the right pane, click the HTTP Transports link.

2. Select the Host Line Entry applicable to the Web container you want to modify.

3. Scroll down the right pane and select Custom Properties.

4. If you don't already have a value in the right pane labeled MaxKeepAliveRequests, click the New button. If you already have the value there and want to change it, click the MaxKeepAliveRequests setting.

5. A new screen will appear with three empty boxes. In the Name field, enter the directive property **MaxKeepAliveRequests**.

6. In the Value field, enter in the setting for this option (e.g., **125**).

7. Click Apply and OK, and then save your settings. You'll need to restart your application server for the changes to take effect.

Keep-Alive I/O Time-out

The keep-alive I/O time-out setting allows you to control how long keep-alive connections should wait for I/O before timing out and closing the keep-alive. This setting is closely coupled with the previous two settings, MaxKeepAliveRequests and MaxKeepAliveConnections. The time interval between I/O or data flow over a keep-alive connection constitutes the trigger for this setting.

If the value of the keep-alive I/O time-out is reached, that particular keep-alive connection will be closed. This helps prevent the available connection list from filling up and running out of free connections for new or additional customer requests. However, the opposite can also happen, whereby lengthy transactions may hold open a keep-alive for a longer period of time, in which case you don't want the connections to be closed prematurely.

Like most of these types of settings, it's a balancing act. On one side you have resource exhaustion, a situation in which you may be running out of free connections if the keep-alive I/O time-out is set too high, and on the other side, you have transactions failing or poorly performing as connections are prematurely closed on them. In most cases, applications with Web components will be able to complete their transactions in under 10 seconds. If, however, you have slow links, overloaded servers, or an unusual application transaction characteristic, this setting will be important.

You can use the Resource Analyzer or Tivoli Performance Viewer tool to understand if your Web transactions are triggering I/O time-outs on your keep-alive connections. In the Web Container drop-down of these tools, ensure that you are collecting data on the "aborted connections" data collection element.

If you see that the aborted connections value is greater than 5 to 10 percent of the total closed connections, you may need to look to increase the keep-alive

I/O time-out setting. As a guide, for normal operations, the default setting of 5 (seconds) is usually sufficient. I've seen cases in which this setting has been required to be set higher than 15 seconds, but this is unusual.

The basic rule for this setting is to ensure that you have it correctly tuned for your application. There is no golden rule or magic calculation you should use other than testing and analysis. You can perform a sanity check by saying that with, for example, 100 connections available in your Web connection request pool and an idle time-out of 5 seconds, you can't exceed 1,200 lengthy transactions per minute (100 connections times 5 seconds, over 60 seconds). So, if you bank on the fact that all your connections will be completed within 50 percent of the I/O time-out, that being 2.5 seconds, you can say that your application environment is good for 2,400 requests per minute or 40 transactions per second (2,400 requests per minute divided by 60 seconds).

The point of this is that if you set your value too low, but your application does in fact have a long I/O interval as a normal operation, you'll need to increase the number of connection requests possible through your Web container and/or increase the I/O time-out value. If you don't do this, you'll have a bottleneck in your environment because it won't be able to process the required transaction rate.

As a guide, it's possible to set this value to 0, meaning that there will be no time-out whatsoever. However, like most infinite value settings, although it may be helpful from an operational point of view to set nonconstraining values, it does over time open the door to problems such as zombie connections. These types of issues will ultimately exhaust all available connections in your pools (this is analogous to a memory leak—it isn't initially a problem, but over time it becomes one).

To make the changes to this setting in WebSphere version 4, follow these steps:

1. From the Web Container Service dialog box, select the Transport tab.

2. In the Keep-alive time-out directive entry section, enter your desired value.

3. Select OK and then Apply. You'll need to restart your application server for the changes to take effect.

To make the changes to this setting in WebSphere version 5, follow these steps:

1. From the Web Container section in the right pane, click the HTTP Transports link.

2. Select the Host Line Entry applicable to the Web container you want to modify.

3. Scroll down the right pane and select Custom Properties.

4. If you don't already have a value in the right pane labeled ConnectionKeepAliveTimeout, click the New button. If you already have the value there and want to change it, click the ConnectionKeepAliveTimeout setting.

5. A new screen will appear with three empty boxes. In the Name field, enter the directive property **ConnectionKeepAliveTimeout**.

6. In the Value field, enter the setting for this option (e.g., **5**).

7. Click Apply and OK, and then save your settings. You'll need to restart your application server for the changes to take effect.

Summary

In this chapter, you examined the recommended settings and optimization techniques for the WebSphere EJB and Web containers. Although the containers themselves don't have a large number of available tuning options, their importance in your application environment's overall performance should be evident. Nothing can beat good testing and proper use of the Resource Analyzer or Tivoli Performance Viewer tool to help you tune these settings to the correct values.

This chapter's aim wasn't to provide you with the exact answer with regard to settings; rather, it was intended to serve as a guide for what to change in your environment to get better performance and what upper and lower thresholds you should consider for those settings.

Developing High-Performance WebSphere Applications

THIS CHAPTER EXPLORES A range of hot-list items that developers who develop applications for WebSphere application servers (the majority of application servers, in fact) should consider using to ensure that performance and scalability management is maintained.

It's almost amusing to watch the antics of developers and architects on projects. Quite often, the architect is stereotyped as someone who really doesn't know the details of what he or she is talking about, except at 50,000-foot level. The developer is often stereotyped as someone developing an application against a specification without considering the big picture. Both of these stereotypes are true in some ways, but false in others. My own belief is that a true architect was a developer in a previous life or may still in fact be in a developer-type role (e.g., lead developer, technical lead, etc.). I don't believe you can architect something that you don't have a fundamental understanding of. Also, I don't believe you can be a Java/J2EE architect without knowing how to code and understanding what it is that you preach. I've seen too many cases in which an "architect" has designed a system and has represented it as a construction of pretty boxes and other shapes on single slide of a PowerPoint presentation.

The reason I've included this chapter is to try to help educate readers of this book about some fundamental design considerations that can make a big difference in the performance of an application operating under WebSphere. This chapter consists of 20 rock-solid performance boosters (broken out by tier) for enterprise J2EE applications that run under WebSphere. This list is by no means exhaustive—entire books have been written on just this topic. What I've tried to do here is present some of the heavy hitters.

NOTE Most of the design considerations presented in this chapter can be implemented on other J2EE application servers.

It's important to note that this chapter doesn't attempt to explain how to code the specific recommendations. Many of the recommendations are fairly fundamental best practices, but far too often I see them missed or forgotten. I believe this is partly due to the nature of a Java-based application development environment, in which timelines are tight, the language allows for a lot of corner cutting, and there are a number of ways to implement any single component.

My purpose here is to explain what the recommendations are and why you should use them (e.g., what the benefits are), in the context of helping to ensure that your WebSphere environment is well tuned and that the applications that run within it are optimized and coded smartly.

To summarize, each section lists the recommendation and gives it a rating from 1 to 5 for the performance and/or scalability benefit it offers an application operating within a WebSphere environment (with a rating of 1 being the highest benefit and 5 being the lowest benefit) and another rating from 1 to 5 for the implementation complexity (with a rating of 1 being a relatively straightforward implementation and 5 being a complex implementation effort). These ratings indicate the level of change required for an application and the level of complexity the application's developers will need to adjust to.

The Top 20 List of Performance Development Considerations

Table 10-1 lists the top 20 rock-solid performance development considerations this chapter covers.

Table 10-1. Top 20 WebSphere Application Performance Considerations

Consideration	Targeted Tier
Avoid constant use of large session objects	Web tier
Invalidate HTTP sessions when they aren't required	Web tier
Use the init() servlet method if doGet() and doPost() aren't required	Web tier
Use <jsp: usebean()> carefully	Web tier
Don't use the single-threaded model with servlets	Web tier
Reuse EJB homes where possible	Business tier
Consider Pass-by-Reference rather than Pass-by-Value	Business tier
Use a multithreaded logger instead of system.out.println()	Business tier
Use container threading services and avoid manually spawning threads	Business tier

Table 10-1. Top 20 WebSphere Application Performance Considerations (Continued)

Consideration	Targeted Tier
Avoid lazy initialization of objects	Business tier
Avoid overusing Java niceties	Business tier
Avoid stateful EJBs where possible	Business tier
Use constants	Business tier
Assume remote objects, but write for local	Business tier
Use Abstraction	Business tier
Use WebSphere data sources	Data tier
Release JDBC resources when you've finished with them	Data tier
Use container-managed persistence only for high-read database access	Data tier
Use Data Access Objects for general database access	Data tier
Use prepared SQL statements where possible	Data tier

Let's now take a look at each consideration in more detail. Considerations appear under the appropriate tier.

Web Tier Performance

The *Web tier* refers to all Web containers, Web servers, and components. This includes Java components such as

- JavaServer Pages (JSP) pages

- Servlets

- Standard classes and beans

- Session Manager settings

Avoid Constant Use of Large Session Objects

As you've learned in previous chapters, sessions are a key element of any Web-based WebSphere application environment. It's possible to overuse sessions by filling them up with unnecessary information, not releasing unwanted elements after use, or using them for incorrect purposes. The effect is exaggerated when session persistence is used to achieve additional levels of redundancy.

Essentially, in the case of persisting the session object because accessing the session object requires serialization and deserialization for each update and read, respectively (to and from the session persistence layer), the J2EE application incurs significant overhead if sessions become too large. This impact is further realized if you use persistent sessions, in which you persist sessions to a database in order to gain availability.

To summarize,

- Don't use sessions for storing large amounts of data for all users.

- Try to keep session object sizes at around 4KB for 95 percent of all session objects. This allows for some large sessions, which may be required to store specific data (e.g., 100KB of data to store an uploaded text file).

- Don't load everything into a session object. Only load the specific information you need in your session at any one time. Too often I've seen situations in which environments load large amounts of data into session objects, only to need very specific amounts of data.

- Consider using a database to store information specific to user sessions if you find that you need to constantly go over the 4KB session object size. Performance will degrade as you go above 4KB to 6KB for session object size, depending on overall system load.

Performance and scalability benefit:	1
Implementation complexity:	3

Invalidate HTTP Sessions When They Aren't Required

HTTP sessions are often used in Web applications. One of the common implementation errors that developers make is not cleaning up sessions that are no longer required. This is a side effect of the thought that because you don't need to manage memory in Java (unlike in C, C++, and so on), you don't need to clear off unused objects.

Because WebSphere can maintain only a certain number of sessions at any one time in memory (a configurable counter), and the fact that there's a finite amount of memory available per application Java Virtual Machine (JVM), you'll want to ensure that you provide your JVM and other application threads the maximum amount of memory available or required by them. By also not invalidating the HTTP sessions forcefully, the JVM garbage collection will spend more time clearing out heap space for other application threads, which impacts overall JVM performance.

To summarize,

- Ensure that your users are provided with a "log off" function that calls the invalidate() method.

- Carefully model your users' online and pause times. You maybe able to decrease the period until WebSphere times out and ultimately forces all timed-out sessions to be invalidated. The default WebSphere setting is 30 minutes (1,800 seconds).

Performance and scalability benefit:	3
Implementation complexity:	2

Use the init() Servlet Method if doGet() and doPost() Aren't Required

Basic servlets consist of the init(), doGet(), and doPost() methods, which are used for different purposes when a servlet is called. The init() method is called each time a call to initialize a servlet is made, whereas the doGet() and doPost() methods are only called when those types of HTTP transactions are requested through the HTTP headers in a user request.

Quite often, a servlet isn't required to perform any function based on input. For this reason, there's no need to use a doGet() method call—this will incur overhead that isn't required. Consider placing heavy or expensive transactions in the init() method instead of in the doGet() and doPost() methods. A classic example is to place bindings to data sources in the init() method, which will alleviate a rebind on each doGet() or doPost() method call. This will increase performance within your application.

To summarize, question the use of doGet() and doPost() method usage in servlets if the servlets aren't expecting any input but are required to return information.

Performance and scalability benefit:	3
Implementation complexity:	2

Use <jsp: usebean()> Carefully

This JSP tag allows developers to directly call a JavaBean from within the JSP code. Quite often, developers use this approach in JSP pages to fill small variables or values into JSP output such as simple integers (e.g., account balances).

This tag, however, will create a new instance of the specific JavaBean if the JavaBean object doesn't already exist. Creating the new bean is an expensive JVM operation and, unless required, it should be used only to obtain a reference to an existing Java object.

Performance and scalability benefit:	3
Implementation complexity:	2

Don't Use the Single-Threaded Model with Servlets

A design approach exists with servlets that allows the servlets to be developed using a single-threaded model. This approach is sometimes used to ensure the protection of specific variables within a servlet's context; however, it does introduce a performance and scalability implication by limiting the number of servlet threads that can be running concurrently.

If specific variables need to be managed per client thread, consider using the session object for small variables or other forms of data storage, such as memory caches and/or databases.

Performance and scalability benefit:	2
Implementation complexity:	2

Business Tier Performance

The *business tier* is the core WebSphere tier, and it's typically associated with EJB containers and the like. The business tier consists of the following Java components:

- One or many EJB containers and EJBs

- Non-Web container Java classes

- Operational Java components

- Design pattern considerations

Let's now take a look at the business tier development performance considerations.

Reuse EJB Homes Where Possible

As you've seen in previous chapters, EJB homes are the points at which other Java client components hook into EJBs running within the EJB container.

Each initialContext lookup to obtain the EJB home is a JVM-intensive operation. For that reason, EJB homes can be both cached and reused with multiple Java components, thereby greatly reducing the cost of requesting the context of an EJB home for each request.

Other implementation considerations include developing helper or locator classes that are called by Java clients that maintain a list of EJB homes. This approach works well for high-volume applications in which EJB homes are looked up frequently.

Performance and scalability benefit:	2
Implementation complexity:	4

Consider Pass-by-Reference Rather Than Pass-by-Value

Pre-EJB 2.0 (i.e., WebSphere version 4), there was no direct way to avoid deploying an EJB client and an EJB to the same server and having to communicate out via the network using RMI. Some vendors, including IBM, provide a feature known as Pass-by-Reference that facilitates method calls via local interfaces, between EJB clients and EJBs. This effectively makes the EJBs appear local and avoids the overhead of going out via the network and RMI stack for communications. This recommendation is only valid for WebSphere version 4, as WebSphere version 5 supports EJB 2.0, which includes a feature to set EJBs to listen locally rather than remotely (or both).

Implementing this change is as simple as modifying the IBM extension deployment descriptor after launch via the ORB properties configuration dialog box (within the Application Server properties menu in the WebSphere console) or via the Application Assembly Tool (AAT) prior to deploying the application EJB components.

Performance and scalability benefit:	2
Implementation complexity:	1

Use a Multithreaded Logger Instead of system.out.println()

One of the painful aspects of operational management is trying to balance the trade-off between good tracing and logging information, and too much information (which usually drives down performance).

The Java.IO classes are solid in functionality, but they do suffer from performance issues pertaining to their fairly heavy use of object synchronization. This can also lead to a heavy usage of disk I/O due to the nature of the I/O mechanism used by the `system.out.println()` class. For this reason, consider employing a third-party logging application. Probably the most popular Java-based logger available is the Jakarta log4j application. It's a multithreaded, collapsible logging system for J2EE and Java application environments.

Use `system.out.println()` only for specific messages relating to the containers in your applications. For application debug and informational messages, use log4j, which you can configure to log only certain types of data. You can also activate and deactivate log4j during runtime. And best of all, it's fast and free!

Performance and scalability benefit:	2
Implementation complexity:	3

Use Container Threading Services and Avoid Manually Spawning Threads

Pre-J2EE days meant that the onus of threading within Java application environments was on the Java developer. One of the powerful features of J2EE is the container. The introduction of the container meant that it (the container) would manage and handle all threading allocation and management within its scope, as opposed to having developers manually develop this form of plumbing.

It's still possible to develop applications and manually create and spawn threads that are unmanaged by the container, but this can place a great deal of overhead on your application server. As each thread consumes JVM processing cycles (and memory), the JVM, through the J2EE threading framework, is constantly monitoring and managing thread pool allocation. If threads are being spawned outside the thread manager's scope, then performance problems will arise.

In summary, unless you have very specific reasons for doing so, don't spawn your own threads. Use the containers to manage thread allocation for your applications.

Performance and scalability benefit: 2

Implementation complexity: 3

Use Lazy Initialization of Objects

Lazy initialization is the process or design of your application code to not load up objects until they're required. For example, don't initialize an object outside an if statement. Instead, initialize the object within the specific if branch that you may require it for.

Lazy initialization also refers to a manner of the activation of entity EJBs. Typically, entity EJBs are activated with all their data references referenced. This may not be the desired result if you only want to load the entity EJB in order to get a specific reference to data.

By using the lazy initialization approach, you're able to activate the EJB to get the specific data reference from the entity EJB when you require it, rather than having all the data retrieved by default, at activation.

Performance and scalability benefit: 2

Implementation complexity: 3

Avoid Overusing Java Niceties

The Java language has a raft of smart features and nice coding syntaxes. Many of these features and syntaxes come with performance trade-offs, however. If your application environment is small or your volumes just aren't high, then your mileage with these considerations may not warrant a look.

Here are some of the more common Java language and feature niceties that you should avoid:

- Consider using the conditional syntax of "? :" instead of if-then structures.

- Use StringBuffer instead of concatenating the String type. Concatenating strings causes the JVM to have to copy and overlay objects in memory.

- Avoid creating objects early. A classic example is when you create a variable in front of an if-then loop. Only one of the if-then branches may ever use it, if at all. This consumes memory and should be avoided. Place these variables and other object creation directives in the actual if-then clause requiring them.

- Attempt to size objects such as hashTables and Vectors. This helps the JVM pre-allocate object memory. Heap allocation of these types of objects works by doubling their size each time memory is required to be increased.

- Be conscious of unused objects floating around that consume heap space. Objects will lie around for a period of time until garbage collection occurs. For example, the toUpper() and toLower() methods create objects in memory when used, but the objects remain in memory until garbage collection, after the method call is completed.

Performance and scalability benefit:	3
Implementation complexity:	1

Avoid Stateful EJBs Where Possible

Stateful EJBs are good in theory—on their own—but they're a problematic component type to work with. From a WebSphere perspective, stateful EJBs don't support workload management failover. This is a big problem for scalable and high-performing WebSphere environments.

For the most part, the functionality of a stateful EJB can be supported through the use of session objects or persisting information to a database or data store. The very nature and the limited EJB caching capability of a stateful EJB means that there's a fair degree of overhead to the EJB container when it attempts to passivate dormant or idled stateful EJBs and later activate them.

In summary, where possible avoid stateful EJBs and consider using other stateful constructs such as session objects and databases. Use stateless EJBs to perform data population. In Chapter 9, you explored the process of sizing and tuning the EJB cache. This will help you gain some performance advantages if your application design mandates that you use stateful EJBs.

Performance and scalability benefit:	3
Implementation complexity:	3

Use Constants

Like many programming languages, variables and constants are commonplace in code. In Java, a *variable* is an object that is provided to hold some form of data of a specific data type. A *constant* is a variable that is constant and doesn't change for the duration of its lifetime.

Always use constants for variables that don't change within the life cycle of the application. The application's performance can benefit greatly, thanks to the JVM's capability to optimize compilation of constants over that of standard variables. For example, here's a standard variable:

```
String myString = new String("WebSphere");
```

and here's a constant:

```
Static final String myString = "WebSphere";
```

Heavy use of constants over variables during some Java programming usages can result in a tenfold increase in performance.

Performance and scalability benefit:	2
Implementation complexity:	1

Assume Remote Objects, but Write for Local

It's important to develop applications in EJB (or any other distributed J2EE technology) form with the mind-set that although the component you're developing can be used remotely from other locations (e.g., from another WebSphere server via RMI), there's always a great deal of overhead associated with remote calls. A transaction here and a transaction there aren't going to bring your application to its knees; however, many transactions will show a performance degradation if the reliance and efficiency of the remote call is overused.

Local method calls within a stand-alone Java application will see response times of between 1 and 10 milliseconds, whereas a remote call to a local EJB method will see response times of between 200 and 1,000 milliseconds. A remote call to another host will see response times of anywhere between 500 and 5,000 milliseconds. Therefore, it's important that you develop your remote invocation components in a way that's highly efficient and assumes remote calls will be made. Following this approach will also help to ensure that local access is optimized.

NOTE WebSphere version 5 supports the new EJB 2.0 local interface specification that allows application components local to the
EJB container to access methods inside EJBs without the overhead of being serialized and deserialized via the RMI protocol.

Performance and scalability benefit:	2
Implementation complexity:	3

Use Abstraction

Abstraction is a fairly loosely used term in application design, but when abstraction is used and implemented correctly, it provides many benefits. Abstraction,
in the context of developing J2EE applications, directs application design in such
a way that all remote callable components should be accessed via a form of
abstraction such as a façade (e.g., the Façade pattern).

Abstraction provides a level of robustness, and ultimately scalability, in your
application's design. You can scale up, change, and alter your back-end components but, if abstraction is used and implemented correctly, your Java clients will
still be able to access the modified back-end components (e.g., EJBs) via a
façade, which helps with platform robustness and scalability.

A slight runtime performance trade-off is involved, depending on your
abstraction implementation approach. Every additional level of abstraction,
while introducing an additional level of robustness and component compartmentalization, does incur a slight performance hit. Without abstraction,
however, your application platform will become brittle and will be affected by
changes made to application components at almost every level.

Performance and scalability benefit:	2
Implementation complexity:	2

Data Tier Performance

The *data tier* within a WebSphere environment relates to all components associated with the database itself or Java components that communicate with the
database.

Use WebSphere Data Sources

It's possible to develop your applications without WebSphere configured and managed data sources. To gain the maximum advantage of a centrally managed application environment, however, it's crucial that you use WebSphere data sources (and ultimately WebSphere connection pool managers).

When you use the WebSphere managed components, the application's JVM and containers are centrally aware of the state of all transactions, queries, connections, and threads within the applications' runtime. This ensures that your applications are running in a contiguous environment, rather than an environment that is compartmentalized with differing, nonaware components.

Using these data sources also enables you to support connection pooling and other WebSphere extension–based services, and it lets you monitor the state of all communications and transactions using the PMI and Resource Analyzer/Tivoli Performance viewer interfaces.

Performance and scalability benefit:	1
Implementation complexity:	2

Release JDBC Resources When You've Finished with Them

It's a common problem to find application code in which JDBC resources that were once created and used during an application's database transaction are left open and unused well after the database transaction has been completed. Like any other objects, these JDBC connections, statements, and result objects consume memory. The memory consumption is even more evident if you have large result sets coming back from your database—those remain in memory after the database query's completion.

Not only does this consume valuable JVM memory, but it also consumes resources from the connection pool managers' list of available free database connections. By not closing these connections off, you place further load onto your database and resources by not freeing up connections for other application threads. It's imperative that your application code closes down its objects, preferably in the following order:

- Result sets

- Statements

- Connections

The problem is somewhat analogous to developers' misconception that JVM will eventually clean up old and unused objects. In this case, it's incorrectly believed that the pool manager will eventually clean up these objects (especially the connection object); however, this takes time, and if every database query acted in this fashion, you'd quickly run out of database connections in your connection pool. Be sure that your application code also closes down connections and statements in failure situations, after your application receives or throws an exception.

Performance and scalability benefit: 1

Implementation complexity: 2

Use Container-Managed Persistence Only for High-Read Database Access

Container-managed persistence (CMP) is a solid J2EE technology that takes the notion of having your application server manage all your application plumbing for you to another level. CMP allows you to define a schema using deployment descriptors and entity EJBs, and have the EJB container manage all the database queries, transactions, and persistence layer for you. You don't need to develop any SQL calls—instead, you use CMP methods such as `findByPrimaryKey(value)` to locate specific database entries.

CMP is a fairly new technology and it's still evolving. Therefore, there are still a number of potential problems with it if it isn't implemented correctly. With the more recent EJB 2.0 specification, CMP has become a lot better than its EJB 1.1 predecessor, but there's still a ways to go before it provides the same level of broad performance as native JDBC.

Because of the nature of CMP and how it functions, it's well suited to application environments that are high-read, low-write. With each change to the database contents, the CMP beans will need to re-obtain the updated table data from the database. Tuning and configuration items can alter this and the CMP behavior. However, for the most part, CMP is best suited for high-read database environments and best avoided for anything write intensive. (Consider DAOs and native JDBC for write-intensive environments.)

Performance and scalability benefit: 2

Implementation complexity: 4

Use Data Access Objects for General Database Access

I discuss the *Data Access Object* (DAO) design pattern in Chapter 12 in the context of database performance optimization. Essentially, a DAO is based on an object-oriented pattern. The DAO provides a façade for developers to access database data without having to involve themselves in database connection plumbing and the performance aspects of database connectivity.

The DAO still uses WebSphere connection pooling and data sources, but it provides a level of abstraction for developers to communicate with. This helps to ensure that database accesses are managed and robust rather than having multiple forms of database accesses occurring via different class implementations across an application.

The DAO is essentially an intelligent and structured way of accessing a database layer that uses JDBC as the underlying protocol. In a non-CMP/BMP environment in which frequent database accesses occur, a DAO implementation is a sound option for performance with a high degree of robustness.

Performance and scalability benefit: 2

Implementation complexity: 3

Use Prepared SQL Statements Where Possible

If you have SQL statements in your application that are repeatedly called to the database, you may find that the use of *prepared statements* provides a higher performing approach. Prepared statements work by allowing the database to cache a common SQL statement and subsequent similar queries to the database and it involves only the passing of bound variables. For example, select name from user_table where color = "pink" is the same as select name from user_table where color = "red" except for the variable.

The parsing of a database query is an expensive task for the query processor to perform. The concept behind SQL prepared statements is that only the variables should change and, therefore, subsequent queries made are the same and don't need to go through the database's query parser engine for compilation. This increases performance and greatly reduces overhead.

The prepared statements' capability is supported by the SQL classes within WebSphere—specifically, the PreparedStatement() method is used instead of the standard Statement() method for building up and parsing in queries to the database.

Performance and scalability benefit: 1

Implementation complexity: 2

Summary

In this chapter, you've seen 20 hot-list items that I consider to be low-hanging fruit (i.e., easy, low risk, and quick win) when it comes to well-performing and well-scaled application development. As I noted at the beginning of the chapter, there are thousands of best practices and recommended approaches for Java/J2EE application development. That said, the 20 items I covered in this chapter will provide you with a good starting point and serve as a checklist for your performance management. Your mileage may vary with each item, so be sure to study each in detail before you implement it.

CHAPTER 11

WebSphere Database Performance and Optimization

As you've seen during earlier chapters of this book, the database is probably the next most important component within a WebSphere application environment after the application server itself. In this chapter, you'll learn ways to improve the overall performance of your WebSphere integration with a relational database.

WebSphere Database Overview

A vast proportion of WebSphere-based environments globally operate with some form of backend database. The reason why isn't complex. Consider for a moment the crux of most WebSphere application environments. They provide a service to customers and end users, typically via a Web medium (some via other means such as thick Java clients) in one of three categories:

- Order and sales

- Services and provisioning

- Information presentation

Order and sales WebSphere-based applications are sites such as Amazon and eBay. Services and provisioning cover features such as Internet banking and Business-to-Business (B2B) commerce, and information presentation covers services such as those provided by Google, Webcasts, and Internet news sites. If you consider each of these examples, you should be able to picture how and where you'll integrate a database.

Don't get me wrong—they're not a necessity, but databases are common WebSphere environment components. Remember, you may be running a WebSphere 5 system that doesn't need to run a database for a repository—you may want to run a Lightweight Directory Access Protocol (LDAP) server instead. Some of the previous examples may work fine with an LDAP implementation.

Either way, it's important to understand how to optimize WebSphere and a relational database to ensure that you maximize your end-to-end performance. Remember, the sum of the overall WebSphere environment's performance is only as good as the lowest performing component.

Databases Supported

WebSphere supports a number of databases for using either the WebSphere 4 repository or both versions of WebSphere for application storage. Table 11-1 and Table 11-2 list the directly supported versions of various databases. Depending on the drivers and platforms, your mileage may vary given that there are numerous other databases and data servers available (for example, nonrelational ones such as object-oriented databases).

Specifically, Table 11-1 lists all the IBM-certified relational databases for WebSphere 4.

Table 11-1. WebSphere 4–Supported Relational Databases

Database	Supported Versions
Oracle 8*i*	8.1.7
Oracle 9*i*	9.0.1, 9.2
Informix Dynamic Server	7.31, 9.21, 9.3
SQL Server Enterprise 2000	2000 with Service Pack (SP) 2
SQL Server Enterprise 7	7 with SP 2 or SP 4
IBM DB2 Workgroup Edition	7.2 with FixPack 5, 6, 7, 8, or 9
IBM DB2 Workgroup Server Edition	8.1 with FixPack 1 or 2
IBM DB2 Enterprise Edition	7.2 with FixPack 5, 6, 7, 8, or 9
IBM DB2 Enterprise Server Edition	8.1 with FixPack 1 or 2
IBM DB2 Enterprise Extended Edition	7.2 with FixPack 5, 6, 7, 8, or 9
IBM DB2 for iSeries	5.1
IBM DB2 for 390 systems	6.1, 7.1
Sybase Adaptive Server Enterprise	12.0

Table 11-2 lists the certified databases for WebSphere 5.

Table 11-2. WebSphere 5–Supported Relational Databases

Database	Supported Versions
Oracle 8*i*	8.1.7, 8.1.7.4
Oracle 9*i*	9.2, 9.2.0.2, 9.2.0.3
Informix Dynamic Server	7.31, 9.3, 9.4
SQL Server Enterprise 2000	2000 with SP2
SQL Server Enterprise 7	7 with SP4
IBM DB2 Workgroup Edition	7.2 with FixPack 7, 8, or 9
IBM DB2 Workgroup Server Edition	8.1 with FixPack 1 or 2
IBM DB2 Enterprise Edition	7.2 with FixPack 7, 8, or 9
IBM DB2 Enterprise Server Edition	8.1 with FixPack 1 or 2
IBM DB2 Enterprise Extended Edition	7.2 with FixPack 7, 8, or 9
IBM DB2 for iSeries	5.1, 5.2
IBM DB2 for zSeries	6.1, 7.1
Cloudscape	5.0.10, 5.0.12, 5.1.21
Sybase Adaptive Server Enterprise	12.0, 12.5

The relational database mix of available servers is somewhat the same between the two versions of WebSphere.

 CAUTION   The Cloudscape 5.0.10 and 5.0.12 database server versions as provided in Table 11-2 aren't supported in a production environment. Version 5.1.21 is supported as a production database server.

Although not officially supported by IBM, many other databases work with WebSphere. Just make sure your database is truly American National Standards Institute (ANSI) SQL-92 compliant and that it can support recent versions of Java Database Connectivity (JDBC)—see the "JDBC Database Integration" section. I've worked with databases such as MySQL, mSQL, and PostgresSQL as well as a number of nonmainstream databases and data stores such as NCR Teradata and Progress Software's ObjectStore.

Remember, at the end of the day, you're communicating to the database via some form of JDBC (the preference) or Open Database Connectivity (ODBC). The performance is therefore bound to four components:

- The chosen database itself

- The network between the database and application tier

- The JDBC or ODBC driver performance

- The WebSphere pool manager configuration

You'll now look at optimizing the communication between WebSphere and the database.

J2EE Database Integration

In the Java 2 Enterprise Edition (J2EE) world, there's many ways to do everything! The same goes for database connectivity. I'll discuss the two types of integration in the following sections. First, you'll look at the four common ways to communicate to a database from within your application code. That is, how do you implement SQL queries to your relational database? Second, you'll look at two connectivity driver types that are commonly used within WebSphere environments.

So, you'll now look at the SQL implementation methods used within WebSphere, learn about the pros and cons of each, and understand when, where, and how you should use them.

Persistence Layer Implementation

The two primary ways of utilizing the J2EE capability of default persistence layering are with Container Managed Persistence (CMP) and Bean Managed Persistence (BMP). Both are commonly used globally, and both have specific pros and cons, including areas that you should investigate for performance optimization.

Container Managed Persistence (CMP)

CMP is a fairly contentious subject when it comes to J2EE and database connectivity. Essentially, CMP is a WebSphere-managed, or container-managed, persistence layer that manages the SQL statements and data persistence between the business components—in other words, the entity Enterprise JavaBeans (EJBs)—and the database.

The reason why CMP is contentious is that it's a "black box" to the developer and, to a large extent, the system manager. In theory, it's rock solid. If you've performed any Java development work before that requires a fair amount of SQL code, you know that implementing SQL code can be cumbersome at times. The concept behind CMP is that the developer writes against a series of J2EE EJB Application Programming Interfaces (APIs) that allow interrogation of the database via an abstract layer. For example, if a developer wanted to find a specific entry in a database, he would create an entity EJB and include methods such as `findByPrimaryKey`, which would allow him to search the database for a particular row via the call `findByPrimaryKey(primary_key)`.

However, in practice, entity EJBs, when incorrectly implemented, can be a performance killer on the database and WebSphere application server tiers. Unlike most other J2EE components, the entity EJBs are "sessionized" within the context of a client (or user) transaction. The entity EJBs are then cached (just the wrapper, not the object data itself) at the end of each client transaction, which is a key component of EJB life cycles (in other words, session, stateless, and entity EJBs). Clearly, however, this depends on the EJB caching strategy and general cache options (for example, the time in cache).

In the past (pre–EJB 2.0), the problem with container-managed entity EJBs was that there was significant overhead associated with the synchronization of the persistence layer (between the entity EJBs and the database). The EJB 2.0 specification that arrived with J2EE 1.3 (within WebSphere 5) provides a great deal better performance over that of the entity beans in EJB 1.1 (within WebSphere 4). Local EJB interfaces, new in EJB 2.0, have played a bit part in this performance improvement.

Even so, you can tune a number of items within WebSphere to help improve CMP performance. In Chapter 10, I'll discuss the specific details of code-level EJB performance tuning. In this chapter, you'll see what you can do with CMP entity EJBs, once they're deployed, in a production environment.

Before getting into the EJB container tuning of CMP, though, you'll look at BMP.

Bean Managed Persistence (BMP)

BMP, unlike CMP, requires that the developer creates the persistence layer using entity EJBs. The developer needs to implement all the database SQL routines and various finder methods within the entity EJBs.

Out of all the various data persistence layer mechanisms, the BMP technology is probably the most involved to develop and manage. The performance, overall, is somewhat the same between CMP and BMP (assuming both have been implemented correctly); however, BMP provides an additional level of flexibility over that of CMP because the developer can code the persistence layer the desired way.

From my experience, BMP is higher performing than CMP for high write-based environments, and CMP, for the majority of situations, outperforms BMP for high read-based environments. This is only because of the default implementation nature of CMP and the way in which the container-managed persistence layer retrieves the relational data from the database. CMP has a caching-like data persistence architecture, more so than that of CMP. You can make BMP perform in the same fashion because, by its nature, BMP uses many of the same ideologies as CMP. The major difference is that the developer has to implement the persistence management.

BMP, overall, is good for circumstances where your developers may want to implement a nonstandard persistence layer—one that isn't specifically handled by CMP.

Tuning Your CMP and BMP EJB Environments

In Chapter 9, I discussed EJB caching. As a refresher, EJB caching is the technology, as part of the J2EE EJB specification, pertaining to the container's support of caching EJB communications between client transactions. In essence, the WebSphere EJB containers support three types of EJB caching known as Option A, Option B, and Option C. You'll now look at these in the context of entity EJBs.

Option A caching assumes that the particular entity EJBs have exclusive access to the underlying data store—the database. During active client transactions, no changes to the underlying data structure can be facilitated.

Option A shouldn't be used with any form of WebSphere clustering or workload management. Introducing one of these groups of high-availability technologies means you may introduce changes to the data store, effectively "breaking" the active entity EJBs. Using this caching option (Option A) with a truly read-only entity EJB paradigm will result in a dramatic improvement in performance. The challenge is to ensure that the entity EJB constructs are in fact read-only.

Option B caching, unlike Option A, allows for shared access to the underlying data store or the database. After each client transaction, the entity EJB synchronizes data back to the database (via the ejbStore() method), and the instance of the entity EJB remains active and is returned to the contain pool after a client transaction has completed.

The final option, Option C, is similar to Option B in that it allows shared access to the database or data store between other entity EJBs. The difference, however, is that at the end of each transaction, the container passivates the EJB. *Passivation* is when the EJB method closes down an instance of an EJB. In this option, when the next client transaction requests an EJB from the pool, the container creates a new entity EJB.

From this, you can choose from the three options per entity EJB implementation type. I find the most efficient way to modify this setting is to edit the IBM extension's EJB Java Archive (JAR) descriptor for your specific EJBs. It's possible, and recommended if you're less familiar with this area of WebSphere, to do this at deployment time through the assembly tools provided by WebSphere.

Each EJB is detailed in a file called ibm-ejb-jar-ext.xmi. This file is the IBM extension deployment descriptor for EJBs deployed in WebSphere.

NOTE   This file will only be present if you've initially created it when deploying an EJB JAR application.

The file contents will look similar to the following line:

```
<beanCache xmi:id="BeanCache_5" activateAt="TRANSACTION" loadAt="TRANSACTION"/>
```

Each EJB you deploy and configure with EJB caching will have a similar entry in this file per EJB JAR. BeanCache_5 represents the iteration of EJB cache entries in that particular file. Unless you know or are confident with what you're editing, it's best to change these settings via the assembly tools.

Table 11-3 defines the three configuration items available.

Table 11-3. Options for Configuring Entity EJB Cache Settings

Option	Activation Settings	Load Settings
Option A	Once	Activation
Option B	Once	Transaction
Option C	Transaction	Transaction

Option C is the default option for these settings. That is, if you don't specifically configure the EJB caching, Option C is used.

Note that you must use each setting in the combination that's mentioned in Table 11-3. That is, if you manually edit the IBM extension's deployment descriptor and change the EJB cache setting to, let's say, Option B, you must set it as follows:

```
<beanCache xmi:id="BeanCache_5" activateAt="ONCE" loadAt="TRANSACTION"/>
```

You can't mix and match the activateAt and loadAt settings.
Use these tips to identify what setting works best for you:

Option A is only possible on single-channel, single-instance, noncloned WebSphere environments. It's quite fast given that the bean isn't returned to the EJB pool, meaning that an ejbLoad() isn't called on each client transaction, greatly improving performance.

Option B, as a general rule, is the next best option. It can be used in workload management–based (clustered) environments. Although each client transaction incurs an `ejbLoad()` call to obtain cached EJBs from the pool, there's no `ejbActivate()` called. Essentially, this option greatly reduces the number of methods called to the EJB container constructs over that of Option C.

Option C is the safest, or most generalized, caching method. Each time a call to an entity EJB is requested, the container must create a new entity EJB instance. Given that the EJBs aren't sitting in memory the whole time (unlike Option A and B), this option uses less memory. However, there's a performance hit if you're using entity EJBs frequently.

At the risk of sounding like a broken record, these are only guidelines and are recommendations based on my experience. In other words, test, test, test. If you have a simple, nonclustered environment, Option A is the best choice. If you have clustering or workload management active and your developers utilize entity EJBs frequently, Option B is the best. If you have clustering or workload management active yet don't rely on entity EJBs, Option C is the most memory friendly.

Embedded SQL

Embedded SQL is a quick-and-dirty (albeit sometimes completely legitimate!) way of compiling SQL queries and commands within your application code. As you can probably guess, SQL code is simply hard-coded into the deployed application classes. There's no management of the persistence mechanism, but it can use features such as connection pooling and the like. The primary reason why I recommend you push your developers away from this method is just as much about performance is it is good (or best) practice.

For small applications that conduct only one or two queries, you can use basic SQL queries without too much of an impact. An example is a simple `select` or `insert` statement such as this:

```
SQL>  select phone_number from user_table where user_ID = '123456';
```

The problems start to arise when you have many or complex queries and SQL commands being used and high-volume environments. Trying to maintain and write Java code with unmanageable amounts of static SQL commands is impossible. If you're constrained to using embedded SQL commands, then my recommendations are somewhat straightforward.

NOTE I discuss these concepts in more detail in Chapter 10.

Prepared SQL Statements

You could safely assume that a system using embedded SQL commands would be a smaller size than a system using CMP or Data Access Objects (DAOs). However, small systems can expect failures in the same fashion as large systems. In some cases, the costs of failures in smaller systems are, unit for unit, greater than that of large systems. This is because problems occur longer after deployment because the load and volume of usage is typically lower. Therefore, it's important to use common sense regarding performance.

Specifically, use prepared SQL statements. It's easier to maintain a handful of prepared SQL statements rather than a large collection of them. Prepared SQL statements work when only the statement, without the data, is passed to the database layer. This causes the database to see that the statement has been issued and compiled previously (a previous request) and, therefore, doesn't need to parse and compile the statement again. The key with databases is to minimize the disk seek time and parsing and compilation time by pushing requests into cache.

Smaller environments can benefit greatly from this approach, and you won't have to purchase a large environment. I'll discuss this in a little more detail in Chapter 10.

As a guide, use prepared SQL statements for SQL statements that will transact fewer than 15 or so similar queries or calls to the database. If you find that you'll have many of the same SQL calls made to the database by your applications—more than 20—prepared SQL statements will start to become better performing than standard SQL statements.

Having WebSphere manage connections for less time to the database means that overall performance is increased (less overhead on the pool manager), fewer threads are used, and memory utilization is decreased by transactions completing faster. It's possible to see a 70–90 percent improvement in speed for smaller WebSphere environments and a 50–70 percent improvement for larger WebSphere environments when using prepared SQL statements.

SQL Statement Management

Given that the use of embedded SQL commands implies hand development of code, it's important that your developers do in fact follow the rules discussed in Chapter 10 about closing all connections and statements at the end of each SQL query set. In more advanced configurations, your developers may implement helper beans or use DAOs where all the database connectivity plumbing work is taken care of (the connection, closure, and so on).

If this isn't the case, then you'll need to ensure that statements are closed. By not doing so, one of two things will happen (and probably both). First, by not closing statements, your WebSphere application server's Java Virtual Machine (JVM) will show signs of memory leaks. Statements have "handles" open to them (they're essentially objects, remember), and by not declaring them closed, they remain open, even if the statement has finished processing.

Second, by not closing the connections to the database or the pool manager, you'll quickly find that you'll run out of available connections to the database. Over time, if you're using a pool manager, it'll help by closing idled or orphaned connections (see Chapter 9) when they're unused for a defined duration. However, if your developers aren't using pool managers and not closing connections, you'll run out of connections to the database (or more correctly, the database will run out of available connections).

The following code shows an example of proper object closure:

```
// establish new connection object
connection conn = null;
// set the JDBC class
Class.forName("some.driver.string");
    // build up the JDBC connection URL
    conn = java.sql.DriverManager.getConnection("jdbc:some_jdbc_connection_url");
    Statement stmt=conn.createStatement();
    ResultSet rs = stmt.executeQuery("select * from username; ") ;
        // position us in our resultset object
        rs.last();
    int count = rs.getRow();
    rs.first();
    while (!rs.isAfterLast()){
        out.println(rs.getString(1)) ;
        out.println(rs.getString(2)) ;
        out.println("\n") ;
        rs.next();
    }
    // close result set object
    rs.close();
    // close statement
    stmt.close();
    // close conection
    conn.close();
```

Don't worry too much about understanding this code; it's provided merely as an example. The important aspects are the last three Java commands:

- The first command, `rs.close()`, closes the result set object that was used to store the results of the query. This primarily reduces memory consumption.

- The second command, `stmt.close()`, closes the `stmt` (or statement object) that was used to build the query. This also reduces memory consumption by cleaning up unwanted objects.

- The last command, `conn.close()`, closes the JDBC database connection. This reduces memory as well as removes an active connection to the database, preventing it from connection exhaustion.

Using prepared SQL statements and closing objects and connections to the database are the essential WebSphere performance winners when using embedded SQL.

As noted, I discuss more SQL generic performance guidelines in Chapter 10. Later in this chapter, you'll look at specific database tuning options you can employ to help SQL queries perform better.

 TIP If you're placing SQL statements into your Java code, best practices suggest placing object dereference methods (for example, `resultset.close()`) into your `Finally` clause. If you're using other forms of JDBC code development such as DAOs, you can build these closure methods into factory classes or part of your value object management.

Data Access Objects (DAOs)

DAOs are essentially a *pattern* in object-oriented design. In the context of databases and database access, DAOs provide a high level of abstraction to the developer. This means you can have a core developer write the actual database connection logic within a DAO construct, and the regular business developers can simply communicate to the database abstraction layer.

The abstraction layer is presented by the DAO, assuring you that any performance and optimization logic implemented by the core developer in the DAO data source logic will be used inherently. Figure 11-1 highlights how this works.

Essentially, Figure 11-1 shows how the interaction between a developer bean or some other Java component communicates to a database of any sort via the DAO.

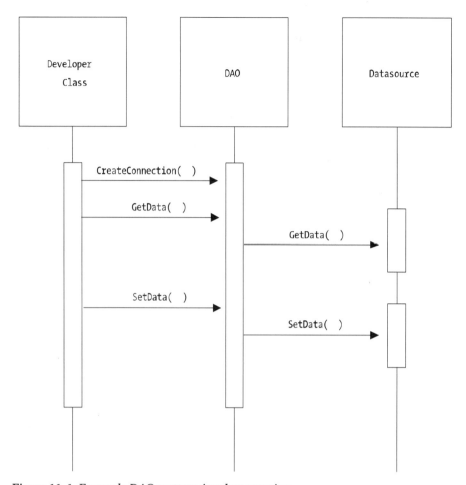

Figure 11-1. Example DAO pattern implementation

Apart from being about insulating business component developers from the plumbing and having a centralized interface to get data to and from a database, it also shows a very abstracted model. If you wanted or needed to change your database vendor from, let's say, Sybase to Oracle, you'd only have to get your core developer to change the one location in the DAO where the database connectivity may occur. Typically, this is handled within WebSphere JDBC pool manager, and as such, all that would need to be changed is the Java Naming and Directory Interface (JNDI) name of the data source.

This is a high-level look at DAOs—a topic that's beyond the scope of this book. However, from a conceptual point of view, the concept should be one with which you're familiar.

In terms of ensuring performance, the key to performance in a DAO-based environment is in the connection manager. Because a DAO predominantly would use a JNDI context lookup to find a predefined connection manager for a specific data source, the pool manager is the essential performance factor. Later in this chapter, you'll look at what you can do within WebSphere JDBC connection pool managers to optimize database connectivity.

 NOTE For those with good eyes or an interest in patterns, Figure 11-1 doesn't show the complete DAO pattern. A key component missing is the ValueObject element.

JDBC

JDBC is the standard J2EE/Java database driver used to communicate and interrogate a relational database. Java 2 Standard Edition (J2SE) JDBC 3.0 supports the SQL-99 command set, meaning that it's compatible with all the major relational database vendors and more.

JDBC in itself is any one of four driver types, known as JDBC type 1 through 4. Each driver level is a different incarnation or implementation of the JDBC. Each driver has its own reason for existence, along with its pros and cons.

You'll now take a quick moment to look at the four different JDBC types.

JDBC Type 1

JDBC type 1 is a JDBC-ODBC bridge. This version of driver is rare to use or find and in fact isn't supported under WebSphere.

The complexity in this driver is that all JDBC calls made to the driver are bridged to an internal ODBC driver, which then converts the calls to the native database vendor implementation driver before sending them onto the database. Figure 11-2 shows how the communication to a type 1 driver works.

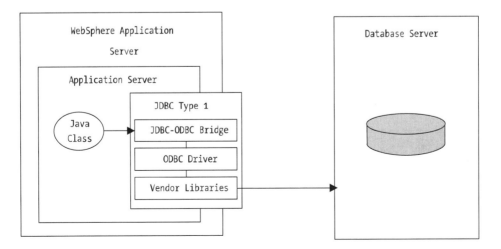

Figure 11-2. JDBC type 1 driver implementation

As you can see, there's a fair amount of abstraction in this type of driver. It should be obvious that there will be performance implications for the multiple levels of abstraction and command translation within the driver.

Overall, this driver shouldn't be used because of its inherent performance issues.

JDBC Type 2

JDBC type 2 drivers are quite common within application environments. WebSphere supports this form of driver, also commonly known as a *thick* driver. In essence, the thick driver implements local or vendor-specific APIs in the driver, which provide a high level of performance over that of type 1 drivers.

This driver, given that it implements vendor-specific or native APIs within the driver library, can take advantage of vendor-specific features and functions. In the case of Oracle, a thick JDBC driver incorporates Oracle Call Interface (OCI) libraries within the driver.

Having the vendor-specific APIs in a type 2 driver means you can take advantage of load balancing and failover of your WebSphere applications as well as other advanced features. I'll discuss some of these in more detail later in this chapter. Figure 11-3 shows the type 2 JDBC driver implementations.

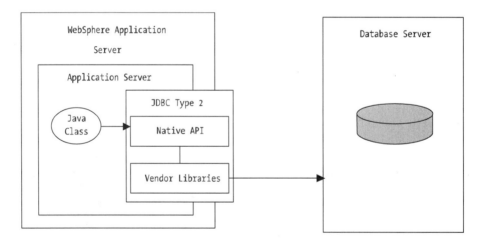

Figure 11-3. JDBC type 2 driver implementation

As you can see, unlike a type 1 driver, the type 2 implementation provides fewer layers to extend through, which ultimately provides far greater performance, with the added advantage of gaining vendor-specific capabilities such as Oracle OCI feature sets.

JDBC Type 3

Type 3 drivers are less common than types 2 and 4 but more common than type 1 drivers. Although the type 3 driver is nowhere near as common as types 2 and 4, it does have some smart features. But, again, with more layers, it's more involved to manage and support.

Suited well to client/server implementations where thick Java clients such as those using Java Swing or Abstract Window Toolkit (AWT) are used, this implementation of JDBC uses a three-tier approach. Figure 11-4 highlights this model.

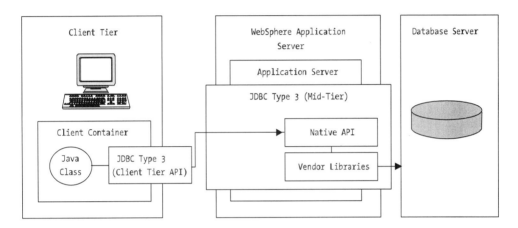

Figure 11-4. JDBC type 3 driver implementation

As you can see from Figure 11-4, the driver is split into three tiers. Interestingly, the middle tier may actually operate a type 1 or 2 driver while on the first tier, and then the pure-Java driver will ferry the JDBC-based request to the middle tier, which in turn will push it to the database.

This driver, because it can use existing type 1 and 2 driver implementations, provides the ability to use load balancing, failover, and other advanced features.

It also provides you as the WebSphere manager or operations architect with the ability to facilitate logging and auditing, given that the driver's client component can be written from scratch or modified from existing reference implementations.

The only performance issue with this model of driver is that because there are more tiers and more layers of technology to traverse, returning data sets will take longer to arrive on the client end. As such, large result sets will not perform as well with a type 3 driver as they would with a "thinner" driver.

JDBC Type 4

The JDBC type 4 driver, more commonly known as the JDBC *thin* driver, is a fully supported driver under WebSphere 4 and 5. Most major database vendors provide this form of driver, which is effectively a native Java-based driver.

For the majority of implementations, this driver is the highest performer. Because calls to the database layer don't have to be translated into an ODBC call or some other form of propriety protocol, the overhead is kept to a minimum.

Unfortunately, however, for the most complex environments where technologies such as advanced failover, load balancing, and so forth are required, this driver will not be able to provide vendor-specific capabilities. Although some vendors do incorporate connection-based failover into a type 4 driver, for the majority, the type 4 driver is a basic, high-performing JDBC interface to the database layer. Figure 11-5 shows just how simplistic this form of driver is.

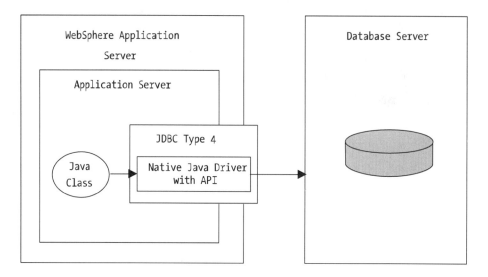

Figure 11-5. JDBC type 4 driver implementation

Still, type 4 drivers have a number of aspects that can affect performance. I'll discuss optimization in more detail later in the chapter when discussing connection pool managers.

ODBC

From an architectural purist's perspective, ODBC-based drivers are a less pure form of database connectivity. ODBC is a standard introduced by Microsoft many years ago to provide a programmable interface to its various SQL-compliant databases (Microsoft Access and, more recently, SQL Server).

Nowadays, if you're using databases with Java environments, the rule of thumb is that you don't use ODBC for database communications. Instead, you choose either type 2 or type 4 JDBC-based drivers. However, you can bend this rule where some more specialized data services vendors don't favor either JDBC or ODBC or they have limited support for JDBC, in which case you'll need to use ODBC.

If this is the case, then you're not out in the cold by yourself! WebSphere does support ODBC integration through its resource groups. The specific tuning and optimization of these types of interfaces is driver specific.

In most cases, refer to your ODBC driver vendor's documentation to understand what the driver settings should be and how they should be configured.

WebSphere Database Tuning

As you move from the database driver implementations and various programmable-level constructs such as DAOs, CMPs, and so forth, you'll learn about some specific aspects of optimizing your WebSphere platform for several of the leading database vendors products.

Specifically, in this section, you'll explore the optimization and tuning recommendations for the two most common database products used with WebSphere:

- Oracle 8*i* and 9*i*

- IBM DB2

Something I find as a useful tool is a checklist of configuration and design considerations. From a database implementation perspective, the following ten items make up my performance checklist for database-to-WebSphere implementation (in no order of priority):

- Use prepared SQL statements where possible.

- Plan and design your data file layout architecture.

- Memory, memory, memory: Databases like memory for buffers.

- Use connection pooling.

- Manage your persisted sessions properly—tune, test, tune, test.

- Design and test your data persistence mechanism carefully (for example, CMP and BMP).

- Use indexes—always.

- Locate your databases within one hop of your WebSphere application servers for performance.

- Don't share database instances for different workload characteristics.

- Always implement some level of high availability.

It's important to note that this is in no way an exhaustive list in the same way this book isn't a database administrator's reference manual! However, you need to consider many specific WebSphere (J2EE) factors when optimizing WebSphere and databases. At the same time, you can consider other database architectural and administrative factors. However, what I'm covering here are design considerations that impact WebSphere performance.

Also, it's important to note that in this chapter, I'm discussing only the implementation aspects of interfacing WebSphere with databases, not application development best practices (please see Chapter 10 for information about this). You'll look at some key points for implementing or architecting a WebSphere implementation with one of the aforementioned vendor databases.

You'll explore generic Relational Database Management System (RDBMS) performance guidelines for integration to WebSphere environments and then each of the two databases in terms of specific optimization configuration parameters. Then, you'll look at ways to monitor the two databases and understand what constitutes poor performance, as well as learn how to diagnose where the problems are.

You'll now look at the specific key optimization and design points for the two databases discussed earlier—Oracle and DB2.

Generic Database Performance Architecture with WebSphere

All relational databases typically follow the same rules when it comes to planning and architecting high-performance, high-availability implementations. In this section, you'll look at these rules and learn how WebSphere benefits from each of them. Although databases all follow similar rules in terms of what produces high performance, the implementation of those rules is different between each database.

Common to all database platforms is their sizing requirements. Most, if not all, will invariably have similar requirements when it comes to the sizing of databases. Essentially, it's not a database requirement but a set of guidelines for the type of workload an RDBMS will put onto a server.

If someone asks me what factors they should consider when implementing a database for a WebSphere-based environment, I typically ask the following questions:

- What are you going to be using your database for?

- What sort of transaction or SQL query rate do you expect to have to your database?

- How dependant is your WebSphere-based application on database performance and usage?

- What sort of SQL transactions are you looking to support—complex or small?

- What sort of scalability are you expecting from your database platform?

You should ask yourself these same questions.

The Purpose of the Database

What are you going to be using your database for? Are you running WebSphere 4, which will need table spaces for the administrative repository plus potential table spaces for application data?

If you're not in need of an RDBMS for your application and just in need of a WebSphere-based repository sitting on the RDBMS, then your database requirements will be minimal. On the other hand, if your WebSphere-based applications will be performing high transaction rates to multiple database instances or table spaces, then your design model is completely different.

The answer to this question will determine just how complex and how much effort you'll need to spend to ensure that your WebSphere-based applications will perform optimally.

Transaction Rate

What sort of transaction or SQL query rate do you expect to have to your database? You may have a complex database environment with many database instances; however, if your SQL or transaction rates are low, then your database size won't need to be complex.

Complex sizing means expensive hardware, and complex database and data architecture means expensive design work. You don't have to have a complex infrastructure platform if you have a complex data requirement (and vice versa).

However, you can safely assume that if your SQL or transaction rate is high, you'll need to invest in both hardware and solid database architecture.

Reliance on the Database

How dependant is your WebSphere-based application on database performance and usage? You need to understand what would happen if your database became unavailable. What would happen to your application? Would it stop operating and serving customers? Does it frequently use the database, or does it operate via an in memory WebSphere caching mechanism where data is sourced from?

If your application must have a database available at all times, then your platform architecture will need to consider high-availability services. You'll need hot-standby servers, highly available solutions, or active clustered solutions.

Type of Transactions

What sort of SQL transactions are you looking to support—complex or small? Although similar to the second question, this question explores the type of transaction your database will be serving.

As you saw in several of the earlier chapters, you can break down transactional characteristics into two groups. First, you can have a high transaction *rate* but a small or lightweight transaction *characteristic* (for example, select * from usertable where username = "me";). Or, you can have a high transaction *rate* with a large or heavyweight transactional *characteristic* (for example, the same previous SQL query but with several table joins and conditional WHERE clauses). On the other hand, you can have a low transaction *rate* with a small or lightweight transactional *characteristic* or a large or heavyweight transactional *characteristic.*

This sounds somewhat simple, but it's an important consideration to remember. High transaction rates will typically require faster disks and will benefit from more disks (spindles) because the overall I/O rate will be high, regardless of the transaction characteristic. Typically, well-tuned buffers will also be advantageous, and therefore memory will be important.

Scalability

What sort of scalability are you expecting from your database platform? This question looks at the long-term lifespan of your environment. If you don't believe you'll need to scale up in the future, you can reduce your hardware costs by not purchasing servers with room for expansion.

The same applies to how you lay out your database architecture. For example, raw partitions provide additional performance over that of native or "cooked" partitions; however, they're cumbersome to manage.

If you're looking at a fairly static system architecture, you may be able to go with raw partitions to gain the extra performance, considering that your operational overhead won't be large if you're not looking to scale and change your database architecture often.

Scalable systems require scalable designs, and scalable designs are typically more complex and more costly to implement.

Generic WebSphere Database Sizing

Sizing a database is a fairly complicated undertaking in itself, and it's one of those "how long is a piece of string" situations. I'll highlight some key points about sizing an RDBMS that synergize well with WebSphere platforms.

Most databases perform well with lots of memory and lots of disk drives. As a rule, you can never have enough disk drives in a relational database platform. These are the three types of database usage you may require with WebSphere:

First, for WebSphere 4, you'll want to operate a WebSphere repository on your database that's efficient but doesn't need to be massively high performing. If you don't happen to need a database for anything other than the WebSphere repository, then your life is easy. Even with a multinode WebSphere cluster operating many WebSphere domains, the load on the WebSphere administration database (the repository) will be minimal to low.

The second form of database usage is for WebSphere session persistence. In this situation, the performance of your database has a direct result on the attributed performance experienced by your end users. If your database is underpowered or not performing, then you'll find that your session management will be a major bottleneck of your environment.

The third form of database usage is for the applications that operate under WebSphere. This is all the custom or third-party applications deployed into the WebSphere environment that use a database for storing information, logs, configuration information, and so on.

The WebSphere repository database performance has the lowest overall impact on a WebSphere environment, with the application database having the highest impact.

You should consider the following key items carefully when implementing high-end databases:

- Disks and disk configuration (including controllers)

- Memory and memory configuration

- System configuration, including Central Processing Units (CPUs) and backplanes

- The network

You'll now learn about each of those.

Disks and Disk Configuration

You explored the science of disks and disk controllers in Chapter 6. You'll now look at some more database-specific considerations that will help you with database sizing. The key to database sizing for your application database is to spread the database files as much as you can. Distribute load across many spindles to reduce single-disk bottlenecks.

Even with the more advanced disks available on the market being able to push theoretically more than 300 megabytes per second (MBps) over a data bus, a single disk performing this operation will still result in poor performance for many concurrent requests.

Consider your usage type based on Table 11-4 (later in the chapter). Although this is a guide, be sure to model your database sizing requirements carefully before implementing the end solution.

For both performance and redundancy, be sure to split your data buses as much as possible. For example, although SCSI and Fibre Channel can both support a fair amount of devices on each bus, consider only loading each bus up by 50 percent to facilitate both overhead (peak contingency) and promote redundancy.

Refer to Table 11-4 for a breakdown of various I/O types.

Memory and Memory Configuration

Memory is really just a high-speed (albeit volatile) version of a disk drive. Given that the access speed of memory is in the order of 10 nanoseconds (ns) as opposed to 10 milliseconds (ms) for disk drives, the more you can reference your data out of memory or buffer, the better.

All the major databases provide methods of caching queries, caching results, and caching frequently accessed data into memory. You'll look at some parameters for the leading databases that provide this functionality shortly.

There's no rule of thumb to capture all types of database memory requirements. Proper sizing and modeling is the only way you can understand your requirements. Therefore, the only guide is to ensure that your cache and buffer hit ratios are as high as possible and that you continue to monitor them.

In Oracle, the Shared Global Area (SGA) is a key to the amount of memory your database has available to it; in DB2, it's known as the *buffer pool*.

For each of the leading database vendors, you'll look at how to tell if your database environment is choking for memory. Also, refer to Table 11-4 for a high-level overview of differing database transaction characteristics.

System Configuration

The system configuration boils down to the type and number of CPUs in your database environment. All the processing of queries and updating of database files as well as administrative functions such as logging and locking and so forth need to be processed by the CPU(s).

If your WebSphere application database is of a high Decision Support System (DSS) workload, then it's going to be more CPU hungry than a WebSphere application that uses a database in an Online Transaction Processing (OLTP) workload.

Therefore, you need to make this decision based on your requirements, your modeling, and your future scalability. Chapter 5 showed ways to understand your performance and sizing of different technologies, and Chapter 4 showed the different families and types of CPUs available.

Network

Only in a large database workload environment will the network be an issue. Again, nothing will provide you with better supporting information than proper modeling. As a general rule, the faster the network between the WebSphere application servers and the database server tier, the better or more efficient transactions will be.

On a small or low-end WebSphere application environment, the overall response times for a database connected via a 10 megabyte per second (Mbps) network versus that of a 1 gigabit per second (Gbps) network will be marginal. It's only when the transaction rate or the transaction characteristics start to increase in number and size that this will be an issue.

Nowadays, 100Mbps switched is the default standard for any server. This will provide most small- to medium-sized systems with enough bandwidth at high loads.

Summary Matrix

Table 11-4 summarizes the four main areas of database sizing between the most common flavors of database workloads:

- DSS

- Batch-based workloads

- Online Analytical Processing (OLAP)

- OLTP

Table 11-4. Workload Summary Matrix

Database Type Network Workload	Disk Workload	Memory Workload	System Workload
DSS	High I/O rate	High memory usage	Medium to high—dependant on size of DSS database Low network requirements
Batch based	High I/O	High memory usage	Medium to high Low to medium network requirements
OLAP	Generally low I/O Rate	High memory usage	Medium to high Medium network requirements
OLTP	Medium to high I/O	Medium to high memory usage	Medium to high—generally lower than DSS

Table 11-4 shows the four main areas discussed and summarizes the areas within a database architecture that make up the difference between low and high performing. It's not possible to quantify what high memory or high I/O rate means because they're somewhat arbitrary guides. You should consider these guiding principles when looking at performance or the design of a WebSphere-based application database.

Before you look at specific database vendor performance considerations, you'll take a moment to rehash file system designs and options with databases.

Database Data Layout and Design

Both Oracle and DB2 support a number of different file system types. You can divide them into three groups:

- Standard Unix file systems

- Advanced or journaling file systems

- Raw devices

As you'd expect, each has its advantages and disadvantages. Standard Unix file systems such as the Berkeley System Distribution (BSD) and Unix File System (UFS) provide a satisfactory file system for smaller, lower-end systems.

For Windows-based servers, the equivalent would be a FAT32-type file system.

Advanced file systems are file systems that offer journaling and logging, which provide improvements in reliability and performance on an order of magnitude of the standard file systems. Veritas File System, IBM Journaling File System (JFS), Network File System (NTFS), Compaq Advanced File System, and Solaris UFS-8 are some examples.

Raw file systems are disks with no formatted file system on them. In theory (and in some practice), raw file systems offer greater performance over that of nonraw or formatted file systems. Because there's no middle layer to go through for I/O, the performance is greater.

This is usually the case, however, because more advanced files systems are starting to support features such as Direct I/O, which come close to the performance of raw partitions. Because of the operational and management overhead of supporting raw partitions, you're better off using a file system that supports Direct I/O than one with raw partitions.

If you're fairly confident that your system isn't going to grow in size and if changes to your existing or initial database requirements aren't going to overly high, consider using raw partitions. If you're looking to have a fairly dynamic database environment, consider using one of the more advanced file systems and, where possible, using Direct I/O.

Oracle 8i and 9i

The Oracle database is one of the leading database implementations available. I'll cover both versions 8*i* and 9*i* because of their wide installation base globally and common use with WebSphere 4 and 5.

The two products are somewhat similar at a high level. Like any comparison with a new and older version of enterprise software, Oracle 9*i* comes with more features than Oracle 8*i* and, in most cases, outperforms Oracle 8*i*.

Figure 11-6 shows a high-level overview of the Oracle architecture. Note that this includes only the standard Oracle 8*i*/9*i* database architecture and doesn't include the Real Application Clusters (RAC) product.

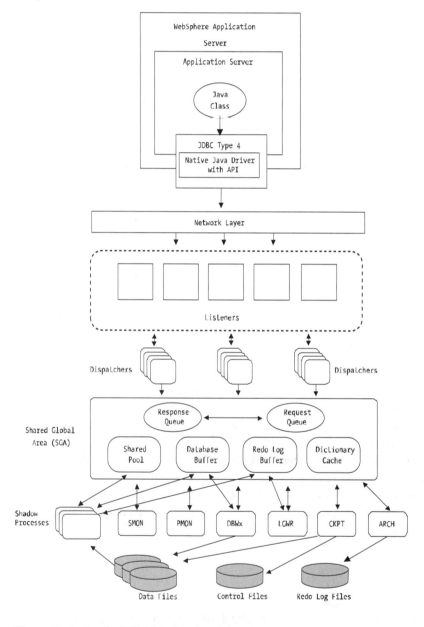

Figure 11-6. Oracle 8i/9i high-level architecture

Each database has a centralized buffer or memory area to store cached data to aid in performance. Other supporting processes govern log files, data I/O, and other management functions but are essentially controlled or mastered by a centralized entity, the SGA.

As you'll see shortly with DB2, Oracle's performance hinders around memory and cache or buffer space. Tuning and optimizing this area of the database will yield the best results. The I/O or speed at which I/O can take place to and from the data files on the disk is the next best area to consider tuning. Oracle 9*i* also allows you to integrate the Oracle 9*i* RAC layer that provides a true active-active database cluster solution, providing ultra-high levels of database availability.

A multitude of available configuration items within Oracle can help performance. Unfortunately, this isn't an Oracle performance optimization manual. Table 11-5 summarizes each of the parameters that you can tune in an Oracle system.

Please don't change your init.ora file based on each of these listed items. Changing it without knowing what you're changing may have dire effects on your system's performance. Use these a guide and talk to your Database Administrator (DBA) or reference your Oracle manuals for more information.

Table 11-5. Oracle System Configuration and Tuning Parameters

Parameter/Feature	Description
db_block_buffers/ db_cache_size	The amount of memory set aside within the Oracle SGA for buffer cache. More is best.
db_block_size	The default block size for the specific database. I recommend 8KB–16KB for standard database loads.
log_buffer	The log buffer size. This is important because if it's too small, the log writer will be constantly active. Use 1MB–2MB as a guide when sizing.
parallel_max_servers	This sets the size or the amount of query servers. It helps with parallelism of queries. As a guide, set this to four times the number of CPUs in your system.
hash_area_size	This sets the maximum size in bytes of the per-user hash join space. Carefully issue changes to this setting based on the number of pooled connections you have from the JDBC connection manager within WebSphere.

Table 11-5. Oracle System Configuration and Tuning Parameters (Continued)

Parameter/Feature	Description
Shared_pool_size	This is the size, in bytes, of the SGA for your database instance. The setting of this value will be a result of your sizing and memory requirements as a whole.
Sort_area_size	This sets the maximum size in bytes of the area in memory of sorts. If your WebSphere-based application is performing many sorts within the query sets, this parameter will be helpful.

As you can see, you can use a number of settings to help with WebSphere performance.

Several tools are available that can help with Oracle performance monitoring. I'll touch on them in Chapters 13 and 14. However, immediate tools you can use that'll provide the current state and status of the aforementioned parameters are two scripts that come with Oracle.

These tools, called utlbstat and utlestat, provide a good snapshot of the performance and associated optimization metrics. They provide you with a start and end script that activate a number of timers and settings. When you run the completion script, utlestat, you'll get output in a report.txt file.

If you're familiar with using the Oracle sqlplus tool, connect to your database as the sysdba user and run this command:

```
alter system set timed_statistics = true;
```

This command will turn on the Oracle-timed collection statistics. The overhead is minimal, and according to Oracle, the impact is negligible to production performance.

Once you've run the previous command, run the utlbstat command as follows:

```
SQL> @ORACLE_HOME/rdbms/admin/utlbstat;
```

Leave this command running, and you'll see some output.

Let your database operate normally for a defined period, and then stop the collection by issuing this command:

```
SQL> @ORACLE_HOME/rdbms/admin/utlestat;
```

The report.txt file will be created, which will have statistics you can study to gain insight into the performance of your application database.

IBM DB2

IBM DB2 is what I'd consider the other industry database heavyweight. As IBM's RDBMS platform, you can imagine that there are some nifty performance features available for interfacing with WebSphere. The DB2 product suite is fairly large, but many of the parameters are generic across the various platforms.

Like the Oracle section, I'll present some of the key tuning parameters and considerations that impact the way WebSphere communicates to DB2. This is a somewhat generic shopping list of items that you should use while planning and designing your overall environment or as a reactive checklist when there are problems.

Shortly you'll look at DB2 system configuration and tuning parameters that help to improve WebSphere-to-DB2 performance.

Figure 11-7 shows the DB2 architecture at a high level. Similar to Oracle, DB2 has a number of individual processes that make up the core engine.

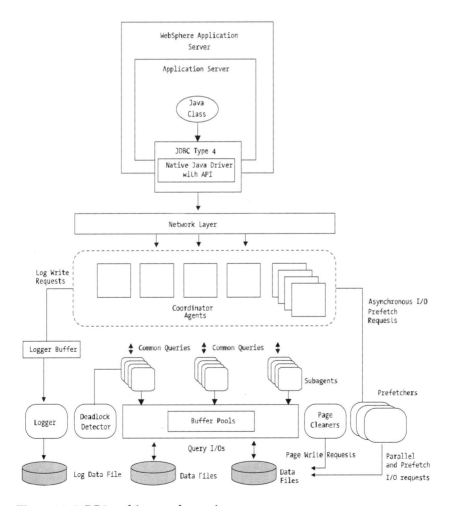

Figure 11-7. DB2 architectural overview

As you can see from Figure 11-7, DB2, like Oracle, is a fairly complex beast. The major components are the agents, subagents, logger, buffer pools, page cleaners, prefetchers, and the data files themselves.

The agents are the master controlling elements within the DB2 engine. These agents coordinate where all the requests need to go—whether it's to a prefetch agent to start populating the buffer pool with data or whether it's to a subsequent SQL query looking to retrieve information from the buffer pools.

The buffer pool is analogous to Oracle's SGA. It provides all the buffering and caching of data from the disks because, as discussed at length, the more you can retrieve your data and queries from cache or buffer, the faster the overall system response time will be.

Therefore, the optimization of the buffer pool is essential.

Like Oracle, DB2 likes well-optimized memory and buffer configurations. Table 11-6 summarizes the recommended DB2 parameters and commands that help to focus on performance via the use of efficient memory and buffer configurations.

Again, use this table as a guideline, but don't take each setting for granted. Because the details of these settings are beyond the scope of this book, take the time to understand and research what each setting means and does. Most of these settings are quite common; however, these specific groupings of settings best support WebSphere performance. You can change these settings via the DB2 CLP tool or via the DB2 Control Center application.

Table 11-6. DB2 Optimization Parameter Recommendations

Parameter/Feature	Description
MinCommit	This setting allows you to change the frequency and kickoff of a commit. Changing this setting may reduce CPU load and disk I/O. Use the command `update db cfg for <insert DB_NAME> using mincommit <new setting>`. Refer to Chapters 13 and 14 and the previous section of this chapter to understand what commands you can use to monitor this setting.
MaxAgents	This setting allows you to tune the number of active connections into the DB2 database. This setting should be tuned in conjunction with your queuing model, focusing on your JDBC connection pool manager. Also, you should ensure that MaxAgents is at least the same value as MaxAppls. Consider your maximum connections from all your JDBC providers, multiplied by the number of application servers using the JDBC providers and then by the number of clones.

Table 11-6. DB2 Optimization Parameter Recommendations (Continued)

Parameter/Feature	Description
BuffPage	This is a DB2 setting that affects the buffer hit ratio of your DB2 database. The buffer hit ratio should be no less than 95 percent. Use this in conjunction with the following three settings.
SortHeap	This setting tunes the query engine for applications that may conduct a lot of sorting within their SQL queries. This can help with databases to reduce CPU loading.
Query Heap	You can use Query Heap (variable `query_heap_sz`) similarly to SortHeap to provide more buffer space for queries. If you have a high transaction rate, this value can help to improve performance of inbound queries.
Logbufsz	This setting allows you to cache or buffer data for a period before writing to logs. Increasing this value can decrease I/O loading to disks.
Pckcachesz	This value allows you to tune the amount of buffer allocated to both static and dynamic SQL statements. Tuning this value can improve the efficiency of SQL queries, especially for high transaction rate platforms.

Table 11-6 isn't an exhaustive list, but it does provide a guide for tuning DB2 for WebSphere-based application environments.

Monitoring Oracle and DB2 for Performance Issues

You can use a number of tools to understand the current load and state of your database. I'll explore this in more detail during Chapter 13, but Table 11-7 provides an overview of the best-suited applications.

Table 11-7. Database Platform Monitoring Tools

Tool	Monitoring Purpose	Targeted Database
iostat	The `iostat` command monitors disk activity, including utilization. This is useful when there are disks being overly utilized or bottlenecking overall performance.	DB2 and Oracle on Unix platforms

Table 11-7. Database Platform Monitoring Tools (Continued)

Tool	Monitoring Purpose	Targeted Database
netstat	The netstat command provides the capability to understand the number of active Transmission Control Protocol (TCP) or User Datagram Protocol (UDP) connections to your database. It can help reveal socket exhaustion or overloading of inbound network activity.	All databases, all operating systems
vmstat	The vmstat command provides a number of features to help understand the status of the system load, memory swapping, and disk load. This is useful when your system is bottlenecking in a single-view application.	Available on Unix operating systems for DB2 and Oracle
Windows Performance tool	The Performance tool in Windows NT, XP, 2000, and 2003 provides a graphical view of the state of disk, CPU, network, and swapping within your Windows-based server environment.	Available for DB2 and Oracle on Windows-based platforms

As noted, you'll explore each of these, and more, in detail in Chapter 13 when you see how to actually use the tools and understand their output.

WebSphere Connection Pool Manager

The WebSphere connection pool manager is an essential component to the connectivity of your WebSphere-based applications to the application database. Essentially, the connection pool manager is the management construct in which your JDBC drivers operate.

The concept behind a pool manager is to provide you with a pool of already connected interfaces to a database or any remote system. Pooling is a key part of performance management. The reason is that connections and disconnections are expensive, both from a network and a system resource utilization point of view.

Each time a connection has to be established, there's overhead in opening a network connection from the client, opening a network connection to the server, logging into the remote system (in this case, a database), and, at the completion of the transaction, closing the connection.

The pool manager removes all the middle ground overhead by pre-establishing a defined number of connections to the database and leaving them open for the duration of the application server's uptime. As new application session or client transactions need to make SQL queries, by coding in references in your application code to call the pool manager classes rather than manually establishing a new connection, you'll notice a great improvement in performance.

You'll also be able to stretch the longevity of your database platform by reducing its load. So, the pool manager is the governing logic within your application server JVM that controls the opening and closing of connections, pooled connection management, and other JDBC-related parameters.

Figure 11-8 shows how a pooled connection infrastructure operates.

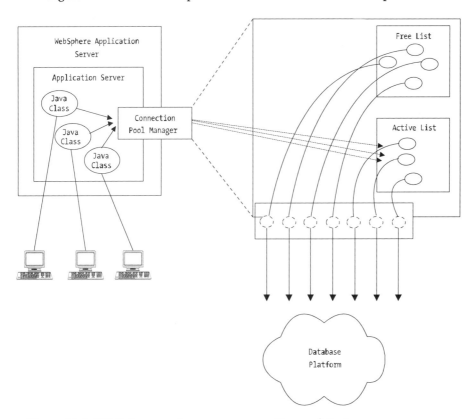

Figure 11-8. WebSphere pool manager connection architecture

Figure 11-8 shows a WebSphere application server, three active clients, an expanded view of the connection pool manager, and an interface layer to a database. In the figure, there are seven connections allocated to the JDBC connection pool. That is, the sum of all active and free connections. As you can see, all seven connections are actively connected to the database, but only three are "in use" by application clients.

If a fourth client logged in, a connection object from the free list would move to the active list, and the reference or handle to that connection object would be provided back to the client application. This is the basic form of a connection pool manager.

Within WebSphere, you have JDBC connection pool resources. Both WebSphere 4 and 5 have similar options that allow you to alter the characteristics of your JDBC connections. I touched on this topic in Chapters 5 and 6 when I discussed queuing models and how to set the JDBC minimum and maximum number of connections to your backend database within the bounds of a queuing model. Putting the queuing model aside for the moment, you'll now see the important settings for the JDBC connection pool manager.

Table 11-8 lists the main areas within the JDBC connection pool manager where configuration can be tuned to gain performance.

Table 11-8. JDBC Connection Pool Manager

Setting	Description
Minimum Connections	The initial startup (bootstrap) number of connections each instance of the JDBC pool manager will launch.
Maximum Connections	The maximum number of connections available to applications within the particular JDBC pool manager.
Connection Timeout	Interval after which an attempted connection to a database will timeout.
Idle Timeout	WebSphere 4 setting allowing you to tune how long an unallocated or idled connection will remain active before being returned to the free pool list.
Orphan Timeout	WebSphere 4 setting allowing you to configure how long an application can hold a connection open without using it before being returned to the free pool list.
Unused Timeout	WebSphere 5 setting, similar to the Idle Timeout setting for WebSphere 4.
Aged Timeout	WebSphere 5 setting to remove connections from the active list after a defined period of time. This value disregards any I/O and other settings.
Purge Policy	WebSphere 5 setting allowing you to define what will happen when a StaleConnectionException is received from the pool manager.

You'll first explore the generic WebSphere settings.

General WebSphere JDBC Connection Pool Tuning

The three primary settings common to both WebSphere 4 and 5 are the following:

- Minimum Pool Size/Minimum Connections

- Maximum Pool Size/Maximum Connections

- Connection Timeout

Although these settings may appear to be simplistic from the outset, there are a number of hidden effects based on how you set them.

Minimum Pool Size

The Minimum Pool Size setting is the value for the startup minimum number of connections available in the pool. This is the current specification for this setting but may change in future releases of WebSphere. This setting provides the number of connections in the active pool at which the data source connection manager will stop cleaning up. Ultimately, after a period of time, or via thorough system modeling, you should be able to understand what this setting should be.

As a safe value, set this value to half the value of the Maximum Connections setting.

Maximum Pool Size

The Maximum Pool Size setting is a little more involved.

This setting needs to reflect a value that represents the maximum number of connections to the database, at any one time, from each application server or clone in your environment.

Don't confuse this with being a total number of connections to the database for your particular application servers. Each application server or application server clone will instantiate it own instance of the JDBC connection pool associated with your defined context (in other words, the JNDI context associated with each particular JDBC data source). Therefore, if you have a JDBC connection pool or data source with 30 connections as a maximum, each of your application servers or application server clones will obtain an instance of the JDBC connection pool or data source with 30 connections maximum.

That means, an application with four application server clones would have a maximum of 120 concurrent database connections available to it.

This is an important point. As a rule of thumb, try not to exceed 75 connections per application server unless you have very small and very short transactions (in other words, a low transaction characteristic). The reason is this: Each connection in the data source requires a thread. If you remember from earlier chapters, some equations relate to how many threads should be active per application server per CPU. Therefore, if you have an application server requiring more than 100 connections concurrently, this would require more than 100 threads to be configured for the application server container.

More than 100 threads on a single JVM isn't a bad thing; however, if you have heavyweight transactions, then this is going to cause you grief unless you can spread out your load (distribute it) via more clones and application servers.

Therefore, follow the rule of thumb that states each application server instance (clone) will have a maximum of 75–100 JDBC connections, with each application server instance (clone) having 75–100 threads active. Therefore, more than 100 threads means you need to distribute your load more effectively with more clones.

NOTE   This is a rule of thumb; there will be instances where this rule doesn't apply. Use this as a guide where other modeling doesn't suggest otherwise.

You should also ensure that you don't hit deadlocks in your JVM by ensuring that there are always sufficient threads available. As each active JDBC connection consumes a thread, if you have 50 threads and tried to get 50 JDBC connections concurrently, your JVM would suffer a deadlock and start to fail. IBM recommends to always set the number of threads to be one more than that of the JDBC Maximum Connections setting. However, I recommend you set the number of threads to be 10 percent higher than the JDBC Maximum Connections setting.

This caters to any unforeseen or loose threads within your JVM. Therefore, for an application server that has a maximum connection pool of 75, your JVM Thread setting should be approximately 82.

Connection Timeout

Connection Timeout is a setting that helps to ensure your application can be coded to handle poorly performing database servers. This setting should be set to a relatively low value of between 10 and 30 seconds so that end user response times aren't exceptionally high.

The default setting is 180 seconds, which is way too long for an end user to be expected to sit and wait. If your connection to the database times out after 180 seconds, then you have bigger issues on your hands than a high (or low) Connection Timeout setting!

As a guide, don't set this value to be less than 10 seconds. There may be some form of deadlock occurring within a database that can take a few seconds to clear. If this happens, you don't want your connection to time out after a few seconds because this can overload the database and the current problems it may be trying to resolve.

WebSphere 4 JDBC Connection Pool Tuning

Table 11-8 lists two specific WebSphere 4 settings that you can tune to optimize the performance of the data source:

- Idle Timeout

- Orphan Timeout

You'll now look at these two settings in more detail. Figure 11-9 shows where you configure the JDBC connection pool.

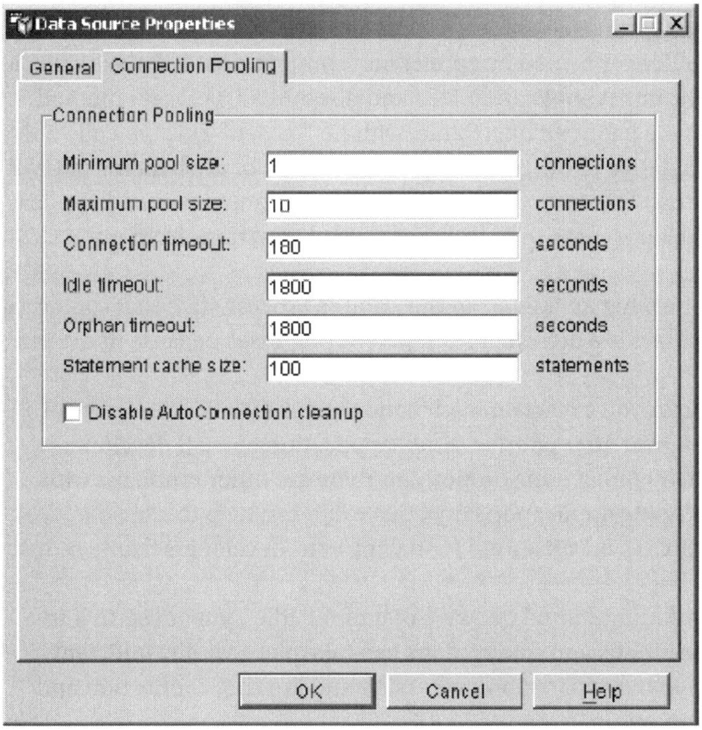

Figure 11-9. Configuring the WebSphere 4 pool manager connection

Idle Timeout

The Idle Timeout setting allows you to tune the JDBC connection pool data source so that connections that are idle or unallocated can be returned to the pool for another process to use. This setting helps to ensure that there are sufficiently free connections available in the pool for your applications to use, rather than allowing connections to remain open and wait for activity. Occasionally, this may be a desired requirement to have long-standing connections active; however, database accesses aren't asynchronous, so you should expect response times within a minute for online-based applications, even for large queries.

Idle Timeout should be set higher than your connection timeout value yet lower than your Orphan Timeout value. As a guide, this setting should be between two times and three times the value of the Connection Timeout setting. This provides a proportionally set value for idle timeouts, based on your perceived (or modeled) connection startup (timeout) time.

Also consider tuning this value if you notice that active connections are starting to build up in the pool manager that don't reflect the number of concurrent users on your systems or the SQL query rate isn't representative of the number of active connections.

Orphan Timeout

The Orphan Timeout setting allows you to tune the data source to cater for connections that are no longer owned by application components. If, for example, a particular thread within an application fails and doesn't call a `close()` method, the connection may be left in an open state, with no "owner." This typically only applies to BMP and native JDBC-based applications. One of the benefits of CMP is that the container will manage the handlers between connection and application clients quite well (for more than 90 percent of all situations from my experience).

This state is somewhat analogous to the Zombie Process state that can occur in Unix where processes are detached from parent processes because of a crash or failure.

This setting allows you to reclaim connections back into the free list pool that may be also left over after poorly written application code. If developers aren't closing off their connections properly, or there are other problems with their data source binding application code, this value can help to alleviate wasted resources (but it's no substitute for having your developers fix the root problem!).

As a guide, this setting should be twice that of the Idle Timeout setting to ensure that all connections and transactions can take place within sufficient time while not impacting application processing and limiting connection and query failure prematurely.

WebSphere 5 JDBC Connection Pool Tuning

WebSphere 5 introduced and replaced some of the WebSphere 4 JDBC connection pool settings. It's possible, and required under some circumstances, to use the version 4 data source structure, especially for EJB 1.1 beans.

However, for EJB 2.0 and other compliant J2EE components that can use the newer version 5 JDBC pool manager, there are three new settings that can help increase performance of your database accesses. Figure 11-10 shows the JDBC data source configuration area within WebSphere 5.

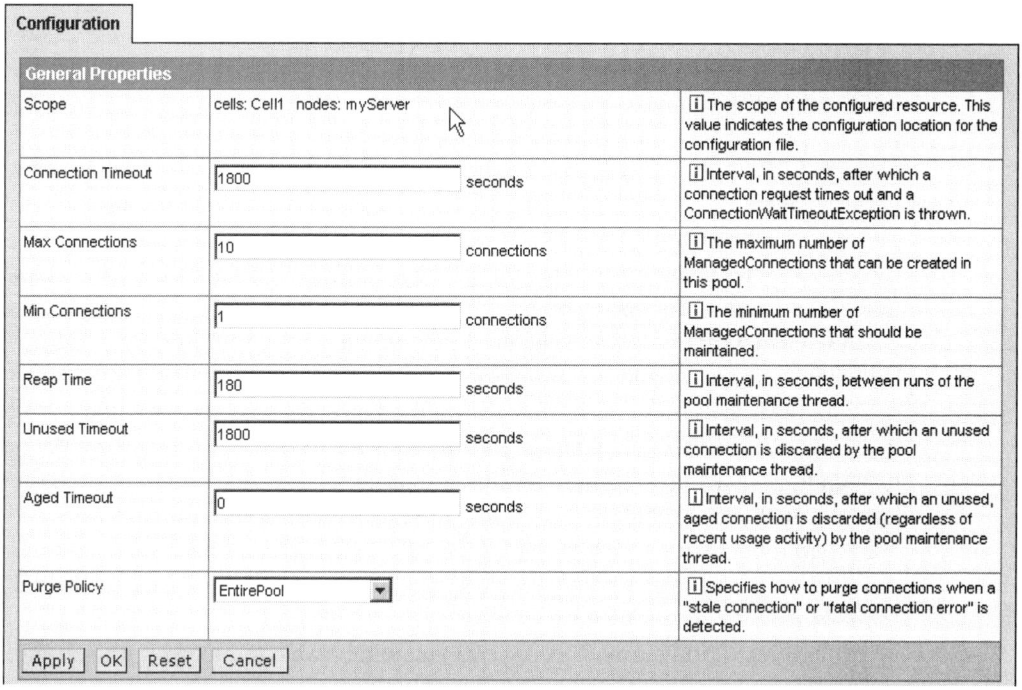

Figure 11-10. WebSphere 5 Pool Manager Connection dialog box

As you can see, the configuration window for WebSphere 5 is somewhat different than in version 4. The new configuration settings available for WebSphere 5 are as follows:

- Unused Timeout

- Aged Timeout

- Purge Policy

You'll now look at each of those in more detail.

Unused Timeout

The Unused Timeout setting gives you the ability to set a timeout for when an unused or unallocated connection is returned to the free pool list. This setting is almost identical to the WebSphere 4 Idle Timeout value. For that reason, I recommend you use the same principles to configure it. That is, set this value to be two to three times that of your Connection Timeout value.

Consider tuning this value if you notice that active connections are starting to build up in the pool manager that don't reflect the number of concurrent users on your systems or the SQL query rate isn't representative of the number of active connections.

Aged Timeout

The Aged Timeout setting is a new setting in WebSphere 5 that, although similar to the Orphaned Connection Timeout setting in WebSphere 4, it does provide greater scope to clean out any unwanted or old connections. However, you can use the same policy as a guide for this setting. Set Aged Timeout to be two times that of the Unused Timeout value.

If you're changing this setting "cold turkey," be sure to monitor it carefully. Unlike the Orphan Timeout setting, the Aged Timeout setting will kill off a connection, regardless of its state, after the defined interval has been reached.

You want to avoid having large transactions terminated by this setting. A backup litmus test for setting this value is to understand what length of time the largest transaction will take to complete in your environment. Although it's a hard item to measure (many variables can affect it), it should help you understand what the value should be; set the Aged Timeout to be two times the value of the longest transaction you may have during peak load.

Your Stress and Volume Testing (SVT) should be able to help you understand this value.

Purge Policy

The Purge Policy setting is another new WebSphere 5 setting. It provides an additional WebSphere-based controlling mechanism to handle StaleConnectionExceptions and FatalConnectionExceptions.

This setting allows you to reset all your connections in your pool manager quickly when there are critical problems on your backend database. You need to be careful of this setting. There are two options:

- Purge Entire Pool

- Purge Failing Connection Only

You need to be aware that if a single connection attempt throws a StaleConnectionException—meaning that there are no new connection threads available—all existing connections not in use will be dropped from the pool's concurrently active list. There is, however, a chance that active connections maybe dropped prematurely.

This may be helpful for situations where you want to restart all queries from scratch when there may be a number of malformed connections to the database. If, for example, connections are building up and new connections are timing out and receiving StaleConnectionException messages, setting this value to Purge Entire Pool allows your pool manager to start from a "clean slate."

All connection requests after a purge need to issue a new getConnection() call to the data source provider. This ensures that only those requests that are required will re-establish themselves to the database.

This setting has pros and cons. It gives you the ability to have WebSphere reset all connections (new attempts and actives) in the event that there are resource exhaustion problems with the database, network, or some other component that cause a banking of database connections. Yet, it also has a potential of starting a flip-flop effect where subsequent database connection requests are met with exceptions, and a continuous purging cycle starts.

By setting the value to Purge Failing Connection Only, you may just be hiding the larger problem. If this setting is configured, you'll find that as each connection met with an exception is purged, additional connection requests will potentially be thrown exceptions, causing the cleanup period to be exaggerated from subseconds to potentially seconds or even minutes.

I recommend staying with the default setting of Purge Entire Pool unless you have a specific application need to only reset the active connection (for example, long multiphase transactions).

Summary

In this chapter, you looked at what WebSphere expects from data sources, databases, and the types of application connectivity available for connecting WebSphere to data sources.

Database technology is a science in itself. However, you should be able to gauge from this chapter the importance and number of available options for configuring WebSphere to operate optimally with database technologies.

To understand how to monitor the performance of your database, see Chapter 13, where you'll look at various tools to help you understand where bottlenecks may be occurring in your WebSphere environment.

CHAPTER 12

Legacy Integration: Performance Optimization

LEGACY SYSTEMS INTEGRATION is a fast growing area of Java 2 Enterprise Edition (J2EE) application integration. In this chapter, you'll look at and pinpoint the areas within your WebSphere-based application and platform environment that can affect legacy systems integration.

Legacy Integration: What Is It?

The rapid emergence of the Internet and the "e-world" during the past decade split the legacy technologies from that of J2EE and Web-based technologies, such as Common Object Request Broker Architecture (CORBA), Common Gateway Interface (CGI), and so on. Specifically, a vast percentage of the world's large back-office systems were running legacy processing engines. Mainframes of all types and midframe systems such as VAXes and AS/400s, were commonplace during the mid-1990s.

With the Internet came entrepreneurs and people who saw the power in taking those back-office systems and interfacing them with the Web. Businesses further saw the power in providing customers with self-service capabilities such as online ordering and sales. Many of these systems were previously handled with proprietary and legacy systems that just weren't designed to cope with the volume transactions that the Web presented.

Legacy systems in companies before the Internet boom would work with loads of hundreds or, at the most, thousands of users. Also, most of this was from 8 a.m. to 6 p.m. The Internet threw all this out the door and provided a completely new paradigm for computing.

The Internet offers 24/7 operational and service availability and has user loads anywhere from the hundreds to the millions. Application computing has changed forever.

The problem we're faced with now is that companies want to get the most from their expensive, legacy, and sometimes proprietary systems. Companies, rightly so, don't want to throw away what has been working well for years. So,

453

you're now faced with the challenge of integrating non-online systems such as mainframe and batch-based platforms into an environment that demands response times in milliseconds and works in the world of objects!

Many technologies are available that cater to this type of computing paradigm. Integrating a legacy system to a WebSphere-based application is no longer the nightmare it once was. Therefore, legacy integration is the act (art) of interfacing a WebSphere/J2EE-based application to a non-J2EE-based environment. *Legacy* refers to systems of older, sometimes less extensible, technology. One of the most common forms of legacy integration is where a WebSphere J2EE application is interfaced with a COBOL-based application on a mainframe via something such as MQ Series.

Figure 12-1 provides an example of a common integration of a legacy system with a WebSphere-based computing platform.

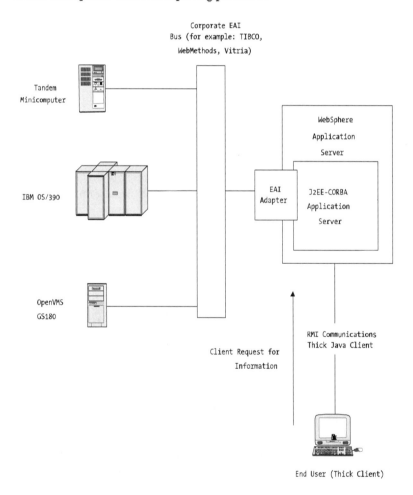

Figure 12-1. Example integration of a WebSphere/J2EE application with a legacy application

As you can see, at a high level, there's nothing complex about the topology. There are definitely many ways to approach this. What I'll discuss in this chapter isn't necessarily the topology considerations but the performance considerations of legacy integration. Remember that many legacy systems are asynchronous and, without proper consideration, will cause complete havoc with J2EE-based applications because of the threading and synchronous model that Java applications follow.

Design Considerations for Legacy Integration

There's a plethora of legacy systems in data centers around the globe. Some of these are old workhorses, and some of these are the more recent and sophisticated systems such as Portal Infranet, Seibel, and SAP. Obviously, I can't discuss all of them—that would entail a series of books! However, what I'll cover are some of the more common approaches being used globally to interface nonproprietary systems to WebSphere.

NOTE   When I say *nonproprietary*, I'm referring to systems that are custom developed.

Generally, the most common way to interface WebSphere-based J2EE applications is via the Java Message Service (JMS). However, Extensible Markup Language (XML) via Simple Object Access Protocol (SOAP) is fast becoming a more distributed flavor of legacy integration over that of JMS.

Essentially, you could use JMS for short hop communications—such as Local Area Network (LAN) or high-speed Wide Area Network (WAN)—or where the legacy system can talk via JMS. You'll find that many legacy systems are starting to appear with Web Service engines so that you can communicate with them via XML over SOAP—or XML Remote Procedure Call (XML RPC), the opensource flavor.

As you've seen throughout the book, Web Services are a growing yet immature technology. I have no doubt that Web Services will eventually provide foundational intersystem communications; however, while it's still an emerging technology with many of the core stack and standards yet to be ratified, you should be cognizant of other, possibly equally sound, distributed computing communications technologies.

JMS can use MQ Series from IBM that provides the low-level queue communications. You can use this form of communication internally to your application or for true legacy systems interconnection. Essentially what you want is system and application interoperability and its continuous evolvement. It'd appear that as each new interconnection technology matures and comes onto the market, critics find holes and limitations in it and move on to design another technology.

I'm a firm believer in the mantra of "Use the best tool for the job." If you find that plain-old socket communication is sufficient for your needs, then why implement something complex such as CORBA? Don't be afraid to use anything that fits the job well—the only caveat is to be sure that whatever technology you use, you consider future scalability and capability needs. Don't lock yourself into something limited that you'll only throw out later.

You'll now look at the more common legacy systems interconnection methods.

CORBA Integration

CORBA 1.0 was released in 1990 and is one of the most powerful and popular distributed communications architectures available. Inherently used in online systems operating C++ and Java runtimes, it can also be used in non-object-oriented technologies such as COBOL and C. CORBA provides a non-language-affiliated distributing computing architecture that gives it its distributed computing flexibility.

Unlike Java Remote Method Invocation (RMI)—which is used for Enterprise JavaBean (EJB) communications, among other things—CORBA is truly platform *and* language independent.

CORBA operates using an application protocol known as Internet Inter Orb Protocol (IIOP) as its primary application protocol. The power and flexibility of CORBA are further realized because variations of CORBA can communicate over protocols that aren't based on Transmission Control Protocol/Internet Protocol (TCP/IP) such as Asynchronous Transfer Mode (ATM). Overall, CORBA allows disparate systems to communicate with one another using myriad protocols and communications technologies.

Because CORBA is language independent, it also enables you to communicate between different systems running different runtime bases. Integrating CORBA into your application environment isn't hard. In fact, many subsystems of WebSphere use CORBA-like communications and communicate using IIOP.

 NOTE There's a difference between RMI-IIOP and IIOP in Java-speak. RMI-IIOP is where RMI communications are handled *over* IIOP instead of plain RMI. IIOP by itself is typically associated with pure CORBA communications.

Figure 12-2 shows how a CORBA implementation may look within a WebSphere platform.

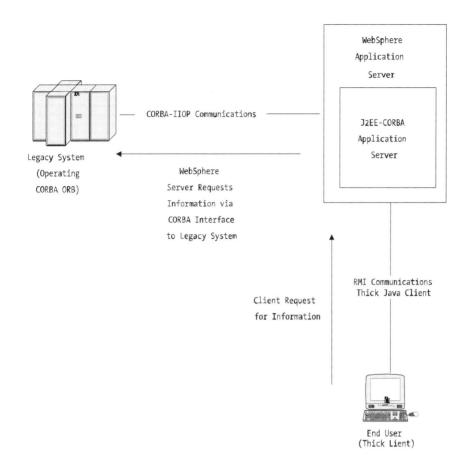

Figure 12-2. Example CORBA and WebSphere implementation

This figure shows a basic WebSphere implementation operating a CORBA interface to a legacy system. The legacy system in this example could be literally any form of host—mainframe, Unix, Windows, or something in-between.

A classic example of this type of implementation is where an object-oriented CORBA implementation may have been implemented some years back before Java really gained enterprise acceptance. In this case, it may have been more cost efficient to leave the existing legacy system where it was and simply interface with it using a CORBA interface from the WebSphere platform. What's important to note is where WebSphere starts to communicate with the CORBA legacy system.

Consider that your J2EE-based application server needs to be well designed because inbound communications will be RMI/RMI-IIOP and outbound requests will be pure IIOP. Both these protocols utilize the centralized Object Request Broker (ORB).

The ORB is essentially the listening server for these types of distributed communications. In CORBA, the ORB is the distributed server. In J2EE, the ORB provides the same concept of technology except there's less reliance on it for RMI-IIOP communications because the RMI layer is more tightly integrated at the Java Virtual Machine (JVM) level via the appropriate Java classes.

You now look at Figure 12-2 at another layer down. Figure 12-3 shows an example transaction taking place from a request from a client (via RMI), which in turn triggers a request to the legacy CORBA system via IIOP.

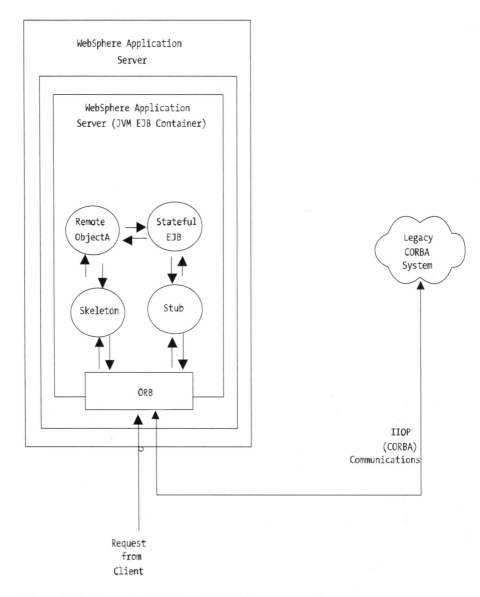

Figure 12-3. Example CORBA and WebSphere transaction

In a situation such as the one presented in Figure 12-3 where you may have a single application server servicing the requests, it may be advantageous to compartmentalize your components and ensure that your developers or application architects are splitting the Java RMI and CORBA components. Having both contained within a singular application server, under load, could introduce performance problems because the ORB needs to service requests for both the RMI communications and the IIOP/CORBA communications.

For each transaction, you're effectively doubling your threading overhead. Of course, you can contain all this within a singular application server if you want to avoid having to communicate to another EJB container within another application server. Using local transactions within WebSphere does decrease your RMI call overhead (except network calls, all calls to remote objects are referenced internally to the same application server).

NOTE Be aware that local transactions aren't J2EE compliant. By default your WebSphere application server will have local transactions disabled.

If you need to have all the components within a shared application server, be sure to model and tune the number of threads allocated to the ORB. You'll find that you may quickly run out of threads within your ORB if you haven't modeled this correctly.

Again, my recommendation is to compartmentalize your components. It's better to take a small hit on overhead for the network RMI calls between application servers than it is to keep your CORBA components within the same application server. This provides a best practice approach at compartmentalizing your components—creating somewhat of an abstraction layer.

Like RMI/RMI-IIOP communications, CORBA communications can become network intensive if there's a high transaction rate occurring. Ensure that your network sizing has adequately accounted for your CORBA overheads, especially if you're trying to route IIOP traffic through firewalls. Because the IIOP payloads (as opposed to the IP packets) contain information about source and destination ORB servers, IIOP can wreak havoc with Network Address Translation (NAT) and similar forms of firewall routing.

In fact, nowadays, it's possible to tunnel and encapsulate many application protocols such as IIOP within more simplistic network technologies such as Hypertext Transfer Protocol (HTTP). In addition, many products provide CORBA proxy servers. These aid security devices as well as route CORBA traffic from public to private or between nonvisible subnets without the pain of double-NAT firewalls and so on.

Always ensure that there are enough network ports and sockets available on both the client and server side of the transaction loop. Also, consider using connection pools for your communications to help alleviate the overhead of starting up and shutting down IIOP communications. Avoid having a new IIOP connection established for each client connection because this will quickly saturate the CORBA server's (and possibly your client's) TCP network services.

Generally, if you're in a position to influence the architecture of the application and your traffic needs to go via a firewall, consider some form of proxy so that you don't have to deal with the complexities of IIOP through firewalls. This may be either one of the aforementioned CORBA proxy server products or a secondary WebSphere application server tier that communicates with the primary WebSphere application server tier via some other protocol that's more firewall friendly (for example, SOAP, sockets/RPC, or RMI).

MQ Series Integration

MQ Series is a powerful host for a multihost architecture used for distributing computing. As discussed earlier during the chapter, MQ Series was originally developed by IBM to allow its host-based systems to be able to communicate with one another.

MQ also inherently provided an implementation that allowed disparate platforms to be able to communicate with a degree of service quality and robustness. The basic architecture behind MQ Series is that it's a message-based (listen and publish/subscribe) architecture. Communications between systems is conducted via an asynchronous queue system. Hosts place messages onto specific queues that are either subscribed or listened to by other systems. Listening servers monitor the configured queues for messages addressed appropriately.

Once a message has been received on a queue, the receiving MQ client or server acts on the message contents like any other form of distributed communications.

Unlike most other forms of distributing communications, MQ Series is an asynchronous architecture. Messages are placed onto queues by clients. After placing a message onto a queue, the client listens for a resulting message on the queue.

The development paradigm is slightly different from most other architectures, so developers need to change the way in which they think about sending and receiving data within their applications.

As an example, the following pseudo-code is an example of how this may be implemented:

```
Public static ActivateQueue();
{
    While true {
        NewMessage = getMesssage();
            PutMessageOnQueue(hostname, queue name, newMessage);
```

```
        MQResult = ListenToQueue(transactionID);
    }
    // do something with queue results
}


public static PutMessageOnQueue(string, string, string);
{
            transactionID = SendMessagetoQueue(message);
            return transactionID;
}


public static ListenToQueue(int);
{
    while true {
        // mq code to listen to queue rsults
        sleep 5;
    }
    return result;
}
```

Ignoring the syntax, the basic flow of this code should provide an example of one way to implement MQ asynchronous transactions. There are many ways you can do this; this merely provides an example.

The need for thread-aware application design with MQ transactions is obvious. Because you have no result guarantee and there may be a need to resend the put message onto the queue if a timeout has been reached, the application will need to retry the request. If threading isn't implemented correctly in an environment where the returned MQ data is large or the remote system (MQ Server) is under load, the MQ transaction could take some time to complete.

Generally, using the MQ series will mostly be limited to mainframe or similar legacy host systems. There are other platform distributed architectures available that suit online systems better; however, with MQ, you'll be typically talking to batch-based systems.

The whole architecture of a batch-based system is typically asynchronous. The distributed communications as well as the internal system processing scheduler operate using a queue architecture. Therefore, you need to consider these factors.

With no real control over when results of queries will be returned, you face an interesting model with which to work. Although MQ architecture is out of the scope of this book, it's important you understand it at a high level. In Figure 12-4, there's a five-stage process where a client request initiates an MQ call to a host-based server. Step 2, as depicted in the figure, places a query onto the query queue. The listening-based host server picks up the addressed message and commences processing (step 3).

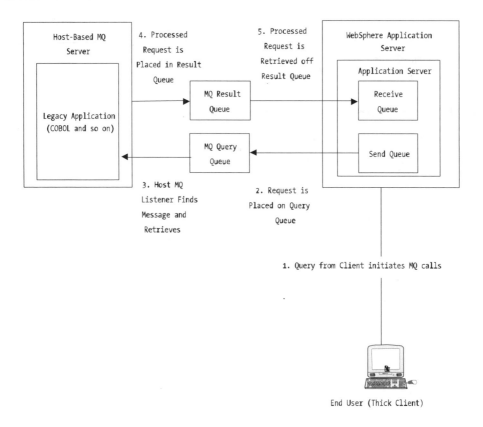

Figure 12-4. MQ Series communications with WebSphere

The result of the query is placed on another queue, which in this example is called the *result queue* (step 4). The calling J2EE-based application then in turn is also listening on the result queue for the query result (step 5). The result is obtained and processed accordingly within the J2EE-based WebSphere application. Although this is a simplistic view of how the technology works, it should provide you with an idea of the transaction flow.

I recommend that if you're requiring communication with an MQ-enabled legacy host system, consider using WebSphere/J2EE based on JMS for more simple environments. I'll discuss this later in the chapter, but JMS provides a cleaner and more robust way of communicating to an MQ-enabled host system.

However, there are factors you need to consider when using JMS if you're looking for high-availability configurations. I discussed this in more detail in Chapter 8. If you're bound to communicate using native MQ Series components without the advanced features such as MQ queue managers for high availability and clustering, consider the following:

Have a low-latency network architecture: Having a low-latency network environment helps with the performance of the messaging-type architecture of MQ Series. If you need a wide area or highly distributed messaging mechanism, consider using Web Services with MQ. I'll discuss this in later sections.

Design your MQ queries tightly: Don't overload your MQ Series host systems. Chances are that it'll be more costly to upgrade these legacy systems than it is for Unix or Wintel environments. Make an effort to ensure that your developers only obtain the data they need in queries rather than getting everything back in a query and filtering it.

Consider preemptive MQ queries: Given the asynchronous nature of MQ Series, the nature of the put and receive messages can introduce unwanted delays in your customers and users sessions. Consider prefetching data you think you may require during the user's session from the legacy MQ host to save delays.

Be aware of thread exhaustion with pending MQ results: Because your applications may be waiting around for results back from MQ hosts, be sure that your WebSphere-based applications don't starve the thread pool of available threads.

Always ensure that your MQ-based applications are using connection pools. It's important to use these pooled connections to help with the performance of both the remote MQ host as well as the local WebSphere-based application server. Code examples for this are provided and discussed in Chapter 11.

Web Services Integration

Web Services are a quickly maturing distributed computing paradigm that provide an efficient and platform agnostic communications approach. Web Services provide a truly decoupled distributing computing architecture. Previous distributing architectures are well suited to specific same-host-to-same-host paradigms; however, through typical Information Technology (IT) industry perseverance, people have extended those architectures to fit their needs rather than developing something from scratch that's truly distributable.

For example, CORBA, although good for distributed communications for the specific host types that it's available on, does fall short for complex environments where firewalls and or WANs are involved. It's what I call a *heavyweight* application protocol. The costs of communication startup and message transformation are quite high compared to that of something such as Web Services.

Web services will, more and more, become the way that distributed, disparate, legacy, and J2EE-based applications will communicate. Unlike previous distributing computing paradigms, Web Services are a model that follows a dynamic, loosely coupled application communications architecture, based on services rather than implementation type.

That is, with Web Services, you interface to the service you want to use. This is different from other distributing computing architectures because you implement the interface once with a Web Service provider and, via that singular interface, can instantiate any exposed data into objects. There's no need to create separate interfaces for separate object or query types.

Web Services typically use SOAP. Usually, SOAP operates over the standard HTTP or HTTPS port, which makes it easy to "massage" through a corporate firewall. Figure 12-5 provides a high-level diagram of how Web Services integrate within WebSphere.

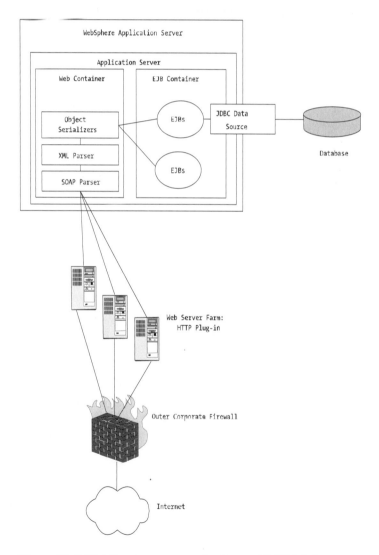

Figure 12-5. Web Service communications with WebSphere

Figure 12-5 highlights how Web Services may be implemented within a WebSphere application server. As you can see, the main area for integration is a Web container, and as such, you can apply many of the rules and recommendations covered in Chapter 7 to Web Services.

In fact, Web Services, from the point of view of the systems or WebSphere architect, isn't that different from any other form of Java Server Page (JSP) or servlet communications. Although the actual logic that handled much of the Web Service communication is different, the same fundamental WebSphere processes and engine dynamics are being used in the same way that JSPs and servlets are using them.

However, again, like the previous legacy distributed application architectures discussed in this chapter, the full architectural overview of Web Services is beyond the scope of this book. The purpose here is to discuss Web Services from a performance implementation perspective.

I'll discuss Web Services based on a HTTP Web Service stack:

- Web Service directory—Universal, Description, Discovery, and Integration (UDDI)

- Web Services description—Web Services Description Language (WSDL)

- XML-based messaging—SOAP

- Network—HTTP

The following are some Web Service performance and scalability tips:

- **Try to use standard SOAP data types**: Using remote data types, for example, will decrease performance and scalability of your WebSphere application using Web Services.

- **Consider whether you need XML validation**: WebSphere application server performance can be increased with XML validation turned off.

- **If using WSDL, consider caching this document type**: Reduces reread frequency during a Web Service transaction and increases overall application performance.

- **Use internal rather than external schema sites**: Improves application performance.

You'll now look at each of those items in more detail.

Using Standard SOAP Data Types

SOAP provides several simple data types for use in SOAP envelopes:

- Int (Integer)

- NegativeInteger

- String

- Float

It's also possible to implement your own data types. For example, if you have a need to access a data type such as a binary format (for example, bitmap, image, raw data, and so on), you can reference an external or nonstandard data type by referencing a different xsd element type. For example:

```
<message name = "getImageCount">
 <part name = "imageCount" type = "xsd:int "/>
</message>
<message name = "getImage">
 <part name = "name" type = "xsd:string"/>
 <part name = "size" type = "xsd:int"/>
 <part name = "image" type = "xsd:http://www.myWebServiceSite.com/imageMapType"/>
</message>
```

As you can see, in the last part directive, there's a data type of http://www.myWebServiceSite.com/imageMapType. This data type is obviously on an external site.

This introduces an element in your WebSphere environment that's probably out of your operational control. The server running that site may be slow, poorly managed, or not highly available. Also, the route path in-between your site and the remote site could be high latency or overloaded. Either way, this introduces a point of performance contention in your environment.

As much as possible, use the standard data types and only use external schema reference sites if required.

NOTE   See the "Internet vs. External Schema Site" section for more information on this robust improvement approach.

XML Validation

XML validation is another aspect of Web Services that can introduce overhead. When a remote application requests data from an exposed Web Service, the serving or calling application can validate the request and receive streams against the service's Document Type Definition (DTD). Although validation is a satisfactory step in providing an error-free application environment, if you know the data types that are being presented, you can usually pretty safely assume that the data being returned will always be of the type you're expecting.

I say this because, generally, the data being requested via the Web Service will be sourced from a database or some form of data store. In this case, the database and data store loading and retrieval is already mastered by a level of data validation. For example, if you created a relational schema for a database that had a data field named MyValue with the data type Integer(2), you could safely assume that if you retrieved that data from that field, you'd get back an integer with two digits.

Therefore, if you're querying a Web Service from a system that you know, trust, or operate yourself, you could possibly do away with this level of data type validation.

Caching of WSDL

It's not uncommon to find this same problem cropping up with standard XML-based or EJB specification DTDs in Java code. Sometimes beans are provided from open-source sites or from packages provided by vendors that reference remote DTDs on external sites such as http://java.sun.com.

This is great for managing changes to application components but awful for performance! You can find the same issue with the WSDL in Web Services. Quite often, WSDL definition files are located on the Web, especially if they're from public Web Service sites.

For high-volume environments, this isn't a good move. Quite similar to the next section's issue, the number-one rule in gaining performance for XML or Web Service environments is to build in some form of XML, DTD, or WSDL caching. I've seen cases where the WSDL is loaded into shared memory and available to all calling applications as well as loading the WSDL into a database and periodically synchronized with the live or Internet-based WSDL template. In the case of the in-memory WSDL concept, a relatively straightforward caching mechanism could read the schema into memory during the application server's bootstrap, and all WSDL lookups could be performed from there.

It's possible to even use the Java Naming and Directory (JNDI) tree to store information such as this. Given that JNDI is distributed between clustered or workload-management-aware WebSphere servers, it provides a straightforward way of exposing this type of data to your Web Service server applications.

The bottom line is this: You want to minimize the end-to-end transaction time for your application server's transactions. By bringing in the WSDL to be local, you reduce the chance of your WebSphere-based application performing badly because of Internet performance or the potential poor performance of the site hosting the remote WSDL template.

Internet vs. External Schema Sites

Similar to the previous recommendation, hosting DTD schemas on remote sites isn't a good solution for a high-performance, high-volume application. Because there's usually a lot of latency between Wide Area Internetworks, the end-to-end transaction time for your customers or users making Web Services calls can vary widely. By using remote, organization-managed components, you're compromising your overall environment from either a security or stability point of view.

Although it'd be hard for it to occur, if a site housing a remotely exposed XML schema was compromised and the XML schema modified, it could easily cause problems with your Web Service transactions if the robustness of the remote system development and testing or even security methodologies were questionable. You don't want to spend countless hours and who knows how many millions of dollars on a high-availability infrastructure and have it completely degraded by components that are out of your sphere of influence.

My recommendation is that all remotely provided XML, WSDL, and other DTD schemas and templates are mirrored locally and are checked through some form of manual validation or automated checking tool. Your application should only reference a copy-managed instance of those schemas locally to your WebSphere environment, and, through a synchronization validation process, you should only introduce the updated schemas once testing and self-validation have taken place.

This flies in the face of one of the key ideals behind Web Services in that exposed services are on the Internet to be used. However, until Web Services become more mature and tighter controls are implemented, my recommendation is that you don't risk your site's integrity. House locally, and validate any changes.

As the Web Service stack becomes more mature, sites will start to expose business data. Without mature security, transaction support, and service quality, Web Services currently shouldn't be used "out of the box." One option to get around this current standards and stack limitation is to consider implementing a homegrown XML parsing-based implementation with homegrown security (in other words, authorization and authentication) such as XML-RPC, with SSL-based Web Servers if you're exposing content.

Batch Components and External Applications

Many components within a WebSphere environment, both locally and on remote legacy systems, may not be all that clever in terms of distributed computing but may in fact be simply batch-based tools operating behind the scenes. This includes things such as native Java code, Perl applications, C applications, and even shell scripts. You'll now look at some of the more common forms of batch components and some considerations for ensuring performance.

Many systems implement system-level batch scripts. In Unix, this is typically shell scripts (for example, sh, bash, zsh, csh, ksh, and so on), and for Windows systems, this is DOS batch scripts. These types of scripts are used predominately for simple tasks that just don't warrant their own full-blown application and may typically consist of many other smaller applications.

Mostly, these scripts are called via the exec() method in Java where it's important for the developers to handle the exit codes of those scripts carefully. In the following sections, you'll see some important considerations for running batch scripts and external applications within your WebSphere application environment.

Make Your Scripts Thread-Safe

If you have a J2EE-based application that's fairly dependant on a script such as one of the aforementioned Unix shell or batch scripts, consider placing it in another thread and compartmentalizing it from the rest of the running Java applications. Because these scripts tend to be dangerous and can quite easily bring down an entire system with an incorrect command or entry, you want to be sure that the Java application code can handle errors and critical failures of these scripts.

Compartmentalize Your Scripts

Remember also that these types of scripts run close to the operating system, similar to that of the JVM from within they're called. Therefore, because the script isn't insulated or managed by the container or a JVM, it has the potential to do damage to your system's performance.

Manage the Operating Priority

Consider running your scripts with a lower operating system priority (in Unix) to ensure that you don't have runaway processes. This will eliminate the possibility of a single process consuming too much Central Processing Unit (CPU) power.

Consider Having a Script Manager Factory

If you have 1,000 users online, with all sessions kicking off a particular script, you'll have that many scripts running within the operating system. Imagine the Input/Output (I/O) overhead if you were running a find command for a particular file from all 1,000 scripts! Your WebSphere performance would quickly turn to mush.

Additionally, if your script location (or the script itself) is exposed to users, it won't take long for some unwanted hacker to "Trojan horse" that script for something else. Never (ever!) expose your operating system directly to the end users. Whether it's intranet or Internet based, if you do need to run scripts as part of your application, always implement a script factory to place a layer of abstraction between your present runtime and your operating system.

If you have to run something such as this within your WebSphere environment, consider a manager class of some sorts that executes these scripts and monitors how many are active at any one time. This type of JavaBean would could be set to only maintain or allow the concurrent execution of "x" many scripts at any one time or only kick off more scripts if the overall system load is less than, let's say, 40 percent. The same class would be responsible for passing results back and forth to the calling objects.

This approach ensures that there's some element of management and control of these scripts. Although it's not perfect, it does provide a reasonable level of operational integrity.

Don't Use All Your Memory!

If you have 8 gigabytes (GB) of memory in your WebSphere server, and 6GB is already consumed by operating system processes and WebSphere components, you want to make sure that whatever scripts you're kicking off don't exceed 2GB—the available memory left in the server! Doing so will force processes such as JVMs to start using swap memory, which will bring the system's performance to a halt.

Perl is a good example where you may need to do large file manipulation. Perl developers typically have to read the file into memory to be able to manipulate it back and forth, and therefore, the amount of memory consumed by the Perl processes will be the sum of the file plus the Perl runtime and some additional overhead.

Don't Use Java Native Interface (JNI)

Unless you have a specific or architecturally sound reason to do so (and this goes for all batch components), don't use Java Native Interface (JNI). JNI on its own is a sound piece of Java technology; however, it breaks the EJB specification when used from within an EJB container and can lead to many problems that the JVM can't handle.

Fatal errors within a JNI-called application can easily cause a JVM to crash. Although WebSphere is configured by default to restart the JVM (the application server) after a crash, it means that while the restart it occurring, customers and users can't use the application. Or, if you're running multiple application servers, the performance of the overall system will be degraded.

For this reason, and as discussed in Chapter 6, consider operating any batch or external (non-customer-facing) application components on separate tiers. This way, you can be confident that if you need to run these types of components, live customers won't be greatly affected if they fail and cause a JVM to crash.

Java Application Clients (JACs)

Java application clients are Java applications that you run from the command line. These are useful to be called from other non-Java applications (such as shell scripts) that may need to obtain data from a Java-based object repository.

For example, imagine you had a shell script that needed to create directories for log files but the name of those directories were based on unique ID numbers that were created and mastered by a J2EE-based application. By using a JAC, you're able to load specific WebSphere and J2EE-based Java Archives (JARs) and access WebSphere running applications.

In this example, you could operate a Java Application Client (JAC) that obtained the Java Database Connectivity (JDBC) data source context from an operating WebSphere environment, then run a query against the database via the JDBC connection pool, and return the result. Of course, it's probably easier to run a direct JDBC connection from the JAC and bypass the WebSphere JNDI context lookups, but the example suits this discussion!

JACs run in their own JVM. As such, the JAC is constrained by the same attributes as normal Java and J2EE applications are—that is, by JVM heap and various other profiling settings.

It's important that if you're running many JACs in your application environment, you don't have each of them firing up with a large amount of Java heap space. As you can appreciate, if your application architecture saw that you had a JAC launch on a regular basis with Java heap allocation sizes of the initial being 128 megabytes (MB) and the maximum being 384MB, it'd only take a handful of active JACs to consume all available memory!

The key here is to ensure the following:

Ensure that proper modeling of memory heap allocations are performed. In my experience, JACs don't typically need much more than an initial heap of 16MB to 32MB and a maximum heap of 32MB to 64MB. Occasionally, greater memory will be required, but in this case, set the initial to always be something low such as 16MB and the maximum to be what you think your maximum JAC memory requirements will be. Monitor this application code carefully to ensure that you don't have memory leaks.

Be sure that the JAC calling mechanism is controlled and tested. You don't want an error to occur within the calling mechanism that in turn goes into a loop and launches a new JAC every second.

Finally, test, test, test.

Summary

As you've seen in this chapter, legacy and batch integration, although simplistic, can sneak in a few performance "curveballs." Regarding batch components, it's worth remembering that although it's important to keep it simple, batch components aren't always the best method of servicing unusual requirements.

Developing a lot of these batch type components within Java, although it may take longer and will operate slightly slower with a one-to-one component view, will, at the end of the day, operate less efficiently when the system is under load. Keeping everything operating as a J2EE Java application means that the WebSphere containers are in charge and are doing what they're designed to do.

Legacy components are slightly different. Most of the common legacy integration technologies available come with best practices and well-proven Java Application Programming Interfaces (APIs). This provides a tighter level of integration with the WebSphere core engine and ultimately provides better performance overall.

The bottom line is this: Follow the rules discussed in Chapters 6–9 when I talked about topologically architectures and high-availability concepts and integrate the key points from this chapter into your legacy systems interface design.

CHAPTER 13

Performance Management Tooling

IN PREVIOUS CHAPTERS, I DISCUSSED ways to implement WebSphere applications and environments with performance and availability in mind. In this chapter, you'll explore some methods and approaches for monitoring and analyzing system and application data so you can understand the performance and load characteristics of your WebSphere servers and applications.

Overview of Performance Tooling

Performance tooling is the fairly broad name given to the process of selecting, implementing, and using performance analysis tools to monitor and probe your applications and servers for information on their load and performance status. In this chapter, you'll look at how to measure some key performance aspects of your systems and correlate those findings with the perceived performance of your WebSphere applications.

That is, you'll look at several key areas of a server that can impact the performance of a WebSphere application. I'll discuss this from both a proactive and reactive point of view. In other words, if your WebSphere applications appear to be running slowly, what steps will you take to understand what's going within your WebSphere application?

Many of you may already know about some or all of these tools if you come from a system administrative background. However, what I've tried to do in this chapter is match the tools to the problem area they can fix and provide examples of what the tools' output really means with regard to your WebSphere applications.

Specifically, you'll see a range of commands and utilities that are useful in determining system and application load characteristics. The first part of the chapter discusses the tools that are best suited to diagnosing and understanding the system state (load, utilization, and so on). At the end of these sections, you'll explore which tools are best for diagnosing potential performance issues and learn how to read the results of the diagnosis. I'll use tables to summarize possible causes to your performance problems. Each scenario will include one or more possible reasons for the performance problem and a guide to hunting down and diagnosing the performance issue.

Essentially, performance tooling is a part of the performance management methodology. It's when you use tools and applications to understand what's going on within your WebSphere application. Essentially, without performance tooling, you'll never know what may be causing a system to operate inefficiently. Many of the tools used for performance tooling are available as part of each operating system or are readily available on the Internet.

In this chapter, you'll look at the following:

- Monitoring system utilization—for example, Central Processing Unit (CPU), memory, and swap space

- Monitoring disk Input/Output (I/O) utilization

- Monitoring network performance and utilization

- Monitoring hot spots within WebSphere applications

At the end of this chapter, you should be able to run tools and understand, either reactively or proactively, the state of your applications via the state of your servers.

Monitoring System Utilization

System utilization is the broad term given to the notion of overall system load. As I've touched on in earlier chapters, system load is caused by a myriad of factors—some of which are obvious, some of which aren't.

All the sections in this chapter that discuss system-based performance tooling in fact refer to overall system utilization. However, in the spirit of breaking down each form of hot spot within a system, you'll consider system utilization to be CPU, memory, and swap utilization in a performance context.

Each operating system has its own representation of system load and requirements, and each operating system has a different representation of what's high load and what's low load. In a WebSphere application server environment, any application that's performing badly could be caused by system overutilization. Then again, the WebSphere application itself might be causing the system utilization to be too high. This could constitute either a poorly written application or a poorly designed platform (in other words, one that's undermodeled).

As you've seen in earlier chapters, the Java Virtual Machine (JVM) is somewhat similar to a mini–operating system that sits on top of the core operating system. It manages its own threads and memory allocation and therefore is susceptible to CPU bottlenecks and poorly performing memory. *Poorly performing memory* refers to situations where your physical Random Access Memory (RAM) is depleted and swap memory or virtual memory is used excessively.

Generally, there's nothing wrong with your server operating system using swap and virtual memory as long as it's not used for runtime applications. Most of the time, the operating system will swap out unused applications to disk in order to free up the real physical memory for running and active processes.

Another way to look at it is to consider the performance (or lack thereof) of a JVM that's operating within swap or virtual memory and is continually performing garbage collection. The performance of the application would be abysmal.

CPU and System Load: Unix

Common with all Unix-based systems are a number of key load and performance identifiers that can be attributed to system load:

- Load average

- Number of waiting processes (similar to load average)

- CPU utilization (percent available, percent used, and by what)

- Memory usage

- Swap usage and utilization

The uptime command on Unix is an important tool to gauge an approximate load rating of the server:

```
/> uptime
 12:10pm  up 62 day(s), 23:11,  13 users,  load average: 0.07, 0.20, 0.23
```

Essentially, what this is showing is a bunch of information related to system usage. The information that you're most interested in is in the last three columns, which shows the load average of the server for the past 1, 5, and 15 minutes.

The load average value isn't exactly a highly accurate rating, but when used as a "measuring stick," it can be helpful. For example, if you've found that during a Stress and Volume Testing (SVT) run a particular WebSphere system operates with a one-minute load average of 6, with 70 percent CPU utilization, then you can use the load average along with the CPU utilization as a baseline.

TIP You can further improve the value of this type of baseline analysis by understanding the system's load at other system utilization ratings, such as 50 percent, 60 percent, and 80 percent. By using simple extrapolation, you should be able to plot the characteristics of the environment at these different system utilization ratings, with them appearing as a near linear line on a graph.

If, then in production, you notice that the load average is, let's say, 12, you can generally state that something isn't operating correctly.

As you can see, this load average by itself is just a measurement—it shows or proves nothing in terms of understanding what part of the system is running "hot."

What Is the Load Average?

The *load average* is an indicator that reports the average number of processes waiting in the Run queue. The Run queue, in Unix, is the controlling mechanism of the operating system that manages what processes and jobs run when, where, and how (in other words, the queue priority and the CPU and process priority). As you'll see in a moment, the vmstat command can also help you better understand what causes a load average to go high.

There's also no real rule that states what constitutes a high load average and what constitutes a low load average. As a guide, however, I tend to work with the notion that a system is operating within normal capacity if the load average doesn't exceed a value of 4 for every one CPU in the system. Therefore, if you have a 32-CPU system, a load average of 128 wouldn't be a major issue. It'd suggest that there's a lot of things going on within your server, and typically this type of load would be more representative of a database server or financial system.

On the other hand, if you had a load average of 18 on a single- or dual-CPU system, you'd have a major performance problem with your WebSphere applications.

Drilling Down to a High Load Average

So, you've notice your WebSphere environment operating sluggishly, you've run the vmstat command, and you've found that the load average is slightly high—what do you do next?

The vmstat command is your friend in this case. It shows a great deal about a Unix server's status. When you run it, a typical output will look similar to the following. This does vary, however, from Unix flavor to Unix flavor, but the basic elements are universal:

```
/> vmstat
procs      memory               page              disk          faults      cpu
 r b w    swap   free   re mf pi po fr de sr dd dd s0 -   in   sy   cs us sy id
 2 0 0  4078832 1321240 36 391 24 3 5 0 12  7 12  0  0  440  234  697 17  9 75
```

This output is showing you a snapshot of your overall system. The important columns to look for are the first three columns, the free size under the memory group (the fifth column), the sr column, and the last three columns.

NOTE   In many Unix systems, a single line of vmstat output is usually incorrect because the application needs at least two inputs to correctly perform the calculations to obtain items such as CPU utilizations. Always run vmstat with at least two to five output lines via the command vmstat 1 5 (1 represents frequency, and 5 represents setting it to run five times).

The first three columns are another representation of your load average. The first column is the Run queue, identified by the r. The second column is the I/O blocking average. If you constantly have a figure greater than zero in this column, your disks may be suffering under load.

The w column represents the swapped or waiting processes. This will be high if many processes on your system have a potential shortage of physical memory.

The sr column is the scan rate of the paging daemon. This will be different between Unix systems, but the figure basically represents how often the paging daemon is scanning the free page list for free pages. If this figure is constantly higher than 120 per 30 seconds, then you may have a shortage of memory and the system is starting to swap constantly. This is a sure sign of the need for additional RAM.

The last three columns show the state of the CPU (or CPUs if you have a multi-CPU system). The us field is the percentage of CPU utilization of processes consumed by user-based processes. This includes WebSphere and the WebSphere-managed JVMs.

The cs column indicates the number of context switches occurring during the test interval period. *Context switches*, in the vmstat output, refer to the number of both voluntary and forced context switches occurring within the CPUs during that period. A context switch is the associated event for when a process releases its time slice of a CPU. Generally, only one process can operate on the CPU at any one time, so if this value is high, then this can indicate that your system is overloaded and that various processes aren't getting sufficient time on the CPU.

It's difficult to give you a rule of thumb on this figure, but what you should do is capture this value during idle periods and during SVT and baselining and then use it as a guide to when there may be excessive context switching.

The switching itself of the processes on and off the CPU(s) occurs for two reasons. First, the process may have used up its delegated time slice on the CPU and is forced off the processor (an involuntary context switch). Second, the process voluntarily switches off the CPU in order to call or access an external interface such as disk or network interface.

Generally, if this figure is high, compared with your idle or baseline measurements, your processes may be struggling to get sufficient time on the CPU. This is a sure sign that either something in your environment is running out of control (such as in a broken process looping) or too much is going on within the system for the number of CPUs you have.

The sy column represents the system processes. This accounts for kernel activity. If this is high, then it indicates a lot of time is being spent on disk and network I/O, interrupts, and system calls. You should ensure that sy doesn't equal or exceed that of the user field. In fact, a healthy system shouldn't see a ratio any higher than 5:1 for user-to-system CPU utilization.

Determining Memory Usage: Real and Swap

Like the general Unix command and tool sets, Unix memory analysis is similar between competing Unix flavors. A number of tools can help you understand the current memory and swap usage. The most common tool available on all Unix flavors is the top command.

The top command is a handy tool that shows you a whole range of information when run by itself. A typical top output may look like the following:

```
last pid: 19972;  load averages:  0.00,  0.00,  0.01
57 processes:  53 sleeping, 3 zombie, 1 on cpu
CPU states:      % idle,     % user,     % kernel,     % iowait,      % swap
Memory: 512M real, 90M free, 18M swap in use, 278M swap free
PID USERNAME    THR PRI NICE  SIZE    RES STATE   TIME  CPU    COMMAND
18536 was       11  25   2    39M    19M sleep   0:02  0.00%  java
18517 was       10  34   2    39M    19M sleep   0:02  0.00%  java
18508 was       10   0   2    38M    17M sleep   0:01  0.00%  java
18553 was       11  16   2    37M    14M sleep   0:01  0.00%  java
18522 was       10  14   2    37M    14M sleep   0:01  0.00%  java
18506 was       19   0   2    34M    12M sleep   0:01  0.00%  java
13713 was        1  47   4    25M    20M sleep   0:14  0.00%  squid
  342 was        5  58   0  6376K  2056K sleep 0:10  0.00%  dtlogin
20515 root       1  46   4  3072K  1960K sleep 11:26 0.00%  sshd
 3168 root       1  58   0  3072K  1160K sleep 0:09  0.00%  rpc.ttdbserverd
25705 root       1  41   4  2904K  1800K sleep 0:05  0.00%  rpc.ttdbserverd
```

This top output is from a small Solaris server. You can tell this by the Solaris-specific items running in the command column.

The server is only running 512 megabytes (MB) of memory, of which 90MB is free. You can also see from the Memory line that 18MB of swap is in use.

If you're just after memory information, then you can run the top command and use Grep to extract only the memory line. For example, you can use top | grep "Memory". This will produce a line such as this:

```
~/hosts>/usr/local/bin/top | grep Memory
Memory: 2048M real, 1384M free, 853M swap in use, 3714M swap free
```

NOTE AIX Unix from IBM has a Monitor command that can provide details and statistics on memory usage.

An important fact to note about the output of the top command is that it also allows you to break down and show the Java processes running within your server. This will ultimately be the WebSphere components and your JVMs that are operating your application servers.

With the previous top output, you're able to see that there are six Java processes running, all of which have approximate memory footprint sizes of 25MB and 39MB (from the SIZE column). This SIZE column shows the total memory consumed by that process, including swapped memory. The RES column shows the total amount of memory resident in memory, not swapped. These values should be capped at the maximum heap size for your JVM when viewing an output such as this.

Another method of obtaining a listing of the top processes running is to use the Unix ps command, which lists all processes running within your Unix server. There are two forms of ps. One is known as the standard SYS 5 Unix ps, and the other is the Berkeley (also called UCB) ps. Typically, the UCB ps is located in the /usr/ucb/ directory with the standard SYS 5 ps in /usr/bin or /usr/local/bin.

If you have the UCB version of ps, you can get a faster snapshot of the system state. For example, the following output is from a WebSphere server running multiple application servers. This output shows the top ten processes on the system from WebSphere (the command to obtain this is /usr/ucb/ps auxw | head -10):

```
USER        PID   %CPU %MEM     SZ    RSS TT  S START      TIME    COMMAND
wasadmin    7376  4.9  10.112759041215920 ? S 21:52:07 61:37   /opt/WebSphere/.../java
wasadmin    4018  0.8  9.812325841172632 ?  S 10:22:06 26:09   /opt/WebSphere/.../java
wasadmin   28974  0.6  9.712352161162848 ?  S    Aug 20 263:17 /opt/WebSphere/.../java
wasadmin    1540  0.5  4.3652048512112 ?     S    Aug 11 420:23 /opt/WebSphere/.../java
wasadmin   22633  0.4  6.8920232818184 ?     S    Aug 25 93:22  /opt/WebSphere/.../java
wasadmin    1548  0.3  6.3884312755032 ?     S    Aug 11 302:15 /opt/WebSphere/.../java
wasadmin   26404  0.3  6.7927128808720 ?     S    Aug 29 37:10  /opt/WebSphere/.../java
wasadmin    1524  0.2  3.5512856412232 ?     O    Aug 11 188:54 /opt/WebSphere/.../java
```

The value in this output is that it shows you a snapshot of the top ten processes on your Unix server. Each process, all of which in this example are JVMs, is shown with its Process ID (PID), its CPU utilization, memory utilization, and a swag of other information such as start time, memory usage, and state. This is helpful output to determine if you have a particular JVM that's operating poorly or consuming too many system resources.

If you do happen to have a WebSphere Java process that's consuming a large amount of CPU utilization (as depicted by a high value in the %CPU column), you could track back to WebSphere and understand which Java application that is by using the PID.

Via the WebSphere Command Program (WSCP) or wsadmin tools (WebSphere 4 and 5, respectively), you can list the running state of each WebSphere application (for example wscp> ApplicationServer show <*app_server_name*> for WebSphere 4). Within those listings, a PID value is available. That PID corresponds to the Unix PID. Combining those items allows you to then find which PID is the offending or high-utilization process.

Swap Space

All operating systems, Unix and Windows alike, use a form of swap or virtual memory. In Unix, it's referred to as *swap space*. Swap space is essentially an overflow bucket of memory that the operating system can use to place less frequently used applications into when other, higher-priority applications require more physical memory.

The golden rule is to not use swap space for active processes. Doing so means that you reduce your memory access performance from 8–60 nanoseconds for main memory to around 1,300 nanoseconds for disk-based swap plus operational overheads!

As soon as your active processes start to use swap for normal operations, your WebSphere application's performance will drop like a paperweight. It's a sure sign of insufficient memory in your server if this starts to occur.

Swap configuration is one area of Unix that has different commands for each flavor. For AIX, Linux, and Solaris, the following commands will display swap configuration:

- **Linux:** free

- **Solaris:** swap -l

- **AIX:** lsps -a

You can also obtain swap information by using the aforementioned `top` command. The `top` command will provide you with a reading of your real memory and swap space usage via the command `top | grep "Memory"`.

Here's an example:

```
~/> top | grep "Memory"
Memory: 2048M real, 1384M free, 853M swap in use, 3714M swap free
```

In this example, the server has 2 gigabytes (GB) of real memory, of which 1,384MB is being used, and approximately 4.5GB of swap space allocated, of which 853MB is being used.

Swap should always be at least double the size of your real memory. This provides the ability to core dump into the swap partition (if your Unix version supports this) as well as a good guide for configuring your swap bucket.

CPU and System Load: Windows NT/2000/XP

Since Windows NT became available on the market, the Windows server operating systems have come with a powerful performance monitoring tool. This tool, known as the Windows Performance tool is a graphical tool that provides information on just about every aspect of the Windows operating system.

Using this tool from a system and CPU utilization point of view, you're able to obtain a snapshot of various aspects of the state of your server. Similar to the previous Unix sections, you'll look at the following system-based states:

- Overall server load

- Queued processes

- CPU utilization (percent available, percent used, and by what)

- Memory usage

- Virtual memory usage and utilization

CPU and Overall Server Load

In the Windows server Performance tool, there are several options that provide the ability to monitor a Windows server's CPU utilization. Within the Performance tool (usually found by Start ➤ Settings ➤ Control Panel ➤ Administrative Tools ➤ Performance), you're able to set up a tooling session where you can monitor, graph, and save information on the performance status of your server. The tool also allows you to save historic information relating to snapshots of your system's performance to view later.

Figure 13-1 shows main console screen of the Performance tool.

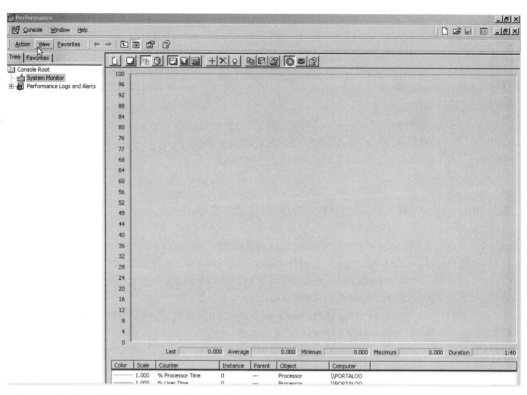

Figure 13-1. The Performance tool console

To set up and perform analysis on the utilization of the system, you need to choose which settings or components of the system you want to monitor. You do this by clicking the plus (+) button at the top of the console, as shown in Figure 13-2.

Figure 13-2. Adding a new monitor

At this point, you'll see a dialog box that allows you to select which elements you want to monitor. Follow these steps to set up active monitoring on your CPU:

1. Because you want to monitor CPU utilization in this example, set the Performance Object drop-down menu to Processor.

2. Once you do this, you want to select three options in the counters list: % Privileged Time, % Processor Time, and % User Time. You can select all three at the same time by pressing Ctrl and then clicking each of them with your mouse.

3. Now click the CPU you want to monitor (if you have a multi-CPU system) or select _Total from the right list, as shown in Figure 13-3.

4. Click Add and then Close.

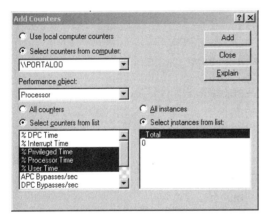

Figure 13-3. Selecting the monitor agents

You'll return to the Performance tool's console, and the monitoring will commence. The key is to avoid excessive CPU utilization. If your server's CPU utilization for the % User Time counter is constantly higher than 60–70 percent, then there are performance issues with your size of server or an abnormal process event is occurring. If your % User Time is high, then this typically means a running process is consuming too many CPU cycles.

It's possible to then drill down and view the WebSphere Java process similar to Unix if you find that your CPU is constantly utilized:

1. Open the Add Counters dialog box again (using the plus button shown in Figure 13-2).

2. Change the Performance Object option from Processor to Process.

3. On the right side of the dialog box, you'll then see a list of all active processes. Select the Java process that corresponds to your particular JVM.

4. On the left side of the dialog box, select % Processor Time (as shown in Figure 13-4).

5. Click Close.

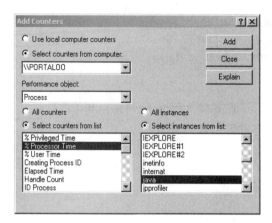

Figure 13-4. Adding the % Processor Time counter

You'll then return to the main console where you can view the JVM process usage against the CPU utilization. If there's a correlation between the troughs and peaks of the CPU utilization and the JVM process usage, then you'll know you've found the problem JVM.

It's also possible to view the data in a report format as well as a historical format. Looking at Figure 13-5, select between the three icons that provide a different view of the data, highlighted by the circle.

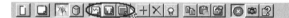

Figure 13-5. Buttons to give you different views of the data

The three different views that are available allow you to switch between a Historical Graph view, a Total Summary view, and a Log Report view. Typically, the Historical Graph view is the most valuable view for understanding the state of your system's performance and resource load.

Memory Usage: Real and Virtual

Similar to Unix, Windows NT/2000/XP/2003 has virtual-like memory that allows the operating system to swap out unused processes into lower-priority memory. Although it's an important part of ensuring that you have enough overflow buffer and your applications don't run out of memory, it's also just as important to be sure your active applications don't try to run from virtual memory. Like Unix, this will quickly bring your server to a grinding halt.

To model the usage of memory and virtual memory, follow these steps:

1. Open the Add Counters dialog box, and in the Performance Object drop-down box, select Memory.

2. In the counters list, select Pages/sec and then click Add.

3. Select Available Mbytes in the counters list, and then click Add.

4. Click Close.

You'll return to the main console, and the new display should start to appear. At this point, you'll see the two monitoring lines continue across the screen.

The key item to watch here is how frequently the Pages/sec counter is higher than 100. If the value is constantly higher than 100, then there's many hard page faults occurring, typically pointing to a lot virtual memory in use. This can greatly slow down the performance of your applications. As your Available Mbytes counter approaches zero free, your Pages/sec average value will increase constantly. The CPU utilization will follow closely behind!

You can do a quick test by loading a Java application within WebSphere and monitoring this screen while you have users access the WebSphere application. As your load increases, memory consumption increases and page faults start to kick in (causing Pages/sec to increase). To a point, it's okay to have spikes every once in a while, but if it's a constant and the averages are high for both CPU utilization and the Pages/sec counter, then there's a shortage of memory in your server.

Monitoring Disk I/O

Disks are an important part of any server platform. Used for the storage of your logs, application data, database files, binaries, and even swap space, their speed is a key input to your platform's overall performance.

You'll now look at how to diagnose "hot" disks and determine their utilization. It's worth highlighting that many high-end disk vendors (for example, vendors that produce controllers and disks, external arrays, and the like) quite often supply software that provides monitoring capabilities for their specific products.

In most cases, if your disks are host connected, then you'll be able to use the standard Unix and Windows tools discussed in this chapter, as well as the proprietary vendor software.

Disk I/O: Unix

Disk I/O in Unix follows a fairly standard design and is somewhat common between all Unix flavors. As discussed in earlier chapters, hard disks are limited by a range of factors that depict their so-called performance level. To summarize, a disk's performance is gauged by a number of factors that, when combined, produce a maximum and sustained transfer rate as well as a maximum and sustained I/O rate. What makes up these factors is everything from rotational speed, onboard cache memory, control and architecture type, and the way in which the data is written to disk.

You can use a number of commands on the three Unix-like platforms discussed throughout this book. The most common one is the iostat command. The iostat command is a common Unix application available on AIX, Linux, and Solaris that provides an ability to understand what's going on within the disk subsystems.

NOTE The iostat command has many different display and output options. The options used here provide the best all-around results. However, you may find that other parameters suit your environment better.

The following is some sample output from an iostat command:

```
~>iostat -xnM
                        extended device statistics
    r/s    w/s    Mr/s    Mw/s wait actv wsvc_t asvc_t  %w  %b device
    4.0    2.9    0.0     0.0  0.0  0.0    2.3    4.0    0   2 c0t0d0
    6.7    5.0    0.0     0.0  0.0  0.1    1.4   11.7    1   8 c0t2d0
    0.0    0.0    0.0     0.0  0.0  0.0    8.3  153.2    0   0 c0t3d0
```

What this command output shows you is a Unix server (specifically, Solaris) that has three disks attached to it (note the three targets, each with a single disk on them in the device column).

Looking at the key data elements on the output, you can tell that the first disk is servicing about seven I/Os per second. You can draw this from adding the r/s, or reads per second, and the w/s, or writes per second, columns.

The next two columns refer to the sum of data transferred—read or written. This is a helpful indicator if you suspect that your Small Computer System Interface (SCSI), Advanced Technology Attachment (ATA), Integrated Device Electronics (IDE), or Fibre Channel bus is running out of bandwidth. By summing up these two columns for all disks on the same bus, you can get an approximate total bus transfer rate.

The next column, wait, refers to how many I/O requests are queued. It's possible to use this number and understand how much the response time of the disks are contributing to the queuing of I/O request.

The next column, actv, shows the number of active I/Os taken off the I/O queue in the time frame of the command's run and processed.

The next two columns, wsvc_t and asvc_t, are the average response time for I/Os on the wait queue and the average response time for active I/Os, respectively.

The last column of interest is the %b column. This infers the overall utilization of that particular disk. In the previous example output, the first disk is only 2 percent utilized, the second 8 percent, and the third 0 percent.

Picking a Hot Disk

Using the iostat command, you're able to identify where a specific disk may be performing badly within your environment and may be impacting overall performance.

A hot disk could be the cause of poor performance within a WebSphere application environment if there's a lot of disk I/Os occurring, such as I/Os to an application log file or reading dump data. Another cause of a high disk I/O is constant or high use of swap space by your operating system. The most obvious sign of a hot disk is the %b column. If it exceeds 50 percent, then your disk will start to become a bottleneck.

The first two columns that refer to the reads and write I/Os per second should also be considered as a guide. As mentioned in Chapter 5, generally, for SCSI and Fibre Channel disks, you can extract 10 I/Os per second from the disk for every 1,000 Revolutions Per Minute (RPM) that the disk can produce. That is, for a 10,000RPM SCSI disk, you can work on achieving 100 I/Os per second. A 7,200RPM SCSI disk will provide you with approximately 70 I/Os per second. As also discussed in Chapter 5, the way to get beyond these I/O limitations is to stripe your disks.

In the previous example, these drives are specifically 7,200RPM drives. The I/O rate for the second drive is approximately 12 I/Os per second. This equates to approximately 17 percent utilization of the disk. However, you'll see that the %b column only says 8 percent utilization. What this means is that although there are 12 I/Os per second occurring, the size of the I/Os are very small and there's an additional amount of headroom available.

Another key performance indicator is the response time and depth of queued I/Os. The actv, or the number of active I/Os taken off the queue (to be processed), should be no more than 1. Generally speaking, this field will become close to 1 as the %b field, or disk utilization, nears 50 percent—give or take.

Table 13-1 summarizes the key hot disk indicators and what they mean in terms of negative disk performance.

Table 13-1. Telltale Signs of High Disk Utilization

Measurement	Meaning	Fix
Asvc_t field greater than 30 milliseconds (ms)	As the number of I/Os increases, the response time to perform I/Os to the particular disk increases.	Redistribute load over disks, purchase faster disks, or consider striping.
Act_v greater than 1	As the number of I/Os queues up, this element will increase. A rate of 1 corresponds approximately to 50 percent of %b.	Redistribute load over disks, purchase faster disks, or consider striping.
%b greater than 50	%b shows the average utilization of the disk I/O to this particular device. This takes into consideration all the previous measurements as well as the number and frequency of writes and reads per second.	Redistribute load over disks, purchase faster disks, or consider striping.

Disk I/O: Windows NT/2000/XP

Disk performance in a Windows server environment has the same implementation considerations as for Unix. Striped disks are always the key in distributing load off single spindles, and this is no different for Windows servers. Similar to monitoring the CPU utilization, monitoring the performance of disks within a Windows server can be done via the Performance tool.

From the details in the previous sections about CPU and system utilization, you know you can open the Add Counters dialog box and select various disk monitoring options.

NOTE The details discussed in the Unix section (such as I/O rates, disk utilization, and limitations) are all applicable to a Windows world. The disks, and in many cases the controllers, are the same (there are just specific driver differences).

The types of disk performance indicators you want to monitor are the same as for the Unix world:

- **Queue Length**: How many I/Os are waiting on the queue

- **% Disk Time**: How much time is the disk(s) taking to service the I/O requests

In the Unix section, you learned about the `iostat` tool. Many of the same `iostat` outputs—such as reads and writes per second, read and write kilobytes/megabytes per second, and so forth—can all be modeled using the system performance tools.

In the Add Counters box, you want to add the two settings, Queue Length and % Disk Time, from the counters list. Once these are selected and your desired disks are being captured (remember, you can add those two options for multiple disks), close the dialog box to start the monitoring.

Figure 13-6 shows graph depicting a Windows XP–based server, charting both Queue Length and % Disk Time.

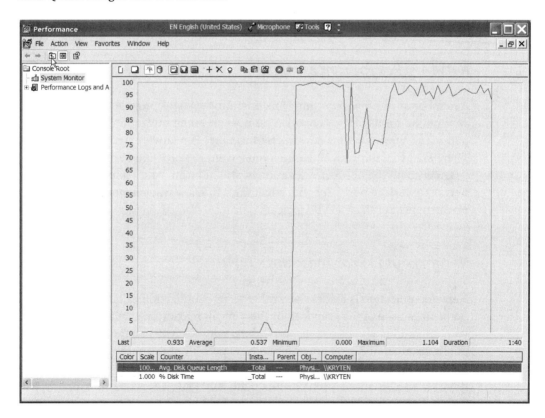

Figure 13-6. Graphing Queue Length and % Disk Time

The important points to monitor here are that the % Disk Time counter shouldn't be more than 50 percent over long periods and the Queue Length counter should remain less than 1 for 75–85 percent of the time. High bursts are fine as long as they don't constitute the norm and don't exceed 15–25 percent as a maximum.

Monitoring Network Performance

Network performance is the third of the "big ticket performance items" mentioned in this chapter. Because WebSphere is by nature a distributed computing platform, network connectivity is an important aspect of the overall WebSphere performance model.

This is more important for local area networking communications. That is, components such as database servers and Web servers must be able to communicate to one another with little latency and high throughput.

In the following sections, you'll look at system tools that allow you to monitor and diagnose network bottleneck issues within your WebSphere application server environment.

Network Performance: Unix

A number of commands within Unix operating systems provide an output or view on the status of the network interfaces and their utilization. In fact, this part of monitoring a Unix system's performance is relatively straightforward. There are two groupings of features you'll want to know about. First, you'll want to know about the network utilization in and out from your WebSphere server network interface ports. Second, you'll want to know what errors are occurring on the network (physical and logical).

Network Utilization: Unix

Network utilization is just like any other form of utilization calculation. It's the percentage used of the practical (or theoretical) maximum available. That is, if you have a 10 megabits per second (Mbps) network, you can theoretically support a throughput rate of approximately 80 percent of the network capacity. In reality, however, your mileage will vary considerably because of your network interface card quality, switch or hub quality and load, distances, wire quality, packet and protocol overhead, and so on.

As a rough guide, using 10 percent of the Mbps ratio will give you a fairly practical throughput rate. For example, a 100Mbps network would mean that you can reach 10 megabytes per second (MBps). Therefore, if you were transferring at 300 kilobytes per second (KBps), which is 0.3MBps, over a 10Mbps network, you'd be operating at a rate of approximately 33 percent of the network capacity.

For Linux, Solaris, and AIX, it's possible to use the `netstat -i` command to obtain network performance statistics. You'll look at this command in more detail shortly for errors; however, it's limited when it comes to calculating network traffic in and out (it only shows packets in and out for most Unix operating systems).

So, what you need to monitor is the ability to capture periodically the amount of traffic transferred in and out of a network interface.

Therefore, for three Unix operating systems, the following commands are available on each Unix flavor to obtain the network traffic in and out:

- **AIX**: You can use `entstat` (in usage, it's `entstat -d entx`). This tool shows a range of network interface statistics for Ethernet-based interfaces on AIX.

- **Solaris**: You can use `netstat` (in usage, it's `netstat -k | grep bytes`). Using the `netstat` command and an undocumented feature of Solaris `netstat`, you can obtain network bytes in and out of an interface. You'll only care about the `rbytes` and `obytes` (receive and send) elements.

- **Linux**: Linux, by its nature, has a number of tools to use. The more popular methods are to use the Internet Protocol (IP) firewall accounting polices included in the kernel or to use a third-party GNU product such as IPTraf.

You'll now look at how to calculate the utilization rate of a network. As I've said, it's very straightforward. Based on a ten-second interval and what you know about the practical speed of a 100Mbps network, you can assume that over ten seconds, the practical maximum that can be transferred (half-duplex) is approximately 89MBps.

So, if you had a network that at the epoch of your test was baselined at "x" for inbound bytes and "y" for outbound bytes, then obtained the reading for epoch +10 seconds, and took the derivative of those results over the practical maximum of our network, you'd have a utilization figure. Table 13-2 shows the results.

Table 13-2. Example Network Utilization Calculation

Test	In Bytes	Out Bytes
Epoch + 0	857,660,792	2,605,030,577
Epoch + 10	858,013,025	2,605,091,769

The difference between the first and second test for the in bytes is 352,233KB and 61,192KB for the out bytes. Therefore, the utilization of the network (in other words, the difference of epoch + 0 in and out and epoch + 10 in and out) is 44 percent. Over time, this test could be refined and fed into a tool such as Multi Router Traffic Grapher (MRTG), discussed in Chapter 14, for graphing or exported to Microsoft Excel for analysis.

The key with this test is to use one of the Unix tools to obtain the in and out bytes, place them in a script, and loop the script indefinitely for monitoring and historical analysis. The script might look like this:

```
#!/bin/ksh
logfile=/tmp/networkStatistics.log
while :
    <run your network data collection script here> >>$logfile
    sleep 10
done
```

It seems simple, but it'll provide you with the raw data to graph and model.

NOTE   You could send the output from this script to MRTG to plot the utilization over time.

So, what constitutes a high utilization? From my experience, as soon as a network starts to exceed 40 percent utilization, there will be performance loss.

This is evident with the ping tool that, although not the most scientific of tools, does provide a fairly good gauge of when a network is underperforming. On a local area network, pinging a remote machine (such as the database server) will produce a timing result that should be no higher than 5ms for Ethernet networks. Beyond this, there's something in the network that's not right. Where the ping tool falls down is that the undesired result could manifest from the remote server being underloaded or a network or router being overloaded. Use the ping tool as a secondary tool and be careful not to place all your bets on it.

To summarize, although these tools are helpful and can help you get an understanding of what the state of play is with your network, they need to be used constantly. Running these network utilization tools on an ad-hoc basis starts to decrease their reporting value. What you want is to be able to have an always-running test that's logging and tracking the network utilization so you can build up a historic view of how your network performs. By having the historic view of the network's performance, you can then go and run the scripts on an ad-hoc basis if you want to get a snapshot of the current utilization and compare it with averages or historic utilization information.

Finally, many Unix vendors have centralized management software packages that come with network monitors and utilization trackers (AIX has the Tivoli Performance tool, and Sun has Sun Management Center). It's worth taking a look at these tools to see if they fit your needs.

Network Errors: Windows and Unix

Errors on a network are going to be caused by a huge range of issues. The most common form of error is the physical error. This type of error is typically caused by poor or faulty cabling, by bad connectors in your Fibre or CATx network cabling, or by running your cabling via noisy electronic interference—for example, Universal Power Supplies (UPSs), air-conditioning units, lift motors, generators, and so on.

There are also the software-based errors. These are sometimes caused by the physical errors or are a side effect to the physical errors but can be attributed to the operating system's network stack, driver problems, collisions, and other anomalies.

When looking at your network performance reactively (probably because of an overall application performance issue), you should check if there are any reported errors with your network interfaces. The netstat command on all operating systems will allow you to output a high-level view of all network-related errors. For example, using the netstat command on Unix with the -i parameter will show the interface statistics on your server. On Windows-based platforms, you can use the netstat command with the -e parameter.

The output will show columns labeled *Ierrs* and *Oerrs* for AIX and Solaris, respectively, *TX-ERR* and *RX-ERR* for Linux and for Windows, respectively, or an output entry called *Errors* for both received and sent data.

There's no golden rule for error figures. As long as your error rate isn't constantly increasing, there's no error or problem with your network. If it's increasing, there's an issue somewhere within your network infrastructure—either local to your server or somewhere out on the wire (for example, cabling, the switch or hub, and so on).

Table 13-3 highlights some additional commands that will provide more information in your environment to probe for network-related errors.

Table 13-3. Example Network Utilization Calculation

Command	Operating System	Purpose
kstat -p -s "*err*"	Solaris 8+	Shows all network-related errors on all interfaces.
netstat -d *interface_name*	AIX 4.2+	Shows all network-related errors on specific interfaces (*interface_name*).

Table 13-3. Example Network Utilization Calculation (Continued)

Command	Operating System	Purpose
netstat -i interface_name	Linux	Shows all network-related errors on specific interfaces (interface_name). Other commands exist in Linux depending on your kernel build that provide more information.

To test and view a Windows-based server for network errors, you'll want to use the Performance tool once again. Figure 13-7 highlights the Add Counters dialog box with the Packets Outbound Errors and Packets Received Errors counters being selected.

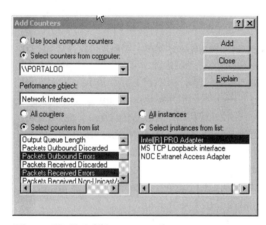

Figure 13-7. Adding network error counters

The output of the Windows server performance console is fairly self-explanatory. Similar to the Unix environments, a random error every once in a while isn't a major problem. It's only a problem if you monitor the console and see a constant rise in errors.

Be sure not to confuse these types of errors with collisions. To determine this, you'll need to obtain a more advanced application or tool to break up the different types of errors into the likes of carrier, collisions, protocol, and so forth or use the TCP and IP Performance Monitoring counters available. These two elements will provide TCP and IP monitoring that includes factors such as connection failures, correct datagrams, and socket retries. This may be helpful if you're trying to diagnose problems with your WebSphere application server dropping connections from a remote system (for example, running out of available local sockets).

If you're on a network that's based on a switched infrastructure (switched as opposed to shared via a hub) and you see errors increasing, chances are that the problem is a legitimate concern. Collisions are rare on switched networks but are common on shared networks.

A Word About Autosensing Configurations

Many network interface cards and switches support a setting known as Auto-Negotiate or Autosensing configuration. This allows your network hardware to determine the optimal settings of your network infrastructure and autoconfig-ure the settings.

Although this is great for desktop or laptop computer network environments, for server environments this is a poor networking implementation or design. Using autonegotiated configurations can lead to performance and availability issues under high-load environments or when networking manufacturers' equipment isn't fully compatible with one another.

Always configure your network interface cards and network switches to force a particular network configuration, including duplex settings and network fabric speed.

Network Utilization: Windows

As you saw previously, activating monitoring for network analysis under a Windows environment is straightforward. Looking at Figure 13-7 again, in order to activate network utilization monitoring, instead of selecting the Packets Outbound Errors and Packets Received Errors counters, select Bytes Total/sec counter.

This counter will give you an approximate utilization reading of your network interface. Be sure to change the scale of your plotting to 1 to ensure that you can match the network traffic against a 100 percent graph.

Networking in Windows is no different from Unix. In other words, network utilization shouldn't exceed 40 percent for sustained periods of time, and you should look at additional network interfaces or a faster network infrastructure if this limit starts to become a common occurrence.

Figure 13-8 shows example output from the Performance tool where a WebSphere application server is running in a Windows 2000 Server environment. The lab network for this example is a 10Mbps shared network environment.

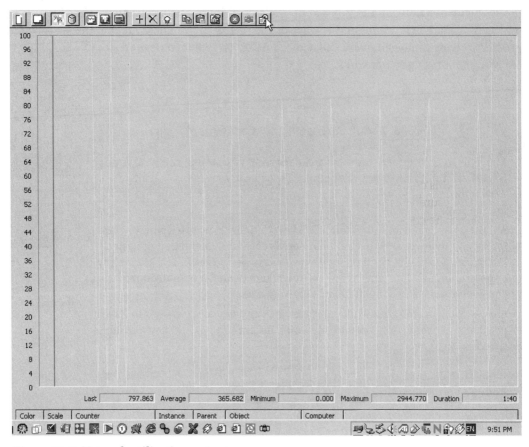

Figure 13-8. Network utilization output

If you look at the bottom of the figure, you'll see these four key values:

- Last

- Average

- Minimum

- Maximum

These values are helpful to get the accurate reading of the network's utilization statistics. You'll also see a fifth element, Duration. This final field is useful if you're tracking against a time factor. For example, it's useful to determine the number of collisions over a specific period of time.

TIP Remember to use the Log Report view of the Performance tool. This will allow you to view multiple systems at the same time (multiple WebSphere servers in a cluster, for example) to compare, log, and study the network statistics in a list format.

Monitoring WebSphere Application Performance

So far within this chapter, you've explored some system and environment performance measurements. In previous chapters, I discussed in detail how to tune and optimize the core WebSphere product and deployed applications. What I haven't yet discussed is how you monitor and track WebSphere performance and fix performance problems. In Chapters 6 and 14, I discuss profiling and benchmarking.

Let's first ponder for a moment what I'm talking about when I say *performance problems*. As touched on during Chapters 1 and 2, performance is typically associated with fast application response times. Consider also that, at the most basic level, a performance issue will be caused by insufficient resources for a task. Although these insufficiencies may be caused by poorly written code that's suffocating system resources, the symptom is still a resource constraint.

Table 13-4 gives you an overview of some of the more common symptoms for poor performance within a WebSphere server. Following Table 13-4, you'll see how to understand and determine if these symptoms are occurring.

Table 13-4. Common Symptoms for Poor WebSphere Server Performance

Symptom	High-Level Possible Cause
High CPU utilization	Overutilization of objects, poorly written code, or high network or I/O activity.
High disk I/O utilization	Overuse of log files, lack of memory driving swap usage higher, persistence of objects to disk (serialization), or poor disk design.
High network utilization	Overuse of remote method invocations, undercapacity network topology, poorly designed data architecture (in other words, data and information transferred between multiple nodes could be broken down into more succinct packages).

You'll now take a closer look at some of these causes and symptoms and how to identify them. The next section lists some characteristics of poor performance, followed by what the possible causes may be, and then offers pointers to understand how to determine the root cause.

This list of performance problems isn't exhaustive. The problems are provided to give an example of common performance problems within WebSphere environments and encapsulate much of what I've discussed throughout the book. It also should help to summarize what tools to use to determine the possible root causes of the various issues.

High CPU Utilization of JVM

You've explored throughout the book a wide range of ways to decrease JVM overutilization of the CPU. However, in this section, you'll explore a number of "what if" scenarios, and I'll attempt to explain what to look for when there's a CPU overutilization problem, including what may be the cause.

Noticing whether a CPU is being heavily utilized is straightforward. You explored this earlier in this chapter. However, why would a JVM cause a CPU to be heavily used? There are many alternatives and possibilities. Table 13-5 describes some possible causes of high CPU use and lists several steps to explain how to determine the cause.

Table 13-5. High CPU Utilization: Cause and Effect

Effect	Possible Cause	Determination Path
Overuse of objects	Excessive object instantiation or poorly written code not closing object handles.	Resource Analyzer/Tivoli Performance tool, method and class invocation and usage rate, or Java profiler.
High usage of block I/O	CPU needs to manage I/O interrupts while they're called. If load of these requests is high, CPU usage will increase.	Check for block I/O requests through disk I/O activity and network I/O activity using system performance tools (see earlier sections).
Excessive garbage collection	Memory leaks caused by not dereferencing objects in memory.	Use the Resource Analyzer/Tivoli Performance console to monitor memory usage within JVM and garbage collection counters. Another option is to use verbose garbage collection and track the output in the standard out log file. You can graph all these outputs to model the frequency and duration of garbage collection.

Poor Database Transactional Performance

As discussed, your database is often a key component to your overall application environment in terms of performance. Several key components affect and make up a transaction within the database tier. These include areas such as Java Database Connectivity (JDBC) drivers, the database itself, the network, and the pool manager.

You'll now look at some possible causes, effects, and resolution paths for these problems. Table 13-6 gives an overview of database transactional performance.

Table 13-6. Poor Database Transactional Performance: Cause and Effect

Effect	Possible Cause	Determination Path
Poorly performing transactions	SQL code and JDBC configured incorrectly implemented	Use database vendor monitoring tools to determine if there are poorly written SQL statements or queries.
Poorly performing database	Misuse or nonuse of indexes, overly utilized CPUs, database server is swapping into swap or virtual memory, saturated network, or overly utilized disk subsystem	Use system monitoring tools discussed earlier in this chapter to track down the performance bottleneck.
Poorly performing persistence layer	CMP or BMP for high write environments, nonuse or poor implementation of Data Access Object (DAO) persistence layer.	Use database monitoring tools to monitor specific offending queries and database load, and use Resource Analyzer/Tivoli Performance management console to investigate database pool usage and utilization.

Poor Network Performance

The network is possibly the next most important aspect of your WebSphere environment. You can have ten high-end machines running your WebSphere cluster, but if they're connected or interconnected via a low capacity or poorly designed network infrastructure, then your overall application environment will run poorly.

You'll now look at two key areas of your environment that can be affected by network performance issues. Networking performance issues are fairly black and white—the network is either performing or it's not; if it's not, it's either insufficient or has overloaded bandwidth.

Table 13-7 addresses two key areas of network performance with some possible methods to help identify where the problems are. Again, these are only examples, and they don't cover all aspects of network performance.

Table 13-7. Poor Network Performance: Cause and Effect

Effect	Possible Cause	Determination Path
Poor performance between tiers	Insufficient or overloaded bandwidth	Use system monitoring tools as discussed earlier in this chapter (for example, netstat and Windows Performance tool).
Poor performance between distributed components (for example, Enterprise JavaBeans)	Insufficient or overloaded bandwidth, or serialization of large amounts of Remote Method Invocation (RMI) encapsulated data	Use Resource Analyzer/Tivoli Performance management consoles to understand the time taken for your various methods and classes to run and return results.

Summary

In this chapter, you looked at some of the key areas that can affect WebSphere application performance and looked at what tools are available for Windows (NT/2000/XP), Linux, Solaris, and AIX.

Throughout the discussion, you saw how to read and interpret the output from these tools to understand what the data means and at what point you should be concerned. This is important for you to build up historic metrics to determine how your environment isn't only performing but also how it's matching any Service Level Agreements (SLAs) you may have with your WebSphere environment.

Further, you explored several approaches to plot the output from the server monitoring tools and WebSphere components for proactive and historic element monitoring. In Chapter 14, you'll explore the implementation of several monitoring tools that provide historic graphing capabilities.

By this stage in the book, you should be able to architect a robust and highly available topological architecture, implement scalable and high-performing server and network components, implement high-performing application code, tune and optimize WebSphere, and proactively manage your WebSphere environment.

CHAPTER 14

Profiling and Benchmarking WebSphere

IN THIS CHAPTER, you'll look at how to profile WebSphere and applications operating under WebSphere. I already discussed how to monitor WebSphere to optimize it, but in this chapter, you'll peer through the other end of the looking glass at the art of benchmarking.

Profiling and Benchmarking, Revisited

Profiling is all about measuring a component of a system, commonly against a predefined set of measures. For example, you may go out one day and purchase a whiz-bang new home stereo system. After bringing it home, you want to crank it up and hear how it sounds. Before you do that, you want to make sure your neighbors won't be knocking on your door complaining about the noise, so you pick a spot outside your house to listen to the music at various levels.

Over the course of an afternoon, you play your sample music and run outside to listen to the noise level. Each time, you go back into the living room and crank up the music one extra notch. You do this until you feel the music is too loud for your neighbors, and you (sadly) mark that spot on the amplifier volume dial.

In a sense, this is *profiling*. You're attempting to profile different levels of music (statistical data) and its effect on your neighbors. If, however, you were trying to see how loud your stereo would go, this would be a form of *benchmarking*. Benchmarking is the measurement of performance for a particular component (for example, an application, a disk drive, a processor, or a stereo).

Profiling and benchmarking an application aren't that different. Essentially, profiling an application is about statistically analyzing various subcomponents, sometimes against pre-existing baseline measurements or, other times, simply to obtain statistical data about how the application measures up. Application benchmarking, on the other hand, is when you want to understand how the application performs.

Why Profile and Benchmark?

Profiling is an essential tool to understand the performance or desired performance of your applications. You can also use it to help diagnose problems such as memory leaks and resource overuse by drilling down to the methods and interface calls made within your classes and objects. Because Java is an object-based environment, profiling is essential.

Profiling can come in many different forms. It includes everything from the most basic form of monitoring the high-level network calls between communicating devices to thread and memory analyzers that help you understand what's going on within an application at the lowest level.

You probably at some stage have faced an irate customer or end user complaining about "poor performance." Alternatively, you may have noticed a performance degradation of your applications through some form of proactive alarming or monitoring. You can use profiling and benchmarking to isolate where these problem are occurring.

I'll use an example of a WebSphere-based application that's running poorly. End users are complaining about poor performance when retrieving information from a particular application screen. To understand this, you can take the problem to your staging or Stress and Volume Testing (SVT) environment and run some simulated tests.

You first run some benchmarking at a reasonable production load to understand how the application response times compare when under load. Your average benchmarked response time for the application is 10 seconds to log in, go to a particular screen, and request details that happen to go off to a backend database and retrieve information. Noticing that there's some performance degradation in that particular area of the application, you decide to profile the application to start to build up some empirical data to quantify what you're seeing.

Using a profiling tool such as JProbe (discussed later in this chapter), you're able to monitor and profile what the application is doing. In this example, by profiling the application using JProbe, it's possible to look at each component (object/class, method call, interface call, and so on) and understand the average time taken to complete each thread, memory consumed, number of calls, and so forth.

After running JProbe on the example application for some time, you'll build up a statistical profile of how the application operates. What JProbe may show about the example application is that a particular method call in a JavaBean that queries the database is taking 150 percent longer than any other bean in the application. Another example of where profiling and benchmarking is important is in ongoing capacity management and planning.

Using a combination of both forms of tooling, you're able to produce baseline capacity forecasts of various aspects of your environment. That is, it's not uncommon for Java 2 Enterprise Edition (J2EE)/WebSphere system managers to run benchmarking on particular functions of their applications on a periodic basis to understand and validate any skewing in their overall WebSphere platform.

These skewings can be caused by slight variations in the environment such as extra operational processes running in the background on servers impacting performance, extra network load causing method calls to various remote systems to take longer to complete, and so forth.

You'll now look at when and how you should tackle profiling.

A Practical Approach to Profiling

You need to first understand what it is you're trying to achieve; there are a number of reasons why you may want to profile your application:

- To reactively analyze a problem with an existing application (for example, a suspected memory leak, poor performance, and so on)

- To do proactive/periodic analysis to benchmark and profile an application or an application's key components

- To do preproduction or development phase testing to gain statistical analysis on the operations of an application

- To baseline or qualify existing capacity model estimates and calculations

In earlier chapters, you looked at performance management and what constitutes a performance improvement. Profiling and benchmarking are key aspects of performance management. In Figure 14-1, you'll see benchmarking and profiling listed on the left of the performance management model.

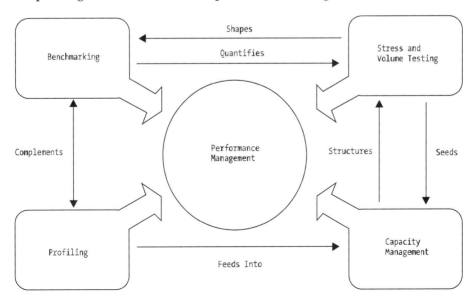

Figure 14-1. Performance management methodology

Although this figure shows what initiatives make up performance management, it doesn't indicate at what stage of your application environment's life cycle each stage should be undertaken. It should be obvious that SVT should be done *before* going live in a production environment. As you saw earlier, you should carry out SVT in a production-like environment when there are new major capabilities or infrastructure changes.

On the other end of the life cycle, profiling, shouldn't be performed in a live production environment either. Although profiling will give you a profile of your environment and application characteristics under load, it'll impact your customers or end users if you're conducting the profiling in a live environment. The same problem applies with benchmarking.

As also discussed in Chapter 2, constant and proactive monitoring and analyzing of your WebSphere environment should be a high priority within your operational processes.

So how does this relate to profiling? Look at it this way: performance management, as discussed, is about taking control and proactively managing the performance, scalability, and optimization of your WebSphere environment. In other words, profiling is the process that provides you with a key statistical measurement of the specific components within your platform in order to model and analyze the platform trends. That is, are things getting slower (lower performing), or are things getting faster (higher performing)?

Benchmarking is more of a quantitative measurement that looks at overall performance. You may use a broad-sword approach and benchmark your application every hour to model the key performance indicators such as access and response time, login time, transaction completion time, and so forth. You can then feed this data into your performance management process, which is mastered or governed by a capacity model of some sort. It's all very theoretical, so refer to Figure 14-1 to see how all these processes fit together.

Capacity management is the key to all things related to performance and scalability. Without this, you have no process, and you have no structure. When considering a profiling and benchmarking approach to your WebSphere environment, you should always start out with a plan of what it is you're trying to achieve. This forms the basis of capacity management. Whether this is in the form of a spreadsheet or some other medium doesn't matter; however, Table 14-1 summarizes the basic format of a capacity management approach.

Table 14-1. Performance Management: Activity Phase

Management Phase	Development Phase
Benchmarking	Development and systems integration environments
Profiling	Systems integration, quality assurance, and production shadow environments
SVT	Production shadow or preproduction environments

As mentioned, you'll need to understand what it is you're trying to achieve. That is, what do you want to measure and manage? Are you looking to measure a static environment to manage performance within a fixed, known set of boundaries? Or, are you looking to measure a dynamic environment that changes from day to day based on marketing campaigns, product releases, and organic growth?

The following key points should make up your approach:

Plan approach: What is it you're trying to measure and why? As I mentioned earlier, you need to understand what your motive is for managing your capacity of your environment. Is it cost, performance, scalability, or process driven?

Create plan and model: After planning your approach, invest time and effort into creating your environment capacity and performance models. The best tool to use in this case is a spreadsheet. They can be powerful tools for modeling and statistical analysis purposes. The model should be a representation of the approach you created. The approach should therefore include the key inputs, key items to measure (in other words, processor, network, disk capacity) and how you plan to measure. For example, what's the frequency of your sampling of performance input or profiling? The model should include a performance, capacity, and scalability baseline from initial benchmarking and profiling or, better still, proper SVT.

Implement approach: Roll out your approach, including your measurement, profiling, and benchmarking tools to start feeding into your capacity model. At this point, you'll iterate on a defined period or frequency, inputting the data from profiling and benchmarking into your model.

This is a high-level approach, but it gives you an idea of the steps involved and where profiling and benchmarking fit into a capacity management process.

Tools Available

There are many profiling and benchmarking tools available on the market today. From open-source and General Public License (GPL) tools to large-scale enterprise software suites, there's a tool to suit everyone's needs.

Given that there are so many tools, you can only explore a handful in this book. I've provided a description of tools that I've used or currently use when I work with profiling and benchmarking in WebSphere-based environments. There are four tools I find to be good all-around profiler tools (regarding cost, performance, and features).

Much of the tools' usage is beyond the scope of this book; however, I've provided some guidelines to help get you started. I've also provided links to the Web sites where you can download either full or evaluation copies of each of the packages, as well as documentation, information, FAQs, and more.

You'll now look at each of the profilers in some more detail.

JProbe

JProbe is a software profiling package from Quest Software (http://www.quest.com) that provides powerful memory, threading, and profiling capabilities. You can download a 15-day demo copy from Quest so you to evaluate the package. This section provides an example of a basic application being profiled by JProbc.

Consider for a moment that you have a basic class that iterates and appears to be causing you performance difficulty. With JProbe, it's possible to look at the profile of an application from several different angles. Figure 14-2 shows a JProbe screen that displays the initial or standard profiling screen, which indicates an application's overall profile metric. That is, it shows the characteristic, overall, of your application.

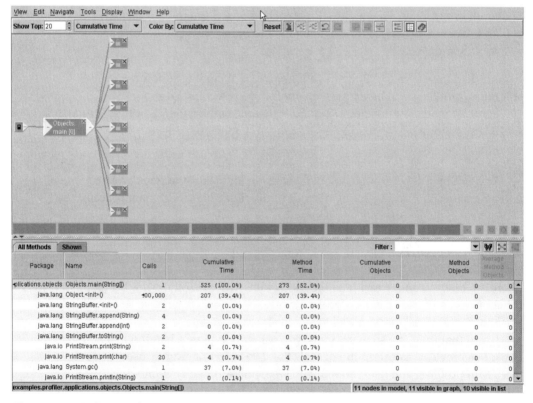

Figure 14-2. Using JProbe

Figure 14-2 shows a basic profiling exercise that has been conducted. At the bottom of the screen, there's a listing of the methods and objects that were called and used within this particular class profiling. To the right of that, there's a breakdown of the time spent within each method or object. Other components within the JProbe suite will allow you to understand, of the objects and methods invoked, what their memory consumption was and what their thread usage patterns were.

Using the thread profiler tool from JProbe, it's possible to take the information from the standard profiler tool (Figure 14-2) and drill down and understand which objects from which components are consuming the most memory. Figure 14-3 shows an example of a screen from the memory profiler.

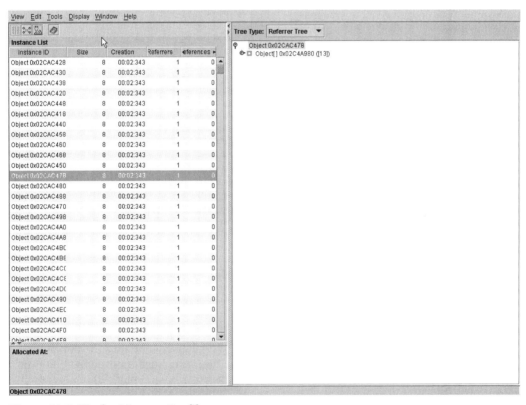

Figure 14-3. JProbe: Memory Profiler

In the left pane of Figure 14-3, you can see a list of all the objects that were created during the execution of the particular Java application in question. As you can see, the profiler shows the size of each object created and the creation time, and it can list the number of references and referrers that indicate the number of times this particular object has been used. Additional control buttons at the top of Figure 14-3 allow you to actually have the profiling tool analyze the results and determine if there are possible memory leaks present.

The tool will also highlight where those memory leaks are stemming from via a graph, as shown in Figure 14-4. Note at the bottom of Figure 14-4 how the summary dialog box indicates where it believes a leak is stemming from. Note also at the top right of the screen that the analyzer has determined the path of the memory leak.

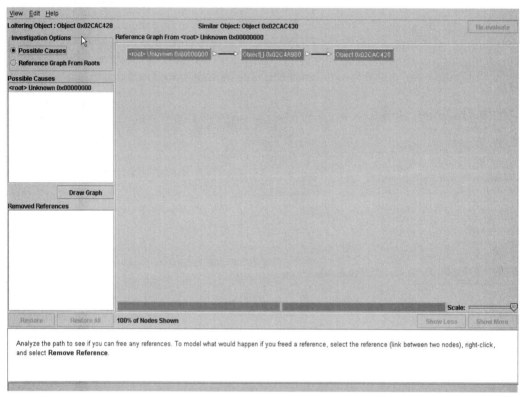

Figure 14-4. JProbe: extended memory profiler

JProbe also allows you to remotely monitor an active application via additional components that come with the suite. Furthermore, JProbe supports a plug-in for most leading Integrated Development Environments (IDEs), including IBM's WebSphere Studio Application Developer (WSAD). Furthermore, it has direct plug-in support for WebSphere, allowing you to analyze your live applications operating under WebSphere rather than via statically running them such as in the examples provide in Figures 14-2, 14-3, and 14-4.

Table 14-2 summarizes JProbe.

Table 14-2. JProbe Specifications

Feature Set	Capability
WebSphere version supported	Version 3.*x*, 4.*x*, and 5.*x*
Live system testing?	No
IDE support	WSAD and all other major IDEs supported via plug-ins
Operating systems supported	Windows NT, XP, 2000, 2003, AIX, Solaris, Linux
Memory profiler?	Yes
Thread profiler?	Yes
Static profiler?	Yes
Wizards and theorizers?	Yes

HPjmeter

HPjmeter is a Java Virtual Machine (JVM) profiler from Hewlett-Packard that provides a slightly different approach than JProbe yet essentially performs a similar function. You can download HPjmeter and its licensing arrangements from `http://www.hp.com/products1/unix/java/hpjmeter/index.html`.

HPjmeter works by hooking into the particular JVM that operates your WebSphere application servers—(typically the IBM Java Development Kit (JDK)—using a command-line JVM option, `-Xrunhprof`.

NOTE If you're running a nonstandard JDK/JVM with your implementation of WebSphere, other command-line options that HPjmeter uses are `-prof`, `-eprof`, `-Xeprof`, `-Xrunprof`, and `-Xrunhprof`.

HPjmeter reads the JVM output from `-Xrunhprof` or the equivalent command-line option and allows you to analyze a plethora of technical information about the application that runs within the particular JVM. HPjmeter allows you to analyze threads, memory usage, CPU, and process utilization within your applications. Figure 14-5 depicts the HPjmeter user interface.

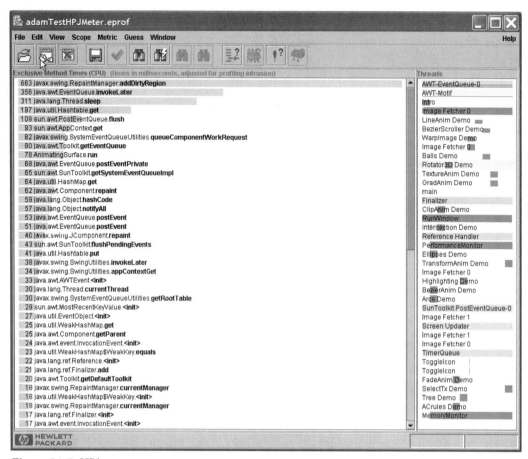

Figure 14-5. HPjmeter

One of the sound ways to use a nonlive profiler such as HPjmeter is to perform snapshot analysis. That is, when your application first goes into production, you should always create a series of baselines. These baselines will consist of performance and component utilization (for example, heap usage, thread allocation, and so on) measured against predetermined application loads, such as 10 percent, 40 percent, 60 percent, and 100 percent.

Then, with the HPjmeter tool, run it periodically over production-sampled data and compare it with the baseline snapshots you acquired before going live in production. This provides a side-by-side comparison between the baseline and the new results of your profiling. HPjmeter has the facilities to assist with comparison between data snap shots.

Overall, HPjmeter supports all JVMs that come with and are supported by both WebSphere 4 and 5. Table 14-3 summarizes its features.

Table 14-3. HPjmeter Specifications

Feature Set	Capability
WebSphere version supported	4.*x* and 5.*x*
Live system testing?	Partial (need to view data once created by JVM output)
IDE support	Supported via updating JVM bootstrap configuration in your IDE
Operating systems supported	All operating systems that support Java and Java Swing Graphical User Interface (GUI) classes
Memory profiler?	Yes
Thread profiler?	Yes
Static profiler?	Yes
Wizards and theorizers?	Yes

Resource Analyzer/Tivoli Performance Tool

The Resource Analyzer and Tivoli Performance tool come with WebSphere 4 and 5, respectively—and provide detailed information about the operational status of your applications running within WebSphere. As you saw in earlier chapters, both these tools are powerful. In the context of profiling, although both tools do provide profiling-like capabilities, they're more attuned to providing snapshot analysis of your live production environment (as discussed in detail during Chapter 14).

For example, if you were experiencing a problem with your production environment's performance, by using either of these tools, you can drill down to component level within each application. At this point, you're able to set each Java component within your application to a defined level of analysis. That is, you can choose to have the tool analyze and track your Java Database Connectivity (JDBC) connections, pool management, and performance while correlating the live status of the Web container threads. Figure 14-6 shows the Resource Analyzer, and Figure 14-7 shows the Tivoli Performance tool's Performance Viewer.

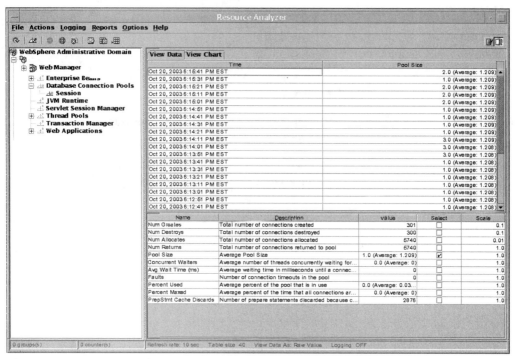

Figure 14-6. Resource Analyzer

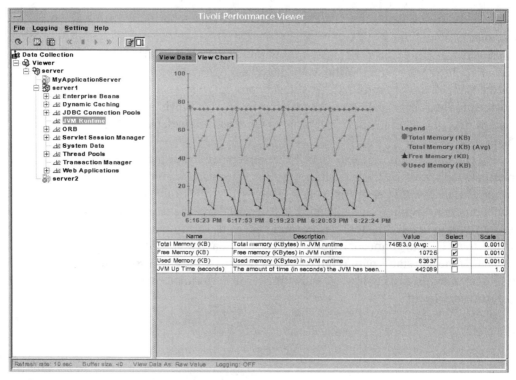

Figure 14-7. Tivoli Performance Viewer

Both these tools provide similar capabilities. Both tools also offer a logging capability that allows you to log, or capture, snapshots in real time and compare them.

Unlike HPjmeter and JProbe, these two WebSphere tools don't provide deep analysis and heuristic functionality. What the two WebSphere-based tools do provide is the ability to allow you to monitor specific application components in live production environments at a level that suits your needs. They're designed to assist you in monitoring your WebSphere environment and as aids in benchmarking. You can use them to analyze the various components and aspects of your WebSphere environment at a feature level, for example, data sources, Web container, Object Request Broker (ORB) threading, and so on.

You'll find that the Resource Analyzer and Tivoli Performance tools are better for performance analysis and looking at environment-related performance factors than pure application profiling. However, because both tools allow you to view snapshots of your application's performance from an environment perspective, they can both give a different angle of potential performance issues with your applications that standard profilers can't (for example, why look at object utilization and object call rates when the problem may be connections to a database?).

Table 14-4 summarizes the two tools and their features from a profiling perspective.

Table 14-4. Resource Analyzer and Tivoli Performance Tools

Feature Set	Capability
WebSphere version supported	4.*x* and 5.*x*
Live system testing?	Yes
IDE support?	No
Operating systems supported	All operating systems that support WebSphere Application Server
Memory profiler?	No
Thread profiler?	Partial
Static profiler?	Partial
Wizards and theorizers?	No

WSAD Profiler/Jinsight

If you're using IBM WebSphere Studio Application Developer (WSAD), then you actually have a powerful profiling tool built-in to your IDE. WSAD is among the best Java/J2EE IDEs available on the market. It has sophisticated testing and profiling suites, smart debugging, and a powerful distributed application development interface—the IDE itself.

Those who are using the predecessor to WSAD, IBM Visual Studio for Java, will have a limited built-in profiling tool. Instead, you can obtain a product from the IBM alphaWorks site (http://www.alphaworks.ibm.com) called Jinsight. Jinsight is another powerful tool that allows you to profile your Java applications. It also includes memory analysis, thread analysis, and other forms of profiling analysis. In the past, Jinsight was used in conjunction with Visual Studio for Java users.

From a development perspective, the WSAD profiling tools are extremely powerful. Given the profiling engine is embedded within the IDE itself, you can integrate the WebSphere testing environment, the debuggers, the code sampling, and the WSAD profiling all within a single application. Figure 14-8 shows the WSAD Profile view. As you can see from the example application that as been profiled, you can obtain a fair degree of information from this output.

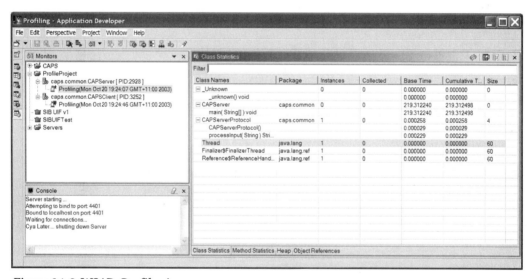

Figure 14-8. WSAD: Profile view

It's important to note that the profiler in the WSAD application isn't a live profiler such as JProbe and HPjmeter but more of a development aid. It's important to remember this because timings and other performance-related data will ultimately change once your application is deployed into a real production environment with real production-sized hardware. You may find that specific parts of your application are performing badly within WSAD because of the size and capacity of your development workstation hardware.

In most cases, taking application and profiling metrics within a live production environment will yield different results. Therefore, use the WSAD profiler as a tool to gauge the application's performance. However, you should never rely on it for hard performance and profiling metrics.

Table 14-5 summarizes the WSAD profiler.

Table 14-5. WSAD: Profiler View

Feature Set	Capability
WebSphere version supported	4.x (WSAD 4.x) and 5.x (WSAD 5.x)
Live system testing	Partial (in IDE only)
IDE support?	Yes
Operating systems supported	All operating systems that support WSAD (for example, Windows, Solaris, Linux, and AIX)
Memory profiler?	Yes
Thread profiler?	Partial
Static profiler?	Partial
Wizards and theorizers?	Yes

Summary

As you've seen during this chapter, profiling and benchmarking can be as limited or involved as you deem necessary. A complete undertaking of any of the initiatives within the performance management model will be involved and quite possibly complex initiatives. They are, however, one of those things that tend to be scrutinized by nontechnical managers who think conducting some form of fuzzy "profiling" is a waste of time.

As discussed in Chapters 1 and 2, building business cases for this type of initiative is about as important (and time consuming!) as it is to actually run the tests once you know what it is you're trying to achieve.

In essence, profiling is all about structure. Approach profiling as you would any other form of detailed testing, and plan your goals and approach thoroughly.

Index

Numbers and Symbols

% Disk Time
    graphing for a Windows XP-based
        server, 489–490
% Processor Time counter
    adding for the WebSphere Java
        process usage, 483–484
32-bit computing vs. 64-bit computing,
    91–92
64-bit architectures
    high-end server platforms with, 91
64-bit computing vs. 32-bit computing,
    91–92

A

abstraction
    using in WebSphere application
        design, 406
ACK directives
    settings for in IBM AIX, 268
active-active clustering
    typical configuration and function of,
        297–298
active-active databases
    configuration example, 223
    connection timeout settings for
        failover configuration, 364
    failover techniques in WebSphere,
        362
    function of, 222–223
active-standby clustering
    typical configuration and function of,
        295–296
active-standby databases
    connection timeout settings for
        failover configuration, 364
    failover techniques in WebSphere,
        361–362
    function of, 220–222
Add Counters dialog box
    selecting counters in to test and view
        network errors, 494
    selecting disk monitoring options in,
        488–490
administration console
    hosted by the deployment manager
        in WebSphere 5, 73
Administration Repository database
    in WebSphere 4, 306
administration server

function of in WebSphere 4, 69
administration service
    function of in WebSphere 5, 76
administrative consoles
    in WebSphere, 53
administrative functions
    in failover techniques in WebSphere,
        306
administrative repository
    configuration issues, 357–358
    use of in WebSphere 4, 68–69
administrative services
    function of in WebSphere 5, 76
affinity-based routing
    types of within the EJB-based server
        groups, 336
Aged Timeout
    setting in JDBC connection pool
        manager, 444
    setting in WebSphere 5, 449–450
AIM (Apple, IBM, Motorola) consortium
    processor designs produced by, 109
AIX. *See* IBM AIX
AIX swap space command, 480
AIX Unix
    Monitor command for memory
        usage information, 479
AMD AthIon 64 (ClawHammer)
    function of, 89
AMD Athlon, Athlon XP, and Athlon MP
    processors
    function of, 87–89
AMD Duron processor
    function of, 87
AMD Opteron
    function of, 89–90
Apache Axis project
    open-source series of APIs available
        from, 74
application architecture
    special considerations for protocols
        or logic, 173
Application Assembly Tool (AAT)
    enabling the default EJB caching
        setting when deploying, 340–341
application availability
    impact of buggy software or unstable
        hardware on, 239–240
application binding
    failover support for in WebSphere,
        359–360

application database (or databases)
    example of a connection to, 359
    function of, 62
    impact of on a WebSphere
        environment, 431
application environment
    multichannel topologies in, 204–218
    security considerations in, 169–170
application implementation
    example CPU choices, 94
application level
    configuring session management in,
        327
application server
    capacity considerations in multi-Web
        server, multiapplication server
        topologies, 208–209
    function of the EJB container within,
        61–62
    as key component of WebSphere
        implementation, 58–59
    steps for accessing the Web container
        for any, 384–385
application servers
    additional topology considerations,
        227–228
    developing high-performance appli-
        cations for, 395–410
    example of a compartmentalized
        approach, 228
    geographically distributed, 227
    location recommendation for
        WebSphere-to-database net-
        working, 143
    vs. server groups, 65
application server topology
    additional considerations, 227–228
applied affinity
    used for clients requesting IORs via
        the LSD, 336
associative referencing
    of level 2 cache in UltraSPARC III,
        99–100
ATA (Advanced Technology
    Attachment), 120–121
ATA-IDE standard
    ratified by ANSI, 120–121
AthIon 64. *See* AMD AthIon 64
    (ClawHammer)
Athlon processors
    function of, 88-89
Auto-Negotiate or Auto-Sensing
    configuration
    warning about using, 495
availability
    as key measure of high-performance
        computing, 33

understanding your needs for, 46–47
    what it is, 35–36
availability and scalability
    a primer, 34–43
    ten rules to live by, 49
availability matrix
    understanding, 39–40
availability measurements
    list of commonly represented and
        associated downtime, 39
availability, performance, and scalability
    costs of, 43–49
Average value
    in Performance tool network
        utilization output, 496
Axis. *See also* Apache Axis project
    Web Services provided by, 74

B
bandwidth. *See* bus bandwidth
Basic method
    setting in Oracle Transparent
        Application Failover, 369
batch components and external
    applications
    problems with using JNI on its own,
        470–471
    within a WebSphere application
        environments, 469–472
batch scripts
    importance of compartmentalizing,
        469
    making thread safe in WebSphere
        application environments, 469
    managing the operating priority of,
        469
batch tier servers, 119
batch-based workloads
    workload summary matrix for, 434
BEA JRocket JVM
    vs. other JVMs, 289–290
    Wintel platform optimized JVM,
        289–290
Bean Managed Persistence (BMP), 27
    vs. Container Managed Persistence
        (CMP, 415–416
    function of in J2EE database
        integration, 415–416
    in multiple JVM environments, 186
benchmarking and profiling. *See*
    profiling and benchmarking
Berkeley ps
    example output from, 479–480
Berkeley System Distribution (BSD), 435
BGP. *See* Border Gateway Protocol (BGP)

Big Brother
monitoring and alerting tool, 245
BMP. *See* Bean Managed Persistence
(BMP)
Border Gateway Protocol (BGP)
rerouting traffic to a secondary
router with, 353
smart routing protocol, 277
using to distribute traffic to multiple
locations, 309
BSD. *See* Berkeley System Distribution
(BSD)
BuffPage parameter
setting in IBM DB2, 441
building block rules
for WebSphere application environments, 155–157
bus bandwidth
calculating performance of, 135–136
business availability
matching with percentage availability, 38–39
business availability index
understanding, 36–39
understanding data redundancy, 37
understanding no redundancy, 37
understanding organization redundancy, 38
understanding people redundancy,
38
understanding system redundancy,
37
business improvements
measuring, 14–19
business tier
avoiding overuse of Java niceties in,
403–404
importance of avoiding stateful EJBs
where possible, 404
importance of reusing EJB homes
where possible, 401
importance of using constants in,
405
importance of writing local method
calls for, 405–406
performance in WebSphere applications, 400–406
using abstraction in, 406
using a multithreaded logger instead
of system.out.println(), 402
using container threading services
instead of manually spawning
threads in, 402–403
using lazy initialization of objects in,
403
using Pass-by-Reference rather than
Pass-by-Value, 401

Bytes Total/sec counter
for checking utilization of a Windows
network interface, 495–497

C
cache cleanup interval
setting for the EBJ container, 383–384
cache size
setting in the EBJ container, 383
Call-by-Reference
setting in the Application Assembly
Tool (AAT), 155
Call-by-Value
calling EJBs via, 155
capacity management
basic format of this approach, 506
Carrot model
showing correct queuing
configuration, 280
cell
defined, 71
vs. WebSphere 4 domain, 70
cells
reducing management overhead
associated with, 72
channel
defined, 173
checklist
for database-to-WebSphere
implementation, 427–428
choke tier
in a 3-tier firewall topology, 169–170
CISC or x86 processors
cost of vs. RISC-based processors, 97
Cisco PIX firewalls
HSRP capabilities supported by, 353
ClawHammer. *See* AMD AthIon 64
(ClawHammer)
client tier API
in JDBC type 3 driver implementation, 425
CloneID directive
use of in WebSphere 4 and 5 plug-in
files, 313
clones
function of in WebSphere 4, 66–68
vs. server groups, 66–67
cloning
extending load-balancing capability
of WebSphere with, 67–68
and workload management
flowchart in WebSphere 4, 68
closed queuing model
function of, 279
cluster. *See* WebSphere cluster
environment

ClusterAddress directive
  code example showing use of, 321
  forcing requests to an external load
    balancer with, 320–322
clustered active-standby configuration
  example of, 221–222
clustering
  to achieve performance improve-
    ment, 293–299
clustering systems
  using other active-standby or IP
    takeover, 369–370
clusterware
  use of in active-standby databases,
    220–222
  using to cluster components,
    294–295
clusterware solutions
  well-known and WebSphere sup-
    ported, 294–295
CMP. *See* Container Managed
  Persistence (CMP)
code example
  for declaring the ConnectTimeout
    setting and value, 322–323
  for handling database errors in appli-
    cation code, 361
  of HTTP plug-in configuration file,
    55–56
  for implementing MQ asynchronous
    transactions, 460–461
  of a JDBC URL configuration file, 367
  for mapping WebSphere 4 dual
    instance Web container configu-
    ration, 314–315
  for mapping WebSphere 5 dual
    instance Web container configu-
    ration, 315–316
  of Oracle TNS names configuration
    file for Transparent Application
    Failover, 368
  of Oracle TNS names configuration
    file for server failover, 366
  for referencing an external or non-
    standard data type, 466
  of server cluster directive, 314
  of server group directive, 314
  showing proper object closure in
    databases, 420–421
  showing use of ClusterAddress
    directive, 321
  of WebSphere 4 HTTP plug-in
    configuration file, 311–312
  WebSphere 4 key CloneID changes,
    316
  of WebSphere 5 HTTP plug-in
    configuration file, 312

WebSphere 5 key CloneID changes,
    316–317
cold disaster recovery sites
  typical configuration and function of,
    301
COMM_FAILURE message, 339
Compaq/HP TruCluster
  clustering solution, 295
comparison chart (CPU)
  x86/IA-64/x86-64 platform (Intel and
    AMD), 90–91
COMPLETE_STATUS message, 339
Complex Instruction Set Computing
  (CISC)-based processors vs. RISC-
  based UltraSPARC processors, 96
component architecture
  WebSphere 4 and 5, 51–79
component modeling
  in multiple JVM environments, 185
components
  reasons for splitting into their own
    tiers, 194–195
concurrent and registered users
  effect of on response times, 236
configuration and tuning parameters
  for Oracle systems, 437–438
configuration repository
  function of in WebSphere 5, 77
configuration settings
  use of administrative repository for
    in WebSphere 4, 68–69
conn.close() command
  closing the JDBC database
    connection with, 421
connection pool manager. *See also*
  WebSphere connection pool
  manager
  provided by WebSphere, 215–217
connection pool managers
  closing connections in WebSphere
    applications with, 362
Connection Timeout
  setting in WebSphere 4 and 5,
    446–447
Connection Timeout setting
  in JDBC connection pool manager,
    444
ConnectTime
  setting in WebSphere 5, 332–333
ConnectTimeout setting
  in WebSphere 5, 322–323
ConnectTimeout setting and value
  code example for declaring, 322–323
Container Managed Persistence (CMP)
  in J2EE database integration,
    414–415
  in multiple JVM environments, 186

Container Managed Persistence (CMP)
vs. Bean Managed Persistence
(BMP), 415–416
container threading services
using instead of manually spawning
threads, 402–403
container-managed persistence (CMP)
using only for high-read database
access, 408
containers
the EJB container, 374–377
high-level application server framework view, 372
an overview, 371–372
within WebSphere, 372
what they do, 373–377
context switches
in vmstat output, 477
cookies
popular means of session management in WebSphere, 327–328
CORBA
example implementation within a
WebSphere platform, 457
example transaction with
WebSphere, 458
having all components with a shared
application server, 459–460
key communications status
messages, 338–340
CORBA integration
platform and language indepen-
dency of, 456
CORBA Object Request Broker (ORB)
services
requests serviced by the application
server, 59
CORBA.INTERNAL exception, 340
cost comparisons
for optimization vs. upgrade for pilot
application, 17
cost impact factors
that help determine downtime costs,
45
CPU and overall server load
measuring in Windows, 481–484
CPU and server comparison matrix
for selecting model for your needs,
104
CPU and system load
key load and performance identifiers
in Unix, 475–481
CPU comparison chart
x86/IA-64/x86-64 platform (Intel and
AMD), 90–91

CPUs
determining best for your needs,
105–108
for development and desktop needs,
92–93
for server and high-end server needs,
93
CPUs and servers
best for medium production
environments, 106–107
best for small production
environments, 105–106
Curl
command line tool for probing
Internet services, 245
Curl/Perl/Lynx
software for custom building stress
and volume testing suites, 246
customer administration application
in a single-channel 3-tier topology,
178–180

D

DAO. *See* Data Access Objects (DAO)
Data Access Objects (DAO)
example pattern implementation,
422
function of in object-oriented design,
421–423
using for data tier general database
access, 409
data redundancy
understanding, 37
Data Replication Service (DRS)
provided by WebSphere 5, 63
data source
defined, 193
data source provider
queue modeling item to monitor, 284
data sources
as components of a WebSphere
queue, 280
data stores and repositories
in WebSphere 5, 77–78
data tier
importance of releasing JDBC
resources when finished with
them, 407–408
performance in a WebSphere
environment, 406–409
using prepared SQL statements
where possible in, 409
using WebSphere data sources in, 407

data types
  in a WebSphere environment,
    272–273
database
  as component of a WebSphere
    queue, 280
  overview, 411–412
database and other external interface
    pooling
  in multiple JVMs with multiapplica-
    tion servers, 215–217
database availability options
  database replication, 306
  database server clustering, 305
  in database server tier, 305–306
  hot-standby databases, 306
  stand-alone database instances, 305
database connection script
  using to plot database connection
    usage, 248
database datasource
  effect on performance, 8
database errors
  handling in application code,
    361–362
database failover events
  summarizing, 369–370
database platform
  determining scalability needed for,
    430–431
  Oracle and DB2 monitoring tools,
    441–442
database replication
  database availability options, 306
  in geographically distributed
    technologies, 226–227
database server clustering, 294
  database availability option, 305
database server failover
  considerations when using Oracle 8*i*
    OPS, 9*i* OPS, and 9*i* RAC,
    365–369
  in WebSphere applications, 356–370
database server node
  recommendation for WebSphere-to-
    database networking, 144
database servers
  having multiple for redundancy or
    high availability, 363–364
database server software
  in single-channel topologies,
    175–176
database server tier
  database availability options in,
    305–306
  in JDBC type 3 driver
    implementation, 425

database tiers
  topological considerations important
    to, 218–223
database transactional performance
  determining cause of poor, 499
database transaction load
  considerations, 180–183
database workloads
  most common flavors of, 434
databases
  code example showing proper object
    closure, 420–421
  data layout and design, 435
  determining your reliance on, 430
  effect on performance, 8
  factors to consider when implement-
    ing, 429–431
  key items to consider when imple-
    menting high end, 432
db_block_buffers/ parameter
  for Oracle system configuration and
    tuning, 437
db_block_size parameter
  for Oracle system configuration and
    tuning, 437
db_cache_size parameter
  for Oracle system configuration and
    tuning, 437
DB2. *See* IBM DB2
Decision Support System (DSS)
    workload
  CPU availability needed for, 433
  workload summary matrix for, 434
delay acknowledgment
  settings in IBM AIX, 268
delay acknowledgment ports
  setting in IBM AIX, 269
deployment descriptor
  for your J2EE application, 372
Deployment Manager
  function of in WebSphere 5, 73, 202,
    306
design considerations
  for legacy systems integration,
    455–472
Direct Attached Storage (DAS) devices
  function of, 128
directional flow rule
  used by the Mirrored Waterfall
    Performance Methodology,
    27–30
disaster recovery
  typical configuration and function of,
    299–301
disaster recovery solution
  implementing, 300–301

disk I/O
monitoring, 485–490
performance in Windows NT/2000/XP, 488–490
telltale signs of high disk utilization, 488
disk I/O performance
calculating disk transfer time, 134–135
disk layout approaches
in system and hardware tuning and optimization, 272–275
for Unix file systems, 273–275
disk performance
the true effects of striping disks, 136–137
disk speed
effect of in a WebSphere environment, 130–131
disk storage technologies
costs associated with, 137–140
current and future performance overview, 131
effect of disk speed in a WebSphere environment, 130–131
implementation costs, 138–139
importance of architectural complexity in selecting, 140
management and support costs, 138
overall performance, 131–137
questions to ask for choosing the right architecture, 132–133
summary, 140
upgrade and scalability costs, 140
disk systems
comparing, 120–130
disk technologies
comparing, 120–130
% Disk Time
graphing for a Windows XP-based server, 489–490
disks and disk configuration
database-specific considerations for, 432
distributed storage architecture
example of, 128
DLPAR. *See* dynamic logical partitioning (DLPAR)
DMZ firewall
function of, 353–354
doGet() method
importance of questioning the use of, 399
domain vs. WebSphere 5 cell, 70
domains
using with SunFire range of servers, 107

doPost() method
importance of questioning the use of, 399
DoS attacks
mitigating chances of with separate network, 351
downtime
calculating the cost of, 45–46
causes of, 41–42
costs of to various industries, 43
example cost impact factors, 45
DSS workload. *See* Decision Support System (DSS) workload
dual application server configuration
example of in WebSphere, 313
dual Web server
single application server topology, 190–197
thick model example, 191
thin model example, 190
dual Web server, single application server topology
advantages of, 195–196
common uses for, 190–197
disadvantages of, 196–197
final considerations for using, 197
dual-channel topologies vs. single-channel topologies, 174
dual-CPU configuration
UltraSPARC III CPU connections to, 101
Duration value
in Performance tool network utilization output, 496
Duron processor
function of, 87
dynamic logical partitioning (DLPAR)
in IBM PowerPC platform (pSeries), 147
Dynamic System Domains (DSDs)
function of in Sun SPARC platform, 145–146

E

e-cache
in UltraSPARC II processors, 98
EIDE (Enhanced Integrated Disk Electronics)
introduction of, 121
EJB and Web containers
performance in WebSphere, 371–394
tuning and optimization, 377–394
EJB caching
types supported by WebSphere EJB containers, 416–418
EJB caching settings
caching options A, B, and C, 340–342

how option A works, 341
option B and C for caching entity
EJBs, 341
options for configuring, 417–418
EJB container
cache size settings in, 383
as component of a WebSphere
queue, 280
differences in between WebSphere 4
and 5, 334
different levels of WLM availability
for configuring, 305
example view of, 375
function of in WebSphere, 61–62
function of the passivation directory
in, 381–382
insulation and implementation, 62
overview, 334
queue modeling item to monitor, 284
setting the cache cleanup interval
for, 383–384
setting the interactive pool cleanup
variable in, 382–383
steps for accessing for any application server, 379
steps for accessing the settings in
WebSphere 5, 380–381
tuning in WebSphere 4, 378–380
tuning in WebSphere 5, 380–381
tuning the performance of, 381–384
vs. Web container performance tuning, 374–375
in WebSphere high availability
environment, 304–305
WebSphere queue settings, 286
workload management, 334–336
EJB container failover and high
availability, 334–342
container overview, 334
workload management, 334–336
EJB container failovers
key CORBA messages thrown to EJB
clients, 338–340
operation of in WebSphere 4 and 5,
336–340
EJB Container Service
dialog box in WebSphere 4, 379
options in WebSphere 4, 380
EJB container services
in WebSphere 5, 381
EJB container tuning, 377–384
in WebSphere 4, 378–380
EJB environments
tuning your CMP and BMP, 416–418
EJB home interface
role of, 375–376

EJB module
function of, 64
EJB object interface
vs. EJB home interface, 376
function of, 376–377
EJB request routing
four primary forms of, 335
EJB server affinity settings
that override WLM settings, 305
EJBs
clusterable available in WebSphere 4
and 5, 341–342
distinction between session and
entity, 376
pros and cons of using in your
designs, 194–195
embedded HTTP server
within the application server, 60–61
embedded SQL
compiling SQL queries and
commands with, 418
EMC
advanced clustering solutions by, 351
EMC Celera HighRoad
as solution for applications using
NFS, 349
Enhanced Integrated Disk Electronics
(EIDE)
introduction of, 121
enterprise application deployment
descriptor
for your J2EE application, 372
Enterprise Archive Resource (EAR) file
components bundled into, 372
Enterprise Integration Layer (EIL) tier
servers, 119
Enterprise JavaBean (EJB) container
effect on performance, 8
entity EJB cache settings
options for configuring, 417–418
entity EJBs vs. session EJBs, 376
entstat -d *interface_name* command
for showing network-related errors in
AIX 4.2+, 493
errors. *See* network errors; physical
errors; software-based errors
expenses
associated with the pilot application
project, 16–17
Extensible HTML (XHTML)
Web container processing of static
content from, 59–60
Extensible Markup Language (XML)
legacy systems integration with over
SOAP, 455

external load balancers
in WebSphere 5, 320–322
external systems
WebSphere's reliance on available,
343–344

F

F4800 servers
choosing for medium production
environments, 106–107
F6800 servers
choosing for medium production
environments, 106–107
fabric controller
shared by IBM Power4 processor
cores, 113
failover and high availability
considerations
in WebSphere, 291–342
failover techniques with WebSphere,
301–307
administrative functions, 306
database server tier, 305–306
EJB container, 304–305
network components, 306–307
Web container, 304
Web server tier/HTTP servers,
303–304
failover types
in Oracle Transparent Application
Failover, 368
failovers. *See* EJB container failover
Fast Ethernet vs. Gigabit Ethernet, 164
FCAL-based storage systems. *See* Fibre
Channel Arbitrated Loop (FCAL)-
based storage systems
federated API view, 371
Fibre Channel Arbitrated Loop (FCAL)-
based storage systems
architecture, 127
costs of vs. other SCSI technologies,
127
function of, 126–128
file system types
supported by Oracle and DB2, 435
FIN_WAIT_2 state
command for viewing current
settings, 263
problems with Sun Solaris
WebSphere-based applications,
263
findByPrimaryKey(primary_key) call
searching a database for a particular
row with, 415
Fireplane
function of in Sun SPARC platform,
145–146

Fireplane crossbar
function of, 101
firewall and load balancing environment
other considerations for, 355–356
firewall devices
hardware based, 353
firewall environment
network diagram of, 167
reasons for housing static content on
the frontend, 170
thin Web server configuration, 168
firewall location
in relation to backend application
and database server, 170–172
firewall rules
to consider before opting for thin or
thick Web server, 166–169
firewall topology
example of 3-tier, 169
firewalls
as critical components of business
systems, 352–353
example showing overhead associated with, 167
importance of having backups for,
353–354
FireWire disk technology
function and future of, 129–130
formula
for figuring overhead when adding
JVMs to environments, 186
four-processor systems
function of, 101
Front Side Bus (FSB)
in Intel Pentium 4 processors, 85
frontend Web servers
in multiapplication JVM, dual Web
server, single application server
topology, 201–202
funnel, or carrot-shaped, model
of correctly configured WebSphere
application environment, 29–30

G

garbage collection
defined, 156
example logging of, 250
example monitoring graph, 160
historic logging example, 251
importance of a dedicated CPU for,
156
monitoring, 159–160
obtaining information from log files
for, 250
use of in JVM's to clean unused items
for heap, 158

garbage collection architecture
in BEA JRocket JVM, 289–290
Gartner Research
introduction of Total Cost of
Ownership (TOC) by, 20
generic database performance
architecture
with WebSphere, 428–431
generic WebSphere database sizing
key points about, 431–435
workload summary matrix, 434–435
geographically distributed application
servers
function of, 227
geographically distributed databases
function of, 226–227
geographically distributed technologies,
224–227
geographically distributed Web servers
example of, 225
Gigabit Ethernet
vs. Fast Ethernet, 164
speed of, 351
global routing example, 310
global routing example failover
scenario, 310
grid computing
in the Sun SPARC platform, 146–147
Grinder
profiling and load testing tool, 243
GX controller
function of, 113

H
hardware and system tuning and
optimization
for WebSphere-based platforms,
271–277
hardware clustered solution
architecture and function of, 295–298
hardware clustering
available for LDAP environments,
345
primary forms of, 295
service availability provided by,
294–298
hardware upgrade
pilot application costs associated
with, 16–17
hash_area_size parameter
for Oracle system configuration and
tuning, 437
HBAs (Host Bus Adaptors). *See* Host Bus
Adaptors (HBAs)
heap
defined, 158

high availability
horizontal clustering for in
WebSphere, 307
methods for achieving WebSphere
platform, 293–307
recap of topologies suitable for, 307
WebSphere clustering for, 307
high availability and failover
fundamentals
in WebSphere, 292–293
High Availability Cluster
Multiprocessing (HACMP)
clustering solution, 295
as solution for applications using
NFS, 349
high CPU utilization of JVM
determining cause of poor
performance of, 498
high load average
drilling down to, 476–478
high-availability database server topologies, 218–223
architectural considerations and best
practices for, 219–223
high-availability extension
example of for multiple JVMs with
multiapplication servers, 215
high-performance WebSphere
applications
developing, 395–410
horizontal and vertical scaling
advantages of combined, 153–154
horizontal clustering
for high availability in WebSphere,
307
horizontal scaling
example of with WebSphere, 151
vs. vertical scaling, 152–153
with WebSphere, 150–152
Host Bus Adaptors (HBAs)
adding to upgrade system performance, 10
hot disaster recovery sites
typical configuration and function of,
300–301
hot disk
picking with the iostat command,
487–488
Hot Standby Routing Protocol (HSRP)
by Cisco, 353
hot-standby databases
database availability options, 306
function of, 219–220
HPjmeter profiler
function of, 511–513
specifications, 513
user interface, 512
Web site address for downloading, 511

HSRP. *See* Hot Standby Routing Protocol (HSRP)
HTTP plug-in
function of, 54–58
HTTP plug-in configuration file
code example for declaring the ConnectTimeout setting and value, 322–323
code for mapping to WebSphere 4 dual instance Web container configurations, 314–315
code for mapping to WebSphere 5 dual instance Web container configurations, 315–316
default virtual host section of, 56–57
example of in WebSphere, 54–56
noncontext configuration section of, 56
Route directive section in, 57–58
ServerGroup directives in, 58
UriGroup directive declaration section of, 57
HTTP plug-in directive
for setting ConnectTime, 332–333
for setting RetryInterval, 331–332
HTTP plug-in topology
example in WebSphere, 55
HTTP server
function of with WebSphere, 53–54
third-party HTTP server platforms, 54
HTTP server clustering, 294
HTTP servers/Web server tier
in a WebSphere high availability environment, 303–304
HTTP sessions
importance of invaliding when they aren't required, 398–399
HTTP Web server
WebSphere queue settings, 285
HTTP Web server plug-in
code example of a WebSphere 4 configuration file, 311–312
code example of a WebSphere 5 configuration file, 312
function of, 311–329
Hypertext Markup Language (HTML)
Web container processing of static content from, 59–60
HyperTransport bus
incorporated in the AthIon 64, 89

I

IA-32
defined, 83
IA-64
defined, 83

IBM AIX
command for getting network interface statistics in, 491
delay acknowledgment settings in, 268
setting delay acknowledgment ports in, 269
TCP hash table size settings, 271
TCP maximum listen backlog setting, 270–271
TCP send and receive buffer attributes, 269–270
TCP TIME_WAIT settings, 267
tuning and optimization, 266–271
IBM DB2
architectural overview, 439
key tuning parameters and considerations, 439–442
major components of, 440
optimization parameter recommendations, 440–441
vs. Oracle9*i* Real Application Clusters (RAC) system, 222
IBM Edge components, 78
IBM JVM
setting object allocation parameters for, 289
tuning and performance options, 289–290
IBM platform
processor architecture, 110–115
IBM Power4 platform. *See* Power4 platform (IBM)
IBM Power4 processor. *See* Power4 processor (IBM)
IBM Power4 processor cores
function of, 113–114
IBM Power4 processors, 116
IBM PowerPC 604e processor
architecture and function of, 111
IBM PowerPC 750 processor
architecture and function of, 111–112
IBM PowerPC 970 processor. *See* PowerPC 970 processor
IBM PowerPC platform (pSeries)
features of, 147
IBM PowerPC platform
summary, 119–120
IBM PowerPC processors
comparison chart, 115–116
IBM RS64-III and RS64-IV processors
architecture and function of, 112–113
IBM Secureway Directory Server
supported by WebSphere, 344
IBM servers
advanced clustering solutions for, 119
IBM WebSphere. *See* WebSphere

IBM WebSphere 4. *See* WebSphere 4;
    WebSphere 4-specific component
    architecture
ibm-ejb-jar-ext.xmi file
    IBM extension deployment descrip-
        tor for EJBs, 417
Idle Timeout
    setting in WebSphere 4, 447–448
Idle Timeout setting
    in JDBC connection pool manager,
        444
IIPJMeter profiling tool (Hewlett-
    Packard), 244
implementation costs
    associated with disk storage tech-
        nologies, 137–140
infrastructure design
    in WebSphere, 81–147
init() servlet method
    using if doGet() and doPost() aren't
        required, 399
initial heap
    defined, 158
in-process routing
    for EJB containers, 335–336
Instruction Issue Unit (IIU) feature
    function of on the UltraSPARC III
        processor, 100
integrated cache
    available in Intel Xeon MP processor,
        86
Intel Architecture-32 (IA-32)
    defined, 83
Intel Architecture-64 (IA-64)
    defined, 83
Intel Itanium 2
    function of, 86–87
Intel Itanium and Itanium 2
    function of, 86–87
Intel Pentium 4 1.7-2GHz processor
    function of, 84
Intel Pentium 4 2.26GHz-3.2GHz
        processor
    function of, 85
Intel Pentium 4 2GHz-2.6GHz processor
    function of, 84–85
Intel Pentium III Xeon 900 MHz
        processor
    function of, 84
Intel Xeon MP processor
    function of, 86
Intel Xeon processor
    function of Pentium III and 4
        versions, 85–86
    memory supported by, 91–92
intelligent routing
    in network configurations, 276–277

interactive pool cleanup variable
    setting in the EJB container, 382–383
internal private network 'mesh'
    function of, 163–164
International SPARC Organization
    creation of SPARC Compliance
        Definition by, 95
Internet Inter-ORB Protocol (IIOP)
    function of, 168
Internet Inter Orb Protocol (IIOP)
    used as primary CORBA application
        protocol, 456
Internet vs. external schema sites
    effect on Web Services transaction
        performance, 468
iostat command
    for monitoring Unix server disk I/O,
        486–487
    picking a hot disk with, 487–488
iostat tool
    for monitoring Oracle and DB2 for
        performance issues, 441
IP failover clusterware
    using with built-in LDAP
        master/replica availability fea-
        tures, 345
iSCSI technology
    benefits of, 122–123
    example of high-level implementa-
        tion, 123
    function of, 122–124

J

J2EE application integration. *See* legacy
    systems integration
J2EE database integration
    Container Managed Persistence
        (CMP), 414–415
    persistence layer implementation,
        414–427
J2EE environment
    Web container as component of,
        59–60
J2EE-based application
    NFS as a solid data sharing technol-
        ogy for, 347–350
J2EE-based application server environ-
    ment
    container as key component of,
        371–372
    key areas that affect application
        performance, 27
JACs. *See* Java application clients (JACs)
Java
    management of memory allocation
        and deallocation by, 158

Java 2 Enterprise Edition (J2EE) applications
the need for performance in, 1–5
Java application clients (JACs)
effect on memory consumption, 471–472
Java Application Clients (JACs)
failover support for in WebSphere, 306
Java components
in WebSphere business tier, 400
Java Database Connectivity (JDBC) and pooling
requests serviced by the application server, 59
Java Database Connectivity (JDBC) pool
effect on performance, 8
Java IIOP vs. RMI-IIOP, 456
Java Message Service (JMS), 27
interfacing WebSphere-based J2EE applications with, 455–456
requests serviced by the application server, 59
Java Naming and Directory Interface (JNDI) services
requests serviced by the application server, 59
Java Native Interface (JNI)
problems with using it on its own, 470–471
Java Server Pages (JSPs)
Web container processing of, 59–60
Java Virtual Machine (JVM)
effect on performance, 8
Java Virtual Machine (JVM) profiler
HPjmeter from Hewlett-Packard, 511–513
Java/J2EE environments
performance degradation caused by garbage collection in, 249–250
Java/JVM memory and object management
management of application queues with, 27
JavaMail components
provided by WebSphere, 215
JavaMail services
requests serviced by the application server, 59
Java/Swing-based Graphical User Interface (GUI)
WebSphere version 4 managed by, 53
JBOD (Just a Basic Old Disk), 136
JCA container
function of in WebSphere 5, 75
JDBC
function of, 423–426

JDBC Application Programming Interface (API)
support for exception messages to perform events, 359
JDBC connection pool data source
setting the Idle Timeout to tune, 448
setting the Orphan Timeout to tune, 448
JDBC connection pool manager
main areas to tune to gain performance, 444
WebSphere queue settings, 286–287
JDBC Connection Pool Manager settings
tuning in WebSphere, 27–28
JDBC connection pool tuning
in WebSphere 5, 449–451
JDBC pool manager
cause of a StaleConnectionException on, 216
JDBC resources
importance of releasing when no longer needed, 407–408
JDBC type 1 driver
as JDBC-ODBC bridge, 423–424
JDBC type 2 drivers
implementation of, 424
JDBC type 3 drivers
implementation of, 425
JDBC type 4 driver (JDBC thin driver)
implementation of, 425–426
JDBC URL configuration file
example of, 367
JDBC-based database interface
provided by WebSphere, 215–216
JDBC/Container Managed Persistence (CMP), 27
Jinsight
Web site address for downloading, 516
JMS server
function of in WebSphere 5, 75–76
JProbe profiling tool (Quest Software), 243
extended memory profiler screen example, 510
getting an application operation statistical profile with, 504–505
memory profiler screen example, 509
plug-in support for most leading IDEs, 510
specifications, 511
using, 508–511
Web site address for downloading, 508
JRocket JVM. *See* BEA JRocket JVM

<jsp: usebean()> tag
    importance of using carefully in
        applications, 400
JVM (Java Virtual Machine)
    garbage collection monitoring,
        159–160
    memory characteristics, 157–161
    multiapplication single-channel
        topology, 183–190
    obtaining verbose garbage collection
        from, 249
    operating system thread to JVM
        thread ratio, 93
    other memory issues to consider,
        160–161
    rules of thumb to follow for, 159
    threading characteristics, 161–162
    tuning, 287–288
JVM environments
    advantages of multiple, 188
    considerations for multiple, 184–186
    disadvantages of, 189
JVM implementation vendors, 158
JVM tuning and performance options,
    288–290
JVP Performance Interface (JVMPI)
    requests serviced by the application
        server, 59

K
keep-alive connections
    setting maximum number of,
        389–390
keep-alive I/O time-out
    setting value for, 392–394
    steps for making changes to in
        WebSphere 4, 393
    steps for making changes to in
        WebSphere 5, 393–394
keep-alive requests
    setting maximum value for, 390–392
Kernel threads
    function of, 93
kstat -p -s "*err*" command
    for showing network-related errors in
        Solaris 8+, 493

L
Last value
    in Performance tool network utiliza-
        tion output, 496
lazy initialization
    using in the WebSphere business tier,
        403
LDAP environments
    forms of clustering in, 345

high-availability implementation,
    346
implementation and performance,
    345–347
LDAP farm
    using LDAP master/replica tech-
        niques to configure, 346
LDAP server clustering
    available for LDAP environments,
        345
LDAP servers
    options and considerations, 344–345
    supported by WebSphere, 344–347
legacy integration. *See* legacy systems
    integration
legacy systems integration
    design considerations for, 455–472
    example CORBA and WebSphere
        implementation, 457
    example of, 454
    performance optimization, 453–472
    via XML over SOAP or XML RPC, 455
    what it is, 453–455
legacy systems integration components
    as part of a WebSphere queue, 280
level 3 cache component
    function of, 113
lightweight connections
    teardown of vs. Remote Method
        Invocation (RMI) connections,
        270–271
Lightweight Directory Access Protocol
    (LDAP) server clustering, 294
Lightweight Processes (LWP)
    function of, 259–260
limp home modes
    used by some load balancers, 354
Linux
    disabling the TCP Selective
        Acknowledgment setting, 256
    getting network interface statistics in,
        491
    and Lightweight Processes (LWP),
        259–260
    optimization and tuning checklist
        for, 255–260
Linux swap space command, 480
Linux TCP/IP stack
    features that can impede
        performance, 255
    optimization, 255
Linux-based WebSphere application
    server
    deactivating the TCP
        Acknowledgment feature, 256
    deactivating the TCP keepalive
        feature in, 256–257

disabling the TCP time stamping feature, 256

increasing the amount of open files, 258–259

increasing the socket buffer memory allocation, 257–258

live production shakeout, 15

load average
defined, 476

load balancer
needed in front of Web HTTP servers, 303–304

load balancers
as critical components of business systems, 352–353

routing mechanism approach, 355

in WebSphere-based applications, 354–356

load balancing
achieving redundancy with DNS round-robin configuration, 308–309

using cloning to extend in WebSphere, 67

load balancing and firewall environment
other considerations for, 355–356

load testing and profiling applications
for WebSphere application environments, 243–244

LoadBalanceWeight directive
function of in failover configurations, 317–318

LoadBalanceWeight setting
example of function of in WebSphere 5, 318–320

LoadRunner, Mercury Interactive
stress and volume testing tool, 246

local network environment
main categories of within a WebSphere environment, 162–164

log_buffer parameter
for Oracle system configuration and tuning, 437

Logbufsz parameter
setting in IBM DB2, 441

logical partitioning (LPAR)
in IBM PowerPC platform (pSeries), 147

Lotus Domino Enterprise Server
supported by WebSphere, 344

LPAR. *See* logical partitioning (LPAR)

LVD (Low Voltage Differential) SCSI
function of, 121–122

LWPs (Lightweight Processes). *See* Lightweight Processes (LWP)

Lynx
command line Web browser, 245

M

master repository
function of in WebSphere 5, 77–78

MaxAgents parameter
setting in IBM DB2, 440

Maximum Connections setting
in JDBC connection pool manager, 444

maximum heap
defined, 158

Maximum Pool Size
setting in WebSphere 4 and 5, 445–446

maximum TCP buffer size
command for determining current setting, 264

Maximum value
in Performance tool network utilization output, 496

MC/ServiceGuard
clustering solution, 295

as solution for applications using NFS, 349

measurement without impact, 31–32

memory
steps for modeling the usage of real and virtual, 484–485

memory allocation
in JVMs, 158–159

recommended for every CPU within a system, 161–162

memory and memory configuration
importance of proper sizing and modeling, 432–433

memory leaks
cause by poor SQL statement management, 419–421

example garbage collection monitoring graph showing, 160

as nastiest of all Java-based problems, 161

messaging interfaces
requests serviced by the application server, 59

method directive
settings in Oracle Transparent Application Failover, 368

Microsoft Excel
using for plotting and analyzing tuning data, 247

Microsoft Web Application Stress tool
stress and volume testing tool, 246

Microsoft Windows Internal Clustering
clustering solution, 294

as solution for applications using NFS, 349

mid-tier
    in JDBC type 3 driver implementa-
        tion, 425
MinCommit parameter
    setting in IBM DB2, 440
Minimum Connections setting
    in JDBC connection pool manager,
        444
Minimum Pool Size
    setting in WebSphere 4 and 5, 445
Minimum value
    in Performance tool network utiliza-
        tion output, 496
Mirrored Waterfall Performance
    Methodology (MWPM), 27–30
    function of in WebSphere environ-
        ments, 232
    other issues with the methodology,
        30–31
    the waterfall model, 28–29
Monitor command
    for getting memory usage informa-
        tion, 479
monitoring and probe impact
    matrix, 242
monitoring and testing
    defining methods of for WebSphere
        applications, 240–243
    table of various testing types, 242
    words of wisdom for, 240–242
monitoring tools
    database platform, 441–442
monitors and probes
    for testing your WebSphere environ-
        ment, 244–245
Moore's law, 115
mount points
    creating for Unix file system data
        types, 274
MQ Series
    communications with WebSphere,
        462
MQ Series components
    things to consider when using native,
        462–463
MQ Series integration
    basic architecture behind, 460–463
Multi Router Traffic Grapher (MRTG)
    monitoring tool (graphing), 245
    tool for analyzing and graphing
        utilization data, 492
multiapplication JVM, dual Web server,
    single application server topology
    function of in WebSphere 4 vs.
        WebSphere 5, 201–202
    function of server groups in, 201–202
    use of in thick models, 197–204

multiapplication multi-JVM topology
    example of, 184
multichannel topologies, 204–218
    vs. single-channel topologies, 174
multi-JVM applications
    advantage of, 216–217
multiple application JVMs
    example of with multiple application
        servers, 212–213
multiple application servers
    example with multiple application
        JVMs, 212–213
multiple JVM environments
    advantages of, 188
    considerations for, 184–186
    disadvantages of, 189
    formula for figuring overhead when
        adding JVMs, 186
    other considerations, 186–188
    persistence issues in, 185–186
multiple JVMs with multiapplication
    servers, 211–218
    advantages of, 217
    database and other external interface
        pooling, 215–217
    disadvantages of, 217–218
    example of high-availability exten-
        sion, 215
    extensions to for improving
        redundancy, 214–215
    final considerations for using, 218
    non-Web-based application consid-
        erations, 213–214
multiple Web server topologies
    function of, 224–226
multiprocessor-based systems
    Athlon MP processor designed for, 89
multithreaded logger
    using instead of a
        system.out.println(), 402
multi-Web server, multiapplication
    server topologies
    advantages of, 210
    application server capacity
        considerations, 208–209
    costs involved in, 210
    database considerations, 209
    disadvantages of, 211
    example of, 205
    final considerations for using, 211
    function of, 205–211
    single points of failure in a
        WebSphere environment, 206
    split-brain WebSphere configuration,
        207–208
MWPM. *See* Mirrored Waterfall
    Performance Methodology
    (MWPM)

N

names services server
    function of in WebSphere 5, 75
NAS (Network Attached Storage). *See*
    Network Attached Storage (NAS)
Net Present Value (NPV) vs. Total Cost of
    Ownership (TCO), 23
netstat command
    finding the number of TIME_WAIT
        state connections with, 389
netstat -i command
    obtaining network performance sta-
        tistics with, 491
netstat -i *interface_name* command
    for showing network-related errors in
        Linux, 494
netstat tool
    for monitoring Oracle and DB2 for
        performance issues, 442
network
    effect of a large database workload
        environment on, 433–434
Network Attached Storage (NAS), 122
    function of, 125–126
network components
    function of, 163
    support for in WebSphere, 306–307
network configuration
    intelligent routing in, 276–277
    system and hardware tuning and
        optimization for, 276–277
Network controllers and interfaces,
    140–145
network errors
    commands for probing additional,
        493–494
    selecting counters to test for, 494
    in Windows and Unix, 493–495
network infrastructure availability,
    352–370
    overview, 352–353
network performance
    determining cause of poor, 499–500
    monitoring, 490–497
    monitoring in Unix, 490
network technology
    importance of using fastest possible
        in networks, 351
network utilization
    example calculation for, 491–492
    key values in Performance tool
        output, 496
    monitoring in Unix, 490–493
    script for monitoring, 492
    in Windows environments, 495–497

networks
    main categories of within a
        WebSphere environment,
        162–164
New Heap
    managing in Sun HotSpot JVM, 288
NFS
    configuration issues, 348
    example of basic implementation,
        348
    implementation and performance,
        347–350
    options, 347–350
    options for using in a WebSphere
        environment, 348
NFS cluster
    importance of failover time within,
        351–352
NFS implementation
    considerations when looking at
        highly available, 350–352
    example of basic, 348
    example of highly available, 350
    file locking and I/O management in,
        352
NFS server availability
    for exposing server files to other
        servers, 347–352
NO_IMPLEMENT exception, 340
NO_RESPONSE message, 339
node
    contents of in WebSphere 5, 72–73
node agent
    in WebSphere 5, 73
None type
    in Oracle Transparent Application
        Failover, 368
nonraw file systems vs. raw file systems,
    435
non-Web-based WLM topology
    advantages of, 202–203
    differences in topology design
        considerations, 202
    disadvantages of, 203–204
    final considerations for using, 204
non-Web-based workload management
    topology
    considerations for, 202
Novell eDirectory server
    supported by WebSphere, 344
NPV. *See* Net Present Value (NPV)

O

object request broker (ORB)
    as component of a WebSphere
        queue, 280

as key part of EJB container's overall
performance, 377
Object Request Broker (ORB)
utilized by RMI/RMI-IIOP, 457–460
ODBC database interface
provided by WebSphere, 215
ODBC-based drivers
function of, 426–427
Oetiker, Tobias
MRTG and RRDtool created by, 247
OLAP workload. *See* Online Analytical
Processing (OLAP) workload
Old Heap
managing in Sun HotSpot JVM, 288
Online Analytical Processing (OLAP)
workload
workload summary matrix for, 434
Online Transaction Processing (OLTP)
workload
CPU availability needed for, 433
open files
increasing the amount of, 258–259
increasing the amount of in Linux
2.2+, 259
increasing the amount of pre-Linux
2.2, 258–259
open queuing model
function of, 279
Open Shortest Path First (OSPF)
routing mechanism, 354–355
smart routing protocol, 277
using to distribute traffic to multiple
locations, 309
operating systems
performance tuning checklists for,
252
operating system thread
to JVM thread ratio, 93
operating system tools
custom-built profiling packages, 244
operational alarms
monitors and probes associated
with, 244–245
operational availability vs. service
availability, 292–293
operations methodology
performance methodology
intersection with, 2–3
Opteron. *See* AMD Opteron
models available, 90
Opteron (x86-64)
defined, 83
optical fiber cable
use of for high-speed FCAL
implementations, 126
optimization
the methodology of in WebSphere
environments, 232

optimization and tuning
checklist for, 251–287
costs associated with for the pilot
application, 16–17
importance of trend analysis strategy
in, 249
planning after analysis and review,
18–19
optimization and tuning checklist
for WebSphere environment running
under Linux, 255–260
for Windows NT, 2000, XP, and 2003,
252–255
optimized system
definition of, 1–5
example of pre- and post-upgrade
support costs for, 10–11
Option A caching
function of in EJB environments,
416–418
Option B caching
function of in EJB environments,
416–418
Option C caching
function of in EJB environments,
416–418
Oracle 8*i* and 9*i*
configuration and tuning
parameters, 437–438
example showing high-level
architecture, 436
Oracle 8*i* and 9*i* databases
function of, 435–438
Oracle Connection Time Failover (CTF)
function of, 365
Oracle Connect Time Failover (CTF)
function of, 366–367
vs. Oracle Transparent Application
Failover (TAF), 367
Oracle Parallel Server (OPS)
availability of, 222
Oracle TNS names configuration file for
Transparent Application Failover
code example, 368
Oracle Transparent Application Failover
(TAF)
function of, 367–369
Oracle Transparent Application
Failover(TAF) vs. Oracle Connect
Time Failover (CTF), 367
Oracle Transparent Application Failover
settings for method directive in, 369
Oracle Transparent Network Substrate
(TNS) names configuration file for
server failover
code example of, 366

Oracle9*i* Real Application Clusters (RAC)
system vs. hot-standby and
active-standby configurations, 222
Oracle-timed collection statistics
commands for turning on and off,
438
ORB (Object Request Broker)
as component of a WebSphere
queue, 280
ORB plug-in
use of for WLM of non-Web-based
topology, 202
organization redundancy
understanding, 38
Orphan Timeout
setting in WebSphere 4, 447–448
Orphan Timeout setting
in JDBC connection pool manager,
444

P

Packets Outbound Errors counter
adding to test for network errors,
494–495
Packets Received Errors counter
adding to test for network errors,
494–495
parallel_max_servers parameter
for Oracle system configuration and
tuning, 437
Parallel-ATA (P-ATA). *See* P-ATA (Parallel
ATA)
passivation directory
function of in EJB container tuning,
381–382
rules of thumb for using, 382
P-ATA (Parallel ATA) vs. S-ATA (Serial
ATA), 128
Pckcachesz parameter
setting in IBM DB2, 441
people redundancy
understanding, 38
percentage availability
matching with business availability,
38–39
performance
costs associated with resolving
problems with, 6–7
as key measure of high-performance
computing, 33
managing, 5–7
operations engineering and, 2
a proven methodology for managing,
24–30
quantifying, 1–5
what constitutes an improvement in,
7–8

performance analysis tools
for monitoring system load and
performance status, 473–500
performance and scalability. *See*
performance management
performance checklist
for database-to-WebSphere
implementation, 427–428
performance improvements
business benefits of, 17
in perceived user or customer
response time, 8–9
performance management
activity phase, 506
the aim of, 25–26
the business bottom line, 13–14
costs for mitigating performance
issues, 6–7
example showing methodology, 505
importance of, 4–5
key components that affect
performance, 8
measurement without impact, 31–32
the method of, 26
model for, 6
a proven methodology for, 24–30
testing, 26
performance management tooling,
473–500
overview of, 473–474
performance methodology
operations methodology intersection
with, 2–3
performance monitors
time needed for analysis and review
of, 18–19
performance testing
setting your expectations, 233–234
a WebSphere platform, 233–251
Performance tool
importance of using the Log Report
view of, 497
using for collision testing on shared
networks, 494–495
Performance tool console
main screen of, 482
performance tooling. *See* performance
management tooling
performance tuning
decrease in operational costs
associated with, 11–13
effect of on ability to handle more
users, 9–11
importance of, 9
performance tuning checklist, 251–287
for Windows NT, 2000, XP, and 2003,
252–255

PerformaSure, Quest
stress and volume with application
management tool, 246
persistence
issues of in multiple JVM environments, 185–186
physical architecture. *See* topological
architecture
physical errors
in Windows and Unix networks, 493
pilot application, 14–17
costs associated with, 16–17
importance of stress and volume
testing in, 15
pilot phase
of the application development life
cycle, 15
ping tool
testing network utilization with, 492
pipeline services
in Sun UltraSPARC processors, 100
platform costs
pre- and post-upgrade examples,
10–11
platform derivatives
some common that WebSphere relies
on, 343–344
platform resiliency
primary goals for, 206
plus (+) button
at top of the Performance tool
console, 482
Polyserv Matrix Server
as solution for applications using
NFS, 349
pooled connection request
failover support for in WebSphere,
360
pooling, 27
portal
in a single-channel 3-tier topology,
178–180
Power4 platform (IBM)
examining, 109–115
overview, 109–110
Power4 processor (IBM)
architecture and function of, 113–114
vs. PowerPC 970 processor
architecture, 114–115
Power4 processors (IBM), 116
PowerPC 604e processor, 115
PowerPC 750Cxe processor
architecture and function of, 112
PowerPC 750FX processor
architecture and function of, 112
PowerPC 750 processor
architecture and function of, 111–112

PowerPC 750 series processors, 116
PowerPC 970 processor, 116
architecture and function of, 114–115
vs. Power4 processor architecture,
114–115
vs. the UltraSPARC III processor, 115
PowerPC platform
selecting for your environment size,
116–119
summary, 119–120
PowerPC RS64-III and RS64-IV
processors, 116
Preconnect method
setting in Oracle Transparent
Application Failover, 369
prefer local algorithm
function of for EJB container, 335
PreparedStatement() method
using in WebSphere application
design, 409
PrimaryServer directive
using to help support failover
configurations, 317
process affinity
for EJB containers, 305
process semaphores
setting in Sun Solaris WebSphere-
based applications, 265–266
processor cores
function of, 113–114
% Processor Time counter
adding for the WebSphere Java
process usage, 483–484
production environments
best CPUs and servers for large,
107–108
best CPUs and servers for medium,
106–107
best CPUs and servers for small,
105–106
most simplistic WebSphere topology
for, 174–178
selecting the right CPU for a large,
118
selecting the right CPU for a
medium, 117–118
selecting the right CPU for a small,
117
selecting the right CPU for large
Power4-based, 118
profiling
a practical approach to, 505–507
profiling and benchmarking
applications running under
WebSphere, 503–517
to isolate where problems are
occurring, 504–505

key points that should make up your
approach, 507
revisited, 503
tools available, 507–517
profiling and load testing applications
for WebSphere application environments, 243–244
proprietary clustering (software
clustering)
function of, 293–294
ps command. *See* Unix ps command
Purge Entire Pool option
in Purge Policy in WebSphere 5,
450–451
Purge Failing Connection Only option
in Purge Policy in WebSphere 5,
450–451
Purge Policy
setting in JDBC connection pool
manager, 444
setting in WebSphere 5, 449–451

Q

quasi-stateless technology
NFS as, 349
Query Heap parameter
setting in IBM DB2, 441
querying databases
failover support for in WebSphere,
360–361
queue configuration baselining
for WebSphere queues, 283–284
Queue Length
graphing for a Windows XP-based
server, 489
queue sizes
determining, 282–283
queues
effect on performance, 8, 27–28
queuing models
supported by WebSphere, 279
queuing network
tuning WebSphere to operate with,
279–287

R

RAM disk technology
function of, 130
raw file systems vs. nonraw file systems,
435
recvspace attribute
setting for TCP send and receive
buffer, 270
redundancy
five progressive levels of in an organization, 36–39

redundancy paths
recommended for WebSphere-to-
database networking, 143
regedit. *See* Registry Editor tool (regedit)
Registry Editor tool (regedit)
changing setting within the registry
with, 252–255
changing the TCPTimedWaitDelay
value with, 254–255
relational database platform
key points about sizing, 431–435
Remote Method Invocation (RMI)
connections
teardown of vs. lightweight connections, 270–271
repositories and data stores
in WebSphere 5, 77–78
repository database failover
configuration issues in WebSphere 4,
356–358
resiliency. *See* availability
Resource Analyzer tool
checking for I/O time-outs with,
392–393
example screen, 514
features from a profiling perspective,
515
function of, 513–515
vs. HPjmeter and JProbe tools, 515
for monitoring and testing
TIME_WAIT state, 390
for monitoring operational aspects of
applications, 244
for monitoring thread values in
WebSphere 4, 387–389
response time
decrease in perceived for user or customer, 8–9
response times
effect of concurrent and registered
users on, 236
example of an end-to-end measurement, 235
testing of for an application, 234–236
RetryInterval
setting in WebSphere 5, 331–332
tuning, 325
Return on Investment (ROI), 19
an overview, 23–24
vs. Total Cost of Ownership (TCO), 23
RISC-based processors
cost of vs. CISC or x86 processors, 97
RISC-based UltraSPARC processors vs.
Complex Instruction Set
Computing (CISC)-based processors, 96
RMI-IIOP, 168
vs. Java IIOP, 456

ROI. *See* Return on Investment (ROI)

round-robin load distribution model, 317–318

Route directive section
in the HTTP plug-in configuration file, 57–58

RRDtool
monitoring tool (graphing), 245

RS64 processor family
architecture and function of, 112–113

rs.close() command
closing the result set object with, 421

rules
building block for WebSphere application environments, 155–157

Run queue
in Unix, 476

S

sales and order management application
in a single-channel 3-tier topology, 178–180

SAN (Storage Area Network) technology. *See* Storage Area Network (SAN) technology

S-ATA (Serial ATA)
function of, 128–129
vs. Parallel-ATA (P-ATA), 128

scalability
as key measure of high-performance computing, 33
understanding your needs for, 47–48
what it is, 34–35

scalability and availability
a primer, 34–43
ten rules to live by, 49

scalability and performance
considerations for scalability and performance, 157–164

script factory
considerations for implementing, 470

SCSI disk technologies
common implementations, 121

SCSI-2 disk technology
function of, 121–122

SecondaryServer directive
using to help support failover configurations, 317

Secure Socket Layer (SSL). *See* SSL (Secure Socket Layer)

security services server
function of in WebSphere 5, 75

Select type
in Oracle Transparent Application Failover, 368

sendspace attribute
setting for TCP send and receive buffer, 270

Serial ATA (S-ATA). *See* S-ATA (Serial ATA)

server affinity, 184
using in split-brain WebSphere configuration, 207–208

server cluster directive
code example of, 314

server group directive
code example of, 314

server groups
vs. application servers, 65
association with WebSphere 4 components, 66
vs. clones, 66–67
improvement of concept of in WebSphere 4, 65–66

server sizes and configurations
deciding on an operational preference for, 172

ServerGroup directives
in an HTTP plug-in configuration file, 58

service availability vs. operational availability, 292–293

Service Level Agreement (SLA), 15
costs associated with for the pilot application, 16–17

session database
function of, 63
as key part in WebSphere availability strategy, 362–365
use of for session persistence, 51

session EJBs vs. entity EJBs, 376

session failover and persistence, 323–326
performance and operational considerations when implementing, 324

session identifier types
supported in WebSphere 4 and 5, 327

session management
configuration levels in WebSphere 5, 327
with cookies, 327
example of with WebSphere, 325
example with WebSphere in a failover scenario, 326
with SSL ID session linkage, 328–329
with URL rewriting, 328

session management scope
new supported in WebSphere 5, 327

Session Manager
configuring to support a session identifier type, 327

session persistence
    option differences between
        WebSphere 4 and 5, 363–364
    three forms of standard with
        WebSphere 4 and 5, 363
    use of session database for, 51
session state
    considerations for multiple JVM
        environments, 185
Session type
    in Oracle Transparent Application
        Failover, 368
shared memory synchronization
    role of Solaris process semaphores
        in, 265–266
shared_pool_size parameter
    for Oracle system configuration and
        tuning, 438
Simple Object Access Protocol (SOAP)
    legacy systems integration via XML,
        455
    standard data types for use in SOAP
        envelopes, 466
Single Instruction/Multiple Data (SIMD)
    instructions
    added to the PowerPC 970 processor,
        115
single-channel 3-tier topology
    advantages of over the 2-tier model,
        181
    contexts in, 179
    database transaction load considera-
        tions, 180–183
    disadvantages of over the 2-tier
        model, 182
    example of high level, 178
    final considerations for using,
        189–190
    final recommendations for using, 183
    how it works, 178–183
single-channel topologies
    advantages of, 176–177
    combined application server and
        database server in, 175–176
    components of, 174–178
    disadvantages of, 177
    vs. dual or multichannel, 174
    example of a high level, 174
    example of a high-level 2-tier, 175
    example of high-level 3-tier, 178
    final considerations for using,
        177–178
    multiapplication JVM, 183–190
    in WebSphere, 173–204
single-threaded model
    importance of not using with
        servlets, 400

SLA. *See* Service Level Agreement (SLA)
SOAP. *See* Simple Object Access Protocol
        (SOAP)
socket buffer memory allocation
    increasing, 257–258
soft costs
    associated with TCO, 21
software clustering (proprietary cluster-
        ing)
    function of, 293–294
software-based errors
    in Windows and Unix networks, 493
Solaris. *See* Sun Solaris
Solaris process semaphores. *See* process
        semaphores
Solaris swap space command, 480
sort_area_size parameter
    for Oracle system configuration and
        tuning, 438
SortHeap parameter
    setting in IBM DB2, 441
SPARC Compliance Definition
    creation of, 95
SPARC RISC platform (Sun
        Microsystems)
    examining, 94–102
    overview, 95
    platform architecture, 95–102
SPARC v9 processors
    comparison chart, 102–104
SPARC V9 RISC architecture
    UltraSPARC II and III processors
        based on, 96
SPARC-based server platform
    selecting for your needs, 104
split-brain WebSphere configuration
    failure issues with, 207–208
    in multi-Web server, multiapplica-
        tion server topologies, 207–208
    non-Web-based application
        considerations, 213–214
spreadsheet applications
    plotting and analyzing tuning data
        with, 247
SQL Query Analyzer
    capturing performance management
        testing results with, 26–27
SQL statements
    management of, 419–421
    using prepared vs. embedded SQL
        commands, 419
    using prepared where possible in
        data tier, 409
SQL transactions
    determining type you're looking to
        support, 430

sqlplus tool
  use of in Oracle, 438
SSL (Secure Socket Layer)
  considerations in system and
    hardware tuning, 277–279
  increasing the number of requests
    per connection, 277–279
SSL ciphers
  availability of, 279
SSL crypto interface adapters
  for increasing SSL-based perfor-
    mance, 278
SSL ID session linkage
  session management with, 328–329
stand-alone database instances
  database availability option, 305
stand-alone databases
  function of, 219
stateful EJBs
  importance of avoiding where
    possible, 404
sticky routing
  using in split-brain WebSphere
    configuration, 207–208
stmt.close() command
  closing the statement object with,
    421
Storage Area Network (SAN) technology
  function of, 124–125
  overview of high-level implementa-
    tion, 124
storage technologies. *See* disk storage
  technologies
stress and volume testing
  importance of, 15
  of your WebSphere applications,
    245–246
Stress and Volume Testing (SVT)
    environment
  testing your applications in, 504–505
stress testing vs. volume testing,
    245–246
striping disks
  calculating performance of, 136–137
Structured Query Language (SQL)
    statement controls
  effect on performance, 8
stub, 59
Sun HotSpot JVM
  managing the minimum and maxi-
    mum heap sizes for, 288–289
  tuning and performance options,
    288–289
Sun Microsystems
  SPARC platform architectures,
    95–102
  SPARC platform overview, 95

Sun Microsystems SunCluster
  clustering solution, 294
  as solution for applications using
    NFS, 349
Sun ONE Directory Server
  supported by WebSphere, 344
Sun server models
  CPU and server comparison matrix,
    104
Sun Solaris
  command for getting network
    interface statistics in, 491
  networking tuning and optimization,
    260–266
  setting TCP keepalive settings,
    261–262
Sun Solaris operating system
  as next best for your WebSphere
    implementation, 108–109
Sun Solaris WebSphere-based
    applications
  changing the TCP keepalive settings
    in, 261–262
  enabling or disabling the TCP time
    stamp, 264
  FIN_WAIT_2 problems with, 263
  maximum TCP buffer size, 264
  process semaphores, 265–266
  setting size of TCP connection hash
    table in, 265
  setting the TCP TIME_WAIT interval
    for, 262
Sun SPARC-based server platform
  selecting for your needs, 104
  summary, 108–109
Sun SPARC platform
  feature of, 145–147
  grid computing in, 146–147
  hot-swappable components, 146
Sun SPARC v9 processors
  comparison chart, 102–104
Sun UltraSPARC II
  architecture and function of, 97–98
  best-use model for, 102
Sun UltraSPARC IIe
  architecture and function of, 99
  best-use model for, 103
Sun UltraSPARC IIi
  architecture and function of, 98–99
Sun UltraSPARC III
  architecture and function of, 99–101
Sun UltraSPARC IIi
  best-use model for, 102–103
Sun UltraSPARC III
  best-use model for, 103
  key components of, 100
  vs. UltraSPARC IIi, 99

Sun UltraSPARC IIIi
    architecture and function of, 102
    best-use model for, 103–104
Sun-based server models
    identifying, 96
SunFire Enterprise class servers
    hot-swappable and hot-pluggable
        components in, 146
    from Sun Microsystems, 95
SunFire range of servers
    choosing for medium production
        environments, 106–107
    hot-swappable and/or redundant
        parts in, 106–107
    recommendation for large produc-
        tion environments, 108
swap space
    in Unix, 480–481
SX processors, 83
sync() method call
    manually persisting session data
        with, 364–365
system and hardware tuning and
        optimization
    disk layout approaches, 272–275
    network configuration, 276–277
    for WebSphere-based platforms,
        271–277
    for Windows-based file systems, 275
system configuration
    effect of workload on, 433
System Interface Unit (SIU)
    in UltraSPARC III processor, 100
system performance
    impact of buggy software or unstable
        hardware on, 239–240
system redundancy
    understanding, 37
system utilization
    monitoring, 474–485
system.out.println()
    using a multithreaded logger instead
        of, 402

T

TCI. *See* Total Cost of Investment (TCI)
TCO. *See* Total Cost of Ownership (TCO)
TCP connection hash table
    setting size of in Sun Solaris
        WebSphere-based applications,
        265
TCP connection time-out
    problems associated with changing
        settings, 330–331
TCP hash table size settings
    in IBM AIX, 271

TCP keepalive feature
    deactivating on your Linux-based
        WebSphere application server,
        256–257
TCP keepalive settings
    command for checking current, 261
    for the Sun Solaris WebSphere-based
        applications, 261–262
TCP maximum listen backlog setting
    function of in IBM AIX, 270–271
TCP port number assignment
    changing maximum with the Registry
        Editor tool, 253
TCP Selective Acknowledgment
    disabling in Linux, 256
TCP send and receive buffer attributes
    setting in IBM AIX, 269–270
TCP TIME_WAIT interval
    setting for Sun Solaris WebSphere-
        based applications, 262
    setting in IBM AIX, 267
TCP time stamp
    enabling or disabling for Solaris
        WebSphere applications, 264
TCP time stamping feature
    disabling on your Linux-based
        WebSphere application server,
        256
TCPTimedWaitDelay value
    changing with the Registry Editor
        tool, 254–255
technical tests
    warning about running behind the
        scenes, 242
testing
    performance management, 26
testing tools
    monitors and probes, 244–245
    recommended for WebSphere
        environments, 243–244
    for your WebSphere environment,
        243–246
thick Web server WebSphere topology
    example of, 191
    example of component mapping for,
        192
    overview of example components,
        193
thin Web server WebSphere topology
    example of, 190
thread size value
    setting, 387–389
    steps for setting in WebSphere 4, 388
    steps for setting in WebSphere 5, 388
threading characteristics
    of JVMs, 161–162

threads
    effect on performance, 8
time stamps
    placing in logging entries within your
        database, 241
TIME_WAIT state
    settings between Web tier and
        application server, 389–390
    steps for setting in WebSphere 4, 390
    steps for setting in WebSphere 5, 390
timing markers
    warning about writing them into
        your code, 240–241
Tivoli Performance tool
    checking for I/O time-outs with,
        392–393
    features from a profiling perspective,
        515
    function of, 513–515
    vs. HPjmeter and JProbe tools, 515
    for monitoring and testing
        TIME_WAIT state, 390
    for monitoring thread values in
        WebSphere 5, 387–389
    Performance Viewer screen, 514
    using to monitor and test queues,
        283–284
tnsnames.ora file
    example that has the CTF extensions
        in it, 366
tools
    for testing your WebSphere environ-
        ment, 243–246
top command
    for determining memory usage on
        Unix servers, 478–480
    getting your memory and swap space
        usage with, 480–481
    using Grep with, 479
topological architecture, 154–164
    blueprints, 165–229
    common elements to consider in,
        165–173
    considerations for scalability and
        performance, 157–164
    and example of a building block for,
        156–157
Total Cost of Investment (TCI), 19–24
Total Cost of Ownership (TCO)
    cost comparisons for different imple-
        mentations, 21–23
    inception of, 20
    vs. Net Present Value (NPV), 23
    an overview, 19–23
    vs. Return on Investment (ROI), 23
    a two year comparison, 22–23

tracing services
    requests serviced by the application
        server, 59
transaction affinity
    for EJB containers, 305
transaction characteristics
    effect of on response times, 236–238
    graph comparing lightweight vs.
        heavyweight, 237
transaction management
    effect on performance, 8
    in multiple JVM environments, 185
transaction rate
    considerations when implementing
        databases, 429–430
    effect on WebSphere environment,
        238–239
    example of, 239
transactional affinity
    for following container transactions,
        336
Transparent Application Failover (TAF)
    function of, 365
trend analysis
    importance of for WebSphere appli-
        cation environments, 249
tuning
    measuring the effects of, 246–251
tuning and optimization
    of EJB container, 377–384

U

UCB ps. *See* Berkeley ps
UDDI Registry
    function of in WebSphere 5, 74
UFS. *See* Unix File System (UFS)
Ultra Port Architecture (UPA)-con-
    nected bus, 98
Ultra160 and Ultra320 SCSI technolo-
    gies
    function of, 122
Ultra320 and Ultra160 SCSI technolo-
    gies
    function of, 122
UltraSPARC CPUs
    most commonly found models, 96
UltraSPARC II
    architecture and function of, 97–98
    best-use model for, 102
UltraSPARC IIe
    architecture and function of, 99
    best-use model for, 103
UltraSPARC IIi
    best-use model for, 102–103

UltraSPARC III
  best-use model for, 103
  key components of, 100
UltraSPARC IIi
  vs. Sun UltraSPARC III, 99
  vs. UltraSPARC II, 98
UltraSPARC III
  vs. UltraSPARC IIi, 99
UltraSPARC IIIi
  architecture and function of, 102
  best-use model for, 103–104
Unix
  monitoring network performance in,
    490
  monitoring network utilization in,
    490–493
Unix CPU and system load
  key load and performance identifiers,
    475–481
Unix File System (UFS), 435
Unix file systems
  disk layout approaches in a
    WebSphere environment,
    273–275
Unix memory analysis
  for determining real and swap
    memory usage, 478–480
Unix ps command
  for getting a list of top processes
    running, 479–480
Unix servers
  determining memory usage on,
    478–480
  getting garbage collection informa-
    tion from log files on, 250
  monitoring disk I/O for, 485–487
  using vmstat command to find load
    average in, 476–478
Unused Timeout
  setting in JDBC connection pool
    manager, 444
  setting in WebSphere 5, 449–450
uptime command
  getting a server load rating with,
    475–476
UriGroup directive declaration
  section of the HTTP plug-in
    configuration file, 57
URL context
  of the HTTP plug-in configuration
    file, 57
URL rewriting
  session management with, 328
USB disk technology
  function and future of, 129–130

user application data sources and
    databases
  supported by WebSphere, 358–362
user capacity
  handling requests for additional,
    18–19
user experience monitors
  monitoring and testing applications
    with, 241
user load
  effect of on response times, 236–238
utility network
  function of, 164
utility tier servers, 119
utlbstat tool
  for Oracle performance monitoring,
    438
utlestat tool
  for Oracle performance monitoring,
    438

V
V series servers
  choosing for production
    environments, 105–106
V100 server
  best use for, 103
V120 server
  best use for, 103
V880 server
  for small production environments,
    106
  UltraSPARC III CPUs supported by,
    101
vendor-specific deployment descriptor
  for your J2EE application, 372
Veritas
  advanced clustering solutions by, 351
Veritas Cluster Server
  clustering solution, 294
  as solution for applications using
    NFS, 349
Veritas Volume Replicator (VVR)
  using to perform geographic
    synchronization, 226
vertical and horizontal scaling
  advantages of combined, 153–154
  example of an environment, 154
vertical clustering
  for high availability in WebSphere,
    307
vertical scaling vs. horizontal scaling,
    152–153
virtual hosts
  capability in WebSphere, 52–53

vmstat command
    for finding load average, 476–478
vmstat tool
    for monitoring Oracle and DB2 for
        performance issues, 442
volume testing vs. stress testing,
    245–246

W

waterfall model, 28–29
Web Archive file
    Web module as WebSphere represen-
        tation of, 63
Web container
    as component of a J2EE environ-
        ment, 59–60
    as component of a WebSphere
        queue, 279–280
    effect on performance, 8
    vs. EJB container performance
        tuning, 374–375
    example implementation within
        WebSphere, 60
    example of how it operates, 373
    failover process, 330–333
    function of, 373–374
    key items that should be tuned,
        386–387
    overview of, 311
    queue modeling item to monitor, 284
    steps for accessing for any applica-
        tion server, 384–385
    steps for accessing in WebSphere 5,
        385–386
    tuning in WebSphere 5, 385–394
    tuning the number of threads
        processed by, 387–389
    in a WebSphere high availability
        environment, 304
    WebSphere queue settings, 285
Web container failover, 329–333
    failover process, 330–333
    primary causes for failure in a typical
        environment, 329
Web container failover and high avail-
    ability, 311–333
    Web container overview, 311
Web Container Service dialog box
    in WebSphere 4, 385
Web container services
    example of in WebSphere 5, 385–386
Web module
    function of, 63

Web module level
    configuring session management in,
        327
Web server
    as component of a WebSphere
        queue, 279–280
    implementation, 308–310
    overview, 308
Web server failover and high availability
    model for, 309
    in WebSphere, 307–310
Web servers (thin vs. thick models)
    considerations for opting for one
        over the other, 166–173
    effect on performance, 8
Web servers
    example of geographically distrib-
        uted, 225
    in high-level 2-tier WebSphere topol-
        ogy, 175
Web servers (thin vs. thick models)
    in your WebSphere topological archi-
        tecture, 165–173
Web server tier/HTTP servers
    in a WebSphere high availability
        environment, 303–304
Web Service engine
    function of in WebSphere 5, 74
Web Services
    based on a HTTP Web Service stack,
        465
    diagram showing integration with
        WebSphere, 464
    future of in legacy systems integra-
        tion, 455
    performance and scalability tips, 465
    using standard SOAP data types,
        465–466
    XML validation in, 467
Web Services Description Language
    (WSDL). See WSDL (Web Services
        Description Language)
Web Services integration
    function of for distributed communi-
        cations, 463–468
Web site address
    for downloading Jinsight, 516
    for Quest Software JProbe profiling
        tool, 508
Web tier
    example of abstraction layer for, 171
    performance development consider-
        ations for, 397–400

Web-based User Interface (UI)
 effect of images and components on response times, 238–239
WebSphere
 administrative consoles, 53
 availability model, 35–36
 base configurations provided by for testing and example purposes, 52
 basic J2EE application operating under, 198–199
 building block rules, 155–157
 the business bottom line, 13–14
 causes of downtime, 41–42
 clusterable EJBs available in versions 4 and 5, 341–342
 combined horizontal and vertical scaling with, 153–154
 common components between versions 4 and 5, 51–64
 database performance and optimization, 411–451
 databases supported by, 412–414
 deployment and network architecture, 149–229
 dual Web, single application server, dual JVM topology, 200–202
 EJB and Web container performance, 371–394
 example of dual application server configuration, 313
 example of horizontal scaling with, 151
 example of session management in a failover scenario, 326
 example of session management with, 325
 example Web container implementation within, 60
 external system availability, 343–370
 failover and high availability considerations, 291–342
 failover techniques with, 301–307
 function of HTTP server with, 53–54
 generic database performance architecture with, 428–431
 high availability and failover fundamentals, 292–293
 horizontal scaling with, 150–152
 infrastructure design, 81–147
 JDBC connection pool tuning, 445–447
 key components that affect performance, 8–9
 MQ Series communications with, 462

performance of Java 2 Enterprise Edition (J2EE) applications, 1–5
profiling and benchmarking, 503–517
scalability and availability, 33–50
session identifiers supported in versions 4 and 5, 326–329
split Web and EJB container JVM configuration, 199–200
SQL implementation methods used within, 414–427
SSL ID-based tracking supported by, 329
types of database usage you may require with, 431
vertical scaling with, 152–153
virtual host capability of, 52–53
Web server failover and high availability in, 307–310
Web Service communications with, 464
WebSphere 4
 administration console, 378
 administrative repository, 68–69
 administrative repository considerations, 356–358
 cloning and workload management flowchart, 68
 cloning in, 66–68
 code example of key CloneID changes, 316
 configuring the pool manager connection in, 447
 EJB Container Service dialog box in, 379
 EJB container tuning in, 378–380
 function of administration server in, 69
 function of EJB container failover in, 336–337
 IBM-certified relational databases in, 412
 improved concept of server groups in, 65–66
 JDBC connection pool tuning, 447–448
 managed by a Java/Swing-based Graphical User Interface (GUI), 53
 parameter to help improve ORB performance, 389
 repository database failover, 356–358
 session persistence options, 324
 steps for making changes to keep-alive I/O time-out values, 393

steps for making changes to keep-alive requests, 391

steps for setting the thread size value in, 388

Web container performance tuning, 384–385

Web module introduced in, 63

XMLConfig tool in, 65

WebSphere 4 and 5
  component architectures, 51–79
  three forms of session persistence standard with, 363

WebSphere 4-specific component architecture, 64–69

WebSphere 5
  code example of key CloncID changes, 316–317
  ConnectTime setting, 332–333
  ConnectTimeout setting in, 322–323
  contents of node in, 72–73
  EJB container services in, 381
  EJB container tuning in, 380–381
  external load balancers in, 320–322
  function of administration service in, 76
  function of administrative services in, 76
  function of deployment manager in, 73
  function of EJB container failover in, 337–338
  function of JCA container in, 75
  function of JMS server in, 75–76
  function of names services server in, 75
  function of security services server in, 75
  function of UDDI Registry in, 74
  IBM-certified relational databases in, 413
  JDBC connection pool tuning, 449–451
  key components of, 69–79
  managed by a Web-based console, 53
  network deployment component architecture, 71
  new configuration settings available for, 449–451
  new session management scope supported in, 327
  node agent in, 73
  RetryInterval setting in, 331–332
  session persistence options, 324–325
  standard deployment component architecture, 70
  steps for accessing EJB container settings in, 380–381

steps for accessing the Web container settings, 385–386

steps for making changes to keep-alive I/O time-out values, 393–394

steps for making changes to keep-alive requests, 391–392

steps for setting the thread size value in, 388

tying ConnectTime setting with other setting in, 332–333

Web container tuning, 385–394

weighted load distribution in, 318–320

WebSpherc 5.0.1
  changes to weighted load distribution in, 320

WebSphere 5-specific component architecture vs. WebSphere 4-specific component architecture, 69–79

WebSphere application environments
  batch components and external applications within, 469–472
  categories of services provided by, 411–412
  effect of large database workload on your network, 433–434
  example of correctly configured funnel or carrot-shaped model, 29–30
  ROI from reducing processing overhead, 23–24
  running batch scripts and external applications within, 469–472
  using iostat command to pick a hot disk in, 487–488

WebSphere application performance
  high CPU utilization of JVM as cause of poor, 498
  monitoring, 497–500

WebSphere applications
  available stress and volume testing tools for, 246
  availability as key performance indicator, 36
  avoiding use of large session objects in, 397–398
  business tier performance in, 400–406
  database server failover in, 356–370
  defining the methods of monitoring and testing, 240–243
  developing high performance, 395–410
  importance of not using single-threaded models with servlets in, 400

importance of using <jsp: usebean()> tag carefully in, 400

importance of using constants in, 405

importance of using WebSphere data sources in, 407

importance of writing local method calls, 405–406

insulating from failover delays, 361–362

invalidating HTTP sessions when they aren't required, 398–399

monitors and probes for testing, 244–245

a practical approach to profiling, 505–507

purpose of, 34

questioning use of doGet() and doPost() methods in, 399

stress and volume testing, 245–246

tools for monitoring performance of, 473–500

top 20 performance development considerations, 396–397

using container-managed persistence only for high-read database access, 408

using Data Access Objects for general database access in, 409

using init() servlet method in, 399

WebSphere application server level

configuring session management in, 327

WebSphere application servers

common symptoms for poor performance of, 497–500

developing high-performance applications for, 395–410

having all CORBA components with a shared, 459–460

how Web Services may be implemented within, 464–465

importance of not using all of your memory for scripts, 470

WebSphere application server topologies

database server tier as important component of, 305–306

WebSphere availability

understanding, 40–43

WebSphere availability index

measuring for components within your environment, 44–45

WebSphere bin directory

WebSphere Control Program in, 65

WebSphere business tier. *See* business tier

WebSphere cluster environment, 78–79

WebSphere clustering

typical configuration and function of, 298–299

WebSphere cluster networking

using for a multinode or multiapplication server environment, 141–142

WebSphere Command Program (WSCP)

listing the running state of each application with, 480

WebSphere connection pool manager

function of, 442–445

how a pooled connection infrastructure operates, 443

for WebSphere-based applications, 442–451

WebSphere Control Program (WSCP)

function of in WebSphere 4, 64–65

WebSphere database. *See also* database

performance and optimization, 411–451

tuning and optimization, 427–442

WebSphere database architecture

database considerations, 209

WebSphere database tuning

for two most common database products, 427–442

WebSphere EJB container

function of within the application server, 61–62

WebSphere environment

options for using NFS in, 348

WebSphere environments

ability to scale down infrastructure with an optimized, 13

building block rules for, 154–164

considerations for scalability and performance, 157–164

data tier performance in, 406–409

disk storage recommendations for larger implementations, 133–134

example of end-to-end response time measurement, 235

HTTP plug-in as key component of, 54–58

importance of knowing what you are changing, 232–233

indicative operational costs, initial outlay, 12–13

key areas susceptible to failures, 40

main categories of networks within, 162–164

the methodology of optimization in, 232

the need for speed in, 231–233

network requirements for, 141–145

networking as a key component in, 140–145

optimization and tuning checklist for one running under Linux, 255–260

primary causes for Web container failover, 329–330

primary reasons for using multiple JVMs in, 183

recommended testing applications for, 243–244

selecting the right CPU for yours, 116–118

summarizing storage technologies in, 130–140

tools for testing, 243–246

tuning the JVM, 287–288

using Microsoft Excel for analyzing tuning data, 247

WebSphere high availability environment

EJB container in, 304–305

example of a complex, 302

levels of, 302–303

Web container in, 304

WebSphere HTTP plug-in

contents of configuration file, 54–56

example of topology, 55

five main sections of configuration file, 56–58

function of, 54–58

WebSphere implementations

cost comparisons for, 21–23

cost items to be included in, 20–21

failover and high availability considerations, 291–342

key indicators of performance improvements in, 7–8

overview of key components of, 149–150

WebSphere Java process

steps for drilling down and viewing, 483–484

WebSphere JDBC connection pool tuning

primary settings common to WebSphere 4 and 5, 445

WebSphere physical implementation

single Web server, single application server topology, 178–183

WebSphere platform

comparing versions in, 79

example CORBA implementation within, 457

exploring advanced features, 145–147

improving performance for greater user capacity, 18–19

methods for achieving high availability, 293–307

performance testing, 233–251

performance, tuning, and optimization, 231–289

testing response times for an application, 234–236

topological architecture, 154–164

WebSphere queue

EJB container queue settings, 286

JDBC connection pool manager queue settings, 286–287

Web container queue settings, 285

WebSphere queues

Carrot mode showing correct queuing configuration, 280

determining sizes for, 282–283

essential components for, 279–281

an example queuing model, 283

HTTP Web server queue settings, 285

as part of performance and capacity management, 279–287

queue configuration baselining, 283–284

queue modeling items to monitor, 284

reasons for using them, 281

updating and configuring, 284

WebSphere repository database

impact of on a WebSphere environment, 431

WebSphere Resource Analyzer tool

capturing performance management testing results with, 26–27

using to monitor and test queues, 283–284

WebSphere topological architecture blueprints, 165–229

and example of a building block for, 156–157

example of a high-level, single-channel, 2-tier topology, 175

example of a high-level, single-channel topology, 174

major network types within, 163

WebSphere-based applications
    factors to consider when implement-
        ing a database for, 429–431
    IBM DB2 parameters, 440–441
    optimization and tuning checklists
        for, 251–287
    products that provide solid, robust
        NFS solutions for, 349
    using baselining and profiling for
        performance optimization, 242
WebSphere-based environments
    factors to consider when implement-
        ing a database for, 429–431
    profiling and benchmarking tools for,
        507–517
WebSphere-based J2EE applications
    interfacing with Java Message Service
        (JMS), 455–456
    the need for performance in, 1–5
WebSphere/J2EE application
    example showing integration with a
        legacy application, 454
WebSphere-to-customer (or Web server)
    networking
    recommendations for, 144–145
WebSphere-to-database networking
    basic recommendations for, 142–144
weighted load distribution
    changes to in WebSphere 5.0.1, 320
    in WebSphere 5, 318–320
weighted round-robin routing algorithm
    used within WebSphere 5's EJB WLM
        routing, 335
Windows 2000 Active Directory (with
    LDAP extensions)
    supported by WebSphere, 344
Windows NT/2000/XP
    CPU and system load performance
        monitoring for, 481
Windows NT/2000/XP/2003
    performance tuning checklist for,
        252–255
    real and virtual memory usage,
        484–485
    steps for modeling the usage of real
        and virtual memory, 484–485
Windows Performance tool
    example showing network utilization
        output, 496
    measuring CPU and system load
        with, 481
    monitoring network utilization with,
        495–497
    for monitoring Oracle and DB2 for
        performance issues, 442

selecting the monitor agents in,
    482–483
steps for setting up active monitoring
    on your CPU, 482–483
Windows server environment
    disk storage technologies, 488–490
Windows server operating system
    performance tuning checklist for,
        253–255
Windows-based file systems
    system and hardware tuning and
        optimization for, 275
WinRunner (Mercury Interactive)
    profiling and load testing tool, 243
WLM availability
    different levels of for configuring EJB
        containers, 305
workload management. *See* load
    balancing
    and cloning flowchart in WebSphere
        4, 68
    of EJB container in WebSphere,
        334–336
    and EJB containers, 340–342
    requirements for user sessions to
        participate in, 329
Workload Management (WLM) pool, 67
workload summary matrix
    for generic WebSphere database
        sizing, 434–435
WSAD profiler/Jinsight
    features of, 517
    function of, 516–517
WSAD Profile view, 516
wsadmin tool
    listing the running state of each
        application with, 480
WSCP. *See* WebSphere Control Program
    (WSCP)
WSDL (Web Services Description
    Language)
    caching of to improve performance,
        467–468

X

x86 architecture
    companies produced by, 82
x86 or CISC processors
    cost of vs. RISC-based processors, 97
x86-64 (Opteron)
    defined, 83
x86/IA-64/x86-64 platform (Intel and
    AMD)
    architecture, 82–84
    CPU comparison chart, 90–91

examining, 82–94
overview, 82
x86/x86-64/IA-64 processors
    what makes them fast, 83–84
-Xgcthreads parameter
    setting for IBM JVM, 289
XML. *See* Extensible Markup Language
    (XML)
-XML parameter
    setting for IBM JVM, 289
XML validation
    use of in Web Services integration,
    467
XMLConfig tool
    function of in WebSphere 4, 65

-XX:NewRatio bootstrap parameter
    Sun HotSpot JVM, 288
-XX:NewSize bootstrap parameter
    Sun HotSpot JVM, 288
-XX:NewSizeMax bootstrap parameter
    Sun HotSpot JVM, 288
-XX:SurvivorRatio bootstrap parameter
    Sun HotSpot JVM, 288

Y

Young Heap
    managing in Sun HotSpot JVM, 288

forums.apress.com

JOIN THE APRESS FORUMS AND BE PART OF OUR COMMUNITY. You'll find discussions that cover topics of interest to IT professionals, programmers, and enthusiasts just like you. If you post a query to one of our forums, you can expect that some of the best minds in the business—especially Apress authors, who all write with *The Expert's Voice*™—will chime in to help you. Why not aim to become one of our most valuable participants (MVPs) and win cool stuff? Here's a sampling of what you'll find:

DATABASES
Data drives everything.

Share information, exchange ideas, and discuss any database programming or administration issues.

INTERNET TECHNOLOGIES AND NETWORKING
Try living without plumbing (and eventually IPv6).

Talk about networking topics including protocols, design, administration, wireless, wired, storage, backup, certifications, trends, and new technologies.

JAVA
We've come a long way from the old Oak tree.

Hang out and discuss Java in whatever flavor you choose: J2SE, J2EE, J2ME, Jakarta, and so on.

MAC OS X
All about the Zen of OS X.

OS X is both the present and the future for Mac apps. Make suggestions, offer up ideas, or boast about your new hardware.

OPEN SOURCE
Source code is good; understanding (open) source is better.

Discuss open source technologies and related topics such as PHP, MySQL, Linux, Perl, Apache, Python, and more.

PROGRAMMING/BUSINESS
Unfortunately, it is.

Talk about the Apress line of books that cover software methodology, best practices, and how programmers interact with the "suits."

WEB DEVELOPMENT/DESIGN
Ugly doesn't cut it anymore, and CGI is absurd.

Help is in sight for your site. Find design solutions for your projects and get ideas for building an interactive Web site.

SECURITY
Lots of bad guys out there—the good guys need help.

Discuss computer and network security issues here. Just don't let anyone else know the answers!

TECHNOLOGY IN ACTION
Cool things. Fun things.

It's after hours. It's time to play. Whether you're into LEGO® MINDSTORMS™ or turning an old PC into a DVR, this is where technology turns into fun.

WINDOWS
No defenestration here.

Ask questions about all aspects of Windows programming, get help on Microsoft technologies covered in Apress books, or provide feedback on any Apress Windows book.

HOW TO PARTICIPATE:
Go to the Apress Forums site at **http://forums.apress.com/**.
Click the New User link.